American Tragedy

★

OTHER BOOKS BY DAVID KAISER

Economic Diplomacy and the Origins of the Second World War

Postmortem: New Evidence in the Case of Sacco and Vanzetti
(with William Young)

Politics and War: European Conflict from Philip II to Hitler

Epic Season: The 1948 American League Pennant Race

AMERICAN TRAGEDY

Kennedy, Johnson, and the Origins of the Vietnam War

DAVID KAISER

THE BELKNAP PRESS OF
HARVARD UNIVERSITY PRESS
Cambridge, Massachusetts
London, England

Second printing, 2000

Library of Congress Cataloging-in-Publication Data

Kaiser, David E., 1947–
American tragedy : Kennedy, Johnson, and the origins
of the Vietnam War / David Kaiser.
p.   cm.
Includes bibliographical references and index.
ISBN 0-674-00225-3 (alk. paper)
1. Vietnamese Conflict, 1961–1975—United States.
2. United States—Politics and government—1961–1963.
3. United States—Politics and government—1963–1969.
4. Kennedy, John F. (John Fitzgerald), 1917–1963.
5. Johnson, Lyndon B. (Lyndon Baines), 1908–1973.   I. Title.
DS558 .K35 2000
959.704′3373—dc21
99-052925

Designed by Gwen Nefsky Frankfeldt

Contents

★

Illustrations follow pages 182 and 374

The traits of American character were fixed; the rate of physical and economical growth was established; and history, certain that at a given distance of time the Union would contain so many millions of people, with wealth valued at so many millions of dollars, became thenceforward chiefly concerned to know what kind of people these millions were to be. They were intelligent, but what paths would their intelligence select? They were quick, but what solution of insoluble problems would quickness hurry? They were scientific, and what control would their science exercise over their destiny? They were mild, but what corruptions would their relaxations bring? They were peaceful, but by what machinery were their corruptions to be purged? What interests were to vivify a society so vast and uniform? What ideals were to ennoble it? What object, besides physical content, must a democratic continent aspire to attain? For the treatment of such questions, history required another century of experience.

—Henry Adams, *History of the United States During the Administrations of Thomas Jefferson and James Madison*

President Kennedy questioned the wisdom of involvement in Vietnam since the basis thereof is not completely clear. By comparison he noted that Korea was a case of clear aggression which was opposed by the United States and other members of the U.N. The conflict in Vietnam is more obscure and less flagrant. The President then expressed his strong feeling that in such a situation the United States needs even more the support of allies in such an endeavor as Vietnam in order to avoid sharp domestic partisan criticism as well as strong objections from other nations of the world. The President said that he could even make a rather strong case against intervening in an area 10,000 miles away against 16,000 guerrillas with a native army of 200,000, where millions have been spent for years with no success.

—White House meeting, November 15, 1961

Our generation has a dream. It is a very old dream. But we have the power and now we have the opportunity to make that dream come true.

For centuries nations have struggled among each other. But we dream of a world where disputes are settled by law and reason. And we will try to make it so.

For most of history men have hated and killed one another in battle. But we dream of an end to war. And we will try to make it so.

For all existence men lived in poverty, threatened by hunger. But we dream of a world where all are fed and charged with hope. And we will help to make it so.

The ordinary men and women of North Vietnam and South Vietnam—of China and India—of Russia and America—are brave people. They are filled with the same proportions of hate and fear, of love and hope. Most of them want the same things for themselves and their families. Most of them do not want their sons to ever die in battle, or to see their homes, or the homes of others, destroyed.

Well, this can be their world yet. Man now has the knowledge—always before denied—to make this planet serve the real needs of the people who live on it.

—President Lyndon Johnson, April 7, 1965

To history has been given the task of judging the past, of instructing men for the benefit of future years. The present attempt does not aspire to such a lofty undertaking. It merely wishes to show how things happened in their own right.

—Leopold von Ranke, *History of the Latin and Teutonic Peoples*

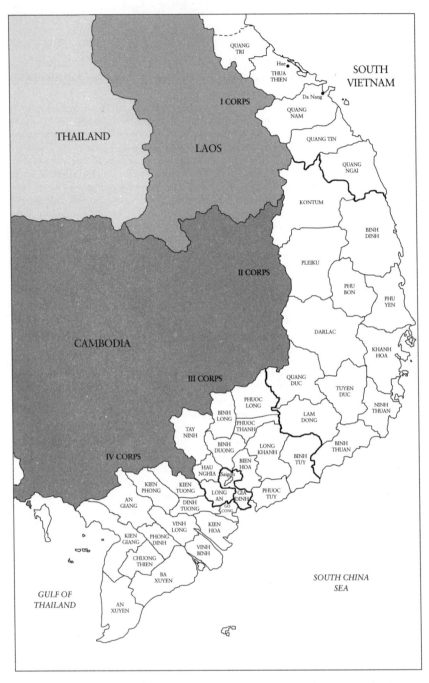

Provinces and Military Corps Boundaries of South Vietnam

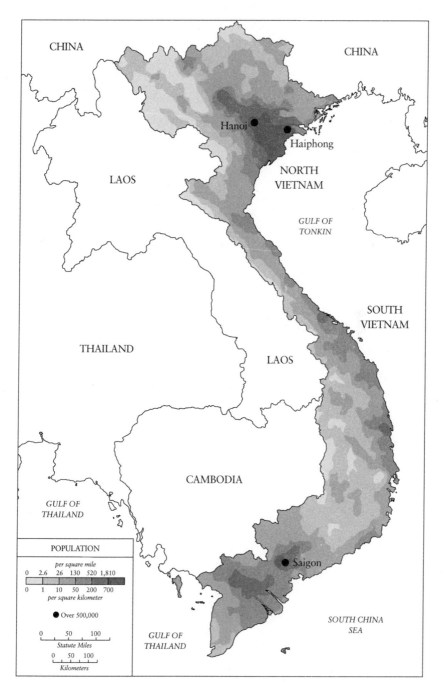

Population Density of Vietnam

INTRODUCTION

★

In the early 1960s the government of the United States probably enjoyed more prestige than at any other time during the twentieth century. The broad national consensus established by the New Deal and the Second World War had been strengthened by the Cold War, sustained economic growth, and progress toward civil rights for all Americans. American opinion showed particular unity with respect to the nation's role in the world and the need to contain Communism. These views had already involved the United States deeply in Southeast Asia, and the decision to fight in South Vietnam in 1965 certainly reflected contemporary conventional wisdom.

By the spring of 1968, when the escalation of the war finally reached an upward limit, this national consensus no longer existed, and by the spring of 1975, when Saigon fell, Americans' confidence in their government had fallen to a new low. Although the *international* consequences of the most unequivocal military defeat in the history of the United States turned out to be considerably less serious than policymakers had predicted, the lost war nonetheless remains the greatest policy miscalculation in the history of American foreign relations. And while its consequences did not compare to the those of Germany's miscalculations in 1914 and 1939, or that of the Confederacy in 1861 or even the British in 1775, they nonetheless included profound effects on American society and politics that persist to this day. The war in Vietnam remains a pivotal event in American history not because of its consequences in international politics, but because it brought an era of American history—the postwar consensus—suddenly and dramatically to an end.

Although the genesis of the war was the subject of large-scale treatments in both the 1970s and the 1980s, only in the 1990s have American archives opened their doors to reveal the genesis of American policy.[1] This book is the first treatment based upon a nearly complete documentary record, giving due weight to both long-term causes and short-term decisions, and telling the story of the early stages of the conflict itself.

Two thousand four hundred years ago, Thucydides the Athenian first explored the distinction between the long-term and immediate causes of conflicts in his history of the Peloponnesian War. The long-term causes of the American involvement in Vietnam, it is now clear, go back to the middle years of the Eisenhower administration, which decided upon a militant response to any new Communist advances virtually anywhere on the globe. The Vietnam War occurred largely because of Cold War policies adopted by the State and Defense Departments in 1954–1956 and approved secretly by President Eisenhower—policies that called for a military response to Communist aggression almost anywhere that it might occur, and specifically in Southeast Asia. These policies ensured that when American clients came under attack from Communist and other forces in Laos and South Vietnam the Pentagon and the State Department would propose American military action. They also ensured that military planners would rely upon nuclear weapons to make such action effective, and some continued to do so well into the Kennedy and Johnson administrations. Ironically, while Eisenhower's supposedly cautious approach in foreign policy has frequently been contrasted with his successors' apparent aggressiveness, Kennedy actually spent much of his term resisting policies developed and approved under Eisenhower, both in Southeast Asia and elsewhere.[2] He also had to deal with the legacy of the Eisenhower administration's disastrous attempts to create a pro-Western rather than a neutral government in Laos—a policy he quickly reversed, thereby avoiding the need for American military intervention there.

Following the lines of policy Eisenhower had laid down, middle- and lower-level State and Defense Department officials began submitting one proposal for military intervention after another as soon as crises in Laos and South Vietnam became serious in 1960–1961. But while the military continually laid plans for action in Indochina, American war plans took relatively little account of the actual strategic situation there or of the capacity of American conventional forces to affect it. War plans were consistently designed to deal with conventional Communist aggression, but the threats that developed in Laos and South Vietnam in 1960–1964 were political in Laos and largely unconventional within South Vietnam. The Pentagon's plans for Southeast Asia involved action against North Vietnam from the air, from the sea, and on land, and consistently foresaw Chinese intervention and escalation to general war as a possible result. When American advisers became actively involved in the Vietnam War in 1962, a few civilians, junior officers, and foreign observers raised basic questions about the nature of the war and American strategy, but the American military never changed its basic approach to the conflict.

The underlying causes of the Vietnam War, we shall find, were the growing Communist insurgency in South Vietnam, on the one hand, and the State and Defense Departments' reflexive proposals for implementing the Eisenhower administration's policies on the other. The more immediate causes of the war, however, and specifically the American decision in late 1964 and early 1965 definitely to begin it after declining to do so in 1961–1962, show the influence of both personality and chance. The appointed senior foreign policy leadership of the Kennedy and Johnson administrations—Secretary of State Dean Rusk, Secretary of Defense Robert McNamara, National Security Adviser McGeorge Bundy, and most of the Joint Chiefs of Staff—never questioned the assumptions of the Pentagon and State Department, and supported intervention in Southeast Asia from 1961 on. But President Kennedy resisted the proposals for intervention in both Laos and South Vietnam that reached him, largely because of broader strategic and political questions that the bureaucracy and his cabinet seemed to ignore. The Kennedy administration did dramatically increase American involvement in South Vietnam, raising the American military presence from about 600 personnel in 1960 to 17,500 in 1963. That increase, however, which took the form of a larger advisory presence and the introduction of helicopter, tactical air, and other forms of combat support, represented a compromise between the President, who sincerely wanted to help the South Vietnamese government cope with the Viet Cong but rejected war as a way to do so, and his bureaucracy and cabinet members, who wanted the United States to intervene directly in 1961.

As Kennedy repeatedly explained, he doubted—rightly as it turned out—that American intervention in Southeast Asia would enjoy much support from the nation's most important allies, or from Congress, or from the American people. Again and again he questioned whether Indochina was an appropriate place for the United States to fight. While keenly interested in the problem of Communist insurgency, he believed that threatened nations themselves bore the principal responsibility for combating it, and he wanted to assist them by means other than direct American military intervention. And Kennedy also looked for ways to improve relations with the Soviet Union and America's image in the Third World—efforts which were slowly succeeding by the end of his last year in office, but which rapidly came to a halt thereafter as the United States began the war in Vietnam. We shall never know what Kennedy would have done with respect to Vietnam had he lived to serve a second term, but it is clear that the Vietnam War would have begun three or four years earlier than it did had he taken his subordinates' advice to send troops.

This book also deals fully, for the first time, with the Kennedy administration's relationship to the government of Ngo Dinh Diem and to its overthrow. The administration's attempts to help the South Vietnamese government cope with the emerging Viet Cong failed, largely because neither Saigon nor the American military knew how to deal with a guerrilla war. Nor, it is clear, was Diem an effective leader unwisely abandoned by his American patrons. A bipartisan consensus had adopted Diem as the preferred South Vietnamese leader under the Eisenhower administration, but he lacked the skills necessary to unite non-Communist South Vietnamese, and his support had already declined significantly by 1961. This book shows, with the help of extensive new documentation, that the counterinsurgency effort in South Vietnam was failing even before the Buddhist crisis of 1963, and that Diem and his brother Ngo Dinh Nhu had themselves to blame for their overthrow. It also shows how Robert McNamara and the Pentagon helped hide the true situation from the President, the rest of the government, and the American people, thereby putting off the need to reevaluate American policy. Kennedy died believing, mistakenly, that the war was still going well.

When in the months after Kennedy's death it became clear that the situation within South Vietnam was deteriorating, the Pentagon renewed proposals for a conventional war against North Vietnam. President Johnson, unlike President Kennedy, never really questioned his subordinates' proposals, and agreed in principle by March 1964 to take action against North Vietnam. But Johnson also wanted to avoid an obvious change in policy or a major war until after his reelection, and his administration marked time for most of 1964, with the exception of the Gulf of Tonkin incident in early August and the retaliatory strike and congressional resolution that followed. After the election, the bureaucracy immediately prepared, and the President approved, a plan for an open-ended war against North Vietnam designed to create an independent, non-Communist South Vietnam. These plans took very little account of the insurgency in the South itself, and essentially ignored the questions of allied support and American public opinion that had dissuaded Kennedy from such moves. The Joint Chiefs of Staff attempted to get the government to commit itself in advance to the use of nuclear weapons if necessary, but this question was left open. In an effort to avoid disturbing his legislative agenda, Johnson concealed even the existence of these war plans for as long as possible. Meanwhile, the Johnson administration essentially lost interest in other critical aspects of foreign policy such as Soviet-American relations.

The American war in South Vietnam—including both bombing and ground forces—began in late February and early March 1965. And although Johnson's deceptive presentation of his decisions fooled both the American people at the time and many subsequent historians, this book shows clearly that he was implementing one basic decision for a major war that had been reached in December of 1964. Knowing that it was embarking upon a much longer and larger conflict than the American people seemed ready to support, the administration decided disastrously to conceal its probable scope and duration for as long as possible, while pretending that negotiations might bring the conflict to an end at any moment. The strategy worked only too well. The initial bombing and troop commitments did not disturb Johnson's legislative agenda, but when the scale of the commitment and the failure to achieve American aims became apparent during the next three years, support for the war began to evaporate rapidly.

Other myths must also be laid to rest. The Johnson administration did not decide upon the war out of fear of a right-wing backlash, or because of a belief that Congress or the American public demanded it, or as a means of saving the Great Society. The strength of the American political right had fallen to an all-time low in early 1965, and an important segment of the right—conservative Southern Democrats—had no real interest in the Vietnam War. While both the Congress and the public could be expected generally to *support* military action against Communism, neither had shown the slightest *enthusiasm* for such a course, and both would have been delighted to have been spared this rather dubious venture. Instead, as newly released taped telephone conversations show beyond doubt, Johnson, Rusk, McNamara, and Bundy undertook the war and overrode the well-founded doubts of some important subordinates simply because they believed it had to be done and had confidence in the nation's ability to do it. They did so even though America's leading allies, the world's leading neutrals, and the Secretary General of the United Nations all tried to discourage them from escalating the war.

Nor did the American failure in the war stem from the civilians' failure to follow military advice to escalate more rapidly. The build-up of 1965–1966 closely followed the recommendations of General William Westmoreland, the commander in the field. It began slowly and gradually mainly because the primitive logistics of South Vietnam could not support more rapid deployments. Meanwhile, General Westmoreland opposed the immediate all-out bombing of North Vietnam because he wanted to secure his position in South Vietnam first. The general, who became the key architect of American strategy, also seems to have accepted the idea that the war could be won conventionally. The loss of the war stemmed not from a failure in civil-military relations but from a failure of either the civilian or the military leadership to understand the nature of the conflict and to define realistic American objectives and strategies.

This book is the first to explore an enormous amount of published and unpublished documentation on the years 1961–1965 that has become available during the last seven years, including seven thick volumes of *Foreign Relations of the United States* devoted to Vietnam itself, thousands of unpublished documents in the Kennedy and Johnson Libraries, many more volumes on other aspects of Kennedy administration foreign policy, the papers of General Westmoreland, numerous Pentagon documents declassified at my request, tapes of several critical meetings during the Kennedy administration, and tapes of President

Johnson's telephone conversations showing his state of mind during the first nine months of his presidency. Although some key documents remain classified, and although the CIA apparently has no intention of ever releasing some important documentation about its relations with the Diem regime, the documentary record of American policy is now relatively complete.

This book is also the first to make a thorough attempt to place the issues of Vietnam and Laos within a broader international and domestic context. Nothing seems more significant, in this respect, than the relative priorities given to Vietnam by the Kennedy and Johnson administrations. Under Kennedy, other issues—Berlin, Cuba, the Congo, relations with leading neutrals, and above all relations with the Soviet Union—generally took up far more of the President's time and attention than Vietnam. Under Johnson, Vietnam within six months emerged as by far the most important issue in foreign affairs, and Johnson undertook the war without giving much consideration to the damage it would do to other aspects of American foreign policy. The importance of Vietnam could only be evaluated within a broad and sophisticated international perspective, something which Johnson did not possess.

While I have provided by far the most thorough and best-documented account yet of the American decision to go to war and added a great deal to our understanding of the South Vietnamese role in the war and of Viet Cong tactics, I have had to rely upon others to understand the role of North Vietnam. Even William Duiker, the foremost authority on the North, who graciously provided me with an unpublished chapter of his new biography of Ho Chi Minh, would agree that our knowledge of Hanoi's policy and strategy in the early 1960s is quite limited. I look forward to the day when Vietnamese and American historians fill this gap. In this war, as in so many others, the secrets of the loser have come to light far more rapidly than those of the winner. The story of Hanoi's policy and strategy will be fascinating and important, but it may well add relatively little to our understanding of American policy, since American leaders knew so little about what their enemy was thinking or doing. Nor, in this case, are researches in the archives of America's major allies likely to help much, since none of them collaborated with the United States in the design of its policy.

My understanding of the war, meanwhile, has been greatly enhanced by the work of William Strauss and Neil Howe, the authors of a provocative new theory of generations and eras of American history.[3] One need not delineate the entire theory in order to understand its relevance to the war in Vietnam.

To a truly remarkable degree, the Vietnam War was the work of a particular generation of Americans—those born in roughly the first quarter of the twentieth century—who came to power for the first time under the Kennedy and Johnson administrations, and included nearly all their senior civilian and military leaders. Whether or not these leaders were the "best and the brightest" of their contemporaries, as David Halberstam argued, they certainly embodied the dominant characteristics of what Strauss and Howe named the "GI generation." Their strengths included an exemplary willingness to tackle difficult and costly tasks, a faith in the institutions of the government of the United States, a great capacity for teamwork and consensus, and a relentless optimism. Their weaknesses, alas, included an unwillingness to question basic assumptions, or to even admit the possibility of failure, or to understand that the rest of the American population was less inclined to favor struggle and sacrifice for their own sake. In sharp contrast to Americans born before 1901 and after 1924, the GI generation that led the nation into the war contained almost no doubters about the wisdom or the success of the enterprise. This, as much as anything else, probably accounted for the decision not only to enter the war but also to persevere for eight fruitless years.

No generational archetype, however, is utterly hegemonic. That John F. Kennedy, the first President of the GI generation, was the most skeptical senior official of his administration regarding the wisdom of war in Southeast Asia gives the war its particularly tragic character. During his short presidency, Kennedy's cautious approach to the use of American power and his interest in accommodation with America's adversaries distinguished him from most of his senior subordinates. Kennedy's attempts to inspire his countrymen showed an understanding that Americans needed new kinds of challenges, and his eventual choice of the space race, civil rights legislation, and the nuclear test ban and détente suggest that he wanted to move in new and less threatening directions. Lyndon B. Johnson, on the other hand, despite some serious misgivings about the war in Vietnam, saw no alternative to fighting it. He accepted it as one challenge among many, and declared publicly that his generation was destined to lead both America and the world into a new era of prosperity, freedom, and peace. Instead, his decision to fight a hopeless war accelerated the inevitable end of the postwar consensus, and began anew the process of redefining the goals of American political life.

The American decision to fight the war in Vietnam remains a highly dramatic one because the war was a logical, but not essential, consequence of the previous thirty years of American history. The consensus regarding the need to defend South Vietnam during these years was broad, but never complete, and both Kennedy and Johnson enjoyed freedom of action in deciding upon policy toward Southeast Asia. Just as the war might easily have begun in 1961, it might not, under somewhat different circumstances, have begun in 1965 at all. As it turned out, a dedicated and accomplished generation of Americans succumbed to the defects of their greatness, leaving it to others to unravel the mystery of how it had all begun.

"I lived through the whole of it," Thucydides wrote of the Peloponnesian War, "being of an age to understand what was happening, and I put my mind to the subject so as to get an accurate view of it."[4] Even now, 2,400 years later, the special passion that informs his work when he discusses the victories and defeats and the heroes and villains of his own city are unmistakable. I lived through the whole of the Vietnam War, and while it was far less of a catastrophe for the United States than the Peloponnesian war was for Athens, no living American remained unaffected by it, and its effects upon the American people have persisted through the remainder of the twentieth century. And thus, while I have written this book as a professional historian, at the end of story I shall also try to discuss its impact on those who lived through it, to place it within a larger historical context, to pay tribute to many Americans whose responses to the war still deserve the thanks of their countrymen, and to try, to the limited extent that any one person can, to help heal some of the wounds that it opened up and that have lasted until this day. A government's decision to fight a mistaken war demands very special kinds of heroism, and Americans displayed them all. The history of every great nation is replete with tragedy, and Americans can view their own both clearly and without undue anger or shame, especially if they can see it as one part of a broader story.

1

The Eisenhower Administration and Indochina

1954–1960

★

The presidency of Dwight D. Eisenhower was a particularly critical period in the formation of American policy toward the less developed regions of the world in general, and toward Southeast Asia in particular. Under Eisenhower, the European powers disengaged from most of their formal colonial empires, leaving new strategic problems behind. Under Eisenhower, the Pentagon grappled seriously for the first time with the problem of defending large parts of Asia from Communist aggression. The Eisenhower administration, moreover, made militant anti-Communism the principle of its foreign policy, committing itself actively to support anti-Communist forces while opposing both leftist and neutral factions virtually all over the world. A rigid organizational structure institutionalized these policies.

Since the Second World War, the U.S. government had built a large and complex national security bureaucracy, including both older institutions like the State Department, the Army, and the Navy, and new ones like the Central Intelligence Agency, the Joint Chiefs of Staff, the Office of the Secretary of Defense, and the National Security Council. Beginning in 1946, these institutions assumed a host of enormous responsibilities all over the world, usually in an attempt to prevent the spread of Communism. Beginning with President Eisenhower, each new President found himself perched atop a massive, intricate organizational pyramid, driven by years and years of organizational momentum toward established goals. Presidents approved policy, but bureaucracies designed it, codified it, and carried it out, playing an increasingly great role in both the formation and the execution of American foreign policy.

In recent decades a number of prominent historians, led by Stephen Ambrose, have painted a relatively restrained picture of Eisenhower's foreign policy. Scholarly studies written before much original documentation had been released also repeated the public line of the Eisenhower administration that "massive retaliation" was the keystone of its anti-Communist strategy.[1] Documentation now undermines this picture. Although Eisenhower concluded the Korean War and managed to avoid involvement in any other actual war during his eight years in office, his administration profoundly reshaped the American government's views of its worldwide interests, the threats to those interests, and the means by which the United States would defend those interests. In particular, it formally defined two extreme tenets of the Cold War as policy: that the United States had to resist any further Communist expansion, if necessary unilaterally, and that the United States should avoid formal recognition of Communist gains whenever possible.

The Eisenhower administration also developed a complex organizational structure to plan, approve, and execute strategies for meeting these extraordinary new worldwide responsibilities. Working under the National Security Council (NSC), the Planning Board continually wrote and revised statements of basic national security policy and policy toward various regions of the world. The Operations Coordinating Board supervised the implementation of these policies, and occasionally pointed out the need to revise them. These policy statements, in turn, provided the guidelines for military planning in the Pentagon, foreign policy in the State Department, and covert activities pursued by the Central Intelligence Agency.

The real roots of the Vietnam War lie in the policies the Eisenhower administration adopted toward Southeast Asia after 1954—policies that exercised an enormous influence not only under Eisenhower but under Kennedy and Johnson as well. Essentially, the Eisenhower administration did everything it could to build up pro-American, anti-Communist regimes in Southeast Asia, while preparing to meet renewed Communist aggression with American military force, including atomic weapons. These policies did not succeed. In Vietnam, America's chosen instrument, Ngo Dinh Diem, had seriously undermined the confidence both of his own people and of the American government by 1961 (see Chapter 3). More significantly, the Eisenhower administration policies toward little-known, remote Laos created a serious crisis during 1960, leaving the incoming Kennedy administration literally at the brink of a potentially major war.

In the late winter and early spring of 1954, while Viet Minh rebels surrounded the French garrison at Dien Bien Phu in northern Vietnam, the Eisenhower administration seriously considered intervening to defeat the Communist revolutionary forces. After several weeks of deliberations, Washington decided against war for several different reasons. Congressional leaders had expressed unwillingness to intervene without the support of European allies, and the Conservative British government of Winston Churchill and Foreign Secretary Anthony Eden was more interested in détente with the Communist powers than in war in Southeast Asia. The French government refused to grant full independence to the Indochinese states, a condition that the United States regarded as essential to defeating the Communist revolutionaries. Lastly, while Admiral Arthur Radford, the Chairman of the Joint Chiefs of Staff, enthusiastically supported intervention—including, very possibly, the use of nuclear weapons—the Chief of Staff of the Army, General Matthew Ridgway, very strongly opposed it, arguing that even hundreds of thousands of troops would not secure a decisive outcome. By July 1954 Washington had resigned itself to a cease-fire in Indochina that would leave at least part of Vietnam in Viet Minh control, and had pledged to respect the Geneva Accords that embodied these terms.[2]

The crisis over Indochina, however, led to the development of new American policies toward Southeast Asia, and new definitions of American interests. Secretary of State John Foster Dulles secured a mandate to establish the broadest possible alliance against any *further* Communist advances in Asia during the crisis, and he pursued it enthusiastically. On August 12, 1954, the NSC first discussed two alternative forms of a Southeast Asia Treaty Alliance to protect Indochina, among other areas. In both cases, Britain, France, Australia, New Zealand, the Philippines, Thailand, and the United States would assume obligations toward Cambodia, Laos, and South Vietnam. Under alternative A, the treaty would "involve the agreement of the participants that there should be immediate retaliation against Communist China if Communist China, directly or indirectly (such as through the Viet Minh) commits armed aggression against any free nation of Southeast Asia, including Laos, Cambodia, and South Vietnam." Alternative B would simply "commit each member to treat an armed attack on the agreed area as dangerous to its own peace and safety and to act to meet the common danger in accordance with its own constitutional processes."[3]

The administration chose the less sweeping alternative. Eisenhower remarked that "any President would be foolish to get the country into war without the consent of Congress," and Dulles acknowledged that the treaty's language purposely differed from that of the NATO treaty, which did give the President the right and the duty to respond to an immediate attack upon an ally. Eisenhower also took care to retain freedom of action in cases of Communist "subversion" within the treaty area.[4] The SEATO Treaty signed on September 8 by the United States, Australia, Britain, France, New Zealand, Pakistan, and the Philippines included Laos, Cambodia, and South Vietnam within the area the signatories gave qualified pledges to defend. It committed each signatory to act "in accordance with its constitutional processes" against overt aggression, but it obliged them only to "consult" in response to Communist subversion. The Southeast Asia Treaty Organization as a whole would act together only in the event of a unanimous resolution by all signatories. In short, it left all its signatories with considerable freedom of action either in response to an overt attack or in response to Communist subversion. Since the Geneva Accords prohibited Laos, Cambodia, and South Vietnam from joining any alliances, they could not sign, and the treaty thus raised the interesting legal question of whether the signatories had the right to pledge themselves to the defense of nations not party to the agreement. In fact, both Cambodia and, much later, Laos eventually renounced the protection of the treaty.[5]

The SEATO Treaty, however, was merely one instrument of U.S. policy toward the region, not the basis of that policy. On December 22, 1954, after several more lengthy discussions in the NSC, President Eisenhower approved NSC 5429/5, "Current U.S. Policy in the Far East," which essentially committed the United States to defend the SEATO area alone if necessary. "The primary problem of U.S. policy in the Far East," it began, "is to cope with the serious threat to U.S. security interests which has resulted from the spread of hostile Communist power on the continent of Asia over all of Mainland China, North Korea and, more recently, over the northern part of Vietnam." Should Communist aggression strike any of the territory covered by the Manila Pact (SEATO Treaty) prior to its coming into effect, the statement continued, the United States should take appropriate actions, "including a request for authority from Congress to use U.S. armed forces, if appropriate and feasible. When the Pact is in effect, the United States should be prepared to opposed any Communist attack in the Treaty area with U.S. armed forces if necessary and feasible, *consulting the Congress in advance if the emergency permits.*"[6]

Six months later, on June 9, 1955, the NSC, after a brief discussion of the all-Vietnam elections scheduled for 1956, authorized the Planning Board to review these provisions as they applied to South Vietnam, and the Planning Board instructed the Department of Defense and the JCS to prepare an appropriate response to possible "Viet Minh" overt aggression against South Vietnam, action undertaken "possibly in connection with the election issue." Specifically, the board asked for studies of U.S. military operations "required—with the use of nuclear weapons and alternatively without such use—(1) to repulse the aggression and punish the aggressor or (2) to destroy the Vietminh forces and take control of North Vietnam," and estimates of the length of time required to reach those objectives.[7]

Defending South Vietnam posed a more general problem that had preoccupied American planners in one way or another since the Second World War: how to win decisive victories, especially in local wars, against numerically superior opponents. Beginning in the late 1940s, nuclear weapons had emerged as the cheapest option for American defense, and despite Truman and Eisenhower's failure to employ them in Korea, nuclear weapons figured very prominently in the Eisenhower administration's defense planning. In public, Secretary of State Dulles in 1954 had announced a policy known as "massive retaliation," implying that the United States might strike at the heart of Communist power in response to local war, but the reality of defense planning did not reflect this at all. Instead, the military—faced with severe restraints upon manpower—planned increasingly to use tactical and strategic nuclear weapons to win local wars. Thus, in January 1955, the President had approved NSC 5501, "Basic National Security Policy," which declared a need for ready, mobile forces sufficient to deter aggression, or "to punish swiftly and severely any such local aggression." Such forces should be "properly balanced, sufficiently versatile, suitably deployed, highly mobile, and equipped as appropriate with atomic capability, to perform these tasks."[8]

The Joint Chiefs submitted their first proposal for South Vietnam to the Planning Board on September 9, 1955.[9] They assumed, as did numerous other strategic appreciations, that in the event of "Vietminh aggression," the South Vietnamese forces alone could provide only "limited resistance." They then foresaw immediate U.S. naval and air attack upon "Vietminh forces," followed by "early movement forward of mobile U.S. forces" to conduct "joint and combined operations in the Tonkin [Red River] Delta area [of North Vietnam]," followed by "a major campaign of pacification" to reconquer the North. The time required, they continued, would depend upon the South Vietnamese, warning time, the season of the year, and "restrictions imposed on U.S. military operations," but they hoped to finish within a year. This optimistic estimate took too little account of South Vietnam's almost nonexistent logistical base, which had weighed heavily with General Ridgway in his recommendation against intervention in 1954 and which delayed an American build-up considerably in 1965. "Use of atomic weapons," the Joint Chiefs wrote, "should result in a considerable reduction in friendly casualties and in more rapid cessation of hostilities." Any restrictions on the use of atomic weapons, they argued, would delay the accomplishment of the objective and could force the United States to deploy greater forces than could be justified for this task.[10] In the wake of the Korean War, the Chiefs appeared to side with MacArthur rather than Truman in arguing that any new Asian war had to employ all available means.

Forced by the Eisenhower administration to plan for worldwide contingencies with relatively limited budgets, the Pentagon relied increasingly upon nuclear options. This strategy became official in NSC 5602, a revised "Basic National Security Policy" approved on March 15, 1956. "It is the policy of the United States," it read, "to integrate nuclear weapons with other weapons in the arsenal of the United States. Nuclear weapons will be used in general war and in military operations short of general war as authorized by the President." Additional language indicated that forces must retain some non-nuclear capability to intervene and took account of allied sensitivities regarding the use of nuclear weapons in local wars, but "if confronted by the choice of (a) acquiescing in Communist aggression or (b) taking measures risking either general war or loss of allied support, the United States must be prepared to take these risks if necessary for its security."[11] Allied opinion would not, as in Korea, constrain American action.

Worried that North Vietnam might attack when the imminent deadline for South Vietnamese elections passed, the Joint Chiefs addressed the issue of Southeast Asia in late May 1956. Admiral Radford proposed a plan using relatively few American ground forces but providing for the immediate deployment of nuclear weapons. The Commander-in-Chief Pacific (CINCPAC), Admiral Stump, immediately replied that more American forces would be required to assault and conquer North Vietnam. Lieutenant General Samuel T. Williams, the commander of the Military Assistance Advisory Group, Vietnam (MAAG), raised other objections, citing the danger of Chinese Communist intervention, obstacles to air operations, and inadequate communications.[12] Meanwhile, State Department officials, led by Policy Planning Director Robert Bowie, worried about the administration's increasing reliance upon nuclear weapons.[13]

When the NSC discussed the issue on June 7, Radford completely disregarded the opinions of his two subordinates in the field, and proposed the introduction of American ground forces amounting to only four regimental combat teams. In addition to American naval and air units—armed, like at least one army unit, with nuclear weapons—he proposed "specially trained U.S. advisory personnel . . . for assignment as advisors with combat units down to the regimental level and as technical advisors with logistics support organizations." The Chief MAAG would become the SEATO commander. Although Radford acknowledged that the Viet Minh troops were superior, man for man, to the South Vietnamese, he introduced several assumptions designed to show that the South Vietnamese could, in fact, stop the aggression with relatively little help. Terrain and lack of air power, he argued, would make it difficult for the Viet Minh to mount an offensive in strength. In addition, once American and SEATO forces intervened, "the quickness of support and the attendant publicity will firm up the spirit of the Vietnamese people so that they will fight with determination and confidence." SEATO support—which Radford acknowledged might involve only token forces—would have a tremendous psychological impact. "For political reasons," he said, "victory should be won by the

Vietnamese backed as much as possible by other Asians. What we should seek to attain is an Asian victory over Asians."

South Vietnamese forces, Radford said, would fight at Quang Tri just south of the 17th parallel, but would probably fall back to Tourane, where they would find "U.S. support in the form of specially trained U.S. ground forces, with atomic support." After friendly forces took the offensive, Radford reserved the option of trying to establish "Vietnamese control over all of Vietnam," depending on the development of the situation.[14] As he had in the spring of 1954, Radford was arguing that American nuclear weapons, without large ground forces, might be decisive. In so doing, we may once again remark, he was ignoring the advice of his commanders in the field. He even added that the same forces could deal with aggression "with or without atomic weapons." The same forces would be required initially in either case, he continued, "since there were no known fixed military targets in North Vietnam that could not be destroyed by conventional bombing." But if the Chinese Communists intervened openly, we would have to use atomic weapons against Chinese air and logistic bases at once.

Senior civilian colleagues reacted to Radford's presentation without raising any of the more difficult questions that it presented. Secretary of State Dulles welcomed the presentation both militarily and politically, although he anticipated that the United States could expect help only from Thai, Filipino, Australian, and New Zealand forces. Later, Dulles remarked that "if the peoples of the area of Southeast Asia could have any idea of the nature of the discussion which was now taking place in the NSC, the effect of such knowledge would be altogether revolutionary. It would, in fact, change the whole attitude of these nations." Dulles, Eisenhower, and Radford discussed how the United States might discreetly make its intentions known, without a security leak.

Assistant Secretary of State for Far Eastern Affairs Walter Robertson suggested that nuclear weapons would have the gravest impact on Asian public opinion, and should only be used in the gravest of situations. Radford immediately and firmly disagreed. Reuben Robertson, the Acting Secretary of Defense, rejoined that South Vietnamese President Diem had recently "shown no concern with respect to the possible use of atomic weapons in resistance to Communist aggression. He shared the view as to the great value of a show of strength." Radford pointed out that "some sort of tense situation might develop between

North and South Vietnam around the first of next July, when the elections were scheduled to take place under the Geneva Agreements, but which, of course, Free Vietnam refused to be bound by."[15]

The meeting of June 7, 1956, was apparently the last time the NSC discussed specific military plans for Southeast Asia until early 1961. The North Vietnamese did not attack when the deadline for elections passed, and, as we shall see, internal subversion, rather than overt aggression, became the main problem in South Vietnam. Yet the NSC continued periodically to approve statements of policy toward Southeast Asia and statements on general national security policy, the use of nuclear weapons, and the requirements of local wars.

Thus, on August 30, 1956, the NSC, after a lengthy discussion, approved NSC 5612/1, "Statement of Policy on U.S. Policy in Mainland Southeast Asia." Stating that "the national security of the United States would be endangered by Communist domination of mainland Southeast Asia," NSC 5612/1 made a sweeping statement of policy toward "the SEATO area," a term clearly designed to include Cambodia, Laos, and South Vietnam, which, as we have seen, fell under the SEATO Treaty, although their governments had not signed it. It made clear that the United States would intervene to protect Laos or South Vietnam as a matter of policy, not treaty obligation.[16] In May 1957, a new NSC paper on basic national security policy (NSC 5707/8) revised the language on nuclear weapons in ways tending further to increase their importance: "It is the policy of the United States to place main, but not sole, reliance on nuclear weapons; to integrate nuclear weapons with other weapons in the arsenal of the United States; to consider them as conventional weapons from a military point of view; and to use them when required to achieve national objectives.[17] Advance authorization for their use is determined by the President."

"The prompt and resolute application of the degree of force necessary to defeat local aggression," the paper continued, "is considered the best means to keep hostilities from broadening into general war." Other language carefully kept the ultimate decision for war in the hands of the President, but the paper tended to ensure that military planning would increasingly rely upon the use of nuclear weapons.[18] In April 1958, NSC 5809, a revision of NSC 5612/1, restated the basic American policy toward Southeast Asia in essentially identical terms, repeating that the United States would intervene to assist any state willing to help itself, regardless of the attitude of its allies, and applied the language of NSC 5707/8 to the situation in Southeast Asia:

> Because these countries do not have the capability of creating armed forces which could effectively resist large-scale external aggression, the United States will be required to provide a basic shield against Communist aggression. For the foreseeable future, local will to resist aggression will depend on a conviction in Southeast Asia that the United States will continue its support and will maintain striking forces adequate to counter aggression in Southeast Asia *with the capabilities described in current basic national security policy.*[19]

All this language survived intact in NSC 6012 of July 25, 1960, the next revision of "Statement of Policy in U.S. Policy on Mainland Southeast Asia."[20]

Since these statements always referred to the need for congressional authorization before American military power might be introduced into Southeast Asia, one can argue that they left the President with sufficient freedom of action to deal with Communist aggression as he saw fit—a point raised in at least one meeting by Eisenhower himself. Yet they inevitably convinced the national security bureaucracies that the United States had established certain objectives—objectives extending well beyond American treaty obligations—and that, under certain circumstances, the United States would act militarily to secure those objectives with any weapons that proved necessary. Equally important, such statements virtually ordered the American military to plan for the use of nuclear weapons. Henceforth, when the Army, the Navy, and above all the Air Force stated that they were ready to perform a particular mission, they were assuming that such weapons would be available as needed. The Eisenhower administration's decision to oppose Communist aggression in various remote parts of the world—including Indochina—could not be separated in practice from its reliance upon nuclear weapons.

In addition to their guidelines for military planning, the statements of "Basic National Security Policy" and "U.S. Policy in Mainland Southeast Asia" also laid down guidelines for diplomacy and covert action designed to affect the political development of various Southeast Asian states. Within Indochina, South Vietnam actually presented the most straightforward political problem. Having helped install Ngo

Dinh Diem, a staunch anti-Communist and pro-American ruler, in 1954, the United States frequently attempted to affect his behavior, but did not seriously consider encouraging alternative political leadership during the late 1950s. In Cambodia and Laos, American policy clashed with political realities, with fateful results. In Laos, in particular, the Eisenhower administration by late 1960 had helped create a major political crisis, triggered a civil war, and indirectly promoted Chinese, North Vietnamese, and Thai intervention. This in turn brought more critical provisions of American security policy into play, and led the United States in late 1960 to the brink of war in Southeast Asia.

During the 1950s, as more and more Asian and African nations began moving toward independence and a non-aligned, neutral bloc began to emerge, Secretary of State Dulles took a strong public position against neutralism. "The principle of neutrality," he said on June 9, 1956, ". . . pretends that a nation can best gain safety for itself by being indifferent to the fate of others. This has increasingly become an obsolete conception, and, except under very exceptional circumstances, it is an immoral and shortsighted conception."[21] Had it been merely a politically inspired rhetorical flourish, this view need not have created major problems in American foreign relations, but it was more. NSC policy statements embodied the principle that neutralism—defined not simply as non-alignment but as a willingness even to entertain diplomatic relations with Communist powers—was dangerous. Under Eisenhower, the American government—including both the State and Defense Departments and the CIA—generally tried to support factions within emerging nations that would unequivocally reject contacts with Communism and support the West throughout the world.

This policy had serious unfortunate effects in Indochina. Although as we have seen the Geneva Accords of 1954 forbade Laos, Cambodia, and South Vietnam to join any military alliance, the Eisenhower administration nonetheless expected them to maintain firm opposition to Communism. Prince Norodom Sihanouk, the Cambodian leader, never lived up to the administration's expectations in this respect. Thus, for example, on February 10, 1956, Assistant Secretary of State for Far Eastern Affairs Walter Robertson told the Cambodian ambassador that "as a friend of Cambodia . . . he sincerely regretted that Cambodia had embraced a policy of neutrality," which "gave the impression of support [for Communism] and assisted a regime which was dedicated to the suppression of individual liberties and the institution of a system of enslavement of the individual," and suggested that Cambodia follow the example of its unfriendly neighbor Thailand rather than that of India.[22] More significantly, these concerns found their way into NSC 5612/1, "U.S. Policy in Mainland Southeast Asia," adopted in September of the same year, which called upon government agencies to "encourage individuals and groups in Cambodia who oppose dealing with the Communist bloc and who would serve to broaden the political power base in Cambodia." Eighteen months later, NSC 5809 of April 2, 1958, included the same provision.[23]

Exactly how various agencies of the United States government carried out these instructions is not yet entirely known.[24] Clearly, however, Sihanouk during 1958–1959 faced, and successfully dealt with, a series of attempts by his eastern and western neighbors, South Vietnam and Thailand, to overthrow his government.[25] And on February 10, 1960, the Operations Coordinating Board, the NSC group charged with monitoring the implementation of the policy statements approved by the NSC, took note of these developments and proposed a change in policy. Sihanouk, the group noted, "has emerged with added power and prestige from the abortive coup plots and subsequent subversive activities mounted against him in 1959 by ostensibly anti-communist elements. In the process many of these elements were eliminated and the revelation of their *real or fancied association with the United States and other free world countries* undermined Cambodian confidence in U.S. motives and became an obstacle to the pursuit of our objectives."[26] NSC 6012 of July 25, 1960, replaced the offending language with a new paragraph that acknowledged that Sihanouk was there to stay.

The situation in Laos was far more complicated from the beginning, and far more significant for American policy toward Southeast Asia. In the wake of the 1954 Geneva Accords, the Laotian government—which functioned constitutionally far more effectively than the government of either Cambodia or South Vietnam—had to deal with the Communist Pathet Lao, which, with Viet Minh help, had taken over the two northernmost provinces of Laos. Prince Souphanouvong, the leader of the Pathet Lao, was the half-brother of Prince Souvanna Phouma, another leading figure favoring neutralism. Souvanna Phouma, who became Prime Minister in January 1956, decided to try to reconcile the Pathet Lao and the government and integrate their small forces into the Royal Laotian Army. To increase his leverage, he visited both Peking and Hanoi, two neighboring Communist capitals that were then trying to improve relations with neutral countries. In both capitals, he rejected requests to exchange diplomatic missions, although he agreed to Chinese demands to ban American bases and American military advisers, while allowing a French mission to remain.[27] In Washington, meanwhile, NSC 5612/1 of September 5, 1956, instructed government agencies: "In order to prevent Lao neutrality from veering toward pro-Communism, encourage individuals and groups in Laos who oppose dealing with the Communist bloc."[28]

Souvanna took another dramatic step in December 1956, agreeing with Prince Souphanouvong to form a coalition government with Pathet Lao representation, in exchange for allowing the government to take over the administration of the two Pathet Lao provinces.[29] The parties implemented the agreement over the next eighteen months, leading to elections in May 1958.[30] But Souvanna's policies never won the confidence of the U.S. government. In January 1958—before the Laotian elections—Souvanna visited Washington. Secretary Dulles lectured him about world Communism, and suggesting that Souvanna's first-hand knowledge of the Pathet Lao had to be supplemented with American understanding of the clever methods of international Communism. In reply, Souvanna argued that many Pathet Lao were not Communists, noted that they had surrendered their two northern provinces to government authority, and compared the situation to postwar developments in Finland. Dulles was not impressed.[31]

The U.S. mission intervened heavily in the Laos elections of May 1958, even supplying identified American Air Force aircraft to fly new equipment to rural areas in Operation Booster Shot, and Washington expressed disappointment when a few Pathet Lao won some places in the assembly.[32] Souvanna promptly invited the International Control Commission (ICC) to withdraw from Laos, and it eventually did. (The Geneva Accords of 1954 had created tripartite International Control Commissions composed of Western, communist, and neutral members to monitor the observance of their provisions in both Laos and Vietnam.) In June the old-line conservative Laotian politicians, including Prince Phoui Sananikone, formed a new party, the Rally of the Lao People (RLP). Immediately thereafter a younger group of anti-Communists, including some army officers, formed the Committee for the Defense of National Interests, or CDNI, to promote anti-Communism and clean government. Despite the limited strength of the NLHX, the U.S. Embassy warned that it might take over the whole country in general elections scheduled for 1959. The Embassy began working hard to promote a new government without any Pathet Lao sympathizers, and in August Souvanna gave way to Phoui Sananikone, who appointed such a government.[33]

Various agencies of the U.S. government now went on the offensive. On September 8, 1958, the Commander-in-Chief Pacific (CINCPAC), Admiral Harry D. Felt, proposed a "cold war plan" for Laos aimed at securing a favorable outcome in elections planned for late 1959. In December Brigadier General John A. Heintges, the chief of the Program Evaluation Office in Laos—the American military mission—submitted a plan for increasing the size of his mission and improving the training and logistics of Laotian forces. In January 1959 the American government agreed to finance a pay increase for the Laotian army. In the same month, in an ominous development, Prime Minister Phoui Sananikone spoke to the National Assembly about military incidents along the North Vietnamese border, and secured special powers to meet this threat. In March Crown Prince Savang Vatthana, a very pro-American figure, asked for new guarantees of American military help against North Vietnam and China, and received new oral assurances but no formal promise. And in May a Pathet Lao brigade flatly refused integration into the National Army, and the Phoui government asked for a new increase in military aid with which to deal with this problem. Hanoi and Peking, meanwhile, began asking for the return of the ICC.[34]

In late June 1959 the French and the Americans reached agreement on a new training program for the Laotian army. Meanwhile, the Pathet Lao and the North Vietnamese and Chinese Communists called for the reestablishment of the ICC. On the night of August 29–30, the Pathet Lao made mortar attacks on several Laotian army posts along the Nam Ma river, some miles away from the North Vietnamese frontier, and the Laotian army garrisons along the river fled. Joseph Alsop, an influential and hard-line American columnist who happened to be in Laos, inflated the incident, as Bernard Fall later showed very clearly, into a major attack supported by North Vietnamese artillery.[35] Alsop's reporting apparently helped Washington take the situation seriously, although the survivors of the attack eventually admitted that they had not seen any enemy infantrymen.

The incident, in fact, led Washington to think seriously about implementing war plans for Indochina. On September 4 the Joint Chiefs of Staff told the Secretary of Defense that urgent, effective reaction might be necessary to save Laos, and Chief of Naval Operations Admiral Arleigh Burke told State Department representatives that "it was possible we might have to move over the weekend. It may be a question of CINCPAC having to execute its plan or witnessing the fall of Laos." President Eisenhower, in Scotland, received word of American preparations to intervene. By September 9, however, the U.S. Ambassador to Laos, Horace Smith, was reporting that the area of the attack now seemed to be entirely quiet. By mid-September serious doubts regarding reported North Vietnamese participation in the attack had emerged. And on September 18 a CIA Special National Intelligence Estimate refused to confirm any North Vietnamese involvement at all, and blamed the Communist resumption of guerrilla warfare on "a stronger anti-Communist posture by the Laotian Government and . . . recent US initiatives in support of Laos." If the United States joined the conflict, the CIA estimated the chances of North Vietnamese or Chinese intervention in response at better than even.[36]

No further real or imagined flare-ups of fighting with the Communists occurred during 1959, but a highly significant political crisis erupted during the last week of the year. During 1959, friction had increased between Prime Minister Phoui Sananikone and the old-line Laotian politicians on the one hand and the young army officers of the CDNI on the other. On December 15, Phoui formed a new cabinet without army or CDNI participation, and the National Assembly endorsed it. General Ouan, the commander of the FAL (Royal Laotian Army), now planned to give Phoui an ultimatum demanding his resignation, and King Savang Vatthana, who had assumed the throne in October, apparently supported him. The State Department on December 22 advised Ambassador Smith to stand aside, tending to blame Phoui for the trouble and hoping for a more united anti-Communist government. Smith dissented two days later, courageously questioning the Department's "continuing unstinted though largely unrewarded support [of the] CDNI, some key members of which patently pursuing and have pursued personal not Lao national interests and certainly not those of US."[37] On Christmas Day Smith warned that, given the CIA's close ties to the CDNI, no one would believe that the United States, at the very least, could not have stopped the coup if it had tried. The State Department refused to change its position, and the army carried out the coup on December 30.[38]

Three days later, on January 2, 1960, Ambassador Smith fired off another cable, complaining that the CDNI officers had disregarded his opposition to the coup entirely and argued that he did not speak for the other Americans in Laos. They had specifically predicted, in fact, that the ambassador was about to lose a power struggle with the CIA station.[39]

One can hardly avoid the conclusion that the CIA had transformed Laotian politics and brought about a military coup. For the time being, apparently, cooler Laotian heads prevailed, and a new civilian government took power during January. Smith reported that the King had decided to block General Phoumi Nosavan's seizure of power, but Phoumi became the Minister of Defense in the new government, with Khou Abhay, a weak figure, as Prime Minister. Phoumi apparently drew support, encouragement, and ideas from his first cousin once removed Marshal Sarit, the Prime Minister of Thailand, who believed that military government was the answer not only for Thailand but for most of the underdeveloped world.

During the next few months the American mission concentrated on trying to unify the shattered anti-Communist block, preparatory to the general elections that had finally been scheduled for April 1960. Meanwhile, the Pathet Lao apparently managed to extend its control over new parts of the countryside. In the elections, the government won an overwhelming victory, with the CDNI and other pro-government candidates dividing the seats about equally, totally shutting out the pro–Pathet Lao NLHX. Both Laotian and foreign observers reported that the elections had been rigged. The U.S. Embassy reported that the new Prime Minister, Tiao Somsanith, would suffer from his reputation as a "front man" for Phoumi.[40]

Laotian politics blew up in the Eisenhower administration's face on August 9, when Captain Kong Le, the American-trained commander of the Second Paratroop Battalion, seized control of Vientiane while virtually the entire government was at the royal capital, Luang Prabang.

Phoumi immediately fled to Bangkok. Within a few days, Souvanna Phouma, the neutralist leader, had once again become Prime Minister with Kong Le's support.[41] Phoumi's American-sponsored attempt to create a pro-American government had united the Pathet Lao and Laotian neutralists.

American Ambassador Winthrop Brown, who had replaced Horace Smith in June, soon proposed that the United States accept Souvanna as Prime Minister and work for a reconciliation between him and Phoumi. Washington agencies, however—especially the CIA and the Pentagon—took an entirely different line. On August 18 CIA Director Allen Dulles told the NSC that, given Souvanna's earlier dealings with the Pathet Lao, "it was his personal view that this was the first step of a possible Communist takeover of Laos." On August 19 the Joint Chiefs recommended assistance, including airlift, to help Phoumi regain control of the government, and the next day Chief of Naval Operations Admiral Arleigh Burke—a staunch and aggressive anti-Communist and a veteran of the Korean truce talks—estimated that with even "a small detachment who is well trained and who is loyal to him," Phoumi "can win whatever fight may develop."[42]

The State Department took a middle position, suggesting talks between Souvanna and Phoumi, but also instructing Brown to warn Souvanna against a coalition including the Pathet Lao. Souvanna, however, explained to Brown on September 5 that he might have to open up relations with Peking and Hanoi, since the previous government had abandoned neutrality by exchanging embassies with Saigon and accepting a representative from Nationalist China. He also said that he would have to call new elections, since everyone knew the last ones had been rigged. A few days later Phoumi met Souvanna in Luang Prabang and agreed to become Deputy Prime Minister, but on September 10, after returning to Savannakhet on the Thai border, he told American representatives that he had made the deal only to get out of Luang Prabang safely. Now Prince Boun Oum, a right-wing politician, was about to proclaim a revolution and a new government.[43]

On September 15 Allen Dulles welcomed Boun Oum's new regime, which had declared martial law, and reported that Phoumi wanted immediate help. President Eisenhower "agreed that the U.S. should support Phoumi." The Joint Chiefs and CINCPAC Admiral Felt recommended that Phoumi be given immediate aid and encouraged to crush the Kong Le coup. Cooler heads temporarily prevailed, and the State and Defense Departments on September 16 instructed Ambassador Brown to ask the King—a pro-Western but not very powerful figure—to appoint yet another new government, including Phoumi and, possibly, Souvanna in a minor position. Brown replied that this would not work, and recommended working through Souvanna. But State, in reply, insisted that whatever his personal shortcomings, Phoumi was now our man.[44]

The political crisis continued during the next two weeks, and fighting broke out both between Pathet Lao and FAL forces and between Phoumi and Kong Le forces. On October 3 the Joint Chiefs, with State and Defense concurrence, authorized CINCPAC immediately to provide Phoumi with supplies and airlift. Brown, who had not been consulted, commented on October 5 that there was now "little or no chance" of salvaging even the southern part of the country by backing Phoumi in opposition to Souvanna, warned of intervention by Communist powers, and reported that his CIA chief and chief military representative agreed that the United States should support Souvanna. At an NSC meeting the next day, no one gave the slightest credence to these views. Repeating his usual mantras, Allen Dulles noted that Souvanna Phouma had indicated a willingness to negotiate with the Pathet Lao and "to resume diplomatic relations with the USSR," and that Phoumi might head off a "neutralist government leaning toward Communism."[45]

The King, however, still refused simply to dismiss Souvanna Phouma, and on October 8, after an interdepartmental meeting, Washington informed Brown that he should offer Souvanna U.S. support in exchange for certain conditions, including the end of talks with the Pathet Lao, while CINCPAC would begin supplying Phoumi's forces at Savannakhet. Meanwhile, Washington stopped aid to Souvanna, without which he could not pay units of the FAL loyal to him. Washington also decided to send Assistant Secretary of State for Far Eastern Affairs J. Graham Parsons, Assistant Secretary of Defense John Irwin, and Admiral Herbert Riley on a special fact-finding mission. By October 20 Washington had agreed to renew aid to Souvanna, while trying to stop his talks with the Pathet Lao. The U.S. government, however, was not presenting a unified front. On October 17 Irwin and Riley met with Phoumi and Prince Boun Oum at Savannakhet and told them that the

United States would support a march on Vientiane to recapture the Laotian government.[46]

Ambassador Brown now recommended forcing Phoumi to submit to Souvanna, but the Pentagon on October 28 convinced Parsons and Undersecretary of State for Political Affairs Livingston Merchant to abandon Souvanna. They wanted to bring enough members of the National Assembly from Vientiane to Luang Prabang to vote Souvanna out of office and replace him with Phoui Sananikone, the pro-American neutral whom Phoumi and his friends had ousted from power at the end of 1959. Brown fought this change in policy for two weeks, but on November 10 State laid down the law after another big interdepartmental meeting. "We have no faith whatsoever in Souvanna Phouma," said State's telegram, "and believe he is taking Laos rapidly down the road to PL take-over." They instructed Brown to begin planning the coup. Before he could do so, Phoumi's own forces seized Luang Prabang on November 10, forcing Souvanna to flee.[47]

Limiting American support to a handful of anti-Communist army officers, the Eisenhower administration had ignored Laotian political realities, disregarded the advice of its own embassy, and, now, presented Souvanna and the rest of Laotian neutrals with a choice between surrender and a coalition with the Pathet Lao. Souvanna chose the latter course, agreeing on November 20 with his half-brother, the Pathet Lao leader Prince Souphanouvong, to form a National Unity cabinet *excluding* Phoumi and Boun Oum. When that news reached Washington on November 21, Secretary of State Christian Herter immediately called President Eisenhower, who was in Augusta, Georgia, and told him he felt "we ought to take the wraps off Phoumi right away." "The Secretary mentioned paying the Phoumi troops directly and the President said he would tell the troops they would get one-half pay now and the rest when they 'licked the other fellow.' The other point was to provide Phoumi with CAT planes." CAT referred to Civil Air Transport, the American-manned airline and direct descendant of the Flying Tigers of the Second World War that flew missions for the CIA all over the Far East and later became Air America. Herter, essentially, was proposing American intervention in the Laotian civil war. "The President asked if it didn't appear that Phoumi was the nearest thing to representing a government. The Secretary said this was so, particularly since Souvanna Phouma was playing with the Pathet Lao. The President agreed to the points being included in the cable to Vientiane."[48]

In the eyes of the American President and Secretary of State, a government willing to talk to its own Communist citizens had now become, not merely impolitic or unacceptable, but illegal. American policy took no account of the actual situation the Laotians found themselves in, or, more critically, of the Communist powers' impressive capacity to respond in kind. Events now moved rapidly to create one of the more serious crises of the Cold War. On November 22 Souvanna demanded that the United States cease its direct aid to Phoumi, and the State Department, disregarding Brown's advice, refused to do so. On December 1 Allen Dulles reported that while Phoumi had begun moving forces toward Vientiane, Souvanna had dispatched subordinates to Hanoi and Peking. The Soviet ambassador to Cambodia had visited Souvanna in Laos promising oil and supplies, and five Soviet IL-14s— reportedly the same planes that had already supplied Lumumba in the Congolese civil war—had arrived in Hanoi, whence to fly into Laos. Meanwhile, CINCPAC, over Ambassador Brown's violent objections, received authority to supply Phoumi as it saw fit. On December 7 Brown bluntly warned that our policy was leading to a civil war in which the United States would support one side and virtually the whole world the other. Souvanna left Laos for Phnom Penh, the Cambodian capital; Quinim Pholsema, a reputed leftist who had visited Hanoi, remained in charge in Vientiane; and the State Department foresaw a showdown between Phoumi and the Pathet Lao.[49]

On December 12 American policy won an apparent victory as the King finally dismissed Souvanna and replaced him with Boun Oum. Two days later a Joint Chiefs–State Department meeting agreed to remove all restrictions on the use of CAT airlift for Phoumi's troops and equipment, and to consider the use of Thai forces if necessary. After the meeting General Andrew Goodpaster, Eisenhower's military aide, telephoned the President at Walter Reed Hospital, where he was undergoing a routine examination, to report, and to warn him that Thailand wanted a promise of American support should China or North Vietnam intervene.[50]

The President said that, in the situation described, he wanted to be as firm as we can be. He thought we should act vigorously, now that we have the cover of legality, in that we are responding to the request of a legally constituted government. He noted that we are committed through the SEATO pact to maintaining the security of the area of Laos, even though

Laos is not itself a member. He said he was completely in favor of the use of Thai transport aircraft, and U.S. aircraft as well.[51]

Eisenhower again suggested a bonus for Phoumi's troops.

With help from CAT and Thai planes, Phoumi's forces took Vientiane on December 18—Phoumi's first and, as it turned out, last great military victory. Two days earlier, on December 16, North Vietnam had warned that Thai intervention might force it to intervene in response.[52] The NSC discussed the situation again on December 20, and Allen Dulles "predicted a strong Communist reaction to recent events in Laos." The Soviets were air-dropping supplies to Kong Le's forces north of Vientiane, and perhaps building up the Pathet Lao forces as well. Soviet IL-14s were arriving in Hanoi, the Chinese Communists were airlifting supplies to Nanning near their Laotian border, and Hanoi was airlifting supplies to Dien Bien Phu. "Mr. Dulles believed that the Communists would do whatever was necessary to get rid of the anti-Communist regime in Laos," and that they might well set up an alternative government. Secretary of State Herter then raised an important but hitherto neglected point: that neither the French nor the British, whom he had just talked to in Paris, supported Phoumi.[53]

Emboldened by the initial success of the new proxy war, CINCPAC Admiral Felt on December 23 suggested supplying Phoumi with the air capability necessary to stop Communist supplies, beginning with ten T-6 aircraft then in Thai hands. The State and Defense Departments accepted this suggestion, as did Ambassador Brown, now loyally carrying out Washington's policy.[54] Politically, however, Laotian developments did not encourage Washington. Phoumi's forces had removed the Laotian treasury from Vientiane and threatened to expel the French military mission. Rumors suggested that Phoumi really wanted to partition Laos, leaving Thai influence supreme in the southern part of the country. Indeed, the Laotian National Assembly had not even given its approval to the Boun Oum/Phoumi government. Boun Oum, who had earlier declared the Assembly dissolved, did not want to ask it for a mandate.[55]

On the last day of 1960 General Lyman Lemnitzer, Chairman of the Joint Chiefs, reported on the situation to President Eisenhower, the acting secretaries of State and Defense, and Allen Dulles. Three Pathet Lao columns, he said, were on the march in the northern and central parts

of the country, including one coming from the North Vietnamese border. (Lemnitzer apparently lumped Kong Le's forces together with the
Pathet Lao.) No North Vietnamese forces had yet been identified, but
Eisenhower nonetheless commented, "we cannot afford to stand by
and allow Laos to fall to the Communists. The time may soon come
when we should employ the Seventh Fleet, with its force of Marines."
Lemnitzer confirmed that Naval, Marine, and Army forces had been
alerted. Merchant, however, stressed that "open [Communist] intervention must be proved before we can do much overtly," and focused
on the need to work within Laos, to legitimize the Boun Oum government, and to secure some international support. In fact, the French and
British ambassadors had made clear on December 23 that they did not
want to support the Boun Oum government at all in its present form,
and that they wanted to delay legitimizing it until it had broadened its
base.[56]

Eisenhower authorized some strategic reconnaissance, but withheld
permission for overflights of China. Lemnitzer then raised the issue of
stopping the Russian airlift, and Eisenhower authorized the use of B-26
planes in Thailand, apparently with third-country pilots.[57] After a brief
discussion, the President also agreed that if the Chinese shot down a
Thai aircraft, we would have the right to retaliate. Eisenhower then
"stressed the necessity to obtain identification of Viet-Minh or Chinese
forces, so definite as to convince not only us but also our allies . . . If
war is necessary, *we will do so with our allies or unilaterally,* since we
cannot sit by and see Laos go down without a fight . . . As the group
left, the President reemphasized that we must not allow Laos to fall to
the Communists, even if it involves war in which the U.S. acts with allies or unilaterally."[58]

The President's warlike statements, like the whole policy that had
created the new situation in Laos, closely reflected the basic national
security policies and policies toward Southeast Asia that he had approved during the previous five years. In further meetings on the situation on January 2, 3, and 5, 1961, however, Eisenhower and his subordinates encountered new problems, and the President began to show
some ambivalence. On January 2, after Secretary Herter reported that
the French opposed the U.S. position, Eisenhower remarked that "if it
weren't for the neighboring countries and the effect on them, we ought
to let Laos go down the drain." A moment later Herter asked Lem-

nitzer "what should be the political objective of operations in Laos in case we had to intervene," and Lemnitzer replied that U.S. forces would "hold the two main cities and leave the Laotians the protection of the countryside." But the President "said he held the conviction that if we ever resort to force, the thing to do is to clear up the problem completely. We should not allow a running sore like the British had in Egypt or the U.S. had in Korea." On January 3 the principals learned that the Thai government was still holding back and the British favored a peaceful settlement. Eisenhower remarked that "if the Communists establish a strong position in Laos, the West is finished in the whole southeast Asian area," but he agreed that peaceful options had to be explored.[59]

On January 5 Lemnitzer had to report to the NSC that limited operations in Southeast Asia would be very difficult and highly vulnerable because of wretched logistics and communications. "Even now," Eisenhower commented, "we did not know what we could do about Laos because of the attitude of our allies."[60]

During the next two weeks small-scale fighting proceeded slowly and inconclusively in Laos, while Western, neutral, and Communist powers all floated various diplomatic solutions to the crisis. On January 19 Eisenhower had a now-famous meeting with President-Elect John F. Kennedy and their senior foreign policy advisers.[61] The contradictions in various accounts of that meeting seem less significant in light of the documentation that has now been published on the previous weeks and months. Secretary Herter briefed Kennedy on the situation at some length, describing the emerging differences between the United States and Great Britain, which was working for a political settlement and refusing to recognize the Boun Oum government. In response to a direct question from Kennedy, Herter endorsed the idea of a new coalition government, provided that it did not include Communists. Eisenhower took the same line, referring specifically to "the example of the coalition with the Communists which was set up in China at the time General Marshall was sent there." Both said that, in the last analysis, SEATO intervention should be preferred to a coalition including the Communists, and seemed to indicate that unilateral intervention would be an appropriate last resort.

On the eve of his departure from office, Eisenhower was sticking to the broader policies of his administration since 1954—policies which had brought the United States close to intervention in the Laotian civil war. NSC statements of policy had foreseen unilateral American intervention, if necessary, to save Laos, Cambodia, or South Vietnam from Communism at least since 1955, and these statements had guided our military planning. The same statements had ordered the American government to encourage pro-Western elements and discourage neutralism—policies which, in Laos, had led directly to our support of Boun Oum and Phoumi, in opposition to our major European SEATO allies. And, as Kennedy found out within a few months, Eisenhower's military policies—also approved by the NSC—had led the military to plan intervention in Southeast Asia based upon the possible use of nuclear weapons to deal with various contingencies. We shall see that even four years later Eisenhower remembered those plans and continued to endorse them.

One cannot know exactly what Eisenhower would have done had he remained President. He was an intelligent and thoughtful man, and he may well have approved some plans which he would have hesitated to implement. Partly because he decided against intervening in Indochina in 1954, and largely because of his cool handling of various crises in other parts of the world, Eisenhower in recent decades has acquired the reputation of perhaps our most prudent Cold War President. Certainly this new reputation rests upon considerable evidence, and this is not the place, in any case, to reevaluate the entire foreign policy of the Eisenhower administration. Yet this survey of U.S. policy toward the new states of Indochina from 1955 through 1960 raises very serious questions about Eisenhower and his administration.

Eisenhower belonged to the Lost generation—born between 1883 and about 1901—which had a difficult path through life.[62] Growing up characterized as bad kids, they struggled through a difficult young adulthood—marked, in Eisenhower's case, by the need to pursue his military career in an era of shrinking forces—only to face the Depression and the Second World War in middle age. While this gave Eisenhower and his contemporaries a certain healthy skepticism, it also left them willing to face the most horrifying possibilities with relative equanimity, rather than to reevaluate the assumptions upon which they were based. Truman, Acheson, Eisenhower, and Dulles—all Lost—showed very little interest in easing tensions with the Soviet Union, or in creating a world in which nuclear weapons could be brought under control. Their successors from the GI generation—especially Kennedy, Nixon, and eventually even Reagan—were far more ambitious in their plans for a new, more peaceful future.

In essence, the policy statements developed and approved by Eisenhower's National Security Council had committed the United States to a series of extraordinarily militant and risky policies—policies which in Indochina took little account of political and military realities. Washington's exclusive support of heavily pro-Western elements alienated the United States from many neutralists who were in no sense Communists and who, indeed—as subsequent events later showed—could, with proper handling, become staunch American allies. And the government's endorsement of grandiose military objectives such as the defense of Laos and South Vietnam against aggression from North Vietnam—possibly supported by Communist China—led to military planning that called for nuclear weapons to fight limited, local wars. In January 1961 these rather frightening chickens suddenly flocked home to roost.

Historians may eventually conclude that the pendulum of Eisenhower's reputation has swung too far in one direction. They shall in any case have to resolve an apparent contradiction: that Eisenhower, who remarked more than once that the era of military power was over, nonetheless encouraged American military planners to rely heavily upon nuclear weapons in a variety of contingencies, and tried to make them available to America's allies as well.[63] They shall also have to deal with the anti-neutralist policies pursued by his two secretaries of state—policies which he certainly did little to discourage. With respect to Southeast Asia, another paradox emerges clearly. Eisenhower himself declined to fight a war there in 1954, but he approved war plans for the region just a year later, and his policies left his successor facing an immediate decision between war and peace.

Eisenhower clearly understood some of the critical dilemmas of the Cold War. The prospect of an endless, costly arms race troubled him deeply, and he continually worried about the conflict between American defense needs and economic health.[64] But his administration never pursued a diplomatic offensive that might have led to détente and a long-term reduction of tensions, instead putting nearly all its effort into political offensives and plans for war. One tantalizing explanation for Eisenhower's ambivalence has been suggested by George F. Kennan, whom Dulles fired from the State Department in the first few months of the Eisenhower administration, but who observed the new President closely while consulting on several critical issues:

> Dwight Eisenhower . . . was in fact, and remains in the light of history, one of the most enigmatic figures of American public life. Few Americans have ever had more liberally bestowed upon them the responsibility of command; and few have ever evinced a greater aversion to commanding. His view of the presidency resembled more closely the traditional pattern of the European head of state than that of his own country.
>
> He had the reputation—and I dare say it was correct—of never reading anything he could possibly avoid reading. His recreations, for which he always seemed to have ample time, were healthy ones but seldom reflected any serious intellectual preoccupations . . .
>
> For all these reasons, there was a tendency in some quarters to view Dwight Eisenhower as an intellectually and politically superficial person whom chance, and the traditional love of the American voter for the military uniform, had tossed to the apex of American political life. The impression was quite erroneous. He was actually a man of keen political intelligence and penetration, particularly when it came to foreign affairs. Whether he used this understanding effectively is another question; but he had it. When he spoke of such matters seriously and in a protected official circle, insights of a high order flashed out time after time through the curious military gobbledygook in which he was accustomed both to expressing and to concealing his thoughts. In grasp of world realities he was clearly head and shoulders (this required, admittedly, no very great elevation) above the other members of his cabinet and official circle, with the possible exception of Foster Dulles, and even here he was in no wise inferior.
>
> Dwight Eisenhower's difficulties lay not in the absence of intellectual powers but in the unwillingness to employ them except on the rarest of occasions. Whether this curious combination of qualities—this reluctance to exert authority, this intellectual evasiveness, this dislike of discussing serious things except in the most formal governmental context, this tendency to seek refuge in the emptiest inanities of the popular sport—whether this came from laziness, from underestimation of himself, or from the concept he entertained of his proper role as President, I would not know. But it is my impression that he was a man who, given the high office he occupied, could have done a great deal more than he did.[65]

2

No War in Laos
January–June 1961

★

"Let the word go forth," John F. Kennedy declared in his inaugural address on January 20, 1961, ". . . to friend and foe alike, that the torch has been passed to a new generation of Americans, born in this century, tempered by war, disciplined by a hard and bitter peace, proud of our ancient heritage, and unwilling to witness or permit the slow undoing of those human rights to which this nation has always been committed." And indeed, Kennedy's cabinet and staff were composed almost entirely of members of what is coming to be called the "GI generation," born roughly between 1901 and 1924, and shaped by the critical decades of their youth.[1] Having fought the Second World War as soldiers, they looked forward to taking over the strategic direction of the Cold War. Kennedy himself had begun a calculated pursuit of the presidency immediately after the Second World War, in 1946, when he ran for Congress in metropolitan Boston. In November 1960 he had narrowly defeated another GI, Richard Nixon, despite Nixon's advantage of representing the incumbent party in an era of peace and prosperity.[2]

Kennedy's father, a highly successful businessman and a prominent member of the Roosevelt administration, had originally promoted his son's political career. Having failed himself to achieve high elected office, Joseph P. Kennedy had initially put his hopes in his oldest son, Joseph Jr., but Joe Jr. had died on a highly dangerous mission in Europe during the Second World War. His second son, Jack, had abandoned thoughts of an academic career and stepped into his brother's shoes after the war. Elected to the House in 1946 and the Senate in 1952, he emerged after 1956 as a leading presidential contender. He had traveled widely and spoken often on foreign policy, most notably in 1957, when a Senate speech expressing sympathy for the cause of the Algerian rebels had won worldwide attention, especially among emerging nations in the Third World. Kennedy had announced a sweeping domestic program during the 1960 campaign, but he certainly came into office more concerned with foreign than domestic affairs, and he immediately found himself facing crises on several fronts.

Although Kennedy was President for only three years, he remains the most compelling American political figure of the second half the twentieth century. The atmosphere of his presidency; his shocking and still hotly debated assassination; a steady stream of revelations about his personal life; an apparently inexhaustible market for fantastic rumors about his life, his death, and his career; and the subsequent lives of his brothers, his widow, his children, and his nieces and nephews have all kept his mystery alive, but they have also obscured the man, and the President, that he actually was. Only in the last ten years has the release of extensive documentation enabled us to follow his foreign policy in detail.[3] The picture that emerges is far more complex than the image most older Americans remember. On the one hand, Kennedy, as many observers immediately understood, wanted great things both for himself and for his country. On the other hand, he was a brilliant natural diplomat who enjoyed the details of foreign policy and who was frequently more sensitive to the dangers of rash action than the contemporaries he chose as his leading subordinates. Nowhere was this difference more apparent than with respect to Southeast Asia.

During the first four months of the Kennedy administration the Laotian crisis competed for center stage with the crisis in the Congo, where Premier Patrice Lumumba's death was announced on February 13, and the worsening confrontation with Cuba, which climaxed in the disastrous invasion at the Bay of Pigs in the third week of April. Meanwhile, Yuri Gagarin made the first orbital flight around the Earth; French generals in Algeria tried and failed to overthrow Charles de Gaulle; freedom riders were beaten in Alabama; and the United States, the Soviet Union, and Britain failed to make any progress on a nuclear test ban. Despite an initial flurry of interest, Vietnam remained a relatively minor issue throughout this period and rarely intruded upon the horizon of the American public, but Laos brought the nation to the brink of war and raised critical issues about American goals and strategies in Southeast Asia.

Publicly the climax of the Laotian affair occurred at Kennedy's televised press conference on March 23. The President dramatically threatened SEATO intervention in Laos and detailed the extent of Communist advances with the help of three maps. But in May the parties in Laos agreed to a cease-fire, and a fourteen-nation Geneva Conference reconvened under the co-chairmanship of Britain and the Soviet Union to discuss the situation. In early June in Vienna, Kennedy and Soviet Premier Khrushchev agreed in principle on the restoration of a neutral Laos—the only agreement they managed to reach during their stormy meeting. Meanwhile, the President had successfully shifted the emphasis of American policy from the defense of the Boun Oum government—politically and diplomatically if possible, and militarily if necessary—to the pursuit of a negotiated solution and a new government. The new policy reflected his approach to most of his pressing international problems, an approach which much some of his senior aides and much of the bureaucracy did not share.

Kennedy took office with the intention of changing both the style and the direction of many of Eisenhower's foreign policies. During his first few weeks in office he fundamentally changed the structure of foreign policy making. Influenced partly by Robert Lovett, formerly President Truman's Secretary of Defense, the Kennedy administration quickly abolished the National Security Council Planning Board, which had written the Eisenhower administration's statements of national security policy, and the Operations Coordinating Board, which had supervised the implementation of those policies. Kennedy and his National Security Adviser, McGeorge Bundy, evidently decided that this machinery had grown too cumbersome. Rather than relying on broad policy statements, the Kennedy administration began by appointing ad hoc task forces to deal with specific crises. Literally in its first few days in office, it created four interagency task forces to address the crises in Laos, Cuba, the Congo, and Vietnam.

More significantly, as we shall see, Kennedy did not want to be bound by the kinds of statements of policy that the Eisenhower administration had turned out. Indeed, it would have been extremely difficult to make the changes that he made in policy toward Laos within the framework of existing policy documents. Substantively, Kennedy used the Laos crisis to show that his administration, unlike Eisenhower's, understood and supported genuine neutralism—a theme he had already sounded in foreign policy speeches as a senator. To do so, however, the new President had to halt the enormous bureaucratic momentum which his predecessor had set in motion, and to impose, gently but firmly, a new set of priorities upon the bureaucracy and the senior leadership that he himself had appointed. With respect to Laos, it took about five months to bring the government around to his views.

The Laos Task Force, headed by Assistant Secretary of State for Far Eastern Affairs J. Graham Parsons, included Deputy National Security Adviser Walt Rostow, who had assumed White House responsibility for Southeast Asia; Paul Nitze, the Assistant Secretary of Defense for International Security Affairs; and a representative of the International Cooperation Administration, soon to be renamed the Agency for Intentional Development. After a busy weekend, the task force presented its findings to a high-level meeting on Monday, January 23—findings which did not essentially differ from Eisenhower administration policy. While noting the critical problems that military intervention would face—the possibility of Communist retaliation, led by the North Vietnamese, and the lack of allied support within SEATO—it counted on either increased military aid or military action to achieve American objectives. It firmly supported the King, the Boun Oum government, and Marshal Phoumi Nosavan's forces, and seemed to assume that Souvanna Phouma and Kong Le had formed a firm alliance with the Pathet Lao. Recommending an increase in aid to the government forces, it also listed a variety of American military actions, including full-scale military intervention, which might enable the Boun Oum government to reestablish its authority. At some point, it foresaw a warning to the Soviets to cease their airlift, coupled with a plan for a political settlement and a neutral Laos.

The meetings of January 23 and January 25 showed Kennedy to be a skeptic regarding military intervention, although he as yet had no alternative policy to propose. When in the first meeting Secretary of State Dean Rusk proposed trying to create a SEATO force to block the Communist threat, the President took a more pessimistic line, noting "the unsatisfactory military situation, the geographic propinquity of Laos to the Communist bloc and the unsatisfactory internal and international situation," and adding that he did not see how the United States could save the situation unless one or more of these problems could be solved. Two days later he told the Joint Chiefs of Staff (JCS) that "he regarded the step of committing American troops as the last step to be employed," and asked for a memorandum describing how many forces we could put in Laos within thirty days, and how quickly the Viet Minh—the North Vietnamese army—might respond. Not satisfied with JCS Chairman General Lyman Lemnitzer's reply that the United States could interdict enemy supply lines, Kennedy on February 6 repeated his request, and Lemnitzer finally submitted a memo on February 16 reporting that the North Vietnamese could introduce 110,000 men and the Chinese about 50,000 within thirty days.[4] And on the same day, in his very first press conference, Kennedy stated in response to an apparently inspired question that the United States wanted to establish in Laos "a peaceful country—an independent country not dominated by either side but concerned with the life of the people within the country."[5]

A week later, Kennedy listened carefully to a lengthy first-hand report on the situation from Ambassador Winthrop Brown, who had returned from Laos for consultation. Kennedy, who always wanted to hear about crises from the men on the spot, began their hour-long conversation by asking Brown about the morale of the Laotian army. Brown replied rather pessimistically that the army was plagued by factionalism and a shortage of first-class officers, and that he did not think the United States could find a satisfactory solution to the problem with purely military means. Asked what should be done, Brown endorsed State Department plans for a commission of neutrals that would arrange a cease-fire and certify Laotian neutrality—an idea, he said, which might end the split between the United States on the one hand and the British and French on the other. He explained that the British and the French regarded the neutralist Souvanna Phouma as the only hope for unifying the country, and that the British would not object to Pathet Lao participation in the government. Kennedy, in reply, expressed concern over our differences with London and Paris, and repeated his reservations regarding the military situation. Endorsing the idea of a neutral commission and a possible political settlement, he asked whether the Communists would be likely to agree. Brown replied that the SEATO military measures now under consideration—including the dispatch of an American unit to Thailand—might have a bad effect upon Communist, allied, and neutral opinion.

Kennedy concluded by asking for Brown's opinion of Souvanna, Phoumi, and Boun Oum. Brown described Souvanna as a sincere and patriotic anti-Communist, but suggested that he might view Sou-phanouvong and the Pathet Lao too naively. He described Phoumi as "ambitious, unscrupulous, hard-driving, egotistical, moody, proud, a fast-talker but a slow thinker who was nonetheless intelligent," and Boun Oum as a "Lao Falstaff" and a "figurehead" in the government—characterizations most unlikely to inspire confidence.[6]

Kennedy, the British philosopher Sir Isaiah Berlin remarked several years later, "listened with extreme intentness . . . I've never known a man who listened to every single word that one uttered more atten-tively. And he replied always very relevantly. He didn't obviously have ideas in his own mind which he wanted to expound, or for which he simply used one's own talk as an occasion, as a sort of launching pad. He really listened to what one said and answered *that*."[7] Kennedy obvi-ously drank in Brown's report, and it helped move him toward a mid-dle position of trying to strengthen Phoumi's bargaining position while making overtures for a peaceful settlement. On February 8, in another meeting of senior officials at the White House, the President expressed opposition to moving any troops into Thailand, but approved an air-lift of military supplies and a mission of seventy-two American mili-tary trainers to counter the Soviet airlift and support Phoumi's new offensive into the Plain of Jarres. But the offensive was designed to strengthen the government's bargaining position, and Washington also decided to approach Moscow and ask for help in arranging a peaceful settlement and in persuading Souvanna to join the Boun Oum govern-ment.[8]

These steps, however, did nothing to reverse the situation. Rusk gave Soviet Ambassador Menshikov the American proposal for a commis-sion of neutral nations on February 20, and eight days later Menshikov simply restated the Soviet position that Souvanna was the legitimate head of the Laotian government, and called once again for a fourteen-nation conference in Geneva.[9] On the same day Walt Rostow reported to Kennedy that Phoumi's offensive had stalled, although Rostow re-mained hopeful about the future.[10] And the next day Rusk reported to Kennedy that only Malaya among the three chosen nations had ac-cepted the Laotian King's invitation to serve on the commission.[11] On March 1 Admiral Felt cabled from CINCPAC, "It needs to be repeated again and again that the only way to save Laos now is by successful military action."[12]

When Admiral Felt returned to Washington and briefed the President and senior officials on March 9, Kennedy once again stressed the problems of existing American policy. He ordered an approach to French President de Gaulle to try to coordinate Franco-American policy, and asked several skeptical questions about another planned Laotian government offensive and the state of Phoumi's forces. He also quoted from Lemnitzer's memo estimating that the North Vietnamese and Chinese had fifteen and eight divisions, respectively, within easy reach of Laos. When a State Department representative mentioned the possibility of a fourteen-nation conference, Kennedy asked for the list of the fourteen nations—Laos, Russia, Britain, France, Communist China, North Vietnam, Cambodia, South Vietnam, Thailand, Burma, India, Canada, Poland, and the United States. He remarked "that it looked like all were in favor of Souvanna except us, and perhaps Thailand and South Vietnam, and that this did not look like a very good lineup. He also said that perhaps the first item on the agenda with this lineup would be to cuss out the U.S." Later he identified allied support for Souvanna—in opposition to the United States—as a critical problem. But Defense Secretary McNamara continued to defend new military steps, and when the President asked if anyone at the table disagreed with him, no one spoke up. Policy remained on track, and the President approved additional preparatory military measures.[13]

The President's increasing interest in a negotiated settlement made no impression upon Secretary of State Dean Rusk. Rusk, who had served as Assistant Secretary of State for Far Eastern Affairs during the Korean War and consistently took a hard line toward Asian Communism, had been a safe, consensus choice for his position, and essentially favored the Dulles policy of backing firmly pro-American elements against both Communists and neutralists and resisting talks with Communist powers. Moscow gave Washington a promising signal on March 10, when Ambassador Llewellyn Thompson had an interesting exchange on Laos in Moscow with a well-briefed Nikita Khrushchev. Khrushchev praised Kennedy's support for Laotian neutrality as a change and a step forward, but rejected the commission of neutral nations and dismissed Boun Oum as "a drunkard and a libertine." He spoke strongly on behalf of Souvanna, whom he compared to Prince Sihanouk of Cambodia and Indian Prime Minister Nehru. On the same day Phoumi and Souvanna met in Cambodia. They agreed in principle on a neutral Laos, but failed to agree on the calling of an immediate conference. But Rusk, chairing a meeting on March 12, simply accused Khrushchev stalling to help a new Pathet Lao offensive, which the *New York Times* had reported during the previous two days. Rusk specifically called for new plans, including intervention by Asian ground forces and, if necessary, by American forces. His view remained the same after a long talk with Soviet Foreign Minister Gromyko on March 18.[14] *New York Times* stories on March 18 and 19, quoting American sources, said that Rusk and Kennedy backed the Laotian government "to the hilt" and were looking for ways to stop the Communist offensive, including "even more forceful action."

Existing policy was pushing the United States toward military intervention, and on Monday, March 20, the President learned exactly what that might mean. Deputy National Security Adviser Walt Rostow proposed using a small American force to seize the Mekong River Valley towns on Laos's western border as a bargaining chip. The Joint Chiefs, in reply, rejected any small force, arguing that any commitment had to include perhaps 60,000 men, air power, and, if necessary, nuclear weapons to save American forces should their airhead be surrounded. The Chiefs had thoroughly absorbed the Eisenhower-Dulles doctrine of treating nuclear weapons as conventional weapons, but the President was apparently appalled.[15] Although the meeting reached no decision, Rostow told Wallace Carroll of the *New York Times* that the administration had "resolved to face all the risks of a test of wills with the Soviet Union rather than let Laos fall under Communist control . . . [Kennedy] is now represented as determined to take whatever steps are necessary to save Laos from Communist domination and accept whatever risks are involved in such a policy." The story led the *Times* the next morning.[16] On the same morning, in preparation for another meeting, Rostow wrote the President a note suggesting that the United States immediately move all necessary troops into Thailand, whence they might go into Laos as needed.[17]

But despite Rostow's bellicose words, Kennedy definitely began the slow process of crafting a new policy and securing allied, press, and congressional support for it—all, ironically, without fundamentally changing the views of most of his senior foreign policy team. An afternoon meeting of March 21 ended with agreement to move forward on two opposite fronts. On the one hand, the government decided to press the British to agree to station a SEATO force in Thailand, as Rostow had suggested, and to go forward with new military aid to Phoumi. In the Pacific, Admiral Felt raised the readiness of an American Joint Task Force to just below the stage of imminent intervention.[18] But those at the meeting also agreed to tell the Soviets that if the Pathet Lao stopped its offensive and created a de facto cease-fire, the United States would accept a Soviet-British invitation to a fourteen-nation conference—a very important concession. On March 23 Kennedy himself made a strong statement in a televised press conference. Showing the extent of recent Pathet Lao gains in a series of maps and detailing the scale of the Soviet airlift since December 13, he referred to the involvement of North Vietnamese combat specialists and demanded a cessation of "the present armed attacks by externally supported Communists." A SEATO conference beginning in four days in Bangkok, he said, would "carefully consider" the necessary response if these attacks did not stop. But he also stated that "if in the past there has been any possible ground for misunderstanding of our desire for a truly neutral Laos, there should be none now," and supported the British proposal for a cease-fire and negotiations. The next day, in New Delhi, Ambassador-at-Large Averell Harriman explained the new policy to Nehru, who promised to help, and former President Eisenhower publicly supported Kennedy.[19]

Kennedy's statement lent itself to varying interpretations. *Time,* always ready to sound the Cold War alarm, especially in Asia, referred in its lead article to an emerging "contest of wills" between Kennedy and Khrushchev, saw an implicit warning of readiness to fight, and enthusiastically listed the military units available to rush into Laos, including large contingents expected from Thailand, South Vietnam, the Philippines, Pakistan, and even Cambodia.[20] But the *New York Times* put a decidedly cautious, diplomatic slant on Kennedy's statement. The main news story on March 24 noted that his emphasis on neutrality clearly distinguished his policy from his predecessor's, and also pointed out that Britain, France, and New Zealand all seemed unenthusiastic about SEATO intervention. Arthur Krock, a venerable columnist with long-standing ties to the Kennedy family, argued that the United States should never have extended the policy of the Truman Doctrine to Laos, which was neither vital nor defensible, and suggested that the Eisenhower administration had brought about the crisis by undermining Souvanna Phouma. And Krock's fellow columnist, Kennedy's contemporary James Reston, offered the clearest clues to the President's thinking. Kennedy, he stressed, was seeking a compromise, but geography usually decided the outcome of Cold War skirmishes around the world. "The Communists may influence Cuba," he wrote, "but they cannot hold it. We may by bold maneuvers influence events in Laos and even save its independence for a while, but the odds are against us."[21] About two weeks later, on April 5, Reston made the same comparison again.[22]

Three days after his press conference, on Sunday, March 26, Kennedy flew to Key West, Florida, to meet with British Prime Minister Macmillan for the first time. The two men received a full Pentagon briefing on SEATO Plan 5, the planned operation to seize the Mekong River towns. Macmillan bluntly warned the President against such an operation, and recorded happily that Kennedy "was evidently in control of the Pentagon, not the other way around," and that he "did *not* want to go it alone."[23] The next morning's papers reported that the two men agreed on the need for a cease-fire, a revived International Control Commission (ICC), and a conference—a major shift in the American position.

Meanwhile, at a SEATO meeting in Bangkok, Dean Rusk was seeking a firm commitment from all the SEATO allies to act in support of the Laotian government, although he recognized early on March 27 that France would almost surely refuse.[24] Stories out of Bangkok took a strong and optimistic line, suggesting that even the French would support military action, if need be,[25] and Rusk's own draft resolution, cabled to Washington on March 27, stated that the SEATO Council "has noted with grave concern the continued offensive of rebel elements in Laos who are continuing to be supplied and assisted by Communist Powers in flagrant disregard of the Geneva Agreements." But on the same day Kennedy saw Gromyko in Washington, and Gromyko described the pending British proposal as "a basis for pacific settlement acceptable to both sides," and stressed the need for both U.S. and Soviet restraint. Kennedy used this opening to shift his own government's policy, but without highlighting his differences with his own Secretary of State. He now cabled Rusk that he was more hopeful of achieving a settlement, and asked for a SEATO resolution "strong enough to hold

SEATO together but not so strong as to seem to challenge the Soviets immediately after my conversation with Gromyko." He amended Rusk's draft as follows:

> The SEATO Council declares the firm resolve of member countries of SEATO not to acquiesce in any takeover of Laos by an armed minority supported from outside. The Council notes with approval the present efforts for a cessation of hostilities to be followed by peaceful negotiations, and it believes that this proposal offers a sound basis for progress toward a neutral and independent Laos. But if these efforts fail and there continues to be an active military attempt to conquer Laos, members of SEATO will be prepared to take whatever action may be appropriate in the circumstances.

In closing, Kennedy suggested that Rusk offer a clear commitment of support to Marshal Sarit of Thailand and argue that American firmness had contributed to Gromyko's cooperative attitude. The resolution adopted used his suggested language.[26] The next day Arthur Krock of the *New York Times* reported that senior State Department officials were disappointed by the Bangkok resolution, but noted that it conformed to Kennedy's public statements. He also recalled what Kennedy had said about Indochina in 1954: "Without the whole support of the people, without a reliable and crusading native army with a dependable officer corps, a military victory, even with American support, is difficult if not impossible."

During the next few weeks Kennedy continued to redefine American policy along diplomatic, pro-neutralist lines, in the face of a stream of hard-line proposals from State, Defense, the Joint Chiefs, and the National Security Council (NSC) staff. When both National Security Adviser McGeorge Bundy and Dean Rusk expressed grave reservations about Souvanna Phouma during the first week in April, Kennedy once again noted that London, Paris, and the Communist states supported him, and asked the British Foreign Secretary, Lord Home, to extend an invitation to Souvanna to visit Washington.[27] Determined to get the change in policy into the public domain, Kennedy went to the State Department on April 6 and gave a press backgrounder himself. The problem, he said, was that the Royal Laotian government "has not maintained the fighting with the vigor we might have hoped. We have given supplies and training yet they have not either maintained or improved their position . . . If the government collapses and the United States intervenes, we are subject to intervention by the Viet Minh and possibly by Red China. The geography is difficult. The French had 400,000 men and could not hold. I was in Hanoi in 1951 and saw for myself." The next day, speaking to *Washington Post* correspondent Chalmers Roberts at the White House, he argued that "to get a coalition government would not be a bad outcome. After all, he said, there had been Pathet Lao in the government before and you, the press ought to point that out." On both occasions, however, Kennedy said the United States would intervene if necessary to prevent a complete collapse.[28] The *Times* of April 8 reported that Souvanna would be "a key player, though not necessarily the first minister." And on April 10 Souvanna, in Paris, accepted an invitation to come to the United States.

The Pathet Lao, however, continued their advance, and the Washington bureaucracy continued to propose intervention. The Laos Task Force met on April 13, and Rostow, its NSC representative, immediately wrote Kennedy a memo arguing that the Soviets and the Pathet Lao were trying to delay the cease-fire until the Western position had collapsed, and recommending the implementation of SEATO Plan 5—the plan to occupy the river towns—at once, even if the British refused to go along. Kennedy compromised at a top-level meeting that evening, authorizing the use of new aircraft in Laos, an increase in military aid, and the use of two Thai artillery batteries should the Soviets fail to agree on the cease-fire by April 15, and the immediate transformation of the American Program Evaluation Office into an overt military mission. The Soviets replied to the British on April 16 expressing broad agreement on a cease-fire and a conference, but haggling over certain critical points of timing continued for several days.[29] Meanwhile, plans for Cuban exile action against Castro dominated the front page of the *New York Times*, and Kennedy specifically stated on April 12 that the United States would not use force to overthrow Castro. On the day before, Yuri Gagarin had made the first manned orbit around the Earth.

During the second half of April the Bay of Pigs landing failed disastrously, and recriminations among the White House, the Central Intelligence Agency, and the Joint Chiefs began leaking into the press. Meanwhile, officials in Washington and eventually even Ambassador

Brown in Vientiane began to panic as the Pathet Lao continued their advance despite a joint Anglo-Soviet call for a cease-fire on April 24.[30] But when the President read Ambassador Brown's desperate telegram to a meeting of senior officials on the afternoon of April 26, a new consensus emerged. "In assessing the possible character of a large-scale involvement in Laos," McGeorge Bundy's minutes read, "the President was confronted with general agreement among his advisers that such a conflict would be unjustified, even if the loss of Laos must be accepted. As to whether an intervention in Vientiane would provoke strong military response, there was some uncertainty, but on balance it seemed wise to avoid a test if possible." Because the threat of intervention was "the only card left to be played in pressing for a cease-fire," however, the President refused to decide against it as yet. Instead, the government sent messages to the British and French and prepared for an appeal to the United Nations. Meanwhile, Kennedy asked McNamara to prepare plans to put American troops in Thailand and South Vietnam should Laos fall.[31]

The NSC met briefly the next morning, and agreed to brief the congressional leadership on the situation. The meeting that followed included the President, McNamara, Undersecretary of State Chester Bowles, and the Joint Chiefs, led this time by Admiral Arleigh Burke; Majority Leader Mike Mansfield of Montana, Minority Leader Everett Dirksen of Illinois, Majority Whip Hubert Humphrey of Minnesota, Foreign Relations Committee Chairman J. William Fulbright of Arkansas, Georgia Democrat Richard Russell, New Hampshire Republican Styles Bridges, Iowa Republican Bourke Hickenlooper, and Massachusetts Republican Leverett Saltonstall from the Senate; and House Speaker Sam Rayburn. Kennedy began by reading Ambassador Brown's telegram once again, and Bowles reported on U.S. efforts to secure a cease-fire. McNamara indicated that 11,000 Americans could land in Laos within a week, but added—echoing Eisenhower administration policy—"that it was the opinion of the Joint Chiefs of Staff that if United States forces became engaged in Laos and the North Vietnamese or Chinese Communists came to the support of the Pathet Lao we would not be able to win by conventional weapons alone." The President continued that virtually all of Laos might imminently fall, and that the British and the French appeared unwilling to act unless Vientiane fell. He also repeated what Lemnitzer had told him earlier in the year, that "the Communists could put into Laos five men to our one." Bowles added that the Chinese had "flatly stated that they would enter Laos if we did so."

The congressional leadership unanimously rejected intervention. After a long pause, Mansfield—a careful student of Asian affairs—said that after thinking about Laos for a long time, he felt "that the worst possible mistake we could make would be to intervene there." Both Fulbright and Humphrey agreed. When Kennedy asked what we should do, Admiral Burke acknowledged that intervention would probably mean war with China and campaigns in North Vietnam and China, apparently with nuclear weapons, but argued in response to questions from Saltonstall and Bridges that "we must hold Laos or face the loss of Southeast Asia," including Thailand and perhaps South Vietnam. Kennedy himself later said that the United States might have to move troops into Thailand and South Vietnam to shore them up, and General Lionel McGarr, the senior American military adviser in South Vietnam, briefly discussed the situation there (see Chapter 3).

Kennedy then gave the floor to Deputy Undersecretary of State U. Alexis Johnson, who argued that Thai morale might easily collapse "if SEATO and the U.S. together are not able to handle the Laotian situation." Mansfield once again argued that intervention in Laos would raise the possibility of using atomic weapons, and that "the whole thing would be a rather fruitless operation." He even blamed our own airlift for the failure to reach a cease-fire. Dirksen also questioned our ability to defend Laos, and added that "the situation in South Vietnam would be very difficult even if we could hold Laos . . . We would be fighting a war 11,000 miles from home and when we got through we would have nothing to show for it." He remained unmoved when Admiral Burke asked where, in any event, we would fight. Bridges agreed that while we might have to take a firm stand somewhere, "this should not be where we dissipate our resources, endanger our other capabilities, and where people won't fight for themselves." Saltonstall remarked that Burke's discussion "had convinced him that it would not be useful to send troops into Laos." And Russell, the leader of the Southern Democratic bloc, commented "that Laos was an incredible fantasy from the beginning. We should fight the first time and place where we have a commitment and an ally willing to fight for itself . . . his view was that we should get our people out of Laos and write the country off." If Admiral Burke thought that Thailand and South Vietnam would fight, he added, "we should put our troops in those countries and take our stand there." Kennedy agreed that we might put troops into Thailand.

When Bridges asked whether we might blockade Cuba, Kennedy replied that the Soviets might retaliate by blockading Berlin. "It had been estimated by the JCS," he added, "that an invasion of Cuba would take 60 to 90 days to mobilize and prepare the necessary force. This all pointed to the necessity of our being better prepared, with emphasis on conventional warfare," and on the need "to handle the weak countries threatened with covert means." Speaker Rayburn questioned whether Laos was worth such a large war; Humphrey discussed possible further difficulties and suggested neutralizing all Indochina, including South Vietnam; and Hickenlooper, while favoring a stand in Thailand and South Vietnam, argued "that it appeared we had lost Laos," which "was no place to fight a war." Concluding, the President stressed the need to keep the meeting confidential, since "the only card we really had in the situation was the threat of U.S. intervention and the uncertainty of the other side in this regard."[32]

In retrospect, this critical meeting revealed a large and highly significant gap within the American political and military leadership. On one side, the Joint Chiefs had become thoroughly accustomed, under Eisenhower, to the idea of intervention in remote areas backed by nuclear weapons, and the loyal organization men who ran the civilian bureaucracies, including McNamara of Ford Motor Company, the absent Rusk from the Rockefeller Foundation, U. Alexis Johnson the career Foreign Service officer, McGeorge Bundy of Harvard, and Rostow from MIT, all seemed to favor a firm response to any Communist moves. These civilians were all from the GI generation, and to varying degrees they saw themselves as continuing the struggle against aggression and tyranny that had dominated their youth. But most of the congressional leadership came from the earlier Lost generation, which had grown up before the United States had begun trying to control developments on every continent, and which had remained skeptical about the need to deploy American forces in remote regions, partly because of the cost involved.[33] And while Kennedy was in some ways the archetypal GI, he was a politician, not a bureaucrat, to the depths of his being. Having been elected to the Senate in the latter stages of the

Korean War, he understood how little the country shared his government's interest in Southeast Asia.

It still took eight more days, however—until May 5—for the Laotian factions to agree upon a cease-fire, and despite the attitude of the congressional leadership, the President had to deal with almost daily proposals for intervention until then. The Joint Chiefs, with some support from Rusk, pushed hard for intervention on April 29, in a meeting attended by the President's brother Robert but not by the President himself, and the NSC met later that day. "In today's meeting of the National Security Council with the President," James Reston reported, "there were officials who, in their anger and frustration, were flirting with military moves which would transform the fiasco in Cuba into a disaster in Laos." But Kennedy, Reston said, "is not going to side with the jingoists who want him to smash into Cuba with the Marines or lunge into a war in the Laotian jungles, where geography and logistics greatly favor the limitless manpower of the Chinese Communists."[34]

Still, the message failed to get through to the President's men. On May 1 Ambassador-at-Large Harriman, on a special mission to Vientiane, reported a panic, and proposed that SEATO at least move troops into Thailand to provide a bargaining chip. On the same day Kennedy received a long memo from Rusk, drafted by U. Alexis Johnson, suggesting that the Laotian government be instructed to request a limited SEATO intervention, purely to stabilize the situation, should no cease-fire occur. More seriously, in an NSC meeting, Secretary of Defense McNamara reversed himself and advocated moving into the southern Laotian panhandle, "recognizing that if we do we must be prepared to win," presumably even if this required the use of nuclear weapons. Kennedy concluded by deciding to consult the British and French once again, and asked the Chiefs and other leading officials to provide individual opinions on intervention to him the next day.[35] McNamara and Roswell Gilpatric, his deputy, weighed in the next day, May 2, with a paper that provided two alternatives: a non-intervention course, including movement of troops into Thailand and South Vietnam should the talks fail, and an intervention course, moving U.S. troops into Laos to protect "a number of key communication and population centers," while readying ourselves to respond to enemy escalation. "After weighing the pros and cons set forth above," they concluded, "we favor 'Intervention Course,'" after setting a 48 hour deadline for a cease-fire." Of the Chiefs, General Lemnitzer, Admiral Burke, and General Decker of the Army essentially shared their view, while Air Force Chief of Staff Curtis LeMay wanted to prepare for all-out war with China. Only Marine Corps Commandant General David Shoup opposed intervention.[36]

Discussing these papers on May 2, Kennedy temporized again, asked for a new State-Defense paper, and shifted the discussion to the problem of reassuring Thailand of American support whatever happened in Laos.[37] The State-Defense paper—drafted jointly by Alexis Johnson of State and William Bundy, the Deputy Assistant Secretary of Defense for International Security Affairs—recommended intervention, if necessary with American forces alone, if a cease-fire was not reached, and accepted the risk of intervention by North Vietnam or China.[38]

The President never considered the paper, because events in Laos took a more favorable turn. The opposing factions initially agreed on a partial cease-fire, and Laotian talks to implement one began on Friday, May 5, clearing the way for the beginning of the Geneva conference one week later. And on the same day the President announced at a news conference that Vice President Johnson would undertake a "fact-finding mission" to allied capitals in Southeast Asia. In response to a question, Kennedy confirmed that Johnson would investigate at least the possibility of sending American troops to South Vietnam, and press stories stated that American troops might also go to Thailand.[39]

The President made a further attempt to redefine policy in a meeting with the *New York Times* columnist and old family friend Arthur Krock on May 5. Repeating that there was no alternative to a coalition in Laos, Kennedy said that General MacArthur "had prophesied to him that eventually [Southeast Asia] would go Communist by popular choice. But . . . whether or not that is true, our policy must be to avoid a positive, formal withdrawal and help protect the area as long as the governments and peoples want this."[40] On Sunday, May 7, James Reston, who probably saw Krock's notes, argued in the *New York Times* Week in Review that our commitments in Southeast Asia now went far beyond our capacity to meet them, and that President Kennedy knew that "it will probably be a long time, involving more embarrassments and defeats, before this policy can be brought into balance without war."

During the next six weeks Kennedy discussed Laos, among many other matters, with de Gaulle, Macmillan, and Khrushchev on his European trip, while continuing slowly to bring his own team around to his policy. Rusk himself attended the first week of sessions at the Geneva conference, from May 12 through May 19. His May 9 instructions, which Alexis Johnson drafted and Kennedy approved, reserved the American position on a new coalition government, specifically refused to accept Souvanna as Prime Minister, doubted that agreement would be reached, called for plans to secure southern Laos for the Boun Oum/Phoumi forces, and called for keeping military plans and preparations "in a high state of readiness" to deal with the situation should a cease-fire break down.[41] Kennedy tempered this line on May 11, however, insisting on the best possible understanding with the British and French, and thus implicitly pushing Rusk toward support for a coalition.[42] Faced with confident Communist adversaries and critical American allies and neutrals at Geneva, Rusk specifically rejected a three-party coalition and estimated that "an acceptable agreement will not result from this conference."[43] But Rusk now turned the talks over to Ambassador-at-Large Harriman—the only administration official, it turned out, who understood what Kennedy wanted.

On May 30 Kennedy met with French President Charles de Gaulle in Paris, and they discussed both Laos and South Vietnam at length. Determined to distinguish himself from his predecessor, Kennedy began by acknowledging that the United States found itself in a difficult situation in Laos because of past mistakes. De Gaulle recommended that Washington support Souvanna and accept the presence of some Communists in the government. Kennedy agreed that Souvanna "may be the best available solution"—a position well in advance of the Geneva delegation's instructions—but expressed the fear that the military situation might make him a captive of the Communists. De Gaulle replied that we might be able to reduce the Communist influence upon him.

"More generally speaking," de Gaulle continued, "Southeast Asia, and that applies to Laos, Vietnam, Cambodia, and even Thailand, is not a good terrain for the West to fight on. The best thing to do is to encourage neutralism in that area, the more so that the Soviets themselves do not have any strong desire to move in. They will, however, tend to follow every time the West moves in." Kennedy replied that he faced the problem of the possibly unwise SEATO commitments made by Eisenhower and Dulles. Simply to abandon the SEATO nations, he said, would have grave consequences in many countries. De Gaulle, citing France's experience, claimed to understand the difficulties, but added that France had preserved some influence in Indochina only after completely renouncing military action, "which seemed to the Asians to be equivalent to a desire to rule them." One could, he said, maintain Western influence by seeking neutrality, even a slightly marginal neutrality. One should neither make military commitments, he said, nor give too much money, which made governments corrupt and unpopular. "This is what is happening at the present moment in South Vietnam." Kennedy acknowledged that South Vietnam might collapse, but asked de Gaulle again to think of the consequences for other nations.

Turning to the Geneva conference, Kennedy repeated that Souvanna "may be the best choice," but raised the issue of the ICC and Soviet demands that it function unanimously. De Gaulle recommended returning to the original 1954 Geneva Accords, with an Indian as chairman of the ICC. When Kennedy asked what we should do if the Pathet Lao took over Laos, de Gaulle replied that France would not intervene, but would try to encourage Cambodia and Thailand. De Gaulle rejected the argument that only a threat of intervention could secure a ceasefire, but promised not to say so to the press. Later Kennedy mentioned that he had visited Saigon and Hanoi in 1951, "and he saw the scope of the French effort. France had a lot of troops and good troops in Indochina. He understands as a consequence that any intervention in that part of the free world [would] have to be a major operation." De Gaulle replied that "the worst thing that could happen to the West would be a military defeat." Summing up, he recommended returning to he Geneva Accords of 1954, and encouraging Souvanna, Sihanouk, and the King of Thailand—but not Ngo Dinh Diem.[44]

In preparation for his upcoming Vienna meeting with Khrushchev, Kennedy received a memorandum from Harriman. Harriman began by pointing out that new Pathet Lao attacks in the Pa Dong area, and their refusal to allow the ICC to investigate, were threatening the cease-fire, and that the Russian delegates were refusing to give the ICC new instructions. He proposed that Kennedy attempt to resolve the cease-fire issue directly with Khrushchev, and that the President try to define the "neutrality" that both sides claimed to want. It should, Harriman argued, call for the withdrawal of all foreign troops, including Viet Minh and Chinese Communists; a government run by sincere neutrals; adequate machinery for supervision; and, as an essential first step, new cease-fire instructions.[45]

To judge from his conversations with Khrushchev on June 3 and June 4, Kennedy took these suggestions to heart. His meeting with Khrushchev was designed to explore the possibilities for the resolution of disputes between the two Cold War rivals. Frustrated by the Bay of Pigs debacle, Kennedy went ahead with the meeting despite the lack of any progress on a nuclear test ban or any new proposal to make on Germany or Berlin, where Khrushchev had already begun making threats. The new President, it is clear, hoped both to establish a personal relationship with his Soviet counterpart and to begin reducing tensions around the world on the basis of a frank mutual recognition of interests, spheres of influence, and neutral zones. In the short run, this policy was doomed because of Khrushchev's own determination to go on the offensive on several fronts, especially in Berlin and with regard to Soviet nuclear armaments, but Kennedy stuck quite firmly to these goals throughout his tenure of office. At Vienna Laos was the only success that he scored.[46] The rest of the meeting was a very difficult experience for the new President and left him convinced that only firm action in Germany would persuade Khrushchev to abandon his plans.

Kennedy introduced the Laotian situation into the discussions, acknowledging once again that "US policy in that region had not always been wise." Attempting perhaps to be too sympathetic to his adversary, he noted that the Pathet Lao had the advantage of favoring change— the basis, he remarked, of his own election as President—and also received assistance from the Viet Minh. "The problem now from a historical standpoint," he continued, "is to find a solution not involving the prestige or the interests of our two countries." Both countries claimed to want a "neutral and independent" Laos, and he suggested Burma and Cambodia as examples of neutral and independent countries. Khrushchev agreed, but this represented roughly the limit of their agreement. The Premier denied that the North Vietnamese were involved in Laos; accused the United States of having started military action from Thailand; and insisted that the ICC could not become "a kind of supragovernment administering the country." The next day the President went further, saying that he was "anxious to get the US military out of Laos," and that he "had not supported, and had been even reluctant to consider a landing of Marines, because he recognized that such action would entail retaliation and counteraction and thus peace in that area might be endangered." Khrushchev continued to argue that, while the cease-fire was important, the three Laotian parties should in any case meet at once to form a truly neutral government.[47]

The two men spent the most critical portions of the meeting in bitter, frightening exchanges over the future of West Berlin, but the communiqué reaffirmed their agreement on the goals of an effective cease-fire and a neutral and independent Laos, and the President clearly regarded this as the meeting's one real success.[48] At a press conference on June 8 Kennedy commented that if the two countries could not agree on the faraway problem of Laos, it would be difficult to see what they could agree on.[49]

Meanwhile, in Geneva, public arguments over the powers of the ICC and the representation of the three Laotian factions had prevented any real progress. Pa Dong fell to the Communists on June 7, and the Western delegations briefly boycotted the talks, trying to force the Soviets to agree to new instructions for the ICC.[50] But no new major fighting broke out during the next few days, and meanwhile, on June 8, Harriman met with Souvanna for the first time. The Laotian prince made a generally good impression upon the veteran diplomat, vehemently expressing opposition to Communist control and requesting American help in getting Phoumi and Boun Oum to agree to a neutral government.[51] On June 12 reports from Geneva suggested that the three Laotian factions had agreed to meet in Zurich to discuss a new government, and on June 16 Harriman reported that the Pathet Lao seemed to have halted their offensive and suggested to Washington that the United States undertake more realistic diplomacy. "Having chosen the conference route," he argued, "we must accustom ourselves to accept less than perfect solutions to each of the problems as they arise unless we are prepared to turn back to the alternative of force." If the Zurich meeting did not produce a single Laotian delegation, he argued, the United States should persuade the Royal Laotian government to attend the conference together with the other two factions, even though Thailand and South Vietnam disagreed. The conference, he argued, could produce an advantageous result, "providing of course a reasonable balanced government of national unity is agreed to."[52] During the next week the three princes agreed to talks on a coalition government, strongly implied that Souvanna would become the Prime Minister, and renounced the protection of any military alliance, including SEATO.[53]

By the middle of June 1961 President Kennedy faced a tremendous new crisis over Berlin, stalled test ban negotiations, a big congressional battle over foreign aid, and continuing problems in the Congo and Cuba. The Laotian situation was hardly encouraging, but Kennedy had successfully and critically shifted American policy from political and military support of pro-American elements to a broad-based attempt to form a neutral government together with neutrals, allies, and, he hoped, the Soviets as well. He had done so not by flatly ruling out American military intervention in Laos—although he had given several revealing indications to journalists and foreign leaders that he viewed the prospect with the greatest distaste—but rather by taking advantage of diplomatic opportunities offered by other powers, especially the British, and avoiding rigid diplomatic positions. He had essentially finessed the beliefs of his Secretary of State, who favored a very different policy, and substituted his own military judgment for the Pentagon's. And in Averell Harriman he had found a diplomat who understood his goals and wanted to help achieve them.

The new Laotian policy, however, still faced considerable opposition within the government, and had repercussions elsewhere. The State and Defense Departments and the Joint Chiefs of Staff still fundamentally doubted that diplomacy could secure a satisfactory outcome in Laos, and the change in policy had sent a shock wave through several other Asian allied capitals—especially Saigon. Within a few more weeks the bureaucracy would be churning out proposals for intervention once again. And this time they would involve South Vietnam as well as Laos.

3

A New Effort in Vietnam
January–August 1961

★

In South Vietnam as in Laos, the Kennedy administration inherited a crisis from the Eisenhower administration, but one of a rather different nature. South Vietnam was larger, richer, and more accessible than Laos, and the United States had jumped into South Vietnamese politics with a vengeance in 1954, establishing the new regime of Ngo Dinh Diem. Diem seemingly provided what the Eisenhower administration sought, but never found, in Cambodia and Laos: a committed anti-Communist regime and a firm bulwark against Communist subversion. Because Diem's government faced no critical threats between 1955 and 1960, and because Washington took relatively little note of the guerrilla war against it that began to grow in strength after 1957, Vietnam engaged little of the attention of the National Security Council (NSC) in the late 1950s.

Within South Vietnam, however, the situation looked very different. Diem continually lost support among non-Communist Vietnamese during the late 1950s, as he relied more and more upon his family, his secret Can Lao Party, and his police forces to govern. Americans in Vietnam saw grave flaws in Diem's regime from the beginning, and their doubts increased as the years went by. Since Diem worked according to his own beliefs—beliefs which differed fundamentally from American democratic ideals—trust between him and his American patrons rapidly evaporated. Meanwhile, American military authorities made some highly questionable decisions regarding the organization and deployment of the South Vietnamese armed forces. Like the crisis in Laos, all these problems were coming to a head when John F. Kennedy replaced Eisenhower on January 20, 1961.[1]

After years of military aid to the French, the American involvement in Vietnam had begun in earnest in the spring of 1954, as Dien Bien Phu came under siege and fell and various powers prepared for the Geneva conference on Indochina. In June of that year the French-supported Emperor, Bao Dai, appointed Ngo Dinh Diem as Prime Minister of the State of Vietnam, the entity to which the French had granted theoretical but not practical independence in the latter stages of the Indochina War. Diem, a Catholic nationalist who had recently spent several years in the United States, probably won the post in recognition of the growing U.S. role in the region. Diem enjoyed the backing of Francis Cardinal Spellman of New York, and of Democratic Senator Mike Mansfield, a long-standing authority within Congress on Asia and Asian problems. His appointment turned the State of Vietnam away from France and toward the United States, which wanted to hold on to as much of Vietnam as possible and set up a regime parallel to the Federal Republic of Germany, the Republic of Korea, and Nationalist China.

Diem did not solidly establish himself in power for more than a year. The South Vietnamese political scene included two religious and political sects based in regions around Saigon, the Hoa Hao and the Cao Dai, as well as an urban sect, the Binh Xuyen, that ran gambling, prostitution, and the drug trade and enjoyed extraordinary influence over the police. It also included at least two nationalist political parties, known as the Dai Viet Party and the VNQDD. Diem struggled during late 1954 and early 1955 against an alliance of the sects and the French government, which retained a military mission and some influence in South Vietnam.

During the first half of 1955 General J. Lawton Collins, Eisenhower's choice as ambassador to Vietnam, lost faith in Diem, owing to the Prime Minister's repeated refusal to conciliate any of his non-Communist opposition. But Diem already had a following in Washington, and he had impressed Secretary of State John Foster Dulles in a face-to-face meeting in February. Closely advised by Colonel Edward Lansdale of the CIA, a veteran of anti-Communist counterinsurgency operations in the Philippines, Diem precipitated a clash with the Binh Xuyen in

Cholon, the Chinese suburb of Saigon, on April 28, just as Washington was preparing to abandon him. His support rallied around him, and he emerged from the crisis stronger than ever.[2]

Diem's relationship with his American patrons in subsequent years included elements of dependence, independence, and, crucially, co-dependence. Although Americans were careful never to say it in so many words, the South Vietnamese regime could never have existed in anything like its actual form without American aid. Having financed much of the French military effort in the final stages of the Vietnam War, the United States financed the South Vietnamese Army from the beginning. It furnished military equipment directly and financed South Vietnamese trade and budgetary expenditures simultaneously through the Commercial Import Program. Under that program, the United States provided dollars to the Saigon government, which auctioned them off for Vietnamese piasters to importers. The importers pur-chased foreign consumer goods—some, but not all, from the United States—and the government spent the piasters on its army and on certain nonmilitary items. American aid to Vietnam—nearly all of it grants—totaled $322.4 million in fiscal 1955 (July 1, 1954, to June 30, 1955), and increased for two years, peaking at $392.7 million in fiscal 1957. It fell drastically and remained at about $250 million per year for the next three years, and fell again to $215.5 million in fiscal 1961. These sums accounted for well over half of the annual South Viet-namese government budget. Only Nationalist China among Southeast Asian nations received comparable sums, and Thailand received be-tween one-fifth and one-tenth as much. Without continuing American aid, the South Vietnamese government would have ceased to exist.[3]

Despite his financial dependence, however, Diem never showed the slightest tendency to follow American advice. In response to never-end-ing pleas from a succession of American ambassadors that he broaden his government's base, he invariably replied that Vietnam was an un-derdeveloped country lacking in qualified personnel, and that the op-position had nothing to contribute but criticism. He and his brother Political Counselor Ngo Dinh Nhu became increasingly suspicious of American attitudes toward them—not without reason—and tried in many ways to limit the extent of American influence, or even of Ameri-can knowledge of events within the country. Nhu eventually expelled the Michigan State University Group, which had helped train Vietnamese police and security forces, because he believed—apparently with some reason—that it served partly as a CIA front.

Diem and Nhu professed their own political theory, personalism, which stressed the duties of the citizen to the state. The American Embassy reported that this philosophy—very loosely based upon certain strains of French Catholic thought from the 1930s, but also designed to use Confucianism to find a Middle Way between Western democracy and Communism—had little real following in the country. To govern, Diem, Nhu, and their brother Ngo Dinh Canh, the boss of the northern part of the country, relied almost entirely upon their family, their security forces, and the Can Lao Party, a secret organization of supporters that monopolized government contracts and taxed other forms of economic activity. In 1959, Ambassador Elbridge Durbrow, a veteran of the American Embassy in Moscow, reported bluntly that the Can Lao, "like the Kuomintang, has created an authoritarian organization largely modeled on Communist lines." By 1959, the party was trying to infiltrate the military, as well, and American observers agreed that it took a cut of every major economic transaction.[4]

Although these policies progressively alienated more and more educated South Vietnamese, they successfully established and maintained the regime's authority within the major urban areas. They enjoyed much less success in the countryside. A land reform program produced few results. During 1954–1955, Diem's Anti-Communist Denunciation Campaign harassed, jailed, and sometimes executed many Viet Minh activists, as well as many innocent bystanders, and drove the Viet Minh underground. The Communists eventually struck back, however, with an intimidation and assassination campaign of their own directed against government officials. In addition, the Communists successfully infiltrated many military units previously maintained by the Hoa Hao and Cao Dai sects, which had continued to operate independently despite the bribes Diem had paid to their leaders. During the war against the French, the Communists had built a very strong organization among many of the most heavily populated provinces of the Mekong Delta, both north and south of Saigon, and established two large secure areas of their own in remote regions: War Zone C, in Tay Ninh province along the Cambodian border, and War Zone D, in Phuoc Thanh province northeast of Saigon. The Diem government seems never to have established control over much of the Mekong Delta, and by 1957 the Communists—now known as the Viet Cong—were clearly increasing in strength, and were once again mounting major attacks.[5]

Meanwhile, the U.S. Military Assistance Advisory Group (MAAG) was helping organize and equip the South Vietnamese Army in ways that did very little to attack Communist strength in the countryside. The first two chiefs of the MAAG, Lieutenant General John O'Daniel and Lieutenant General Samuel T. Williams, tried to shape the South Vietnamese Army to deal with a conventional attack from North Vietnam, and refused to regard guerrilla warfare in the countryside as the Army's primary mission. Their views reflected mainstream American military doctrine. The American Army now regarded guerrillas as partisans, that is, irregular forces supporting enemy main force units, not as insurgents supporting themselves from the populations and struggling for political authority. They instinctively planned to deal with guerrillas by attacking the main force units that they believed the guerrillas needed for support.[6]

With American encouragement, the South Vietnamese Army was organized into seven divisions, most of them stationed near the northern and northwestern borders of South Vietnam, with a few based in the outskirts of Saigon. Diem consistently gave the latter troops the most loyal commanders, since they might either protect him or carry out a coup. Diem also assigned many forces to the command of local province chiefs, who in turn used them to guard provincial and district capitals—much to the despair of General Williams, who complained that these missions made it impossible for the South Vietnamese to undergo necessary training. Virtually none of the Army of the Republic of Vietnam (ARVN) occupied the heavily populated regions of the Mekong Delta north and south of Saigon, where the Communists were strongest.[7] In any case, formal American plans counted on the ARVN to provide only "initial resistance" to a Communist attack.

In theory, local village security was the responsibility of Self-Defense Corps, or armed local militiamen, and the Civil Guard, a more mobile force designed to patrol the countryside and come to the aid of villages under attack. By 1957 Diem wanted to transfer the Civil Guard from the authority of the Ministry of the Interior to the Ministry of Defense, and vastly improve its training and equipment. But American Embassy officials opposed this move, fearing that Diem wanted to build a private army, and pointing out that the transfer of authority would force the United States to fund the Civil Guard as well as the ARVN. The Embassy also opposed increased funding and equipment for the Self-Defense Corps, which were known to be heavily infiltrated by the Viet Cong.[8]

A series of minor crises struck South Vietnamese–American relations during 1959 and 1960. With the Eisenhower administration yielding to pressure to cut foreign aid, General Collins in 1959 returned to South Vietnam for a brief visit and suggested reducing the ARVN below 150,000 men—an idea Diem violently rejected. In July 1959, a series of articles in the Scripps-Howard newspapers charged waste and mismanagement of American aid, leading to two congressional visits to Saigon—visits which Diem deeply resented. In August 1959, Diem staged obviously rigged elections for the National Assembly, and when the only serious opposition candidate whom he allowed to run won a resounding victory in Saigon, the government trumped up charges of electoral fraud to prevent him from taking his seat. In late April 1960, eighteen prominent South Vietnamese figures issued the Caravelle Manifesto, attacking the nature of Diem's rule and calling for liberalization. According to an interview later given by Ambassador Durbrow, Diem's suspicions that Americans had contributed to the manifesto were correct.[9]

These crises coincided with a renewed Communist offensive. During the first half of 1959 the Central Committee of the Vietnamese Communist Party had decided to undertake a renewed struggle against the Diem government, although the precise roles of political and military struggle remained unclear. The Communists had increased their recruiting in the South and had begun infiltrating more cadres from the North. Communist guerrillas staged impressive local actions in coastal Quang Ngai province and in Kien Hoa province in the Mekong Delta in late 1959 and early 1960.[10] In an important step, the party formed a National Liberation Front to carry on the political struggle in December 1960, and in the following month the Politburo decided upon an intensified military effort centered in the Mekong Delta and in the Central Highlands. While unaware of the details of these moves, American authorities certainly knew that the situation in the countryside was deteriorating.[11]

For more than a year Durbrow had been vainly imploring General Williams, who was chief of the MAAG in 1959–1960, to shift the emphasis of the South Vietnamese Army toward pacification and counter-insurgency. In reply, Williams insisted that fighting against guerrillas did not differ from fighting against regular soldiers, and continually protested that Diem assigned too many troops to pacification, making it impossible to provide them with necessary training.[12] General Lionel McGarr, who replaced Williams in September 1960, took the insurgency much more seriously, but when the MAAG completed a counter-insurgency plan on October 27, it reflected the continuing ambivalence of American military thinking. On the one hand, it recognized that the Viet Cong (VC) was trying either to overthrow the Diem government or to establish effective control over much of the Mekong Delta with guerrilla tactics, and it reported that the Capital, 1st, and 5th military regions now included large numbers of VC sympathizers and neutrals. Nonetheless, the MAAG continued to protest that 70 percent of the ARVN was committed to pacification, most of it in static and guard duty missions. It recommended once again that four full divisions guard the northern and western borders while an improved Civil Guard took a greater role in the interior, and it again endorsed the expansion of the ARVN by 20,000 men.[13] Durbrow continued to oppose the ARVN increase.[14]

By the summer of 1960 Durbrow and others at the Embassy had apparently decided that Diem simply had to make fundamental political changes in order to survive. A CIA Special National Intelligence Estimate of August 23, 1960, reported that Diem faced both increasing opposition within "urban groups and government circles," and the Viet Cong insurgency. Criticism by opposition elements, the CIA stated, "focuses on Ngo family rule, especially the roles of the President's brother, Ngo Dinh Nhu, and Madame Nhu; the pervasive influence of the Can Lao, the semi-clandestine apparatus of the regime; Diem's virtual one-man rule; and growing evidence of corruption in high places." These trends—combined with the growing Communist insurgency—would, "if they remain unchecked . . . almost certainly in time cause the collapse of the Diem regime," although not, probably, within the next year.[15] Echoing this analysis, Durbrow in September asked for permission to talk frankly to Diem and suggest that Nhu leave the country on a diplomatic or intelligence mission, and warned that the United States might have to find alternative leadership. Although Diem's old patron

General Lansdale tried to head off this démarche, the State Department agreed.[16]

Durbrow presented his demands on October 15 and October 20, and Diem received the suggestion that the Nhus go abroad grimly. He blamed the Communists for rumors about Nhu, spoke of giving Nhu important new responsibilities, and cited the worsening military situation in Laos as a further reason to increase his Army from 150,000 to 170,000 men.[17] These issues were still unresolved when events dramatically confirmed the depth of Diem's domestic political problems. On November 10 rebel South Vietnamese paratroopers surrounded the presidential palace. Rather than attack and take control of the palace and Diem himself—as they easily might have done—they began negotiating with him regarding the broadening of the government, freedom of the press, and a more active anti–Viet Cong campaign. During the negotiations Durbrow and McGarr put pressure on both sides to compromise, while a CIA operative, George Carver, monitored the proceedings from the coup leaders' headquarters. Meanwhile, Diem reached friendly units in the countryside over the telephone, and the rebels promptly surrendered and accepted asylum in Cambodia when the units arrived.[18]

Although the coup certainly vindicated Durbrow's reporting, it weakened his position. The coup plotters' demands resembled Durbrow's own recent recommendations in many respects, some of the officers had been close to American advisers, and Nhu orchestrated a press campaign blaming both the French and the Americans for the coup. Back in Washington, Lansdale now argued that the ambassador had to go, and on November 27 Durbrow finally agreed to allow Lansdale to visit South Vietnam.[19] Lansdale's plans immediately created controversy. While he credited himself with unique influence upon Diem, the rest of the American government regarded him as a dangerously loose cannon whose activities—fictionalized in two best-selling novels—had generated far too much publicity.[20] Durbrow had another stormy meeting with Diem on December 24 and warned Washington again that new leadership might be necessary, but on December 31 the State Department replied that we had gone as far as we could in pressuring Diem at the present time.[21]

On January 4, 1961, the Embassy finally forwarded a draft counterinsurgency plan for South Vietnam to Washington.[22] Politically, the report incorporated Durbrow's most important reservations regarding the Diem regime, and endorsed his recommendations as expressed in his several unsuccessful approaches to Diem during the last few months of 1960. Militarily, it reflected an attempt to implement long-standing American concepts more effectively. While noting the growth of the Viet Cong, especially in military regions 1 and 5, it continued to stress the need to defend South Vietnam's borders against outside aggression while dealing with the insurgency. It endorsed Diem's proposed 20,000-man increase in the Army and new increases in the Civil Guard, and supported putting the Civil Guard under the Department of Defense. It spent very little time on the details of maintaining security within villages.[23]

After spending the first two weeks of 1961 in South Vietnam, Lansdale submitted a report on January 17 that put Vietnam on the agenda of the Kennedy administration. He began bluntly, arguing that the approaches of both the South Vietnamese government and the American Embassy had to change fundamentally to avert imminent defeat, and suggested that the United States needed to send "the best people you have, people who are experienced in dealing with this precise type of emergency, and send them to the spot to remedy the situation." Lansdale obviously had himself in mind, either as ambassador or as a special political operative. In shocked tones, he reported that the Viet Cong now controlled most of military regions 1 and 5, the heavily populated, economically richer areas north and south of Saigon. He made no specific military recommendations, but put his faith in a new political strategy: an "unusual American" of great sympathy should go to Saigon and be given the task of "creating an opposition party which would coalesce the majority of the opposition into one organization," helping it design a program of sound ideas, and persuading it "to play the role of loyal opposition while President Diem is in power and the nation is in such great danger."[24] This was not, in fact, very different from what Durbrow had tried to do by sponsoring the Caravelle Manifesto. Diem had already made clear to Lansdale that he had no intention of allowing the opposition to organize, and he would have regarded Lansdale's plan merely as an attempt by the Americans to groom his successor. Indeed, Lansdale himself may actually have been thinking along those lines, since the report referred to the need to "support Ngo Dinh Diem until another strong executive can replace him legally." Essentially, Lansdale was counting on his own relationship with Diem to work a miracle.

Lansdale's report initially reached General Andrew Goodpaster, Eisenhower's military aide, and Goodpaster passed it along to Walt Rostow, the MIT economist who had just become Deputy National Security Adviser. Rostow, who was about to assume responsibility for Southeast Asia and various other underdeveloped regions within the NSC staff, gave the report to Kennedy, who remarked that Vietnam seemed to be "the worst one we've got." On January 28—just one week after his inauguration—Kennedy gave Lansdale an opportunity to discuss his report at the White House.[25] Secretary of State Rusk began the meeting by having Assistant Secretary of State for Far Eastern Affairs J. Graham Parsons brief the President on the counterinsurgency plan. With typical perspicacity, Kennedy immediately asked why an increase in the army from 150,000 to 170,000 might be critical against a force of 10,000 guerrillas, and Parsons replied that the South Vietnamese Army had to defend both against the guerrillas and against external invasion. Kennedy expressed interest in starting a guerrilla war against the Communists in North Vietnam, and Allen Dulles reported that several teams had been infiltrated.

Lansdale then conveyed the key points of his report at some length, with particular reference to relations with Diem, and the President offered to write a personal letter to Diem to assure him of our support. The meeting discussed sending Lansdale to Saigon as ambassador, and Kennedy accepted Rusk's suggestion for an interdepartmental task force to deal with South Vietnam, parallel to another one just established to deal with Cuba.[26] But later that day Parsons met with Rusk, explained that Lansdale was a "lone wolf and operator" who resented the State Department, and effectively killed the idea of sending him to Saigon as ambassador, while conceding, apparently, that Durbrow had to go. Instead, Frederick Nolting, a Foreign Service officer now posted at NATO headquarters, was chosen on February 17.

Lansdale wrote Diem on January 30 informing him that he had reported personally to Kennedy, and repeating his own main suggestions, which Diem declined to adopt.[27] But the Vietnam task force does not seem to have met for some time, and in Saigon, Durbrow, now a lame duck, began another long but unsuccessful struggle to secure the political changes called for in the counterinsurgency plan from Diem, in return for American financing for the planned increases in the ARVN and Civil Guard.[28] No agreement had been reached by April 9, when Diem won reelection, announcing that he had received over 90 percent of the vote in a race against two virtually unknown candidates.

Faced with Lansdale's report, the problem of Castro's Cuba, and the threat of Communist subversion elsewhere, Kennedy was already pushing the government for new strategies against guerrilla warfare. Secretary of Defense McNamara informed Kennedy on February 20 that the United States had "too little ability to deal with guerrilla forces, insurrections, and subversion."[29] Discussing this issue in a meeting with the Joint Chiefs of Staff (JCS) on February 22, Kennedy ran into the doctrinal conservatism of the American military. When he asked specifically about the mission of the Army's Special Forces, General George Decker, the Chief of Staff of the Army, said they would be used in "cold war, limited war, and even general war, if it occurred." Later, the JCS insisted that some Special Forces had to remain in Germany, in order to move behind Soviet lines into the Warsaw Pact countries in the event of general European war. Decker also told Kennedy that only three members of the Vietnam MAAG were "skilled in guerrilla warfare operations." Kennedy asked whether more Special Forces might go to Vietnam to train both guerrillas that might operate in North Vietnam and counterguerrilla forces. Marine Corps Commandant General David Shoup told the President that while the Marines could easily operate as guerrillas themselves, they preferred not to train other people. Kennedy replied "that it is not always possible for us to take direct action and that, for most of the problems that face us now, we will have to satisfy ourselves with training the people of these various countries to do their own guerrilla and anti-guerrilla operations." A moment later he elaborated his view:

> The President then mentioned that Ambassador [Llewellyn] Thompson told him that it is his opinion that, in the future, no Soviets will actually cross their own borders to enter into these operations and, therefore, for the time being, we will have to prepare other forces to protect themselves. The President added that we will have to do more to help those countries (with whom we are associated) to do more for themselves. He mentioned the *threat* that 15,000 men from North Vietnam will be enough to overwhelm South Vietnam, and that Vietnam "will fall this year." The Presi-

dent felt that, if this threat had any basis of realization, certainly we must face up to it promptly.

Kennedy then asked whether the forthcoming SEATO meeting might discuss guerrilla and counterguerrilla activity, and commented "that the Malayan example was a very successful one and might be applied to some of our trouble spots. Again he mentioned Cuba, Vietnam, and possibly Iran."[30] Although the Pentagon paid more and more attention to South Vietnam during 1961, it never fundamentally altered its conventional approach to counterguerrilla warfare. In May McNamara informed Kennedy that we could not increase our own conventional forces to meet "the indirect aggression carried on by the Communists in many parts of the world," since our forces were not organized to deal with these threats.[31]

Meanwhile, Walt Rostow emerged as another major figure trying to energize and militarize policy toward both Vietnam and Laos. Rostow, who had recently published *The Stages of Economic Growth,* laying out a model of Third World development, believed that the United States was waging a global struggle against the Soviet Union similar to the Second World War, in which he had served as an intelligence officer. He was perhaps the epitome of a GI-generation intellectual, proud of the challenges he and his contemporaries had overcome, eager to face new ones, and utterly committed to the linear forward progress of the human race. "In the field where I worked—Laos and Vietnam—" he explained in a confidential interview in 1964, "when I had taken a good hard look at the situation, in those first days and weeks, I concluded that this was the worst mess I had seen since 1942," when Britain seemed on the verge of losing the Middle East and Germany was winning the battle of the Atlantic. "I saw no way that we could protect vital US interests without the application of American force."[32] He also wanted the government to move immediately to address the problem of guerrilla warfare, with special reference to South Vietnam. Rostow's energetic pursuit of new solutions gave Vietnam a higher profile for the rest of the year.

On March 29, when Rusk was in Bangkok for the SEATO meeting and the Laotian cease-fire negotiations had reached a critical stage, Rostow wrote Kennedy suggesting a coordinated political and military effort to strengthen South Vietnam, including a vice presidential visit to

Saigon, and argued that the United States should find ways to bring new assets to bear, including armed helicopters, other new weapons, and Special Forces.[33] In a long series of memos and meetings during the next two weeks, Rostow prodded the Pentagon to beef up American counterguerrilla activity, reiterated his suggestions for high-level visits, and told State Department officials that current thinking favored abandoning the restrictions on American aid in the Geneva Accords.[34] Meanwhile, Lansdale on April 19 gave McNamara a wide-ranging memorandum reiterating most of the suggestions in his report and offering to lead a special three-man staff for the new ambassador. Armed with Lansdale's memo, McNamara at a cabinet meeting on April 20 secured Kennedy's renewed agreement to the formation of a Vietnam Task Force led by McNamara's deputy, Roswell Gilpatric. The task force, which also included Lansdale, Rostow, Deputy Undersecretary of State U. Alexis Johnson, and representatives of the JCS and of the CIA, had an April 28 deadline for submitting its report.[35]

The task force's meetings and its three successive draft reports both expanded the existing effort Vietnam and raised critical new military questions.[36] The CIA secured agreement to increase its presence in South Vietnam, partly to improve "the population's participation in and loyalty to free government in Vietnam," but also for "operations to penetrate political forces, government, armed services and opposition elements to measure support of government, provide warning of any coup plans, and identify individuals with potentiality of providing leadership in event of disappearance of President Diem." The Agency apparently believed that Diem's survival could not be counted upon, and Rostow agreed.[37]

The Pentagon, meanwhile, secured approval of recommendations it had been pressing for weeks: immediate agreement to the 20,000-man increase in the South Vietnamese Army; an increase in the size of the MAAG, despite the Geneva Accords, to train the new ARVN forces, the Self-Defense Corps, and the Civil Guard; new equipment for the Civil Guard; a Combat Development and Test Center in South Vietnam to develop new techniques against the VC; and improved border surveillance by land, sea, and air. The President approved these recommendations, which seemed to respond to his February request to the JCS, at an initial NSC meeting of April 29, even before the completion of the final draft, and reiterated his approval on May 11. All the drafts also called for an American economic mission to work out South Vietnam's financial contribution to the new ARVN increase.[38] Lansdale and the State Department essentially fought to a draw over the issue of abandoning pressure upon Diem, and the authority of Ambassador-designate Nolting was reaffirmed.[39]

But while the task force worked, an entirely new and much more serious element was introduced into the situation. Responding to Communist gains in Laos and the opening of the Geneva conference, both the Pentagon and the State Department weighed in with suggestions for major new American political and military commitments. They focused on a potential conventional military threat to South Vietnam through southeastern Laos—a threat that did not become a reality for years, but that became the basis for an endless stream of proposed American actions. In fact, the potential conventional threat through Laos immediately overshadowed the President's emphasis on the need for counterguerrilla techniques. On April 28 Assistant to the Secretary of Defense Colonel Edwin F. Black, a member of the task force who had already visited Vietnam on Lansdale's behalf, argued that a settlement that left southern Laos in unfriendly hands would open three mountain passes from North into South Vietnam, posing a new threat "to the entire western flank of South Vietnam." This, he said, "requires the prompt organization of two new G.V.N. divisions and vastly accelerated U.S. training program for the entire G.V.N. Army." To train these forces, he suggested establishing two U.S. training commands in the Central Highlands, totaling 3,200 Army and Marine personnel, and shifting the First Special Forces Group from Okinawa to Nha Trang.[40]

The second draft of the task force report incorporated these suggestions, and asked the JCS and CINCPAC for recommendations for the deployment of U.S. forces for several possible purposes. In another departure, State proposed that Ambassador Nolting begin discussions with Diem on the possibility of the conclusion of a direct bilateral alliance and "a formal rejection of the Geneva Accords." The task force meeting on May 4 discussed the possible dispatch of American troops at some length.[41] On May 8 Roswell Gilpatric asked General Lemnitzer, Chairman of the JCS, for recommendations for the use of American forces, and on May 11 the Joint Chiefs replied, "assuming the political decision is to hold Southeast Asia outside the Communist sphere, the JCS are of the opinion that US forces should be deployed immediately to South Vietnam," rather than wait, as in Laos, until war had already broken out.

Having encountered enormous problems trying to support an intervention in Laos, the Chiefs wanted to lay the foundation for combat action in South Vietnam at once. They recommended "sufficient forces" to accomplish five purposes: to provide a visible deterrent to North Vietnamese or Chinese action; to release Vietnamese forces "from advanced and static defense positions to permit their fuller commitment to counterinsurgency actions"; to help train the Vietnamese; to "provide a nucleus for the support of any additional major US or SEATO military operation in Southeast Asia"; and to indicate our firmness to all Asian nations. A few days later, CINCPAC specifically suggested stationing an American Army division in the "High Plateau region," or Central Highlands, and sending naval and air units.[42]

Administration officials began discussing these broader strategic issues publicly during the first week in May. On May 4 Rusk, in a news conference, linked the growing threat to South Vietnam to Pathet Lao gains in Laos, and suggested that we might provide more unspecified help. Senator Fulbright, after meeting with the President, stated that while he still opposed intervention in Laos, we might dispatch troops to Thailand or South Vietnam, if those countries wanted them.[43] The NSC, meeting on May 5, agreed that Diem needed reassurance that we were not abandoning Southeast Asia, but tentatively decided against introducing troops unless the Geneva conference on Laos had broken down.[44] And later that day, in a press conference, President Kennedy announced that Vice President Johnson would undertake "a special fact-finding mission" to Asia. He dodged a question regarding the possible dispatch of American forces to South Vietnam, but later declared, "There is a limit beyond which our efforts cannot go . . . In the final analysis, then, the responsibility rests with the people involved to maintain the support of the people, to identify their government with the people." Kennedy never abandoned this view.[45]

On May 11 Kennedy approved the objectives of the task force report: "to prevent Communist domination of South Vietnam," and "to create in that country a viable and increasingly democratic society." He confirmed his April 29 approval of the initial set of military actions, asked for further study of the additional 30,000-man increase in the South Vietnamese army and of various proposals for the use of U.S.

forces, and authorized Nolting to explore a possible new bilateral arrangement between the United States and South Vietnam. Lastly, he approved the proposed actions in the economic, psychological, and covert action fields, including the opening of contact with opposition groups and the concurrent expansion of the CIA station.[46]

Like so many subsequent plans for South Vietnam, the task force report had received little or no input either from the Embassy in Saigon or from the South Vietnamese government. Diem's reaction considerably reduced its impact. Vice President Johnson had the honor of presenting Washington's new plans to Diem, together with a personal letter from President Kennedy, on May 13. Johnson's trip, to Saigon, Manila, Taipei, Hong Kong, Bangkok, New Delhi, and Karachi, was designed mainly to reassure our more militant anti-Communist Asian allies that our agreement to a Laotian conference did not signify a fundamental change in policy. To Diem, the big news was the Americans' final approval of the 20,000-man ARVN increase and support for the Civil Guard, which, he did not fail to point out, he had requested several years previously. An enthusiastic Johnson, indeed, went even further, inviting Diem to propose further ARVN increases of up to 100,000 men. Diem gave Johnson a memorandum on the need for American financing of the in-country costs of the ARVN increase, and agreed that an American economic mission might study the question. Regarding political and economic changes, Diem repeated, as he had many times before, that they "must be appropriate to Vietnam as country which is underdeveloped and subject to Communist subversion." Diem also welcomed the increase in MAAG personnel and responsibilities, the need for improved border control measures, and a research and development facility for new weapons.[47]

From Diem's point of view, the agreement represented a victory in the long battle for his 20,000 additional men. On May 15 he wrote Kennedy expressing great satisfaction with Johnson's visit, and particularly with Johnson's request for Diem's suggestions on how to meet the crisis. "I was most deeply gratified by this gracious gesture by your distinguished Vice-President," he wrote, "particularly as we have not become accustomed to being asked for our own views as to our needs."[48] Washington's broader proposals, however, went nowhere. Diem told Johnson that he wanted American or SEATO troops in South Vietnam only in case of new, overt aggression, and pleaded in a private conversation with the new U.S. ambassador to Thailand, Kenneth Young, "that all American military personnel—and all Americans—exercise tact and restraint in Vietnam in this critical and delicate period."[49] General McGarr actually received the impression that Diem would favor American combat units to provide training, but in late May Nguyen Dinh Thuan, Diem's leading palace assistant, told Nolting that this was not correct.[50] And on May 26 Nolting reported that "Task Force Saigon"—the new designation for the South Vietnam country team, parallel to the task force in Washington—opposed including South Vietnam within SEATO or signing a new, bilateral treaty with the South. Diem, he argued, had been reassured about American intentions by Johnson's visit, and his military plans—drawn up with "indirect US planning guidance"—assumed that the United States would intervene within seventy-two hours if war began. In addition, the Embassy did not believe it could justify such a major violation of the Geneva Accords of 1954.[51]

On June 9, however, Diem submitted a blockbuster request in another letter to Kennedy. Citing the need to defend against the new North Vietnamese threat through southeastern Laos, he asked for two more increments of ARVN forces: the 20,000 already agreed to, in order to prevent forces in the far north of South Vietnam from being outflanked and forced to withdraw; and an additional 100,000 over the next few years. Diem asked for extensive new American aid to help pay for these increases, stressed the primacy of military needs, and defended his policies toward Cambodia.[52]

Ambassador Nolting, meanwhile, was abandoning his predecessor's policy of carrots and sticks. Although some American officials hoped that the Johnson visit and increased aid might induce Diem to make some of the changes that they had demanded for so long, the new ambassador seems to have decided almost at once to interpret Diem's behavior in the most optimistic light possible, and thus to dampen any efforts to change Diem's behavior. "In general," Nolting commented on May 31, "I have no doubt that US is doing wise thing in giving full backing to this regime. By our attitude here, at home, and abroad, I think we may be able to start a trend toward a broader backing for this regime in this country."[53] Such, alas, did not prove to be the case. On June 2 Nolting reported that four leading members of the South Vietnamese diplomatic corps were quitting in disgust. The ringleader,

Dang Doc Khoi, told an Embassy officer that Diem had made no real changes, and had now kicked Vice President Nguyen Ngoc Tho upstairs "so as to remove restraining hand which he had exercised on corruption in economic field as Secretary of State for National Economy." Diem's sham changes, he said, fooled no one, and Army morale remained low.[54]

Nolting defined his position more clearly in July, when Sterling Cottrell, the new director of the Vietnam Task Force, asked him some now familiar questions. Was Diem really carrying out reforms? How successful were recent military operations? Nolting replied on July 14 that he himself had been seeking answers to such questions for weeks. His extremely lengthy reply said at least as much about the corner into which the ambassador was painting himself as it did about Diem.

The ambassador began, curiously, with a long paragraph answering a question which the State Department had not thought it necessary to ask: "What is Vietnamese Government (which means President Diem) striving for? Are his philosophy, objectives, and moral values sound in terms US interests in world?" Nolting commented that he was now convinced, after many hours of discussions, that Diem was "no dictator, in the sense of relishing power for its own sake," and that he did not

> fundamentally enjoy power or the exercise of it. He is, nevertheless, an egoist in the sense that he believes (in my judgment, with some justification) that he can govern in South Vietnam, in general and in detail, better than anyone else now available; and that he knows more about the Communist movement in this area and how to combat it than anyone else. His own strong convictions, energy, and his faith in himself are both a strength and a weakness—a strength in providing a counter-dynamic to communism, a weakness in causing overconcentration of governmental power and authority, consequent lack of governmental efficiency, and in offering a vulnerable political target. His philosophy of government, summed up in the term "personalism" . . . is certainly in my judgment sound and right, and compatible with US interests . . . Thus, I think the United States should have no hesitation on moral grounds in backing Diem to the hilt.

Then Nolting stated the principle that became his mantra during the next two years: "Where we think he is wrong, we can bring about ameliorations and improvements, gradually in proportion to the confidence which he has in us and in his ability to make concessions without slipping." But having argued, in effect, that Diem was not a fascist or a totalitarian, Nolting shrank from saying that his philosophy was having a beneficial effect or keeping pace with the growth of Communism. Indeed, he declined even to endorse the effects of the increased American effort to date:

> Strong and evident US support has brought to the government side a certain number of fence-sitters, and has also probably considerably reduced the likelihood of a military coup d'état. It has at the same time made Diem an even more vulnerable target of Communist attack, which has, I fear carried some people into the enemy's camp ... I do not think it is true that US support has given President Diem's government as yet an increase in popularity among the Vietnamese people ... If the situation drags on in an inconclusive manner for many more months, either a military coup, or an open proclamation of a Communist Government and widespread civil war, is likely.

The key to progress, he argued, lay in "sufficient military and security forces" to protect the countryside. "I do not believe that the net security situation is any better now than it was 2 months ago," he wrote. "In our attempt to help create a new and winning psychology," he added, "I have taken a much more optimistic line in conversations with other diplomats and with press here than that reflected above, and I think we should continue to do so, giving benefit of the doubt wherever possible to optimistic assessment." Regarding the promised reforms in the military chain of command and the new Vietnamese central intelligence organization, Nolting put his faith in increasing Diem's confidence in the United States, which would enable the United States to change some of his ways.[55]

Whereas Nolting's counterpart in Laos, Winthrop Brown, had gently but firmly let Kennedy know that the United States could not rely upon Boun Oum and Phoumi Nosavan, Nolting had rapidly persuaded himself that Washington had no alternative but to make the best of Diem. Yet since he as yet lacked any evidence that this policy might work, he was increasingly casting himself in the codependent role of the spouse of an alcoholic who decides that since criticism has not worked, tolerance may.

Nolting's admitted policy of talking optimistically in the press probably contributed to a series of upbeat *Time* and *Newsweek* stories on military progress in Vietnam during July and August.[56] But given such appraisals, Washington was not likely to approve Diem's new requests without some concessions in return. After the Stanford economist Eugene Staley led a special economic mission to Saigon, Washington eventually agreed to increase the ARVN to 200,000 men over the next eighteen months, with the United States bearing somewhat more than half of the cost. But the joint program that Kennedy approved on August 11 also imposed several conditions upon the increase, including "a mutually agreed upon geographically phased strategic plan for bringing Viet-Cong subversion . . . under control" and Vietnamese economic reforms. It also failed to specify the total amount of new American aid during this period. Diem, on August 8, received the proposals rather coolly for this reason, but Nolting's report put the best possible face on his reaction.[57] *Time,* going well beyond Nolting, actually reported that Diem seemed to be a changed man. While in the past he had refused to accept U.S. political advice, "Every recommendation in the Staley report has already received his concurrence in advance."[58]

By late June, Berlin had definitely replaced both Southeast Asia and Cuba as most important crisis Washington faced. At Vienna, Soviet Premier Nikita Khrushchev had threatened once more to sign a separate peace treaty with East Germany, terminating, he argued, the occupation rights of the Americans, British, and French in West Berlin, and leaving access to West Berlin in the hands of the East German regime. East Germany, he said, would have every right to block that access, and should the Western powers try to force their way through, war would result. On June 28 Kennedy received a report on Berlin from former Secretary of State Dean Acheson that called for an absolutely firm line in response to Khrushchev's threats, and a massive conventional build-up in Europe to back it up. A month later, on July 25, Kennedy announced an increase of 217,000 American forces to meet the crisis, and proposed a large fallout-shelter program for the United States. On August 13 the Berlin Wall went up. Meanwhile, the administration struggled to develop some non-nuclear military options in Europe in the event that Khrushchev actually carried out his threats.

These momentous events, combined with the continuing crisis in the Congo, tension with Cuba, fighting between Tunisia and France at Bizerte, and various domestic legislative battles, temporarily eclipsed the problems of Laos and South Vietnam, but debate over policy toward Southeast Asia continued. At the White House, Walt Rostow, still in the grip of his 1942 analogy, believed that the Soviets might decide to test the West simultaneously in both Berlin and Southeast Asia, and feared the consequences of the situation in Laos for South Vietnam. At State, U. Alexis Johnson, who as Deputy Undersecretary of State was exercising principal responsibility for Southeast Asia, shared Rostow's pessimistic view of the Laotian situation, and wanted to prepare for the failure of the talks. Johnson, a career foreign service officer, had just completed a tour as ambassador to Thailand. Much earlier, in 1950–1951, he had been Rusk's main subordinate responsible for Korea while Rusk served as Assistant Secretary of State during the Korean War. His was one of the very few appointments that Rusk had made on his own initiative. He immediately emerged as Rusk's most important subordinate on Southeast Asia.[59] At Defense, the Joint Chiefs also protested that the conference was leading to another defeat for American prestige. As a result, a steady stream of proposals for military action reached Kennedy during the early summer of 1961.

Rostow never stopped pushing for more action in Southeast Asia. On June 20 reports of Kennedy's intention to name retired General Maxwell Taylor as his personal military representative had reached the newspapers, and Rostow on June 21 suggested for the first of many times that Kennedy send Taylor to South Vietnam to survey the situation. On June 23, replying to a memo from Alexis Johnson, Rostow called for plans to seal the border between southern Laos and Vietnam, followed by "naval, air or other direct action against North Vietnam from the seaward side" in response to North Vietnamese intervention.[60]

The State Department also took a worried and aggressive view of developments in Laos. Although Ambassador-at-Large Harriman was encouraged by his recent talks with Souvanna Phouma,[61] Washington officials still believed that any coalition led by Souvanna would be "Communist-dominated," and they saw that the conference was not likely to accept an International Control Commission (ICC) with powers sufficient to police Laotian territory. On June 24 Sterling Cottrell, the Vietnam desk officer at State and the head of the Vietnam Task Force, specifically proposed that the United States reject a Souvanna government and a weak ICC, maintain its position in Geneva, and prepare to seize the Mekong Valley under SEATO Plan 5 with American, Thai, and South Vietnamese forces when the cease-fire broke down. Rusk apparently endorsed this course, although McNamara hesitated to go that far.[62] By the time the NSC met to consider Cottrell's paper on the evening of June 29 Marshal Phoumi Nosavan, the commander of the pro-American Royal Laotian Army, was in Washington to discuss the situation with the President and the Secretary of State. Harriman had returned as well.

The NSC meeting began with Dean Acheson's presentation of his proposals for the Berlin crisis, which estimated the chances of war over Berlin as perhaps greater than 50 percent and called for a large conventional build-up. Kennedy deferred any immediate decisions and asked the departments involved to study Acheson's proposals. Later Rusk turned to Laos, predicted that a neutralist government would be "difficult, if not impossible, to establish," and suggested that the United States should prepare to invoke SEATO Plan 5, possibly within seven to ten days. But Kennedy immediately returned to the issues he had raised during the winter and spring, asking General Lemnitzer to comment on the state of the Laotian armed forces, and adding "that he was suspicious of relying on airstrips in Laos any longer."[63] More to the point, he asked that Ambassador Brown "maintain close relationships with the British and French to determine their reactions and their willingness to respond with the United States"—a willingness he knew to be very limited indeed. And when Harriman reported that Souvanna would probably become Prime Minister, Kennedy quickly agreed, and suggested that Souvanna visit the United States.[64]

Marshal Phoumi Nosavan must have been rather confused by his conversations with Rusk that evening and Kennedy the next day. Rusk stressed that intervention in Laos could lead to World War III, but declared that the United States might indeed take this step under certain unspecified circumstances, and expressed unwarranted confidence that America's principal allies would join in. Then, although he had just heard Kennedy accept the idea of a Souvanna government, he warned Phoumi against "the path of premature concessions leading to the formation of a coalition Government which would in fact be dominated by the Communists," and added, in words worthy of John Foster Dulles, that "from the American point of view, the so-called neutralists in Laos are in fact the allies of the Communists." Rusk even accused

Phoumi, in effect, of treating the other factions too amicably at the three-power Laotian talks.[65]

Phoumi got a rather different message the next morning from the President. In response to Kennedy's questions, he said that if the cease-fire broke down, he "could not hold out without supplementary assistance if the enemy received additional aid from the Viet Minh." When he bluntly asked Kennedy what our attitude would be if he accepted Souvanna as Prime Minister, Kennedy replied that it would depend on the distribution of portfolios, and that we certainly would want Phoumi to remain minister of defense. When Kennedy asked him whether a Souvanna government would remain neutral, Phoumi replied that "he thought it would be quite difficult," given Souvanna's association with the Communists. Kennedy in turn replied that the British and the French had more confidence in him. Kennedy concluded with an interesting historical analogy:

> The President realized how difficult the negotiations would be and reminded Phoumi what Talleyrand faced at Vienna when he represented a France which had no power and was in complete collapse after losing a war. Yet Talleyrand succeeded in obtaining a stronger France out of these negotiations. The President added, of course, that France was in a much worse state then [sic] Laos is today. Therefore Phoumi, the President said, should conduct his negotiations with perseverance. He hoped that Phoumi might achieve a favorable solution.[66]

Harriman returned immediately to Geneva and began discussing the details of a coalition with Souvanna, making clear that the United States would look carefully at the men around him. Meanwhile, Phoumi, who had apparently heard only what he wanted to hear in Washington, returned to Vientiane "visibly encouraged and with the feeling that the US would back him militarily," and demanded that the King, not Souvanna, lead the new government. He passed along plans for SEATO military action in Laos to American military advisers. On July 18 the State Department informed Ambassador Brown in Vientiane that Phoumi was distorting what Rusk and Kennedy had said,[67] but the bureaucracy continued to discuss war plans. In a memo for Rusk, Rostow expressed skepticism that the United States would get a satisfactory Laotian settlement without a convincing military posture, and suggested plans to act directly against North Vietnam, both from the air and amphibiously from the sea.[68] On July 12 the Joint Chiefs, who were smarting somewhat from stories partially blaming them for the Bay of Pigs debacle and from Taylor's appointment as the President's special military representative, took the offensive in a highly political memorandum for McNamara. The cease-fire promised in return for the conference, they argued, had never occurred; both Thailand and South Vietnam opposed the positions we were taking; we had effectively conceded political equality to the three Laotian factions; and should present trends continue, "the outcome will be a Laos more Communist than neutral," and "US prestige will have suffered another serious blow." "U.S. failure to exercise active leadership of SEATO, particularly since August 1960," they continued, "is not understood and is considered by many in Asia as a sign of weakness."

The Chiefs referred to a plan "approved at high levels of State and Defense" for intervention of American and SEATO forces in Laos, presumably the plan for Thai–South Vietnamese–American action, and suggested that an opportunity to implement it had been lost after a June 7 cease-fire violation. They asked McNamara to seek a high-level government decision to withdraw from the conference at the next breach of the cease-fire, and to undertake military operations within Laos either with SEATO allies or unilaterally in order to make it possible to secure a unified, independent, and neutral Laos through negotiations. McNamara does not seem to have passed the memorandum on. The Chiefs in the early 1960s frequently based their recommendations on overtly political arguments which in other times would have been regarded as the province of other departments.[69]

On July 16 General Taylor also asked the Chiefs for new military plans. He laid out three tasks for allied and American forces: to secure the Laotian panhandle and parts of the Mekong Valley; to launch offensive air and guerrilla operations from the panhandle; and to apply military pressure against North Vietnam, both from the air and from the sea. Following part of the argument of his 1959 book, *The Uncertain Trumpet,* Taylor argued for "maximum use of indigenous ground forces, employing largely Laotian, South Vietnamese and Thai troops," combined with American naval and air assets, and, perhaps, ground troops to guard American bases.[70] Working with little staff, Taylor had laid out the strategic rationale that guided his thinking during his mission to South Vietnam later in 1961, and, more critically, during his tenure as ambassador to South Vietnam in 1964–1965.

After meeting with Alexis Johnson and Taylor to discuss various possible military actions,[71] Rostow on Friday, July 21, gave Kennedy a long, complex memo on the situation in Southeast Asia asking for new decisions on military planning. Kennedy, who was leaving as usual for the weekend and preparing for his major Berlin address the following week, returned it with the notation, "Too difficult to read,"[72] and Rostow submitted a slightly revised version four days later, listing various questions of when and how the United States might intervene as points for decision, and suggesting once again that General Taylor visit Southeast Asia.[73] Rostow and his staff took the possibility of intervention sufficiently seriously to query the CIA regarding probable Communist and friendly reactions to various courses of action, including both the occupation of the southern Laotian panhandle and the seizure of Hanoi and Haiphong. CIA estimates that the southern Laotian occupation would not make the Communists more forthcoming in Geneva and that most friendly Asian nations would view the occupation of Haiphong with alarm did not deter them.[74]

Taylor, Rostow, and Alexis Johnson were increasingly stressing the growing danger to South Vietnam posed by the Communist position in southern Laos, and the need to act against it.[75] On July 27 Taylor and Rostow jointly alerted the President that Rusk would make a new presentation the next day. They demanded an integrated strategy for all Southeast Asia, and proposed three alternatives: the most graceful disengagement possible; finding a political pretext for an attack upon Hanoi; and—as they assumed, the preferred alternative—"to build as much indigenous military, political and economic strength as we can in the area, in order to contain the thrust from Hanoi while preparing to intervene with U.S. military force if the Chinese Communists come in or the situation otherwise gets out of hand."[76]

Kennedy heard the presentation on Friday, July 28, three days after his dramatic television address to the nation calling for 217,000 men, $3.4 billion in new defense appropriations, and fallout shelters for the American people to meet the threats posed by the Berlin crisis. During the intervening few days, he had apparently been orchestrating a press campaign to suggest that these measures actually aimed at reaching a new Berlin agreement with the Soviets, involving concessions on both sides.[77] Southeast Asia had disappeared almost entirely from the front pages. Now, once again, Kennedy found, in effect, that the bureaucracy had yet to adopt the policy that he had selected three months before.

With Rusk present—but, oddly, without any representatives from the Pentagon—Alexis Johnson laid out the State Department position. He implied that we were unlikely to secure our main objectives in Geneva, an ICC strong enough to secure Laotian neutrality and a government not dominated by the Communists. He proposed that without securing these objectives the United States not abandon Boun Oum and Phoumi, and even welcomed the stiffening of Phoumi's position since his visit to Washington. Should the talks break down on these points, he proposed the seizure of southern Laos by forces from any SEATO nations willing to contribute. Meanwhile, he continued, "there was discussion of meeting any substantial intervention by the Viet-minh with a direct air and naval operation at Haiphong or Hanoi."

Kennedy's responses again revealed very different views of both the political situation and the proposed military options. Regarding Phoumi, he expressed the suspicion that the Marshal wanted the conference to break up, forcing the United States to intervene. He also "expressed his feeling that we should have to take a Souvanna government, sooner or later"—a decision he had reached in late April—although Rusk, responding, held out the hope that the King might lead the government. Then, obviously recalling earlier meetings, Kennedy zeroed in on the military issues involved:

> Questions from the President showed that the detailed aspects of this military plan had been developed. It was not clear how great an effect action against Haiphong or Hanoi would have on Northern Vietnam, nor whether it would be easy to hold what had been taken in a single attack. Similarly, no careful plan has yet been developed for an operation to take and hold Southern Laos. Planning is proceeding, and General Taylor is in close touch with General Lemnitzer. But the President made clear his own deep concern with the need for realism and accuracy in such military planning. He had observed in earlier military plans with respect to Laos that optimistic estimates were invariably proven false in the event. He was not persuaded that the airfields and the existing situation in Southern Laos would permit any real operation to save that part of the country, and he emphasized the reluctance of the American people and of many distinguished military leaders to see any direct involvement of U.S. troops in that part of the world. In reply it was urged that with a proper plan, with outside support, and above all with a clear and open American commitment, the results would be very different from anything that had happened before. But the President remarked that General de Gaulle, out of

painful French experience, had spoken with feeling of the difficulty of fighting in this part of the world.

The President also noted that the British, who were reducing their military commitments east of Suez, would be "most reluctant to participate" in such a scheme, and that international opinion would not as yet understand the need to retaliate against the North. Johnson, while avoiding asking for any immediate decision, asked whether "it could be understood that the President would at some future time have a willingness to decide to intervene if the situation seemed to him to require it." Kennedy

> in reply offered no decision, but he made it very plain that he himself is at present very reluctant to make a decision to go into Laos. He believed that the negotiations in Geneva should be pressed forward, that we should not get ourselves badly separated from the British, that the American people were not eager to get into Laos, that nothing would be worse than an unsuccessful intervention in this area, and that he did not yet have confidence in the military practicability of the proposal which had been put before him, though he was eager to have it studied more carefully.

Kennedy did approve the recommendations of the Staley report on Vietnam without making any precise financial commitments, and he authorized General Taylor to visit South Vietnam at an appropriate time. A few days later he asked the State Department for a weekly report from Harriman on the progress of the Geneva talks.[78]

John Kennedy's whole life—professional and personal—was extraordinarily compartmentalized, and no one document, meeting, or relationship ever revealed all his feelings about anything or anybody. Thus, in May he had referred to Phoumi as "a total shit" in a conversation with a friend and fellow Navy veteran, the journalist Ben Bradlee, but when he met Phoumi himself he had compared him respectfully to Talleyrand.[79] He customarily expressed himself more frankly to both journalists and other foreign leaders than to his own subordinates, disliked confrontations, and tended to avoid dismissals. Such standard operating procedures generally allowed the President to exercise decisive influence at truly critical moments and gave the impression of a smooth-running team, but frequently did not allow him to get through to subordinates who did not share his assumptions. Thus, his statements of July 28 had very little effect upon the bureaucracy, and within a month he faced a new round of proposals for military action.

On August 3, as the flow of East German refugees to West Berlin became a flood and McNamara asked Congress for a fallout-shelter program, Alexis Johnson wrote William Bundy, the Deputy Assistant Secretary of Defense for International Security Affairs, predicting a breakdown of the Geneva talks and asking once again for plans to occupy southern Laos and take the offensive against North Vietnam from South Vietnam and from the sea. Rostow, writing to Kennedy on August 4 on behalf of himself and Taylor, creatively interpreted the President's recent statements as having endorsed new military plans, either to induce the enemy to reach a satisfactory settlement or to act against the Hanoi-Haiphong area from the air, from the sea, and possibly on the ground, with appropriate plans to meet Chinese Communist intervention, should the talks fail to secure American objectives. Later that day he again asked the President for "the ablest military mission we can muster," to develop a "geographically-phased strategic plan" for the whole area. Kennedy on August 7 merely asked Rostow and Taylor for a report on the status of the Geneva talks, and said that he assumed he would shortly be receiving military plans along the lines indicated.[80]

After another round of discussions of plans for military intervention with limited U.S. participation,[81] Rostow on August 17 wrote the President, Alexis Johnson (for Rusk), and Robert Kennedy that he did not think that such a scheme would work without American participation at least at the level of SEATO Plan 5. Repeating his doubts that the other side would agree to a satisfactory settlement, he proposed going ahead with a revised plan, beginning with the appointment of an American SEATO military commander. Forcing the pace, he proposed announcing that appointment by September 15. He was not deterred by the Berlin crisis, which had entered a new and more frightening phase on August 13, when East German and Soviet troops surrounded West Berlin and began building the Berlin Wall, and which had led Kennedy to send Vice President Johnson and General Lucius Clay to Berlin to boost morale. (McGeorge Bundy, not Rostow, was overseeing policy toward Berlin at the White House.) In conclusion, Rostow appealed to Kennedy's sense of history, comparing his proposed plan to the enunciation of the Truman Doctrine in 1947, arguing that SEATO forces could easily handle North Vietnam and the Pathet Lao, and stating his belief that Communist China would not intervene.[82]

These new Washington initiatives took relatively little account of actual developments either in Southeast Asia or in Geneva. When the State Department on August 8 asked the Saigon Embassy whether Diem could join in an effort to clean out the Laotian panhandle, Nolting replied that Diem had no large forces available for such a mission. He also doubted that Marshal Sarit, the Thai leader, would favor a major effort in that area, rather than along the length of the Mekong.[83] Meanwhile, the Geneva talks were making considerable progress. In early August, Harriman and the British and French delegates formally agreed to accept Souvanna as Prime Minister, provided that no Pathet Lao member or sympathizer held a key position, and provided that the ICC had the power to make investigations and supervise the withdrawal of foreign forces. Harriman on August 12 reported a "noticeably less acrimonious attitude on part of bloc representatives, particularly the Soviets."[84] Washington, however, doubted Moscow's good faith. With Rostow on vacation, his staffer Robert Johnson wrote McGeorge Bundy on August 23 that he suspected the Russians of preparing a trap, and that State Department officials agreed with him. Meanwhile, the State Department informed the White House that Phoumi was emerging as the biggest obstacle to a political agreement.[85]

The two opposing lines of U.S. policy—negotiation and military planning—finally collided in three meetings on August 23, August 28, and August 29, when John Steeves's new Southeast Asia Task Force unveiled the plan for SEATO military action which Rostow had described to Kennedy. In the first meeting, Harriman, who had returned to Washington for consultation, rejected the assumption that a Thai–South Vietnamese–U.S. move into southern Laos would strengthen the American position in Geneva, arguing that it would probably wreck the talks. While accepting that military action might become necessary and agreeing to put more American military advisers into Laos, he recommended waiting for a military provocation on the scene, bringing the British into the planning process at once, and conveying our resolve to the Soviets by a firm statement, not provocative acts like the establishment of a SEATO headquarters in Thailand and the movement of American forces. As of August 25 Alexis Johnson still expected one more good "college try" in Geneva to fail, whereupon the United States would implement a revised SEATO Plan 5 for seizing the Mekong River towns. On the same day the *New York Times* reported that the administration was thinking of suspending the Geneva talks because of lack of progress on guarantees of neutrality.[86]

The paper Rusk gave Kennedy in preparation for a large top-level meeting on August 29 incorporated a new objective, the dissolution of the Pathet Lao forces, and assumed, as Rusk had from the beginning, that the Geneva conference would probably fail to reach our objectives. It proposed a military exercise and the establishment of a headquarters in Thailand in about six weeks, even if the negotiations continued and the Communists did not substantially violate the cease-fire.[87] At the meeting in the Cabinet Room, in which Robert Kennedy and Harriman joined the entire senior State, Defense, and White House national security team, Rusk began by suggesting that Souvanna's proposed cabinet, and particularly the eight men he wanted to represent his own faction, was entirely unacceptable, and that although we should attempt to move him toward our own position, we should also "be prepared, if the world situation permits, to take military action." Kennedy went right to the heart of the matter, asking whether "there were eight potential cabinet candidates who were pro-Souvanna but not actively involved with the Pathet Lao." Alexis Johnson replied revealingly that the "center group" should instead include individuals who were "not pro-Souvanna." Kennedy then asked Steeves to describe in detail the background of each of Souvanna's candidates—a task that tested Steeves's tongue, as well as his knowledge.[88] The group discussed various options, and Kennedy asked for a new approach to Souvanna.

Harriman then suggested bluntly that the United States had to secure Souvanna's friendship with economic and political support, something Souvanna had already received from the Soviets, and that Washington should make him dependent upon the Laotian army, as well as upon Kong Le's forces. This—although Harriman did not say so—actually represented an alternative to insisting upon the dissolution of the Pathet Lao, for which the State Department representatives continued to press. Rusk endorsed this strategy, and Kennedy suggested that Harriman consult our men in Vientiane regarding possible cabinet candidates. Harriman readily agreed, and introduced another new and critical distinction: "It was important that, in these negotiations, we distinguish between individuals who were anti-American but neutralist and those who were pro–Pathet Lao." Should we fail to reach agreement with Souvanna, Harriman continued, we would do better to convince him to step aside altogether, leaving behind a face-off between the Pathet Lao and the Royal Laotian government, rather than backing one faction against two. "The President," according to McGeorge Bundy, "in approving this pattern of negotiations, made clear that we would like nothing better than 'to get out of Laos, if we can.' We have no objective there other than to reach an acceptable settlement which does not hand the country over to the Communists." Nonetheless, he gave General Lemnitzer the floor to present the new military plans.

Lemnitzer, seconded by Alexis Johnson, now presented the new SEATO Plan 5, and the preliminary plans for actions designed to stiffen the Royal Laotian Army or confuse the Communists. McNamara, however, opposed any commitments to take action until we had reviewed the situation in Laos in light of other problems, especially Berlin. Kennedy typically suggested that we make clear "that we were developing a plan, but were not agreeing now to implement it." When Lemnitzer fell back upon the proposal to hold an exercise in Thailand, Robert Kennedy—who never forgot the Bay of Pigs and the Laos discussions in the spring—asked how many troops would be required, should the Communists respond. Lemnitzer said 13,000 American troops could seize the Mekong River towns. Questioning the general repeatedly, Robert Kennedy recalled that, several months previously, "it had been estimated that the Viet Minh could wipe out forces introduced into Southern Laos in two or three days," and asked why we were now more optimistic. Lemnitzer replied "that there had been no change in view but that SEATO Plan 5 was a flexible plan and could be the basis for taking action going beyond its original concept."

Alexis Johnson noted that if the Communists raised the ante, then rather than pouring in more troops, "we would draw back and attack North Vietnam from the sea and from the periphery of Laos." Rusk, seeming to shift his position in response to the discussion, argued for the importance of finding a peaceful solution in Laos—something he had initially viewed as doubtful. The President agreed: "We didn't want to be put in a position where we were only one man away from agreement with Souvanna on a cabinet." Then, once again, he cited the problems of fighting in Laos: the lack of British and French support, and the severe lack of interest among the American public. When Rusk repeated what Johnson had said—that if war came, we would not build up in Laos as in Korea, but would strike the Communists from the sea and outside Laos—Kennedy "indicated his agreement."

Then, as he often did, Kennedy asked for points requiring immediate decision. Once again he authorized Harriman's approach to Souvanna and talks with SEATO allies purely on a planning basis. The meeting deferred the October SEATO exercise for further study and agreed to go on equipping Meo tribesmen in Laos, and to carry out aerial reconnaissance over enemy positions.[89] Kennedy, however, was not through. "The President," Averell Harriman minuted later that day, "telephoned me today after the meeting in the White House and wanted to make sure that I would make every effort to get an agreement with Souvanna. He said he agreed we should not be too narrow in appraising the men Souvanna wished to bring into the government, since the alternative to an understanding with Souvanna was not one that he would like to contemplate. I said that I agreed, commenting some men may have been considered by our people to be pro-Communist because they were anti-American."[90]

Harriman was starting to emerge as Kennedy's most important diplomat precisely because of his vast difference in outlook and approach from the President's own contemporaries. Rusk, Rostow, McNamara, McGeorge Bundy, Alexis Johnson, Maxwell Taylor, and all five of the Joint Chiefs all belonged to the GI generation. In theory they almost unquestionably accepted the need to resist Communist expansion wherever it took place, and distrusted negotiation with adversaries; in practice they were exemplary bureaucrats, dedicated to team play, and quite willing to come forward with virtually identical proposals again and again. But Harriman, born in 1890, was a striking representative of the Lost generation: a lone wolf, distrustful of organizations and procedures, who trusted his own instincts and enjoyed nothing more than man-to-man talks with America's foremost adversaries. Enormously wealthy, he had spent his youth as a playboy, but had become President Roosevelt's personal representative in London and ambassador to the Soviet Union during the Second World War. While he was not the kind of man who would make a courageous public stand on principle, he would do anything to execute the wishes of a strong President, and on Laos Kennedy had now given him all the authority he needed to make sure that the President would not have to implement any of the endless stream of war plans that younger men were providing for him. Still, because of the momentum built up by the Eisenhower administration and kept alive by Kennedy's team, the issue of intervention in Southeast Asia refused to die.

War or Peace?
September–November 1961

★

September 1961 was a month of terrible crises. Soviet-American relations—the Kennedy administration's highest priority and most challenging problem—had reached a critical stage. The Soviets shocked the world on August 31 by resuming atmospheric nuclear testing, beginning a long series of tests that culminated in the detonation of a fifty-megaton bomb. Yet another crisis erupted on September 18, when U.N. Secretary General Dag Hammerskjold died in a plane crash on a mission to the Congo and the Soviets tried to use his death to increase their influence over the United Nations. Meanwhile, President Kennedy put increasing pressure on McGeorge Bundy and Dean Rusk to come up with new negotiating positions on Berlin.[1] Laos remained the only issue upon which the two countries had reached even an agreement in principle, and both parties began trying to complete this agreement during September.

In talks with the Soviet representative Georgi Pushkin on September 13, September 29, and October 10, Averell Harriman confirmed agreement on the need for a North Vietnamese withdrawal from Laos, while conceding that Chinese Nationalist troops in Laos would have to withdraw as well. Pushkin and Harriman also moved closer to agreement on the powers of the International Control Commission (ICC), and Harriman indicated that Laos might renounce the protection of SEATO, as the Communists had long demanded. "Moscow agrees with Harriman remark that US/Soviet relations could be different from what now exist," Pushkin commented on October 10. "Harriman has always been considered among those who sincerely want settlement of

US/Soviet differences because such development would be guarantee for maintaining world peace."[2] Harriman also visited Laos, where he found Souvanna considerably more forthcoming than Phoumi. By September 26 Harriman was warning Kennedy that the United States might have to withdraw its support for Phoumi if he continued refusing to negotiate. On September 29 Khrushchev himself wrote Kennedy suggesting that the Laotians themselves be allowed to decide on the personnel of their new government, and agreeing on the need for the withdrawal of foreign forces from Laos.[3]

Kennedy personally took some soundings regarding both Laos and South Vietnam in a long conversation with Prince Sihanouk, the Cambodian Prime Minister, at the United Nations in New York on September 25. Using a technique he frequently employed, Kennedy began by asking for the Prince's advice, and specifically for his opinion of Souvanna Phouma and some of his controversial cabinet nominees. Sihanouk replied that while he could not say that the nominees were actual Communists, they had worked with the Communists for years, and he doubted they would follow a neutral policy. Kennedy eventually asked for Sihanouk's frank opinion "of what was wrong in Vietnam." Diem, Sihanouk replied, had not gained popular support, and survived only because of American assistance. When Kennedy asked for Sihanouk's reaction to SEATO intervention in Laos, the Prince replied categorically that SEATO intervention would be very bad, since it would trigger Chinese and North Vietnamese retaliation, and all Southeast Asia would be overrun. SEATO, he said, could not defend countries unwilling to defend themselves.[4]

Several weeks later, on October 16, Kennedy answered Khrushchev's letter, acknowledging that Souvanna would become Prime Minister but repeating the American position that Souvanna must not fill his eight cabinet positions "in a manner which heavily weights the scales in favor of one side or the other."[5] After returning home, Sihanouk on November 16 declared that the American position in Southeast Asia might have been saved had Kennedy been President four years earlier, but that American mistakes had now made the establishment of a neutral government in Laos much harder.[6]

Rostow and the bureaucracy, however, were still moving in the opposite direction, and during September they went on the offensive again in response to a stream of reports linking new military problems in South Vietnam to developments in Laos. On September 1 Sterling Cottrell, the director of the Vietnam Task Force, passed along Saigon reports to Rusk stating that the Viet Cong had now grown from 10,000 to 15,000 active fighters largely through recruiting among the hill tribes along the Laotian border. Two weeks earlier, on August 17, Cottrell had dispatched William Jorden, a former *New York Times* reporter who had joined the State Department's Policy Planning council, to South Vietnam to gather evidence of North Vietnamese infiltration. On September 5 General McGarr cabled CINCPAC that intelligence reported several thousand Viet Cong now in southern Laos just over the border. The Embassy specifically reported a 1,000-man VC attack in Kontum province in the Central Highlands on September 5.[7] Rostow sounded the alarm over this build-up in another memorandum for Kennedy on September 15, and recommended "the implementation of SEATO Plan 5 now," or the creation of a command and logistics base to implement it—exactly the recommendations that Kennedy had rejected on August 29—and Taylor joined in on September 18.[8] On September 18 Ambassador Nolting cabled his view that a neutral Laos such as Harriman was seeking would not control infiltration into South Vietnam, thereby facing the United States "with the alternatives of sending US forces into SVN or backing down." Nolting recommended telling the Soviets that we could not accept Pushkin's guarantees to control the North Vietnamese, and suggested an informal partition of Laos that would leave the southern part in friendly hands.[9]

Kennedy had scheduled an address to the United Nations on September 25, and Rostow on September 15 suggested that he specifically state that "the territory of Laos is being used systematically to introduce external forces into South Vietnam," remind Khrushchev of his own promises regarding Laos, and ask the world community to "devote constructive attention" to the danger to peace in Southeast Asia.[10] Kennedy's speech did refer to "the smoldering coals of war in Southeast Asia" as one of two major threats to peace, but his discussion of Berlin far overshadowed it. "South Vietnam is under attack," he said, "sometimes by a single assassin, sometimes by a band of guerrillas, recently by full battalions . . . the peaceful people of Laos are in danger of losing the independence they gained not so long ago." Denying that these conflicts were "wars of liberation," he called for measures "to protect the small and the weak from such tactics. For if they are successful in

Laos and South Vietnam, the gates will be open wide."[11] Press accounts, however, paid relatively little attention to these passages.

The Viet Cong made five or six successful large-scale attacks during September: in the Central Highlands north of Kontum on September 5; at the provincial capital of Phuoc Thanh near their stronghold, War Zone D, on September 19, where they executed the province chief; and in several locations around the country, including the Highlands, the northern sections, and the Mekong Delta, between September 19 and September 22.[12] But when William Jorden returned from Saigon on September 27, he took a more restrained view of the infiltration danger. Despite some movement across the borders, he wrote, "We delude ourselves if we visualize the Viet Cong effort in the South as primarily a movement of large, organized units across the GVN borders. It is apparent that the VC rely on local recruitment, both by persuasion and by terror, for the bulk of their organization."[13] Southern Laos was only one of several base areas for the Viet Cong, whose strength was roughly proportional to the density of the South Vietnamese population, *not* to the proximity of an open frontier. Nine months earlier, Lansdale had correctly located the main problem in the Mekong Delta provinces surrounding Saigon. But for various reasons, as we shall see, both Diem and American military planners consistently preferred to focus on the border regions in the north and west of the country. Despite Jorden's conclusions, Rostow on September 29 suggested to a subordinate that Jorden's report become the basis for accusing North Vietnam of aggression in the United Nations, thus laying the foundation for the implementation of SEATO Plan 5.[14] While Rostow claimed to be interested in the threat of guerrilla warfare, his proposed responses were invariably conventional.

On the very same day, September 29, Diem suddenly dropped a new element into the situation in Saigon, when he asked Nolting and McGarr for a bilateral U.S.–South Vietnam defense treaty, such as Washington had concluded years earlier with Nationalist China. Nolting ascribed the proposal to Diem's concern over American policy in Laos and fear that SEATO would never act effectively. He recommended giving the suggestion serious consideration, but pointed out that the step would clearly violate the Geneva Accords of 1954. The State Department, making the same point, spoke of strengthening our commitment under SEATO instead.[15] A few days later, in a speech to the National

Assembly, Diem redefined the conflict in South Vietnam as a "real war," not a "guerrilla war," fought by regular units under orders from the Communist international.[16]

In an "eyes only for Secretary" cable of October 6, Nolting took another big step toward endorsing Diem's position. Contradicting his report of July 14 denying any improvement in the situation, he now said that while things had been improving until September, developments in Laos had reversed the trend. Infiltration from Laos now emerged as the root of all evil—the deteriorating security situation, the apprehension of South Vietnamese military leaders, the danger of a coup, the unavailability of South Vietnamese troops for training, and Diem's refusal to delegate authority. He admitted, however, that some subordinates took a different view.

"Two of my closest colleagues," Nolting wrote, "believe that this country cannot attain the required unity, total national dedication, and organizational efficiency necessary to win with Diem at the helm. This may be true. Diem does not organize well, does not delegate sufficient responsibility to his subordinates, and does not appear to know how to cultivate large-scale political support." Although these colleagues apparently included his deputy chief of mission, Joseph Mendenhall, Nolting still thought all-out support of Diem was the only possible American policy, and that it had an even chance of success, provided the border could be protected.[17] Nolting in effect was calling for intervention in Laos rather than a Souvanna government, as many of his State Department superiors had long proposed.

Meanwhile, the perception of a new crisis in South Vietnam was leading State to consider a variety of significant new alternatives, and even a fundamental change in policy. Thus, some State planners suggested amending the SEATO treaty to remove the requirement that all its signatories consent to a SEATO intervention, but Rusk on September 18 declined to present this proposal to the President.[18] Undersecretary of State Chester Bowles, going in quite a different direction, suggested to Rusk in a memorandum of October 5 that the United States should build upon Harriman's efforts in Geneva to push for the neutralization of all Southeast Asia. Although Bowles later reported that both Harriman and Undersecretary of State for European Affairs George Ball agreed with him, he admitted that the memo had produced "a relatively negative reaction" at State as a whole, and a meeting he proposed between himself, Rusk, Ball, Harriman, and Alexis Johnson never took place. Bowles, in any case, was arguing from a weak position, since his days on the job were numbered. He had antagonized the President and Robert Kennedy at the time of the Bay of Pigs, and he had barely saved his job by leaking news of his impending dismissal in mid-July.[19]

At the same time, all through September, discussions continued among Rostow and his staff at the White House, Alexis Johnson and others at State, and Joint Chiefs of Staff (JCS) planners regarding SEATO Plan 5 and, by early October, a new plan for intervention in South Vietnam.[20] On October 5 Rostow wrote yet another long and stirring memo to Kennedy calling for intervention. "The sense of the town is that, with Southern Laos open, Diem simply cannot cope," Rostow said. Rostow needed relatively little convincing on this point, since his study of guerrilla warfare in Greece during the late 1940s had convinced him that guerrillas possessing sanctuaries over an open border were nearly impossible to defeat.[21] Rostow now suggested a three-pronged political/military offensive to try to expose and deal with the infiltration problem, and concluded with "my old pitch: it is essential that Generals Taylor and Lansdale take a good, hard look at Vietnam on the ground, soon."[22]

The Joint Chiefs had other ideas. They told McNamara on October 9 that forces in South Vietnam should not go on the border, and they secured his agreement, crucially, that "if we cannot go into Laos, we should go into South Vietnam, with SEATO." McNamara asked for an immediate recommendation on the number of troops needed "to eliminate Viet Cong." Nine months into the Kennedy administration, McNamara had emerged as the can-do man of the new team and one of Kennedy's two most trusted cabinet members.[23] He had already tangled frequently with the Joint Chiefs on issues of weapons procurement and, crucially, American reliance on nuclear weapons, an issue very close to the President's heart. On Southeast Asia, he had helped hold the line against a troop commitment during the summer by pleading the priority of the Berlin crisis, but he was now coming around to the Joint Chiefs' position. The Secretary of Defense was beginning to see South Vietnam as a critical military test—one which, typically, he eagerly wanted to meet. Earlier, on August 28, he had told the Joint Chiefs that he wanted to make South Vietnam "a laboratory for the development of organization and procedures for the conduct of sub-limited war," run by an experimental command directly responsible to the Secretary's Office.[24]

The Chiefs made their own recommendations on October 9. SEATO Plan 5 remained their preferred option to ensure the defense of Southeast Asia as a whole, and they rejected piecemeal deployments of SEATO forces along South Vietnam's borders on a variety of very reasonable grounds. As an additional, non-preferred alternative, they proposed deploying one division (9,600 men) of SEATO forces in the Central Highlands (referred to in this and many other contemporary documents as the "high plateau region"), together with headquarters, air, reserve, and support units totaling "about 13,200" men. These men would free up South Vietnamese forces for counterinsurgency operations, but would also be expected to operate across the Laotian border.

The Kennedy administration had expanded American ground forces, and the Chiefs had abandoned Admiral Radford's 1956 plans to defend South Vietnam with a few regimental combat teams armed with tactical nuclear weapons. They estimated that North Vietnamese intervention in response—which the Chiefs tended to doubt—would require more than twelve SEATO divisions to meet, of which the United States would provide only three, plus major air units. "When appropriate," they said—echoing plans in effect for the last six years—"SEATO forces would mount a general offensive against the enemy," possibly through amphibious landings. Should the Chinese intervene, SEATO would require more than fifteen divisions—four of them American—and, very possibly, authorization to use nuclear weapons.[25] The Chiefs had now answered Robert Kennedy's query at the meeting of August 29 regarding what would be required in response to Communist escalation, but their estimates foresaw wildly over-optimistic contributions from unnamed SEATO allies, and confirmed Kennedy's suspicion that the war would become massive and perhaps nuclear.

The President remained unlikely to accept such plans, but one service had also produced a smaller-scale plan tailored to the situation in South Vietnam. In March 1961 the Air Force, under General LeMay, had established the 4400th Combat Crew Training Squadron, nicknamed Jungle Jim, to provide air support to counterinsurgency efforts with older, propeller-driven aircraft. In early September, LeMay had suggested to McNamara that the unit go to Vietnam to develop new special warfare methods, and the Chiefs apparently sold this recommendation to the State Department in early October.[26]

On October 11 Alexis Johnson presented yet another paper on Southeast Asia to Kennedy and his entire senior national security team. Its opening sections on Laos respected the President's position, in that they focused on the Geneva negotiations and did not simply assume, like so many earlier efforts, that those talks would fail. Surveying the situation in Thailand, where confidence in the United States and SEATO had dropped, the report recommended that voting within SEATO be changed from unanimity to majority or three-fourths' rule. Regarding Vietnam, the paper noted that Diem had neither increased his political support nor created an effective chain of command. It combined Rostow's proposals for a "white paper" on North Vietnamese aggression and a request for U.N. observers to verify it with the Chiefs' military proposals of October 9, calling for a division in the Highlands and massive plans to meet North Vietnamese or Chinese escalation. First, however, it recommended the dispatch of a "very high-level military figure" to explore the political and military feasibility of intervention. Any plan, it added, should also result in improved GVN political performance—suggesting that leverage was once again in fashion. The paper also suggested the immediate dispatch of the Jungle Jim Air Force unit to South Vietnam.[27]

Despite Kennedy's repeated, low-key admonitions against fighting a war in Southeast Asia, the bureaucracy could come up with nothing else in response to new problems within South Vietnam, and the President made two limited but rather critical concessions on October 11. First, Kennedy authorized the dispatch of the Jungle Jim squadron to South Vietnam to serve under the MAAG as a training mission, but not for combat. Second, the President finally yielded to Rostow's long-repeated request and agreed to dispatch Taylor, together with Rostow, Lansdale, and various other representatives, to Vietnam that weekend to evaluate the JCS proposal, a more limited troop proposal, or "alternatives in lieu of putting US combat forces in Vietnam." State, meanwhile, would prepare a White Paper and discuss SEATO action in South Vietnam with our allies. The President announced the dispatch of the mission that afternoon, prompting an angry protest from Nolting, who, like the South Vietnamese, learned about the mission through the press.[28]

Rostow, Taylor, and most of the senior leadership team apparently expected the mission to recommend some form of American intervention. Taylor's own October 11 draft of his instructions from Kennedy asked the general "to evaluate what could be accomplished by the introduction of SEATO or United States forces into South Vietnam, determining the role, composition and probable disposition of such forces," and "concurrently" to make suggestions for improvements of South Vietnamese forces.[29] Kennedy, however, had other ideas.

The most critical episode in the drama of Kennedy's quiet attempts to reorient American diplomacy was now coming to a head, not over Southeast Asia, but over Berlin. In the two months since the Berlin Wall had gone up on August 13, Kennedy had attempted without success to redefine the nature of the Berlin crisis. As he repeatedly told his subordinates, he wanted serious negotiations with the Soviets, and might be prepared to sign parallel peace treaties with East and West Germany, to recognize the Oder-Neisse boundary, to give at least implicit recognition to East Germany, and to discuss some kind of denuclearization agreement, in return for new guarantees of Western access to Berlin. He had, however, experienced great difficulty moving the State Department toward these positions. More important, when he and other officials had begun orchestrating a press campaign to prepare public opinion for such a deal, the West Germans and the French, who had not been informed of his intentions, had reacted angrily.

Rusk had finally begun discussions with Soviet Foreign Minister Andrei Gromyko in late September, and their conversation of September 30 seemed to indicate a basis for possible agreement.[30] But on October 2 McGeorge Bundy warned Kennedy that the proposed deal—new guarantees of access in exchange for recognition of the boundaries of the two Germanies, restrictions on nuclear weapons, and a new status for West Berlin—would involve substantial Western concessions in return for a reassertion of existing Western rights. "Unless something more is put into the record before these conversations close," Bundy wrote Kennedy on October 2, "I think we are on a dangerous slope of appeasement, and I am certain that this will be the view of the Germans, the Frenchmen and the Republicans." He also warned, using a phrase of Rusk's, against "buying the same horse twice," and suggested that any new agreement include new guarantees of Western access, and international, rather than East German, supervision or control of at least some of the access routes.[31]

Bundy's memorandum raised the essential dilemma of the Kennedy administration. The President himself, despite his hard-line campaign rhetoric, was trying to ease the atmosphere of the Cold War by reaching new agreements on critical issues. He had, however, chosen his cabinet largely in response to broader political considerations, and most of his senior national security team did not share this priority. Thus, Adlai Stevenson as Secretary of State would surely have better understood the President's approach and could have lent his own considerable prestige to carrying it out, but Stevenson had fatally alienated the Kennedys by making a late, half-hearted run for the Presidency in 1960, and Kennedy had chosen the safe but unadventurous Rusk instead. Now Bundy, who as Republican had been another safe, consensus choice as National Security Adviser, was suggesting that the President might be heading for a kind of diplomatic Bay of Pigs—a bold initiative likely to backfire politically, both at home and abroad. In 1959, when Ben Bradlee had asked him whether he really thought he could be elected President, Kennedy had replied, "Yes, if I don't make a single mistake myself, and if I don't get maneuvered into a position where there is no way out."[32] After his razor-thin victory, Kennedy had apparently continued to follow this rule as he looked ahead to 1964. And with respect to Berlin, Khrushchev, now busily exploding multi-megaton bombs, had hardly given him much to work with in his careful quest for détente.

Seemingly convinced by Bundy, Kennedy took the same position himself with Gromyko on October 6, and leaked the line about purchasing the same horse twice to the press.[33] Subsequent talks bogged down, as Rusk insisted upon promises that Western rights would be guaranteed before serious discussions of broader issues. Despite this tactical retreat, however, Kennedy was still concentrating upon relations with the Soviets, and still disliked the idea of American troops in Southeast Asia. After approving the Taylor mission on the morning of October 11, he entertained the columnist Arthur Krock for lunch. Krock prepared an account of the conversation immediately afterward. Over a Bloody Mary and "a very good lunch," Kennedy began with Berlin, apparently trying to prepare the ground for a new agreement:

> The status quo, which so many of his critics expound, is no policy at all. The situation there is as undesirable for the United States and the West

as it is for the Russians in a good many particulars. It is Mr. Kennedy's "inheritance," "a dangerous mess," and his critics, especially the Republicans, should come up with concrete suggestions to clear up the mess instead of yelling "appeasement" whenever he tries to find out if any compromise is possible—using "compromise" in the dictionary sense of a "settlement reached by mutual concessions."

Then Kennedy turned to Vietnam:

The President had just come from a meeting on the problem in that country. He said the Pentagon generally approved a recommendation by the Chiefs of Staff to send 40,000 troops there. The President said he was not favorable to the suggestion at this time *and therefore was sending General Maxwell Taylor to investigate and report what should be done.* It was a hell of a note, he said, that he had to try to handle the Berlin situation with the Communists encouraging foreign aggressors all over the place. The President said he was thinking of writing Khrushchev, urging him to call off these aggressors in Vietnam, Laos, etc., and asking Khrushchev how he thought he could negotiate with Kennedy if their positions were reversed. The President still believes, he said, in what he told the Senate several years ago—that United States troops should not be involved on the Asian mainland, especially in a country with the difficult terrain of Laos and inhabited by people who don't care how the East-West dispute as to freedom and self-determination was resolved. Moreover, said the President, the United States can't interfere in civil disturbances created by guerrillas, and it was hard to prove this wasn't largely the situation in Vietnam.

I asked him what he thought of the "falling domino" theory—that is, if Laos and Vietnam go Communist, the rest of South East Asia will fall to them in orderly succession. The President expressed doubts that this theory has much point any more because, he remarked the Chinese Communists are bound to get nuclear weapons in time, and from that moment on they will dominate South East Asia.[34]

Krock's column the next day repeated the essentials of the conversation regarding Berlin almost verbatim.[35] This conversation, together with Kennedy's repeated refusal of proposals for war in Southeast Asia, helps correct a myth initially propagated by David Halberstam in his 1972 book, *The Best and the Brightest:* that Kennedy, in a conversation with James Reston immediately after his meeting with Khrushchev in Vienna, specifically referred to Vietnam as the place to demonstrate the credibility of American power. Even Reston himself eventually repeated this story in his memoirs in 1988, but in a much earlier column on June 10, 1979, Reston made clear that the link between Vienna and the increased commitment to Vietnam later in the year was simply an *inference* on his part, and did not reflect what Kennedy had told him. In fact, as we shall see, Kennedy never regarded Southeast Asia as a propitious place to deploy American power.[36]

Two days later, Kennedy gave Maxwell Taylor revised instructions confirming his opposition to direct involvement. Dropping the general's language, which had asked him to choose among different proposals for the use of American and other SEATO forces, Kennedy simply asked for "courses of action which our Government might take at this juncture to avoid a further deterioration in the situation in South Vietnam and eventually to contain and eliminate the threat to its independence. In your assessment," he continued, "you should bear in mind that the initial responsibility for the effective maintenance of the independence of South Vietnam rests with the people and government of that country. Our efforts must be evaluated, and your recommendations formulated, with this fact in mind." Taylor's recommendations should take full account of political, social, and economic elements of the situation, which were "equally significant" to military ones.[37] The press was not entirely under control, and the redoubtable Joseph Alsop had written a blood-curdling column on October 12 predicting the dispatch of American troops to South Vietnam. On October 13, after a meeting with the President, General Lemnitzer cabled Admiral Felt in Honolulu that the President had "expressed concern over build-up of stories to effect U.S. is contemplating sending combat forces to Vietnam," which might well not occur.[38]

The Taylor mission, with Rostow, Lansdale, and various other military and civilian representatives in tow, left Washington on October 15, spent two days in Honolulu, arrived in Saigon on October 18, and departed on October 25, eventually returning to Washington via Bangkok on November 3. Unlike many subsequent American missions to Saigon, it actually made the visit first and drafted its report afterward. And while many of the report's proposals reflected long-standing thinking in Washington, the mission's experiences in Vietnam had a profound effect as well.

By the time the mission left on October 15, the Pentagon had developed a list of twenty military recommendations. They included both the immediate deployment of several American combat units and extensive logistical preparations to deploy many more.[39] *Time* published some of these recommendations on October 21.[40] Of all their proposed measures, only training for the Civil Guard and Self-Defense Corps addressed the political problems of counterinsurgency. When Taylor saw Diem on October 18, Diem asked for tactical aviation, helicopter companies, coastal patrol forces, and logistic support, and these recommendations, as well as the Jungle Jim unit already agreed to, found their way into Taylor's eventual report of November 3.[41]

At the same time, the mission concluded, in essence, that the United States had to go on the political offensive again with respect to Diem. Too many reports now stated that Diem had not made the changes recommended back in the spring, particularly concerning the military chain of command and the need to broaden the base of his government. Even Nolting, while arguing for a careful balance between the ideal and the possible, agreed that increased American aid gave the United States both a right and a duty to demand that Diem take "extensive steps" to strengthen his government politically. The Embassy drew up a long list of reforms to demand, and some of Diem and Nhu's closest collaborators even told CIA operatives that changes simply had to occur.[42]

During his mission, Taylor received very blunt reports regarding the same difficulties from two Vietnamese sources. On October 19 General Duong Van Minh—"Big Minh," as he was often known—the Commanding General, ARVN Field Command, told Taylor that the entire population had lost confidence in Diem, that Diem favored certain religious groups over others, and that Diem still maintained a second chain of command through frequently incompetent province chiefs. The next day, Vice President Tho also indicated that the United States had to bring about changes in "Diem's methods of government and administration." On October 23 Lansdale, who still saw himself as the key to the situation, gave Taylor a concrete suggestion: "to place the right Americans into the right areas of the Vietnamese government to provide *operational* guidance." Vietnamese officials, he suggested, might be invited to request Americans of their choice. When Taylor raised the question of additional American personnel in his last talk with Diem on October 25, Diem asked for more help in *training*, and, coincidentally enough, asked for Lansdale's services in Vietnam. A State Department marginal note suggested that Lansdale's own dispatch remained most unlikely, but the general recommendation for a network of American operating officials at many levels was the main political recommendation of the eventual Taylor report.[43] Given what the mission heard, the report inevitably revived the approach which Ambassador Durbrow had pushed during 1960, but which Nolting had abandoned: that the United States had to force Diem to alter his behavior.

The question of American troops also took a new turn as a result of the visit. Despite Kennedy's clear preference, Taylor in the end recommended a small contingent, initially for political rather than military reasons. While acknowledging the limited impact of such a contingent and the risk of escalation, Taylor saw troops as the only solution to a Vietnamese crisis of confidence both in the Diem government and in the U.S. commitment to South Vietnam.

On October 13—two days after the Washington announcement of the Taylor mission—Ambassador Nolting and General McGarr had had a long conversation with Thuan, Diem's Secretary of State and Minister of Defense. Thuan generally had a much easier relationship with American officials than Diem or Nhu, and often acted as go-between on sensitive issues. He now specifically asked for new aircraft, American pilots for helicopters, and "U.S. combat units or units to be introduced into SVN as 'combat trainer units,' stationed in the north near the 17th parallel and in the Central Highlands." Three days later Nolting again linked these demands to Diem's concern over the possibility of a neutral government in Laos, which the ambassador opposed as well, and recommended some combination of U.S. reinforcements and political reforms to strengthen the South.[44]

When Taylor and Rostow saw Diem for the first time on October 18, Diem asked for air, sea, and logistics forces to help meet the threat posed by the Laos situation, but did not specifically ask for American combat troops. When Lansdale met with Diem's brother Nhu on October 21, Nhu vehemently attacked American policy in Laos and asked for some immediate proof from Taylor of an American intention to act, but not specifically for troops. Meanwhile, the mission heard repeatedly of widespread distress over the recent large-scale Viet Cong attacks, and the government suffered another blow when the body of ARVN Colonel Hoang Thuy Nam, the Saigon liaison to the ICC whom the VC had kidnapped on October 1, was found on October 17 near Saigon. A severe flood in the Mekong Delta also shook the government, and American officials immediately seized upon the disaster as a possible new excuse for the introduction of American forces.[45]

Despite Diem and Nhu's failure to ask for troops, Taylor on October 25, his last day in Saigon, cabled Washington that he intended to recommend "a task force consisting largely of logistical troops for the purpose of participating in flood relief and at the same time of providing a U.S. military presence in VN capable of assuring Diem of our readiness to join him in a military showdown with the Viet Cong or Viet Minh [that is, the North Vietnamese Army]." The 6,000–8,000 men he had in mind, he acknowledged, would have little military effect, but they would "give a much needed shot in the arm to national morale, particularly if combined with other actions showing that a more effective working relationship in the common cause has been established between the GVN and the U.S." He did not, however, broach this proposal to Diem that day.[46] Diem in an interview with a *New York Times* correspondent on October 28 pointedly declined to request American troops, but a few days later, on October 31, Nolting reported that conversations with Vietnamese over the last ten days showed an almost unanimous desire for U.S. forces, arising from a serious decline in morale in the wake of Colonel Nam's death and expanded VC infiltration, which he claimed had underlined the American failure to act aggressively in Laos.[47]

Taylor actually reported in two separate stages. On November 1, before his return, he addressed two "eyes only" cables to the President, summarizing the conclusions and recommendations of the report, and specifically trying to explain his rationale for American troops. Despite the paucity of our strategic reserves, the increased commitment of U.S. prestige that would be involved, the possibility of further demands for American troops, and the increased risks of escalation, Taylor argued, American and South Vietnamese officials agreed that "there can be no action so convincing of U.S. seriousness of purpose and hence so reassuring to the people and Government of SVN and to our other friends and allies in SEA as the introduction of U.S. forces into SVN." He therefore recommended the introduction of the flood-relief task force. He continued, in a passage that recapitulated many of Rostow's favorite arguments:

The risks of backing into a major Asian war by way of SVN are present but are not impressive. NVN is extremely vulnerable to conventional bombing, a weakness which should be exploited diplomatically in convincing Hanoi to lay off SVN. Both the DRV and the Chicoms would face severe logistical difficulties in trying to maintain strong forces in the field in SEA, difficulties which we share but by no means to the same degree. There is no cause for fearing a mass onslaught of Communist manpower into SVN and its neighboring states, particularly if our airpower is allowed a free hand against logistical targets. Finally, the starvation conditions in China should discourage Communist leaders there from being militarily venturesome for some time to come.

Without the recommended force of 8,000, Taylor concluded, "I do not believe that our program to save SVN will succeed."[48] He accepted the risk of a larger conflict based on arguments about enemy logistical difficulties and vulnerability to bombing that Rostow had been repeating for months—and that General MacArthur had used to discount Chinese intervention in Korea in 1950. The report argued, in effect, that conventional American power could deter or defeat guerrilla war at a relatively low cost. Exactly how Taylor and Rostow persuaded themselves that air action alone might save the situation remains unclear. Rostow made clear in 1964, without altogether explaining why, that he had rejected out of hand the Joint Chiefs' estimates—conveyed to Kennedy earlier in the year—of the fifteen and eight divisions, respectively, which the North Vietnamese and Chinese could deploy within the area in response to American moves.[49]

The official mission report of November 3 looked forward more bluntly to a new war, and Rostow discussed presumed North Vietnamese military vulnerabilities at considerably greater length.[50] The United States, Taylor argued, had to decide how to cope with

> Khrushchev's "wars of liberation" which are really para-wars of guerrilla aggression . . . a new and dangerous technique which bypasses our traditional political and military responses . . . the time may come in our relations to Southeast Asia when we must declare our intention to attack the source of guerrilla aggression in North Vietnam and impose on the Hanoi Government a price for participating in the current war which is commensurate with the damage being inflicted on its neighbors to the south.[51]

And later, in the body of the report, Rostow and Taylor essentially rewrote the scenario proposed by Rostow in papers late in the summer: a new exchange of letters between Kennedy and Diem, the publication of the Jorden report on infiltration, a complaint at the United Nations, a special session of Congress, a resolution of support, and "a quiet message to the U.S.S.R. . . . indicating that we propose to help defend South Vietnam and urging Moscow to use its influence with Ho Chi Minh to call his dogs off, mind his business, and feed his people."

Taylor's report raises several interesting issues. The general's book *The Uncertain Trumpet* (1959) had earned him a reputation as an innovative thinker, but he now proposed to win a guerrilla war by turning it into a conventional one. Essentially, he and Rostow were taking very nearly the same line that John Foster Dulles had taken back in 1954: that the United States should respond to any new Communist aggression in Asia by striking directly at the source, which had then been regarded as Peking. Striking at Hanoi initially seemed less risky, since neither man seemed to take North Vietnam's conventional capability very seriously. Certainly they were not proposing any new political or military strategy to fight guerrillas, but rather an adaptation of conventional strategy to a new situation. And both of them, remarkably, ignored the experience of the Korean War, in which the most unrestrained bombing of North Korea had failed significantly to affect the Chinese and North Korean ability to fight on the ground.

As Taylor, Rostow, and company concluded their work, Washington resolved a new crisis in the Laos negotiations. On October 26 Harriman, who apparently understood that the Taylor mission might revive proposals for military action in Southeast Asia, argued for taking some new risks to reach a settlement. Phoumi, he said, was the major obstacle to an agreement, and Souvanna would indeed enlarge and broaden his proposed cabinet if Phoumi began negotiating seriously. He recommended bypassing Phoumi in order to get things on track. The President still wanted a peaceful settlement that would provide "a reasonable chance" of a neutral and independent Laos, he argued, and such a settlement was virtually within his grasp, provided the United States rejected new military moves in Laos. He continued that commitments from Souvanna and from the Soviets to block the use of Laotian territory as a corridor should help the South Vietnamese problem, which in any event must be solved within South Vietnam and not by military action within Laos. While the introduction of SEATO forces into Laos could lead to very dangerous escalation, the settlement of the Laos question might also lead to progress on Berlin.[52]

The whole direction of American policy in Indochina now hung in the balance. John Steeves, the chairman of the Vietnam Task Force, warned Acting Secretary of State Bowles on November 1 that Harriman was buying the agreement at the expense of yet another major concession—the Russian demand that the ICC could only issue unanimous reports, although it might approve investigations by majority vote. He enclosed a Defense Department memo listing the concessions the United States had made, and recommended recalling Harriman to reconsider our position in light of Taylor's forthcoming report. Bowles, apparently agreeing, told Alexis Johnson to call Harriman in Geneva, but Harriman flatly refused to come home, claiming that the agreement was ready.

Late in the afternoon of November 1 Bowles telephoned Kennedy, who invited him to the White House, where he was meeting with Ambassador to India John Kenneth Galbraith and with former President Truman. Kennedy telephoned Harriman himself, and asked whether the Polish Communist representative on the ICC would be able to silence his Canadian and Indian colleagues. Harriman assured him that he would not, since the agreement provided that the commission's reports would also register differences of opinion. Kennedy authorized him to accept the language while securing additional clarification from the Indian delegation. Later that day Harriman reported that Pushkin, the Soviet delegate, had also agreed that the Soviets and the British, as co-chairmen, should guarantee that their allies would observe the agreement, and that the Soviets and Souvanna were committed to stopping North Vietnamese infiltration. "I am grateful for your faith and support," he told the President.[53]

Having kept the Laos talks on track, Kennedy was ready when Taylor returned on November 3. The day before, he received a memorandum from Senate Majority Leader Mansfield, opposing Taylor's already-rumored recommendation of troops. Mansfield, the Senate's leading authority on Asia and one of Diem's original patrons, was now losing faith. "If the necessary reforms have not been forthcoming over the past seven years to stop communist subversion and rebellion, then I do not see how American combat troops can do it today," he wrote. And on Saturday, after Taylor returned and met the President briefly, the *New York Times* lead story was headlined, "President Is Cool on Asia Troop Aid . . . Kennedy Remains Opposed to Sending of Forces after Hearing Report," and reported, "Officials said it was correct to infer from this that General Taylor did not look favorably on the sending of United States combat troops at this time." Kennedy was making sure that the public perception of Taylor's report reflected his original strictures against troops. On the same day General Taylor told a meeting of the senior national security team, less Kennedy and Rusk, that the President was "instinctively against introduction of US forces," wanted everyone's recommendations on Tuesday, November 7, and wanted Diem to broaden the representation in his government in exchange for further assistance.[54] Kennedy also ordered that Taylor's true recommendations be very closely held, and the *Times* on November 5 repeated that the President opposed American troops and noted that Washington planned to push Saigon to make necessary reforms. The next issue of *Newsweek* also stated that the general had opposed troops.[55]

The Departments of State and Defense, however, seemed still to be basing their recommendations upon the Eisenhower administration policy of military resistance to Communist expansion, if necessary, alone. They paid relatively little attention to Taylor's specific recommendations, and they disregarded Kennedy's strictures against American troops entirely. Instead, seizing upon Taylor's statement that nothing less than his program would save South Vietnam, they now proposed the most sweeping military measures in South Vietnam yet discussed. Pulling and hauling over Southeast Asia continued for ten more days, culminating in a National Security Council (NSC) meeting on November 15. While the news headlines generally focused upon new problems in Berlin, a visit from Indian Prime Minister Nehru, new fighting in the Congo, and Soviet diplomatic pressure upon Finland, the highest officials of the government debated the wisdom of going to war in Southeast Asia.

The Defense Department had taken a back seat with respect to Southeast Asia during the summer and early fall of 1961, but the Berlin build-up had now been completed, and McNamara and his subordinates moved into a leading role. Taking charge at an interdepartmental meeting on Saturday, November 6, McNamara stepped into his can-do persona, wrote off the Taylor recommendations as inadequate to save South Vietnam, and demanded that other forces be made ready for action against North Vietnam: "The forces—6 to 8 divisions—required to meet Communist escalation in SEA are available." After the meeting, McNamara asked William Bundy, the Deputy Assistant Secretary of Defense for International Security Affairs (and older brother of McGeorge Bundy), to draft a memorandum for the President.[56]

William Bundy continued to play an enormous role in the design of Vietnam policy from 1961 through 1968, and the ideas in his paper recurred again and again. He began by recommending that the United States "commit itself to the clear objective of preventing the fall of South Vietnam to Communism . . . The fall of South Vietnam to Communism would lead to the fairly rapid extension of Communist control, or complete accommodation to Communism, in the rest of mainland Southeast Asia right down to Indonesia. The strategic implications worldwide would be extremely serious." Echoing McNamara, Bundy argued that the 8,000-man force would not convince the other side that Washington meant business, and estimated the maximum likely commitment at six to eight divisions, or about 200,000 men. The American commitment in Vietnam eventually reached eight divisions, but by that time the total number of men exceeded 500,000. McNamara discussed these recommendations with General Lemnitzer the next day, Monday, November 6. Disagreements between the Secretary of Defense and the Chiefs on a number of points were already leaking into the press,[57] but McNamara was going along with them on Southeast Asia.[58] No one seems to have considered the logistical problems associated with such proposals. When deployments to Vietnam actually began in 1965, it took more than two years to create the logistics base necessary to support troops on the scale envisioned.

The senior leadership was scheduled to meet with Kennedy late on November 7, but that morning, Rusk said that "those working on [Southeast Asia] have too simplified a view," and he, McGeorge Bundy, and Kennedy decided to postpone the meeting for twenty-four hours.[59] In the interim, a redraft of William Bundy's paper by Alexis Johnson turned it into a joint declaration of the views of Rusk, McNamara, and the Joint Chiefs. The redraft, like some of Johnson's recent papers on Laos, suggested that the Deputy Undersecretary—and perhaps Rusk as well—now understood the President's reluctance to commit American combat troops to the area and his desire to conclude the Laotian talks successfully. While doubting that anything less than American troops would save the situation, the new draft proposed that a combination of "our prompt revamping of the administrative and military command structure of the GVN," new American military equipment, a greater role for the MAAG, and threats to Hanoi to bring about "a sharp diminution in Communist support to the Viet Cong" might achieve "some stabilization of the situation in South Vietnam." An effective warning, however, would require "a clear decision to commit ourselves to the objective of preventing the fall of South Vietnam to Communism and the willingness to commit whatever United States combat forces may be required to accomplish this objective."

Johnson also argued that the immediate introduction of combat forces might easily wreck the Laos talks. The draft, then, recommended committing the United States to prevent the fall of South Vietnam; communicating this decision to the Communist bloc; continuing to work for a Laotian settlement; and implementing the recommendations of the Taylor report, *less* the recommendation for American combat forces.[60] McNamara and Lemnitzer attended a meeting at the State Department that evening, and McNamara came away convinced that the Pentagon had to try to find ways to make new military steps in Vietnam less visible, largely for the sake of the Laos negotiations.[61]

The meeting with the President was postponed again. Both Defense and State produced new drafts of the agreed paper, and all the principals but the President discussed them at the State Department on the afternoon of Thursday, November 9. The State redraft dropped any recommendation for the *immediate* use of combat troops, but foresaw an eventual, initial deployment just south of the 17th parallel. Rusk now leaned strongly "toward introducing administrators, MAAG, etc.—it does not commit US as does combat forces. Reluctant to put in US forces until Diem makes a 100% effort in his area." Harriman, meanwhile, introduced an entirely new element into the situation, proposing "a conference" and a confrontation with the Soviet Union after a deployment was ready, but before it was made. He also confirmed, in response to Rusk's question, that an immediate American deployment in South Vietnam would "blow open [the] Laotian situation."[62] The next morning the *New York Times* reported that the Air Force had already begun flying bombers, helicopters, and fighters into South Vietnam, as part of an expanded aid mission, and noted the dispatch of the Jungle Jim air force unit.[63]

A final redraft was ready for the President on Saturday, November 11. On the surface, it followed the basic line of argument developed over the preceding week, laying out the same drastic consequences of the fall of South Vietnam, adding a sentence regarding the "bitter domestic controversies" that the loss of South Vietnam would unleash, stressing the need for reform of the Saigon government, recommending a clear American commitment to save South Vietnam, but *apparently* deferring the introduction of American combat forces, largely in order to save the Laos talks. Meanwhile, however, and without any interdepartmental discussion that has left any trace behind, the Pentagon had introduced new language at three points of the draft—language which critically redefined the nature of the American role in South Vietnam.

The draft, to begin with, blurred the distinction between combat and non-combat (or advisory) U.S. forces by dividing American forces into two categories:

(A) Units of modest size required for the direct support of South Vietnamese military effort, such as communications, helicopter and other forms of airlift, reconnaissance aircraft, naval patrols, intelligence units, etc., and (B) larger organized units with actual or potential military missions. *Category (A) should be introduced as speedily as possible.* Category (B) units pose a more serious problem in that they are much more significant from the point of view of domestic and international political factors and greatly increase the probabilities of Communist bloc escalation.

The specific, immediate military recommendations of the new draft included the following:

(a) Provide increased air lift to the GVN forces, including helicopters, light aviation, and transport aircraft, *manned to the extent necessary by United States uniformed personnel and under United States operational control.*

(b) Provide such additional equipment and United States uniformed personnel as may be necessary for air reconnaissance, photography, *instruction in and execution of air-ground support techniques,* and for special intelligence.

(c) Provide the GVN with small craft, including such United States uniformed advisers *and operating personnel* as may be necessary for quick and effective operations in effective *surveillance and control* over coastal waters and inland waterways . . .

(f) Provide such new terms of reference, reorganization and additional personnel for United States military forces as are required for *increased United States participation in the direction and control of GVN military operations and to carry out the other increased responsibilities which accrue to MAAG under these recommendations.*[64]

Read carefully, the first three of these recommendations committed American forces to war in South Vietnam, in the air, in support of ground operations, and at sea. The last—replacing earlier language that had referred only to an expanded MAAG—led to the creation of an actual military command headquarters not responsible to the Embassy, in contrast to the situation prevailing in Laos in the fall of 1960, which the Joint Chiefs had tried and failed to reverse under Eisenhower.

Before the meeting to discuss the draft with the President, Rostow wrote yet another long memo for Kennedy asking the President to go beyond the recommendations of the draft and introduce some American forces into South Vietnam at once, rather than exercise restraint out of fear of Communist retaliation.[65] After a brief meeting with Taylor and Rostow, Kennedy met with them, Rusk, McNamara, Alexis Johnson, McGeorge Bundy, Paul Nitze, Robert Kennedy, and General Lemnitzer at noon on Saturday, November 11. Rusk presented the conclusions of the paper. When Rusk specifically listed the recommended military steps under paragraph 3—including those quoted above—Kennedy apparently commented that they sounded "like Laos," and asked about giving them an international character by using some SEATO allied forces. The President's remark seemed to overlook a crucial difference. Americans were performing many of the same functions in the Royal Laotian Army, including flying helicopters and aircraft, but they were acting covertly, apparently under contract to the CIA, rather than as uniformed personnel taking orders from a local American military headquarters.

Then, once again, as he had in April, May, July, August, and October, Kennedy made clear that he differed fundamentally from his advisers' approach to Southeast Asia. Ignoring the draft's statements regarding the domestic consequences of *losing* South Vietnam, he commented that the administration had "a Congressional problem," since "Senator Russell and others are opposed." "Troops," Lemnitzer's notes of the meeting quoted him as saying, "are a last resort. Should be SEATO forces. Will create a tough domestic problem. Would like to avoid statements like Laos & Berlin." Robert Kennedy added that while the President had to make a statement in the wake of Taylor's mission, "We are not sending combat troops. Not committing ourselves to combat troops," and that the effort should be as "much SEATO as possible."

McNamara, stating the view of the Joint Chiefs, said that the proposed actions would not solve the problem, and that further action would be required. Rusk asked for general approval of the paper's approach, but Kennedy specifically refused to approve the commitment of the United States to saving South Vietnam, suggesting that it might lead to war with China. He would, he said, approve the planning for various different uses of American forces; the specific, immediate military steps that the paper outlined; Nolting's approach to Diem, demanding further reforms; and a new exchange of letters with Diem. Again, with respect to the specific military actions approved, he asked that they be "as multilateral as possible."[66] McNamara apparently interpreted the meeting as granting formal approval for the proposals concerning short-term military assistance, and issued orders that day ordering them to go forward.

The meeting apparently left other principals in some uncertainty regarding future action. McGeorge Bundy began drafting a National Security Action Memorandum to reflect the meeting's conclusions, but some confusion remained, and Bundy told Taylor that he felt "the President does not know what he is approving."[67] Meanwhile, a small dissident group within the administration had begun trying to introduce a contrary view. Harriman on November 11 had given a memorandum proposing a different course to Rusk, and Rusk on the next day authorized him to give it to the President. Essentially, Harriman proposed that he follow up on a forthcoming Laotian agreement by opening new Geneva talks on Vietnam, beginning with an approach to Pushkin. "A peaceful settlement," he said, "should be built on the foundation of the 1954 accords. The U.S.S.R. and the United Kingdom, as co-chairmen, should bring together a small group of the powers directly concerned to review the accords to see how compliance can be secured and how they can be strengthened to meet today's needs." In sharp contrast to Rusk, Alexis Johnson, and Rostow, who never seemed to mention the provisions of the 1954 accords calling for elections and reunification of Vietnam and spoke of the accords as though they had divided Vietnam into two independent countries bound to respect one another's independence, Harriman acknowledged that reunification would go onto the agenda of such a conference, and added, "We should not preclude a restudy of the possibility of elections as a matter of strategy."[68] When McGeorge Bundy drafted the National Security Action Memorandum, he apparently worked Harriman's proposal into it. The redraft endorsed *planning* for various categories of military action, but also suggested various diplomatic initiatives, including Harriman's suggestion that the United States propose that all sides return to the 1954 Geneva Accords.[69]

Also in Washington that weekend was Ambassador to India Galbraith, who had accompanied Prime Minister Nehru on an official visit. Kennedy had known the Harvard economist and best-selling author for years, and apparently had asked for his views on Vietnam during the first week in November. Galbraith on November 3 had replied with suggestions similar to, but less daring than, Harriman's, proposing talks to secure a cease-fire in South Vietnam and the admission of both Vietnams to the United Nations. Galbraith suggested that Nehru might approach Ho Chi Minh on America's behalf. Nehru himself, according to James Reston's column of November 8, had warned Kennedy that the dispatch of American troops to South Vietnam would provide the Communists with a very useful propaganda edge.[70] About a week later, on the eve of the presidential meeting on the Taylor report, Galbraith managed to get a copy of the entire report from his friend and fellow Cambridge, Massachusetts, economist Walt Rostow. On Monday, November 13, Galbraith gave the President a digest of the report's most devastating comments about Diem and the South Vietnamese armed forces. Rostow immediately replied, arguing that the situation in South Vietnam was better than the situation in Greece in 1947.[71] On the same day Alexis Johnson told Rusk that "we would have to move quickly to nail down Saturday's decisions," and worried that "Galbraith has been working hard on this."[72]

On November 14 Kennedy himself addressed several questions to Rusk and McNamara in preparation for an NSC meeting the next day. His memo asked them to consider Harriman's proposals for talks, and perhaps to send Harriman back to Geneva at once to discuss them with Pushkin. He also wanted a letter to the co-chairmen of the Geneva conference—the Russians and the British—asking them to consider breaches of the Accords in South Vietnam, since the United States was obviously going to breach it as well. Recognizing that plans now called for a four-star general in Vietnam, he recommended a young general, or perhaps George McGhee, currently the director of the Policy Planning Council at State, who had played a similar role in Greece in the late 1940s. The President specifically recommended looking into the

Greek analogy, and asked for more training in guerrilla warfare and, possibly, the use of lighter weapons.[73] His subordinates failed to follow up any of these suggestions.

The next morning, before the meeting, McGeorge Bundy submitted some advice of his own. Bundy, who had been leaving Southeast Asia largely to Rostow, apologized for providing yet another opinion, but Kennedy had solicited his advice during a swim. He proposed an immediate commitment to introduce limited American combat units, if necessary, in order to secure Diem's cooperation and prevent the program from becoming "half-hearted." Should the commitment be made, he argued, "the odds are almost even that the commitment will not have to be carried out." Lyndon Johnson, Rusk, McNamara, Taylor, and Rostow, he added, all agreed with him.[74]

The NSC meeting that morning, November 15, showed that the combined barrage from Rusk, McNamara, Rostow, and Bundy had not moved the President at all. Rusk began once again by discussing a new draft of November 14, which dropped plans for American combat troops or any declaration that the United States was determined to save South Vietnam, but the President still found the presentation too warlike. He immediately replied in terms suggesting that his subordinates had entirely failed to convince him regarding the nature of the threat and the appropriate action to meet it: "The President expressed the fear of becoming involved simultaneously on two fronts on opposite sides of the world. He questioned the wisdom of involvement in Vietnam since the basis thereof is not completely clear. By comparison he noted that Korea was a case of clear aggression which was opposed by the United States and other members of the U.N. The conflict in Vietnam is more obscure and less flagrant." Then Kennedy indicated that in one crucial respect he made no distinction between Laos and South Vietnam:

> The President then expressed his strong feeling that in such a situation the United States needs even more the support of allies in such an endeavor as Vietnam in order to avoid sharp domestic partisan criticism as well as strong objections from other nations of the world. The President said that he could even make a rather strong case against intervening in an area 10,000 miles away against 16,000 guerrillas with a native army of 200,000, where millions have been spent for years and with no success. The President repeated his apprehension concerning support, adding that

none could be expected from the French, and Mr. Rusk interrupted to say that the British were tending more and more to take the French point of view.[75]

Rusk now repeated the line that Kennedy and Robert Kennedy had rejected four days earlier: "that firmness in Vietnam in the manner and form of that in Berlin might achieve desired results in Vietnam without resort to combat." Kennedy replied that the issues were far less clear in Vietnam. McNamara then introduced another argument whose significance eventually became very great indeed: "that action would become clear if U.S. forces were involved *since this power would be applied against sources of Viet Cong power including those in North Vietnam.*" Kennedy replied bluntly "that it was not clear to him just where these U.S. forces would base their operations other than from aircraft carriers which seemed to him to be quite vulnerable." Lemnitzer said that we would also use Taiwan and the Philippines as bases, and no one commented on the political risks of involving Taiwan in a war on the Asian mainland.

"The President," the record continues, "returned the discussion to the point of what will be done next in Vietnam rather than whether or not the U.S. would become involved." In particular, Kennedy clearly hoped to use the Jorden report on North Vietnamese infiltration to charge the North with violating the Geneva Accords, *prior* to taking American actions that would obviously violate them. He asked State to study this question, but nothing seems to have been done beyond the release of the Jorden report on December 8. General Taylor repeated that much could still be done within South Vietnam, but McNamara, speaking perhaps for the Joint Chiefs, "cautioned that the program was in fact complex and that in all probability U.S. troops, planes and resources would have to be supplied in additional quantities at a later date." Indeed, the Chiefs had already asked to preposition new American forces in the Philippines and elsewhere to meet various possible future contingencies.[76]

Clearly somewhat doubtful, the President asked McNamara if he would take action if SEATO did not exist, and McNamara replied affirmatively. The President asked for justification, and Lemnitzer replied "that Communist conquest would deal a severe blow to freedom and extend Communism to a great portion of the world." Kennedy asked how he could justify fighting in Vietnam while ignoring Cuba, and Lemnitzer quickly replied that the JCS also wanted to go into Cuba.

Kennedy then suggested that neutral nations would not support the United States—at least publicly—and "again expressed apprehension on support of the proposed action by the Congress as well as by the American people. He felt that the next two or three weeks should be utilized in making the determination as to whether or not the proposed program for Vietnam could be supported. His impression was that even the Democratic side of Congress was not fully convinced." Then Kennedy seized upon the excuse of the Vice President's absence to delay any action on the proposed memorandum until he had been able to see him, and asked State to report to him when the directed studies had been completed—presumably a reference to his memo of the day before.[77]

After the meeting Kennedy apparently telephoned Harriman and Taylor, and then had a critical conversation with McGeorge Bundy. Despite his closing comments, the President apparently remained willing to go forward with the military steps—helicopters, air power, naval forces, and other measures—which he had approved at the November 11 meeting, although he was *not* willing to commit himself to further action should these steps fail. He could no longer ignore, however, that his senior national security team saw the situation in Southeast Asia very differently than he did, and he was determined to bring policy more in line with his thinking. Bundy telephoned Rusk at 1:05 PM that day and offered to visit the State Department in mid-afternoon, prior to Rusk's coming to the White House to see Kennedy somewhat later. Bundy arrived with a list of questions that he and Kennedy had jointly prepared.

Although Bundy shared some of Rusk and McNamara's basic views on Southeast Asia, his note to Kennedy on his meeting with Rusk shows that he was now more interested in helping Kennedy make his own views prevail. And in this case, Kennedy had grasped that he could not implement his own policy without one critical personnel change at State: a new Assistant Secretary for Far Eastern Affairs. Bundy began the conversation on that very issue.

"I've told the Secretary frankly," Bundy wrote Kennedy after the meeting, "that you feel the need to have someone on this job that is wholly responsive to your policy, and that you really do not get that sense from most of us. I suggested Averell [Harriman]. He said Averell was needed in Geneva and that Alexis [Johnson] would loyally carry out any policy you directed. I don't think this is the same as having your own man—Alexis isn't that dispassionate—or that much of an executive. Averell is your man, as Assistant Secretary."

Bundy's judgment seems acute. While Alexis Johnson had brought himself around to formal support of the President's Laotian policy, he had never mustered any enthusiasm for it. Harriman was the only member of the team who, like Kennedy, saw Southeast Asia as an area to pursue cooperation with the Soviets, not an area to meet them in a test of wills.

Bundy then suggested replacing Nolting with George McGhee, the former ambassador to Greece now serving as head of Policy Planning at State. Rusk, who always guarded his prerogatives regarding ambassadors very carefully, restated his confidence in Nolting. "I would still consider McGhee," wrote Bundy, "(for one thing, if he thinks it won't work after a good look, he'll tell you, and he has the authority of the victor in Greece)." Rusk did agree that "no routine four-star general will do" as the new Saigon military leader, but that decision, it would emerge, lay far outside his influence.

Discussing the situation in Vietnam, Rusk once again opposed bombing Hanoi, but suggested doing enough inside South Vietnam "to put the result up to Diem." He added, however, that "the good of our actions depends on belief we mean to hold in Southeast Asia." "He knows we may lose," Bundy wrote, "and he knows we want no Korea, but he thinks we *must* try to hold and show determination to all concerned. He suggests you should let this be a Rusk-McNamara Plan and fire all concerned if it doesn't work. He thinks we *must* meet Khrushchev in Vietnam or take a terrible defeat." Attaching accounts of Rusk's recent conversations with the British and French ambassadors, Bundy invited Kennedy to comment on the hard line Rusk had taken.

In conclusion, Bundy proposed taking advantage of the Harriman appointment to kill a few other troublesome birds. "If Averell, or any other strong man, is to [become Assistant Secretary]," he wrote, "it should be in the context of a general game of musical chairs." George Ball could replace Chester Bowles as Undersecretary of State; Bowles could replace Harriman as ambassador-at-large; and Rostow, Bundy tentatively suggested, might take McGhee's job as director of the Policy Planning Council at State, one that Rostow had wanted in the first place. Richard Goodwin, a controversial White House assistant who had been concentrating on Latin American policy, might go to the State Department as well. "Secretary won't do this till you tell him to," Bundy concluded.[78]

Kennedy met briefly with Rusk that afternoon. He apparently confirmed his approval of new military measures combined with a new approach to Diem, since cables embodying the approach went out to Nolting that night. He decided to leave Nolting in Saigon, to make McGhee Undersecretary of State for Political Affairs and clear the way for Rostow's move to State, to replace Bowles with Ball, and to bring Harriman back to Washington as Assistant Secretary for Far Eastern Affairs.

On November 17 a low-key *New York Times* story reported that the President had decided to send "several hundred specialists in guerrilla warfare, logistics, communications, engineering and intelligence" to train South Vietnamese forces, but not to send combat troops. General Taylor and the President, the story said, agreed that the South Vietnamese, with appropriate changes in organization and tactics, could turn back the Communists. The GI-generation leaders of the Kennedy administration were team players above all, and no hint of the State and Defense Departments' enthusiasm for a larger commitment had reached the newspapers. Vietnam was still a relatively minor issue. "President Kennedy has spent most of his time since inauguration coping with a succession of foreign crises," the *Times* commented on Sunday, November 19—"Cuba, Berlin, Laos, nuclear testing, the Congo."[79]

On Sunday, November 26—three days after Thanksgiving—the White House announced the changes at State and the White House, and the press, focusing on the long-awaited demotion of Bowles, immediately christened this the Thanksgiving Day Massacre. In a press conference on November 29 Kennedy explained that Bowles, as ambassador-at-large, could now devote his full attention to the problems of Asia, Africa, and Latin America. "I'm also grateful to Governor Harriman," he added spontaneously, "after holding probably as many important jobs as any American in our history, with the possible exception of John Quincy Adams, for now taking on the job of Assistant Secretary for the Far East."[80]

From March through November of 1961 Kennedy had resisted the bureaucracy's repeated calls for full-scale American military intervention in Southeast Asia. While characteristically careful never absolutely to rule it out, the President had returned again and again to the drawbacks of war either in Laos or in Vietnam: the difficulty of fighting in the jungle, the clear lack of support from America's European allies, the very real lack of congressional support for such a war, and the difficulty of making a convincing case for the American people. But the State and Defense Departments had failed to reevaluate their assumptions, and Rusk and McNamara continued to speak for them—Rusk, certainly, out of long-standing conviction, and McNamara, by October, in an effort to solve the critical problem of guerrilla warfare through some bold new initiative. In Laos, Macmillan and Khrushchev had given Kennedy a diplomatic alternative, and Harriman was almost single-handedly making it work. No foreign leader, however, had presented any diplomatic alternatives with respect to South Vietnam, and the State Department failed to act on Kennedy's November 14 request to follow up Harriman's proposals for talks with the Soviets on Vietnam.

Despite his misgivings about full-scale intervention, Kennedy had always been willing to entertain proposals for strengthening South Vietnam, and he had now approved an increased American military effort, almost certainly without knowing how big it would get. In fact, McNamara seized upon the November decisions to take the Vietnam situation under his wing and try to score a resounding success against Communist guerrillas. During the next eight months the new commitment became public, and the President struggled to define it in an appropriately limited fashion and, eventually, to give it a firm time limit. Meanwhile, developments in Europe, Africa, and above all in Cuba took center stage again.

5

Limiting the Commitment
November 1961–November 1962

★

Only during the first half of 1962 did the real nature of the Kennedy administration's policy toward South Vietnam develop any clarity. The government initially began implementing the November decisions on Vietnam in secret, but the country awoke to its new involvement in the war in February, leading to the definition of a new administration line. The Pentagon continued to oppose the negotiations for a coalition government in Laos, but Harriman managed to bring the talks to a successful conclusion in July. Debates over Vietnam also continued, and in June and July Robert McNamara apparently attempted to clarify the situation by setting a firm time limit on the new American involvement.

As usual, Washington's policies encountered difficulties as soon as the United States tried actually to implement them in Vietnam. On November 17 Ambassador Nolting saw President Diem to explain what the United States now intended to do, and what Washington expected Diem to do in return. Both aspects of his instructions inevitably caused the South Vietnamese President considerable concern. Having been won over to the idea that American troops would demonstrate firm American resolve, Diem was now disappointed to learn that they would not be arriving after all. The American renewal of the issue of political change within the South, however, was far more serious.

As we have seen, the events of 1961 and the Taylor mission itself had apparently convinced virtually all the most involved Americans that the United States had to insist on fundamental changes in the operation of Diem's government and army in order to win the struggle against the Communists, including the insertion of American advisers in key civilian and military positions, improvements in the chain of command, and a broader base for Diem's regime.[1] When Diem received these proposals on November 17, he immediately accused Nolting of trying to turn South Vietnam into a protectorate. Nolting denied this and argued that only such drastic measures could save the situation. A full five days later, on November 22, Thuan told Nolting that Diem had not yet shown him the text of the proposals, but that he was "very sad and disappointed." Nolting interpreted both talks as optimistically as possible, and suggested giving Diem time to make his decision.[2]

During the next few days, Ngo Dinh Nhu unleashed a press campaign against the American proposals, arguing that they represented an attack on Vietnamese sovereignty and comparing the Taylor mission to the 1946 Marshall mission to China, which had worked for a coalition between the Kuomintang and the Communists. When Nolting saw Diem again on November 25, the President denied that the government had inspired the offending articles in the Saigon press, and blamed them on articles in *Time* and *Newsweek* that had suggested that the United States had to exert more influence in Vietnam. Bowing to the inevitable, Nolting suggested that the United States might do better to focus upon improvements in the "efficiency" of the South Vietnamese government, rather than upon the "more nebulous concept of 'political reform,'" or in other words, broadening the government.[3]

The Pentagon, meanwhile, was *not* waiting until after the conclusion of Nolting's negotiations to proceed. On November 22 National Security Action Memorandum (NSAM) 111 formally approved the recommendations for new American military efforts that Kennedy had agreed to earlier in the month, including increased airlift, "instruction in and execution of air-ground support techniques," and the establishment of a new military headquarters with new terms of reference.[4] On November 25 Nolting protested angrily that a new Air Force headquarters had established itself in Saigon without his knowledge or approval.[5] With the increased American involvement already under way, Washington, with critical encouragement from Nolting, decided to take what it could get in his talks with Diem. At a meeting at the White House on November 26, Rusk, Alexis Johnson, and Lansdale took positions somewhat sympathetic to Diem, and Kennedy apparently came down for wholehearted public support of the regime. Johnson and Rostow sent Nolting new instructions scaling back American demands. On November 28—well before Nolting had managed to reach agreement—McNamara essentially settled the question in a telegram to Admiral Felt and General McGarr, scheduling a conference in Honolulu on December 16. The uncertainty of Diem's position and our doubts regarding his willingness to make changes, McNamara said, "must not prevent us from going ahead full blast (without publicity, until political discussions are completed) *on all actions short of large scale introduction of US combat forces.*"[6]

Nolting beat a major tactical retreat during a long conversation with Diem on December 1. After hearing Diem's customary complaints, Nolting simply asked what Diem could do to improve his government's efficiency, on the one hand, and its public image both at home and abroad, on the other. Diem promised to reactivate a National Internal Security Council and create Provincial Councils, and eventually conceded that "certain Americans, on a selective basis and on request, could help strengthen his government." He essentially refused to concede the existence of any problem in his military chain of command, but promised to cooperate closely with American forces. Politically, he refused to promise anything more than additional trips to the countryside and addresses over the radio. He also agreed to more American military advisers and to provincial surveys, although he insisted that these deal with intelligence and military matters, not political ones. Nolting in conclusion accepted Diem's argument that winning the war was the key to the government's "public image," and stated his belief that "the tide can be turned with the limited concessions which Diem is prepared to make now and others that we can obtain on piece meal basis. In sum, I believe that we should proceed with confidence." On December 4 Nolting drew up a memorandum of understanding summarizing this conversation, and the next day Kennedy asked Rusk to inform Nolting that he had "done a good job."[7]

Nolting and McNamara now agreed that Washington must and could content itself with whatever changes Diem was willing to make. Nolting declared frankly at the conference in Honolulu on December 18 that Diem was unlikely to carry out even his very limited commitments "to the degree or as rapidly as we would expect or like," and McNamara agreed that Diem was the only man we had, and that "if we concentrated on fundamental military specifics he thought we could get Diem to cooperate." Shortly thereafter, the commander of the Military Assistance Advisory Group (MAAG), General McGarr, protested that Diem had managed to retain "actual veto power over valid U.S.-proposed measures required to win," but McGarr stood no chance against the McNamara-Nolting alliance.[8] Helped by the sudden new commitment of American forces to Vietnam, Diem had once again forced the United States to give up the idea of leverage.

During November, December, and January new command arrangements put McNamara and the Joint Chiefs firmly in charge of the new American effort. Months before, as we have seen, McNamara had told the Joint Chiefs that he wanted to make South Vietnam "a laboratory for the development of organization and procedures for the conduct of sub-limited war," and to establish an "experimental command" directly under the control of his office to do so.[9] The Chiefs, not surprisingly, opposed this proposal, and Admiral Felt managed to kill another request for a senior American commander who would take over all activities relating to the counterinsurgency effort, including the CIA's intelligence activities, and "report directly to the JCS and thence to me [McNamara] for operational purposes," thus bypassing CINCPAC. Felt on November 14 argued that even the introduction of logistics and support forces could easily trigger Communist retaliation and the subsequent implementation of CINCPAC or SEATO plans under his command. The admiral rejected one of the implied premises of Kennedy's program—that South Vietnam's problems could be solved within South Vietnam. "In the event of overt Communist aggression in South Vietnam, or anywhere in Southeast Asia," he concluded, "the threat must be met by a single coordinated effort under the Commander in Chief, Pacific."[10]

Taking essentially the same line, the Joint Chiefs on November 22 gave McNamara their proposal for the new headquarters: a unified military command, responsible to CINCPAC, and similar to other commands in Korea, Taiwan, and Japan, with operational rather than advisory functions. The four-star general selected to head the command would enjoy equal status with the American ambassador. Maxwell Taylor, who understood that Kennedy wanted to avoid dramatic departures, recommended retaining the present military command structure, but McNamara disregarded his advice. The State Department managed to change the new title of the senior American officer to "Commander, Military Assistance Command, Vietnam," instead of "Commander,

Military Assistance *Forces,* Vietnam," suggesting a slightly less direct American role. McNamara apparently failed in his attempts to secure authority over CIA operations, however, and the final directive made no mention of intelligence.[11]

The men on the spot, Nolting and McGarr, protested that this decision showed an excessively conventional military orientation, but Kennedy approved the agreed terms of reference in Palm Beach on January 3, 1962. The decision, however, was not yet announced.[12] Nolting eventually submitted a letter to Kennedy through Rusk offering his resignation if he could not be assured of his overall authority over the military, but Rusk declined to back him or to forward the letter to the President.[13] The new commander received the right to discuss military matters with Diem and South Vietnamese military authorities, with the obligation merely to keep the ambassador informed. Ironically, the Marines' classic *Small Wars Manual* had argued in 1940 that American ambassadors should direct counterinsurgency campaigns, but Rusk, who made clear again and again throughout his tenure as Secretary of State that he regarded the conflicts in Laos and South Vietnam as offensives by international Communism dictating a military response, did not object to the Pentagon's preeminent role.[14]

CINCPAC's view of the new American commitment—that it might easily become a first step toward greater American involvement in a conventional, long-foreseen war against Asian Communism—also received some implied confirmation in the choice of General Paul Harkins to head the Military Assistance Command, Vietnam (MACV). Harkins seems to have been selected not because he was close to General Taylor—whom the Pentagon would not have consulted on such a question—but because he was already the Army Commander under CINCPAC and had been the commander of forces prepared to land in Laos in the spring of 1961. When McGeorge Bundy heard of the appointment, he commented that Taylor, McNamara, and other Pentagon civilians had repeatedly said that only younger Army officers could provide a really new look—Harkins was fifty-seven—but the decision had been made.[15]

McNamara began putting his stamp on the operation at the first of a series of meetings with Admiral Felt and the senior Americans from Saigon in Honolulu on December 16. He assured the participants that the U.S. military establishment was making a major effort in South

Vietnam, and that the United States would provide practically anything but combat troops.[16] The Joint Chiefs, however, still rejected his one restriction. The fall of South Vietnam, they argued on January 13, 1962, would lead rapidly to the loss of the whole Southeast Asian mainland, including Thailand, and possibly to the loss of Indonesia and neutralist pressure in the Philippines and Japan. Since Diem's failure to take American advice might doom the present effort, they once again recommended additional American deployments.[17] McNamara apparently did not reply.

While McNamara took charge of Vietnam, Laos remained the province of the State Department in general and Harriman in particular. Here, too, new steps toward a settlement revealed continuing controversies within the administration. In early November, Harriman had finally concluded that Phoumi had become the main obstacle to a settlement and was leading the United States toward war. Indications in Geneva, Harriman said, convinced him that China would intervene if SEATO sent forces into Laos, and he now wanted to force Phoumi to reach agreement with Souvanna.[18] By early December Ambassador to Laos Winthrop Brown had given up hope of getting Phoumi into the coalition and was willing to try to destroy Phoumi's influence or bring about his resignation, if necessary, in order to create a new government.[19]

Rusk remained a skeptic about the coalition, essentially taking Phoumi's side in a conversation with his French and British counterparts in Paris on December 11. But on January 6, with Harriman back in Washington, Kennedy approved cutting off aid to Phoumi and Prince Boun Oum in order to force them to accept Souvanna, who in turn had refused to accept Phoumi as Minister of Defense or Interior. The *New York Times* of that morning had reported that Phoumi was threatening to resume fighting, and Kennedy made it clear that he did not want the cease-fire to break down. He overruled the new CIA Director, John McCone, who suggested that Marshal Sarit, Sihanouk, and Diem would be disturbed by sanctions against Phoumi.[20] But military and civilian authorities at the Pentagon continued to call for a much tougher anti-Communist line, and Phoumi continued to reinforce an outpost in Nam Tha, in the northern part of the country, despite its vulnerability to Pathet Lao attack.[21]

The press followed the emerging struggle between Washington and its erstwhile clients Phoumi and Boun Oum rather quietly, and paid relatively little attention to the increased American presence in South Vietnam. During December and January low-key stories in the *New York Times, Newsweek,* and *Time* all reported the arrival of more Americans and their equipment, but Washington made no major announcements. The story broke loose, however, after Washington announced the creation of MACV on February 8. During the next few days, unidentified Washington officials told reporters that the United States was "drawing a line here," and was "determined to put in what it takes to win." On February 13 the Republican National Committee demanded a full report on what was happening in South Vietnam, backing the objective of protecting Southeast Asia but asking whether the United States was moving toward another Korea.[22] The administration clearly had to explain what it was doing.

Led by the President himself, senior officials now tried to establish a new line in a careful series of statements. Asked about the Republican National Committee's complaints at a February 14 press conference, Kennedy reviewed the history of American involvement in South Vietnam, argued that the war was becoming more intense every week, and confirmed that "our assistance has increased as a result of the requests of the [Saigon] government." While confirming that we had sent "training missions" with the right to fire back if fired upon, he added, "we have not sent combat troops in the generally accepted sense of the word."[23] Only four days later Attorney General Robert Kennedy stopped at the Saigon airport in the middle of a world tour and made a considerably stronger statement: "We are going to win in Vietnam. We will remain here until we do win." Then, on February 21, McNamara returned from his third meeting in Honolulu and added a critical theme to the administration's line: optimistic reports of progress. Pentagon spokesmen explained that the South Vietnamese were "hitting the insurgent Communists harder," "pursuing them harder," and demonstrating the ability to clear and hold new areas. And in early March Admiral Felt visited Saigon again and declared that the South had gone on the offensive.[24]

On February 21 the administration leadership briefed the congressional leadership on Berlin, Laos, and Vietnam. Rusk had nothing to report about the recent Moscow talks on Berlin, in which both sides were maintaining their initial positions—a Soviet insistence upon changing the status of West Berlin, and an American insistence on maintaining Western occupation and access rights. McNamara then gave a long, detailed, and generally accurate briefing on the situation in Vietnam and the American commitment. He described the American involvement accurately, with one major exception: he did not explain the real role of the Jungle Jim Air Force unit, which was already flying combat missions with one South Vietnamese riding along for the sake of form. He also referred to Operation Sunrise, just about to kick off in Binh Duong province, as the first large-scale clear-and-hold operation designed to secure the population. Both McNamara and the President stressed that any official acknowledgment of the size of the new American presence would create a problem with the International Control Commission (ICC).

When McNamara took questions, he became over-optimistic. Senator Dirksen, who had obviously been reading the papers, asked what kind of cooperation we were getting from Diem and his family, and McNamara replied that we were getting "very effective cooperation, within the limits of their capabilities. They are accepting the advice of our military advisors." Rusk also said, rather confusedly, that Diem was trying to broaden his political base and we were trying to help him. Senator Russell of Georgia suggested that it might be cheaper to offer rewards for the capture of Viet Cong. When Harriman discussed the Laos negotiations, Senator Mansfield spoke once again against intervention in Laos, and put his trust in a Souvanna government as "the only reasonable solution." Vice President Johnson commented that the administration wanted a bipartisan policy, and invited the Republicans present to offer any suggestions. None of them did, and Senator Dirksen, referring to the criticism of the Republican National Committee, said that "in essence, it was clear that the Republicans fully supported the President's position," and offered to explain to his colleagues that the administration wanted to avoid a formal announcement of everything it was doing so as not to incur the censure of the ICC.[25]

During March 1962 the Laotian talks reached a critical stage, while the *New York Times* and the weekly news magazines increased their coverage of Vietnam to new and disturbing levels. Phoumi continued to refuse his assent to a new cabinet. Washington finally won Marshal Sarit, the Prime Minister of Thailand and Phoumi's cousin, over to the support of American policy, but only in return for a new and important concession. Ever since the Laotian cease-fire the previous spring, Sarit had argued that SEATO no longer served any useful purpose and threatened to pull out of it. Rather than try to strengthen the alliance itself, Secretary Rusk and Foreign Minister Thanat exchanged letters in Washington on March 6 committing the United States to Thailand's defense.[26]

Harriman visited Bangkok and Vientiane several weeks later. Phoumi now said that while he accepted Souvanna as Prime Minister "in principle," he could not accept Souvanna's planned cabinet, and the King agreed. In a last meeting in Vientiane, Phoumi blamed the entire crisis since August 1960 on Souvanna, whom he accused of going over to the Communist side. In both meetings Harriman referred bluntly to Phoumi's military failure, accusing him of having started a war and lost it, and referring to his forces as a "defeated army." In the end he told Phoumi and his men that they were "driving their country to disaster" and pleaded with them to reconsider.[27] Phoumi, Harriman told William Bundy on the telephone, was "much worse than I thought he was—(and you know how I've felt about him in the past)—I've never seen anything like it."[28] Admiral Felt and General Lemnitzer now believed that the chances of a neutral coalition had virtually disappeared, and recommended resuming full-scale support for Phoumi and implementing SEATO Plan 5 should hostilities resume, on the assumption that "the Viet Minh would not fight Americans." But Harriman pushed ahead, apparently without consulting the Pentagon.[29]

The senior leadership in Washington was busy with other issues. During March the President had chaired a series of meetings to define the U.S. position on a new nuclear test ban treaty and on disarmament.[30] Meanwhile, Rusk had presented a new American proposal on Berlin to the Soviets, leading to wide-ranging discussions in Geneva and in Washington and a few glimmers of progress on the critical issues of access to West Berlin and some recognition of East German sovereignty.[31] These stories, together with the climax of the Algerian war for independence, John Glenn's first orbital flight in February, and the American resumption of atmospheric nuclear tests in the Pacific, dominated the news, but more and more stories about the American advisory and combat role in Vietnam appeared, especially under Homer Bigart's byline in the *New York Times*. One of Bigart's first big stories, on February 25, had sketched out plans for American ground combat involvement if the situation worsened.[32] Meanwhile, beginning in late February, both Peking and Moscow denounced the increased American presence, and Peking and Hanoi called for a reconvened Geneva conference.[33] The President became unhappy.

On March 9 Arthur Sylvester, McNamara's Assistant Secretary for Public Affairs, cabled Felt and told him to warn Harkins that stories about the American combat role had upset the President and the Joint Chiefs, and to ask that American officers not give the impression that they were leading combat operations.[34] On Sunday, April 1, the *Times* printed another long article by Bigart, complete with a picture of American soldiers participating in the resettlement of South Vietnamese peasants as part of Operation Sunrise,[35] and Harriman echoed the President's complaints three days later. All public and private utterances by U.S. personnel, he concluded, "must reflect the basic policy of this government that we are in full support of Vietnam but we do not assume responsibility for Vietnam's war with the Viet Cong. This responsibility remains with the GVN."[36] Harriman brought a copy of his memorandum to a meeting with Kennedy and his contact on the National Security Council staff, Michael Forrestal, on April 6, to discuss both Vietnam and Laos.

Despite having approved and announced the new American commitment, Kennedy apparently remained somewhat skeptical. He began by reading a memorandum he had just received from Ambassador to India John Kenneth Galbraith, who was just finishing a brief visit to the United States. In November 1961, after submitting his comments on the Taylor report, Galbraith had received permission from Kennedy to visit Saigon on his way back to India, apparently because the President wanted to give him a chance to develop his skeptical views.[37] Galbraith had reported that the insurgency was strongest in the far south, thus casting doubt on the importance of outside support, and argued based on the balance of forces that Diem's political incompetence was probably the biggest source of the problem. He then had bluntly predicted that Diem would never reform, and suggested that the United States would eventually have to dump him, as the Eisenhower administration had done to South Korean leader Syngman Rhee in 1960.[38] Kennedy, who had known Galbraith for many years and frequently saw him socially, apparently had kept this advice to himself. A few days later

Galbraith had cabled State asking for permission to meet with a North Vietnamese official who was planning to visit New Delhi, but the Department had denied permission.[39]

Galbraith's memo of April 4, which the President read to Harriman and Forrestal, stressed the dangers of the increased American involvement: that the United States might become the new colonial power in the region; that the burning and relocation of villages might have serious negative effects; and that the war might become a new Korea, with serious domestic consequences. He suggested once again that the United States loosen its ties to Diem, take advantage of a forthcoming ICC report on American and North Vietnamese violations of the 1954 accords, and suggest new talks leading to a cease-fire. Meanwhile, he recommended keeping Americans out of combat and away from operations like relocation and defoliation.[40]

Harriman—another old friend of Galbraith's—endorsed only certain aspects of the memorandum. He agreed that the United States should reduce its involvement in military operations "to the absolute minimum," and he showed Kennedy his telegram to Nolting of April 4, with which the President agreed. He also thought the ICC report might provide a basis for talks on reducing the level of fighting. But in his new job as Assistant Secretary for the Far East, Harriman was now committed to trying to build up South Vietnam, and he opposed reconvening the Geneva conference or seeking the neutralization of South Vietnam. He also argued that while Diem was probably a losing horse "in the long run," the United States should not actively seek to replace him.

Kennedy seemed to side slightly more with Galbraith. He had his memorandum forwarded to McNamara, and asked Harriman to prepare instructions for Galbraith dealing with a possible Indian approach to Hanoi regarding a mutual North Vietnamese–American withdrawal from the South. Although Harriman agreed, such instructions do not seem to have gone out. Concluding, Kennedy "observed generally that he wished us to be prepared to seize upon any favorable moment to reduce our involvement, recognizing that the moment might yet be some time away."[41] When the Chiefs replied to Galbraith's memo on April 13, they argued that American policy was "to support the government of President Diem and the people of South Vietnam *to whatever extent may be necessary* to eliminate the Viet Cong threat"—exactly the kind of commitment that Kennedy had always refused to make.[42] Galbraith, they continued, was advocating an unjustifiable reversal of American policy, and they argued that present policy, "as announced by the President, should be pursued vigorously to a successful conclusion."

Galbraith tried again a few days later. Prince Sihanouk of Cambodia, whose relations with Diem had never improved and who feared the spread of the war, had recently joined the Communists' calls for a conference on South Vietnam. Galbraith suggested to Harriman on April 19 that we should not reject a conference, and that our policy should not be beholden to the need to maintain Diem's confidence.[43] On May 1 Kennedy met with State, Defense, and CIA officials on Southeast Asia, and Deputy Secretary of Defense Roswell Gilpatric brought up Galbraith's proposals for a negotiated, neutral government. "Both Harriman and I vigorously opposed this recommendation," Roger Hilsman of the Bureau of Intelligence and Research minuted, "and the President decided against it." The next day, at another meeting, Kennedy apparently declared that diplomatic approaches would await the forthcoming report of the ICC on American and North Vietnamese violations of the Geneva Accords.[44]

On May 5 Galbraith discussed the situation in New Delhi with the Indian representative of the ICC, who suggested that bilateral talks between Washington and Hanoi—not a conference—might indeed begin after the report, which he said would condemn both sides, had been issued. Harriman replied on May 16 that Kennedy was interested in Galbraith's conversation, and that Galbraith should pursue the question of how the Geneva co-chairmen—Britain and the Soviets—might bring about informal talks on "stabilization, compliance [with the 1954 accords], and peace."[45]

Kennedy's concern about overcommitment emerged again late in April, when Undersecretary of State George Ball asked for White House permission to make a speech explaining administration policy. The speech in Detroit on April 30 referred to the war as "a task we must stay with until it is concluded," and referred to worldwide consequences of any American failure to meet American commitments. Marguerite Higgins of the *New York Herald Tribune* reported the next morning that Ball had announced an "irrevocable commitment" and that American retreat or withdrawal was "unthinkable," and Bundy promptly telephoned Ball to report that the President was "disturbed." Bundy later commented that the speech "has a tone and content that we would not have cleared, simply from the point of view of maintaining a chance of political settlement."[46]

McNamara, perhaps Kennedy's most energetic and loyal subordinate, pushed the new administration line and privately tried to shift the emphasis of American policy during his first visit to Vietnam, on May 11. Homer Bigart reported that McNamara was "tremendously encouraged" by what he saw, and did not expect American military personnel to be increased much above current levels, then estimated at around 7,000 men. The administration, he continued, thought that reporters were overemphasizing the involvement of Americans and writing too much about American casualties, thereby giving Congress a distorted picture of American involvement in a shooting war.[47] On the same trip, McNamara convened his fifth conference on the war. At the conclusion of his formal briefings, he asked how long Harkins thought it would take to conclude the American effort. Looking around the room at his staff, Harkins replied that he had not thought about it, and McNamara asked for a plan to complete the training of the South Vietnamese and reduce our forces, to be submitted at the next conference.[48]

McNamara's visit coincided with new and dramatic developments in the Laos crisis. During April the administration had made more efforts to conclude the talks on a new government, despite opposition from the King and Phoumi. On April 9 the ambassador delivered a letter from the King complaining that the United States was forcing Laos to collaborate with Communism by forming the coalition, but the President was unmoved. We would not, he said, send American troops to help the Royal Laotian Government, since neither Congress nor the American people would accept this. If the cease-fire were broken, the end of Laos would result. The President promised all possible help to a new coalition government, which he regarded as the only solution that offered hope against the Communists.[49]

April 1962 saw Kennedy emerge victorious from the biggest domestic crisis of his presidency to date: his successful attempt to force U.S. Steel to roll back a price increase. Meanwhile, Washington secretly increased pressure on Phoumi during the rest of April, but without result. By May 3 the Thai government was moving back toward support of Phoumi's position, threatening not to sign the new Geneva Accords, much to Kennedy's disgust. On May 2, Harriman queried Brown about rumors that the CIA and the MAAG in Vientiane were still backing

Phoumi, and Brown assured him that the American mission was working together, and that the CIA and MAAG men closest to Phoumi had both left Vientiane.[50] But on May 6 Kennedy's hopes of quietly wrapping up the Laotian agreement went up in smoke. After Phoumi's five months of stalling, the Pathet Lao staged a successful attack on his reinforced northern outpost of Nam Tha. Phoumi's troops fled once again, and a full-scale resumption of fighting suddenly seemed possible.

The fall of Nam Tha thrust Laos back onto the nation's front pages and momentarily panicked the highest levels of the administration. McNamara and General Lemnitzer, who were attending a NATO meeting in Athens, received orders to fly to Thailand and investigate the possibility of a Mekong River defense line, which they did, with disturbing results, on May 8–9.[51] On May 8 Kennedy implicitly blamed Phoumi's delaying tactics for the collapse of the cease-fire, but informed high-level Pentagon officials that we might have to make new military moves if the Pathet Lao seemed to be taking over. Then, on May 10, Kennedy learned that Harriman and Roger Hilsman wanted to move the fleet into the Gulf of Siam and move 1,000 men now in Thailand to the Laotian border. Harriman and Hilsman thought this would show the Soviets and the Chinese that the United States meant business and might be necessary to reestablish a cease-fire, and Ambassador Brown broadly agreed. Kennedy, while awaiting the return of Rusk, McNamara, and Lemnitzer from trips overseas, ordered preparatory fleet movements.[52] The next day, May 11, Max Frankel of the *New York Times* reported that the administration was reviewing the situation, "with the emphasis on measures that would not lead to direct U.S. involvement in the fighting," and with the goal of reestablishing our bargaining position and continuing attempts to form a neutral government.[53]

As in 1961, however, both the Joint Chiefs and the State Department seemed to be working on rather different assumptions, and Phoumi's self-inflicted defeat brought the government to the brink of war again. The Joint Chiefs on May 11 denounced the basis of American policy in a memorandum for McNamara, claiming that the Nam Tha attack demonstrated "the futility of relying on [Souvanna Phouma] to provide requisite leadership for a neutral Laos," and recommended implementing their old standby, SEATO Plan 5, should military movements fail to bring about a cease-fire. The next day, May 12, Roger Hilsman produced a paper calling for two additional phases of military action: Phase II, which would move Thai and U.S. troops to the Thailand-Laos border; and Phase III, which would move them into Laos itself, if necessary, to force a cease-fire.[54]

Kennedy, however, still wanted a peaceful solution. He made clear to George Ball late on May 11 that he hoped simply to reestablish cooperation with the Soviets to secure a settlement, and opposed any call for SEATO intervention. But in another conversation just a few minutes later, Kennedy confided his biggest fear. CIA Director McCone and Michael Forrestal had briefed former President Eisenhower that day, and Eisenhower, restating the policy of his own administration and echoing some of his own statements eighteen months earlier, had suggested that if we sent troops into Laos, we should do anything necessary to secure our objectives, including, if required, using tactical nuclear weapons. Now Kennedy told Ball that he feared that Eisenhower—who to date had attacked only aspects of Kennedy's domestic policy—might make a public statement favoring intervention.[55]

On May 12 Kennedy again postponed a decision after a large meeting of the principals at the White House. It was apparently at this meeting that a famous incident occurred, when General Lemnitzer, the Chairman of the Joint Chiefs, began briefing the President on the situation with the help of a large-scale map of Asia. Roger Hilsman, whose pugnacious personality was already making enemies, pointed out that General Lemnitzer's pointer was on the Yellow River, not the Mekong River, and took over the presentation while the President looked on, grinning. After the meeting the Joint Chiefs ordered Admiral Felt to prepare the movement of forces into Thailand, subject to the completion of diplomatic arrangements. On Sunday, May 13, Kennedy authorized preparations to go forward, but reiterated that we would not intervene to back Phoumi, and that we aimed to get Phoumi, the Soviets, and the Chinese back to the conference table. On the same day Eisenhower made clear to McCone and Forrestal that he would not advocate immediate intervention. The next day Kennedy definitely approved the new deployment, with General Harkins becoming the Commander of U.S. Forces in Thailand. Harriman, who obviously took the crisis very seriously as a test of Soviet intentions, opposed reconvening the Geneva talks until the Soviet attitude became clear. According to Michael Forrestal, Kennedy immediately expressed reservations about the decision.

"Mike," he said, "are you sure this was the right thing to do? How will I get them out?" Press stories on the new deployment repeated that American objectives remained unchanged.[56]

The President and the whole senior national security team briefed congressional leaders on May 15, and the briefing turned into a wide-ranging discussion of administration foreign policy. Rusk explained that the deployment was designed mainly to reassure the Thais. Kennedy himself stressed that we still favored a coalition, largely because of the absence of any allied support for intervention, blamed Phoumi once again, and promised "further exhaustive study and consultation" with Congress before any decision to send U.S. forces into Laos. Not one congressional leader, Republican or Democrat, called for stronger action. Dirksen asked what we would do if Laos fell, and Kennedy replied that we would try to make a stand in Thailand.[57]

Huge headlines the next morning reported the dispatch of 4,000 troops to Thailand. Kennedy's public statement reaffirmed the essentials of his policy, and on May 17 the *Times* reported that the administration had never had much faith in John Foster Dulles's brainchild, SEATO, which had divided the major neutrals from the other nations of the region. "The great hazard is of a shooting war in Asia—in the jungles of Asia," Kennedy said in a press conference the next day, "and it is our object to bring about a diplomatic solution which will make the chances of such a war far less likely." He also indicated that we would not demand a Communist pull-back as part of a cease-fire.[58]

The bureaucracy, however, kept pushing more aggressive options. Harriman on May 15 created an interdepartmental working group chaired by his deputy, William Sullivan, to devise responses to a new breach of the cease-fire. In a White House meeting on May 24 Kennedy authorized contingency planning to occupy either the left bank of the Mekong inside Laos or the Laotian panhandle along the South Vietnamese border, while pushing ahead with the negotiations.[59] The initial working paper prepared by the State-Defense-JCS working group called for American troops to occupy the Mekong Valley, either to help bring about a new neutral government, or to prepare for a de facto partition of Laos should the talks fail. The paper anticipated North Vietnamese intervention in return. But at a meeting of senior State, Defense, and White House officials—less Kennedy—McNamara expressed doubts about such a plan and proposed a force of at least

40,000 that might occupy the Laotian panhandle as well—a scheme which General Harkins was already considering.[60] General Lemnitzer argued that we should focus upon hurting North Vietnam, the Communist sanctuary. Specifically, he proposed an amphibious landing at Vinh, within North Vietnam, followed by a march westward to seal off infiltration into Laos and South Vietnam. Rusk and McNamara both agreed, but suggested that a "phased operation" might begin with the occupation of the Mekong Valley.[61]

Military planning continued during the first week of June, but on June 11 the Embassy in Vientiane reported that the three Laotian factions had agreed on a cabinet. Despite the unnerving presence of Quinim Pholsema, one of Souvanna's most left-leaning supporters, as Foreign Minister, Harriman found the cabinet acceptable, and even favored resuming aid to Phoumi.[62] At a meeting of the senior leadership, less Kennedy, on June 12, McNamara secured agreement to about $25 million worth of military construction in Thailand, to ease any future logistical problems. At a June 13 meeting with the President, Rusk still expressed distrust of the Laos talks, and speculated that with Souvanna in Paris and Phoumi on his way to Geneva, Souphanouvong might try a coup. Kennedy quickly shifted the discussion to the implementation of the new agreement and coordination of friendly forces within Laos. He eventually approved McNamara's proposals for Thailand.[63]

After six more weeks of negotiations, Rusk signed the Geneva accord on Laotian neutrality on July 23. One remaining problem was resolved through an unusual channel. On June 18 Robert Kennedy had one of a series of conversations with a Soviet journalist, Georgi N. Bolshakov, who was presumed to be an intelligence agent and who sometimes passed messages to and from Khrushchev. Bolshakov said that Khrushchev would be personally very appreciative if the American troops sent to Thailand during the crisis could now be withdrawn, and Robert Kennedy promised to speak to the President. After doing so, he told Bolshakov on the next day that the United States would begin withdrawing the troops within ten days, but avoided any promise that they would *all* come out. On June 25 President Kennedy conveyed his desire to withdraw some troops to George Ball and to McNamara, and Forrestal explained to Ball that the President had wanted to make a gradual withdrawal for some time. Orders to withdraw 1,000 Marines went out the next day. When Pushkin, the Soviet negotiator, raised the issue of the troops with Harriman and Forrestal on July 3, Harriman referred to press accounts of this withdrawal. The last of the Marines left Thailand later that month, although some Army and Air Force units may have remained.[64]

On July 22 and 23 two remarkable conversations on opposite sides of the world confirmed the directions in which Kennedy wanted to go, and revealed some of the difficulties the administration would inevitably encounter. On July 23, while the Laotian accords were being signed in Geneva, McNamara convened yet another conference in Honolulu, and this time he came prepared to insist upon putting definite *temporal* limitations upon the American involvement in Vietnam. After General Harkins summarized progress in various areas, McNamara took the floor. Six months ago, he began, "we had practically nothing and we have made tremendous progress to date." Now he wanted "a carefully conceived long-range program for training and equipping the South Vietnamese Armed Forces and phase out of major US combat, advisory, and logistics support activities."

McNamara and his staff had obviously done some planning of their own. When the Secretary asked Harkins how long it would take to eliminate the Viet Cong "as a disturbing force," Harkins gave an optimistic estimate of about one year after all friendly elements had become fully operational and begun pressing the Viet Cong. McNamara immediately replied that the program should assume a period of three years. "We must line up our long range program as it may become difficult to retain public support for our operations in Vietnam," he continued, echoing the concerns that the White House had expressed all spring. "The political pressure will build up as US losses continue to occur. In other words we must assume the worst and make our plans accordingly."[65] The conference concluded with a firm decision to devise a three-year plan.

The initial flurry of stories and the initial handful of American casualties in February and March had apparently convinced Kennedy that the American involvement in South Vietnam must be severely limited. The President had repeatedly stated that we were "assisting" the South Vietnamese in their efforts to defend themselves, and had tried to get the press and administration officials to downplay the American role. He had shown more interest in a negotiated settlement than any of his subordinates, and he remained determined to avoid war in Laos—although, typically, he had allowed another round of contingency planning to take place during the Laos crisis. According to McNamara's deputy, Roswell Gilpatric, Kennedy "made clear to McNamara and me that he wanted to not only hold the level of U.S. military presence in Vietnam down, but he wanted to reverse the flow."[66] And while we lack any record of any communication between Kennedy and McNamara, the Secretary of Defense had obviously got the message.[67] In December he had told the first Honolulu conference that the United States would send anything short of combat troops, but in May and once again in July he had emphasized the need to limit our involvement and to wrap it up within a few years. Meanwhile, the administration had successfully sold its limited policy to the Congress, where Vietnam had aroused relatively little interest.[68]

The decision to limit American participation in the war reflected the general guidelines laid down by the Special Group/Counterinsurgency, which had been created in January 1962 under the chairmanship of Maxwell Taylor. In August 1962 Kennedy approved NSAM 182 and an accompanying document, "U.S. Overseas Internal Defense Policy," which listed a variety of roles that the United States might play, ranging from "immunization of vulnerable societies not yet seriously threatened by communist subversion or insurgency" to "assisting the government under attack with military as well as non-military means." The goal, however, was to "minimize the likelihood of direct U.S. military involvement in internal war by maximizing indigenous capabilities." The major effort in counterinsurgency, it continued, "must be indigenous since insurgency is a uniquely local problem involving the aspirations and allegiance of local people."[69] Unfortunately, the American military never really adopted these precepts with respect to the situation in South Vietnam.

On the day before McNamara laid down the law in Honolulu, in Geneva Harriman had met privately, and for the first time, with a North Vietnamese official, Foreign Minister Ung Van Kiem. Harriman may not have asked for authorization to hold the meeting, but the ICC report on American and North Vietnamese violations of the Geneva Accords had now been issued, and Harriman probably regarded the conversation as a first attempt to explore a possible settlement along the lines he had suggested as early as November 1961, and that he had discussed with Kennedy. The North Vietnamese, meanwhile, entertained serious hopes that Washington might be willing to follow up the agreement on Laos with a similar agreement for the neutralization of South Vietnam.[70] Harriman began by recalling that his old boss President Roosevelt had not expected the French to return to Indochina after the war, and suggestively asked the Foreign Minister what would have happened if Roosevelt's policies had been carried out. Kiem replied that he was well aware of Roosevelt's views, that his government had been very surprised when the Americans allowed the French back in, and that the years following were years of suffering and tragedy for the Vietnamese people.

After inquiring after the health of Ho Chi Minh, Harriman turned to the point immediately at issue: compliance with the Laotian accords. Declaring the American intention to carry them out in letter and spirit and to withdraw all military personnel from Laos, he asked whether the North Vietnamese intended to do the same. Kiem assured him that they would, but without referring specifically to the withdrawal of North Vietnamese troops. Pressed by Harriman, he acknowledged that, in response to requests from Souvanna Phouma, Hanoi had provided "military trainers and military specialists" to assist Souvanna's troops—a formulation he might almost have borrowed from President Kennedy. Harriman immediately recognized this as an advance over Pushkin's denials of any North Vietnamese military presence, but failed to get an acknowledgment of "North Vietnamese military units."

Kiem then said that his government thought that the success of the Geneva Accords depended upon the United States, to which Harriman immediately replied that by a remarkable coincidence, Washington thought that it depended upon North Vietnam. Kiem said the United States had to withdraw American forces, Thai forces, Kuomintang forces, Filipino forces, and South Vietnamese forces. In response, Harriman denied only the presence of South Vietnamese forces. The two men then agreed, following Khrushchev and Kennedy in Vienna, that they wanted a neutral Laos along the pattern of Burma or Cambodia.

Kiem then said that he wanted to turn to the question of Vietnam, whose people strongly resented American intervention. Only American intervention, he said, had prevented the elections called for by the Geneva Accords of 1954 and the reunification of the country. The intervention had increased, and was now "mercilessly killing Vietnamese citizens." "While Governor Harriman spoke of President Kennedy's policy which respects neutrality," he said, "and the fact that it has produced an agreement on Laos, the Foreign Minister could not understand how President Kennedy could continue the policy of military intervention in Vietnam." Harriman replied firmly that President Kennedy had responded to Diem's requests for assistance in the belief that, as the ICC had recently confirmed, the aggression against him was led, trained, and supplied by the North. "The way that peace could be brought to Vietnam," he said, "would be for the North Vietnamese to cease their aggression against South Vietnam, and to stop guerrilla activity. *Then the status envisaged by the 1954 Agreements could be reestablished and the possibilities of dealing with other difficulties could be explored.*"[71]

Harriman was obviously trying to hold out the possibility of a new deal that might follow a cease-fire, but Kiem did not bite. The Americans, he said, did not seem to understand the situation: a popular revolt was taking place in South Vietnam without help from the North, and the United States was trying to suppress it. Harriman, noting that he had to meet with Secretary Rusk, declined to pursue the question. Few Americans had more experience in negotiations with Communist powers than he, and he undoubtedly was not disturbed by the immediate failure to discover any common ground. And he did not completely understand, apparently, the ways in which Hanoi both separated and linked the issues of Laos and South Vietnam. On the one hand, Hanoi was prepared to tolerate a neutralist government under Souvanna. On the other hand, as long as the war in the South continued, Hanoi was determined to continue to occupy the Ho Chi Minh trail through Laos and assist the Viet Cong. Kiem implicitly tried to make this clear in a last, fateful exchange:

> Before departing, Harriman wished to return to the first part of the conversation which he and the Foreign Minister had had concerning Laos. He felt that clear undertakings on the part of the US Government and on the part of the North Vietnamese to carry out scrupulously all the provisions of the Geneva Agreements on Laos would result in peace in Laos. He trusted that that would be done and that this sort of cooperation between the US and North Vietnam could make a great contribution toward the peace of Southeast Asia.
>
> The Foreign Minister agreed with this statement, and said that he would remember the first part of the conversation that he and Governor Harriman had had this afternoon. He hoped, however, that Governor

Harriman would not forget the second part of the conversation, and particularly what the Foreign Minister had had to say about American military intervention in Vietnam.[72]

Harriman, in any case, did not favor immediate negotiations. Ambassador-at-Large Bowles, who was planning a trip to Southeast Asia, in mid-July had suggested proposing the mutual withdrawal of "Vietminh troops" and foreign forces from South Vietnam, but Harriman in late July rejected the idea, preferring to wait and test Communist compliance with the Laotian agreement. Michael Forrestal on August 2 also rejected a conference, commenting that no one knew who was winning the war, and suggesting that a conference should await the emergence of a definite military trend, "one way or the other."[73]

Harriman and other American authorities, moreover, did not realize that Hanoi was now enjoying increasingly militant backing from Mao Zedong in Peking. Communist China had only partially recovered from Mao's disastrous Great Leap Forward, but Mao was determined to remain on a radical course. Both domestically and within the Communist world, where his polemics against Khrushchev's "revisionism" had become more and more bitter in the last few years, it suited Mao to take up the struggle against the new American initiative in Vietnam. In February 1962 another high Communist functionary, Wang Jiaxiang, had suggested a moderate policy designed to avoid involvement in another "Korea-style war created by American imperialists," but Mao severely criticized his proposals as revisionist, and prepared to take a far more militant line.[74]

Washington, indeed, had continued to make policy virtually without reference to events in Southeast Asia itself. The creation of MACV and the new advisory, helicopter, and air support represented a compromise in governmental politics, developed after Kennedy repeatedly rejected full-scale involvement. Then, beginning in February and culminating in July, the White House had decided to limit the scope, objectives, and length of the American commitment mainly to avoid adverse political fall-out. Meanwhile, however, the American involvement was having consequences of its own. Americans and South Vietnamese were now trying, without much success, to devise a common, effective strategy against the Viet Cong. Eventually, the consequences of their effort would make themselves felt in Washington as well.

Despite the Laos crisis in May, the possibility of war in Southeast

Asia had receded during 1962, but other situations had become much more serious. The Berlin talks had dragged on through the spring and into early summer. Moscow hinted from time to time that it might agree to Western troops remaining in West Berlin provided that their connection with NATO was dissolved, and the United States indicated some willingness to forbid the two German states to acquire nuclear weapons, but neither side even proposed specific agreements, and by August Washington was preparing for the unilateral signature of a Soviet–East German peace treaty. Then, in early September, Khrushchev told American officials that he planned to wait until after the American congressional elections before signing a treaty, and Tass confirmed this publicly.[75]

Latin America, however—and especially the Caribbean—had become the focus of the Kennedy administration's most intense and dangerous foreign policy initiatives. The administration's policy had two major aspects: a desperate attempt to prevent the emergence of a second Communist or Marxist state in the region, and plans to overthrow the Castro regime. Thus when on May 31, 1961, the Dominican dictator Rafael Trujillo was assassinated, several leading administration figures, including Robert Kennedy and Robert McNamara, wanted to move American troops onto the island at once. With the President in Europe, Chester Bowles, Dean Rusk, and Lyndon Johnson managed to slow things down, and when the President returned, he made the much-quoted statement that "we wanted a democratic regime in the Dominican Republic; failing that we would prefer a friendly dictatorship, and the last thing we wanted was a Castro regime."[76] Later the administration carried out a long, determined campaign, diplomatically and covertly, to prevent the Marxist Chedi Jagan from becoming the head of government of British Guyana when it became independent—a campaign which amazed its British allies.[77]

With respect to Cuba itself, the administration began considering direct military intervention immediately after the failure of the Bay of Pigs, but the President never fully committed himself to it. The Taylor report of June 1961—the official postmortem prepared by Maxwell Taylor—seemed to favor an invasion at some point, but added that the whole world situation would have to be considered. In the fall of 1961 Taylor directed various agencies to plan for the contingency of Castro's sudden death, presumably through assassination. The President in late

November approved what became Operation Mongoose—headed by General Lansdale—an attempt to sabotage the Cuban regime and provoke an internal revolt that would provide a pretext for intervention. But typically, Kennedy on January 18, 1962, told the National Security Council that the time had not yet come when the United States must force a solution to the Cuban problem.[78]

By February 1962 Lansdale was planning specifically for an uprising in October, to be followed, apparently, by U.S. military intervention. CIA Director John McCone warned as early as April that the Soviet Union might introduce missiles into Cuba, and argued for immediate aggressive action against Castro. By August Lansdale was proposing a more aggressive "Phase II" of operation Mongoose, reiterating his hopes for an uprising that would trigger American intervention, and, apparently, pushing for the assassination of the Cuban leadership as well. Although McCone failed to convince either the rest of the administration or his own analysts of the Soviet plans to install missiles, the President by late August was already taking the possibility seriously and linking possible Soviet missiles in Cuba to American Jupiter nuclear missiles in Turkey.[79]

During September Soviet military equipment in Cuba became a major political issue, and the possibility that the Soviets were installing nuclear missiles increasingly preoccupied administration officials. The Pentagon ordered military theater commands to prepare detailed plans for air strikes and an invasion of Cuba, to be readied by October 20. On October 2 McNamara directed the Joint Chiefs to prepare contingency plans to remove *either* Soviet weapons in Cuba threatening American security *or* the Castro regime itself. Two days later Robert Kennedy insisted on intensifying Operation Mongoose.[80]

Just as it had prepared for war in Southeast Asia a year earlier, the Pentagon was now planning for the invasion of Cuba—but in much greater detail, with considerably more presidential interest, and with a deadline of October 20. Evidence does not indicate, however, that the administration had reached any decision to act prior to the discovery of Soviet nuclear missiles in Cuba on October 16. In all probability, Kennedy, not for the first time, had set a long chain of events in motion without having decided where it would lead. The discovery of Soviet missiles might easily have served as a pretext for the immediate execution of the invasion plans, and the Joint Chiefs apparently believed that it would.[81] Instead, when intelligence discovered Soviet missiles, an air strike and invasion eventually emerged as a last resort.

The bulk of the story of the missile crisis lies outside the scope of this book and has been told in detail several times.[82] Yet the crisis demands some attention from any student of Kennedy and Johnson foreign policy, both because of what it revealed about Kennedy and because it influenced much later decisions about Vietnam. Once again, as in Southeast Asia in 1961, Kennedy's views differed fundamentally from those of his closest advisers, and once again, with even higher stakes in play, he insisted upon his own solution.

Between October 16, when intelligence discovered Soviet medium- and intermediate-range nuclear missiles in Cuba, and Monday, October 22, when Kennedy addressed the nation, the administration decided to begin its response with a naval quarantine, rather than an air strike, and to hold further military moves in reserve. McGeorge Bundy and the Joint Chiefs favored the air strike; McNamara and Robert Kennedy argued strongly for the blockade as a first step; and McNamara argued as early as October 19 that the United States would have to pay some price—perhaps its Jupiter nuclear missiles in Turkey and Italy—for Soviet withdrawal of missiles in Cuba. During the week reconnaissance reported work continuing on the missile sites at top speed, while Ambassador Adlai Stevenson at the United Nations tried to secure Soviet agreement to halt construction. On Friday, October 26, Kennedy speculated that the United States would either have to invade Cuba or trade its Turkish missiles to secure Soviet withdrawal. That evening Khrushchev had offered to withdraw the missiles in return for an American pledge not to invade Cuba, but on Saturday he publicly demanded that the United States remove Jupiter nuclear missiles from Turkey in return.

During a long discussion late on Saturday, October 27, the President concluded that Khrushchev's new, public demand for a trade now represented his true position, and argued in contradiction of the views of most of his advisers that the United States should explore a trade. Overruling Bundy, he reasoned that the full-scale action against Cuba planned to begin Monday morning would lead to Soviet retaliation in Europe, and that America's NATO allies would then blame the United States for having rejected the trade. Taylor, meanwhile, reported that the Joint Chiefs wanted to begin an air attack on Monday morning, followed seven days later by an invasion.[83] Later in the meeting McNamara proposed *dismantling* the missiles in Turkey before proceeding with the invasion, but admitted that the Soviets might react elsewhere, perhaps in Berlin. That prompted Vice President Johnson, Undersecretary of State Ball, and CIA Director McCone to look more favorably upon a trade. The discussion in the full Executive Committee or ExCom, however, simply decided to accept Khrushchev's Friday evening offer.[84]

McGeorge Bundy revealed in 1988 that a smaller group had met immediately afterward in the Oval Office to discuss an oral message from Robert Kennedy to Soviet Ambassador Dobrynin. It included Kennedy, Rusk, McNamara, Robert Kennedy, Bundy himself, Roswell Gilpatric, Theodore Sorensen, and former Ambassador to the Soviet Union Llewellyn Thompson—but not General Taylor, the only member of the Joint Chiefs who had participated in the ExCom discussions. The group decided that Robert Kennedy would warn Dobrynin of imminent military action unless Khrushchev withdrew the missiles. And at Rusk's suggestion, they also decided that Robert Kennedy would assure Dobrynin that, although Washington could make no announcement and could not acknowledge any trade, the Jupiter missiles would come out of Turkey after the crisis was resolved. Rusk made this suggestion, in Bundy's opinion, because he understood that Kennedy wanted to give up the Turkish missiles to avoid war—a fact which emerges very clearly from the transcript of the larger meeting, which was recorded. And that night, according to Rusk in 1987, Kennedy authorized an approach to U.N. Secretary General U Thant asking him to propose such a trade, should it prove necessary.[85] Robert Kennedy delivered the message to Dobrynin. In a little-noticed public hint of the administration's thinking, James Reston, on Sunday, October 28, reported that it was "significant" that the White House had not ruled out a trade, and indicated that some deal regarding the Turkish missiles might eventually be worked out.[86] Khrushchev announced the withdrawal of the missiles the next day, in return for an American pledge not to invade Cuba.

Confronted with the greatest crisis of the whole Cold War, Kennedy had chosen nearly the least warlike alternative before him. Knowing that a trade would have been branded by the Republicans as shameful appeasement, he concealed it not only from the public but from most of his administration. The small group that met in the Oval Office on October 27 agreed never to discuss what they had decided, and they kept that resolve for twenty-five years. The world first learned about the trade when Robert Kennedy's memoir, *Thirteen Days,* appeared after his death. Meanwhile, the administration carefully orchestrated the presentation of the crisis to the press and the public. On Monday, October 29—the day after Khrushchev gave in—Reston reported that Kennedy regarded the crisis "not as a great victory, but merely as an honorable accommodation in a single isolated area of the 'cold war' . . . he is rejecting the conclusion of the traditional 'hard-liners' that the way to deal with Moscow everywhere in the world is to be 'tough,' as in Cuba."[87]

The President immediately made clear to his most anti-Communist European ally, Konrad Adenauer, that he would welcome any new overtures from Khrushchev regarding Berlin.[88] Then, in early December, Kennedy—wittingly or unwittingly—distanced himself dramatically from the *idea* of a trade, when Stewart Alsop and the President's friend Charles Bartlett published their famous account of the missile crisis in the *Saturday Evening Post.* The story sensationally quoted a member of the ExCom to the effect that Adlai Stevenson had advocated a "Munich"—a trade of Turkish missiles for Cuban missiles.[89] Kennedy quickly reaffirmed his confidence in Stevenson, but his assurances rang hollow. Bartlett has never revealed the source of the leak, but it seems most likely to have come from outside the very small group that knew the trade had in fact been consummated.

As 1962 gave way to 1963, the President—buoyed by a strong showing in the congressional elections, in which the Democrats held their own in the House and increased their majority in the Senate—hoped to move back in the direction of détente. Southeast Asia had definitely faded into the background, eclipsed by the Cuban crisis and by European and arms control issues. Officially, the Laotian accords had settled the crisis in that country, and the United States was engaged in a three-year training exercise in South Vietnam that would enable the Diem government to deal with the guerrillas more successfully.

Unfortunately for Washington and the United States, however, events within South Vietnam were still moving in the wrong direction. The United States was now deeply involved in a major counterinsurgency effort, but without either the understanding or the influence necessary to bring it to a successful conclusion. The war in Vietnam now had a momentum of its own, quite unrelated to the official American line as defined in Washington. We must now turn to the evolution of the conflict itself.

The War in Vietnam
1962

★

Until now, no one has ever attempted to provide more than an impressionistic account of what South Vietnamese, American, and Viet Cong forces actually did in 1962–1963, with respect to both conventional military operations and the new strategic hamlet program designed to protect the population against the Viet Cong. Newly available American documents provide a clear picture of what the United States wanted and what the South Vietnamese did and did not do—and why—in the last two years of the Diem regime. The war against the Viet Cong was complicated by the existence of three different strategic concepts: one developed and pushed by senior American military leaders; a second, first promulgated by Roger Hilsman of the State Department but also adopted by some American aid workers in the field; and a third, far more important than either of the others, belonging to the South Vietnamese themselves. By late 1963 the Pentagon and the State Department were arguing bitterly about the course of the war, but neither one was really exercising a decisive influence over it.

The American military planned to defeat the Viet Cong (VC) with conventional military operations. Encouraged in late 1961 to step up the war, the American military authorities—led by General McGarr in Saigon and Admiral Felt in Honolulu—proposed dramatic new offensives. They preferred two main types of operations: purely conventional moves against remote Viet Cong base areas in relatively unpopulated regions, and provincial "clear and hold" operations that would combine attacks on the VC with the resettlement and mobilization of the population. The South Vietnamese Army (ARVN), in their view, suffered from its dispersal around the country in static defensive positions, and because Diem himself insisted on giving orders to individual units through the province chiefs, no South Vietnamese general could concentrate troops to go on the offensive against major Viet Cong base areas such as War Zone D north of Saigon. During 1961 McGarr had persuaded Diem to create the Field Command under General Duong Van "Big" Minh, an American favorite and a hero of Diem's battles with the non-Communist sects, but Minh, whom Diem and Nhu distrusted, had never received authority over enough troops to undertake operations.[1]

By late October 1961 McGarr had produced a plan for a major attack on War Zone D. It planned to defoliate about 100 square miles of jungle forest—about one-tenth of the area—in an effort to deny the enemy cover. By early December CINCPAC had also developed a plan for large-scale operations, and had given it to McGarr with instructions to run it by General Minh.[2] McGarr briefed McNamara on the Zone D plan at the very first Honolulu conference of December 18, and McNamara sent it back for further study. The plan, he and others suggested, was too complex and relied too heavily upon defoliants. McNamara showed more interest in the immediate strengthening and more effective arming of the Civil Guard and Self-Defense Corps, which, he believed, had to secure areas after the ARVN swept through them.[3] Despite this, McGarr stuck to the plan, and especially to the defoliation aspects, which had specifically been added to it by the South Vietnamese. But when Big Minh asked Diem for troops to create task forces to conduct major operations in Zone D and elsewhere, Diem and Nhu immediately suspected him of wanting the troops for a coup.[4] Felt on December 23 reemphasized the need for a plan that would put "mobile, hard-hitting forces, efficiently organized and commanded, against VC at proper time and place," but asked McGarr to abandon the Zone D plan for the moment. In order to meet a "vital need for an early GVN victory," he proposed an operation to clear Binh Duong province adjacent to War Zone D instead—a plan that eventually became Operation Sunrise.[5]

McGarr did not give up, and on January 12 he explained his Zone D plans to Diem: a two-division operation to surround Zone D on three sides, followed by a heliborne landing and drive into the pocket from the fourth side. Diem remained skeptical, arguing that a defeat might backfire.[6] Meanwhile, American equipment began to have an impact on the battlefield. Forty-four helicopters arrived in South Vietnam in December and began operations on December 23. McGarr rapidly concluded that they could provide the mobility which, combined with better intelligence and improved communications, would enable friendly forces to "strike the enemy before he disperses" by achieving "complete surprise." Five hundred forty heliborne operations since December 23, he reported on February 8, had proven that helicopters provided the best means to achieve these tasks, and he asked for more.[7] Meanwhile, in late December the White House approved the combat use of American Jungle Jim aircraft, code-named Farmgate, with one South Vietnamese aboard.[8]

In fact, the American military authorities put the highest priority on mobile, medium- to large-scale operations against the estimated 20,000 Viet Cong regular troops that they visualized as operating from secure base areas: Zone D north of Saigon, War Zone C northwest of Saigon in Tay Ninh province on the Cambodian border, the Plain of Reeds in Kien Phong province due west of Saigon, An Xuyen province at the southernmost tip of the country, in the Central Highlands near the Laotian border, and in the Annamite mountains in Quang Nam and Quang Ngai provinces. Over the next two years General Harkins continually advised the South Vietnamese army to attack these Viet Cong strongholds in large-scale operations. American reports on the fighting during 1962 frequently complained that too many South Vietnamese troops remained in static positions, defending towns, villages, and watchtowers against attacks by local guerrillas. In order to free these troops for a more offensive role, the American military had for some time advocated strengthening the Civil Guard and Self-Defense Corps to take over these missions. While they also sponsored some "clear and hold" operations within populated areas, the Americans generally emphasized the purely military aspects of these operations as well, counting on ARVN troops to rid the designated areas of Viet Cong, and leaving the political follow-up to civic action teams, Civil Guards and Self-Defense Corps, and provincial authorities. In areas definitely identified as VC-controlled, Harkins favored the use of napalm to kill guerrillas and defoliants to destroy crops. The Americans also wanted to organize military units among the Montagnard tribes, the non-Vietnamese inhabitants of the highlands, who might patrol the trails that led from Laos and North Vietnam.

Harkins hardly had arrived in Saigon, however, before a determined American critic emerged: Roger Hilsman, the director of the State Department's Bureau of Intelligence and Research (INR). Young, energetic, abrasive, and highly opinionated, Hilsman had fought behind Japanese lines with the OSS in Burma during the Second World War. He believed, not without reason, that he understood the nature of guerrilla and counterguerrilla warfare and the need to fight guerrillas with unconventional means. Hilsman had known President Kennedy during the 1950s, when he had worked for the Legislative Reference Service of the Library of Congress, and had contributed memoranda to his campaign. Kennedy apparently regarded him as an innovative thinker, and in January 1962, when Hilsman was thinking of leaving the government to take an academic job, they discussed the general problem of guerrilla warfare. Kennedy convinced Hilsman to remain in his position as director of INR, and asked him to attend the second Honolulu conference in mid-January 1962 and to visit Vietnam after that. Hilsman leapt at the opportunity, and returned with a long appreciation of the situation as he saw it.[9]

Hilsman's paper of February 2 located the problem squarely within the villages of South Vietnam. Downgrading the significance of infiltration, he pointed out that the Viet Cong were concentrating upon extending their authority in the countryside. The battle for control of the villages, he suggested, could only be won "by denying [the Viet Cong] access to the villages and the people." Hilsman suggested that the frequent American complaint about the ARVN—that it spent too much time on static defense—missed this point, but agreed that the Civil Guard and Self-Defense Corps had to be increased. American "sergeants, lieutenants, and Civic Action teams, including police trainers and public administrators," could work in villages with South Vietnamese troops.

Turning to his more specific strategic concept, Hilsman stated three principles: that the Viet Cong presented a political rather than a military problem; that a counterinsurgency plan had to provide the villages with security; and that "Counterguerrilla forces must adopt the tactics of the guerrilla himself. Conventional military tactics are ineffective against guerrillas." Then, drawing on his own experience, he compared an ineffective, large-scale Japanese action against his own guerrillas in Burma to a recent heliborne operation against the Viet Cong along the Cambodian border in Tay Ninh province. In both cases, the anti-guerrilla forces used large units and tried to trap guerrilla forces, but failed to make contact. In the Tay Ninh operation, Hilsman argued, the South Vietnamese forces had relied on outdated intelligence and tipped the enemy off with a preliminary air bombardment and the pre-positioning of troops, resulting in little contact and very few enemy casualties. "The basic concept of creating a trap," he wrote, "will rarely work against guerrillas. In general, counterguerrilla warfare requires that contact be made with the guerrillas by aggressive patrolling, and at that point troops should be brought up to form a trap by ambushing the trails and roads leading away from the area of contact." He also complained that the operation had killed more civilians than VC, with negative political consequences, and criticized the use of air strikes before ground troops had actually made contact with the enemy.

In place of such operations, Hilsman endorsed the proposals of the British counterguerrilla expert and veteran of Malaya Sir Robert Thompson, and proposed the creation of "strategic villages" in densely populated areas, to organize the villagers against the Viet Cong. Farther away from the population centers, he called for a network of "defended villages" as a "forward security line against Viet Cong expansion." Eventually, this line would move to the Laotian and Cambodian borders. To execute his plan, Hilsman proposed approximately doubling the size of the Civil Guard and Self-Defense Corps, but called for only about 1,000 additional Americans.[10]

Hilsman's memorandum reached Kennedy at a propitious moment. Less than three weeks earlier, the President had told McNamara that he was still "not satisfied that the Department of Defense, and in particular the Army, is according the necessary degree of attention and effort to the threat of Communist-directed subversive insurgency and guerrilla warfare," and he had returned to this issue in the National Security Council on January 18.[11] But the news that a second-level State Department official had critiqued American military strategy disturbed the Joint Chiefs of Staff (JCS), who did not want State Department officials telling them how to fight a war. The Chiefs invited Hilsman to present his findings at a regular State–Joint Chiefs meeting on February 9. They received him politely, but Admiral George Anderson's pointed questions revealed that Hilsman had spent only five days in South Vietnam, and that he had not discussed his findings with General McGarr. When Anderson asked whether Hilsman believed that the U.S. military in Vietnam had not been "sufficiently effective, helpful, imaginative, and resourceful," Hilsman replied that we could not blame the Americans on the spot for a lack of positive action, since they were merely advisers.[12]

A long series of State-Pentagon arguments over tactics and strategy had begun. Interdiction bombing, or the bombing of villages in areas under reputed Viet Cong control, also created controversy almost as soon as the Air Force's Jungle Jim unit began to operate. A raid which accidentally struck a Cambodian village on January 21 led Alexis Johnson to suggest to William Bundy at Defense that restrictions be placed upon the use of bombs, napalm, rockets, and .50 caliber machine guns against villages. Bundy proposed some new guidance on the subject a few days later, but the JCS opposed it. In mid-February, in preparation for the third Honolulu conference, Sterling Cottrell of the Vietnam Task Force suggested to Harriman that the government limit such bombing either to cases in which ground troops were already engaged (Hilsman's original proposal) or to areas specifically approved by the Embassy—a diminution of Harkins's powers under the directive establishing his position. Cottrell also gave Harriman a copy of Hilsman's strategic concept, while warning Harriman not to refer specifically to it for fear of offending the military. Harriman raised the matter politely at the conference, and Nolting and General Anthis, the Air Force commander in Vietnam, replied that all target recommendations came from the Vietnamese. McNamara stressed the need to bomb only when military advantages outweighed political disadvantages, but Harriman agreed that Nolting and Harkins would decide upon individual cases.[13] In fact, however, Harkins took a much more relaxed view of the matter, and several months later, in a July 18 conversation with Diem, he complained that air assets were not being fully utilized. "Where an area is known to be VC controlled," he said, "it might be a good idea to warn the people by means of pamphlets that they must leave. If they refuse to leave then we could assume the village was VC or VC controlled."[14]

The use of defoliants, especially for the destruction of crops, was another source of controversy. Kennedy on January 3 had authorized some experiments with defoliation in South Vietnam, but only along roads and around airfields, to test the effectiveness of such chemicals and improve security. The Diem government, however, immediately wanted to extend the program to food supplies in Viet Cong areas. At the fourth Honolulu conference on March 27, General Harkins and Ambassador Nolting endorsed Diem's request for further authority to destroy crops in VC areas, but State and Michael Forrestal of the NSC staff successfully delayed, stressing the propaganda risks involved and demanding more data on the effectiveness of the chemicals.[15] During July, Nolting, Harkins, the Joint Chiefs, and McNamara all requested authority for crop destruction, but Hilsman and Forrestal opposed it, and Kennedy on August 8 refused it.[16] The argument refused to die, however, and at a State Department–Joint Chiefs meeting on August 24, outgoing JCS Chairman Lemnitzer remarked "that it is strange that we can bomb, kill and burn people but are not permitted to starve them." And after hearing directly from South Vietnamese Defense Minister Thuan, who visited Washington in September, Kennedy on October 2 overruled Harriman, Hilsman, and Forrestal, and agreed to crop destruction, subject to specific American approval. "I believe his main train of thinking was that you cannot say no to your military advisors all the time, and with this I agree," Forrestal wrote.[17] Since Rostow's departure from the White House, Forrestal had assumed the NSC responsibility for Southeast Asia.

Harkins's support for interdiction bombing and crop destruction—which CINCPAC Admiral Felt shared—reflected his approach to the war. He focused above all on reported Viet Cong strongholds in relatively remote areas, and wanted to use all available means against them. Keeping the Viet Cong under constant pressure, he reasoned, would make it impossible for the enemy to make the frequent attacks against outposts, Civil Guards and Self-Defense Corps which they preferred, and eventually would reduce the enemy threat to manageable proportions. More than anything else, the Americans wanted to get the ARVN out of defensive positions and into a more aggressive posture. And in their effort to sell our new effort in Vietnam, American sources began to state for the record that the South Vietnamese had seized the initiative in early 1962. Admiral Felt told reporters that the government had gone on the offensive in early March, and in April he informed the JCS that the South Vietnamese had agreed to keep the enemy off balance and prevent the division of the country in the narrow northern part of South Vietnam. "In other words," he wrote, "Diem is responding favorably to American military strategic advice."[18]

Certainly the South Vietnamese welcomed the equipment the Ameri-

cans had to offer, but the Diem government seized upon both the increased firepower and mobility offered by MACV to implement its own
concept of military operations. South Vietnamese practice did not reflect American theory. And while both MACV and the Embassy concealed much of the truth within a stream of guardedly optimistic reports, lower-level American officers and civilians knew what was
happening, and Harkins and Nolting had plenty of access to the facts
as well.

In Saigon during the first half of 1962, Brigadier General H. K.
Egleston, the Acting Chief of the Military Assistance Advisory Group
(MAAG), distributed a series of papers entitled "Lessons Learned," de-
signed to improve the performance of American advisers and the South
Vietnamese units to which they were assigned. This collection, which
Harkins eventually passed along to his successor, General William
Westmoreland, provides the clearest picture of the actual nature of
South Vietnamese operations that has yet become available.[19]

The "Lessons Learned" series initially described thirteen operations
in various parts of the country from March through June. Two were
partially successful; the other eleven generally failed. Three of them
found no enemy at all, and while eight others reported some contact
and some VC casualties, the American observers repeated again and
again that the government forces had failed to pursue the enemy. The
authors quickly drew conclusions similar to Hilsman's. "Battalion and
larger-sized 'sweep' operations," a report noted on April 11, "are generally unproductive and wasteful in terms of manpower, effort and
materials expended."[20] On June 19, the sixteenth Lesson Learned summarized the first fifteen. Sweep-type operations, it began, should be
avoided, since they reflected a lack of good intelligence. Contact with
the enemy, once established, must not be lost; pursuit must be relentless. Units must use all available fire support, and small unit leaders
must show excellent leadership and aggressiveness. Helicopters had
proved their potential usefulness, but troops had to be "civic action
minded," and avoid destroying homes, stealing food, or molesting
women, even in suspected VC areas. But the report ended on an optimistic note: "Sustained counter-insurgency operations can wrest an
area from VC control."[21]

The "Lessons Learned" series—never before discussed in print—
shows that at least some American advisers had rapidly grasped critical

elements of the nature of the war and the tactics that the conflict required. Yet the available record does not suggest that these insights led
to any real changes. In a long conversation with Diem on July 18,
Harkins recommended one-battalion-sized operations, but the conversation had no apparent effect.[22] Military and published sources list six
large sweep operations during the first half of 1962, none of which
made major contact with the enemy,[23] and at least the same number
during the second half of the year. More than 1,000 ARVN soldiers
swept through Binh Duong and into Phuoc Thanh province in late July,
without discovering any Viet Cong. A relatively successful sweep in
busy An Xuyen province reportedly killed at least sixty VC in mid-Au-
gust and drew a favorable review in "Lessons Learned," but the South
Vietnamese government failed to exploit the success politically.[24] Two
large sweeps targeted the Plain of Reeds in September and October,
with one reporting substantial success, and the other—a huge operation called Morning Star—coming up empty. Diem obviously enjoyed
the increased firepower and mobility that American airplanes and helicopters provided, but he seems to have wanted to use them only to assert the presence and authority of the government in outlying areas,
rather than to risk large numbers of troops in major battles.

Only Viet Cong records, if such still exist, will ever provide accurate
information as to VC casualties. Armies throughout history have customarily exaggerated the casualties they inflict, and the ARVN was
clearly anything but an exception. Newspaper accounts repeatedly described operations in which 50–150 Viet Cong were reportedly killed,
but Americans rarely saw large numbers of bodies. Scattered evidence
suggests the nature of the problem, but does not allow a real estimate
of the extent of it. Thus, in January 1962 *Newsweek*'s skeptical reporter François Sully saw an ARVN unit arbitrarily report twenty-one
enemy dead after an air and artillery strike against a village in Binh
Duong province.[25] In June Joseph Mendenhall, the departing Embassy
Political Counselor, paid a farewell call on Vice President Tho, who expressed his hope "that we do not believe the figures put out by the
GVN on Viet Cong casualties. He said many of these casualties were
not VC at all but members of the population killed by the GVN forces.
If all these casualties were VC, he said, the war would be over."[26] Considerable evidence suggests that the South Vietnamese routinely began
claiming dozens of enemy killed in action after every air strike upon an

identified Viet Cong position, whether they inspected the position afterward or not.

Meanwhile, the Viet Cong, an organization distinguished by its adaptability, had begun altering its tactics. The increased firepower the Americans deployed did force the VC to reduce the scale of their attacks. They had continued making battalion-sized attacks during the spring of 1962, but in the second half of the year they generally abandoned them—a development which American authorities immediately interpreted optimistically. Instead, the VC carried out numerous attacks against outposts and villages, and staged about two ambushes every day, most of them in the Delta around Saigon. Ambushes of convoys greatly disturbed the MAAG, and two long papers in the "Lessons Learned" series discussed means of avoiding them. One of the papers included an "Ambush Questionnaire" to gather more data.[27] A lack of aggressiveness frequently prevented the South Vietnamese from reacting properly to an ambush. In his July 18 talk with Diem, Harkins complained that after an initial VC volley killed 20 of 270 men in a convoy in Binh Duong province—the site of Operation Sunrise—the rest of the men stood around doing nothing.[28] Aircraft flying with ground convoys offered considerable protection, but ambushes continued to plague friendly forces.[29]

By September 1962 General Harkins had been in Saigon for more than six months. In July in Honolulu he had received McNamara's orders to prepare to phase out his mission during the next three years. On September 5 Harkins had a remarkable conversation with Diem, and apparently tried to win the South Vietnamese President over to his own strategic concept—a highly American and conventional one.[30] Harkins began by praising recent successes in the Delta area—presumably a reference to the An Xuyen sweep—and listing the new American helicopter companies, armored vehicles, and aircraft expected during the next few months. One of the two new Vietnamese divisions, the 9th, had completed training, and the second, the 25th, was scheduled to come on line in January. The completion of ongoing training of the Civil Guard, Self-Defense Corps, and paramilitary forces, he continued, would bring a total of 450,000 government forces under arms.

Harkins then suggested that the enemy numbered "slightly over 20,000 hard core VC," with "another 100,000 local guerrillas and an unknown number of sympathizers." This represented a slight increase from the 16,500 guerrillas which Harkins had reported to McNamara in May, after a bitter battle among intelligence officers in Saigon, who had initially concluded that VC main forces numbered more than 40,000 men.[31] The ratio of forces, Harkins argued, was very favorable to the government, and he now proposed that the South Vietnamese plan and execute a "sudden explosion everywhere at the same time," weather permitting. "Perhaps it would not be possible to kill all the Viet Cong," he said, "but it should at least drive them underground."

Harkins obviously hoped to use the promise of ultimate victory to convince Diem to implement certain long-desired reforms. The explosion, he said, would require logistical improvements, the stockpiling of supplies, a much greater intelligence effort, and that constant American demand, a fully unified military chain of command. Units, he said, must receive adequate staffing, and "many units . . . now had only 50 or 60% of their officer and noncommissioned office strength." When Diem asked how much time would be required for the plan and what results could be expected, Harkins replied that he wanted to prepare to implement it "shortly after the first of the year." One year, he thought, would be enough to achieve victory—although he acknowledged that Secretary McNamara had disagreed, and admitted his own chronic optimism. With more than 450,000 men under arms, he thought, success was within reach—and if some military leaders did not approve, Diem would have to find new ones.

Diem simply did not want to risk his army in an all-out attack. Echoing McNamara, he replied that he found it more reasonable to envision reducing the Viet Cong to such an extent within three years, not one, and said that "the VC, he thought, would not accept a defeat of this kind." Harkins said that they would have to accept it. Diem suggested that they might reinforce, but Harkins seemed to think that that would simply allow the South Vietnamese to kill more of them. Diem then turned the conversation toward events in various parts of the country, stressing the danger he saw in Quang Nam and Quang Ngai provinces, where he feared the VC might stream out of their mountain base areas and move to the coast. Harkins continually stressed the need for more aggressiveness.

The "explosion" eventually mutated into the National Campaign Plan, a much more general document that tried, once again, to take ARVN troops, Civil Guards, and Self-Defense Corps away from the province chiefs and place them under a unified command, but did not commit the ARVN to simultaneous offensive operations around the country.[32] Yet American planners also began working seriously on the requirements for simultaneous attacks all over the country, and the idea of the explosion seems genuinely to have reflected Harkins's strategic views. While the general always paid lip service to the importance of counterinsurgency and the strategic hamlet program, he still saw the Viet Cong waiting in base camps and staging areas in relatively remote regions around the country, emerging from them to ambush convoys and terrorize strategic hamlets. The solution, in his view, lay in striking at the Viet Cong where they were, in offensive operations designed to trap and kill them—and he was sticking to this solution in the fall of 1962, even though some of his subordinates clearly shared Hilsman's view that such operations hardly ever worked against guerrillas.

Harkins, in fact, presented the plan to McNamara and Harriman at another Honolulu conference on October 8, calling for a nationwide offensive preceded by "saturation bombing against VC installations, especially in Zone D." Both Admiral Felt and Harkins's Air Force commander, General Anthis, wanted to designate certain VC zones for indiscriminate bombing. Harkins also announced that he had a plan for a three-year phase-out of American personnel, as demanded by McNamara, which would require large new increases in the number of Vietnamese under arms. Both Harkins and Anthis asked for more American pilots to support operations, but McNamara replied that "the original objective was for the US not to carry the burden of combat," and warned that such a request would be received coolly. But in December CINCPAC and the Pentagon secured an increase, with Harriman's concurrence, by arguing that the increased size and aggressiveness of South Vietnamese forces required it, in order to avoid missing promising opportunities.[33]

Immediately after the meeting Harriman wrote Nolting expressing concern about the explosion, which the VC would probably learn about and which might easily kill a great many innocent people. Nolting replied six weeks later, reporting that Harkins knew that the VC might conceal themselves, but that they would be "unable to operate as effectively during and after the operation as before," and that the strategic hamlet program and "clear and hold" operations would continue.[34] In December representatives of CINCPAC and MACV met in

Honolulu, discussed the plan at length, and scheduled its execution phase for some time after February 15, 1963.[35]

Meanwhile, in a very important development unknown to the Americans, the Viet Cong had opened up a vital new source of supply. In July Ho Chi Minh had visited Peking, and the Chinese Communists had promised 90,000 rifles and other weapons to assist the Viet Cong guerrillas—enough to equip 230 infantry battalions. Chinese Communist policy was becoming increasingly militant on various fronts, and Mao, who had given Ho very important assistance in his war against the French, was more than happy to assist him against the Americans as well. Although Rusk during the next year began making accusations of Chinese weapons deliveries to Vietnam, Washington does not seem to have been aware that a formal agreement had been reached.[36] With Chinese help, the Viet Cong was quite capable of matching any improvements in effectiveness the ARVN might manage to make.

And the process of improving the ARVN was slow at best. Harkins—driven partly by McNamara's deadline—was planning huge, decisive operations before the ARVN had become even a marginally effective fighting force. During October the MACV commander received a confidential report with serious implications. The author was an Australian colonel, Frank Serong, who had arrived in early August with thirty of his countrymen to help train the South Vietnamese.[37] Serong had fought guerrillas in New Guinea, Malaya, and Burma, and had managed to familiarize himself with the South Vietnamese situation very quickly. He began his report by declaring, "We can win this war," and arguing that the Viet Cong was now in trouble. More specific portions of his seventy-one-page report, however, painted a devastating picture of the South Vietnamese effort.

Serong, to begin with, spoke bluntly about the long-standing deficiencies of South Vietnamese forces: "The officer in the field believes that all reward and professional satisfaction exists only in Saigon . . . Consequently, except for the rare dedicated fighting man, the aim of the officer is a steady escalation up the formation headquarters to the Promised Land. He doesn't want to fight, because, if he does, he may spoil his record, and his Saigon chances; and he may be killed." The troops, he wrote, were poorly paid, led, fed, and cared for: "It might help, too, if the ration allowance for the soldier were a little higher than that for a dog." The ARVN needed more officers, and the ARVN Officer Candidate School staff, he said, were "completely unsuited to their task of producing fighting leaders." ARVN officers did not know how to conduct the most rudimentary inspections, and ARVN soldiers needed basic training in the use of their weapons.

Turning to ARVN operations, Serong noted, but also explained, some of the critical problems that had already emerged in the "Lessons Learned" series. Civic action cadres, he reported, did not accompany ARVN units on "clear and hold" sweeps because the ARVN did not want to brief them, lest security be breached. When civic action teams left strategic hamlets after a few weeks—even showcase hamlets like Cu Chi in Binh Duong province, which McNamara had visited personally—"complete disintegration of the established security procedures" followed. Long-range, deep-penetration patrolling had gotten off to a bad start because the unit selected for it had botched the job, leaving other units too frightened to try it. Units simply had to begin pursuing contacts with VC, even though losses would result. Echoing the "Lessons Learned" reports, Serong called for more operations of smaller-than-battalion size, but he added the damning fact that the ARVN did not allow American advisers to accompany such operations.

In general, Serong suggested, American advisers had been too polite. Many waited to be asked for advice and never made a request. The advisers needed to adopt a positive approach, and to threaten to take matters up the chain of command. Serong also commented upon the distribution of American weapons. The .57 mm recoilless rifle and the bazooka, he argued, served no purpose in government operations, but in the hands of the VC, they "could, and do, create havoc." The Special Forces at Boun Enou in the Highlands had distributed 10,000 excellent weapons to the Montagnards, but the Saigon government now wanted some of them recalled.

Serong, in words that would have curled Hilsman's hair had he read them, also criticized the "food control" program in Montagnard areas. "Crop and house destruction in Montagnard territory is madness," he wrote. The allegiance of the Montagnards, upon whom the Americans planned to depend to control the Laotian border, was far more important than any food they might provide the VC. He added that the government did not warn suspected Viet Cong villages that they might be bombed, and that while some suspected villages might not, in fact, be VC-controlled, all of them would be after they were strafed.

Serong's report described an ARVN incapable of virtually *any* effective military operations, impervious to American advice, and wedded to counterproductive tactics. Harkins kept the analysis in his files, but remained trapped by the pressures of his two major constituencies as well as his own doctrinal limitations. On the one hand, he had to convince Diem that he was not undermining his authority by insisting upon doing things the American way; on the other, he had to meet McNamara's deadline for producing dramatic results. Large-scale operations continued apace. On November 20 the South Vietnamese began their biggest sweep yet into the Communist stronghold of War Zone D in Phuoc Thanh province. Harkins had recommended this operation to Defense Minister Thuan on October 5, arguing first for round-the-clock napalm bombing of Zone D, followed by "determined ground actions" to fix the enemy within the Zone, and then, "massive all out attacks using all means at your disposal with the aim of complete destruction of the enemy in Zone D."[38]

In fact, at American urging, the South Vietnamese had combined twenty-two Ranger companies from three provinces—Phuoc Long, Binh Long, and Phuoc Thanh—into a special PBT Ranger unit for operations against Zone D. A March 30, 1963, MACV report noted that two operations in July and September 1962 had gone badly, but that the new unit had made three sweeps through the area in November, late December, and February. They had turned up a good deal of information about the enemy and reportedly killed 245 VC, out of an estimated enemy strength of nearly 8,000 men, at a cost of 51 friendly deaths. Not once, the report stated, had the Rangers actually managed to surprise a Viet Cong unit, and they had regularly been ambushed anywhere that they chose to spend the night. The troops, moreover, had found it impossible to use conventional tactics along trails that could accommodate only one soldier at a time.[39]

On December 7 Harkins issued a draft comprehensive plan for the war. "Overall strategy of [South Vietnamese armed forces] operations," it stated, "should remain unchanged—to retain the overall initiative and keep VC off balance by penetration of strongholds, destruction of food supplies (particularly in the highlands), elimination of specific regular VC units, preparation of areas for civic action, clear-and-hold operations, and ultimate control of insurgency." After most of a year, Harkins continued to emphasize conventional operations against identified Viet Cong units—a strategy whose effectiveness depended upon inflicting heavy casualties. A definitive assessment of enemy casualties can only come from Viet Cong sources, but it seems clear that the South Vietnamese, with plenty of encouragement from the American military, were continuing to run highly conventional operations that had only occasional effectiveness against Viet Cong troops, and no effect—or a negative effect—upon the attitude of the South Vietnamese population and the political strength of the Viet Cong.[40]

The Pentagon apparently shared Harkins's fundamentally conventional approach to the war. At Fordham University on November 7, General Earle Wheeler, the new Army Chief of Staff, pointedly discussed the nature of the war. In Vietnam, he said, the United States was "committed to the support of a military action": "It is fashionable in some quarters to say that the problems in Southeast Asia are primarily political and economic, rather than military. I do not agree. The essence of the problem in Vietnam is military . . . The struggle in Southeast Asia, then, is a military struggle in a military context, with political and economic factors significant but not as significant at this moment, I think, as are the military factors."[41]

Despite their good intentions, the Americans inevitably tended to encourage a relatively high proportion of large-scale operations—all the more so, as we have seen, because they were not *allowed* to take part in small-scale ones. Meanwhile, the strategic hamlet program—the centerpiece of Hilsman's proposed strategy, which Diem and Nhu seemed eagerly to have embraced—was launched upon a most uncertain and hazardous course as well.

As Hilsman recognized and as the CIA analyst Sam Adams discovered several years later, the real source of Viet Cong strength lay among the densely populated villages of South Vietnam, specifically within the Mekong Delta—where the majority of the population lived—and in the coastal plain in the center and north. Some of their strength dated from the war against the French—indeed, the Saigon government had never made its presence felt in certain regions, especially in the southern Mekong Delta—but much of it had been rebuilt with astonishing rapidity in 1960–1961, after the Viet Cong finally received permission from Hanoi to embark on a terrorist offensive again.[42] A substantial portion of their leadership had gone north in 1954 under the terms of the Geneva Accords, but many had stayed behind, and many more had now returned. Intelligence estimates by MACV and by the South Vietnamese government recognized the existence of Viet Cong support in the countryside by listing 100,000 "local guerrillas" in addition to approximately 20,000 main-force guerrillas. The figure of 100,000, which successive estimates held constant through the early 1960s, shows every sign of being arbitrary, and was almost certainly wildly low. According to Douglas Pike, the National Liberation Front—the Communist-led political organization that included the Viet Cong—had 300,000 members by early 1962.[43] When Sam Adams began working on the enemy order of battle in 1966, he inherited the same 100,000-man figure, and after several months of work he had revised it to 500,000, in addition to 100,000 Viet Cong regulars.[44]

As Adams came to realize, MACV, both before and after 1965, consistently underestimated both the size and the significance of the local guerrilla forces and political cadres. The VC main-force units upon which Harkins focused all his attention were simply the tip of a much larger iceberg, and a symptom of the problem the South Vietnamese government faced, rather than the problem itself. The village guerrillas and political operatives provided resources and, above all, manpower to the fighting forces as needed. Indeed, many of them provided supply and medical services, and thereby deserved to be included in the order of battle just as surely as their uniformed South Vietnamese and American counterparts. This reservoir of manpower enabled the VC to maintain or even increase their fighting strength, despite their losses—however large those actually were—on the battlefield. The situation baffled successive American leaders in Saigon, and as late as 1967 General Westmoreland refused to face up to it in a major order-of-battle controversy that eventually led to his lawsuit against CBS in the 1980s.

Ultimately, Viet Cong strength within the villages of South Vietnam—where two-thirds of the population lived—was the source of the insurgency, and ultimately, the government could only reduce it at the village level. The Diem government, however, had never developed an effective security system within the villages. Indeed, it had driven the Hoa Hao and Cao Dai sects, which had provided security in significant portions of the Mekong Delta, into opposition. To assert its presence, the government relied upon isolated military outposts, which became easy targets for attack, and ARVN sweeps or raids into populated areas, which momentarily drove the VC into the countryside but rarely inflicted any significant damage upon them. The government put little faith in the Civil Guard or the Self-Defense Corps, whose loyalty was frequently dubious.[45] In 1960 the Viet Cong had begun assassinating and kidnapping government officials. In at least one critical Delta province, Long An, this campaign had immediately driven local officials into a few well-protected outposts, allowing the Viet Cong to collect taxes, redistribute land, and organize their manpower.[46]

As we have seen, plans developed in Washington during 1961 foresaw strengthening the Civil Guard and Self-Defense Corps in order to free the ARVN for operations against main-force VC units. In late 1961, however, new plans for reducing VC strength in the countryside poured into Saigon. During the autumn Sir Robert Thompson, a British counterinsurgency expert who had helped defeat the Communist insurgency in Malaya, arrived in Saigon to advise Diem. Thompson drafted a counterinsurgency plan for the Mekong Delta—the most populated area of the country, and the center, as Lansdale had recognized earlier in the year, of Viet Cong strength—to be implemented under Diem's direct supervision. American authorities initially reacted angrily to the plan, which they disliked on both geographical and organizational grounds, but Diem and Nhu became enthusiastic about it. Diem on February 3, 1962, signed a decree establishing the Interministerial Committee for Strategic Hamlets, chaired by Nhu.[47] Thompson's plan, which Hilsman also embraced after his January trip to Vietnam, initially confined itself to ten of the most densely populated provinces in Vietnam: Vinh Long, Vinh Binh, Kien Hoa, parts of Dinh Tuong and Long An, Gia Dinh, the southern tip of Tay Ninh province along the Cambodian border, southern Binh Duong province, the southern tip of Phuoc Thanh, most of Bien Hoa, and the southern tip of Phuoc Tuy. It foresaw two types of hamlets: strategic hamlets in relatively secure areas, defended by the Self-Defense Corps and the Republican Youth, Nhu's personal militia; and defended hamlets, into which population would have to be regrouped, in more remote areas or areas under Viet Cong control. It emphasized identifying and controlling the population, improving administration and public services, and very carefully applying military power. The ARVN could keep VC main-force units off balance while security was established.[48] Thompson's plan, in short, aimed to organize the bulk of South Vietnam's rural population under the benevolent hand of the government. If successful, it would have substantially eroded the political and economic base of the Viet Cong.

General McGarr, meanwhile, had developed a plan of his own that differed somewhat in approach but established similar geographic priorities. McGarr foresaw the ARVN moving through successive provinces and clearing them of Viet Cong, *after which* the local Civil Guards and Self-Defense Corps would be trained, the government would move in with civic action teams, and effective control would be established. McGarr, then, seemed to give military operations priority over political work within the villages and hamlets, but he also prepared a map showing a three-year schedule of geographic priorities that largely replicated Thompson's approach. His map reserved roughly the same area of provinces around Saigon for operations during 1962, foresaw clearing the coastal plain all the way north to Hue and most of the southern Delta during 1963, and left a few of the toughest VC strongholds for 1964.[49]

Admiral Felt, however, had other ideas. As we have seen, in December 1961 Felt had urged McGarr to abandon the planned conventional operation against Zone D, and instead had given McGarr a detailed plan for "a timely, aggressive, coordinated military operation to secure early GVN control of Binh Duong Province."[50] The Honolulu conference of January 15 agreed in principle to plan a clearing operation in one province, and one month later the MAAG presented such a plan for Binh Duong province north of Saigon at the third Honolulu conference. The plan itself, code-named Operation Sunrise and dated February 8, seems to have been designed according to relatively conventional strategic principles. Binh Duong, it noted, was "near the vital SAIGON area, controls important highways to N and NW of SAIGON, and links the VC areas in Zone D, TAY NINH PROVINCE and the PLAINE DES JONCS [the Plain of Reeds]."[51]

Thompson had chosen part of Binh Duong for his pacification plan, but Operation Sunrise proceeded according to principles quite opposite to his. Thompson had designated only the southern half of Binh Duong province for pacification and the construction of strategic hamlets, presumably because the northern half was known to be a VC stronghold. Diem himself on January 11 had suggested to McGarr that this would be a demanding and lengthy operation, and that it should only be undertaken as part of a larger plan to clear a belt of provinces west of Saigon.[52] Operation Sunrise, however, focused mainly upon the insecure area north of the town of Ben Cat. The plan directed several battalions of ARVN and Civil Guards "to destroy and harass the VC and relocate the population of 15 hamlets into 5 secure villages along key routes to the north." It confirmed that "the VC have been in control of most of the area for an extended period of time," and estimated their forces at 1,800. "Our best chance of success," it concluded, "involves the use of surprise and deception and conducting a hasty operation to envelop objectives prior to the VC dispersing the population into the dense but familiar jungle." After the ARVN moved the population into new hamlets, civic action teams would remain among them for several months.

The plan was scheduled for mid-February, but was apparently delayed. A month later Hilsman visited Saigon and expressed doubts about Sunrise, pointing out the danger of beginning the strategic village program, as he called it, in such an insecure area. He reported that both Harkins and Nolting shared his reservations and now wanted Diem to cancel the operation, but dared not ask him to do so because the MAAG had designed the operation and had previously proposed, and then abandoned, an operation against neighboring Zone D itself.[53] Apparently Admiral Felt insisted upon the operation once again during his visit to Saigon in early March.[54] In fact, according to Diem, the Viet Cong had already learned about the operation and forced large numbers of people to flee to avoid it.[55]

Despite these problems, Operation Sunrise kicked off on March 26 and drew extensive American press coverage. Homer Bigart of the *New York Times* had a page-one story on it the next day, portraying it as the beginning of Thompson's plan to clear guerrillas from the area around Saigon. Over the next two weeks, Bigart developed a rather skeptical picture of the operation. His first story reported that the encirclement of VC forces had failed to prevent 100 men from escaping into the forest, and that only 70 of 205 families had actually moved voluntarily. While arguing that this "harsh, desperate measure" had worked for the British in Malaya, Bigart said that the British had paid the Malayan peasants to resettle, but that little of the $300,000 that the United States had allocated for the operation seemed to be reaching the villages. Peasants told Bigart they had worked for six weeks without pay, and South Vietnamese General Cao told Bigart that the cost of new housing had been deducted from the planned payments to the peasants.

An MACV paper for a senior advisers' conference in May confirmed much of what Bigart had said.[56] It was Bigart's April 4 story that disturbed President Kennedy, since it showed Americans inspecting a new resettlement hamlet and accused Americans of "taking on a drastic program that was certain in the initial stages to be bitterly resented by the peasantry whose allegiance must be won." As we have seen, Harriman immediately cabled Saigon asking that the American role be toned down.[57] The Embassy, meanwhile, treated Sunrise as the first step in a general pacification campaign.[58]

Secretary McNamara and General Lemnitzer visited a Sunrise hamlet during their whirlwind trip through South Vietnam in May, but the next day the Viet Cong successfully ambushed a convoy between Ben Cat and Saigon.[59] Several reports from Hilsman to Harriman took an upbeat view of the operation during the spring. A "Lesson Learned" of July 31, however, confirmed that 2,900 people had now been relocated, but listed a number of serious problems to avoid in future, similar operations. The new homes, it argued, should be constructed in advance, since the VC inevitably learned about the operation anyway. The government's psychological warfare effort was no match for Viet Cong propaganda. The operation needed funds for unanticipated expenses, and trained civic action cadres. It had failed to take account of the agricultural cycle. Five weeks later a cable from MACV to the Joint Chiefs passed on a chilling detail: that each of the Sunrise hamlets had between 50 percent and 100 percent more adult women than adult men, suggesting that many of the latter had fled to the hills with the VC.[60] And on November 27 a Viet Cong battalion successfully attacked three of the Sunrise hamlets, showing that the area remained insecure.[61]

Operation Sunrise remained the model for provincial clear-and-hold operations, which targeted known VC areas and relocated the population. During 1962 the South Vietnamese also conducted such operations in Binh Dinh, Quang Ngai and Phu Yen provinces along the north central coast and in An Xuyen in the far south, far from the Delta provinces that Thompson's plan had targeted. They also scheduled such operations for Long An and Dinh Tuong, in the heart of the Delta. And according to a document prepared by MACV on the implementation of the strategic hamlet program, the ARVN involved itself *only* in "clear-and-hold" operations of this type, clearing Viet Cong from given areas and relocating the population. The creation of Thompson and Hils-

man's preferred kind of hamlets in densely populated areas was referred to as "province rehabilitation," and the authority for these operations, according to MACV, lay with the province chief, supported
by the Civil Guard and Self-Defense Corps. Neither MACV nor the
ARVN, in short, was taking much interest in the South Vietnamese
population, except in areas definitely identified as VC-controlled and
ripe for coercive measures.[62] When Hilsman visited Saigon in January
1963, Harkins specifically listed six clear-and-hold operations in VC
strongholds.[63]

The strategic hamlet program proper had officially begun on February 3, 1962, when Diem signed the decree establishing the Interministerial Committee for Strategic Hamlets, under his brother Ngo Dinh
Nhu. Within a month word had reached Washington that 784 strategic
hamlets had already been constructed, 453 more were under construction, and 6,066 were scheduled to be built during 1962.[64] On March 16
Diem signed another decree laying out Thompson's plan for the ten
most heavily populated Delta provinces. But William Trueheart, the
Saigon Deputy Chief of Mission, was already worried that Nhu might
try to build hamlets "all over the country simultaneously without priorities," which would "of course, kill everything."[65] And Colonel Lac,
whom Diem appointed to head the Delta (Thompson) plan, told the
Embassy in late May that he had no separate organization but was simply serving on Nhu's committee. Defense Minister Thuan told Trueheart that the Delta would not receive priority, and that the strategic
hamlets program would proceed throughout the country.[66] Events
proved that Nhu planned to use the program to build a nationwide network of supporters, not to regain the support of the population in a
careful, coordinated campaign. Meanwhile, when McNamara and
Lemnitzer visited Saigon in May, Harkins, in one of his most scandal-
ous moves, altered a map of the countryside prepared by his intelligence team so as to reduce drastically the area shown under enemy control.[67]

The Saigon Embassy and the USOM aid mission tried to use American funds as a lever to bring the strategic hamlet program under control. On June 14 Nolting reported that Diem felt such concern over the
South Vietnamese budget deficit for the coming year that he was refusing to allocate funds to finance counterinsurgency. Although Nolting
believed that Diem was overestimating the deficit, he recommended al-

locating $10 million to buy piasters to finance counterinsurgency operations, and another $12 million to purchase equipment, waiving the normal "buy American" requirement for these funds. He characteristically expressed the intention of using the money as a carrot to increase American influence over counterinsurgency efforts, but he added: "We are not, however, going to bypass the Saigon Ministerial machine completely. This is simply not acceptable to GVN, and there should be no illusions that this is what we expect to obtain."[68]

On June 15 the State Department approved the money and the "buy American" waiver. President Kennedy learned about this decision from the June 20 *New York Times,* and asked Michael Forrestal of the NSC staff to find out what was happening. Kennedy, who took the American balance-of-payments deficit very seriously and had submitted his second consecutive deficit budget himself, thought that South Vietnam could make the same sacrifice. Forrestal replied that McNamara wanted the money provided immediately, partly to fund the resettlement of the Montagnards, but argued himself that Diem was blackmailing the United States, and suggested that Kennedy discuss the matter with McNamara before making a decision. The next day State informed the Embassy in Saigon that the waiver of "buy American" authority had been withdrawn, but apparently left the purchase of $10 million piasters in place.[69]

Nolting replied suggesting that the United States purchase $22 million in piasters, not $10 million. On June 29 State told Nolting that Kennedy wanted him to know that he had personally rejected the desired waiver and would not approve the additional piaster purchase.[70] The piaster fund took on new significance, however, when American officials, led by Rufus Phillips of AID's Office of Rural Development, managed to secure direct control of the funds, allowing them to distribute them to peasants as part of the strategic hamlet program.

Indeed, when State asked in mid-July whether strategic hamlets were proceeding according to any plan, the Embassy replied that the new, dollar-generated piaster fund to pay for hamlets could "induce the GVN to come up with coordinated clear and hold operations in those areas which we regard as having highest priority." Diem himself told Nolting on July 19 that he wanted to stress, first, white (secure) areas; then the most populated provinces of the Delta—"roughly the ten provinces of the Delta Plan"; and then the coastal plains of the central provinces, such as Phu Yen, Binh Dinh, and Quang Ngai, where the Viet Cong threatened to cut the country in half. Diem had added, however, that "in some areas, the districts, villages and hamlets themselves are sufficiently rich and enthusiastic to carry out the program largely under their own steam." That, as frequent conversations showed, reflected Diem and Nhu's belief that the peasants should pay for any new construction themselves, or donate their labor.[71] Just a few days later, at the July Honolulu meeting, Harkins reported that "some of the hamlets are not particularly good" and "there has been no national plan for their establishment," yet repeated the official figures of 2,400 finished hamlets and 6,000 projected by the end of the year.[72]

Ngo Dinh Nhu, his brother's most influential adviser, certainly adopted the strategic hamlet program as his own favored child, but his concept of the program differed fundamentally from Thompson's or Hilsman's. On September 11 General Maxwell Taylor, soon to take over as Chairman of the Joint Chiefs, received a briefing of several hours from Nhu during a four-day return visit to Saigon. While Nhu's elliptical language must have challenged the interpreter's skill and Taylor's powers of understanding, a careful reading suggests that Nhu had a clear concept of his goal: to build up an enthusiastic network of government supporters within the hamlets and villages of South Vietnam, which could expel the Viet Cong from the villages and undertake a "guerrilla war" of its own to hunt them down. Nhu apparently counted upon the Self-Defense Corps and his own organization, the Republican Youth, to play this role, moving from the present "counterguerrilla" strategy to a true "political and social revolution" and a more offensive spirit. Yet Nhu also expected the peasants to contribute the necessary work out of enthusiasm alone, and he indicated fairly clearly that he resented his increasing reliance upon the United States. Nhu spoke abstractly and at great length, and only quotation can convey the flavor of his presentation.

> One of the difficulties in implementing his theory of converting the Vietnamese effort from a counter-subversive movement to a straight guerrilla war against the enemy was the question of how to wage a real democratic revolution with cadres who are engaged in anti-revolutionary activities. He hoped that the successful completion of the Strategic Hamlet Program would result in the banishment of fear and would make it possible to instill the revolutionary spirit in the people who were in support of the gov-

ernment. He added that his concept had to be expounded with a certain amount of care because many people within the government might be frightened by it and oppose it.

Taylor replied by asking whether the province chiefs were working according to a plan, and Nhu quickly turned the discussion to one of his favorite themes, self-reliance:

> Reverting to his original theme Mr. Nhu added that efforts were being made to change the attitudes of these government representatives from their orientation towards a counter-guerrilla aspect of their efforts. It was hard for them to understand the difference which exists between counter-subversive activities and direct guerrilla warfare, which is total in nature. The guerrilla counts on no one but himself. Those who have been oriented towards the counter-guerrilla concept have had the benefit of American aid including arms, equipment and all types of supplies. They have been sheltered and when they were sick they were cared for. The guerrilla has no hospital, no supplies and depends only on himself—a reversal of mental attitudes.

Nolting, who understood what Nhu was saying, "commented that this was a hard philosophy and hoped there might be some way in which it can be softened," but Taylor simply asked how Nhu planned to change people's thinking. Nhu stressed the need to develop a guerrilla force based on the ideology of "freedom vs. slavery . . . if we could succeed in this, we could give a step by step political strategy which would be valid for all of the underdeveloped countries, who, lacking this ideology, are obliged to seek neutralism in order to reduce the tension which is placed upon them"—an implied slap at U.S. policy in Laos. A democratic spirit, he assured Taylor, was developing, as evidenced by the complaints he received from peasants. Nhu repeated that about one-third of 16,230 projected hamlets would be completed that year.

Nhu concluded by suggesting that Americans might have become too ubiquitous in South Vietnam, and that he wanted their role to decline. He urged the Americans to seek rest and recreation outside Vietnam—perhaps reflecting the views of his wife, who feared the American impact upon Vietnamese morals—and "referred vaguely to the implications which might follow the progression of the Vietnamese effort from counter-subversive to all-out guerrilla activities, implying that this might be bad for the Americans."[73] Years later, Harkins, who was also present, recalled that Taylor couldn't understand what Nhu was talking about.[74]

Nhu's basic goal—to develop an enthusiastic, armed network of government supporters inside the hamlets of Vietnam—was sound, but numerous reports indicated a failure to achieve it. Sterling Cottrell, Harriman's deputy and the new State Department point man on Vietnam, wrote Nolting on the very day that Taylor saw Nhu. Quoting a CIA report, he asked whether the regime was arming the Self-Defense Corps adequately (a constant concern of McNamara's), whether peasants were building new hamlets without pay, whether relocation into new villages was necessary, and whether the United States was seen as replacing the French in a colonial role. Nolting, who always resented interference from Washington, took weeks to reply to these critical questions. He confirmed that the government hesitated to provide weapons to villagers for fear that they might be lost to the enemy, and that "the poorest inhabitants are bearing the brunt of unpaid work on strategic hamlets." Regroupment of people did not always take place, he said, but in Sunrise it was both necessary and successful.[75]

More pessimistic views came from the U.S. Consul in Hue, John Heble, who reported that "in Central Vietnam the strategic hamlet program is mostly pure facade," since Ngo Dinh Canh, the boss of the region, was feuding with his brother Nhu and didn't take it seriously. The program often began and ended with a fence around part of the hamlet, and the villagers complained bitterly about unpaid work. Canh, moreover, was focusing on building up his own paramilitary force, the Popular Force, a group parallel to Nhu's Republican Youth. Heble provided a rare piece of real and significant intelligence: that in many hamlets approximately one-third of all adult males actively sympathized with the VC. In November Taylor's aide, Commander Worth Bagley, informed him that some White House, State Department, and Pentagon officials had serious doubts about the progress of the strategic hamlet program. Bagley was not convinced by a reassuring memo to Taylor from Marine General Victor Krulak, Taylor's Special Assistant for Counterinsurgency Affairs, and recommended attempts to get better information about the program.[76]

In a memorandum for McNamara of November 17, Taylor acknowledged that of the 3,353 strategic hamlets reported complete, "probably not more than 600 can be viewed as fulfilling the desired characteristics in terms of equipment, defensive works, security forces and, possibly most important, government." Now, however, the memo stated, "properly conceived hamlets" were increasing at 300 per month. The memo, which Krulak apparently had drafted, said nothing about Taylor's own conversation with Nhu, and concluded optimistically, "There would seem to be no reason for modifying the views expressed by General Harkins and Ambassador Nolting regarding the long-term virtues of the program," which was only now "beginning to mature." It added that the Viet Cong's attacks upon the program, which the memo carefully documented, "suggest that the Viet Cong perceive its potential." The memo did not include a new paragraph, suggested by Bagley, calling for improved reporting on the actual situation.

Indeed, the memo included a map showing Viet Cong attacks against populated areas, by province, from August through October. To an impartial observer, the map simply demonstrated that the Viet Cong remained strong throughout all the populated areas of the country, and especially in the Delta provinces immediately around Saigon, where Thompson wanted to put priority attention, and in the northern coastal plain. Attacks on hamlets averaged more than one per day overall, with 77 attacks reported against non-strategic hamlets and 44—a proportionately greater number—against strategic hamlets. Fourteen attacks had occurred against hamlets within the approved clear-and-hold relocation operations in Binh Duong (Sunrise), Phu Yen, Binh Dinh, and Quang Ngai provinces. The memo provided no information as to the success of these attacks, but the ARVN's sweeps into supposed VC base areas did not seem to be doing much to make the countryside more secure.[77] These attacks, moreover, were only the beginning. "We must figure out a way to destroy [the strategic hamlets]," Ho Chi Minh told the North Vietnamese politburo in November 1962. "If so, our victory is assured."[78] Following Ho's orders, the Viet Cong prepared for a major offensive against the hamlets during the following year.

As 1962 drew to a close, Vietnam and Southeast Asia had receded from the public's consciousness. The official line held that American help had turned the situation within Vietnam around, and Ambassador Nolting and General Harkins eagerly restated it as often as possible. In Washington, McNamara, Taylor, Hilsman, and Forrestal were most actively interested in South Vietnam, and all of them hoped and believed that Diem's government might, in fact, address its problems and win the war. At the turn of the year, however, two dramatic events highlighted some of the enormous political and military difficulties that the Diem regime still faced: Senator Mike Mansfield's visit to Saigon in December, and the Battle of Ap Bac.

Mansfield's visit—which he undertook at Kennedy's request[79]—reopened the question that Nolting had been trying to close for at least a year: whether Diem could survive politically at all. When Diem had refused to make any basic changes in his regime after the Taylor visit, Nolting had effectively concluded that it was the job of the United States to secure Diem's confidence, not the other way around, and had refused to entertain any discussion of alternative leadership. In reality, however, Diem's position was anything but secure, and fundamental questions about his future continually reached Washington and even surfaced in the press.

Thus, in February 1962 Diem terminated the Michigan State University contract to train South Vietnamese police, a program that had begun in 1955. Diem and Nhu complained that some of the professors had used their positions to collect intelligence, and especially protested articles in *The New Republic* by two of the professors suggesting that the regime could not survive. Wesley Fishel of the university, who had returned to Vietnam after a long absence to try to save the program, gave a devastating report on the situation there to Michigan State President John Hannah in February, and Hannah forwarded it to Kennedy himself. Citing the increasing influence of Nhu and Madame Nhu, Fishel argued that Diem's support was nearing the vanishing point. Of 118 Vietnamese friends with whom Fishel had talked during his stay—none of them part of the political opposition, and most of them strong Diem supporters only three years earlier—only three or four now supported Diem with any enthusiasm. Diem, Fishel argued, would never allow capable Vietnamese to reach positions of authority.[80]

Just a few days later, on February 27, events dramatically underlined Diem's problems, when two Vietnamese Air Force pilots bombed the palace in an attempt to assassinate Diem, Nhu, and Madame Nhu, all of whom survived without injury. Diem told Nolting that derogatory articles in *Newsweek* had helped inspire one of the pilots,[81] and refused to allow Vietnamese pilots to drop bombs for several weeks. Later that month Homer Bigart of the *New York Times* reported that an opposition leader had written an open letter to Diem calling upon him to free prisoners and legalize the opposition, and that an American professor in Saigon had been searched, interrogated, and detained because he had met one of the palace bombers. On March 23 Bigart—one of America's most respected reporters—and *Newsweek* correspondent François Sully received orders from the South Vietnamese government to leave the country on the next available plane. The Embassy apparently managed to get the orders rescinded.[82]

Both Colonel Howard Burris—Vice President Johnson's military aide—and General Taylor's aide Commander Bagley received a stream of discouraging intelligence reports from Vietnam during the spring. Burris in April reported that several different groups were plotting against Diem, who seemed "certain" to be overthrown, and Bagley repeatedly argued that Diem was simply not taking enough American advice.[83] In mid-June the South Vietnamese ambassador to the United States, Tran Van Chong—Madame Nhu's father—told Senate Majority Leader Mike Mansfield's aide Frank Valeo that Diem was hopeless and likely to be overthrown by the military. Chief of Naval Operations Anderson wondered openly about the consequences of Diem's overthrow as well.[84]

Homer Bigart completed his six-month assignment in South Vietnam in July. On July 25 his summary assessment appeared in the *Times*. Despite the massive American effort, he wrote, victory seemed far away because of Diem's inability to win the support of the people. Bigart discussed Diem and Nhu's interference in military operations at length, even implying that it jeopardized American lives. The article discussed most of the problems that troubled American officials, such as forced labor in strategic hamlets, Diem's refusal to allow Americans to disburse aid in the provinces, and the ARVN's fondness for conventional tactics. He also described in detail how Americans had effectively given up on forcing Diem to reform after the Taylor mission. Frequent statements of confidence from high American officials had robbed Nolting of any leverage. Bigart concluded with a brief history of Diem's ups and downs. "Should the situation disintegrate further," he wrote, "Washington may face the alternative of ditching Ngo Dinh Diem for a military junta or sending combat troops to bolster the regime." He doubted, however, that the Americans could do much better than the French.[85]

On August 16 Joseph Mendenhall, who had recently returned from a long tour as Political Counselor in Saigon, wrote a State Department superior along lines similar to Wesley Fishel's. Security had deteriorated drastically since 1959, Diem and Nhu would never change, and the United States should "Get rid of Diem, Mr. and Mrs. Nhu and the rest of the Ngo family." He recommended encouraging a military coup and laid out a lengthy scenario for doing so.[86]

Mendenhall's report never left the State Department, but on October 18 President Kennedy wrote Majority Leader Mike Mansfield asking him to lead a bipartisan group of senators on a trip to Berlin and Southeast Asia. Mansfield had been a congressional authority on Asia since the 1940s, and he had been one of Diem's original sponsors. Between December 1 and December 3 he had long talks with Diem and with Nhu, who once again laid out his concept of strategic hamlets. At the airport, Mansfield refused to read a statement given him by the Embassy saying that he was encouraged by evidence of progress, thereby becoming the first American visitor not to make such a statement in recent memory.[87] He submitted his report to the Congress on December 18, and it was published on February 24.

In retrospect, Mansfield's report shows far more sophistication than any other contemporary American appreciation of the situation, both with respect to what he discovered in Indochina and with respect to the options open to the United States. While acknowledging the optimism and enthusiasm of South Vietnamese and Americans, he noted that he had been hearing about "new concepts" since the French Navarre Plan of 1953, and that the situation in Vietnam seemed to have deteriorated significantly since 1954, despite all the American help. The countryside remained insecure, Diem had grown older and more tired, and Nhu, who seemed obsessed with political power, was stepping into the breach. If the anti-guerrilla offensive and the strategic hamlet program failed, he suggested, the United States would face pressure to take over the war itself—"an alternative which I most emphatically do not recommend"—and would risk stepping into the French role, with a significant danger of North Vietnamese or Chinese escalation.

Having established a substantial probability that the American effort would fail, Mansfield suggested that its success was critical only if "it is essential in our interests to maintain a quasi-permanent position of power on the Asian mainland as against the Chinese." If this was not deemed essential, he suggested very clearly—although without actually saying so—that the United States might move toward neutralization of the entire area.[88]

While acknowledging the difficult situation that persisted in Laos, and criticizing certain American government agencies (though not the ambassador) for apparently believing that the Laotian settlement was doomed, Mansfield paid particular tribute to Sihanouk in Cambodia, whose "internal stability [was] exceptional for contemporary Southeast Asia"—"an illustration of what can be achieved in the lush lands of the region in conditions of peace, with a vigorous and progressive indigenous leadership and a judicious and limited use of outside aid." On the other hand, Mansfield noted that the Thais opposed the policy of neutralization in Laos, and that American actions in Thailand seemed to mirror their skepticism. The United States was constructing jet airports in eastern Thailand—the results of McNamara's $20 million allocation agreed on during the summer—and although American troops had withdrawn, others were planning to return to build a fuel pipeline across the country. Mansfield clearly believed that the level of American aid to Thailand could not be justified, and concluded that the United States might indeed discover "that it is in our interests to do less rather than more than we are now doing" throughout the whole region. "If that is the case, we will do well to concentrate on a vigorous diplomacy which would be designed to lighten our commitments without bringing about sudden and catastrophic upheavals in Southeast Asia."[89] When Mansfield saw Kennedy in Palm Beach, Florida, and gave him his report, the President rather angrily commented that it did not tally with the opinions of his subordinates.[90]

The North Vietnamese and Viet Cong leaders, meanwhile, had been disappointed in their hope that the Laotian accords might lead to a similar settlement in South Vietnam. They continued, therefore, to try to escalate the conflict within South Vietnam, with particular attention to the strategic hamlet program, but hoped to avoid provoking the United States into outright intervention.[91]

The Battle of Ap Bac on January 2, 1963—coming right on the heels of Mansfield's report—provided a wake-up call of another sort. At the time, the battle tended to undermine the general impression of military progress that the American government was trying so hard to create. Newly available documentation shows that the battle and its aftermath also revealed the extent of the dilemma that American military advisers faced, and the gulf between their reports and reality.

The Battle of Ap Bac was undertaken by General Huynh Van Cao, who as commander of the Vietnamese 7th Division had operated in the Delta just southwest of Saigon during 1962. It has received unusual attention from the time it took place because the 7th Division's senior American adviser was Lieutenant Colonel John Paul Vann, one of the most famous American participants in the war, who discussed the battle freely with the press at the time. Since the spring of 1962 Cao—then a colonel—had been running heliborne operations into the Plain of Reeds, the huge Communist stronghold in Kien Tuong and Kien Phong provinces along the Cambodian border. While some of these operations had some success, they seldom measured up to Cao's press releases. Neil Sheehan of UPI reported on May 13, 1962, that 300 Communists had been killed on the Plain, but the next issue of *Newsweek* scaled enemy casualties down to 20, with 27 friendly killed.[92] Two months later, on July 21, Vann and Cao trapped about 150 VC regulars on the Plain, but Cao's lethargy allowed most of them to escape. While Cao claimed 131 killed and the government eventually raised the number to 150, Vann himself counted only about 40 dead and officially stated that enemy dead "did not exceed 90." After this operation Vann concluded that Cao and his fellow officers generally preferred to avoid combat. A parallel theme, lack of aggressiveness, had already been cited in several of the MACV "Lessons Learned" series.[93] On September 18 the 7th Division apparently killed 158 guerrillas with the help of a new American weapon, armored personnel carriers.[94] On October 5, however, a VC ambush shot down two helicopters and killed 12 South Vietnamese Rangers and an American near the edge of the Plain of Reeds. The government arbitrarily claimed 100 enemy dead from a retaliatory air strike, but the Viet Cong held their positions and did not flee into the open.[95] After that, Cao cut back Vann's role in planning operations. Then Cao became a general and took over command of the newly created IV Corps, responsible for the whole southern Mekong Delta.

The Battle of Ap Bac occurred because of a radio intercept that located a Viet Cong force in the hamlets of Tan Thoi and Bac just west of My Tho, in Dinh Tuong province in the heart of the Delta. A 7th Division battalion, two battalions of Civil Guards, and a company of M-113 armored personnel carriers set off to encircle the hamlets in a classic exercise of American-sponsored tactics and firepower. They did not know that over 300 guerrillas were inside. The Viet Cong, according to a document captured later, had been altering their training and tactics to counter American firepower, and they wanted a big victory to restore their morale.

The battle went wrong from the beginning.[96] Well-prepared Viet Cong shot down three American helicopters as they landed South Vietnamese troops, and two more as they tried to rescue the men. Lieutenant Colonel Vann, trying to direct the operation from a spotter plane, told the M-113s to rescue the survivors from the helicopters, but the M-113s' commander refused to move. The emotional Vann eventually asked an American adviser to shoot the South Vietnamese commander and take control himself. Eventually the M-113s advanced, but they halted before determined, disciplined fire from Viet Cong guerrillas. Then, late in the day, General Cao refused to reinforce the attack, allowing the enemy to slip away during the night. A paratroop force missed its drop zone and incurred heavy casualties. In the end, the Viet Cong, who stood and fought a major action against the ARVN and its American firepower for the first time, lost 18 dead while killing about 80 South Vietnamese and three Americans.[97] The next day General Cao staged an attack into the now-empty village, and friendly artillery fire killed several South Vietnamese soldiers and just missed a few American reporters. The reporters found Vann not long after, and received a blunt, earthy account of the battle, including his characterization of it as "a miserable damn performance" by the South Vietnamese.

Reports of the loss of the helicopters reached Washington during January 2 (the battle had begun on the late afternoon of January 1, Washington time) and provoked immediate queries to Saigon. On January 3 Deputy Secretary Gilpatric forwarded a Joint Chiefs' report for President Kennedy. "It appears," the Chiefs said, "that the initial press reports have distorted both the importance of the action and the damage suffered by the US/GVN forces. Although unexpectedly stiff resistance was apparently encountered, contact has been maintained and the operation is being continued." They reported 65 GVN killed in action, and "Viet Cong known losses" of 101 killed. The next day the Army headquarters in Hawaii characterized the action more correctly as "one of the bloodiest and costliest" battles of the war, and correctly reported Viet Cong losses as "unknown."[98] On January 4 Harkins put the best face possible on the matter in a cable to General Dodge, the Commander of U.S. Army Pacific in Hawaii, which the White House

1

In Washington in May 1957, President Dwight Eisenhower and Secretary of State John Foster Dulles met their most important Southeast Asian ally, South Vietnamese President Ngo Dinh Diem.

★

2

The majority of the Joint Chiefs (2), as well as Deputy National Security Adviser Walt Rostow (3), repeatedly urged President John Kennedy to intervene in Laos, but the President got a very different picture in a long conversation with U.S. Ambassador to Laos Winthrop Brown (4). (Joint Chiefs left to right: Air Force General Curtis Lemay, Admiral Arleigh Burke, Army General George Decker, Chairman General Lyman Lemnitzer, and Marine Corps Commandant General David Shoup.)

★

3

4

11

In early 1962 President Diem reviewed leading South
Vietnamese Air Force officers (11) after two renegade pilots
tried to assassinate him by bombing the presidential palace.
Meanwhile, his troops tried to strike Viet Cong base areas in
American-equipped and American-advised operations (12).
Later that year Senate Democratic Majority Leader Mike
Mansfield—shown here with his Republican counterpart,
Everett Dirksen (13)—visited Southeast Asia and warned
Kennedy that Diem's leadership had deteriorated since 1954.

12

13

16

In August 1963, as black and white Americans assembled on the Mall in the great March on Washington (16), South Vietnamese Buddhists demanded basic political rights in Saigon. The Xa Loi pagoda is in the background (17).

17

18

19

20

21

Ngo Dinh Nhu, Diem's brother, political counselor, theorist, and head of the Strategic Hamlet program, inspected the fortified village of Cu Chi (18). During 1963 Nhu and his outspoken, photogenic wife, Madame Nhu (19), clashed with the American Embassy over policy toward the Buddhists and the proper role of American advisers. In September 1963 President Kennedy suggested in a televised interview with Walter Cronkite (20) that the Nhus might have to leave the Diem government in order for Diem to avoid defeat in the war against the Viet Cong. Later in September Kennedy met with the Laotian neutralist Prime Minister Souvanna Phouma (21).

22

On November 2, 1963, after Diem had repeatedly refused to dismiss Nhu, Diem (above) and Nhu were assassinated following a successful military coup.

★

eventually received. He acknowledged some of the criticism that had reached the press, even saying, "The statement that it was a miserable performance can be taken either way. In some cases they could have done better, and I think they should have." He said nothing specifically about the failure of the armored personnel carriers, and denied that the government troops had simply hit the mud and stayed there. He admitted that "some of the VC slipped out overnight" but claimed, falsely, that government troops were still in contact with them and calling for air and artillery support. "The [hard-core VC] battalion," he wrote wrongly, "will be out of business for some time, I think, as over 101 are now dead."[99]

The battle drew unprecedented attention in the United States, including long stories in *Time* and *Newsweek,* all evaluating the South Vietnamese performance negatively and quoting an unnamed American's reference to a "miserable performance." Perhaps the most provocative reaction came from the *New York Times* columnist Arthur Krock. On January 8 Krock suggested that Ap Bac merited a "fundamental review" of administration policy; quoted an April 6, 1954, speech in which then-Senator Kennedy had suggested that no amount of American military aid would suffice in Indochina unless the South Vietnamese people could fight for their independence; and argued that Ap Bac showed that the South Vietnamese still lacked the will to defend themselves. The President might have to find an alternative to our existing policy, a product of "starry-eyed diplomacy and . . . ingenuous commitments." Krock once again quoted many of the arguments against military involvement that Kennedy had made to him back in October 1961.[100]

Harkins's further responses to the battle reveal exactly how he saw his mission. Lieutenant Colonel Vann's remarks to the press had caused most of the trouble from the South Vietnamese government's point of view, and the Diem government and General Cao immediately retaliated by blaming the battle's outcome on Vann. Harkins initially asked General Charles Timmes, the MAAG chief since March 1962, to relieve Vann—presumably to pacify Diem—but Timmes refused. Neil Sheehan—then a UPI correspondent—concluded that Harkins had convinced himself that Ap Bac really was an ARVN victory, but another new source indicates that the general was informed that Diem himself acknowledged and approved the failure to press the battle.

On March 14, 1963, the Australian Colonel Frank Serong submitted his second report to Harkins, and raised the continuing problem of ARVN morale. "One consequence of Ap Bac . . . ," he wrote, "was that it gave the President [Diem] an opportunity to restate certain views he has been known to hold on attack policy."

> I am aware that this point has been discussed between COMUSMACV [Harkins] and the President, and that the President has given an assurance that he is not sponsoring a passive policy. Perhaps semantics and translation have clouded the issue. Be that as it may, I have specific contrary evidence.
>
> He has stated that Ap Bac was a clash of opinion between Vietnamese commanders and American advisors, the latter wanting to "sacrifice" three CG companies in a "useless" attack against a known VC strongpoint, the former resisting the "useless bloodshed" of Vietnamese soldiers. He has supported the VN standpoint.
>
> What his motivation has been will never be known—it may not be clear to the President himself—perhaps face, perhaps a desire to score a point or two before a third party. Whatever the motivation, the fact is now well known in the RVNAF officer corps, and substantiates a point of view that their commanders have expressed earlier, and which they have used to excuse their own timidity—that the President will not accept casualties.
>
> This policy is tragic . . .[101]

By early 1963, then, Harkins should have known that Diem's philosophy stood in the way of the kind of offensive approach that he believed was necessary, and that Diem had no intention of allowing him or any other Americans to direct the war. He owed his superiors a truthful accounting, but circumstances had put him in a difficult position. Harkins, like Nolting, had apparently grasped the essential American dilemma in South Vietnam: that Diem simply would not tolerate American criticism, or even allow Americans that he perceived as unfriendly to remain in Vietnam. Any hope of influencing Diem depended upon retaining his confidence and respecting his ultimate authority.

The Ap Bac controversy also reflected an important generational divide, one that became more and more critical as the American involvement in Vietnam grew. Harkins, Nolting, Felt, Wheeler, and McNamara all belonged, of course, to the GI generation. In their youth they had seen American firepower reduce America's enemies to rubble, and almost nothing could shake their faith that any new war must turn out the same way. Today's problems would be solved tomorrow; if their success came slowly, more resources would do the job. Nothing could really challenge their confidence in ultimate victory. Now, however, they faced criticism from the next-younger Silent generation—including Vann, Sheehan, and the *New York Times* reporter David Halberstam—who had been too young to experience the Second World War as adults. The Silents had grown up both respecting and, inevitably, resenting the overwhelming authority of the GIs, and here in Vietnam they could clearly see that GI prescriptions were not working. The Silents did not challenge the premises of American policy directly, but they could see that its execution was failing.[102] Vann was the first of a great many American officers of his generation who understood that the American strategic concept in Vietnam was wrong, but who never managed to prevail against the authority of the GI victors of the Second World War. And for Silent-generation journalists, the opportunity to challenge their elders' wisdom in print was the chance of a lifetime.

7

A Gathering Storm
January–July 1963
★

The Kennedy administration moved forward on several important fronts during the first half of 1963. In the aftermath of the great triumph of the Cuban missile crisis, the administration tried to reach agreement with the Soviet Union on the critical issue of nuclear testing, and a sudden breakthrough finally occurred in June. In that same pivotal month of American history, the President finally took a decisive step to bring the crisis over civil rights under control, introducing the most sweeping legislation on the subject since Reconstruction. Officially the line on Southeast Asia remained relatively optimistic, and General Harkins moved loyally to implement McNamara's 1965 deadline for the withdrawal of the bulk of American forces. But beneath the surface two important sources of dissent from existing policy began to emerge. On the one hand, civilians like Hilsman, Forrestal, and Harriman continued to argue that current strategies had at least to be modified for progress to continue. On the other, the Joint Chiefs began to suggest that the war could be won only by direct action against North Vietnam.

Roger Hilsman, still the director of the State Department's Bureau of Intelligence and Research, and Michael Forrestal, the National Security Council staffer responsible for Southeast Asia, visited South Vietnam from December 31, 1962, through January 9, 1963. Hilsman had been giving optimistic press briefings on Vietnam during the second half of 1962,[1] and the Hilsman-Forrestal report of January 25 took a generally optimistic line as well. Citing the construction of 4,000 strategic hamlets, the arming and training of the Montagnards, an increase in government-controlled territory, and a more aggressive Vietnamese military as evidence that the war "is clearly going better than it was a year ago," it also referred to recent Viet Cong successes and called for more improvements to *accelerate* progress. Significantly, it declared that "the strategic objectives of the war in South Vietnam, as in most guerrilla wars, are basically political"—just the opposite of what General Wheeler, the Army Chief of Staff, had said two months earlier—and listed offensive military objectives against regular guerrilla units as the *third* military objective, behind the protection of key installations and the reinforcement of villages under attack. General Harkins clearly would have disagreed with that provision.

Continuing, Hilsman and Forrestal cited the lack of any overall national plan, the proliferation of inadequate or insecure strategic hamlets, the lack of coordination between civilian and military efforts, and the lack of an amnesty program. Quoting "some American military advisors," their report suggested that the South Vietnamese might still be running too many large-scale operations and relying too heavily on air power, particularly "interdiction" bombing against remote VC targets. It then commented on the problem of poor press coverage, largely blaming Diem but adding that while the My Tho operation—the battle of Ap Bac—"contained some mistakes, it was not nearly the botched up disaster that the press made it appear to be."

An eyes-only annex for the President went marginally further. "The American military mission," it said, "must share some of the blame for the excessive emphasis on large-scale operations and air interdiction." Hilsman and Forrestal bluntly recommended a more aggressive use of American leverage against Diem, and suggested replacing Nolting with a more prominent and effective ambassador at an appropriate moment. Neither one, clearly, believed the optimistic picture of Diem's behavior that Nolting had given them.

The Joint Chiefs were not convinced things were going well either, but they favored a very different strategic concept. On February 1 the Hilsman-Forrestal report collided with another report by General Wheeler, who had visited South Vietnam in January with a Joint Staff team. The Joint Chiefs had sent the mission on January 7, apparently with the hope of widening the war. An Air Force paper for General LeMay's use at their meeting of that day argued that the increasing strength of the VC showed that "*WE ARE NOT WINNING,*" and stressed the military problem of trying to destroy the guerrillas despite an endless supply of replacements. "We should consider now the application of selected, measured sanctions against the North Vietnamese," it continued, ranging from the infiltration of agents to bombing and a blockade.[2] After the mission left, Commander Bagley, long-time aide to General Taylor, recommended to his boss—now the JCS Chairman—that the return of the Wheeler mission become an opportunity to re-evaluate both the question of the political situation in South Vietnam and the possibility of acting directly against the North.[3]

While Wheeler's team was in Vietnam, General Harkins submitted his "Comprehensive Plan for South Vietnam" to his superior, CINCPAC Admiral Felt. The plan promised to fulfill McNamara's July 1962 directive to complete American involvement by the end of 1965, but only by *increasing* various elements of American support and activities during the interim period. The plan foresaw further increases of approximately 20 percent in all categories of Vietnamese armed and paramilitary forces by 1965. Although current plans reduced military assistance from $187 million for fiscal 1962 to $130 million for fiscal 1963, the new plan proposed an increase to $234 million for fiscal 1963 (July 1963–June 1964). Harkins had already asked that the American Air Force within South Vietnam be *doubled* in order to carry out the National Campaign Plan. Before terminating the American effort, Harkins argued, Washington first had to increase it. And, read carefully, his plan called for phasing out American combat support by the middle of 1966, not the end of 1965.[4]

The Wheeler report—an enormous document that Wheeler briefed to the President on February 1—endorsed current programs and strategies. While concluding that victory was now "a hopeful prospect," it declined to predict victory within any specific period of time. Bowing graciously to Hilsman, Wheeler acknowledged that "in a counterinsurgency campaign, there are few major judgments that are wholly military," and agreed that in early 1962 the ARVN had made too many large-scale sweeps. Regarding press relations, he regretted that reporters still insisted, "contrary to facts," that Ap Bac was a defeat, and recommended the dispatch of "mature and responsible" newsmen to South Vietnam.

The report hedged on the critical question of widening the war. It repeatedly emphasized the importance of infiltration and outside assistance to the Viet Cong, estimating infiltration at 500 per month (a figure not validated by contemporary MACV documents, as we shall see). It cited external assistance to the Viet Cong as one of the two greatest problems facing the Vietnamese, and one "that must be solved by methods more practicable than surveillance of the country's borders." It complained that "we have not given Ho Chi Minh any evidence that we are prepared to call him to account for helping to keep the insurgency in South Vietnam alive, and that we should do something to make the North Vietnamese bleed." But for the time being it recommended an increase only in South Vietnamese paramilitary capabilities, to enable South Vietnamese troops to carry out "raids and sabotage missions in North Vietnam, coordinated with other military operations . . . to consume communist resources and prevent the North Vietnamese from giving unimpeded attention and support to the insurgency in South Vietnam."[5]

Michael Forrestal hoped to raise some of his and Hilsman's questions before Kennedy in a meeting with McNamara, Rusk, Taylor, Wheeler, and other senior officials on February 1, but as he wrote Kennedy days later, "the rosy euphoria generated by General Wheeler's report made this device unworkable," and the meeting became "a complete waste of your time for which I apologize." Instead, Forrestal decided to raise some of the issues through various other channels.[6] He got nowhere. Convinced that the United States could not wholly rely upon Diem for the long term, Forrestal suggested to Harriman on February 8 that the Embassy should increase its contacts with the opposition. Harriman wrote Nolting along these lines on February 18, and Nolting on February 27 replied with a ringing defense of his preferred policy, "Sink or swim with Ngo Dinh Diem." Any attempt to build up new leadership, he said, "would ruin the carefully-built base of our advisory and supporting role here, which must rest on persuasion and confidence in our integrity." Forrestal commented, "Everything is just dandy in Saigon!" and began thinking about the choice of a new ambassador when Nolting's term ran out in the spring.[7]

Then, on March 22, Harriman sent a long airgram to Nolting questioning the wisdom of extensive interdiction bombing and even daring to point out, for the first time, that such bombing was not really authorized by NSAM 111 of November 22, 1961, which had limited American personnel to "instruction in and execution of air-ground support techniques." This question might more logically have been addressed to the Pentagon, but as Harriman recalled two years later, Rusk still regarded Vietnam as McNamara's preserve, and generally refused to confront him about it.[8] Harkins denied on March 30 that interdiction bombing was an "indiscriminate killer" and argued that the elimination of the enemy's political strength required the use of force against its military capability. General Anthis, the Air Force commander, objected even more strongly, arguing, "If we wish to serve the interests of the Communists, this is the step to take." After typically delaying his final reply for more than a month, Nolting on April 25 defended the practice and denied the existence of any evidence that bombing might be harmful politically. If anything, he argued, it made neutrals flee VC-controlled areas in favor of government-held areas.[9] But despite his unfailing optimism, Nolting refused to endorse the premises of the new Comprehensive Plan. While agreeing to see the plan put into effect, he opposed any definite decisions on phasing out the American effort, which he wanted to occur gradually and not until the South Vietnamese could take over. That process might not begin until after 1965.[10] Harkins also rejected the criticisms of the Hilsman-Forrestal report in a message to Felt, who forwarded Harkins's views to Washington.[11]

Harkins, Nolting, Felt, and Wheeler's report cited an increasingly familiar litany of improvements in Vietnam: the greater firepower and aggressiveness of South Vietnamese forces, an increase in small-unit operations, the success of the strategic hamlet program in bringing more of the population under government control, the training of thousands of Montagnards within Civilian Irregular Defense Groups (CIDG) by American Special Forces,[12] and the increasing confidence between the Diem government and the American mission. They also welcomed the new Chieu Hoi, or "Open Arms" program, designed to encourage Viet Cong to defect—a step Americans had long urged upon Diem. Harkins and Nolting obviously felt that they were doing the best they could, and Nolting in particular repeated time and time again that the United States had to act so as to reassure Diem of its support. Criticism, he said, fostered coup plotting and encouraged the enemy.[13]

The ambassador and the MACV commander persisted despite ample contrary information at their disposal. Harkins himself received a devastating survey of the war from the outspoken Australian Colonel Serong in March 1963. Taking a considerably more severe tone than he had in October, Serong identified several trends that threatened to lose the war. During February 1963 a weekly MACV "Headway Report" had noted a continuing drop in incidents of all kinds initiated by the Viet Cong. Incidents had fallen from 434 per week in April 1962 to 300 per week during the last four months of 1962, and to 202 per week during January and February 1963.[14] Serong, however, cautioned that the VC must have chosen to slow the tempo. He emphasized that the VC were growing, not shrinking; that their organized military manpower represented simply "the visible part of the iceberg"; and that only shortages of logistics, particularly ammunition, were holding them back. Regarding strategic hamlets, Serong argued that the government's program had counterproductive results. Feeling pressure from Nhu to meet statistical goals, local officials had built hamlets in insecure areas, requiring more and more ARVN troops to protect them, and tying down more and more of the ARVN in static defense. In particular, he argued, while the government organized many hamlets along main transportation arteries, it was doing little or nothing *between* these major arteries. VC could still congregate in the interior areas and attack the new hamlets. Serong reserved particularly harsh words for MACV's showcase project, Operation Sunrise, and implicitly for other "clear-and-hold" operations:

> Another malpractice, which further weakens the system, is the Operation Sunrise technique. Here, in a conceptual monstrosity the aim of which is still unclear, a major SH complex was formed by leaping over a VC infested area. With perhaps a too ready cynicism, I believe that the real reason for this leap was that the intervening space was judged a nut too difficult to crack, so we went for the easier job a little further on. Whatever the reason, it left us with a built-in ambush to negotiate every time our troops attempted the Ben Cat road.
>
> Later, the error appeared to have been recognized, and a program was begun to make good the space between Thu Dau Not and Ben Cat. I believed the lesson had been learned, and prepared to forget that problem. To my utter dismay, I now find plans in preparation for more "Great Leaps Forward."

Although the situation was somewhat better, he said, in "the smaller SH complexes initiated on the coastal plain in the center and north of the country," where geography bunched the population even more tightly together, the program as a whole was increasing the vulnerability of the government, not increasing its strength.[15] Most hamlets, he argued, met less than 20 percent of the "book requirements" for effective hamlets, and remained reservoirs of men and materiel for the VC. The enemy, he also stressed, had *not* been weakened, and the recent observed lull in enemy activity was due partly to a shortage of ammunition and mainly to the Viet Cong's own tactical decisions. By late 1963, he predicted, the ARVN would no longer be able to concentrate in sufficient numbers to deal with larger VC units in remote areas. This was not all. As Hilsman and Forrestal had said, different American agencies—MACV, the USOM aid mission, and the CIA—were pursuing different strategies (as was Nhu) and needed either a coordinating czar or a directorate of operations. He proposed a specific plan, concentrating military force around Saigon and clearing the critical Long An province and establishing a "white area," visible evidence of success.

Serong also made some disturbing comments on the Montagnard question, where most reports saw great progress. Large numbers of Montagnards had apparently moved into areas of government control during the last few months, and the United States, working through the CIA's Operation Switchback, had begun arming and training them to police the remote highland areas and, eventually, to try to control the Laotian border. Recently, however, the South Vietnamese government had asked the Americans to retrieve some of the weaponry they had given to the Montagnards. Why, Serong asked, did they take measures contrary to the goals of this program?

> The reason is that their aim is not our aim. Our aim is the production of a strategic pattern, fitting into an overall strategic concept whose target is the destruction of the VC Com Z in the High Plateau, and eventually control of the border. There is ample evidence available now to show that President Diem and Counsellor Nhu do not share that aim, or at best regard it as secondary. Their aim in the High Plateau is the subjugation of the Montagnard, their destruction as an ethnic entity, and the incorporation of the Montagnard people and the Montagnard land in an integrated Vietnamese community.

The United States should not, he argued, "allow ourselves to be used as a catspaw in an operation that has an excellent prospect of finishing as genocide (Though undoubtedly a most paternal, loving and well-intentioned genocide—call it 'genocide by ineptitude.')."

Harkins himself was still trying to influence Diem. On February 23, in a long letter for Diem, he called yet again for the decentralization of the ARVN command structure and warned that the Viet Cong must not be allowed to rest or regroup, but must be relentlessly pressed between now and the coming of the rainy season in a few months, lest the enemy regain the initiative. On March 11 he wrote Thuan complaining that, despite numerous American complaints, the number of small, vulnerable outposts in the Delta manned by Civil Guards still seemed to be increasing, not decreasing. He specifically wanted an investigation of the province chief in Kien Tuong province on the Cambodian border, but when Thuan asked Diem about this on April 13, Diem replied that the government was over-investigating its officials already.[16]

On April 1 the controversial John Paul Vann submitted his final report as senior adviser of the 7th Division. Echoing Serong, he argued that the far-flung hamlet program was tying up too many troops, and suggested concentrating on Long An province. Passing on the results of a six-month diary of the activities of three ARVN battalions, Vann reported that they had spent 3 percent of their time training, 13 percent in combat operations, 10 percent preparing for and cleaning up after combat, and 74 percent "resting." Vann also said that Vietnamese counterparts were discounting their advisers' advice, and that the most popular advisers were those who were going along with their counterparts and failing to improve the units they advised. Nothing would change, he argued, until advisers won the right to take any dispute to the commander and adviser at the next level of the chain of command. Given that Vann's 7th Division had made a reputation as one of the most active and successful ARVN units during 1962, his statistics seriously undermined the claims of more intensive ARVN operations.[17]

Harkins remained as optimistic as possible with his superiors. On March 20 Admiral Felt apparently queried him about a speech given by Serong, in which the outspoken colonel had evidently enumerated some of the points in his March report. Harkins denied that the government was losing the confidence of the Montagnards, argued that morale in the ARVN was "surprisingly high," discounted reports of indiscriminate killing of villagers from the air (but acknowledged Diem's policy "that all victims of GVN attack are, per se, VC"), and denied that Vietnamese were sabotaging American efforts. While acknowledging Serong's expertise and welcoming his advice, Harkins said he did "not believe that his remarks or opinions, of themselves, are a valid yardstick against which to measure either our accomplishment or the tasks remaining."[18]

Unfortunately for Harkins, his subordinates' doubts were increasingly finding their way into the American press. On March 18 a UPI story—presumably from Neil Sheehan—reported two more uneventful large-scale sweeps in the Plain of Reeds and in Kien Hoa province, and added, "Many American military men here believe these major operations result from a Vietnamese desire not to risk suffering heavy casualties in close-up fighting and possibly 'lose face' as they did in the Ap Bac debacle in early January."[19] On March 30 Peter Arnett of the Associated Press discussed the strategic hamlet program in the Delta in terms reminiscent of his fellow Australian Frank Serong's recent report. Quoting "independent sources," Arnett reported that most hamlets had been built along major arteries, leaving large Communist-dominated areas between them.[20]

On April 1 the *New York Times*—still the only paper with a full-time Saigon correspondent—resumed publication after a four-month New York newspaper strike, and David Halberstam wrote a series of critical stories. On April 13 he rehashed Ap Bac—which had taken place during the strike—argued that the ARVN had been avoiding casualties in recent months, and described how John Paul Vann, whom he did not name, had almost been removed for criticizing the South Vietnamese. On April 18 he quoted a Vietnamese source to the effect that the government had instituted the Chieu Hoi defector program because the Americans wanted it for its international propaganda effect, but not because they took it seriously. On April 19 he reported that a VC battalion had attacked a series of hamlets in coastal Quang Ngai province, and treated government casualty figures skeptically. And on April 21, in his most controversial piece, he reported bluntly that the Communists controlled the four southernmost provinces of the Mekong Delta, Kien Giang, Chuong Thien, Ba Xuyen, and An Xuyen.[21] A few weeks later *Time,* whose coverage was generally optimistic, confirmed some of what he had said about the Delta.[22]

Harkins's and Nolting's other favorite talking point—the improving relationships between the South Vietnamese government and the American mission—came privately and publicly into question in April and May. The piaster fund created to finance the hamlet program the previous summer was running out, and Nolting in March thought he had negotiated new arrangements, under which American and South Vietnamese authorities would each approve the disbursement of funds. But on March 28 Thuan, who remained the main intermediary between the Americans and the Ngo family, informed him that Nhu now rejected the procedure because of the current atmosphere in U.S.-Saigon relations, the fault of the Mansfield report, negative press coverage, and Nhu's belief that American support for the government was wavering. On April 5 Diem himself told Nolting that the number of Americans was creating the impression of a protectorate, and that many younger Americans insisted too much on doing things their own way. In perhaps the frankest exchange of Nolting's tenure, the ambassador asked whether Diem was really working for the people, or merely to perpetuate his regime, and Diem replied by listing the programs he had pushed in the face of American opposition. When Nolting reported that he had seen Americans working effectively among South Vietnamese in An Giang province, Diem rejoined that his own officials there complained that the people now regarded the Americans as the government.

Diem eventually said that the real trouble was the presence of too many Americans advising in too much detail on too many things, and that the United States should gradually cut back the number of advisers and restore "control at the top." Specifically, he refused to let Americans control the GVN's contribution of 1.3 billion piasters, even after Nolting pointed out that Saigon controlled American aid worth 36 billion piasters. Commenting, Nolting declared that only the American effort had led to the "progress" of the last year, and predicted that the government could not win the war without the current advisory presence for at least another year. The ambassador could not have been entirely surprised, since Nhu had raised these issues at least six months earlier.[23]

Nolting's report sufficiently disturbed Washington to reach the agenda of an NSC meeting on April 10, but a somewhat more optimistic report on the previous day led the item to be dropped. In another conversation, Thuan had pledged a large sum of piasters for counterinsurgency, but had refused to allow Americans to share authority to disburse them. When Nolting suggested that Nhu "seemed to expect the Vietnamese peasants to pull themselves up by their own bootstraps when they have no shoes," while the Americans thought they needed some inducement in money or in kind, Thuan did not dissent. Nolting thought, however, that a solution was coming into view.

On April 12 Nhu told CIA Station Chief John Richardson that the American advisory presence should be reduced by between 500 and 4,000 men, and added that the existing arrangements for the counterinsurgency fund smacked of a condominium and could not continue.[24] It is not clear whether Nolting heard about this conversation from Richardson, who generally handled relations with Nhu, but on April 17 Diem dropped his request for a reduction in the American advisory presence in a new conversation with the ambassador. The two men agreed to devise new procedures to keep the American advisory effort within acceptable bounds.[25] But a few days later a CIA cable reported that Diem was building a dossier of American mistakes and preparing to confront Nolting and Harkins with his evidence and demand a reduction of the advisory presence.[26]

In the last week of April Nolting reached agreement with Diem on a new procedure for funding strategic hamlets, despite the argument of Rufus Phillips, USOM's Assistant Director of Rural Affairs and the leading American authority on strategic hamlets, that only U.S. participation and funding made success possible. A few days later Phillips wrote a long memorandum for all his superiors, arguing that, despite some successes, most South Vietnamese authorities still failed to understand the spirit behind the strategic hamlet program, and that "the situation is changing for the better, but still too slowly to produce the type and number of viable hamlets needed to win this war." Phillips offered to resign in protest over the new procedure, but his superiors in Washington insisted that it be given a chance.[27]

Despite his staffer Michael Forrestal's attempts to get him more deeply involved in the Vietnam effort, President Kennedy generally stayed out of the details of Vietnam policy during the first half of 1963. He received a mildly optimistic briefing from the British expert Sir Robert Thompson on April 4, in which Thompson questioned defoliation and crop destruction but endorsed the strategic hamlet program.[28] In late April another problem came directly to his attention. John Mecklin, the head of the United States Information Agency mission in Saigon, had returned to the United States in February for major surgery. He had now recovered, and one of his superiors suggested to Pierre Salinger, Kennedy's press secretary, that he see the President. No aspect of government fascinated Kennedy more than the management of the press, and he always welcomed direct reports from the field. Salinger arranged an appointment for April 29. As Mecklin waited for his appointment in Salinger's office, he remarked nervously that he hoped he could avoid criticism of his superiors. "If you don't level with the President," Salinger assured him, "he doesn't want to talk to you at all."

After inquiring after Mecklin's health, Kennedy asked, "Why are we having so much trouble with the reporters out there?" Mecklin immediately exonerated the reporters, and argued that we could improve coverage only by winning victories against the Viet Cong or taking the newsmen more into our confidence, despite Diem's sensitivities. When Kennedy asked for specific suggestions, Mecklin proposed a halt to over-optimistic public statements and complaints about unfavorable stories, and a greater frankness with newsmen. Afterward Kennedy told Salinger that Mecklin had impressed him deeply, but that he did not think the government could do very much, because of "the highly conflicting interests of the government and the press there"—a reference, perhaps, to their respective efforts to make Diem and his regime look either good or bad. A new directive for Nolting and Harkins very gently advised them to try to be more forthright with American reporters, "particularly on matters which they are almost certain to learn about anyway," and to avoid either excessive optimism or excessive pessimism in public statements.[29]

During April Laos once again supplanted Vietnam as the main story from Southeast Asia for the first time since the summer of 1962. After the signing of the Laotian accord, Souvanna Phouma had indeed become the head of a new coalition government in September 1962, but the North Vietnamese had not withdrawn from their positions along the border, and the three factions faced one another uneasily. Neither side, as Harriman acknowledged privately, had fully complied with the accords, and CIA pilots were still flying missions for the CIA's contract airline, Air America, within Laos.[30] Within two months Phoumi had taken advantage of his new job as Minister of the Interior to arrest several pro–Kong Le neutralist officers, and Americans again suspected him of trying to wreck the coalition. Neutralist troops also clashed with the Pathet Lao on the Plain of Jarres. In January 1963 Hilsman and Forrestal visited Laos as well as Vietnam, and recommended assisting Kong Le's forces in order to bolster Souvanna. In February a Colonel Ketsana, one of Kong Le's supporters, was assassinated, apparently by the Pathet Lao.[31] In late February Souvanna, his left-leaning Foreign Minister Quinim Pholsema, and the Laotian King visited Washington and saw Kennedy. Souvanna expressed some guarded optimism about the political situation, reporting that Phoumi and the neutralists were getting along somewhat better but that the Pathet Lao and Phoumi still distrusted each other intensely and refused to demobilize.[32]

The biggest news stories of early 1963 concerned de Gaulle's rejection of British entry into the Common Market, new Franco-German accords, the American proposal for a Multilateral Nuclear Force, the controversy over McNamara's award of the TFX fighter plane contract to General Dynamics rather than Boeing, and Cuba, where some Russian troops remained and where future American policy remained unclear. Few Americans could have noticed, but the Laotian situation definitely began coming unglued on April 1, when a neutralist soldier assassinated Quinim Pholsema. In light of subsequent revelations about CIA assassination plots, this episode inevitably arouses some suspicion. Souvanna's reliance upon Quinim Pholsema, who had flown to Hanoi to ask for assistance in the midst of the 1960 crisis, had disturbed many Americans during 1960–1961, and he had even taken the Pathet Lao line regarding the withdrawal of North Vietnamese troops during his February 1963 visit to Washington. His assassination seemed at the time to represent retaliation for the assassination of Kong Le's subordinate Colonel Ketsana, however, and probably had nothing to do with the United States, although a Chinese Communist diplomat claimed in April that America was responsible.[33] Within a few days the Pathet Lao ministers had left Vientiane and their troops had moved against Kong Le's forces—supported, according to Kong Le, by North Vietnamese troops. The United States, for the third consecutive spring, was contemplating war over Laos.[34]

On April 4 Averell Harriman became the Undersecretary of State for Political Affairs, the third-ranking State Department official behind Rusk and George Ball, and Roger Hilsman replaced him as Assistant Secretary of State for Far Eastern Affairs. Rusk had quickly suggested either intervention in Laos or direct action against Hanoi, if necessary, to secure the area. State suggested reintroducing troops into Thailand, as in the spring of 1962, and Harriman in an April 10 NSC meeting proposed a diplomatic offensive, taking advantage of Souvanna's own attack upon the Pathet Lao as the aggressor.[35] At an April 19 meeting McNamara and the Joint Chiefs definitely opposed sending American troops either to Laos or to Thailand, preferring merely to send air units to Thailand—presumably to the new American-built jet airfields—and a carrier task force off the coast of Vietnam. Harriman wanted some threat of American military action to take with him to Moscow, where he planned to raise the issue of the violation of the Laotian accords with Khrushchev. At another meeting the next day, Rusk suggested putting SEATO forces into Thailand and into the northern portion of South Vietnam, "in order to be in a position, in Laos falls, to move into North Vietnam." The President, however, had other plans.

Two years into his term, Kennedy was still trying to implement his own ideas regarding certain critical Cold War issues. The White House was in the midst of a long struggle with the Pentagon over nuclear strategy. While the Air Force wanted a first-strike capability that could reduce damage to the United States in a nuclear exchange to "acceptable" levels, Kennedy and McGeorge Bundy felt, as Bundy said in a staff meeting, "that the military planners who calculate that we will win if only we can kill 100 million Russians while they are killing 30 million Americans are living in total dreamland."[36] But while ruling out nuclear war as a realistic option, Kennedy still felt the United States needed a limited military option that would enable Washington to reply to a Soviet move in Berlin or elsewhere. And as he had explained to the National Security Council on January 22, 1963, he had decided in the wake of the missile crisis to make a virtue of necessity, and had designated Cuba as the Soviets' vulnerable spot: "The President pointed out that we must always be an a position to threaten Cuba as a possible riposte to Russian pressure against us in Berlin. We must always be ready to move immediately against Cuba in the event we decide such action would be a more effective response to a Soviet initiative than a nuclear response. We can use Cuba to limit Soviet actions in the way the Russians use Berlin to limit our actions."[37]

Now, on April 19, faced with Communist moves in Southeast Asia, the President remarked at least twice that he wanted to link the continued Soviet presence in Cuba with Communist activities in Laos. The Soviets, he commented, were "continuing the type of harassment effort in Laos that we had stopped by the Cuban exiles," and they were not moving out of Cuba as we wished. In addition to any steps we might take around Laos, he suggested, we might resume low-level reconnaissance in Cuba, "which would place pressure on the Soviets in an area in which they were somewhat weaker." The next day he rejected Rusk's suggestion for forces in South Vietnam, "because of the difficulty of removing them at a later time," but approved the dispatch of a carrier task force to the *South* Vietnamese coast, and asked for a study of possible air action against North Vietnam. Once again he asked "why we need to follow such a careful policy toward Cuba in view of the fact that the Russians appear to be prepared to see the Geneva accords destroyed." CIA Director McCone pointed out that the last American prisoners should come out of Cuba shortly, and Kennedy said this could allow the United States to "act against Cuba" if the Laotian situation kept deteriorating. Kennedy also approved Harriman's mission to Moscow. At the end of the meeting McCone suggested to Robert Kennedy and McGeorge Bundy that while American action against Cuba might bring down Khrushchev, action in Laos would seriously hurt Kennedy, and that the United States should not "save Khrushchev at the expense of Kennedy." Both men assured him that the President understood this fully.[38] Clearly Southeast Asia was still not the place where Kennedy wanted directly to confront Communism.

"Am I talking to the architect of the Geneva Accords?" Kennedy asked Harriman when he telephoned him on April 21. They agreed that Harriman would go to Moscow, although the old diplomat admitted that it might not do much good. The next day the NSC noted the typically very small scale of the actual fighting in Laos, and Kennedy noted the irony that Kong Le, our most dangerous foe just two years earlier, had become the center of our hopes. On April 23 the Joint Chiefs suggested a sequence of military actions to bring about stability in Laos, culminating in air attacks on targets in Laos and North Vietnam. When Harriman saw Khrushchev on April 26, the Soviet Premier reiterated his support for a neutral Laos and agreed in principle to an inspection of the Plain of Jarres by the International Control Commission, but declared, in effect, that he had no control over the ICC or the North Vietnamese. Harriman insisted that Laos remained a test of Soviet-American cooperation, but Khrushchev belittled the country's significance. They issued a brief, noncommittal communiqué, and the crisis cooled down.[39]

In South Vietnam, the contradictions among McNamara's plans, the actual military situation, and Nhu's plans for the future were becoming inescapable as McNamara convened yet another Honolulu conference on May 6. The Secretary of Defense was having a difficult spring, but seemed to be riding higher than ever. He was struggling with Congress over his refusal to authorize a new manned bomber, and his award of the contract to build the TFX fighter plane to General Dynamics instead of Boeing had become the subject of a congressional investigation. He had just secured the President's agreement to relieve Admiral George Anderson as Chief of Naval Operations, apparently because Anderson refused to tailor his TFX testimony to McNamara's specifications, and to reappoint Air Force Chief of Staff LeMay for just one year. According to Anderson, McNamara had stated that the TFX dispute was the greatest crisis of his career, and that he had to be proven right, no matter what happened. To soften the blow, Kennedy appointed Anderson Ambassador to Portugal.[40]

On Vietnam, McNamara was pushing ahead with his plan to wrap up the American commitment in 1965. To make the shrinkage of the American presence a reality, he evidently planned by mid-April 1963 to ask for a withdrawal of 1,000 Americans by the end of the year. Unfortunately, since the submission of the Comprehensive Plan, authorized American strength had risen from 12,200 to 15,600—only 3,000 of whom were advisers. McNamara now planned to ask for a 1,000-man withdrawal by the end of the year at Honolulu in early May. This echoed a suggestion by Sir Robert Thompson during his visit to Washington earlier in the month that some troops be withdrawn while declaring a certain province a "white" area, that is, one clear of Viet Cong.[41] The Secretary did not seem to be paying much attention to press stories that called his optimistic plans into question.

Only days before the Honolulu conference, McNamara and the Joint Chiefs apparently received a well-balanced briefing on the war from the Joint Staff. The briefing described two recent operations in detail. In coastal Quang Ngai province, the ARVN had responded quickly to a coordinated series of VC attacks. South Vietnamese forces had lost 96 men—33 of them killed—while Viet Cong dead "were reported as 383. 263 were counted; about 90 actually seen by US advisers." The other described a battalion-sized enemy attack upon ARVN and Self-Defense Corps forces that destroyed an outpost and reportedly killed 50 ARVN in the Ca Mau peninsula at the southernmost tip of the country—a known VC stronghold where the government was trying to run a pacification campaign. The briefing also included some fascinating comments on the Chieu Hoi amnesty program. The program apparently amounted to regrouping the population of VC-influenced areas into strategic hamlets and counting them as defectors from the Viet Cong.[42]

MACV prepared a similarly realistic briefing for McNamara's Honolulu meeting in early May. During the last six weeks, it read, favorable trends had been reversed, and Viet Cong actions were increasing again, mainly against hamlets and outposts.[43] Harkins, however, disregarded this briefing. A year earlier he had refused to let his intelligence officers show McNamara their map of Viet Cong–controlled areas, and now, when he led off the conference on May 6, he said he felt "that we are certainly on the right track and that we are winning the war in Vietnam, although the struggle will still be a protracted one." Phase II of the National Campaign Plan, an all-out offensive against the Viet Cong, would begin in July. Trueheart reported that the strategic hamlet program was going well, except in IV Corps. Harkins concluded that some recent setbacks had occurred when people dropped their guard—"a natural reaction when things are going well"—and added that the United States should *not* mention any cutback of assistance to the South Vietnamese at this time.

McNamara turned immediately to the Comprehensive Plan. Calling for a reduction in the fiscal 1964 appropriation, he said the planned phase-out was too slow, and that the U.S. presence should be reduced to a minimum before July 1965. He repeated that the United States had to phase down its effort to retain support at home.[44] No one ever questioned the assumptions behind these plans. Upon his return, McNamara said that "the corner has definitely been turned toward victory."[45] Together, Harkins and McNamara had committed themselves, in defiance of the available facts, to the idea of rapid progress that would allow an American withdrawal to begin. In an unrecorded session of the conference, General Krulak, Taylor's Special Assistant for Counterinsurgency Affairs, reported on plans for raids against North Vietnam, but no copy of his report has been found. Working on this track, the Joint Chiefs on May 21 ordered CINCPAC to develop a plan for American-supported South Vietnamese hit-and-run operations against North Vietnam. CINCPAC completed OP-Plan 34 in June.[46]

Just a few days after the Honolulu meeting, on Sunday, May 12, the crisis in South Vietnamese–American relations reached the front page of the *Washington Post*. In an interview with visiting correspondent Warren Unna, Nhu said that he had asked for the withdrawal of half the American presence a full five months previously. Many of the Americans, he said, were gathering intelligence, and he once again accused Americans of responsibility for the 1960 coup attempt. With Harkins's national offensive scheduled to begin on July 1, Nhu also said, "the moment has not come yet for us to launch a general counter offensive." Later he said that the South Vietnamese opposed big operations, which rarely brought much home, and that he wanted to preserve the army for later operations. When Unna asked whether General Cao—the IV Corps commander, and Vann's former counterpart—was a "political general" who tried to preserve his troops, Nhu replied quite accurately that Cao had done a great deal of fighting, but "unfortunately, the Communists became much smarter after being beaten five consecutive times by this general"—a clever reference to Ap Bac. Americans were impatient, Nhu said, and some advisers had lost their lives by exposing themselves too readily. Unna reported that the Honolulu meeting had discussed the withdrawal of a thousand Americans, the first time this news had made it into print, and explained that Saigon feared American influence in the provinces.[47]

Over the next two days Hilsman met with an angry House Foreign Affairs Committee, cabled Nolting asking for immediate, public clarification, and asked his staff for measures to pressure the South Vietnamese government. Nolting managed on May 17 to get Diem's assent to a joint communiqué on the strategic hamlet program which endorsed the current scale of the U.S. advisory effort but anticipated that foreign assistance might drop as progress continued. Nhu, meanwhile, claimed that Unna had misquoted him.[48] On the same day Nolting reported on a two-day trip through the countryside with Diem, arguing that what was happening in Vietnam differed radically from "the reflection of it in the outside world," and claiming "a steady forcing of the Communists to the defensive."[49] Kennedy himself took a question about Nhu's statements in a May 22 press conference, and replied calmly that the United States would be glad to withdraw troops whenever the South Vietnamese so requested. He added that the United States hoped to withdraw some forces by the end of the year, but that "we couldn't make any final judgment at all until we see the course of the struggle next few months."[50]

Meanwhile, Harkins wrote Diem on May 15, summarizing the results of the last year. The letter combined an emphasis upon the positive with a number of indications that many things had to change. He credited the South Vietnamese with 6,000 completed strategic hamlets, including over two-thirds of the population. He complained again that units failed to remain in contact with the enemy, and that too many operations relied on poor intelligence and never made contact at all. But the Viet Cong, he said, were becoming increasingly isolated, like rats in a trap. Bluntly disagreeing with Nhu, he argued that "the time for an all-out offensive is at hand, before the armed forces get stale." Nineteen sixty-three, he said, could be the year of victory.[51]

With Diem increasingly intransigent and McNamara relentlessly optimistic, Harkins continued to push for more offensive action and hope for the best. MACV's own weekly Headway Reports, however, suggest that his strategic appreciation was already out of date when he wrote his letter.[52] Harkins's optimism had not been entirely without foundation. Total Viet Cong activity had dropped during the second half of 1962, and small- and large-scale ARVN operations had increased in number. Events during the spring, however, confirmed Frank Serong's prediction that the decline in VC activity would prove temporary. Viet Cong armed attacks, which had fallen from more than 100 per week during early 1962 to 55 in the second week of March 1963, jumped to 98, 97, and 90 during the three weeks from March 20 through April 11. After falling once again, they jumped to a new high of 128 for April 18–24, fell for the next four weeks, then jumped again to 107 during the last week in May and 113 during the first week in June.

For the most part, the VC avoided contact with the ARVN. The vast majority of their attacks targeted strategic hamlets and Civil Guard and Self-Defense Corps outposts, especially in IV Corps in the southern Delta, where as many as 75 percent of the total attacks occurred. In these attacks, the Viet Cong typically inflicted two or three times as many casualties as they suffered themselves. During the week of April 17–24, these attacks killed 93 South Vietnamese at an estimated cost of 38 VC; during the following week, they killed 101 South Vietnamese and lost an estimated 70 men (many of them in one large-scale attack in Kontum); during the week after that, they killed 67 at an estimated cost of 33, many of them unconfirmed. The countryside in IV Corps, in short, remained chronically insecure, and local government forces could not defend themselves. These attacks also captured numerous weapons.

The Headway Reports also listed several hundred Viet Cong killed every week, most of them, paradoxically, in operations *initiated* by the government, in which government losses were reported to be much lower. Thus, the Headway Report for May 1–8 listed 148 friendly small-unit operations that made contact and, it said, killed 150 VC and captured 29 VC and 47 suspects. The same operations reportedly resulted in 27 ARVN dead and 66 wounded. VC wounded were listed at only 46, and usually were only a fraction of estimated VC dead, contrary to the experience of friendly forces and, indeed, to military experience generally. These figures are especially suspect because the South Vietnamese did not allow advisers to accompany small-unit operations. In three out of four weeks during May, ARVN losses were much lower than Civil Guard or Self-Defense Corps losses, even though the ARVN was more than twice as large as either of the others. While the Viet Cong chewed up the paramilitary forces—especially in the Mekong Delta—the ARVN remained largely immune from attack, and frequently failed to make much contact.[53]

On June 7 a Headway Report counted 113 VC attacks over the preceding week, and specifically described attacks that killed 101 friendly forces and an estimated 48 Viet Cong. VC attacks fell to 87 during the next week, but the Headway Report of June 13 stopped listing them in detail, making it impossible to total up the casualties. The pattern of increasing Viet Cong attacks did not indicate progress. Meanwhile, the same Headway Report included a June 6 special intelligence report from the 2nd Air Division. Since early 1961, it stated, the Viet Cong had captured 13 American .50 caliber machine guns, and perhaps 20 more from ARVN forces. These weapons had now given them a substantial anti-aircraft capability. After hitting only 89 American and South Vietnamese aircraft during the last four months of 1962, they had hit 257 in the first four months of 1963, most of them north of Kontum, in War Zones C and D, and thence southeastward through the Delta. The Viet Cong, in short, were now defending their main base areas effectively against helicopters and air attack, and the battle of Ap Bac, far from being an isolated incident, had heralded a most disturbing new trend.[54]

Harkins, however, continued pushing the South Vietnamese toward a victorious battlefield offensive. In June both General Le Van Ty, the ARVN Chief of the Joint General Staff, and the U.S. Embassy suggested that the time had not come to implement the main-force offensive in Phase II of the National Campaign Plan, which was scheduled to begin on July 1. Rather than face this fact, Harkins on July 6 wrote that the terms "Phase I, II, and III" "have now lost all real validity in the context of evaluating overall national progress." He continued:

> Current and continuing problem facing US military advisors in their military planning role is to determine logical balance of effort in each of several areas of RVN while local balances of VC versus GVN strength vary substantially. Persuading GVN and RVNAF authorities to accept these solutions or to devise and implement equally effective solutions of their own as aggressively and professionally as they possibly can, will determine rate of success in counterinsurgency. Progress here is afoot. There remains no doubts [sic] that military defeat of VC is attainable, barring catastrophic political or social development in RVN.[55]

Lacking any clear indicators of real military progress, Harkins frequently used official South Vietnamese figures for strategic hamlets to suggest that the government was winning the war. But the hamlet program did not fall under Harkins's authority, and he knew relatively little about its actual progress. The Americans participating in the program, who belonged to the Office of Rural Affairs of the U.S. Operations Mission (AID), knew that the situation was far more complex and not nearly so encouraging. A month earlier, on June 1, the Rural Affairs Office, led by Rufus Phillips, had submitted a comprehensive province-by-province survey of the strategic hamlet program. The authors of the report were young, dedicated Americans who believed deeply in their mission, and they declared unequivocally that the program had secured the allegiance of the people and hurt the Viet Cong seriously in certain areas. Where properly implemented, they said, the program had proved itself as "a brilliant advance in the art of counterinsurgency as well as a most effective means of nation-building." "By remaining true to its aspirations and ideals, its high purposes and high courage," they concluded, "the Strategic Hamlet program cannot fail." But success, as Phillips had warned some weeks earlier during the funding crisis, depended upon keeping the program on track in some areas and getting it on track in others.

The report made very clear that the official statistics for completed hamlets, which Harkins used to show progress, could not be trusted. In northern Quang Tin province, it reported, only about one-third of 201 reportedly completed hamlets met the American "six-point criteria," and it was difficult to say how many could actually defend themselves. A guardedly favorable report on Kontum province in the Central Highlands stated that "more defenses are needed, as well as weapons and ammunition, in at least half of the 127 'completed' hamlets," and the report on neighboring Pleiku province declared that much remained to be done "in more than half of the 86 'completed' hamlets in the way of defenses, weapons, and the development of self-government." In Binh Duong, home of Operation Sunrise, the report concluded, "The completed hamlets meet to a fairly high degree the '6-point criteria' for being complete." Many other individual observations confirmed that official figures could not be taken at face value.

In general, the report made no grandiose claims of success, but simply tried to identify provinces in which the province chiefs—who had clearly emerged as the key to success—had *begun* establishing hamlets on a sound basis. It confirmed that the government had set many unrealistic schedules, that hamlets had been built too rapidly within insecure areas, and that many provinces had resisted arming the hamlet militia. It gave a very guardedly optimistic report on progress in northern I Corps, where the initial lack of interest of Ngo Dinh Canh had evidently been overcome. I Corps was remarkably quiet militarily during the first half of 1963, but none of the individual province reports showed tremendous success in the hamlet program. Its most optimistic picture came from II Corps, especially in the Highlands, where the resettlement of the Montagnards was proceeding well, but also in parts of the coastal provinces of Quang Tri and Binh Dinh.

The report gave a more mixed account of III Corps, north of Saigon. While citing good progress in three provinces, it listed a number of chronic obstacles to the effort, including a failure to establish hamlet militia in secure areas, a failure to ensure that the military respected the population, and a general lack of trust in the populace. Lastly, it gave a very negative report on IV Corps, in the southern Delta, including provinces like Dinh Tuong and An Xuyen, where so many ARVN operations had taken place. It had good words for the program in the critical province of Long An, and in Kien Hoa, where the province chief,

Lieutenant Colonel Chau, was already becoming a legend, but these were very much the exception.

Taken as a whole, the report merely indicated that some secure hamlets had been built in some parts of the country and that some province chiefs understood the program. Its comments on provinces like An Xuyen, Dinh Tuong, and Binh Duong showed that extensive ARVN activity did not necessarily help pacify the countryside. And although the report did not say so, it showed a broadly *inverse* correlation between the population density of a province and the success of the strategic hamlet program. The program was doing best in the sparsely populated Highlands, somewhat better in the central and northern coastal provinces, and least well in the Delta, where the bulk of the population lived and the Viet Cong, as we have seen, were most aggressive.[56] David Halberstam had already reported similar conclusions in a long survey of the program on May 5, but nothing so detailed had reached the State or Defense Department, where few if any high officials would have been able to identify *any* of the specific provinces of South Vietnam.[57]

About fifteen years earlier, during the late 1940s, Washington had tried to help another authoritarian Asian client, Generalissimo Chiang Kai-Shek, defeat a Communist insurgency. In early 1948, after years of extensive American aid, Secretary of State George Marshall—a distinguished leader from a much earlier generation—had summarized a critical aspect of the problem before the Senate Foreign Relations Committee. He had begun by detailing the very extensive aid which Chiang had received since the war, and continued: "All the foregoing means, at least to me, that a great deal must be done by the Chinese authorities themselves—and that nobody else can do it for them—if that Government is to maintain itself against the Communist forces and agrarian policies . . . We must be prepared to face the possibility that the present Chinese Government may not be successful in maintaining itself against the Communist forces or other opposition that may arise in China."[58]

Marshall had effectively identified the critical problem inherent in such a situation: that while the United States and its ally, either Chiang or Diem, might share the common *objective* of defeating Communism, their *strategies* might be so different as to rule out effective cooperation—and Washington, in such a situation, had no way of making its strategic preferences prevail. Thanks to Marshall's leadership, the

United States had kept its commitment to Chiang limited. In the spring of 1963, the American leadership was continuing to hope for the best in South Vietnam.

Washington was paying less attention to Southeast Asia. During May the domestic crisis over civil rights reached a climax as the Birmingham, Alabama, police used dogs and fire hoses to suppress nonviolent demonstrations against segregated public accommodations led by Dr. Martin Luther King Jr. The administration, meanwhile, was making a last attempt to secure a comprehensive test-ban treaty with the Soviet Union and Great Britain, despite obstacles both in Moscow and in Washington. On the one hand, Khrushchev steadfastly refused to accept what the administration regarded as the minimum number of on-site inspections necessary to detect illegal underground tests; on the other hand, the Joint Chiefs did not believe that the administration could detect Soviet underground tests. They also wanted more American atmospheric tests to at least reduce the Soviet lead in high-yield nuclear weapons, and American underground tests to work on anti-ballistic missile warheads.[59]

Two major presidential decisions turned June 1963 into one of the pivotal months of the second half of the twentieth century. First, Kennedy decided to strike a new note in a commencement address at American University on June 10. In a speech written in the White House without Pentagon or State Department clearance, Kennedy called specifically, and for the first time, for a whole new attitude toward the Soviet Union and a greater effort for true peace. He asked Americans "not to fall into the same trap as the Soviets, not to see only a distorted and desperate view of the other side, not to see conflict as inevitable, accommodation as impossible and communication as nothing more than an exchange of threats. No government or social system is so evil that its people must be considered as lacking in virtue." Then, picking up a proposal signed a week earlier by twenty-seven senators for a ban on nuclear tests in the atmosphere and under water, Kennedy pledged not to resume atmospheric testing before the Soviets did, and announced that British, American, and Soviet representatives would soon meet in Moscow to discuss a new agreement.[60]

On the very next day, June 11, two black students entered the University of Alabama after the President federalized the National Guard to remove it from the control of Governor George Wallace and prevent it from standing in the students' way. That evening he addressed the nation and promised new civil rights legislation, including laws "giving all Americans the right to be served in facilities which are open to the public—hotels, restaurants, theaters, retail stores, and similar establishments." Speaking calmly and carefully, Kennedy portrayed this legislation—which he had decided to ask for as the only means of bringing demonstrations and violence to an end—not primarily as a moral crusade but as a step that simply had to be taken. With seventeen months remaining until the election of 1964, the Kennedy administration had found new directions both at home and abroad. Meanwhile, the President prepared for a visit to Ireland, West Germany, and Berlin later in the month.

These tremendous events had reduced the Laotian crisis to insignificance, but bureaucratic wheels kept turning. Both State and Defense remained in a relatively militant mood in the wake of the breakdown of the cease-fire. A new perspective on the Laotian crisis had emerged in the wake of Harriman's trip to Moscow: that Peking, now embroiled in a full-scale ideological controversy with the Soviets, was exercising more influence in Southeast Asia.[61] During May the Pathet Lao continued to nibble at the edges of Kong Le's positions, and the State Department still wanted some military options either to preserve the Laotian government or to prepare for a disguised or overt partition of Laos. As Michael Forrestal reported to Kennedy on June 7, both he and Bundy wanted some military response to deter the Pathet Lao. A week later, on June 18, Forrestal gave the President a new State-Defense paper on Laos.

As we have seen, the Geneva Accords of 1962 had yielded important assets to the United States. They had not (and would not) secured the withdrawal of North Vietnamese troops from Laos, and the Pathet Lao had now withdrawn from the coalition government and begun expanding their position militarily. The ICC, in addition, had not been able to fulfill the functions the United States had hoped for. But the accords had produced an uneasy unity between Phoumi and Souvanna. Souvanna and Kong Le were already accepting American help, and within another year and a half Souvanna would emerged as a staunch American ally, quite capable of holding his own against the Pathet Lao. The United States, in short, had the wherewithal to maintain a non-Communist government in control of most of Laos simply by stretching provisions of the Geneva agreement relative to military aid and covert American assistance. Laotian internal politics—really, as we have seen, the cause of the crisis of 1960–1961, and largely the source of the new outbreak of fighting—had evolved favorably from the American point of view.

The view of the new State-Defense paper, however, ignored the Laotian political roots of the current crisis. "The root of the problem in Southeast Asia," it began, "is the aggressive effort of the North Vietnamese to establish Communist control in Laos and South Vietnam as a stepping-stone to control all Southeast Asia." The paper defined a series of American objectives, including reestablishment of the government of national union, a cease-fire along the lines of the one that had been in force before April 1, and the withdrawal of North Vietnamese troops from Laos. If necessary, it suggested abandoning the government of national union—although not Souvanna himself—in favor of an unacknowledged or acknowledged partition of the country. It proposed two phases of action to achieve this: Phase I, focusing on strengthening the Laotian government forces and encouraging them to drive back the Pathet Lao; and Phase II, which included an increased American advisory effort, preparations for American military intervention, South Vietnamese patrols into Laos, and American overflights of North Vietnam.

Should these measures fail, the paper recommended Phase III—overt military action against North Vietnam—to secure a partition of Laos *that would leave the Laotian–South Vietnamese border in friendly hands.* Specifically, the State Department, repeating the proposals of 1961–1962, favored the occupation of several Mekong River towns by American troops, while the Pentagon now wanted to stay out of Laos and move directly to air action against North Vietnam and the mining of North Vietnamese ports. "Taking this final action," the paper read, "will in itself enlarge our objective from that centered on Laos to the cessation of DRV subversive activity in the remainder of Southeast Asia." Once again, the State and Defense Departments wanted to set the United States on the way to war in Southeast Asia. President Kennedy for two and one-half years had resisted their efforts, but he had not changed their thinking.[62]

On June 19—a few days before leaving for Europe—Kennedy discussed the paper with Rusk, McNamara, Harriman, Hilsman, Forrestal, and others. He began by expressing skepticism about the idea of Phase III air strikes against the North, suggesting that they might bring in the Chinese without actually doing much damage. Harriman pointed out that the meeting was asking only for the approval of Phase I actions, the approval of planning for Phase II, and future consideration of Phase III. The meeting agreed that the situation, while apparently deteriorating, was not desperate, and the President asked for immediate new consultations with the British and the French to ask their opinions on measures to be taken before further planning went forward. Kennedy eventually approved Phase I, but concluded, "we are not likely to receive Congressional or public support of U.S. intervention in Laos and we should not kid ourselves about this too much." Six weeks later, on July 30, the President approved a few more actions in support of Laotian forces, while noting that the situation had quieted down considerably. He never approved the more provocative actions of Phase II.[63] The Pentagon, however, ordered CINCPAC to prepare plans to implement Phase III as well as Phase II, and those plans were ready when the situation in Laos heated up again a year later.

Ever since assuming the Presidency, Kennedy had received a long series of proposals for war in Southeast Asia from the State and Defense Departments. Rejecting them all, he had established the goals of a neutral regime in Laos and an effort to assist the South Vietnamese against the Viet Cong. In these meetings, as in so many others, he referred immediately to the Chinese ability to respond in force to American intervention. He questioned the impact of American air power, and he mentioned, once again, the need for consultation with unenthusiastic allies and the lack of public support for war in Laos. Kennedy never saw Indochina as a region in which great work could be done. He had never put a high priority on securing the withdrawal of a few thousand North Vietnamese troops from Laos, he had taken little part in the direction of the American effort in South Vietnam, and he apparently would have liked nothing more than the rough maintenance of the status quo in Laos and South Vietnam for the remainder of at least the first term of his Presidency. Unfortunately for him, even these limited objectives were threatened by late spring 1963. By the time Kennedy left for Europe in June 1963, the Buddhist crisis had begun, and the situation in South Vietnam was beginning to require attention at the very highest levels.

8

The Buddhist Crisis and the Cable of August 24

1963

★

On the evening of May 8, 1963, in Hue, the former imperial capital of Vietnam, a celebration of the Buddha's birthday turned into a demonstration against the Saigon regime, which had forbidden the display of a Buddhist flag. According to a much later report from a South Vietnamese diplomat, the trouble stemmed from an argument between two of Ngo Dinh Diem's brothers: Ngo Dinh Canh, the political boss of northern and central Vietnam, and Ngo Dinh Thuc, the Catholic Archbishop of Hue, who had insisted, with Diem's support, that Canh stop allowing the Buddhists to display their flag. ARVN and Civil Guards came out to meet the demonstration, and the Civil Guards opened fire and, according to most impartial observers, threw a grenade into the crowd. The American consulate reported eight dead and four wounded. Two days later the Buddhist clergy published a manifesto calling for the display of the Buddhist flag, equal status with Catholics, an end to arrests of Buddhists, freedom of Buddhist bonzes (clerics) to preach their religion, and compensation for the victims and punishment of the offenders in the Hue incident.[1]

Although the majority of South Vietnam's population was nominally Buddhist, the number of seriously practicing Buddhists may not have substantially exceeded the number of Catholics. Certainly Diem's regime had relied largely—although not exclusively—upon Diem's fellow Catholics, contributing to the narrowing of its support. Within weeks the Buddhist crisis had become the last and most serious struggle between Diem's regime and the growing non-Communist opposition to it. Unlike the sects he had crushed in 1954–1955 or the opposition politicians who had occasionally dared to challenge him, the Buddhists had an urban mass base. They rapidly learned how to coordinate activities in different cities and, more critically, to communicate with the American press and influence the government in Washington. Pressed by the Americans finally to conciliate the non-Communist opposition—all the more so because Ambassador Nolting went on leave for several crucial months—Diem belatedly made a number of hopeful statements, but Nhu and Madame Nhu consistently undercut them and reduced South Vietnamese and American support for the regime still further.

During the six months from May to November the crisis escalated, briefly took over the attention of the highest levels of the American government, and led ultimately to the overthrow and assassination of Diem and Nhu on November 1–2, 1963. In subsequent decades several authors have cited the coup, which American policy had certainly helped to provoke, as the biggest step toward American involvement in the war.[2] In fact, Diem's fall had profound long-term roots and did not lead inevitably to any particular outcome. The Buddhist crisis was simply the last and most serious phase of the decade-long erosion of Diem's non-Communist support, and it eventually forced the American government to recognize that its collaboration with Diem was not working. Like the controversies over Ap Bac and the American advisory role that had become public during the first half of 1963, the crisis reflected Diem's own limitations—which doomed him in the political struggle against the Viet Cong—and the vast gulf that separated him from his American supporters and turned their relationship into a continual tug-of-war. Kennedy eventually decided that Diem simply could not continue as before, and the evidence suggests that that conclusion was correct.

On May 18, only ten days after the Hue violence, Nolting met with Diem for two hours and asked him to take responsibility for the deaths, offer compensation to the victims, and reaffirm religious equality. Diem replied that the Buddhists had purposely provoked the incident and that the Viet Cong had thrown the grenade, and declined to make any statement as yet. His government on May 29 issued a brief communiqué that merely affirmed freedom of religion but stressed the supremacy of the *national* flag, which had to be flown above any other.[3] On thesame day David Halberstam reported that the Buddhists planned hunger strikes and protests, and the State Department immediately suggested to William Trueheart, who had taken over the Embassy in Nolting's absence, that Diem might be encouraged to modify his line. Two days later, however, as new demonstrations took place in Hue and Da Nang, Thuan told Trueheart that the government feared that concessions to the Buddhists would lead to pressure for talks with the Viet Cong. By June 4 the ARVN had repeatedly used tear gas against demonstrators in Hue and had declared martial law, while the Saigon government declared that some of the leading bonzes were in fact Viet Cong. Halberstam had now reported that some American officials hoped that Diem would meet the Buddhists' demands—exactly the kind of story which, as Nolting had long recognized, would almost certainly have the opposite effect.[4]

The pattern of the crisis definitely took shape during the next few days. During the first week of June Nhu agreed to meet with Buddhist leaders from Hue, and Vice President Tho—a Buddhist—became the head of a commission to mediate the dispute. Thuan also told Trueheart that the government would agree to the major Buddhist demands, including repeal of Decree Law 10, which gave the Catholics some special privileges, new rules for the display of flags, an end to arbitrary arrests, and compensation for the dead and wounded of May 8. Diem made a conciliatory address on June 7. On the very next day, however, Madame Nhu's Women's Solidarity Movement issued a resolution condemning the Buddhists as anti-nationalists "exploited and controlled by Communism and oriented to the sowing of disorder and neutralism," and calling for vigilance toward "those inclined to take Vietnam for a satellite of a foreign power." Roger Hilsman's Far Eastern bureau instructed Trueheart to inform Thuan or Diem that something had to be done to counteract this statement, which had "greatly increased the difficulty of the US role as a supporter of the GVN." Instead, Thuan told Trueheart on June 10 that Diem had ruled out immediate repeal of Decree Law 10. Meanwhile, Neil Sheehan on June 9 and Halberstam on June 10 reported that many Americans in Saigon privately dissociated themselves from government policy, drawing a June 11 blast in the Nhu-influenced, English-language *Times of Vietnam*.[5]

On June 11—the day after Kennedy's American University speech—a Buddhist monk burned himself to death in front of the Cambodian Embassy, after American reporters and photographers had been alerted. On the same day in Washington, Hilsman, with Averell Harriman's clearance, sent a telegram threatening a drastic shift in American policy. It proposed that the government fully and unequivocally accept the five original Buddhist demands, and even proposed language for a communiqué. It also authorized Trueheart to tell Diem that if he failed to take such action within a few days, "the United States will find it necessary publicly to state that it cannot associate itself with the GVN's unwillingness to meet the reasonable demands of the Vietnamese Buddhist leaders." Should Diem refuse, it concluded confidentially, "we will have to re-examine our entire relationship with his regime."[6]

Hilsman and Harriman were ready to give up on Diem, but President Kennedy was not. When Kennedy on June 14 learned about State's new threat, he immediately banned any more threats or formal statements of dissociation without his approval. Still, the crisis deeply concerned the President. As a fellow Catholic chief of state within a non-Catholic country, he was extremely sensitive to the appearance of Diem's religious persecution. Pictures of Saigon police and soldiers suppressing demonstrations, moreover, bore an uncomfortable resemblance to similar pictures of police attacking civil rights demonstrators in the American South. Kennedy did not want to force an immediate crisis, but he now decided to take out some political insurance. For months Michael Forrestal had been trying to persuade Secretary of State Rusk to replace Nolting. Rusk, apparently on his own initiative, now suggested that Kennedy appoint Henry Cabot Lodge, Nixon's vice presidential candidate, whom Kennedy had unseated as a Massachusetts senator in 1952. Despite Forrestal's own objections, the idea appealed to the President, and the appointment was announced late in the month.[7]

Remarkably, the American threat initially worked. On June 16 the government and the Buddhists agreed on the five Buddhist demands, including an investigation of the May 8 incident and punishment of those responsible. Hilsman and Harriman had already suggested to Trueheart that he assure Vice President Tho of American support should circumstances arise in which Diem could no longer function as President,[8] but Trueheart now replied that under the circumstances he saw no need to do so. While his misgivings about the Ngo family had increased, neither he nor his colleagues were impressed by the competition, and Americans were replying to talk of a coup—of which they heard plenty—with expressions of support for the government. The Buddhists, meanwhile, declared a two-week moratorium on demonstrations as part of the accord.[9]

Things quieted down considerably in Saigon during the next two weeks, and Kennedy left Washington for his dramatic trip to West Germany, Berlin, Ireland, Britain, and Italy. Behind the scenes, however, all four major parties—the Saigon government, the Buddhists, the Department of State, and the American press—prepared for another round of struggle. Upon being informed of the planned appointment of Lodge on June 25, Diem told Thuan, "They can send ten Lodges, but I will not permit myself or my country to be humiliated, not if they train their artillery on this Palace." Rumors immediately began circulating that Nhu's Republican Youth were working to undermine the agreement. Diem on June 28 described to Trueheart the Nhus' great contributions to the democratization of the country, and the whole Ngo family gathered in Hue the next day to celebrate the anniversary of Archbishop Thuc's investment. On July 1 the Nhus' English paper, the *Times of Vietnam,* published a highly provocative article implicitly criticizing Vice President Tho and suggesting that a Buddhist failure to resume demonstrations would show that the Buddhists were now satisfied. Halberstam, meanwhile, fanned the flames with stories on June 22 and July 3 suggesting that a coup was likely and reporting that many Americans felt the war effort was going downhill and wanted a change of government.[10]

Since Nhu and Madame Nhu seemed determined to undermine any agreement, Washington again began to wonder whether Diem might dispense with them. According to Trueheart, Washington queried him asking for his characterization of the relationship among the three, and he replied that without wishing to be sacrilegious, he would compare it to the holy trinity.[11] The Saigon CIA station reported on June 28 that Diem would never let go of any of his family members, whose organizations played key roles in his rule, but added that the Buddhists had won the sympathy of students and of the Catholic Church, and that Diem would not be able to crush them by force.[12]

On July 3 Kennedy returned to the United States, and Forrestal wrote him that Trueheart, on instructions from Hilsman, Harriman, Ball, and himself, had warned Diem that if he failed to make another conciliatory statement and new incidents took place, the United States would disavow his policy. Diem on the same day received this warning very briefly and coolly, and when Trueheart raised the *Times of Vietnam* article, denied that he had seen it. The next day, July 4, Hilsman briefed the President at length, passing on reports that Diem did not plan to respect the agreement and predicting coup attempts during the next few months.[13] Washington was still downplaying the crisis. "Once in a while," Max Frankel wrote perceptively in the July 3 *New York Times,* "Washington remembers that there is a war on in South Vietnam. It remembered last week when President Kennedy chose Henry Cabot Lodge to be ambassador to Saigon. It remembered the week before when President Ngo Dinh Diem's dispute with Buddhists almost provoked the administration to denounce him. But for long stretches, the war against Communist-led guerrillas in Vietnam fades from memory here, not because no one cares, but because the men who care most decided long ago to discuss it as little as possible."[14]

On July 7 South Vietnamese police had an altercation with several American reporters covering a Buddhist demonstration, and the reporters telegraphed President Kennedy asking for a formal protest. Nolting returned to Saigon on July 11 and spent seven hours with Diem over the next few days. While he decided not to send a full report of these talks, he resumed his traditional line, reporting on July 15 that Diem's confidence in American intentions had been badly shaken in recent weeks, and that restoring it—and subsequently persuading Diem to take "more positive and sensible political actions"—would take some time. Nolting advised against either repeating or carrying out any threats of dissociation, provided that the situation quieted down. The CIA, meanwhile, picked up several reports of a meeting between Nhu and senior generals on July 11, at which Nhu had promised the generals a bigger role in the war, asked for their loyalty, and criticized the government's gentle handling of the Buddhists.[15]

On July 16 and 17, while Harriman was negotiating the atmospheric test ban in Moscow, police beat Buddhist demonstrators and strung barbed wire in Saigon. On July 17 Assistant Secretary of State Robert Manning had a marathon session with Nhu, who admitted that American correspondents got much of their information from Vietnamese sources but also accused them, with some justice, of trying to replace the government. Nhu also suggested rather tellingly that the United States change the basis of its aid to South Vietnam to something resembling lend-lease, and drew a parallel with American aid to Stalin during the Second World War, which the United States had obviously extended without any "moral commitment." Diem, in a shorter session the next day, was considerably less forthcoming.[16]

On July 18 Diem broadcast new instructions, issued "at the proposal of the Interministerial Committee [on Strategic Hamlets]," which Nhu, of course, chaired. He made only very minor concessions, but Nolting, bidding to reverse the trend of American policy, asked the State Department to issue a statement calling the broadcast "forthright and statesmanlike" and declaring that the way was now clear for the settlement of all religious issues. State refused to do so in a telegram cleared by Rusk himself. Nolting immediately confessed himself "very much disappointed," and argued that thanks to "hard choices, clearly taken" over the past two years—essentially, the decision to support Diem and remain content with whatever he would do—"we have helped build what is admittedly a much stronger defense against Communist takeover than what was thought possible . . . our best bet still lies in encouraging and prodding and helping them to accept and follow through on policies that look reasonably good." Hilsman rejected this perspective on July 23, arguing that Diem was unlikely to take concrete steps and the situation would probably get worse, but advising against trying either to encourage or to discourage a coup. Nolting on July 25 replied more calmly that he still regarded the Diem government as having the best chance of succeeding in counterinsurgency, but even he now advised against "putting all our eggs in one basket or alienating possible successor governments or leaders."[17]

The President and his senior advisers, meanwhile, were focusing on the Moscow test ban negotiations, which culminated in the initialing of an atmospheric test ban by Harriman, Gromyko, and the British negotiator Lord Hailsham on July 25.[18] The President addressed the nation on the treaty the next night, and the action now moved to the Pentagon and the Senate. General Taylor had explained to the National Security Council on July 9 that individual Joint Chiefs did not believe that an atmospheric test ban would serve the nation well, but a draft JCS memorandum a week later had suggested that while the atmospheric ban would be "militarily disadvantageous," "overriding nonmilitary considerations" might yet make it in the national interest.[19] Conservative Republicans and Southern Democrats viewed the treaty suspiciously, and ratification might be impossible without the Chiefs' support.

The test ban—Kennedy's biggest diplomatic achievement—obviously had taken center stage, but for the first time in the two and one-half years of the Kennedy administration, Vietnam had become a continuing major news story. And in an apparent effort both to maintain some support for administration policy and to encourage Diem to resolve the embarrassing crisis, administration officials suddenly began making their most optimistic statements yet about the progress of the war. Kennedy himself, who in May had refused to declare that progress would allow an American withdrawal by the end of the year, commented on July 17 that the military struggle "has been going better than it has been going in many months . . . it is going quite well." He expressed the hope that a solution would be found to this "religious dispute," rejected an American withdrawal that would in his opinion lead to the collapse of all Southeast Asia, and asked for sympathy for the South Vietnamese in their difficult position.[20] The *New York Times* of July 21 quoted administration officials to the effect that enemy attacks had fallen from 120 to 70 a week in the last year, and *Time* on July 19 reported American dismay that the crisis "can only hinder the war effort against the Viet Cong, just when it is beginning to go well."[21]

But while some officials made optimistic statements, the Pentagon was pushing for a widening of the war. Marine Lieutenant General Victor Krulak, General Taylor's Special Assistant for Counterinsurgency Affairs, had given Taylor a moderately optimistic report after a one-week visit to Vietnam in late June, repeating the usual litany of more aggressive offensive operations and completed strategic hamlets. Krulak also reported, however, that CIA Station Chief Richardson and MCAV Commander Harkins both thought that events in Laos were severely affecting the situation in South Vietnam, despite a lack of "abundant hard evidence" of infiltrated weapons and personnel, and noted "strong sentiment . . . for more covert pressure on the Laos corridor and on North Vietnam." Briefing the Joint Chiefs on July 3, Krulak recommended "deep incursions into Laos to cut supply lines and get better intelligence," and Secretary of Defense McNamara told the Chiefs a few days later that he wanted the ARVN to make such border crossings.[22]

And meanwhile, in South Vietnam itself, the Viet Cong were beginning their biggest offensive of the entire war. With the rainy season at its peak in the Delta, VC armed attacks had fallen to 76 for the week of June 26–July 3 and 53 for July 3–10.[23] The next Headway Report, for July 10–17, reported new increases in ARVN operations, but careful readers noted that enemy attacks had jumped back to 77, 59 of them in

IV Corps, the southern Delta. And in the next week they nearly doubled to a total of 124, including a two-battalion attack in Binh Duong province and 105 attacks in IV Corps. They increased yet again to 130 in the last week in July, with 25 attacks in III Corps surrounding Saigon and 12 in hitherto-quiet I Corps against Civil Guard and Self-Defense Corps in strategic hamlets. ARVN operations actually declined.[24] The Viet Cong, once again, were proving what Frank Serong had argued in March: that they slowed down operations when they chose to do so. Halberstam wrote another series of pessimistic military stories late in July, citing continuing problems in the Delta, attacks on Montagnard hamlets in the highlands, and the South Vietnamese abandonment of their own base in the heart of War Zone D. He did not, however, realize how quickly VC activity had increased.[25]

Washington and the public had only a very dim awareness of the military situation, but the Buddhist crisis erupted for all to see in the first week of August. Having failed to move Washington to bless Diem's handling of the affair, Nolting on July 28 told a UPI correspondent that he had "never seen any evidence of religious persecution" during his tour in Vietnam. Harriman—recently returned from Moscow—telephoned Hilsman on August 1 to suggest the ambassador's immediate recall, but cooled down when he realized that Nolting was scheduled to return on August 13 anyway. The Buddhists, who had continued to refuse to meet with the government until it finally took responsibility for the May 8 incident, put tens of thousands of demonstrators into the streets of Saigon, Da Nang, and Hue on July 30, and criticized Nolting's remark, which the controlled Saigon press had publicized heavily. On Sunday, August 4, the *New York Times* carried a Reuters interview with Nhu, in which he bluntly said that he had discussed an anti-Buddhist, anti-American coup with generals to end the government's weak policy, and specifically to crush the Xa Loi pagoda, Saigon's protest headquarters. Madame Nhu, speaking to the Women's Solidarity Movement on the same day, attacked the Buddhists as seditious elements using Communist tactics. On the same day another Buddhist burned himself outside the range of cameras. A few days earlier Madame Nhu had told a CBS reporter that the Buddhists had simply decided to "barbecue" a bonze with "imported gasoline."[26]

On the next day, August 5, *Time* published a cover story that bitingly portrayed Madame Nhu as a master of oriental deception bent on her own self-aggrandizement. It painted her as the real power in the palace, quoted her criticisms of Diem's conciliatory policy toward the Buddhists, and suggested that the regime might not survive. The story—written by the correspondent Charles Mohr, who had frequently clashed with his editors over his dispatches from Vietnam—endorsed, in spades, all the customary criticisms of Diem's regime, although it also quoted the official figures for completed strategic hamlets and questioned the existence of alternative leadership. Coming under the imprimatur of America's leading foe of Asian Communism, Henry Luce, the story showed that Diem had very few friends left.[27]

When Nolting saw Nhu on August 7 to protest the Reuters interview, Nhu said he still favored conciliation, and Nolting replied that if so, Nhu was a most misunderstood man. On the next day the *New York Times* carried a new statement by Madame Nhu that seemed designed to make *Time* look good. Bragging that the Embassy had tried and failed to shut her up, she called for stronger action against the Buddhists and argued that Diem himself depended on the personal followings of Ngo Dinh Canh, Nhu, and herself. She praised Nolting and added, "If [Lodge] is a good American, he will do as well as Nolting."[28]

Washington officials were looking more and more closely at the possibility of a coup. Hilsman on August 6 wrote Undersecretary of State Ball that a coup had become likely, and that if Diem managed to forestall one and repress the Buddhists, he would probably lose so much support as to make the defeat of the VC impossible.[29] Ten days later William Colby of the CIA—the former Saigon station chief—gave Hilsman several assessments from Saigon that showed that even the Agency had jumped ship. In one paper Colby's successor, John Richardson, expressed doubts about his ability to improve Nhu's "domestic or international image," and rated Nhu's own chances of either seizing or maintaining power as poor. A second paper, "Contingency Planning for Succession Crisis," made clear that Diem's support among the military was probably not sufficient to stop a coup. Most critically, the paper advised against the United States taking any position in the early, confused stages of a coup, despite the risk of Diem's resentment of our inaction should he prevail.[30]

Nolting was still trying desperately to resolve the crisis, but Nhu and Diem had turned the ambassador into a stooge. As one CIA report had already suggested, Nhu planned to crush the Buddhists during the period between Nolting's departure and Lodge's arrival.[31] Refusing to believe the worst, the ambassador spent a last, pathetic week trying to get Diem to repudiate Madame Nhu and reaffirm a conciliatory policy. Diem hinted in talks with Nolting that Madame Nhu had gone too far even for him, and said she might take a rest. But Diem showed no understanding of the Buddhists' position, and Vice President Tho, the supposed executor of the conciliation policy, gave an August 13 press conference promising to prosecute *Buddhists* for the affair of May 8, and denying clemency to any Buddhists arrested since June 16. Another Buddhist burned himself to death on the same day.[32] On the morning of August 14 Nolting saw Diem for the last time. Diem "maintained stoutly that neither the American press nor apparently the American government understood the real dimensions or all complexities of the Buddhist problem, nor did we understand the true situation concerning the Ngo family and their individual contributions to the independence of Vietnam. He went into great detail on this, stressing particularly the absolute selflessness of Ngo Dinh Nhu's contribution to the cause." Nolting replied that the U.S. government would be unable to continue their present relationship if Diem did not issue a statement reaffirming a conciliatory policy and making clear that he was running the government, and Diem apparently agreed in principle. In a poignant farewell, Diem said that Nolting's tenure would be one of the best memories of his life, reaffirmed their friendship, and asked Nolting to thank President Kennedy for all he had done for Vietnam.[33]

That afternoon Diem saw Marguerite Higgins, a strongly anti-Communist correspondent for the *New York Herald Tribune* who had been dispatched to Saigon largely to refute current press coverage. "The policy of utmost reconciliation is irreversible," he told her, "and neither any individual nor the government could change it at all." Although the South Vietnamese public never saw the statement, Nolting later interpreted it as meeting his requests.[34]

While Lodge traveled to Saigon via Honolulu, where he met with Nolting, the military situation suddenly became controversial as well. On August 15 a front-page *New York Times* story by Halberstam once again described the Viet Cong build-up in the Delta. Noting that 60 percent of the population lived there, Halberstam reported that two new VC battalions had recently been identified in the area, bringing their total to 23, and that VC losses were falling while government personnel and weapons losses rose. He noted some gains in Kien Hoa and Vinh Binh provinces, but quoted an American that the United States did not yet know how to make the strategic hamlet program work in the Delta. Lastly, he reported for the first time that Ap Bac had marked the beginning of vastly improved enemy response to helicopters, and argued that the VC now dared attack the ARVN, as well as the Civil Guard and Self-Defense Corps.[35]

Kennedy, who saw Lodge off that same day, immediately asked Rusk and McNamara for information on "military operations in South Vietnam." General Krulak responded to McNamara the very next day with a new and rather imaginative explanation of how the Delta problem related to American strategy:

> Halberstam . . . exhibits a lack of understanding of our entire Vietnam strategy. From the start, that strategy involved a purification process, north to south; driving the Viet Cong southward—*away from their sources of strength* and compressing them in the southernmost area of the peninsula. This has proceeded. I Corps is fairly clean; II Corps, not much less so; III Corps, warmer; and IV Corps, still tough.
>
> This was expected. The gradual redisposition of Vietnamese power, from the less to the more critical areas, portrays this. As General Cao, CG, IV Corps, said in June, "We want to see all the Viet Cong squeezed into the Ca Mau Peninsula, and then rot there."
>
> If Halberstam understood clearly this strategy, he might not have undertaken to write his disingenuous article. Perhaps this strategy should be more fully explained to the press.[36]

Pressed by the Commander in Chief, the Pentagon was revealing its own misunderstanding of the war. Krulak seemed to be viewing the war like the campaign in Western Europe in 1944–1945, with the Ca Mau peninsula in the role of Berlin, but the real problem was entirely different. The strength of the Viet Cong throughout South Vietnam, as we have seen, varied directly with the density of the population, and the population was by far the most dense in III and IV Corps. Krulak's new theory does not seem to have originated in South Vietnam, and he had heard nothing like it during a recent visit in late June.[37] A few days later Krulak gave McNamara a more detailed analysis that also reached the President.[38]

Determined to refute Halberstam, both CINCPAC and the Saigon Embassy denied critical facts. CINCPAC on August 17 forwarded an analysis to the Joint Chiefs acknowledging that IV Corps was the most critical area of the war, and affirming that the Viet Cong were making their major effort there. But they added that ARVN operations had increased "several fold" during the same period, with a "more aggressive" combat posture and tactics—in defiance of all the evidence, including conversations with Diem and Nhu, that the ARVN had become less aggressive after Ap Bac. While citing "spurious, unconfirmed" reports of larger VC units and admitting that the hamlet program was going poorly in the Delta, the report declared that "the RVN is carrying the war to the enemy" while the Viet Cong "have been prevented from expanding operations to a campaign involving large Communist units." And on perhaps the most sensitive military point—the increased vulnerability of helicopters—the report resorted to deception. Although June MACV Headway Report had shown that VC anti-aircraft capabilities had nearly tripled during the first four months of 1963, this report stated that "Viet Cong attempts to negate heliborne warfare tactics have not succeeded," and counted "only 404 hits" on helicopters *during a twelve-month period* beginning July 1, 1962. Judging from the earlier report, at least three-quarters of those hits had been suffered during 1963, and the new report said nothing about the last six weeks. Lastly, it denied, ritually, that Ap Bac had been a Communist victory—"in Harkins-Felt opinion."[39] The Saigon Embassy—which under Nolting always cleared military reports with MACV—commented in largely identical terms on August 19, arguing that while IV Corps definitely presented special problems, Halberstam's article was "basically unsound."[40]

Despite the extremely serious political crisis, Halberstam and his Silent generation sources among the American advisers and USOM personnel could not prevail against their GI superiors. MACV, CINCPAC, and the Saigon Embassy convinced both the State Department, the Pentagon, and even the President that the war was basically going well. On the day Halberstam's article appeared, a memorandum from Foreign Service officer Paul Kattenburg to Hilsman apparently accepted the Saigon Embassy's estimate of a favorable trend in both population control and the military campaign during the first half of the year. Five days later, summarizing the analyses from CINCPAC and the Embassy, another subordinate confidently reported to Hilsman that these reports unanimously contradicted Halberstam's central theses.[41] Such estimates allowed the Pentagon to proceed with the initial withdrawal of American forces upon which McNamara had insisted. On August 20 General Taylor forwarded to McNamara CINCPAC's plan for the withdrawal of 1,000 American personnel by the end of the year. The plan called specifically for taking the men out in four increments, "in order to achieve maximum press coverage, and at the same time cause the least impact on US/RVN military operations." It listed units for withdrawal, but according to the Pentagon Papers, some of the units had been specially created from miscellaneous American personnel solely for the purpose of being withdrawn. Taylor added that the Chiefs now believed that no withdrawals should take place "until the political and religious tensions now confronting the government of South Vietnam have eased," and therefore recommended delaying approval of the withdrawal until October.[42] Alas, the political crisis in South Vietnam was reaching a climactic stage at the very moment that Taylor signed off on the plan.

On August 15 two more Buddhists committed suicide in protest. The next day Rusk, in a news conference, said the United States was "deeply distressed" by these events, but made optimistic estimates of the military situation. On Sunday, August 18, the *New York Times* reported that the Catholic rector of the University of Hue and forty-seven faculty members had resigned to protest government policy, and the government of Ceylon asked the United Nations to investigate the persecution of the Buddhists in South Vietnam. On Tuesday, August 20— after another weekend of huge, often violent Buddhist demonstrations in Saigon, Hue, and Da Nang, and a day-long meeting among Diem, Nhu, and senior South Vietnamese generals—Diem proclaimed martial law, effective at midnight. The Embassy reported the next day that the generals had in fact pushed for martial law because of the crisis' effect on the war effort. Troops, police, and units of the Vietnamese Special Forces—a unit under Nhu's direct control, led by Colonel Le Quang Tung—raided and emptied Buddhist pagodas, including the Xa Loi pagoda in Saigon. Reports stated that some monks had been injured or killed.[43]

In Washington, Hilsman at State, Colby at the CIA, and Krulak at the Pentagon spent the rest of the week trying to find out who was actually behind the martial law declaration. On Thursday evening, August 22, as Lodge was arriving in Saigon, Hilsman cabled him that Washington still saw three possibilities: that the military had taken control, that Diem had used the military to strengthen his position, or that Nhu was calling the shots. Lodge replied the next day that the palace seemed to be in control, that Nhu's influence certainly had not diminished, and that the military seemed to be split.[44] But Halberstam on August 23 took an opposite point of view, arguing that Nhu and Colonel Tung's forces had masterminded the crackdown and raided the Xa Loi pagoda.[45] And on Saturday, August 24, Tad Szulc of the *Times* reported that "many policy planners in Washington" looked favorably on a military junta as an alternative to Diem's rule.

General Harkins, meanwhile, had reported that the new chief of the Joint General Staff, General Tran Van Don, had now explained to him that Diem himself had ordered martial law. While promising to watch for any impact of the crisis on the war, Harkins made an even more optimistic estimate of the military situation. "We have accomplished our part of everything we set out to do after your visit in the fall of '61," he wrote Taylor, "—all except ending the war, and that is not far off if things continue at present pace." He said I Corps was "quiescent," "not much" remained to be done in II Corps, III Corps "has its biggest headaches in the provinces around Saigon," while IV Corps "is where the war is being fought." The increase in the number of South Vietnamese operations showed their determination to win, and martial law might be "a blessing in disguise," since some measure of authority had to be established.[46] Thus, on the afternoon of Friday, August 23, State Department officials were contemplating a coup, but General Taylor had just heard that Diem was working with the generals, that the war was going better than ever, and that, in effect, the 1,000-man withdrawal plan he had forwarded to McNamara three days earlier could indeed go into effect, certainly by the end of the year.

President Kennedy—who worked and played hard, taking a nap and a swim every afternoon and spending his evenings socializing and his weekends in Palm Beach, Virginia, or Hyannis Port—presided over an administration of workaholics. The President was back in Massachusetts on Saturday, August 24, but when Hilsman and Harriman arrived at State, they found several new reports. Lodge, to begin with, forwarded two accounts of conversations by Rufus Phillips, the chief American adviser to the strategic hamlet program, the first with General Le Van Kim, General Don's deputy for public relations, on August

23, and the second with Thuan, Diem's Secretary of State and Minister of Defense. Kim bitterly denied that the army had anything to do with the raids on the pagodas, which he blamed on Nhu and Colonel Tung's Special Forces, and complained that the people were blaming the army for the raids. The army was split, he said, and if the United States supported action to remove the Nhus from the government, the army would take it. Thuan, whom Phillips had known since 1955, reported that Diem had just written Madame Nhu a letter in which he ordered her to make no more statements or public appearances, enraging her and her husband. Thuan, too, suggested that the United States encourage the army to remove the Nhus from the government.[47]

On August 24 a CIA telegram reached Hilsman describing a long conversation between Lucien Conein, a veteran CIA operative, and General Tran Van Don, who drew a very different picture from his deputy Kim. Don took responsibility for the decision for martial law, claiming that ten generals had reached it on August 18, and that Diem had endorsed it. He also explained that General Ton That Dinh, the new military governor of Saigon (and III Corps commander), and Colonel Tung both took orders directly from the palace, and added that "the Generals hate Tung's guts." Don also said that he had not known that Colonel Tung's forces were going to raid the Xa Loi pagoda, and asked that the Voice of America absolve the military of responsibility for the attack. Don made some confusing statements, but he gave no evidence of any plan to overthrow Nhu, Diem, or both of them. He explained that Madame Nhu's power came from her role in the palace as Diem's "Platonic wife," while adding that he did not think that Diem had ever had sexual relations with her or, indeed, with anyone else. Another CIA cable reported widespread discontent among more junior officers, who felt that Nhu and Madame Nhu had to be removed from power to win the war but worried that the United States fully supported Diem and even that Americans had planned the crackdown against the Buddhists.[48]

Summarizing these discussions in a telegram that arrived at 2:05 PM, Lodge suggested that Nhu had played a major role in the crackdown, but with considerable support from the generals. The Embassy clearly doubted Don's disavowal of the attack upon the pagodas. He concluded that none of the generals with military strength in Saigon wanted to remove either Diem or Nhu, and termed the suggestion that the generals would act if encouraged by the United States an overly simplistic one. "Action on our part in these circumstances," Lodge concluded, "would be a shot in the dark," and he proposed a course of watchful waiting.[49]

Hilsman had two other sources of information that Saturday: Neil Sheehan in the *Washington Post,* and Halberstam in the *Times.* Both reported the resignation of Foreign Minister Vu Van Mau—never a particularly important figure, since Diem and Thuan handled relations with the Americans—who had shaved his head to show sympathy with the Buddhists. Sheehan's UPI dispatch reported that Nhu had engineered the crackdown and now seemed to be completely in charge, and Halberstam went much further. In a story that seemed designed to have the maximum impact upon American sensibilities, he quoted "reliable sources" to the effect that Nhu had "effectively taken power," and that he was the main advocate of the attacks upon the pagodas. Madame Nhu "was reported to be exuberant, saying this was the happiest time for her since the Government crushed the rebellion of the Binh Xuyen sect in 1955," and real military power, he reported, was in the hands of Colonel Tung—something even General Kim had not alleged. "Sources," he continued, said that the military's apparent leading role was "a facade," and that the population was becoming more bitter against Americans. He denied that General Don had even known the crackdown was coming.

Halberstam then tried to use the crisis to show once and for all that he had been right and Nolting and Harkins had been wrong:

> The entire episode has underlined what some sources here consider to be one of the gravest sicknesses of the vast and talented American mission here—a vast divergence between what the people in the field are seeing and reporting and what the highest American authorities are reporting. Some observers see the heads of the mission so tied to the Ngo family that, as one source said, "their world is completely different from ours. It's like we're in different countries."

The "Man in the News" column, also apparently written by Halberstam, dealt with Colonel Tung, and reiterated that he was now the head of the military—something which not one diplomatic or intelligence report had alleged. Oddly, the same edition also printed Halberstam's first August 21 dispatch on the crackdown, which censorship had held up, and which did not mention the role of Special Forces in the pagoda raids at all.[50]

Telegram 243 from Washington to Saigon, which Hilsman drafted during August 24, echoed Halberstam's line, and demanded immediate action:

> It is now clear that whether military proposed martial law or whether Nhu tricked them into it, Nhu took advantage of its imposition to smash pagodas with police and Tung's Special Forces loyal to him, thus placing onus on military in eyes of world and Vietnamese people. Also clear that Nhu has maneuvered himself into commanding position.
>
> US Government cannot tolerate situation in which power lies in Nhu's hands. Diem must be given chance to rid himself of Nhu and his coterie and replace them with best military and political personalities available.
>
> If, in spite of all your efforts, Diem remains obdurate and refuses, then we must face the possibility that Diem himself cannot be preserved.

The telegram, in order to prevent Nhu from consolidating his position, proposed immediate steps, subject to Lodge's and Harkins's approval. It asked the Embassy to tell key military leaders that the United States would not be able to continue supporting the government unless Nhu were removed, and to promise them "direct support" in any "interim period." It also proposed public statements in both Saigon and Washington absolving the army of blame for the Pagoda raids, and asked for immediate planning to replace Diem, if necessary. "Needless to say," it concluded, "we have held knowledge of this telegram to minimum essential people and assume you will take similar precautions to prevent premature leaks."[51]

At 4:50 PM Michael Forrestal forwarded a copy of the draft to the President, who had already received the most recent cables from Saigon, at Hyannis Port. He advised the President that he himself, Hilsman, and Harriman wanted to dispatch the telegram immediately, and that they were seeking reactions from Acting Secretary of State Ball and from the Department of Defense. CINCPAC Admiral Felt, meanwhile, had telephoned Hilsman twice during the day, essentially endorsed the telegram, and volunteered the concurrence of Harkins, his immediate subordinate. Hilsman eventually found Ball on a golf course and the Acting Secretary cleared the cable. McNamara was vacationing in the West, but Forrestal reached his deputy, Roswell Gilpatric, late in the afternoon. Gilpatric, a corporate lawyer by profession and a conciliator by temperament, replied that the cable sounded like a State Department matter, and told Forrestal he had no objection. Gilpatric then called Maxwell Taylor and gave him the gist of the cable.[52] Hilsman, meanwhile, had discussed the cable with Admiral Herbert Riley, apparently the senior duty officer at the Pentagon, who concurred in its proposed course of action and telephoned General Krulak, the Special Assistant for Counterinsurgency Affairs, to inform him.

At about 7:00 PM Krulak went to the White House, where Forrestal told him that Gilpatric had approved the cable and that it had gone to the President for approval. Krulak then secured a copy and tried without success to reach General Taylor. Between 7:30 and 8:00 Krulak learned from Forrestal that the President had cleared the message, which went out at 9:36 PM.[53]

The August 24 cable reflected Harriman, Hilsman, and Forrestal's belief that Nhu, at the very least, had to go to make American policy a success. Harriman had never felt any commitment to Diem, and Hilsman and Forrestal had become increasingly disillusioned during 1963. The telegram, following Kennedy's instructions, gave Lodge and Harkins the opportunity to reject the proposed course. It reflected a generally held belief—shared by Admirals Felt and Riley, among many others—that South Vietnam could not survive without fundamental changes, including the end of the influence of Nhu and Madame Nhu.

This belief and Hilsman's proposed action were neither novel, nor idiosyncratic, nor without precedent. Two of Nolting's predecessors, General Collins and Ambassador Durbrow, had reached the same conclusion years earlier, and Durbrow had asked Diem to send Nhu abroad late in 1960. Nolting had stood up for Diem and Nhu for two years, but the Buddhist crisis—played out, disastrously, in public and on television before the entire world—had made it virtually impossible for any American to believe in their political survival now. And beginning in 1954 Americans had regarded Diem as the instrument of their policy, and subject, thereby, to their dismissal should they conclude that he could never perform successfully. Diem was far from the first American protégé to lose Washington's confidence. President Syngman Rhee of South Korea had been America's ally throughout the three years of the Korean War, but in the spring of 1953 his intransigence over the conclusion of an armistice had led Washington to think seriously about his removal. At that time Rhee had agreed to the armistice, but seven years later, in 1960, he, like Diem now, had faced riots and demonstrations, specifically after staging a rigged election. In that case as in this one, the United States had told Rhee that it could not remain indifferent to the political crisis and told him exactly what he should do to resolve it. When Rhee refused to follow American advice, his Vice President and cabinet resigned, in much the same way that many of Diem's closest collaborators were now beginning to repudiate him, and after Washington effectively dissociated itself from the aged President, he resigned from office.[54]

Harriman and Hilsman's hasty move, however, assumed far too much about the situation in Saigon, and utterly disregarded the principles of team play and linear progression forward to which the Kennedy administration (and the whole GI generation) were dedicated. The telegram effectively rejected the Saigon Embassy's view of the developing situation in favor of Halberstam's, and Halberstam in this case had allowed himself utterly to succumb to the exhilaration of having been proven right. Far from being on the verge of a coup, most of the South Vietnamese generals had just made a new bargain with Diem. Meanwhile, Harriman, a notorious lone wolf, Hilsman, easily the most abrasive personality of the whole national security team, and Forrestal, who after his father's death in 1949 had been almost adopted by Harriman, had taken advantage of the weekend to secure presidential approval for a course of action which the Pentagon was almost certain to oppose. In addition, this drastic proposal flew in the face of Harkins, Taylor, and McNamara's view that the American involvement was nearing a successful conclusion. None of these three men had really been able to express their opinion before the telegram was dispatched, even though Vietnam since 1961 had been mainly a Pentagon responsibility.

When Krulak finally found Taylor and showed him the telegram on the evening of August 24, the general remarked that it reflected the long-standing desire of Hilsman, Harriman, and Forrestal to dump Diem; that it had not received sufficient interdepartmental staffing; and that McGeorge Bundy, had he been present, would never have allowed it to go out. On Monday McNamara returned, and Taylor took the matter up with him and Robert Kennedy at once. By the next day the Kennedy administration was involved in its bitterest internal clash.

The telegram had critical effects in Saigon as well. After meeting with

Lodge on August 15, Kennedy had summarized American policy in a new formula. The United States, he said, wanted South Vietnam to defeat the Communists, and "anything that helps that policy we are in favor of and anything that hinders it we are opposed to."[55] Kennedy had also told Lodge to take immediate, personal charge of relations with the American reporters in Saigon. When Lodge arrived he discovered that the regime had confronted him with a fait accompli. He also listened respectfully to the many Americans, both within the American mission and in the press, who had had to swallow their frustration with Diem and his regime during Nolting's tenure. During the few days between his arrival and August 25, Lodge had Sheehan and Halberstam to lunch at the Embassy, and Sheehan poured out his heart about the regime, arguing that it could not possibly win the war. When at the end of the lunch Sheehan screwed up his courage and asked Lodge for his opinion of Diem's government, Lodge replied that it was about the same.[56]

Lodge also heard from William Trueheart, who did not believe that the United States could possibly support what Diem had done, and who as we have seen did not believe that Diem could be split from the Nhus. As Trueheart recalled many years later, he thought that the August 24 cable was just what the doctor ordered.[57] Saigon time was twelve hours ahead of Washington time, and the cable—dispatched on Saturday evening in Washington—arrived Sunday morning. But during Sunday, Lodge—and, subsequently, Washington—received two more reports of conversations with Vietnamese generals that showed that a coup was anything but imminent. Harkins on Saturday had seen General Don again, and the general, while expressing himself in favor of adding some generals to the cabinet and making Diem "clean house" and finally delegate some authority, had said nothing about getting rid of Nhu. General Nguyen Khanh, the II Corps commander, raised for the first time a new possibility: that Diem and Nhu might make a deal with Hanoi, or even Peking, rather than submit to the Americans. *In that case,* he said, the generals would overthrow the government, but otherwise they counted on the United States to take unspecified steps to clear up the political situation.[58]

Lodge now emerged suddenly as the most critical player in the drama. Born in 1902, in a gray area between the Lost and GI generations, Lodge, like Harriman, utterly lacked the devotion to team play so characteristic of the younger generation. He had enraged the managers of his 1960 vice presidential campaign by insisting upon his daily afternoon nap, and he was about to become the despair of his younger superiors in Washington by insisting upon defining and executing his own policy. Despite his equivocal intelligence, Lodge decided on August 25 to give up on Diem almost completely. Replying to the August 24 cable, he stated his belief that the "chances of Diem's meeting our demands are virtually nil." By making them, the United States would give Nhu an opportunity to take more preemptive action. He therefore proposed that the United States directly approach the generals and tell them that while the United States would be "prepared" to keep Diem without Nhu, they should make the decision, provided that they released the Buddhists and carried out the June 16 agreement. When Hilsman, Harriman, and Ball received this telegram, they immediately agreed to his proposed modification. Forrestal passed Lodge's reply on to Kennedy in Hyannis Port, but it is not clear that the Pentagon ever heard about this exchange at all.[59]

McNamara returned to his office on Monday morning, August 26. Learning of the August 24 cable, he shared his displeasure with Taylor, with Robert Kennedy, and then, apparently, with the President. According to Forrestal's later recollection, Kennedy became angry at him when he learned that the telegram had *not* been cleared by all responsible authorities, and Forrestal offered his resignation, which the President promptly rejected. As McGeorge Bundy recalled many years later, Kennedy was particularly upset because the ultimate responsibility was in fact his own.[60] The White House convened an emergency meeting of the senior national security team at noon on Monday. For the first time in nearly two years, Vietnam was receiving the concentrated attention of the highest levels of the Kennedy administration.

The Monday, August 26, meeting was the first of a series of daily meetings that lasted through Saturday, August 31. By Monday the new crisis over Vietnam was showing some unpleasant similarities to the worst debacle of the Kennedy presidency, the Bay of Pigs invasion more than two years earlier. Taylor and McNamara—two of the President's three most trusted advisers in national security affairs—believed that one part of the government had gone off half-cocked without proper consultation. As in April 1961, security seemed to have broken down, and the press was covering the sordid details of the crisis in excruciating detail. Worst of all, on the morning of August 26 Saigon time, a

Voice of America broadcast stated not only that Nhu's secret police, rather than the army, had carried out the raids upon the pagodas without the knowledge of the military, but that the United States might cut its aid to Vietnam if the officials responsible were not removed from office.[61]

The new crisis, moreover, had broken out just as the administration's most important initiatives in foreign and domestic affairs were coming to a head. The Senate Foreign Relations Committee was just concluding lengthy hearings on the limited test ban treaty, to which the Joint Chiefs, with considerable encouragement from General Taylor, had given their reluctant assent. Ratification still depended on substantial Republican support, and the administration was not sure it would be forthcoming. On Friday the House had cut $585 million from the administration's foreign aid request, a substantial portion of the total. Meanwhile, the administration's civil rights bill was moving slowly through the House of Representatives, and over 100,000 black and white Americans were preparing to assemble before the Lincoln Memorial on the following Wednesday to ask for its passage. With the election a little more than a year away, Kennedy needed more than ever to maintain an image of calm control of events.

The meetings that took place all week included nearly the entire senior national security team and several Vietnam specialists: Rusk, Ball, Harriman, and Hilsman from State; McGeorge Bundy and Forrestal from the White House; McNamara, Taylor, Gilpatric, and Krulak from the Pentagon; and General Marshall Carter and Richard Helms from the CIA. Kennedy always prided himself on running a smooth ship and conducting business courteously, and the issue of the clearance of the August 24 telegram never directly came up during these meetings. It emerged during the week, however, that McNamara and Taylor wanted to stop the coup, and that the President at the very least feared that the U.S. government was launched on a premature operation. At the beginning of the very first meeting Kennedy commented rather angrily and insightfully that Halberstam's reporting must not unduly influence American actions, and asked for assurances that it would not. Hilsman and Harriman tried to reassure him, but Harriman in effect conceded the truth of the accusation by saying that Saturday's cable had gone out as soon as the effect of the pagoda raids had become known.[62]

During the first two days of meetings McNamara and Taylor

avoided a frontal attack upon the August 24 cable, but argued that the coup was unlikely to succeed. Beginning on Tuesday, August 27, they relied heavily on Nolting, whose presence McNamara had arranged.[63] Ignoring Hilsman and Harriman's views, the ambassador defended Diem and American reliance upon him in the strongest terms, arguing that the generals lacked the courage or the means to overthrow him. This eventually drew a very angry retort from Harriman, who on Wednesday morning stated bluntly that he had always thought Nolting's approach to Diem was wrong. But Nolting's remarks bolstered Taylor and McNamara, and both the Monday and Tuesday meetings of the ExCom—the Executive Committee of the National Security Council, as it had become known the previous October during the missile crisis—decided, with the President's encouragement, to query Lodge and Harkins regarding the feasibility of the coup.

Kennedy on Tuesday also asked about the effect of the political crisis on the war in the countryside. Krulak replied that government operations had declined, but not greatly, and that "Viet Cong operations are continuing at the low level to which they had dropped after the Geneva accords offensive [in May]." One cannot tell exactly how Krulak had reached this conclusion or who had given him his information, but it was not true, since the Viet Cong had actually increased their activity to a new 1963 high for three weeks during July.[64] Had Kennedy been correctly informed about the deterioration of the military situation, his response might have been different, and the Pentagon's failure to pass along its own statistics was an important element in the crisis.

Washington also did not yet understand that the events of August 20 and Lodge's arrival had transformed the situation in Saigon. Years of American frustration were pouring out, and virtually the entire mission had concluded that Nhu—and therefore Diem—presented a hopeless obstacle to the success of American policy. Thus, Harkins, who had been following Admiral Felt's lead in support of the coup since Saturday, immediately cabled a relatively optimistic assessment of the strength of the opposition forces, and Lodge reported on Wednesday, Saigon time, that both he and Harkins still favored a coup.[65] Even the Saigon CIA station chief, John Richardson, jumped on the coup bandwagon on the same day, saying that he believed the generals were prepared to act and had a good chance to win. "If the Ngo family wins now," Richardson reported, "they and Vietnam will stagger on to final defeat at the hands of their own people and the VC." While the generals needed to carry out the coup without obvious American assistance, he continued, "we all understand that the effort must succeed and that whatever needs to be done on our part must be done."[66]

McNamara and Taylor, however, did not give up. On the morning of Wednesday, August 28, Taylor arrived at the Pentagon and apparently found a message from Harkins explaining that Admiral Felt had volunteered his support for the August 24 cable, and that Harkins was supporting Lodge for this reason.[67] Taylor replied with a personal message to Harkins asking for his comments on the planned coup and inviting him to register a belated dissent. "For your information," the telegram concluded, "State to Saigon 243 [the August 24 cable] was prepared without DOD or JCS participation. Authorities are now having second thoughts."[68]

When the ExCom convened again at noon on Wednesday, tens of thousands of black and white Americans were gathered before the Lincoln Memorial listening to a series of speakers, capped by Dr. Martin Luther King Jr., supporting the President's civil rights bill. At the meeting McNamara once again expressed doubts about the success of the coup, and the President commented that although Lodge and Harkins backed "the enterprise," Washington did *not* yet have to decide to go ahead. Eventually, Kennedy asked that Lodge and Harkins be asked their opinion of the generals' chances yet again. In the midst of the discussion Kennedy revealingly asked about exile for Diem and Nhu, "stating that nothing should be permitted to happen to them." Then he adjourned the meeting until 6:00 P.M.

Harkins's reply to Taylor, which arrived at about 2:30 in the afternoon, took Taylor's hint. He expressed doubts about the necessity of removing Diem, but made clear that he agreed that the Nhus had to leave South Vietnam, and suggested that Diem might be given a chance to agree, while doubting, based on past experience, that he would. "The Vietnamese people can't live with [the Nhus], the military can't live with them, and neither can we," he wrote, adding the hopes that there would be little or no bloodshed and that the war would proceed.[69]

At 5:16 P.M. McGeorge Bundy called Rusk to ask him to attend the 6:00 meeting. He was worried by "a real possible split between State and DOD," and he wanted Rusk, not the passionate Harriman, to represent State. He also confided that McNamara and Taylor had not yet indicated the extent of their displeasure over the August 24 cable. The President, Bundy continued, wanted to begin by meeting with Rusk, McNamara, Taylor, and himself, "with B[undy] as notetaker to get a slightly common front on this." This was a technique that Kennedy had used before, most notably, as we have seen, at the height of the Cuban missile crisis.[70] To date, no record of the five principals' meeting has emerged,[71] but McNamara apparently persuaded the President to temporize once again. When the principals emerged, Kennedy announced that three more messages would go out—one each to Lodge and Harkins personally, and one to them both. "We were in doubt about General Harkins' views," he said. "We thought he was for the coup plan, but General Harkins apparently thought that a decision had been made in Washington to back a coup and that his task was to carry out a decision communicated to him." Actually, given Harkins's reply to Taylor, which had arrived during the afternoon, this was no longer the case. Harriman, the oldest and perhaps the toughest bureaucratic fighter of them all, knew he had been outflanked, but couldn't resist a parting shot. "Mr. President," he said as he left, "I was very puzzled by the cable from General Harkins until I read the outgoing from General Taylor." Kennedy controlled himself with difficulty until the room was almost empty, burst out laughing, and remarked, "Averell Harriman is one sharp cookie."[72]

The telegrams showed that McNamara and Taylor were back in charge. The first one for Lodge—drafted at the White House—basically adopted Harkins's proposed objectives and strategy. While noting Lodge's support for the coup, it suggested redefining U.S. objectives. Calling the removal of the Nhus "the center of the problem," it asked Lodge to comment on the wisdom of "one last man-to-man effort" to persuade Diem to eliminate their political influence.[73]

Lodge, who had suddenly emerged as McNamara's real rival, did not budge an inch in his reply the next day:

We are launched on a course from which there is no respectable turning back: The overthrow of the Diem government. There is no turning back in part because U.S. prestige is already publicly committed to this end in large measure and will become more so as facts leak out. In a more fundamental sense, there is no turning back because there is no possibility, in my view, that the war can be won under a Diem administration, still less that Diem or any member of his family can govern the country in a way to gain the support of the people who count, i.e., the educated class in and out of government service, civil and military—not to mention the American people.

Continuing, Lodge rejected Harkins's suggestion for a last meeting with Diem regarding Nhu, arguing that it would simply tip the American hand and invite delay, but reported that Harkins concurred with the rest of the telegram. Harkins himself, in an unusually impressive telegram, argued simply that the United States should continue to support the generals—perhaps through him—but should give Diem an ultimatum regarding the Nhus at an appropriate moment, mainly in an attempt to avoid bloodshed. He acknowledged that Diem might well refuse.[74]

But while the ambassador was determined to try to overthrow Diem, he had to cope with the flaw in the August 24 cable: its assumption that a large group of generals felt betrayed by Nhu and was ready to stage a coup. In Saigon, events during this frantic week told a contradictory story. General Khiem on Tuesday told CIA operative Conein that the coup would take place within a week, but added that General Dinh, the III Corps commander and martial law governor of Saigon, and IV Corps commander General Cao had to be "neutralized"—surely a tall order. But II Corps commander General Nguyen Khanh temporized. Meanwhile, Diem and Nhu counterattacked during the week, declaring repeatedly that the generals had approved the pagoda raids and meeting with a government-sponsored Buddhist organization in an effort to put the Buddhist crisis behind them once and for all. On Thursday General Dinh declared publicly that he had commanded "overall operations" during the pagoda raids. Nhu also reportedly told a meeting of generals that the United States was moving toward a policy of appeasement of the Soviet Union and other Communist countries, as shown by the Test Ban Treaty, and might reduce military and economic aid. South Vietnam, he said, could if necessary stand alone "because of the tremendous success of the strategic hamlet program."[75]

Lodge himself had met with Diem only once since his arrival, but on Thursday, August 28, Diem had received Paul Kattenburg, a Foreign Service officer from Hilsman's Far Eastern Bureau who had served in Vietnam and known Diem since 1953. Like Mike Mansfield, Kattenburg noticed a deterioration in Diem's emotional state. "The impression of growing neurosis cannot be escaped," he wrote. "It was as if words themselves had magic which made them believable as they came out and he then echoed and re-echoed them further." Diem blamed the Buddhist agitation completely on the Communists, an allegation for which the CIA had never found any evidence and which Kattenburg found Diem unable to substantiate. Actually, a recent CIA cable had reported that Hanoi feared that the Buddhist crisis would lead to Diem's fall and his replacement by a more popular government. Attacking the American press and American broadcasts, he defended Nhu, Archbishop Thuc, and Colonel Tung in the strongest terms, expressing the wish that the Americans could provide him with another man like Nhu.[76] For a decade Kattenburg had watched Diem steadily losing ground in his struggle to organize non-Communist Vietnamese against the Viet Cong, and he now understood that Diem's support had reached the vanishing point. He boarded a plane the next morning to return to Washington.

The pro-coup forces also went on a public relations offensive in both Saigon and Washington. All week long, the *New York Times* reporter Tad Szulc wrote that the U.S. government had decided that Nhu, at least, had to go, and that "the United States has almost openly been advocating a military coup d'état in Saigon." Halberstam speculated not only about a coup but about the specific roles of various generals.[77] Kennedy called Hilsman on August 29 after reading Szulc's story, and made clear that he did not want such stories to appear. He accepted Hilsman's assurances that no one was talking to Szulc.[78] Such was the team spirit of the administration that the daily ExCom meetings remained a secret.

Despite Lodge's obstinacy, the ExCom on August 29 sent yet another telegram to Lodge asking about the wisdom of an attempt to separate Diem and Nhu, along with an authorization for Harkins to tell the generals that the United States favored the coup. Bundy also reported that CIA Director McCone favored one more try to convince Nhu to remove himself, perhaps with the help of William Colby. Kennedy at one point asked whether the United States could actually threaten to abandon Vietnam in an approach to Diem, and received no reply. Kennedy then left for a four-day Labor Day weekend at Hyannis Port, but Bundy prepared another telegram under the President's signature, showing it only to McNamara and Rusk. Showing the clear influence of the Bay of Pigs, it informed Lodge that until the very moment the coup began, "I must reserve a contingent right to change course and reverse previous instructions . . . I know from experience that failure is more destructive than an appearance of indecision." Lodge replied the next day that while he respected the President's right, in the event the generals might well unleash the operation on their own.[79]

On the same day, August 29, a new international element further complicated the situation. President Charles de Gaulle of France issued a statement expressing France's willingness to help "Vietnam as a whole" play a greater Asian role "once they could go ahead with their activities independently of the outside, in internal peace and unity and in harmony with their neighbors . . . Naturally it is up to this people, and to them alone, to choose the means of achieving it, but any national effort that would be carried out in Vietnam would find France ready, to the extent of her own possibilities, to establish cordial cooperation with this country."[80] The neutralization of South and North Vietnam had not been discussed within the executive branch for more than a year, although Senator Mansfield had suggested it to Kennedy once again in a carefully argued memo on August 19.[81] In Saigon the French ambassador, Roger Lalouette, was already proposing such a plan, with some help from Mieczyslaw Maneli, the Polish delegate to the ICC.[82]

On Friday, August 30, the *Times* made Roger Hilsman the Man in the News, but evidence came in throughout the day suggesting that Nhu was outmaneuvering the U.S. government and the dissident generals once again. The CIA reported reliable rumors that Nhu would begin arresting dissident generals within twenty-four hours. Lodge's reply to the ExCom's last telegram agreed that removing the Nhus was the prime objective, but added, "This certainly cannot be done by working through Diem . . . He wishes he had more Nhus, not less." Thus, Lodge opposed any new approach to Diem, but added that the mission faced disturbing "inertia" among the generals: "The days come and go and nothing happens." Then, also on August 30, General Khiem declined to meet his CIA contact on the grounds that he was "too busy," and went to the palace instead. According to a report that reached Washington several days later, Nhu told a large group of generals that while the CIA was trying to overthrow him, he could manage Ambassador Lodge, who would come to agree fully with his concepts and actions.[83]

By the time the ExCom met at noon on August 30—without Harriman, Kennedy, or Robert Kennedy—McNamara and the CIA had prepared a counteroffensive. McNamara and Richard Helms seized upon a CIA report of a conversation with the infamous Colonel Pham Ngoc Thao—an inveterate coup plotter and suspected VC agent—to argue that a coup would fail, and Helms said that Nhu was close to reestablishing control.[84] A well-prepared General Carter, the CIA Deputy Director, then suggested that the silence of Madame Nhu, the statements by government-inspired Buddhist organizations, and the release of student demonstrators indicated that Nhu was trying to return the situation to normal. Despite Richardson's cable of only two days before, the leadership of the agency apparently wanted to reestablish its nine-year-old relationship with Nhu. McNamara and Rusk both cited the mounting evidence that the generals did not seem to have a plan, and Rusk even suggested that "maybe the thing to do was to get the generals back to fighting the war." No decisions were taken.

While official Washington slept, Harkins met with General Khiem on the morning of Saturday, August 31, Saigon time. Khiem immediately announced that Big Minh was the key figure, but that Minh had stopped planning. Nhu had in fact called the generals in on August 30 and told them that he accepted everything the United States wanted and had secured the backing of President Kennedy. Harkins said that was news to him. Khiem added that the Nhus were so friendly with CIA Station Chief Richardson that the general wondered whether they were on the CIA payroll. With remarkable naïveté, Harkins in his telegram reporting this conversation inserted here the comment "a new angle indeed." Nhu and many of his organizations had indeed received direct financial support from the CIA for many years. Harkins explained that under the circumstances he declined to give Khiem assurances of U.S. support, but offered to talk to Big Minh. Harkins also asked whether anyone might tell the Nhus that their absence from the scene would solve the problem, and Khiem, with black humor, replied that this would constitute "self-immolation." General Don now planned to propose the inclusion of generals in the cabinet. Lodge telegraphed his own conclusion that "this particular coup is finished."[85]

No senior American understood what had happened. As Rusk had said the day before, they all believed that the crisis had begun a week earlier, when the generals had informed the United States that they wanted to move against the government. But the biggest flaw in the August 24 cable was precisely its assumption that the generals all felt double-crossed by the pagoda raids and wanted to go ahead—something reported by David Halberstam, but not by the Embassy. Coup planning had apparently started *after* August 24, and was far from finished now. On the very same Saturday afternoon Rufus Phillips saw another General, Le Van Kim, in Saigon, and Kim accused Khiem of having misled Harkins. Later, after seeing Minh, Kim also told Conein that Minh hadn't known about Harkins's meeting with Khiem. Minh explained that Nhu had too many forces at his disposal, thanks largely to U.S. aid, and that the generals thought that the United States still supported him.[86]

When the ExCom met at 11:00 on August 31 with the Vice President in attendance, Rusk was ready to resume American collaboration with Diem and Nhu. He began by suggesting that they focus on the specific, harmful things that Diem and Nhu had *done*, not on them as individuals—a line which McNamara soon adopted as well. He quickly proposed that Lodge discuss new measures regarding Buddhists, students, military reforms, the role of American advisers, Madame Nhu's status, relations with Cambodia, and, in short, "a total program to achieve what the Nhus were undercutting." McNamara agreed, and suggested that Lodge and Harkins should immediately get back in touch with Diem. Rusk also asked if anyone doubted that the coup was off. Paul Kattenburg, who had left Saigon only two days earlier, replied that he did, and boldly criticized Harkins for failing to assure Khiem of American support, since the generals needed further reassurances. Rusk and McNamara promptly defended Harkins to the hilt.

Hilsman now tried to lay out the problems Diem was causing. He began by mentioning disaffection among officers, noncommissioned officers, and bureaucrats, and McNamara and Taylor immediately interrupted to say they knew of no evidence of this and would like to see any. Kattenburg backed Hilsman up, arguing that middle-level officers and bureaucrats were "uniformly critical of the government." Then Hilsman noted that Nhu might continue his reported flirtation with the French and with Hanoi and try once again to reduce the American advisory presence, and mentioned the problem of U.S. and world public opinion. He suggested that Lodge might tell Diem we were suspending aid to secure certain changes, and Rusk responded hopefully, suggesting we might now get South Vietnam to cooperate further. Rusk added that he did not think that disaffection with the Saigon government had spread beyond Saigon—an almost unbelievable statement, given the protests in Hue, Da Nang, and elsewhere. USIA Director Edward R. Murrow said that world opinion had definitely turned against us, but McNamara said "we must work out a way of continuing to help the GVN against the Viet Cong."

Since 1954 various Americans had cherished the hope that they might get Diem and Nhu to take their advice. Most of those directly involved now understood that this was impossible. Nineteen months before, Colonel J. R. Kent of the Pentagon had suggested perceptively that a long series of events had convinced Diem that he was always right and the Americans were generally wrong.[87] Rusk and McNamara were ready for another try. Paul Kattenburg, who had watched the Diem-U.S. relationship for ten years and listened to a classic Diem monologue three days earlier, could not contain himself. He conveyed a message which Lodge had specifically asked him to deliver:

> Mr Kattenburg stated that as recently as last Thursday it was the belief of Ambassador Lodge that, if we undertake to live with this repressive regime, with its bayonets at every street corner and its transparent negotiations with puppet bonzes, we are going to be thrown out of the country in six months. He stated that at this juncture it would be better for us to make the decision to get out honorably. He went on to say that, having been acquainted with Diem for ten years, he was deeply disappointed in him, saying that he will not separate from his brother. It was Kattenburg's view that Diem will get very little support from the military and, as time goes on, he will get less and less support and the country will go steadily down hill.[88]

Taylor asked Kattenburg to explain what he meant, and Kattenburg predicted that within six months to a year, "as the people see we are losing the war," they would go to the other side and ask us to leave. Nolting immediately disagreed, arguing that discontent with Diem was confined "to the city, and while city support of Diem is doubtless less now, it is not greatly so." (This in a sense was true, since city support had fallen near the vanishing point by the time Nolting arrived in Saigon.) Nolting insisted that "we have done a tremendous job towards winning the war, working with this same imperfect, annoying government." Rusk declared Kattenburg's view to be "largely speculative," and suggested that the meeting "start on the firm basis of two things: that we will not pull out of Vietnam until the war is won, and that we will not run a coup." McNamara agreed. Rusk, continuing, said he believed "that we have good proof that we have been winning the war, particularly the contrast between the first six months of 1962 and 1963." Just how long Washington could continue ignoring what had happened in July and August remained an open question. Vice President Johnson then weighed in as well, rejecting either a pull-out or a coup, and expressing complete agreement with Rusk, McNamara, and Nolting.

More than fifteen years later, in an interview with William Gibbons, Kattenburg recalled the incident:

> I listened for about an hour or an hour and a half to this conversation . . . and they looked to me absolutely hopeless, the whole group of them. There was not a single person there that knew what he was talking about. It simply looked, to me, that way. They were all great men. It was appalling to watch. I didn't have the feeling that any of them . . . really knew . . . They didn't know Vietnam. They didn't know the past. They had forgotten the history. They simply didn't understand the identification of nationalism and Communism, and the more this meeting went on, the more I sat there and I thought, "God, we're walking into a major disaster."[89]

Kattenburg's Foreign Service career never recovered from his rash intervention, but one other administration official—the President—also rejected returning to business as usual. On Labor Day, September 2, Kennedy gave an interview to Walter Cronkite for the first half-hour broadcast of *CBS News*. In preparation for it, Bundy drafted a statement on Vietnam that stressed Washington's agreement with Saigon on many points, disapproved of recent repressive actions, but concluded, "Our support for the people of South Vietnam against the Communist aggressors will continue as long as it is wanted and can be effective."[90]

Vietnam was still far from the leading story of the day, and Kennedy first took questions on civil rights, his opinion as to his possible Republican opponent, unemployment, and the ratification of the test ban. Then, in calm and carefully chosen language that differed significantly from Bundy's draft, the President answered a series of questions on Vietnam:

MR. CRONKITE: Mr. President, the only hot war we've got running at the moment is of course the one in Vietnam, and we have our difficulties there, quite obviously.

THE PRESIDENT: I don't think that unless a greater effort is made by the government to win popular support that the war can be won out there. In the final analysis, it is their war. They are the ones who have to win it or lose it. We can help them, we can give them equipment, we can send our men out there as advisers, but they have to win it, the people of Vietnam, against the Communists.

We are prepared to continue to assist them, but I don't think that the war can be won unless the people support the effort and, in my opinion, in the last two months, the government has gotten out of touch with the people.

The repressions against the Buddhists, we felt, were very unwise. Now all we can do is to make it very clear that we don't think this is the way to win. It is my hope that this will become increasingly obvious to the government, that they will take steps to try to bring back popular support for this very essential struggle.

MR. CRONKITE: Do you think this government still has time to regain the support of the people?

THE PRESIDENT: I do. With changes in policy *and perhaps in personnel* I think it can. If it doesn't make those changes, I would think that the chances of winning it would not be very good.

MR. CRONKITE: Hasn't every indication from Saigon been that President Diem has no intention of changing his pattern?

THE PRESIDENT: If he does not change it, of course, that is his decision. He has been there ten years and, as I say, he has carried this burden when he has been counted out on a number of occasions.

Our best judgment is that he can't be successful on this basis. We hope that he comes to see that, but in the final analysis it is the people and the government itself who have to win or lose this struggle. All we can do is help, and we are making it very clear, but I don't agree with those who say we should withdraw. That would be a grave mistake. I know people don't like Americans to be engaged in this kind of an effort. Forty-seven Americans have been killed in combat with the enemy, but this is a very important struggle even though it is far away.

We took all this—made this effort to defend Europe. Now Europe is quite secure. We also have to participate—we may not like it—in the defense of Asia.

This was the longest statement on South Vietnam that Kennedy had ever made to the American people during his presidency, and it once again showed a significant difference between the President and his senior advisers. Kennedy had concluded himself that Diem could not win the war on his present course, and he had virtually stated that if he could not, the United States would not be able to prevent a Communist victory. He also commented calmly and courteously on de Gaulle's statement, suggesting that America would appreciate more help in meeting its burdens, but adding that de Gaulle was not an enemy, but "our friend and candid friend."[91]

Kennedy had publicly placed the same restrictions upon the American commitment to South Vietnam that he had insisted upon within the government two years earlier, in 1961. The United States would furnish only assistance, and, implicitly, would *not* regard South Vietnam as a vital American interest—as Rusk, McNamara, and Bundy had asked him to do in 1961—and would live with the outcome if South Vietnam eventually lost the war. His statement also defined a short-term policy: that Diem had to make changes in policy, and "perhaps" in personnel—an obvious reference to the Nhus—in order to win the war. Having decided in December 1961 not to insist upon political change in South Vietnam, Washington now faced political problems that were worse than ever. For the next month the Kennedy administration struggled to resolve its internal differences, and to find a way to make its policy work without a coup.

9

The Coup
August–November 1963

★

To leaders of the GI generation like Rusk, McNamara, and Taylor, who had seen the United States defeat Germany and Japan, help rebuild Western Europe, stop Communism in Korea, establish NATO, create an economy of unparalleled abundance, and send men into orbit around the earth, the Vietnam War remained a relatively minor problem that required no more than persistence upon a sound course. On Tuesday, September 3—the day after Labor Day—McNamara formally approved CINCPAC's plan for a 1,000-man withdrawal by the end of the year.[1] Two more meetings of the ExCom on September 3 and September 6 agreed once again that Lodge should see Diem and try to convince him to release students and Buddhist bonzes, end press censorship, restore damaged pagodas, repeal Decree Law 10, negotiate with the Buddhists, and, possibly, encourage the Nhus to leave the country. Meanwhile, Taylor at the second meeting mentioned that three weeks earlier the Joint Chiefs had believed that they could win the war with Diem, and asked whether that judgment remained valid. McNamara eventually suggested that General Krulak make a whirlwind visit to Saigon to assess the military situation, and later that day Washington informed Lodge that both Krulak and Joseph Mendenhall, who had left the Saigon Embassy the previous year, would visit for the weekend to survey South Vietnamese attitudes. On another front, Hilsman on September 5 met with a subcommittee of the Senate Foreign Relations Committee and encountered widespread skepticism not only about Diem and Nhu but about the whole American effort in Vietnam.[2]

Back in Saigon, the Labor Day edition of the Nhus' English-language paper, the *Times of Vietnam,* ran a huge headline accusing the Americans of plotting a coup, and Lodge saw Nhu together with two Italians, Monsignore Salvatore Asta, the apostolic delegate to South Vietnam, and Giovanni d'Orlandi, the Italian Minister, later that day.[3] Having mended his fences with the generals, Nhu now told Lodge that he wanted to lift martial law, quit government service, and move to the resort town of Dalat *after* "certain U.S. agents who . . . are still promoting a coup d'état have left." In one welcome concession, he indicated that Madame Nhu would leave the country in about two weeks to attend a meeting of the Interparliamentary Union in Belgrade. He denied any interest in de Gaulle's or Ho Chi Minh's proposals for neutralization, but argued that several Viet Cong units wanted to surrender to him—a hint, perhaps, that a deal remained possible. Lodge, however, still rejected his instructions to see Diem to ask for new policies. Nhu and Diem, he argued, had decided to solve their problems without reference to American advice, and he had less chance than ever of exerting American influence.[4] Events quickly proved him right. Nhu erupted on September 6 when Asta and d'Orlandi conveyed Lodge's warning of a congressional aid cut-off and his advice to leave the country for six months. Declaring "I'm the winning horse—they should bet on me," he refused to leave but repeated that Madame Nhu would do so within a few days.[5]

Lodge finally gave in to Washington and met with Diem on Monday, September 9, threatening him with both a congressional aid cut-off and a U.N. resolution by other Buddhist countries condemning his government. When Lodge suggested that Nhu leave the country at least until December to allow the foreign aid appropriation to pass, an aghast Diem replied, "it would be out of the question for him to go away when he could do so much for the Strategic Hamlets." Continuing, Diem pronounced the Buddhist crisis solved, denied that censorship existed, said that the student demonstrations were Communist-inspired and showed that the Communists had abandoned the countryside because of the success of the strategic hamlet program, and told Lodge it was Lodge's job to "disintoxicate" American public opinion. Lodge concluded that Diem did not seem really interested in what he had to say and was "totally absorbed with his own problems here and was justifying himself and attacking his enemies."[6] Thuan, who now feared for his own life, told Rufus Phillips and William Trueheart that Nhu effectively controlled the country and might dispense with American help altogether, and clearly asked the United States to initiate a change of government.[7] Madame Nhu, however, did leave Saigon to attend the Interparliamentary Union meeting in Belgrade.

The CIA, meanwhile, was firmly back in Nhu's camp. On the same day that Lodge met Diem, September 9, an unsigned *New York Times* story with a Manila dateline reported that in the preceding week the Saigon CIA station chief had disbursed a regular monthly payment of $250,000 to Colonel Tung's special forces over his subordinates' objections, declaring, "Gentlemen, it's business as usual." The next morning the station cabled Washington reporting that Diem had successfully dealt with the Buddhists and the generals, and that the war could now resume successfully "in military and civil sectors." Also on September 9, President Kennedy appeared on the *Huntley-Brinkley Report* and took a more moderate line. While reiterating that the United States was trying to bring about changes, he denied any intention to cut aid and acknowledged a belief in the domino theory. "We should use our influence in as effective a way as we can, but we should not withdraw," he said. He declined to comment on CIA activities.[8]

The administration finally lost its GI composure on September 10, when Krulak and Mendenhall reported to the ExCom about their weekend trip to Vietnam, together with John Mecklin, the Embassy public affairs officer, and Rufus Phillips, the AID official responsible for strategic hamlets. Krulak's terms of reference had clearly been carefully designed to produce a report endorsing the thrust of American policy and undermining the case for a coup. As early as July 19 the senior adviser of I Corps had warned MACV that Diem was losing support as a result of the Buddhist crisis, and two other advisers noted the impact of the crisis on the war effort on September 9 and September 11.[9] But Krulak now argued that the war was going ahead "at an impressive pace," that the impact of the political crisis was "not great," and that "excluding the very serious political and military factors external to Vietnam, the Viet Cong war will be won if the current U.S. military and sociological programs are pursued, irrespective of the grave defects of the ruling regime." No one picked up the veiled reference to external factors, which military authorities had raised several times during the year. Krulak did not even report Harkins's view that

South Vietnam could "survive—and flourish—with [the Nhus] gone and Diem still there."[10]

Joseph Mendenhall, the former Saigon Deputy Chief of Mission who had long believed that Diem could not survive, then gave his report. Civil government had broken down in Saigon; among the people the war against the government had taken precedence over the war against the Viet Cong; the Viet Cong were making gains in the rural northern provinces, where Buddhist agitation had spread; and the war "could not be won if Nhu remains in Vietnam."[11]

"The two of you did visit the same country, didn't you?" asked the President.

Trying to discredit his former Deputy Chief of Mission, Nolting immediately pointed out that Mendenhall had believed in 1961 that Diem could not survive, and suggested that "progress" since then invalidated his opinion. Before Mendenhall could reply, Kennedy repeated his question. After a long silence, Krulak ventured that Mendenhall had given a "metropolitan report" while he himself had given a "national report," and drew a dirty look from Taylor, his boss. McGeorge Bundy then weighed in on Mendenhall's side against Nolting, arguing that now it was the government, rather than the Viet Cong, that was causing the trouble.

A young, idealistic, and very brave Rufus Phillips now took the floor. Noting his own long acquaintance with Vietnam and his familiarity with the countryside through the strategic hamlet program, he said that Nhu had lost the confidence and respect of officers and civil servants, and that the South Vietnamese wanted the Americans to force a change in government with deeds, not words. The South Vietnamese, he said, would like to see Diem remain but unalterably opposed Nhu, and he stated his own belief that "we cannot win the war if the Nhus remain"—a belief shared by Thuan, Colonel Lac of the strategic hamlet program, and many others. As Phillips spoke, McNamara repeatedly shook his head, while Kennedy took notes. Phillips then asked specifically that his mentor Lansdale return to Vietnam to organize a campaign to isolate the Nhus and eventually eliminate them from the government. If necessary, he said, the United States could carry on the strategic hamlet program in the provinces alone.

Nearly two years before, McNamara had confidently assumed authority over the war in Vietnam, and had immediately begun claiming that the United States was on the right track. Krulak, the Pentagon's point man for this meeting, now tried again, repeating the American officers' judgment that the war was going well. Kennedy asked Phillips for comment, and Phillips endorsed the judgment that the war was going well in the first three corps areas—certainly an optimistic statement—but said that "it was emphatically not going well in the fourth corps, the Delta region," where the VC had overrun fifty strategic hamlets recently, including 60 percent of the hamlets in Long An province south of Saigon. Once again Krulak stuck to his guns, suggesting that Phillips was disagreeing with General Harkins, and that, on military matters, "he would take General Harkins' assessment." It was evidently at this point that Harriman, who had sat with Krulak on the Special Group for Counterinsurgency, said that Krulak had never been right during the two years that he had known him, and that he regretted to say that Krulak was nothing but a damn fool.[12]

John Mecklin then went even further, arguing that Diem had to go, since the Nhus were "only a symptom," and that the United States had to introduce its own forces to win the war. Rusk, apparently shaken, asked once again what had happened to change the judgment of several months previously that Diem had been winning the war. As the long meeting drew to a close, Kennedy tried to take charge, thanking the four reporters and asking for papers on specific aid cuts to influence the situation and for another meeting the next day. He also complained about repeated leaks of the views of different agencies, and asked that all present stop fighting their battles in the press and instruct Saigon authorities to do the same. Lastly, he discussed the possibility of using Senator Frank Church's proposed new resolution opposing aid to the current regime as a further lever.

The GI-generation leaders of the administration were not about to abandon their course because of the criticism of junior men from the field. At another meeting late that afternoon, without the President, McNamara, Taylor, and McCone recommended returning immediately to the pre–August 20 policy of support for Diem, with Harriman dissenting.[13] Taylor later suggested that the Buddhist and student demonstrations might be Communist inspired and in effect endorsed Diem's repression of them. And in another meeting the next day Rusk argued that American policy toward Chiang Kai-Shek, which he had defended as an author of the 1949 China White Paper, had been mistaken, and that the United States should not make the same error again. When Chiang was encountering "dissidence and opposition," Rusk said, "The U.S. had decided to terminate its support to China, stepped out of the Chinese picture, and the Communist Mao took over . . . we must not yield to the temptation of despairing of Diem and act in a way which would result in the Communists taking over Vietnam."[14] This was a remarkably ahistorical comment, since the United States had *not* in fact terminated support for Chiang, but now that Rusk was in charge himself he apparently refused to face the possibility that Vietnam in 1963, like China in 1949, might be beyond the power of the United States to control. He also suggested discounting what Vietnamese "tell their American friends," an obvious reference to Rufus Phillips, who did not attend this or any further meetings.

But while Rusk, McNamara, and Taylor might write off Phillips, Mendenhall, and Mecklin, Henry Cabot Lodge was another matter. In a cable that powerfully impressed Kennedy and Bundy, Lodge on September 11 not only argued that the political crisis was bound to affect the war but also questioned the assessments provided by junior American officers to generals. The ship of state, he said, was slowly sinking, and he suggested aid cuts to try to force Diem to dispense with Nhu.[15] Although McNamara told Bundy that neither he nor Taylor agreed with the thrust of the message, he added that he would bring the Defense Department into line if Kennedy decided to take Lodge's advice.[16]

And thus, at another ExCom meeting later on September 11, the President gently refused his senior advisers' recommendations to be content with renewed conversations between Lodge and Diem aimed at securing Nhu's departure, without any cuts in aid. Kennedy, who in the midst of the meeting read a new attack on himself by Madame Nhu that came in by wire service ticker, eventually suggested proceeding carefully on several tracks at once: developing plans for pressure upon Diem, writing a personal letter to Diem in an effort to start conversations between him and Lodge, planning the evacuation of American dependents, and promoting a nonbinding congressional resolution of disapproval as another means of pressure.[17] As it turned out, AID had already suspended talks on several aid projects and held up disbursement of funds for the Commodity Import Program, Saigon's main source of funds. The circumstances of this suspension have never been fully explained, but State informed Lodge on September 12 that it would continue.[18]

In a press conference on September 12 the President took humorous digs at his two main prospective campaign opponents, Governor Nelson Rockefeller and Senator Barry Goldwater, expressed opposition to long-range school busing to achieve racial balance, and pushed for ratification of the test ban. Then he took a new and balanced line toward the Diem government, making clear that he still believed it had to change:

> What helps to win the war, we support; what interferes with the war effort, we oppose. I have already made it clear that any action by either government which may handicap the winning of the war is inconsistent with our policy objectives. This is the test which I think every agency and official of the United States government must apply to all of our actions, and we shall be applying that test in various ways in the coming months, although I do not think it desirable to state all of our views at this time.
>
> . . . In some ways I think the Vietnamese people and ourselves agree: we want the war to be won, the Communists to be contained, and the Americans to go home.

Kennedy had put his finger on the critical issue: whether South Vietnamese–American agreement on objectives could also lead to agreement on strategy sufficient to continue an allied effort.[19]

Lodge, who immediately refused yet again to open talks with Diem until Diem had to ask him for something,[20] was now engaged in an all-out war with MACV and the Saigon CIA station. Harkins now argued that the war was being won, not lost, and, echoing Diem, characterized both the Buddhist and student movements as "well-organized, covertly led Communist trick[s]" undertaken in response to Communist military failure.[21] The ambassador and the general also argued over the significance conversations in which both Thuan and Big Minh expressed their despair over the situation, and the Embassy independently expressed the opinion that the political crisis was bound to affect the war effort.[22] Lodge on Friday September 13 also wrote Rusk confidentially, asking for the replacement of CIA Station Chief Richardson, whom he now regarded as a symbol of American support for Diem and Nhu, by Lansdale, who could supervise a change of government. McCone violently rejected this suggestion, offering to replace Richardson, but arguing that the agency had no confidence in Lansdale whatever, and complaining that "this whole thing was built up by him [Lansdale] through Rufus Phillips."[23] Halberstam reported serious disagreements among the American community on Sunday, September 15.[24] The State Department, at Kennedy's request, had asked Lodge to keep disagreements out of the papers, but Lodge regarded leaking as an ambassadorial prerogative.[25] Meanwhile, Madame Nhu's attacks on the United States made daily news, and Monday's papers reported that she planned to visit the United States.

By Monday, September 16, Hilsman had prepared drafts of two alternative cables for Lodge, one a "reconciliation track" and the other a "pressures and persuasion track," and a draft letter from Kennedy to Diem.[26] After two more days of ExCom meetings, a telegram drafted by Bundy gave Lodge authority to suspend American aid to use as he saw fit to try to bring about a long series of changes. These included a forthcoming attitude by Diem toward those who had opposed him, the release and toleration of Buddhist and student activists, "full latitude of expression" for the press, an end to police operations against the non-Communist opposition, cabinet changes, the surfacing of the Can Lao party, the repeal or amendment of Decree Law 10, and, if possible, the departure of both Nhus from Saigon or Vietnam. Lodge promptly commented that nearly every one of these suggestions would certainly strike Diem as politically suicidal, but Rusk and McNamara wanted a final try.[27]

The President, who had refused simply to decide between Lodge and Hilsman on one side and McNamara and Taylor on the other, still hoped to bridge the gap between them, and also to deal with growing doubts about the military situation. On September 16, Halberstam had once again reported that recent Viet Cong attacks showed that the strategic hamlet program was overextended in the Ca Mau peninsula and quoted an American that the government refused to correct the situation. Kennedy had immediately asked McNamara how accurate the story was.[28] Then, rather than bring Lodge home for consultation, Kennedy on September 17 asked McNamara and Taylor to visit Saigon themselves to survey the situation, both "in terms of actual progress of operations and of need to make effective case with Congress for continued prosecution of the effort."[29] Lodge complained that the mission would undermine American policy and later found it "inconceivable

. . . that direct questions asked on a whirlwind tour of the countryside can possibly elicit any new and deep insights into the situation," but he was overruled.[30]

McNamara totally backed the Pentagon/MACV line regarding the military situation. In a September 21 response to Halberstam's article, he claimed 9 million people *resettled* into strategic hamlets, including 4 million in the Delta. His memorandum claimed 60 hamlets in southern-most An Xuyen province, which Halberstam had cited as a VC-con-trolled enclave, and which Phillips's USOM Office of Rural Affairs had recently said "remains under Viet Cong control with the exception of a handful of widely separated government strong points . . . The Strategic Hamlet program has not succeeded." The same USOM report had also discussed serious problems all over the Delta, just as Halberstam had said.[31]

By the time the Taylor-McNamara mission left, it also included Har-riman's deputy William Sullivan from State; William Bundy, who had not been involved in the controversy, from the Pentagon; and Forrestal, representing the Harriman-Hilsman viewpoint; as well as McNamara, Taylor, William Colby, and Krulak. In a final meeting with Undersecre-tary of State Ball, McNamara, Taylor, and Bundy on September 23, Kennedy suggested that McNamara see Diem twice and "press the need for reform and change as a pragmatic necessity and not as a moral judgment." He clearly did not expect the mission simply to endorse the status quo. During the previous week the hard-liner columnist and presidential friend Joseph Alsop had reported from Saigon that Nhu was seriously pursuing negotiations for a cease-fire with the French, the Polish ICC representative, and, indirectly, Ho Chi Minh, and had ac-cused Nhu of losing touch with reality.[32] Hoping to head off Madame Nhu's visit to the United States, Kennedy mentioned her recent attacks on junior American officers. "As long as she had limited her criticism to the President," he said, "her opposition had not been serious but . . . an attack on subordinates of the Pentagon was obviously intolerable." When Taylor suggested that the mission might work out a timetable for finishing the job and tell Diem that we would only remain for so long, with so many forces, the President made no comment.[33]

Whether Nhu had actually opened any serious talks with the enemy seems unlikely. Maneli, the Polish ICC delegate, had been busily pro-moting the idea for months, but by his own account he admitted early in September that he could not tell if Nhu was serious, and Nhu told him—in the midst of a typically bizarre monologue in which Nhu professed to believe in the withering away of the state—that no talks had yet taken place. Maneli himself eventually concluded that Nhu was promoting such rumors to blackmail the United States—although he might eventually have decided to pursue this option under different circumstances.[34]

Kennedy apparently still hoped that Diem might see reason and make some changes.[35] No one within the official family had suggested that the war could not *somehow* be won—either with Diem and Nhu or without them—and only John Mecklin had proposed the introduction of American troops. Some voices outside the administration had called for a broader reevaluation of American policy, and Kennedy was still thinking about other long-term options. Back on August 19 Senator Mansfield had given Kennedy a confidential memorandum suggesting that Vietnam was, in fact, less important to the United States than to the Vietnamese, and that the United States should reserve the right to withdraw its assistance should the Saigon government prove incapable of making use of it.[36] De Gaulle, as we have seen, had specifically proposed the neutralization and eventual reunification of Vietnam on August 29, and the influential columnist Walter Lippmann had welcomed this proposal on September 3. Kennedy, on his own initiative, had referred to this proposal at an ExCom meeting on September 3, but had rejected it, arguing that "neutralization was not working in Laos."[37] The administration had managed to persuade Mansfield not to make a speech endorsing Lippmann's proposals. Similarly, Bundy on September 11 had reported that he had barely managed to dissuade James Reston from calling for an American withdrawal.[38]

Also in early September, Roger Hilsman had told the *Newsweek* correspondent Edward Weintal that the administration might eventually have to accept neutralization. "In private," Newsweek reported on September 23, "some policy makers conceded that the de Gaulle solution might be the only answer in the long run."[39]

Kennedy on September 23 also discussed neutralization with Souvanna Phouma, who had come to Washington from Paris and had publicly endorsed de Gaulle's proposals for Vietnam. Souvanna now explained that in his opinion a lasting solution to Laos's problems depended upon a settlement in Vietnam. North Vietnam, he said, did not want the Laotian government to extend its authority over the whole country because it wanted to continue moving men through Laos into South Vietnam. Kennedy replied equivocally:

> The President told the Prime Minister that the United States would consider the neutrality of Vietnam if conditions indicated this would be successful. However, the necessary ingredients seemed to be lacking, such as a personality who could lead a united Vietnamese people. Moreover, North Vietnam would dominate South Vietnam which would collapse and as a consequence the pressures on Laos and Cambodia would be intensified. General de Gaulle's proposals on Vietnam were fine, but for the future. The President did not see how they could be realized for the present.

South Vietnam could make progress only under a popular regime, Souvanna said, "and this was lacking under President Diem." In response to a question from Kennedy, Souvanna affirmed that fear of American involvement prevented the North Vietnamese from overrunning Laos, and Kennedy promised that the United States "would never accept Communist control of Laos."[40]

The President's Office Files at the Kennedy Library include a memorandum written in the late summer or early fall of 1963 that raises another interesting possibility. Entitled "Observations on Vietnam and Cuba," it suggested that the USSR and the United States were bogged down, respectively, in unprofitable Cuban and Vietnamese predicaments from which they would probably like to escape. It suggested enlisting de Gaulle's help to combine Soviet withdrawal from Cuba with American withdrawal from Vietnam, while working for the neutralization of Vietnam under French auspices. The memo, however, is unsigned and undated, and nothing is known about the reaction it provoked.[41]

Initially the Pentagon apparently regarded the McNamara-Taylor mission as an opportunity to reestablish control over policy. According to Michael Forrestal, Krulak drafted the military portion of the report before the mission left, and Arthur Sylvester, the Pentagon's Assistant Secretary for Public Affairs, leaked the story of Hilsman's role in the unauthorized August 24 cable to the press on the eve of the mission's departure. Hilsman, meanwhile, gave Forrestal a letter for Lodge, advising him to stick to his guns regarding the need for a new Saigon government and arguing that Washington would come around.[42]

In Saigon, however, Lodge arranged a dramatic series of meetings designed to shake McNamara's and Taylor's confidence in Diem. An American professor with extensive experience in Vietnam, P. J. Honey, told McNamara that neither Diem nor Nhu could continue without the other, and that he did not think Diem could win the war. Monsignore Asta, the Vatican's delegate, told McNamara that the regime was a police state based on torture, that the Viet Cong were far stronger than they appeared to be, that Nhu seriously intended to make a deal with the Communists and dispense with the Americans, and that the people no longer believed that the United States opposed Nhu. CIA Station Chief Richardson, reversing himself again, told McNamara to maintain the suspension of aid and that the United States had to force Diem to dispense with Nhu. Vice President Tho said the United States had to stop police state methods, told McNamara and Taylor that the people supported the Viet Cong because of the government, and added that there were no more than twenty or thirty well-defended strategic hamlets in the entire country. And when McNamara and Taylor saw Diem, he spent three hours defending himself along customary lines and refusing to recognize that the regime's actions had created any problems.[43] Lodge, meanwhile, asked for Richardson's recall, arguing that he symbolized long-standing American support for Nhu.

The report that the team cobbled together on the way home and submitted on October 3 reflected a complex, continuing bureaucratic struggle. Restating the official view that McNamara had promulgated six months earlier and that Harkins and Krulak had repeated ever since, it began, "The military campaign has made great progress and continues to progress," and referred initially to "the present favorable military trends." A table of military statistics also showed that VC activity from June through August was at least equal to activity twelve months earlier, but the table did *not* reveal that VC activity had jumped during those months from its lower levels of the first half of the year. Worse, the report disgracefully ignored four new Headway Reports for September that showed a dramatic deterioration in the military situation. The Viet Cong staged 109 armed attacks from August 28 through September 4; 95 from September 4 to September 11, including a new high of 23 in supposedly pacified I Corps; 137 attacks from September 11 to September 18, the highest total since April 1962; and 113 attacks from September 18 to September 25, including 20 more in I Corps and 15 in II Corps.[44] Instead, its careful use of statistics enabled the report to state, falsely, that the "great progress" of the last year and a half had continued "at a fairly steady rate in the past six months."

Attempts by some of the team to inject some realism into Pentagon estimates resulted in the following conclusion: "From a more strictly military standpoint, it should be noted that this overall progress is being achieved against a Viet Cong effort that has not yet been seriously reduced in the aggregate, and that is putting up a formidable fight notably in the Delta and key provinces near Saigon." The Pentagon was claiming "progress" even though the enemy had not lost strength. In truth, the VC had been growing stronger, and its activity was reaching new highs.

Continuing, the report repeated that the political crisis had not affected the military effort, endorsed the scheduled 1,000-man withdrawal, and estimated that the Viet Cong threat could be reduced to insignificance by the end of 1964—that is, within another year—except in the Delta, where all of 1965 might be necessary. Taylor on October 1 gave Diem a farewell letter in which he praised the strategic hamlet program and spoke of military advances, but cited the need for a much greater and more effective effort in the Delta, and for bringing many combat units up to authorized strength. He, too, suggested that the war might be finished in the first, second, and third corps by the end of 1964, and in the fourth by the end of 1965.[45]

The report's discussion of the political situation, however, suggested that Diem had to alter his methods to maintain popular support, and favored real pressures upon him. It discounted the possibility of an early coup, but suggested a covert effort under Lodge's authority to investigate possibilities for alternative leadership. The report concluded with three "Goldilocks" options: immediate reconciliation with Diem (too cold), the immediate promotion of a coup (too hot), or the continued suspension of the Commodity Import Program and an end to support for Colonel Tung's Special Forces while maintaining an air of disapproval (just right). It suggested tying the resumption of aid to agreement upon a timetable of military and political objectives.[46]

National Security Council and ExCom meetings discussed the report on October 2, 3, and 4, eventually approving new public statements and a new instruction for Lodge. Tapes of these meetings, released during 1997, show that the administration remained fundamentally optimistic, while unwilling simply to give up on pressuring Diem.[47]

Astonishingly, McNamara in the first meeting on October 2 referred to nearly all the major Silent-generation critics of the conduct of the war and discredited them one by one. Halberstam and Neil Sheehan, he said, were allowing an "idealistic philosophy" to color their stories. Bundy then mentioned that having read Halberstam's *Harvard Crimson* stories for two years, "I know what you've been up against." Kennedy, remarkably, asked about "this Colonel Vann"—now retired from the Army—and McNamara said Vann was basing his sweeping criticisms of the American effort on the situation in one Delta province. Taylor and McNamara also referred to a "high strung" Australian officer whose views Harkins had discounted. This was probably Serong.

McNamara made clear during the discussion that he did not intend to end the American advisory effort by mid-1965, but rather to withdraw the American combat and support troops, whose functions could be assumed by trained South Vietnamese. "We need a way to get out of Vietnam," he said, "and this is the way to do it." Taylor and McNamara said the strategic hamlet program was working, although they acknowledged a big problem in the Delta. Politically, McNamara indicated that he did not hope fundamentally to change Diem's methods, but rather to get him to do what he was doing "in a less visible way." While Kennedy showed some skepticism about the withdrawal date, he was pleased that both McNamara and Harriman accepted the report, which, Bundy remarked, would end the "civil war" within the government. Then, in a smaller meeting, Kennedy confirmed that Richardson should be replaced, but remarked that Lodge could not possibly have the man he wanted, that is, Lansdale.

A full NSC meeting later that afternoon formally agreed to the report. One change made by the President was apparently never discussed. Refusing—as in 1961—to characterize the security of South Vietnam as "vital to United States security," Kennedy had the statement altered to read, "The security of South Vietnam is a major interest of the United States as of other free nations"—a hint, perhaps, that the United States would not act unilaterally to preserve it, should the need arise.[48]

The administration's public statement specifically attributed to McNamara and Taylor the view that "the major part of the U.S. military task can be completed by the end of 1965" and 1,000 men could be withdrawn by the end of the year. During the mission's return trip Forrestal and William Sullivan had complained that this timetable was unrealistic, but Taylor had argued that the United States had to send a message to the South Vietnamese, and McNamara now insisted that such a declaration would have a good effect on those like Senate Foreign Relations Committee Chairman Fulbright, who were already arguing that the United States was bogged down in South Vietnam. McNamara had apparently told William Bundy that the statement simply had to include that declaration. The statement also called the South Vietnamese political situation "deeply serious" and warned that it might affect the war effort.[49]

The ExCom met again on October 5 to discuss the next steps in Saigon.[50] The leadership decided that Harkins should discuss proposed military changes with Diem immediately, but Rusk and McCone agreed that political changes were necessary as well. Showing extraordinary naïveté, the ExCom seemed actually to believe that Colonel Tung's Special Forces—Nhu's hand-picked security troops—might be put under the control of military authorities. Bundy, critically, raised the issue of American policy toward a possible coup, stating that while the United States did not want to be "in the coup business"—a point the President endorsed—suspension of aid would trigger some plotting, about which the United States would want to be informed. McCone opposed Lodge's involvement in such contacts, but Kennedy authorized contacts by "appropriate officials . . . under the Ambassador's guidance."

In another meeting later that day, McNamara went on the offensive. A cable from Lodge reporting new queries about the American attitude from Big Minh—relayed through Lucien Conein—had arrived, and McNamara argued, in effect, that Conein should return home. Everyone, he said, knew that Conein had been involved in the August coup effort, and "to continue this kind of activity just strikes me as absurd." The August 24 cable and related leaks, he said, were "disgraceful."

Taylor added that the United States was wasting its time with Big Minh, who had declined to reveal his plans in a meeting with Taylor in Saigon. But Kennedy remarked, critically, "As I understand it our position now is, if you do it, it's all right, if you don't do it, it's all right. We're not now going to him and asking him to do it."[51] Thus the meeting left the issue in Lodge's hands, and Bundy eventually told Lodge to get whatever information he could without approving any specific plans.[52]

Lodge's new instructions informed the ambassador that the suspension of the Commodity Import Program would continue, and that certain other aid projects would be delayed; that he should maintain his policy of "cool correctness" toward Diem in an effort to force Diem to start serious talks; that he should also suspend aid to Colonel Tung's forces. The instructions also specified that, when conversations began, they should concentrate on military improvements; on the familiar long list of demands regarding Buddhists, students, the broadening of the government, and the nature of the Diem regime; and on an end to attacks on the CIA and the United States in the *Times of Vietnam* and elsewhere. The cable carefully avoided specifying exactly what Diem had to do end the suspension, but argued that some reduction in the role of the Nhus would be necessary.[53]

A separate cable from Bundy to Lodge dealt with coups. It cut Harkins out of coup planning and made clear that the President, under certain circumstances, would look with favor upon a change in government:

> President today approved recommendation that no initiative should now be taken to give any active covert encouragement to a coup. There should, however, be urgent covert effort with closest security under broad guidance of Ambassador to identify and build contacts with possible alternative leadership as and when it appears . . . We repeat that this effort is not to be aimed at active promotion of coup but only at surveillance and readiness.[54]

Richardson, as per Lodge's request, was now recalled from Saigon and replaced by his deputy, David Smith. But the cable did not fully clarify the situation. While Lodge now felt authorized to deal with any generals who came forward with plans for a coup, the Pentagon and Harkins concluded that, since no alternative leadership existed, the

United States opposed a coup. And indeed, Bundy's cable made a small but significant change from the language of the McNamara-Taylor report, which had recommended that policy be "to seek urgently to identify and build contacts with an alternative leadership *if* and when it appears," and thus had suggested that no alternative leadership was as yet on the horizon.

The announcement that the United States planned largely to end its involvement in Vietnam by the end of 1965 led the *New York Times,* the *Washington Post,* and other newspapers on October 3, and commentators suggested that it was designed to take the issue out of electoral politics.[55] A few days later, on October 7, Madame Nhu arrived in the United States, where officials ignored her and she received generally negative coverage. McNamara and Taylor also received a rough going-over from several senators of all shades of opinion before the Foreign Relations Committee on October 8.[56] Yet they clearly took the new timetable entirely seriously, and Taylor on October 5 instructed Harkins to discuss with the South Vietnamese plans to finish the military campaign in I, II and III Corps by the end of 1964 and in IV corps by the end of 1965, and to withdraw American forces as envisioned.[57]

In the midst of these deliberations, on October 4, the President called Undersecretary Ball to complain about new stories of a State-Defense split—stories for which he blamed Harriman. His candid, informal remarks give another important clue to his thinking.

> You'd better get Averell in, for Christ's sake. The fact of the matter is that Averell was wrong on the coup. We fucked that up. *Even though it may have been desirable,* so that the Pentagon can go on saying the State Department fucked it up, got us into a lot of trouble, so I think there's nobody in the position to be pointing the finger at anybody else. I think if they just stick it in their own eye instead of somebody else's, we'd be much better off. Do you think you can get everybody in and just give them hell?[58]

While Kennedy now believed that a coup might be desirable, he had also decided that Harriman had jumped the gun on August 24—albeit with his consent. Only rarely, as we have seen, did he reveal even this much about his thinking, and his reticence tempts historians and journalists to attribute his behavior to a hidden, perhaps dark agenda. This, however, reflects a critical misunderstanding of the man. Kennedy took a cautious line throughout the crisis because he was not certain either that a change of government definitely would improve the situation or that such a change was possible. What he feared more than anything, from August through October, was an American-sponsored coup that failed.

Kennedy's refusal to say exactly what he wanted also reflects his ironic detachment—an unusual quality among political leaders. "I felt at times," his personal attorney and sometime adviser Clark Clifford wrote many years later,

> that, as he dealt with personal or professional crises, he was able to step away from himself and look at a problem as though it involved someone else. Sometimes, watching him during a discussion on some contentious issue, I felt as if his mind had left his body and was observing the proceedings with a detached, almost amused air. Something within him seemed to be saying, "This may seem supremely, even transcendentally important right now, but will it matter in fifty years? In one year? I must not permit myself to become involved to the point where my judgment is suspect."[59]

In many ways Kennedy was an archetypal GI—quick, eager to do great things, self-confident, cheerful, but relatively unemotional and hardly introspective, least of all about himself. When he asked the nation to complete the work of the Civil War and raise black citizens to full equality, he did so almost diffidently, in a manner similar to that of his fellow GI Henry Fonda in *Mr. Roberts* or *Twelve Angry Men*. Yet he differed from his contemporaries in one critical respect. His objective was rarely anything so concrete as a legislative program or a victorious war, but rather the more elusive goal of maintaining his effectiveness as President. This required an entirely different kind of calculation, and it ensured that he would seldom move very far in advance of public opinion, or take any firm decision before he absolutely had to. And in this case the President's equivocal position reflected a fundamental truth: that Diem's fate was really in Diem's own hands.

Kennedy's detachment, curiosity, and quick intelligence allowed him to deal rapidly with a variety of issues as President, even while maintaining a relatively relaxed routine. His appointment calendar shows him holding meetings during most of the morning, disappearing for lunch, a swim, a nap, and perhaps other forms of relaxation in the early afternoon, returning for more meetings until dinner, socializing in the evening, and spending most weekends away from the White House. As we have seen, his detachment and flexibility were also responsible for some of the tendencies in his administration that have troubled both contemporaries and some historians: his willingness to let different parts of his administration work at cross purposes, his tolerance for subordinates who clearly did not share many of his views, his initially cautious response to the civil rights crisis, and his relatively poor record with Congress. Yet these qualities, combined with his personal grace, also enabled him to maintain his emotional equilibrium during three very turbulent years of American history—and, far more important, helped the vast majority of his fellow citizens to maintain theirs as well.

The Vietnam story quieted down during October. The Soviets resumed harassment of American convoys into Berlin, and the administration's civil rights bill encountered a crisis in a subcommittee of the House Judiciary Committee, where liberal attempts to strengthen it endangered its eventual passage. Khrushchev announced that the Soviets would not race the United States to the moon, but rejected Kennedy's sudden October 20 suggestion for a joint Soviet-American venture. The President took several questions on Vietnam in each of two news conferences on October 9 and October 31. In the first he denied that the CIA had acted independently and said the United States had seen no changes in the South Vietnamese government. In the second he reaffirmed the plan to withdraw 1,000 men.[60]

Beneath the surface, however, a new struggle over policy broke out almost at once. In Saigon, Lodge initially characterized his new instructions as "excellent" and "likely to produce constructive results," but within a few days he reversed himself, arguing that "the only thing the U.S. really wants—the removal or restriction of the Nhus" seemed further away than ever.[61] On October 4 another Buddhist monk burned himself in Saigon, and police beat three American newsmen at the scene.[62] Later Lodge argued in two weekly reports to the President that the government was doing no better than holding its own militarily and was still going downhill politically. He also provided bloodcurdling reports of South Vietnamese arrest and torture of male and female students, and of a rumored assassination plot by Nhu against Lodge himself. Thuan, he reported, was pleased by the continued suspension of commercial imports.[63] The ambassador also indicated on October 14 that he had a new proposal to discuss with Bundy, Rusk, or Harriman, and this led to a decision to have him return to Washington for consultations at the end of October.[64]

Meanwhile, as we have seen, new Vietnamese-American coup contacts had begun even as the administration was deciding upon its new policy. General Don spoke with Trueheart on October 2 and asked to meet Lucien Conein, and Trueheart refused either to encourage or discourage a coup. General Minh told Conein on October 5 that he had to know the American view regarding a change of government. Minh said he wanted only to win the war, for which the present level of American aid would be necessary. Conein refused to comment specifically on several different scenarios. Lodge, after consulting Harkins, suggested to Washington that he tell Minh that the United States would not thwart his plans, offer to view them (except for assassination plans), and promise American support to any government that could secure popular support and win the war. The ambassador downplayed the contact, confessing that he shared Harkins's lack of faith in Big Minh.[65]

Unknown to Washington, the South Vietnamese generals had been plotting apace during October. According to what General Dinh—the III Corps commander and military governor of Saigon—told William Colby just days after the coup, he, Don, and other generals had become disillusioned after the pagoda raids when Diem and Nhu double-crossed them and refused to take them into the cabinet and began arresting students and intellectuals.[66] Available documents do not show how closely CIA operative Conein stayed in touch with Generals Don and Minh, but on October 20 a Colonel Khuong, a member of Don's staff, discussed a coup with an American officer.

The split between Lodge and Harkins now had serious consequences. On October 22 General Don—the chief of the Joint General Staff since August 20—saw Harkins, and Harkins mentioned Khuong's approach and told Don not to undertake a coup, since the war was going well. On October 23 Don told Conein that a coup would occur within a week, apparently offered to provide Lodge with detailed plans, and expressed his concern regarding what Harkins had said.[67] On the same day Lodge queried Harkins about what he had told Don. When Harkins said that he thought Washington opposed a coup, Lodge "explained . . . we had instructions from the highest levels not to thwart any change of government which gives promises of increasing the effectiveness of the military effort, insuring popular support to win the war, and improving working relations with the U.S." Lodge claimed that Harkins expressed regret and promised to give Don a clarification, but on the following day, October 24, Harkins stood up for his interpretation in a cable to Taylor. He argued that a coup would lead to further power struggles and would *not* make the military effort more effective. Meanwhile, Conein told Don that Harkins's statement was contrary to presidential guidance, and asked for coup plans again. The next day Harkins complained about this conversation in another cable for Taylor and, in another meeting with Don, refused to discuss coups at all. That night, Don told Conein that he could not provide the coup plans for security reasons, but promised at least forty-eight hours' notice. Conein declined to promise support for the coup without the plans.[68]

Civil-military relations showed other new strains in Washington and Saigon. On October 22 the State Department's Bureau of Intelligence and Research (INR)—now led by Thomas Hughes—published a study entitled "Statistics on the War Effort in South Vietnam show Unfavorable Trends." Using MACV's own data, this report finally noted—for the first time—the general increase in the scale and effectiveness of Viet Cong attacks since July. The military situation, it concluded, "may have reverted to the point it had reached six months to a year ago."[69] The idea that the war was going well underlay the McNamara-Taylor report, the Pentagon's whole policy, and—perhaps most significantly— its opposition to a coup. The INR report enraged the Pentagon, although it took more than two weeks to produce a formal reply.

On October 28 the Joint Chiefs discussed the military situation and relations between Lodge and Harkins with McNamara, and the next day Taylor pointed out in a cable to Harkins that Lodge's military estimates in his weekly reports to the President appeared to contradict Harkins's views. "Are we correct," he asked, "in believing that the Ambassador is forwarding military reports and evaluations without consulting you?"[70] Harkins replied on October 30 that he had been planning to raise the same question, that he had not even seen Lodge's most recent weekly report to Kennedy, and that Lodge, unlike Nolting, was "forwarding military reports and evaluations without consulting me."[71]

The Don-Conein conversations had set off alarm bells in the White House. McGeorge Bundy, who had suddenly moved into a leading role, told Lodge on October 24 that the White House was concerned about Conein's reference to a presidential directive and the possibility that Nhu might be using Don to entrap the United States. Lodge replied the next day defending Conein's role, and tentatively arguing that Don must be taken seriously. He opposed trying to thwart a coup, "the only way in which the people in Vietnam can possibly get a change of government." On October 28, before leaving on a day trip to the country with Diem, Lodge saw Don at the airport and confirmed that Conein spoke for him. That evening Don and Conein had a long conversation in which Don insisted that the generals did not want American involvement in the coup. Pressed by Conein, he promised the plans four hours—not forty-eight hours—in advance, suggested that Lodge stick to his planned October 31 departure date for his trip back to consult in Washington, and hinted that the coup might take place very close to that time. He provided a partial rundown of the units involved, but denied that General Dinh was on board. The next day, October 29, Lodge told Washington that a coup was imminent, and that the United States should not try to stop it.[72]

The Pentagon and the State Department were still at odds, but the cool, gentlemanly style upon which President Kennedy insisted kept the dispute within polite bounds. On October 28 Taylor and the Chiefs met with McNamara and apparently proposed a change in coup guidance in order to end any encouragement of a coup.[73] Robert Kennedy also emerged in this crisis as an ally of McNamara, Taylor, and McCone, and only six months later he summarized his—and their—view of the conflict in frank, confidential interviews for the planned Kennedy Library that showed much more emotion than any of the meetings in which he participated. Lodge, he said, leaked too much and had angered McNamara, Taylor, and McCone, and he had had "a lot of conversations about Henry Cabot Lodge": "We were going to try to get rid of Henry Cabot Lodge. He was supposed to come home—if that coup hadn't taken place, he was going to come home—and we were trying to work out how he could be fired, how we could get rid of him."[74]

While the administration was composed above all of team players who had loyally tried to compose their differences and compromise in early October, Lodge was a somewhat older, determined lone wolf who knew how to use his position to control events. The ExCom finally met again in the late afternoon of October 29 to review the situation.

Twenty-four hours earlier a telegram from Lodge had described a day-long visit with Diem on Sunday, October 27. Diem, as Lodge hoped, had asked him when the Commercial Import Program might be resumed. (Thuan later told Lodge that Diem had concluded that the South Vietnamese government could not continue without American aid—another sign that the option of a deal with Hanoi was not serious.) Lodge in reply had asked whether Diem would reopen all the schools, free the Buddhists and other prisoners, and repeal Decree Law 10, and Diem in effect had argued that these problems either did not exist or fell outside his competence. When Lodge repeated that the United States could not support acts "against our traditions and ideals," Diem replied, "I will not be a servant."[75] Brother Nhu, Diem said, was "so good and so quiet, so conciliatory and so compromising." Diem made no specific concessions, but Lodge suggested that the conversation might possibly "mark a beginning," all the same.[76]

The ExCom did not discuss this conversation for long. Instead, its meeting was virtually a replay of one of the meetings following the August 24 cable. Colby began by arguing that pro- and anti-coup forces seemed about evenly divided, and the President questioned him at length about various possible scenarios. Rusk said that the United States should try to stop any coup that might lead to a long civil war, but later suggested that the generals might lose heart in the war if the United States bluntly opposed a coup. He proposed that Lodge leave on schedule, and that Harkins be consulted about the strength of the generals. "I don't think we ought to put our faith in anybody on the Vietnamese side at this point," he said.

The President then suggested that Lodge leave Saigon as planned, and that Harkins take charge in his absence. Such a move could easily have made a coup much less likely, something which Kennedy surely understood. "I would say probably the odds are against a coup," he said. McNamara suggested leaving authority jointly in the hands of Lodge, Trueheart, and the CIA station chief, but McCone refused to give his man equal authority. Then, suddenly, Robert Kennedy weighed in against a coup, arguing that the idea made no sense on the face of it, that the situation had not changed over the last few months, and that a coup would put "the future of [Vietnam] and in fact all of Southeast Asia in the hands of one man that we don't know very well." The United States would take the blame for whatever took place, and Diem might invite the United States out of South Vietnam if it failed. He described this as "the minority view," but both Taylor and McCone promptly agreed with him and argued that even a successful coup would set back the war effort. Rusk and Harriman questioned whether Diem could in fact win the war.

The President again asked whether the coup was likely to succeed, and demanded more information. McGeorge Bundy suggested sending a military plane for Lodge to enable him to delay his departure and remain "during the uncertain days immediately ahead." McNamara, who had sat quietly through the meeting, suddenly endorsed this suggestion and argued against having Lodge turn authority over to Harkins. He said that Lodge would resist this step, all the more so since the two men did not seem to be talking and Harkins did not know about the coup planning.

With the generals quite possibly determined to move and without any indication that Diem actually might change, the administration fell back upon the policy of late August, emphasized the potential disaster of a *failed* coup, and once again passed the buck back to Lodge. A redrafted telegram to Lodge, which the ExCom approved after a short break, asked for separate appreciations of the coup's prospects from him, Harkins, and the CIA station chief, and suggested that Conein tell Don that the United States was not convinced he could succeed. The telegram left it up to Lodge to decide whether to leave on Thursday or on Saturday, and added that in his absence "Harkins should participate in supervision of all coup contacts"—in which the general had hitherto refused to take part—"and that in event coup begins, he become head of country team and direct representative of president." The President himself insisted that the generals had to provide proof that they could win, lest they destroy the American position in Southeast Asia.[77]

Lodge's reply arrived the next morning, October 30, and showed the bit firmly between his teeth. He denied that the United States had the power to delay or discourage a coup, insisting, with some justice, that it was a Vietnamese affair. He rejected further attempts to contact Big Minh, and accepted the offer of a military jet to enable him to delay his departure. Regarding the order putting Harkins in charge, he wrote: "It does not seem sensible to have the military in charge of a matter which is so profoundly political as a change of government. In fact, I would say to do this would probably be the end of any hope for a change of government here. This is said impersonally as a general proposition, since Gen Harkins is a splendid general and an old friend of mine to whom I would gladly entrust anything I have."

Lodge also said the generals might need money at the last minute to buy off opposition, and suggested supplying it. "Gen. Harkins," he concluded, "has read this and does not concur."[78] Harkins on the same day sent two angry cables to Taylor. The first strongly opposed a coup against Diem, and the second said that Lodge had only just informed him of Conein's critical conversations with Don; that he could not vouch for the plans; and that he thought the United States needed more information before agreeing. He also disagreed with Lodge's interpretation of Washington's instructions regarding a coup, and complained that Lodge was withholding important messages.[79] Taylor sent Mc-Namara and Bundy copies of Harkins's messages, but State Department officials apparently did not receive them.

At 11:00 AM on October 30 the President met with Rusk, McNamara, Harriman, McCone, Taylor, and Forrestal. No written record of this most critical meeting survived, but the Kennedy Library has recently released a tape. McNamara brought Harkins's cables, and the group for the first time frankly discussed the extent of the split between Lodge and Harkins and Lodge's obvious enthusiasm for a coup, always without abandoning their GI equanimity. They now understood that the rebellious generals did not trust the American military. Kennedy carefully went over the cables, calmly raising key points. Lodge, the President remarked, was "much stronger for it than we are here," "for very good reasons." "I admire his nerve, not his prudence," he said. Then he read at length from Harkins's first cable, which favored a change "in the methods of governing rather than a complete change of personnel." Bundy reiterated that the group wanted Harkins in charge if a coup took place after Lodge's departure, but added that the general should maintain a "hands-off attitude," not try to stop a coup.

Kennedy asked again that Lodge be queried on the balance of forces and provide some assurance that the coup was likely to succeed. Rusk, critically, then broke in to express his opinion that the United States was "on a downward slope at the present time" and that despite the risks of a failed coup, the chances were "very high" that the United States could not succeed without "a real change in the government."

Bundy referred to evidence of political deterioration "on a number of different circuits" and associated himself with Rusk's view. Kennedy asked for the evidence, and McCone read from a new assessment stating that the United States could "no longer be confident of victory over the Viet Cong in the foreseeable future," given the deterioration of Diem's position since May. Rusk and Bundy passed on other unidentified reports. Kennedy asked McNamara for his thoughts, and the Secretary of Defense replied supporting the draft cable but asking that Colby or a similar figure go to Saigon immediately to take over the supervision of Conein from Lodge, in whom he expressed a lack of confidence. Bundy recommended removing both Trueheart and Mecklin to provide a whole new second echelon in Saigon—perhaps a case of blaming the younger messengers, who had refused to confirm their elders' optimistic hopes.

McCone suggested that the cable make clear that the administration was counting on Lodge to say that the coup would not fail. The President replied that Joseph Alsop, whom he called the most loyal man he knew, had told him upon his return from Saigon that Nhu was now hopeless, and referred once again to the new reports that seemed to confirm that things could not go on as they were.[80] Kennedy, Bundy, and Rusk had finally lost faith in Diem.

That afternoon McGeorge Bundy sent a last instruction to Lodge, asking yet again that he try to persuade the generals not to undertake any operation that did not have a real chance of success. The cable stated that Trueheart would remain in charge after Lodge left, but that he should consult with Harkins and the acting CIA station chief regarding further contacts between Conein and generals, and that Harkins would take charge if a coup began after Lodge's departure. It also ordered Americans not to take sides during a coup, but concluded that "once a coup under responsible leadership has begun . . . it is in the interest of the U.S. Government that it should succeed." While fearing a failed coup, the ExCom had decided that the United States could invest no further in Diem's future. "Thanks for your sagacious instruction," Lodge replied. "Will carry out to the best of my ability."[81]

On the morning of November 1, Diem met with CINCPAC Admiral Felt, who was visiting Saigon, and with Lodge. After giving a customary monologue and complaining about American activities and aid cuts, Diem saw Lodge alone. He indicated that he would reopen the universities and perhaps broaden the government "at the proper time." Then he concluded in poignant, characteristic fashion:

> He hoped that when I [Lodge] was in Washington, I would ask Mr. Colby of CIA and former Ambassador Nolting about brother Nhu because the fact was that brother Nhu did not wish power but that he was such a flexible spirit and was always so full of good advice that people would ask him for his advice. When they had a difficult problem, brother Nhu would always find a solution. Mr. Colby had come to President Diem and had said that it was too bad that brother Nhu was living in an ivory tower, he should go out more. Ambassador Nolting had agreed and it was "due to their pressure" that brother Nhu had started going out and making himself known. But then when he did go out, people said he was usurping power and it was then all the bad publicity began.
>
> When I got up to go, he said: Please tell President Kennedy that I am a good and a frank ally, that I would rather be frank and settle questions now than talk about them after we have lost everything. (This looked like a reference to a possible coup.) Tell President Kennedy that I take all his suggestions very seriously and wish to carry them out but it is a question of timing.[82]

Lodge's comments—which he apparently wrote after this conversation had been overtaken by events—suggested that Diem might finally have been willing to make concessions, but gave no hint that he would ever remove Nhu. What exactly he might have done will never be known.

The coup began about two hours later, at 2:00 PM Saigon time on November 1. Rebel units immediately seized several key Saigon commanders, including Colonel Tung, and surrounded the palace. To the great surprise of the Americans, General Ton That Dinh, the III Corps commander, had joined the coup. Conein, who received only a few minutes' notice, went immediately to coup headquarters. The generals surrounded the palace and told Diem and Nhu that they must surrender immediately or face an attack. At 4:30 in the afternoon Diem telephoned Lodge, reported unnecessarily that some units were revolting, and asked for the U.S. government's attitude. Lodge declined to give an American position, but offered to do anything he could to assure Diem's safety. Diem and Nhu then escaped through a secret passage and made their way to the Chinese section of Cholon. At dawn the next morning they contacted General Don at the Joint General Staff and offered to surrender in exchange for safe conduct to the airport. An armored personnel carrier picked them up, but they never arrived. Instead, they were shot and killed inside the vehicle. The coup leaders initially announced that they had committed suicide. The news reached the White House on Saturday morning, November 2, and Kennedy—who as a fellow Catholic immediately discounted the official explanation—left the room in shock.[83]

In subsequent decades some American policymakers and historians—including Eileen Hammer, William Colby, Frederick Nolting, and Lyndon Johnson and Richard Nixon—cited the coup against Diem as the American government's biggest mistake and, perhaps, the most important cause of full-scale American involvement in the war.[84] Nixon went further during his presidency, undertaking unsuccessful attempts to prove—wrongly—that Kennedy had ordered Diem's assassination. Like other simplistic explanations for America's failure in Vietnam, this one substitutes facile, politicized, emotional rhetoric for real analysis in an effort to keep alive the myth—so dear to Nixon and Colby's GI generation—that every problem has a solution.

Without question, the two men most responsible for the overthrow of the Diem government were Ngo Dinh Diem and Ngo Dinh Nhu. Diem in 1954 took power with the financial and political backing of the government of the United States and the support of most of the active non-Communists in South Vietnam. During the next nine years he steadily reduced his domestic support until it scarcely extended beyond his own family. Despite his control of the American-provided military budget, he never established a relationship of confidence with most of his generals. He was nearly overthrown in 1960 and nearly assassinated in 1962. He dealt with all opposition—the sects in 1954–1955, the political parties in the late 1950s, and the Buddhists and students in 1963—by trying to crush it. He never allowed popular province chiefs to remain in office for too long, and he never trusted anyone outside his narrow circle. As late as September 1963 he might have bought some more time simply by taking some generals into the cabinet, but he refused to do so and lost the critical support of General Dinh in Saigon. And while his political support faded, the Viet Cong—frequently taking advantage of his mistakes—added non-Communist adherents to its cause. Lansdale, Diem's most fervent American supporter, had concluded by 1961 that Diem must allow the opposition to operate legally, but Diem refused. And by the fall of 1963 even Lansdale—like his protégé Rufus Phillips—had concluded that Diem could only survive without Nhu. Nothing ever suggested that Diem would take that step, or that Nhu—who controlled the regime's secret police and political machine—would agree to it either.[85]

The Buddhist crisis, then, was merely the last and biggest of a series of challenges to Diem's authority and political skill that called the American policy of relying upon him into question. Two years earlier, at the time of the Taylor-Rostow mission, many responsible Americans had argued that Diem had to make significant political changes in order to survive, but Nolting and McNamara had persuaded Washington to push ahead without them. During the intervening two years the same two men—and McNamara in particular—had told Washington that American policy was working and South Vietnam was winning the war. As late as mid-September the Pentagon had tendentiously refuted Halberstam's latest military analysis, and as the coup took place McNamara was pressuring Rusk to withdraw the INR challenge to the Pentagon's analysis. Not until December did McNamara inform a new President, in effect, that Halberstam and INR had been right. Had Washington not suspended aid to Diem and Nhu, further crises and coup attempts would undoubtedly have occurred in any case, and the Viet Cong would probably have continued to gain.

On November 4, 1963, President Kennedy sat down in the oval office and dictated his own reflections on the coup. Never before heard, they show his thoughts, his style, and his approach to government very clearly. The President spoke carefully, settling accounts for the benefit of future historians.

> One two three four five. Monday, November 4, 1963. Over the weekend, the coup in Saigon took place. It culminated three months of conversation about a coup, conversation which divided the government here and in Saigon. Opposed to a coup was General Taylor, the Attorney General, Secretary McNamara to a somewhat lesser degree, John McCone, partly because of an old hostility to Lodge which causes him to lack confidence in Lodge's judgment, partly as a result of a new hostility because Lodge shifted his Station Chief; in favor of the coup was State, led by Averell

Harriman, George Ball, Roger Hilsman, supported by Mike Forrestal at the White House.

After impartially summarizing his subordinates' views with hardly a trace of emotion, the President turned to his own role. It is interesting that he failed to ascribe any view at all to Dean Rusk.

I feel that we must bear a good deal of responsibility for it, beginning with our cable of early August [*sic*] in which we suggested the coup. In my judgment that wire was badly drafted, it should never have been sent on a Saturday, I should not have given my consent to it without a roundtable conference at which McNamara and Taylor could have presented their views. While we did redress that balance in later wires, that first wire encouraged Lodge along a course to which he was in any case inclined. Harkins continued to oppose the coup on the ground that the military effort was doing well. Sharp split between Saigon and the rest of the country. Politically the situation was deteriorating, militarily it had not had its effect. There was a feeling however that it would. For this reason, Secretary McNamara and General Taylor supported applying additional pressures to Diem and Nhu to move them . . .

This is perhaps the most significant revelation on the tape: that Kennedy, even at this late date, believed the assurances of his trusted subordinates McNamara and Taylor that the military effort was going well. He never learned the truth.

At this moment the President's ruminations were interrupted by one of his children, probably his son John-John, who was nearly three. His father invited him to say something, and the words "Hello," and "naughty, naughty Daddy" are clearly heard. After giving his son an impromptu lesson on the four seasons, Kennedy continued in a more somber vein:

I was shocked by the death of Diem and Nhu. I'd met Diem with Justice Douglas many years ago. He was an extraordinary character. While he became increasingly difficult in the last months, nonetheless over a ten-year period he'd held his country together, maintained its independence under very adverse conditions. The way he was killed made it particularly abhorrent. The question now is whether the generals can stay together and build a stable government or whether Saigon will begin—whether public opinion in Saigon, the intellectuals, students etc., will turn on this government as repressive and undemocratic in the not too distant future.

After a pause, the President suddenly continued more rapidly. "Also we have another test on Autobahn today," he said, referring to the latest Berlin incident. He quickly moved on to other events of the day.[86]

In the end there is no great mystery about the coup, no mysterious assassination plot designed to forestall a premature peace agreement.[87] Although he had long-standing affection for Diem, Kennedy had quickly concluded during the summer of 1963 that Diem could not continue on the course that he was on. If he refused to mend his ways, a change of government seemed almost inevitable. Having appointed Lodge to Saigon both to pressure Diem and to provide critical liberal Republican political cover should controversial events take place, Kennedy was not likely to overrule Lodge's opinion or to replace him, despite the Attorney General's subsequent remarks. At the last critical meeting on October 30, he heard new, pessimistic reports about Diem's performance and cited Alsop's well-founded doubts about Nhu. That meeting reached its decision not to head off a coup on the basis of a realistic assessment of the future. Had Kennedy known the truth about the military situation he might have considered other options, but he did not.

Kennedy refused at any time during the fall of 1963 bluntly to decide that Diem must either stay or go. The policy embodied in the McNamara-Taylor report and Lodge's subsequent instructions—some of which were written by Bundy for Kennedy himself—reflected his views: that the United States should pressure Diem to change, that Washington should not actively promote a coup, but that it might accept or even encourage alternative leadership if and when it emerged. Lodge—of all Americans the most responsible for the coup—eagerly moved the process along, although he did not, and could not, initiate it, and remained ignorant of key aspects of the plan right up until the end. Meanwhile, the McNamara-Taylor report had a most ironic effect. McNamara and Taylor apparently insisted upon its prediction that the American effort might largely be finished by 1965 and its planned announcement of a 1,000-man withdrawal largely as confirmation that their existing policy was working. McNamara had laid down both deadlines in May 1963, and the report simply affirmed publicly what he had already decreed privately. Yet according to several South Vietnamese military leaders, the deadline—as well as the suspension of American aid—stimulated the coup plotters to move. Seeing no way that Diem could win the war by the end of 1965, they decided they had to take drastic action to get the situation back on track before the Americans departed.[88]

In another irony, the general optimism among the President's advisers decisively militated against any discussion of radical alternatives such as negotiation or neutralization. Kennedy on August 29 asked the ExCom, in the midst of a discussion of pressuring Diem, "whether we would really pull out of Vietnam in any event," and apparently received no reply.[89] When Paul Kattenburg on August 31 suggested that things might be much worse than anyone expected, he received a career-threatening response. In another meeting, as we have seen, Kennedy expressed skepticism about de Gaulle's neutrality proposals, although Roger Hilsman had indicated to *Newsweek* that they might eventually have to be implemented. Kennedy in 1961 opted for neutralization in Laos because the pro-American position was so weak both politically and militarily. All through the fall of 1963 his advisers insisted that despite Diem's political problems the military situation was progressing. And no one seems to have realized that the Buddhists were skeptical about the war, as well as about Diem, and would soon form the nucleus of a neutralist movement in South Vietnam.

Kennedy, in any case, never made decisions until he had to, and for the moment circumstances inclined him to hope for the best and try to defuse controversy over South Vietnam. In the broader foreign policy realm, the President in the autumn of 1963 was looking for further progress in Soviet-American relations. Khrushchev had now finally committed himself to détente,[90] but Kennedy still faced the difficulty of making any concessions to Soviet positions on Germany without angering America's NATO allies, especially West Germany. Adenauer had been unhappy with the test ban treaty because it barred West German nuclear development and because East Germany was allowed to sign it, and he would also oppose Khrushchev's proposed nonaggression pact between NATO and the Warsaw Pact. In late July, immediately after completing the test ban talks, Harriman—the only senior aide who had successfully put Kennedy's desire for Soviet-American détente into practice—had bluntly advocated some form of recognition of East Germany, which he thought would help relax tensions and loosen the bonds between Poland and Czechoslovakia on the one hand and the Soviets on the other. (This was the step, of course, which the Nixon and

Ford administrations finally took in the early 1970s, but only after Chancellor Willy Brandt of West Germany had led the way.) A few days later, in a high-level meeting on August 2, Kennedy had invited Harriman to make his case, and had expressed interest in linking a nonaggression pact to new guarantees for the Western powers in Berlin.[91]

At least one seasoned observer was convinced that Kennedy had gotten American foreign policy on a new track. George F. Kennan, who had resigned as Ambassador to Yugoslavia in early 1963 and returned to Princeton, saw Kennedy during October and wrote him on October 22: "I am full of admiration, both as a historian and a person with diplomatic experience, for the manner in which you have addressed yourself to the problems of foreign policy with which I am familiar. I don't think we have seen a better standard of statesmanship in the White House in the present century."[92] The administration, inevitably, was looking ahead to the 1964 elections, and on November 12 a long conference at the White House envisioned a campaign based on peace and prosperity. The economy was growing apace, the tax and civil rights bills were proceeding—albeit slowly—through the Congress, the President's approval rating was over 60 percent, and the emerging Republican ascendancy of Barry Goldwater seemed too good to be true. As Robert Kennedy recalled a few months later, the brothers had confidence that Goldwater would self-destruct, but worried that he might do so before he received the Republican nomination.[93]

The Kennedy administration did not change its policy toward Vietnam during the weeks after the coup. After a brief delay, it formally recognized the new government on November 7. While most of the American press greeted the coup with some relief, the dramatic events in Saigon also triggered some doubts about administration policy in general. Reston on November 6 suggested that Washington take up the idea of negotiations on South Vietnam, perhaps in an attempt to create a "neutral belt" of Southeast Asian states, and a *New York Times* editorial on November 10 advocated neutralization as well. Both Forrestal and Joseph Mendenhall of State—two of Diem's most determined opponents—became alarmed that such talk could hurt the war effort, and began thinking about ways to reassure Saigon.[94] At almost the same moment, Cambodian President Sihanouk on November 6 angrily protested the continuing radio broadcasts of the Khmer Serei opposition from Thailand and South Vietnam, blamed American support, and threatened to renounce all American aid unless the broadcasts ceased by the end of the year. Two weeks later reports appeared that Sihanouk planned to renew his calls for a conference on Cambodian neutrality. Kennedy decided to send Michael Forrestal to see him.[95]

On November 12 the administration announced that Rusk, McNamara, Taylor, and McGeorge Bundy would all meet with Lodge and Harkins in Honolulu on November 20. In a November 14 press conference Kennedy said that the Honolulu meeting would "attempt to assess the situation: what American policy should be, and what our aid policy should be, how we can intensify the struggle, how we can bring Americans out of there." Ritual references to bringing Americans home had now become part of the presidential line.[96] Kennedy also reaffirmed confidence in Harkins, whose usefulness Halberstam had questioned in the *Times* of November 13, but did not follow up Forrestal's suggestion specifically to denounce neutralization proposals.[97] MACV in Saigon formally announced the 1,000-man withdrawal on November 16, adding honestly—and for the first time—that this would leave the American total at 15,500.[98] In Washington the Joint Chiefs planned to discuss "vigorous action toward North Vietnam" in Honolulu.[99]

In Honolulu both Lodge and Harkins gave broadly optimistic presentations and denied any differences between them. Harkins reported a brief, extraordinary flurry of Viet Cong incidents in the week after the coup, but said, according to the record, that "after 6 November [incidents] dropped down to normal and have remained that way ever since." This was false. A Headway Report of November 15 showed that the VC had broken their all-time weekly record for incidents and attacks during the week of November 6–13, and that they were continuing at one of the highest levels of the year.[100] Finally recognizing the strength of the VC, Harkins singled out thirteen critical provinces with "current problems": not only the entire Delta and the area surrounding Saigon, but also Binh Dinh and Quang Ngai along the central coast, where the war had reportedly been going well. He acknowledged that the VC essentially ran An Xuyen province, as Halberstam had long reported. And in an unrecorded session, the principals also discussed proposals for action against North Vietnam.

Although the civilian leadership of the Kennedy administration had periodically discussed action against North Vietnam in connection

with the Laotian situation—most recently in June 1963—the administration had not discussed such action in connection with Vietnam since
1961. We have seen, however, that during 1963 military authorities—
including Wheeler, Harkins, Krulak, and CINCPAC Admiral Felt—had
made clear on a number of occasions that they believed that many of
South Vietnam's problems were external and required a different kind
of solution.[101] These issues came up at the November 20 Honolulu
meeting, and while they did not figure in the formal memorandum of
discussion, they found their way into a new draft National Security Action Memorandum 273. Bundy and McNamara returned to Washington on November 21, and Lodge planned to fly to Washington over the
weekend for consultations. On Friday morning, November 22, Bundy
gave the NSC staff a brief report on his trip, stressing the continuing
Lodge-Harkins split, and implying that the United States might now
need a new ambassador. The meeting then turned to other business.

NEWS CONFERENCE WITH MALCOLM KILDUFF
Parkland Memorial Hospital, Dallas, Texas
1:31 PM, [November 22, 1963,] Dallas, Texas

MR. KILDUFF: President John F. Kennedy died at approximately
1:00 o'clock, Central Standard Time, today, here in Dallas. He died of a
gunshot wound in the brain.
I have no other details regarding the assassination of the President . . .
Q. Was Mrs. Kennedy hit?
A. Mrs. Kennedy was not hit.
Q. Was Connally hit?
A. Governor Connally was hit.
Q. Was Vice President Johnson hit?
A. The Vice President was not hit.

Memorandum for Record
Subject: White House Staff Meeting, 1530 hours, 23 November

Mr. Bundy presided over a brief, sad meeting that marked the end of an
historic era. Although he tried to maintain his composure, his voice broke
on two occasions. The first time was when he was talking briefly and
vaguely about the transition to President Johnson, and the need for everyone's help. During his comments he acknowledged there might be some
uncertainty as to the final relationships because of the personal loyalty to
and adjustment to the ways of President Kennedy in the staff. His voice

broke as he mentioned personal loyalty to President Kennedy. The second occasion he had to gather himself up was when he referred to the future. He remarked that he had already received a memorandum from Komer on how to achieve continuity in his area, and he hoped Komer could make all those things come true.[102] His voice broke again and the tears welled as he thought of the future without President Kennedy.

On each occasion he quickly caught hold of himself, but all of us knew we had before us a man whose personal view of life would be different from what it had been before Friday, and for whom something significant that gave real meaning and purpose to life would be absent in the future. What stood out most was his deep loyalty and devotion to, and belief in the purposes of, President Kennedy. He tried to be brave and confident about the future; he evidenced that his first contacts with President Johnson had been salutary, and that the new President intended in the immediate future to follow President Kennedy's policies. The first particular instance of this will be Stevenson's speech on space in the UN—it is amazing how the processes of government force one to go from the general to the specific and test in practice general policies and beliefs people have adhered to previously, sometimes half heartedly . . .

In continuing President Kennedy's policies, President Johnson will not be able to do everything President Kennedy would have, because President Kennedy could have done things President Johnson cannot, because his reputation has not yet been established. The specific example cited was again a UN matter . . .

We were all deeply shaken by the events, and before Bundy appeared there was a general exchange of comments on the tragic events. Schlesinger . . . remarked that the day after Stevenson had been attacked in Dallas,[103] President Kennedy had asked him to call Stevenson. Stevenson said he, of course, had not been injured but that he was deeply concerned with the undercurrent of hatred in Dallas. He asked Schlesinger to tell the President not to go there. Schlesinger said he did not deliver the message since he knew President Kennedy would say that it was another of Stevenson's exaggerated reactions. And 24 hours later Stevenson called to say his earlier suggestion, upon reflection, was probably overly pessimistic. But it turned out he was correct.

General McHugh talked of the trip. Prior to the shot, it had been a complete success . . . General McHugh had some good words for President Johnson. He said he kept his composure, though very shaken by the events, and immediately took charge of things . . .[104]

10

A Decision for War
November 1963–April 1964

★

The new President, Lyndon Johnson, was fifty-four years old. He had been one of the most powerful men in Washington as Senate Democratic leader from 1952 through 1960, but his role in the new administration had rapidly faded into insignificance, leaving him deeply depressed by the fall of 1963. While the President had always treated him with great respect, most leading administration figures had ignored him, and he and Robert Kennedy distrusted each other intensely. With Texas and the rest of the South up for grabs in light of the civil rights crisis, his presence on the ticket was if anything more necessary for 1964 than for 1960, but he had enjoyed almost no influence, even on domestic issues. While he had undertaken several goodwill trips abroad as Vice President, he lacked expertise or confidence in foreign affairs.[1]

In the weeks immediately following the assassination, Johnson, like the whole nation, was struggling with shock, while trying to reassure his subordinates, his fellow citizens, and himself that the nation would continue upon the course that Kennedy had set. He grew rapidly in this role, and the country rapidly accepted him as President. As early as November 28 James Reston noted "the terrible paradox and tragedy of the moment": "President Kennedy apparently had to die to create a sympathetic atmosphere for his program."[2] Within weeks Johnson was redeploying his formidable legislative skills on behalf of Kennedy's two major domestic initiatives, the tax cut and the civil rights bill, spending hours plotting strategy with the Democratic congressional leadership.

The tax bill had now passed the House, and the civil rights bill was likely to do so early in the new year, but Johnson feared that if civil rights came before the Senate first, a lengthy filibuster might prevent action on either measure before the election. To persuade Virginia's Senator Harry Byrd, the ultraconservative chairman of the Senate Finance Committee, to take up the tax bill at once, Johnson insisted on submitting a fiscal 1965 budget below $100 billion—a reduction of about $1.5 billion from existing plans—even if this required some creative accounting. The first steps of the strategy worked brilliantly, and on February 26 Johnson signed the tax cut, his first major legislative triumph.

Although Johnson's participation in the Second World War had been minimal, his life was in many ways even more tightly bound up in the experience of the GI generation than Kennedy's. He had known economic hardship as a child, he had struggled through college in the 1930s under difficult circumstances, he had been a local administrator of Roosevelt's National Youth Administration, and his whole congressional career had been intimately bound up with major aspects of the New Deal, the war effort, and the impact of the Cold War. Even more than Kennedy, he was a doer rather than a thinker, and he and his contemporaries instinctively reacted to the trauma of Kennedy's death by embarking vigorously upon great new tasks. "Work, that's the answer," a junior member of the new administration advised his devastated sixteen-year-old son two days after Kennedy's assassination, and while this recipe might not be effective for the children of GIs, it served the GIs themselves very well indeed in 1964–1965. Even the older congressional leaders who had blocked most of Kennedy's domestic initiatives were now ashamed to stand in the way of Johnson's efforts to build a Great Society at home and secure freedom abroad.

And while Johnson pushed ahead on the legislative front, he also tried hard to establish himself as an effective leader in foreign affairs. McGeorge Bundy immediately grasped the needs of the new President and tried to meet them. In his very first memo to Johnson on November 23, Bundy provided a remarkably thorough outline of what Johnson might say at his first cabinet meeting, and he continued to provide comments on topics and individuals prior to presidential meetings of a kind that Kennedy never would have needed.[3] Johnson's first important meeting with a foreign head of government took place over Christmas, when he entertained the new German Chancellor, Ludwig Erhard, at the LBJ Ranch in Texas.[4] Johnson failed to move Erhard toward a more flexible policy toward the Soviets and East Germany,[5] but Bundy and Rusk immediately contacted all the leading columnists to assure them that the meeting had gone well, and Bundy passed examples of enthusiastic press coverage up to his new boss.[6]

With respect to the Soviet Union, Johnson seemed to favor more détente but received little guidance on how to proceed. The *New York Times* reported that he sought a "peace offensive" during 1964 but that administration officials reacted coolly to Soviet proposal for a common renunciation of the use of force to alter borders.[7] And indeed, although Bundy on January 13 suggested working toward bilateral agreements with the Soviets, the administration never came up with any important new initiatives in Soviet-American relations during 1964.[8] Here Johnson was falling victim to his predecessor's failure to institutionalize his policies. In seeking détente with the Soviet Union, Kennedy himself had tried to provide the long-term planning, since the State Department—and Rusk himself—generally held to the rigid positions of the 1950s. The one high-ranking State Department official who had shared Kennedy's views and enjoyed his confidence was Harriman, but Harriman apparently lost whatever chance he had of real influence with Johnson in December, when he objected to Johnson's appointment of his fellow Texan (and Ambassador to Mexico) Tom Mann as Undersecretary of State for Latin American Affairs. Johnson already distrusted Harriman, both because of Harriman's loyalty to Kennedy and because of his role in the coup against Diem.

Bundy's frequent memos to Johnson show that the new President remained fundamentally uncomfortable with the process of diplomacy. While Kennedy was never more relaxed or more forthcoming than in his talks with foreign leaders—even relatively minor ones—Johnson intensely disliked that part of his job. Bundy in February 1964 had to work to get his agreement to spend a total of one hour each week with foreign diplomats, and although as Bundy pointed out in May only about half of that time actually was used, the President continued to complain.[9] These problems became worse, if anything, as time went on. Bundy frequently had to beg Johnson to meet outgoing American ambassadors for a few minutes, simply to increase their credibility vis-à-vis their hosts, and in December 1964 Bundy even had to explain, in the wake of a visit from British Prime Minister Harold Wilson, why such visits simply had to take place.[10]

"It was a great contrast," George Anderson, then Ambassador to Portugal, recalled a few years later,

> coming back for the first time to call on President Johnson, presumably to discuss Portuguese-American relationships, and finding that the consultation with the President was a complete farce. I was put in line with two other ambassadors waiting in the Cabinet Room. President Johnson came out. The photographer was there to take the picture shaking hands, on to the next one, on to the next one. Within forty-five seconds, all three of us had our pictures taken and were out of the room. The press indicated that I had been in there, a long consultation with the President. No. Different type of a man, you see, Johnson and Kennedy. Kennedy would have found the time to discuss, and was interested in, Portuguese-American relationships. He took an hour, for example, just before I went over and talked very intelligently. President Johnson probably didn't know anything about it, wasn't interested. He had other things on his mind.[11]

Johnson was extremely intelligent and probably worked harder than Kennedy, but he gave himself less time to think. Kennedy, like his predecessor, lived a comparatively normal life as President, but Johnson's calendar shows that he, like his successor, almost literally never relaxed.[12] Even back at the LBJ Ranch, he occupied himself with a frantic round of visits to Hill Country neighbors. Addicted to the telephone, Johnson made anywhere from twenty to eighty calls a day, blowing off steam, getting information, "stroking," applying pressure, and often, as recently released conversations show, just passing the time. The weekends, when he was in Washington, marked no break in his routine at all.[13] And while he could, and did, brilliantly design long-term legislative strategy and spend hours on the telephone executing it, he lacked the capacity to do the same in foreign policy.

Johnson also worried continually that foreign policy setbacks or leaks might embarrass him, and expressed an utter lack of confidence in the Department of State. He disliked large meetings or widely circulated written documents, which could lead to leaks showing dissent or disloyalty. As we shall see, the Kennedy administration practices of agreed State-Defense recommendations, ExCom meetings, and National Security Council meetings designed to consider policy options lost favor under Johnson. Instead, McGeorge Bundy became the gatekeeper who decided what diplomatic papers would reach the President, while McNamara handled several key problems—including Southeast Asia—largely on his own.

Vietnam was one of the few issues in which Johnson had been involved, and about which he had strong feelings. As we have seen, Johnson in May 1961 had toured the capitals of America's Asian allies to reassure them after Kennedy had decided to enter into the Laos cease-fire talks. A man of powerful emotions who rarely did anything halfway, Johnson had returned tending to identify with the Nationalist Chinese, Philippine, Thai, and South Vietnamese leaders with whom he had met. Indeed, in the opening of his report to the President, Johnson analyzed the impact of the Laotian talks in terms suggesting that the United States was the supplicant, rather than the guarantor, of assistance and support. "Laos," he wrote Kennedy at the end of the trip, "has created doubt and concern about intentions of the United States throughout Southeast Asia. If these men I saw at your request were bankers, I would know—without bothering to ask—that there would be no further extensions of my note.[14]

Having publicly and personally reaffirmed the U.S. commitment to Diem, Johnson remained loyal to him during 1962 and 1963, despite numerous reports from his military aide, Colonel Howard Burris, suggesting that Diem was not doing very well.[15] And he objected very sharply to the August 24 cable and the subsequent coup against Diem, whom he compared to a difficult but irremovable subcommittee chairman.[16] And within days of assuming office Johnson was already speculating—partly, to be sure, for dramatic effect—that Diem's and Kennedy's assassinations were in some strange way connected.[17] He disliked Roger Hilsman, whom he had observed making fun of Dean Rusk at a Washington dinner party, and resented Harriman's and Hilsman's role in the coup.[18] And when Johnson met with Lodge on November 24, he said that he was not at all sure that the United States had taken the right decision with respect to Diem.[19]

Apparently disturbed by Lodge's briefing and worried about trouble during an election year, Johnson—in sharp contrast to Kennedy—immediately designated Vietnam as an area of intense interest. On December 2 he asked Rusk, Taylor, and McCone to assign their most effective men to Saigon, and referred to South Vietnam as "our most critical military area right now."[20] Three days later, in a brief speech at the State Department, Johnson raised Vietnam himself, exhorting his listeners to "let no day go by without asking whether we are doing everything we can to win the struggle there."[21] And because the situation in South Vietnam was deteriorating, a new aspect of Vietnam policy had reached the White House for decision for the first time. It concerned plans for action against North Vietnam, which McGeorge Bundy included in a draft National Security Action Memorandum embodying the results of the Honolulu conference. The conference had specifically discussed possible incursions into Laos, and Bundy's first draft also referred specifically to the development of new plans for action by the South Vietnamese against North Vietnam.[22] The final draft, however, referred merely to unspecified "plans" to be developed involving different levels of increased activity, while evaluating their potential damage to North Vietnam, their plausible deniability, possible North Vietnamese retaliation, and other international reaction.[23]

Kennedy on July 30 had approved several similar actions in connection with the situation in Laos, including, apparently, South Vietnamese incursions into Laos and *planning* for more aggressive actions involving American forces. This, however, was the last he had heard of any such suggestions.[24] Now Johnson had approved another round of planning, while giving his chief subordinates a feeling of increased urgency.

Johnson's behavior with respect to Vietnam in 1964–1965 confused his subordinates, the press, and the public, and it has continued to confuse many historians. Largely because the President was moving on very different tracks privately and publicly, he left behind evidence that can support almost any interpretation. Only gradually did his beliefs and plans become apparent, and because he instinctively told people what they wanted to hear, one must in the end focus upon what Johnson did, rather than what he said, to determine his real beliefs. Johnson clearly did not eagerly seek war in Southeast Asia, but he never questioned the need for the United States to resist the Communist threat to South Vietnam by any necessary means. He certainly wanted to avoid war before the November elections, but he always seems to have been ready to undertake it should the situation become critical enough, and he never seriously considered the alternatives of neutralization and withdrawal. Johnson, in short, accepted the premises of the policies that had been developed under Eisenhower—premises whose consequences Kennedy had consistently refused to accept for three years. And under Johnson the government decided quickly decided in principle to implement some version of those plans to save South Vietnam.

Johnson also increased confusion, both then and in retrospect, because he often refused to state his views as long as possible, especially when he felt in any way pressured. Asked whether the President truly trusted anyone, one of his senior advisers once replied, "I think Lady Bird, most of the time."[25] He resented attempts to influence him, and he sometimes refused to make appointments after they had been leaked to the press. During this same spring of 1964, he kept the possibility of selecting Robert Kennedy as his running mate open for about six months, even though he never had any intention of doing it, and he subsequently delayed announcing his choice of Vice President until literally the last possible second. Johnson certainly knew war in Vietnam would not be popular, and that also encouraged him to delay it as long as possible. He never, however, seriously considered any alternative to going to war.

In South Vietnam, the military situation remained serious in the weeks after the coup. The Viet Cong went on a coordinated, countrywide offensive in the first two weeks of November, making 166 attacks from October 30 through November 6 and a record 233 the following week—most of them against watchtowers and outposts. In two dramatic victories during the last week in November, the Viet Cong infiltrated and overran a Special Forces camp in Hau Nghia province near the Cambodian border, and downed or damaged twenty American aircraft in an An Xuyen operation in which the VC attacked a hamlet, dug in with anti-aircraft weapons, inflicted effective fire upon planes and helicopters, and withdrew without serious losses. MACV apparently managed to keep this larger-scale Ap Bac entirely out of the press. But Viet Cong attacks subsequently fell dramatically, declining to 59 for December 4–11 and 66 and 67 during the next two weeks.[26] Civilian American agencies now unanimously agreed about the deterioration of the situation in the Mekong Delta, which Halberstam had long reported. Lodge confirmed in particular that the VC had overrun most of the hamlets in critical Long An province, and General Don—the chief of the Joint General Staff—personally confirmed that the Diem government had moved the peasants away from their land and extorted forced labor from them while pocketing the money allocated for construction.[27] By December 13 McNamara's own Defense Intelligence Agency was finally acknowledging that the Viet Cong had steadily increased their capabilities during 1963.[28]

When Lodge saw General (and now President) Big Minh on December 1, Minh, who came from Long An himself, showed an excellent grasp of the problems surrounding the hamlet program. Minh wanted to concentrate on critical areas around Saigon, and hoped to bring the Hoa Hao and Cao Dai sects over to the new government. But Lodge, who was worried by Minh's fears that the United States intended to support neutralization for South Vietnam, successfully opposed Prince Sihanouk's new proposal for a conference on Cambodian neutrality—a move aimed specifically at Thailand and South Vietnam, who Sihanouk claimed were still supporting his opposition. In a series of exchanges that carried into mid-December, State authorized Lodge repeatedly to assure the South Vietnamese that the United States resolutely opposed the neutralization of South Vietnam, and Lodge insisted that the United States had to reject the conference on Cambodia to make this declaration convincing.[29]

McNamara was also feeling a need to do something, and he now seized upon the Pentagon's favorite option: military actions against North Vietnam. McNamara met with the Chiefs on December 2, and the Chiefs cabled Admiral Felt and General Harkins asking what could be done to increase South Vietnamese efforts in the Delta, but adding that a lack of detailed information on enemy infiltration was "a prime intelligence deficiency" that affected "our overall Southeast Asia strategy." McNamara also told the Joint Chiefs to "push actions" against North Vietnam together with the CIA.[30] Four days later, on December 6, most of the ExCom met at the White House to review progress in the implementation of National Security Action Memorandum (NSAM) 273, and agreed to "expedite for further consideration plans for phased operations against NVN," Cambodia, and Laos. Then, on the next day, while McNamara was discussing budget plans with the President, Johnson suddenly suggested that McNamara go to Saigon after visiting Europe later in the month. The President—who according to McNamara gave him "quite a lecture on South Vietnam and expressed concern that we as a government were not doing everything we should"—announced McNamara's trip in a press conference that same day, December 7.[31] And in a message to MACV on December 10, Mc-

Namara in effect announced a crucial change in American policy. He was looking forward, he told Harkins, to seeing a plan for South Vietnamese operations against the North designed "to make clear that *the US* will not accept a Communist victory in South Vietnam *and that we will escalate the conflict to whatever level is required to insure their defeat.*"[32] He confirmed his plans to discuss cross-border operations to the Joint Chiefs on December 9.[33]

McNamara was rapidly establishing his influence in the new administration. Although news stories initially speculated that he might lose some of his influence under Johnson and leave after the 1964 elections, the reverse occurred. Johnson wanted to cut the budget, and McNamara within a few weeks submitted revised figures and announced the closure of numerous military bases. The Secretary of Defense rapidly became Johnson's indispensable man, solving problems well outside his official duties. In a conversation on January 6 McNamara promised Johnson to put a USIA White House photographer on the Pentagon payroll, explained why some aid to Indonesia should be authorized, and agreed to help find a speechwriter to replace the departing Theodore Sorensen.[34] By mid-January Reston reported that McNamara was emerging as "the strong man in the Johnson cabinet," and in late March he floated McNamara as a possible choice for Vice President.[35]

McNamara spent December 19–20 in Saigon and made a blunt, sometimes undiplomatic effort to take charge. In a conference with Minh and Don he openly criticized Don's simultaneous tenure as chairman of the Joint General Staff and Minister of Defense and demanded General Dinh's removal as III Corps commander. When Minh complained about Sihanouk's proposed conference, McNamara ended the discussion by suggesting that Sihanouk was reacting to Viet Cong successes in November and December. He also told Minh to start "acting like a Chief of State" and make more speeches, and pushed for the redeployment of a number of battalions to the Delta provinces.[36]

McNamara's report to the President on December 20 painted a grim picture and tried to seize control of both political and military aspects of the U.S. effort. "The situation," he began with uncharacteristic and unprecedented pessimism, "is very disturbing. Current trends, unless reversed in the next 2–3 months, will lead to neutralization at best and more likely to a Communist-controlled state."[37] He blamed the situation upon the "indecisive and drifting" new government and upon Ambassador Lodge. Reopening the battles of the late summer and early fall, McNamara once again accused Lodge of reporting on the military situation without consulting Harkins and withholding important incoming messages. "My impression," he said, "is that Lodge simply does not know how to conduct a coordinated Administration."[38] McNamara did give Johnson his "best guess" that "the situation has in fact been deteriorating in the countryside since July to a far greater extent than we realized because of our undue dependence on distorted Vietnamese reporting." As we have seen, he would have been well aware of this if he had simply paid attention to MACV's own Headway Reports on Viet Cong attacks, instead of trying to silence the INR analysts who had pointed out the truth.

Regarding military moves across the borders, McNamara backed away from operations into Laos, which had drawn sharp protests from American Ambassador to Laos Leonard Unger and from Hilsman,[39] but informed Johnson of covert action plans for "a wide variety of sabotage and psychological operations against North Vietnam from which I believe we should aim to select those that provide maximum pressure with minimum risk." Military authorities were already thinking well beyond covert action. CINCPAC Admiral Felt had already warned that if the South Vietnamese undertook covert operations "the U.S. must be prepared to back up RVN and be willing to commit U.S. forces in the event reaction from the DRV and CHICOMS escalates to a threshold beyond RVN capabilities or *if actions are not sufficiently persuasive.*"[40] General Krulak's own longer report on the McNamara visit confirmed that the military and the CIA had prepared a program of "actions of escalating intensity, ranging from minor propaganda moves to destruction of major resources by raid or bombing," and the plan which McNamara's party carried back to Washington included provisions for increased American support and American forces to counter Communist escalation. Either McNamara or McCone discussed these plans with Johnson on their return.[41]

On January 2 an interdepartmental committee chaired by General Krulak approved a three-phase plan for pressure against North Vietnam. Although no detailed information on Phases II and III has ever been released, they evidently involved the infliction of "increasing punishment upon North Vietnam . . . to create pressures, which may convince the North Vietnamese leadership, in its own self-interest, to desist from its aggressive policies."[42] In early January Johnson apparently saw the whole list of proposed options for action against the North, and on January 16 he approved the execution of at least some operations against North Vietnamese targets, to begin on February 1. The full list of these planned operations has never been declassified, but according to the Joint Chiefs' history of the war, Phases II and III—which the President declined to approve as yet—included air strikes and other operations that could not be denied.[43]

Ambassador Lodge indicated the scope of the planned operations in a January 21 conversation with General Minh, Prime Minister Tho, and others. Although the President had initially approved only psychological and sabotage operations during the next four months, Lodge apparently described a three-phase twelve-month program. Lodge mentioned "the destruction of petroleum reserves and of naval installations" as an "example" of what was contemplated, and argued that the program was designed to convince Hanoi that "South Vietnam, with the tacit approval of the United States, intends to increase the rate and the extent of operations against North Vietnam, thus causing immense destruction on the economic and military installations of North Vietnam, if that becomes necessary." When Minh—echoing CINCPAC—warned that the United States had to be willing to meet various forms of North Vietnamese or Chinese retaliation, Lodge and Harkins tried to reassure him. American authorities in Saigon and Washington now clearly envisioned a program of action against North Vietnam that would eventually include air strikes, with a consequent threat of North Vietnamese retaliation that the United States would have to prepare to meet.[44]

Oddly enough, while the United States was planning the escalation of the war, the struggle within South Vietnam was actually slowing down. After the extraordinary round of VC attacks during the first three weeks of November, many of them directed against small outposts, the weekly average in December fell to about 64 attacks, down from 143 in November, 99 in October, and 119 in September—indeed, the lowest figure for the whole year. The downward trend continued through January (weekly average of 54 attacks), February (49), and March (45). Total *incidents,* however, including terrorism, sabotage, and propaganda, numbered in the 400–500 range in most weeks, compared with 200–300 in the early part of 1963. The Viet Cong were relying increasingly upon terrorism, and in early February they began a terrorist campaign explicitly directed against Americans.

The fall-off in armed attacks remains difficult to interpret. The main focus of Viet Cong activity shifted somewhat from IV Corps, the southern Delta, to III Corps, the heavily populated areas around Saigon—partly, perhaps, because government authority had virtually ceased to exist in large areas of IV Corps. At the same time, the fall-off in activity may have owed something to a paradoxical consequence of the November 1 coup. In preceding months the Viet Cong had managed to take advantage of the Buddhist crisis to rally thousands of non-Communist South Vietnamese to their cause—including the Hoa Hao and Cao Dai sects. Much of this support had evaporated after the coup, creating a possible political opportunity for the new government.[45] And, despite some pressure from subordinates like Communist Party Secretary General Le Duan to escalate the conflict in the South, Ho Chi Minh was actually refusing as yet to send North Vietnamese troops south in an attempt to finish off the Saigon government. Doubting the support of the Soviet Union and fearing a confrontation with the United States, he still hoped that negotiations might produce an American withdrawal.[46]

An exchange with Majority Leader Mike Mansfield also showed a hardening of administration policy. During the last week of December 1963, Johnson called Mansfield's aide Frank Valeo about legislative business, and mentioned that he did not want "another China" in South Vietnam. In a memorandum of January 6, Mansfield suggested to Johnson that the United States did not want another Korea, either. He forwarded a copy of a December 7 memorandum proposing a truce, perhaps on the basis of acknowledging some Viet Cong control of South Vietnam, whereupon Washington might explore possibilities for peace with the help of other nations. Treating such proposals as a threat, Johnson told Bundy to ask McNamara and Rusk for personal "memorandums of refutation" which he could use with Mansfield during the next few days. Both of them totally rejected neutralization, and Rusk claimed, astonishingly, that de Gaulle's "attitude toward the eventual settlement of Vietnam is very close to our own." McNamara described the stakes as so high that "we must go on bending every effort to win." Bundy was less categorical, citing neutralization as a possibility if it became clear that present efforts would not succeed.[47]

The Joint Chiefs, meanwhile, pushed for stronger action. They agreed on January 7 to prepare a categorical statement of American objectives and what would be required to secure them. By January 20 they were discussing specific operations against the North, and on January 22 they submitted a long memorandum to McNamara stating a detailed political and military case for war. Failure in South Vietnam, they argued, would shake the confidence of "Burma, India, Indonesia, Malaysia, Japan, Taiwan, the Republic of Korea and the Republic of the Philippines" in American resolution, and might have the same effect in Latin America and Africa as well. So far, we were "fighting the war on the enemy's terms" by observing self-imposed restrictions, including the non-use of American combat forces and the avoidance of operations against North Vietnam. In conclusion, they recommended putting General Harkins in charge of both the American mission and the fighting of the war; turning the South Vietnamese air force loose against North Vietnam; and committing U.S. forces to the bombing of the North and to combat operations in both South and North Vietnam.[48] Faced with the failure of the counterinsurgency effort, the Pentagon now proposed a conventional war.

Testifying before the House Armed Services Committee on January 27, McNamara seemed torn between a desire to reaffirm Kennedy administration policy and a need to announce a forthcoming change. On the one hand, he implicitly restated the hope that the American advisory presence might be largely eliminated in 1965, and repeated, "This is a Vietnamese war, and in the final analysis it must be fought and won by the Vietnamese." But he concluded that "the survival of an independent Government in South Vietnam is so important to the security of all of Southeast Asia and to the Free World that I can conceive of no alternative other than to take all necessary measures within our capability to prevent a Communist victory." James Reston immediately telephoned his friend George Ball to ask for clarification, and his next column pointedly told President Johnson and Secretary Rusk that "it would be nice to know if any new intervention was being considered."[49] In a February 4 memo for a presidential lunch with Rusk and McNamara, McGeorge Bundy referred to the need for a plan for "pressure on North Vietnam."[50]

On January 30 General Nguyen Khanh, the II Corps commander who had played a relatively minor role in the overthrow of Diem, took over Saigon and put Minh, Don, and Kim under house arrest. The coup replaced the primarily Buddhist leadership of November 1—including Minh, Don, and former Vice President Tho, who had become Prime Minister—with a more Catholic military faction. Khanh claimed, however, that he acted for broader reasons, and specifically to prevent a French-led neutralist coup led by Don, Kim, and General Mai Huu Xuan, with Minh's approval. French sources may conceivably confirm parts of this story, but as yet no hard evidence suggests that Khanh was right.[51] The Minh-Tho government had violently resisted Sihanouk's conference proposals and de Gaulle's calls for neutralization, and had even inspired student demonstrations against the French Embassy. And in the weeks and days before the coup, Lodge had reiterated both his confidence in the new regime and the regime's continuing opposition to a negotiated, neutral solution.[52]

New evidence shows, however, that American military authorities encouraged this second coup, and that Lodge did not stand in its way. McNamara had criticized the new government severely in his report to the President of December 20, 1963, and the government had subsequently rejected his proposal for more American advisers in districts and villages.[53] On January 28 General Khanh warned his adviser, Colonel Jasper Wilson, of the supposed forthcoming neutralist coup, and Wilson passed the word to Lodge and Harkins. Khanh went to Saigon on January 28–29 and spoke to Harkins as well. Harkins described his conversation with Khanh in an oral history ten years later:

> In 1964, on January 28, I got word from General Khanh, II Corps Commander, through my senior advisor, Colonel Wilson, wanting to know if he minded if Khanh had a coup. Well, I was an old coup hand, at that time, and I said that I didn't like coups. He said, "Well, Generals Kim and Don were going to incarcerate 'Big' Minh and take over the government. They had a meeting coming up on Thursday, a Corps Commanders Meeting, and they were going to turn the government back to the French. Now you wouldn't like that General Harkins, would you?" Well, I had nothing to say really, "No, I wouldn't like it at all." So Khanh said, "Do you mind if I have a coup?" and I said, "No, I think you are a very fine general."[54]

Harkins apparently managed to win Lodge over. On the next evening Lodge reported that he, Harkins, and CIA Station Chief Peer Da Silva had effectively concluded that a change of government might indeed serve American interests, since Khanh "is considered to be the most capable general in Vietnam" and "has the reputation of being politically perspicacious." Lodge added that he had authorized Colonel Wilson to promise Khanh a plane at Da Nang to take his family out of the country should the coup fail.[55] In a cable to Taylor, Harkins confirmed that he regarded Khanh as "the strongest character in the military."[56] The coup plotters also removed General Ton That Dinh, the III Corps commander and Interior Minister about whom McNamara had complained in December, from office and arrested him.

After the coup Khanh and his collaborators promised to produce documents proving their charges of pro-French neutralism, but they never did.[57] Nonetheless, Lodge on February 1 decided to put the best possible face on these events, and gave Khanh's charges a guarded endorsement.[58] Although there is no evidence that Minh intended to pursue a neutralist policy, both the Embassy and MACV clearly could have tried to head off the coup but declined to do so. After the coup they preferred to accept Khanh's explanation rather than the alternative explanation of a move based upon jealousy and ambition, with more, similar coups likely to follow.

The coup, in any case, did nothing to slow the militarization of American policy, and in some respects accelerated it. Lodge on February 20 also endorsed action against North Vietnam, citing the need to retaliate against an escalating Viet Cong terrorist campaign that had killed five Americans and wounded fifty since the beginning of February. On the same day Johnson himself asked his senior military team to speed up contingency planning for action against North Vietnam, and the next day a telegram under presidential signature assured Lodge that Rusk and McNamara were already preparing such plans, and that McNamara would visit him in mid-March. And on February 22 the President himself, in Berkeley, California, publicly warned the North Vietnamese, "Those engaged in external direction and supply would do well to be reminded and to remember that this is a deeply dangerous game." Stories from Saigon and Washington reported that Washington was considering approving South Vietnamese sabotage operations against the North—operations that had actually been approved more than a month earlier, and which began by the end of February.[59]

Important personnel changes were now changing the balance of power within the administration. President Johnson had always regarded Assistant Secretary of State for Far Eastern Affairs Roger Hilsman, as a disloyal troublemaker, and he blamed Hilsman and Harriman for the overthrow of Diem. In early 1964 the President shifted Harriman from Asian to African problems. On February 4 McGeorge Bundy wrote Johnson, "we must end the deep-seated lack of confidence which exists between senior people at Defense and the Hilsman office,"[60] and within a few weeks they had solved the problem by replacing Hilsman with Bundy's brother William, McNamara's Assistant Secretary of Defense for International Security Affairs.[61]

McNamara and his subordinates were seriously discussing a possible war with North Vietnam and China. On February 21 the Secretary gave the Joint Chiefs a series of vitally important questions drafted by William Bundy relating to action against North Vietnam. In an effort to prepare both for a limited war against North Vietnam and for a possible general war against North Vietnam and China, Bundy's memo raised five basic questions. First, it asked for an estimate of North Vietnamese and Chinese capability to retaliate, both in Southeast Asia and elsewhere. Second, it asked the Chiefs to list actions against North Vietnam that could be taken either by the South Vietnamese or the United States, to estimate their effectiveness, and critically, to specify what operations would be most likely to bring about the cessation of North Vietnamese support for insurgencies in North Vietnam and Laos, but least likely to lead to "stepped-up conflict and adverse reactions in third countries." The next two questions assumed the worst—large-scale intervention by the North Vietnamese and/or the Chinese, either in Southeast Asia or elsewhere—and asked about the effectiveness of various forms of American retaliation, including the use of nuclear weapons. They also asked to what extent the United States could counter such actions "through air and naval responses only (without the use of ground forces other than those presently deployed.)" The last question asked whether existing contingency plans had to be modified to meet these threats "primarily" with air attacks rather than with substantial ground forces. McNamara requested a reply by Monday, March 2, in light of his anticipated departure on another visit to Saigon on Wednesday, March 4.[62]

The Chiefs discussed the questionnaire on March 1, and their March 2 reply essentially urged civilian authorities to plan for general war in Southeast Asia. The Chinese Communists and North Vietnamese, they warned, could introduce thirteen and nine divisions, respectively, into

Southeast Asia during the dry season. The South Vietnamese, acting alone, had "very limited" capabilities for operations against North Vietnam, and the Chiefs recommended the overt use of American forces. Targets whose destruction would "reduce" the North Vietnamese capability to support the insurgencies in Laos and South Vietnam included airfields, POL (petroleum, oil, and lubricants) storage facilities, bridges, infiltration routes, communications between North Vietnam and China, and "selected industrial facilities and power plants."

With respect to the critical issues of deterring and/or countering Communist retaliation, the Chiefs submitted appendices laying out the forces needed to counter Communist aggression against a variety of areas inside and outside Southeast Asia. They ignored one of McNamara's most important requests: to specify what actions would be most likely to achieve American objectives without leading to escalation or adverse third-country reaction. Instead, they made quite clear that they regarded nuclear weapons as an essential element in plans to deal with possible North Vietnamese or Chinese retaliation:

> In the broad application of land and sea based airpower, nonnuclear attacks may not cause the ChiCom/DRV to cease aggression; however, nuclear attacks would have a far greater probability of causing them to desist . . .
> *The Joint Chiefs of Staff emphasize that in initiating actions against the DRV there must be a readiness and willingness on the part of the United States to follow through with appropriate contingency plans to counter DRV/ChiCom reaction as required.*[63]

The Chiefs added that CINCPAC had "no specific plans based solely on air and naval responses which apply to all the situations contained in this paper." In their meeting on March 1 they had concluded that "in no case is it safe to count on air and naval power alone," but now they promised "to direct the preparation of such plans as required."[64] In conclusion, the Chiefs recommended taking overt military actions against the DRV (Democratic Republic of Vietnam) to make our resolve "to extend the war as necessary" immediately clear. They did not expect Communist China to introduce large numbers of ground troops into Indochina. In a separate memorandum the Chiefs asked McNamara to lift restrictions upon the movement of South Vietnamese troops across the Laotian and especially the Cambodian borders, where, they argued, Viet Cong units were using sanctuaries.[65]

The appendices to the Chiefs' reply show that they, like many civilians, counted heavily upon the psychological impact of American military action to induce the North Vietnamese to stop the insurgency in the South. Drawing upon game theory currently in fashion, they suggested that the threat of destruction of its industrial base might cause Hanoi to back off, and called for "selective" targeting "so as to allay the fear that the US objective is other than the causing of a cessation of DRV support of the insurgency."[66] Laying out the respective advantages and disadvantages of a single sharp blow or an incremental approach, they declined to recommend either one.

Appendix C, devoted to possible enemy reactions, discussed possible Chinese retaliation against Burma, Thailand, South Korea, Taiwan, and Laos, as well as North Vietnamese movement into Laos and South Vietnam. Estimating the entire North Vietnamese Army at 250,000 men—probably a significantly low estimate[67]—they foresaw only two NVA divisions entering South Vietnam in response to American action against the North. To defend *both Laos and South Vietnam*, Annex C to Appendix D foresaw a need for seven Army and Marine divisions and two independent brigades—a force that ultimately proved inadequate for operations within South Vietnam alone. The paper made no attempt to estimate how long the deployment of such a force would take. The annexes also assumed that the Chinese Communist air force would assist the North Vietnamese, and that the United States would have to move against Chinese air bases in return—with what weapons they did not say. The Joint Chiefs, in short, were entirely ready to embark upon war against North Vietnam and the defense of South Vietnam, but they substantially underestimated the size of the enemy and the American forces required to meet it, overestimated the morale effects of American bombing, and generally ignored the logistical problems that would significantly slow down the deployment of American forces.

The Chiefs, meanwhile, said almost nothing about the insurgency in the South. They continued to believe that guerrillas were partisans who depended on the support of conventional armies, not insurgents who lived off the population, and that they could therefore be defeated only by attacking the conventional forces upon whom they relied and denying them secure bases. The Chiefs restated this view in another March 2 memorandum for McNamara: "All our experience in counterinsurgency indicates that when the insurgents enjoy the advantage of such sanctuaries and support across international borders, their elimination will be a most difficult, if not impossible, task."[68] Their implied recommendation of the use of nuclear weapons to stop North Vietnamese or Chinese retaliation harked back to the policies promulgated under the Eisenhower administration. The Chiefs' enthusiasm also reflected some changes in their personnel. In the spring of 1961, when the Kennedy administration discussed war over Laos, General LeMay and Admiral Burke had favored war despite the risk of war with China, but General Decker of the Army had taken a middle position and General Shoup of the Marine Corps had specifically opposed intervention. Now LeMay, Admiral David McDonald, and Marine General Wallace Greene had strongly supported war during the preparation of the Chiefs' response to McNamara, with no apparent dissent from Army Chief of Staff Earle Wheeler.[69]

There seems at this point to have been little disagreement between McNamara and the Chiefs. McNamara had wanted a proposal that would avoid the use of U.S. ground troops, but when he discussed the Chiefs' proposals on March 2, he apparently acknowledged the need for some U.S. ground forces. He hoped to hold them to a minimum, however, "by substituting Chinese Nationalist or other third-country units and particularly by a 'far more massive use of air.'"[70] And in succeeding months remarks by leading civilians showed a willingness to consider the use of nuclear weapons in response to North Vietnamese or Chinese aggression against the South, just as the Chiefs had suggested.

On the same Monday, March 2, William Bundy submitted his first draft of a report on McNamara's forthcoming mission to South Vietnam—a report whose final version was incorporated in NSAM 288, the document that established American objectives in the Vietnam War. He began by defining the U.S. objective as "an independent non-Communist South Vietnam, which must be free to accept outside assistance as required to maintain its security." As Bundy subsequently acknowledged, this objective went well beyond the observance of the 1954 Geneva Accords. Presenting a slightly less alarmist view than the Joint Chiefs, Bundy argued that the fall of South Vietnam would lead to the immediate fall of the rest of Indochina, the "accommodation" of Burma, the fall of Malaysia and probably Indonesia, and increased threats to Thailand, the Philippines, India, Australia and New Zealand, Taiwan, Korea, and Japan.

Rejecting a negotiated, neutral solution as bound to lead to a Communist takeover, Bundy called for American action against North Vietnam along lines that clearly drew upon the experience of the Cuban missile crisis. The United States, he said, should put together convincing documentary proof of North Vietnamese supply and direction of the insurgency in the South, even if this required "a degree of overemphasis," and release it dramatically at the last minute, as in the missile crisis, to provide the basis for a congressional resolution in support of armed action. The United States should then blockade the port of Haiphong and bomb key rail lines from North Vietnam into China, "the road nets to Laos and South Vietnam," training camps for cadres going South, and key industrial targets. Oddly, he did not expect Hanoi to cut off support for the Viet Cong in response, but he thought it "equally unlikely that they would pour major forces across the borders of Laos and South Vietnam." In addition to at least reducing the flow of men and supplies, he counted upon the bombing to stiffen the new Khanh government in Saigon, and to send a message to left-leaning President Sukarno of Indonesia.[71] In essence, Bundy was putting his faith in a sudden, sharp demonstration of American power to reverse current trends. If, however, his assumptions proved wrong and the North Vietnamese simply escalated in return, the United States would face pressure to escalate further.

Bundy in another March 2 memorandum gave another reason for favoring action against the North: to "demonstrate to *Saigon* by more forceful action that we really do mean to preserve a non-Communist South Vietnam." A few days later Lodge confirmed that many South Vietnamese wanted American action against the North, even at the risk of war with China, "thereby taking responsibility for the war out of Vietnamese hands."[72] The dual basis for action against the North—that it might both restrain the enemy and encourage our ally—had now been laid.

President Johnson, however, was suddenly having second thoughts, not so much about the wisdom of escalating the war as about the political consequences of doing so now. Vietnam was not a subject that he discussed frequently during the first year of his administration. His telephone conversations dealt more often with legislative issues, Texas politics, the investigation of his former Senate aide Bobby Baker, and the Panama crisis over U.S. rights to the Canal Zone and the canal. But on March 2, troubled by congressional and press comments about the drift in American policy and leaks of planned American actions, Johnson telephoned McNamara to ask him to prepare a brief statement of administration policy that he could commit to memory. He suggested listing the alternatives of sending in American troops, accepting neutralization with drastic consequences for nations like Thailand and the Philippines, and continuing to improve the training and morale of the South Vietnamese, which he regarded as the best alternative. "Do you think it's a mistake to explain what I'm saying now about Vietnam, and what we're faced with?" he asked. "Well, I do think, Mr. President," McNamara replied revealingly, "that it would be wise for you to say as little as possible . . . the frank answer is we don't know what's going on out there."[73] Johnson also mentioned the need to meet any request from Lodge fully and promptly, so as not to be "caught with our britches down." Johnson on March 4 called Walt Rostow at the State Department—the source, apparently, of some of the leaks—to warn him not to tell the press anything anymore.[74] On the same day, McNamara provided a two-page statement rejecting withdrawal, neutralization, or American ground forces, and reaffirming existing policy.[75]

On March 4 the five Joint Chiefs of Staff discussed the situation with Johnson, apparently for the first time. When he asked for recommendations, Taylor advocated "the progressive and selective attack against targets in North Vietnam." While Taylor, Admiral McDonald, and General Greene favored an incremental approach, General LeMay advocated an immediate "hard blow."[76] Johnson replied that he did not want to lose South Vietnam, but that "he did not want to start a war before November." After General Greene had forthrightly predicted that Johnson would have to choose between escalation and withdrawal, Johnson spoke even more frankly:

He repeated again that the Congress and the country did not want war—that war at this time would have a tremendous effect on the approaching Presidential political campaign and might perhaps keep the Democrats from winning in November. He said that he thought it would be much better to keep out of any war until December; that would be after the election and whoever was going to be President could then go to Congress for a supporting and joint resolution, and the people of the United States to explain to them why we had to risk the chances of another war by expanding our operations in Southeast Asia. The political situation in December would be stabilized.

It occurred to General Greene, who immediately made a record of the meeting, that "what the President was actually doing was indirectly telling General Taylor that he did not want him to return from SVN with a recommendation that the campaign there be expanded to include NVN to the extent that the risk might arise of a Korean-type war, or all-out war with the Communists."[77]

Later that day, describing the meeting in a telephone conversation with McGeorge Bundy, the President reiterated these views:

> And I told them, now let's try to find an amendment that will . . . we haven't got any Congress that will go with us, and we haven't got any mothers that will go with us in the war, and in nine months—I'm just an inherited trustee, I've got to win the election or Nixon or somebody else has [to] . . . *and then you can make a decision that . . .* but in the meantime let's see if we can't find enough things to do . . . to keep them off base, and to stop these shipments that are coming in from Laos, and take a few selected targets to upset them a little bit, *without getting another Korean operation started.*[78]

In order to prevent further coups, Johnson also asked McNamara and Taylor to make clear that General Khanh was "our boy," and he specifically asked for newspaper photos showing McNamara and Taylor holding up Khanh's arms. In order to forestall congressional criticism, he wanted to make sure that Washington had met all requests from Harkins and Lodge since November. He also made clear that he wanted to stop press leaks of plans for military action against the North.[79]

McNamara and William Bundy apparently got the message as well, and on March 5 Bundy submitted a new draft report backing away from any immediate recommendation of action against the North. Such action, he now wrote, would create premature pressure for negotiations while failing to cut off assistance, and would be a poor risk without a stronger Saigon government.[80]

While Johnson obviously wanted to delay action, neither he nor McNamara was certain that he could, and the administration gingerly continued to prepare public opinion. James Reston on Sunday, March 1, suggested that the administration was "divided" on widening the war, but adopted the Pentagon argument that men and supplies from North Vietnam were critical and that the United States had to "change the rules" of the war to be successful.[81] McNamara reported increasing numbers of Chinese weapons in South Vietnam in a March 6 press conference, just before his departure. While Johnson himself hoped to keep policy on the existing track, he knew he might have to face war when McNamara returned. After Taylor and McNamara had left he warned his old friend Senator Richard Russell that he might face a tough decision soon: "Now on Vietnam, when they come back here they're going to make a choice. They're going to want to go in, or something else, and I don't see how we can do anything unless . . . I think what we're going to have to do is have McNamara and about three or four people sit and listen to them . . . You're going to be one of the three or four in meetings, so you go to sleep thinking about it tonight."[82]

While in South Vietnam from March 9 through March 12, McNamara and Taylor toured the countryside with General Khanh, raising his hands as ordered by the Commander in Chief and trying, as McNamara acknowledged, to assure the South Vietnamese that Khanh enjoyed "the full and complete support of President Johnson and our whole government."[83] Privately, Khanh promised an ambitious program of national mobilization, and he and McNamara agreed that further actions against North Vietnam could be helpful *after* Khanh had strengthened his government. Saigon correspondents indicated that South Vietnamese paramilitary operations against the North might now begin—news that was already several weeks old.[84] McNamara's press chief, Arthur Sylvester, told correspondents that McNamara had *not* come to plan escalation by the United States or South Vietnam, except perhaps into Laos, and that "McNamara does not believe there is any real advantage in attacking the North."[85]

As the visitors returned home, William Bundy produced a new draft report, lauding the Khanh government for its ability and responsiveness to American advice—a judgment which CIA Director McCone refused to endorse—and emphasizing action within the South. "On balance," he recommended against overt American or South Vietnamese action at the moment, but he proposed making ready to begin "border control" actions within seventy-two hours, and "graduated overt military pressure" within thirty days. Significantly, however, the report looked forward to action against the North either in the event of an emergency or after the situation in the South had *improved,* in order to avoid "a very length campaign based on a war-weary nation." The final report omitted McCone's dissenting, pessimistic footnotes, apparently with the excuse that McCone had had a chance to register his dissent with the President personally.[86]

Despite the President's reluctance to act, the Joint Chiefs continued to argue for stronger action. After seeing Bundy's report, they declared on March 14 that its recommendations would not turn the tide, and recommended immediate action against the North. But on March 16 McNamara simply told them that the President had adopted the report, accepted their memorandum without comment, and declined somewhat contemptuously even to ask for their advice. Only Taylor attended the NSC meeting the next day, and Greene and LeMay were furious when they found that they had not received McCone's dissenting footnotes.[87] At the March 17 NSC meeting that adopted the report, Rusk and McNamara clearly anticipated action against the North at some point in the future.[88] Publicly, however, the administration insisted that policy had not changed. "New Vietnam Policy: More of the Same," the *New York Times* headlined its Week in Review on March 22, reporting that advocates of stronger action had lost out, "at least for now." And the decision to temporize did not reflect any willingness to consider alternatives to war. "I think that nothing is more important than to stop neutralist talk wherever we can by whatever means we can," Johnson cabled Lodge, adding that he had personally made this point with both Mansfield and Walter Lippmann.[89]

By the middle of March 1964 the senior leaders of the American government—including Johnson, McNamara, Rusk, and McGeorge Bundy—definitely believed that action against the North could improve the situation in the South. They had also officially adopted the objective of "an independent non-Communist South Vietnam . . . free to accept outside assistance as required to maintain its security." McNamara, Bundy, and the Chiefs had wanted action at once, but Johnson had raised the issue of the election in his meeting with the Joint Chiefs. Lodge commented that the United States should at once develop a plan to use its power to pressure and dissuade North Vietnam from seeking a Communist victory, but the President replied that present policy reflected the consensus judgment of Lodge himself, Khanh, and McNamara in Saigon that action against the North at present "would be premature." The immediate problem, he said, was "to develop the strongest possible military and political base for possible later action." He urged Lodge to let him know if he believed immediate action was required.[90]

In response to NSAM 288, the Joint Chiefs asked permission to redeploy forty-eight B-57 jet bombers from Japan to Clark Air Force Base in the Philippines, presumably to allow them to begin retaliatory strikes within seventy-two hours or graduated pressure on the North within thirty days. They also asked CINCPAC to develop a new Operations Plan (OPLAN) 37–64, designed to allow the South Vietnamese to put pressure on the North with only deniable assistance from the United States, and a plan for action against North Vietnam and China that would emphasize—but not be limited to—air and naval power. During March and April Generals LeMay and Greene kept pushing for stronger action.[91] The J-3 (Operations) division of the Joint Staff submitted a Commander's Estimate, "Alternate Courses of Action, Vietnam," on March 30, which recommended three phases of action culminating in the American bombing of the North. It also foresaw the immediate deployment of two brigades—one Army and one Marine—to Thailand and South Vietnam to cope with possible enemy retaliation. On April 14 LeMay and Greene once again argued for the immediate implementation of three phases of action against the North.[92]

In planning an increased American role in the war, the Pentagon was thinking in completely conventional terms. Hilsman—the prime advocate of an unconventional approach—had now left the government, but his erstwhile ally Michael Forrestal made one more attempt to reopen the question of American tactics at a March 30 meeting of the White House NSC Staff. The occasion was the MACV Headway Report of March 23, which began by noting the slow progress of a new pacification plan, and then described friendly "Significant Operations." These included four highly conventional, relatively large-scale operations, each designed to trap a large VC force, and all relying heavily on air support and firepower, including napalm—exactly the kind of operation which Hilsman had vigorously critiqued in his strategic concept more than two years earlier. The enemy, Forrestal argued, "was not as readily identifiable as these operations made him sound."

When Maxwell Taylor's aide Colonel William Smith, who regularly attended these meetings, asked what alternatives the civilians had in mind, Forrestal replied by citing a newly translated book, Roger Trinquier's *Modern Warfare,* which used the French experience in Indochina and Algeria to describe how counterguerrilla warfare should be conducted. Chester Cooper, another NSC staffer, suggested that the Saigon government had to win some "dramatic victories" in the next few months to increase morale. Later Cooper admitted that he didn't know how to win dramatic victories without an identifiable enemy. McGeorge Bundy commented that the military "thought of the war in Vietnam too much in terms of regular conventional warfare with an identifiable enemy and specific military objectives. In fact the problem was quite different. The result of this type of military thinking was that all the Chiefs except General Taylor wanted to go North." Bundy asked for a memorandum raising these questions with McNamara, but Forrestal warned that McNamara would simply produce some "Krulak statistics" to show things were going well. In a memorandum for Bundy later that afternoon, Forrestal proposed solving the problem by replacing Harkins with his deputy General William Westmoreland, which McNamara refused to do before Lodge's departure. "Chet Cooper is completely right," Forrestal concluded. "This is a Greek tragedy, and the curtain is slowly descending." The memo Bundy requested from Cooper and Forrestal apparently never appeared.[93]

The tragedy lay in the United States government's utter inability to abandon its conventional approach to the war. Forrestal's questioning of the military's orientation was entirely to the point, but despite his reading of Trinquier, he clearly had no idea himself of the kind of small-scale, widespread military presence that would be necessary to make a counterguerrilla war work.

Since the President had delayed widening the war, the administration had to focus upon the other specific recommendations of NSAM 288, including new increases in South Vietnamese forces, new and better aircraft and armored personnel carriers, a new civil administrative corps, and guerrilla forces to act against the North and in Laos. An interdepartmental committee on Vietnam, established under the chairmanship of Harriman's former deputy William Sullivan, tried to monitor the implementation of these recommendations, but real progress proved almost impossible to achieve. No one in Washington dared to do anything about the problem of the American civilian and military leadership in Saigon. Although Johnson frequently doubted Lodge's administrative capacities, he had become exquisitely sensitive to Lodge's opinions as the ambassador emerged as a leading Republican presidential candidate, winning the New Hampshire primary with write-in votes on March 10. On at least five occasions from February through April Johnson asked for and received confirmation from subordinates that the administration had made every effort to meet all of Lodge's requests. The President repeatedly told Lodge that he wanted all his advice and would do anything he suggested.[94] Lodge sensed Johnson's obsessive concern, and he tried to assure Forrestal in May that while the President had a right to his advice, he did not invariably have to take it.[95]

The situation regarding Harkins was even stranger. "I do not know anyone," McGeorge Bundy wrote the President in a top secret, eyes-only memo on January 9, "except perhaps Max Taylor, in the top circles of your government who believes that General Harkins is the right man for the war in Vietnam now." Although McNamara had said nothing about Harkins in his December report to Johnson, Bundy now reported that the Secretary of Defense had been "shocked by the quality" of much of Harkins's staff in December, and "still more shocked by finding that Harkins and Co. have been dead wrong about the military situation for months." But Taylor and the Pentagon, Bundy explained, were standing behind Harkins because of the attacks on him by Lodge, Hilsman and the press. McNamara now planned to appoint General William Westmoreland as his deputy and bring Harkins home after some months, but he did not even dare confide this plan to Taylor. Bundy suggested that Johnson speak to both McNamara and Taylor, if need be, to expedite the switch, but nothing happened.[96] Because Johnson did not dare remove Lodge, he could not remove Harkins either. Meanwhile, the Lodge-Harkins feud persisted, and visitors to Saigon found that the two were not communicating.[97]

Partly for this reason—but mainly because of the political turmoil in the South Vietnamese government and the preeminent position that the Viet Cong had secured for itself in much of the countryside over the last few years—the government was making no progress in securing the support of the people. Ten critical provinces around Saigon now rated a separate section in MACV's weekly Headway Reports. After Khanh's coup the province chief in key Long An province was replaced, and the new chief promptly became involved in a power struggle with the local military commander that lasted more than a month. On March 14 MACV reported that hamlet militia all over the country, who had been forbidden to levy local contributions since November, were turning in their weapons and refusing to fight. Their numbers had declined by 60 percent in the critical provinces. A mid-February report noted a terrible shortage of recruits for the Civil Guard and Self-Defense Corps in Binh

Duong, the site of Operation Sunrise, and in the critical Delta prov-inces, where 50 percent of all recruits had to be brought in from other parts of the country. "A general do nothing policy continues in most of the critical provinces," the report continued. Hamlet construction had come to a halt, and the training of civil cadres had ceased in Novem-ber.[98] The Viet Cong were becoming more and more active in the key central and northern coastal provinces of Binh Dinh and Quang Ngai. According to David Nes, Lodge's new Deputy Chief of Mission, he and Westmoreland made some progress in the early spring by forming a new pacification committee, but Lodge disbanded it when it became too powerful, leaving the American effort in a chaotic state.[99]

Military planning, meanwhile, was proceeding on very optimistic as-sumptions. The Chiefs, with the exception of General Wheeler of the Army, generally assumed that bombing could force North Vietnam to stop supporting the insurgency in the South and allow the South Viet-namese to bring it under control. While they foresaw the need to pre-pare to deal with North Vietnamese or Chinese retaliation, they had not grasped the seriousness of the situation within South Vietnam or the scale of the American ground effort that might be required to hold it together. The Commander's Estimate which they endorsed on April 14 assumed that South Vietnamese government forces were adequate "to control the major centers of population and occupy selected rural areas thereby permitting the government an opportunity to win the people."[100] Only the issue of the *timing* of agreed actions divided the ci-vilians and the military at this time.[101]

When Washington finally decided to escalate the war in February 1965, it did so according to concepts prepared by the Pentagon and by MACV in Saigon. The administration tried to sell the idea that a dem-onstration of American power might lead to early negotiations, rather than acknowledge the true scope of the administration's plans and the task it had undertaken. MACV by then had made quite clear how many American forces might be required, and the civilians had shown a willingness to do what was necessary. What made the American build-up gradual in 1965 was not a civilian strategic concept but rather the inability the infrastructure of South Vietnam to absorb American troops more quickly and the need for a huge build-up of American forces before the United States could take the offensive.

11

To the Tonkin Gulf
April–August 1964
★

By the spring of 1964 Lyndon Johnson had established himself as a
highly effective President in his own right, especially in domestic affairs. The passage of the tax bill and progress on the civil rights bill
gave an impression of impressive new momentum toward critical national goals, and foreign affairs were noticeably calmer and quieter
than in 1961 or 1962. But both the style and the substance of American
foreign policy began to change during the first six months of the Johnson administration, even though Rusk, McNamara, and Bundy remained at their posts. Kennedy's attempts to recognize the aspirations
of the Third World—even when voiced by somewhat unsavory national leaders—began to fade into the background. The first visible
shift occurred in December 1963, when Johnson appointed Ambassador to Mexico Tom Mann—a conservative, pro-business Texan—
Undersecretary of State for Latin American Affairs, a job Mann had
held under Eisenhower.[1] A month later, rioting broke out in Panama
protesting the sovereignty granted the United States "in perpetuity"
under the 1903 treaty that had allowed the United States to build the
canal. In conversations with intimates like Senator Russell of Georgia,
Johnson expressed his belief that local Communists were behind the rioting and should be met with a tough line.[2] The crisis dragged on for
months while Johnson steadfastly refused to promise to negotiate a
new treaty. Then, in March, Brazilian generals, apparently with the approval of American authorities, overthrew the leftist Brazilian President Joao Goulart, ending democracy in Brazil for more than twenty
years.

Policy also shifted toward Indonesia. For three years Kennedy had courted President Sukarno—who at home balanced his large domestic Communist party with a pro-Western army—and his administration had supported the transfer of West New Guinea from Dutch to Indonesian sovereignty and successfully mediated the dispute between the two nations. By the end of 1963 a new crisis was brewing over British plans to create the Federation of Malaysia, to include Malaya, Singapore, and the northern part of Borneo. Sukarno, who had designs on northern Borneo himself, regarded the federation as an exercise in neo-colonialism. In the week before his death, Kennedy had decided to visit Indonesia in the spring of 1964. Johnson understandably canceled the visit, and in December he dealt a severe blow to American-Indonesian relations by bowing to congressional pressure and refusing to certify that aid to Indonesia served the national interest. While he was persuaded in January to continue some aid and to send Robert Kennedy on a visit to Indonesia that temporarily defused the crisis, his telephone conversations show that he did not take the issue very seriously.[3]

In February, when British Prime Minister Sir Alec Douglas-Home visited Washington, Rusk and Foreign Secretary R. A. Butler agreed that the United States would support Britain on Malaysia in exchange for general British support for the American position on Vietnam.[4] Five months later, in July, the new Prime Minister of Malaysia, Tunku Abdul Rahman, visited Washington, and the United States came down squarely on his side of the controversy and offered military training and assistance. This, as Ambassador to Indonesia H. P. Jones explained several years later, marked the end of good relations with Sukarno, and helped set off a spiral of recriminations and Indonesian shifts leftward that culminated in a civil war in the fall of 1965.[5]

Policy also changed with respect to the most critical area of Africa, the former Belgian Congo. Working through the United Nations, the Kennedy administration for three years had tried to form a stable central Congolese government, and during 1963 U.N. peacekeeping forces had defeated the rebellion in Katanga. U.N. Secretary General U Thant wanted to withdraw the U.N. forces, however, and at the time of Kennedy's death their withdrawal was scheduled for mid-1964. When a new rebellion broke out against the Congolese government at that time, the Johnson administration apparently made no effort to get the U.N. to stay, but instead tried to enlist the Belgian government's help in stabilizing the situation—a major departure from the Kennedy administration, which had refused to follow the Europeans' lead. When that failed, Washington turned to white mercenaries under contract to the CIA to crush the rebellion, a most unpopular move throughout most of the continent.[6]

In a remarkably prophetic memorandum for McGeorge Bundy on February 25, his staffer Robert Komer expressed concern over the deterioration of American relations with a number of neutrals, including Indonesia, Egypt, and India. "A hard line now," he wrote, "may increase the chances that—in addition to the Vietnam, Cuba, Cyprus, Panama and other current trials—will be added come summer Indonesia/Malaysia, Arab/Israeli, India/Pak crises which may be even more unmanageable . . . the net effect of adding several additional minor crises to the present list will be further flak that LBJ can't handle foreign policy, and is reversing the Kennedy line." Within a few years the three crises Komer mentioned had indeed mutated into actual wars.[7] Johnson was not personally responsible for these changes in approach, except perhaps with respect to Panama, where he allowed his wounded pride to make him more intransigent. Instead, his lack of direction was simply allowing the bureaucracy to follow its own instincts.

Meanwhile, the administration's policies in Southeast Asia were leading to new splits with European allies. As we have seen, Washington at the moment of Johnson's accession faced two new diplomatic initiatives: de Gaulle's proposal for the neutralization of North and South Vietnam, and Sihanouk's demand for a conference designed to guarantee Cambodian neutrality. The State Department initially concluded, on December 1, 1963, that the United States would have to agree to such a conference, but Lodge protested so bitterly regarding its potential effects on the Minh government—which suspected that a conference on the neutralization of South Vietnam would follow—that Washington quickly backed away from the proposal. Washington tried to substitute a declaration by Saigon, Bangkok, and Washington of a willingness to respect Cambodia's neutrality, and even rejected British proposals for a conference. This did not satisfy Sihanouk, especially after South Vietnamese troops—accompanied by Americans—attacked and bombed a Cambodian village just over the border on March 19, but Rusk insisted to the British that the United States could not agree to a conference without Thai and South Vietnamese consent.[8] In 1961

Washington had agreed to the Geneva conference on Laos despite the opposition of its clients in Bangkok and Saigon, but now it was refusing a conference intended simply to reaffirm the neutrality of Cambodia because of their opposition.

French President de Gaulle, meanwhile, continued his calls for the neutralization of all Vietnam. In late January he made another dramatic diplomatic move, recognizing the Communist government in Peking, a step which Rusk violently attacked in a talk with the French ambassador.[9] When de Gaulle had first made these proposals in late August, Kennedy had reacted negatively but politely. Now, in late February, Lodge complained that de Gaulle's statements were demoralizing many South Vietnamese, and asked Washington to ask the French President to qualify his statement significantly. When Ambassador Charles Bohlen saw de Gaulle on April 2, the general agreed that the United States should not immediately withdraw, but rejected Bohlen's argument that "military stabilization" had to precede any talk of neutralization. Arguing that South Vietnam had no real government, de Gaulle repeated that only neutralization could avoid a Communist takeover. The only alternative for the United States, he argued prophetically, was to broaden the war to include North Vietnam and possibly China—a course which he did not support.[10]

The Johnson administration, of course, had already decided upon eventual action against the North, but the President wanted to avoid any moves until he had been elected. Unfortunately, developments in both South Vietnam and Laos refused to wait, and the United States in the late spring and early summer faced repeated pressure to do something. In Saigon, General Khanh wanted immediate action against North Vietnam to rally support for his government, and in Laos, new moves by both the right and the left reignited the civil war. These twin crises brought the administration to the brink of war again in late May and early June, but the President's caution once more carried the day.

Khanh asked for immediate action to Rusk when the Secretary of State made his first visit to South Vietnam in mid-April, and proposed a sweeping program of domestic mobilization and action against North Vietnam to Lodge on May 1.[11] Washington tried to find ways to placate the general during the next two weeks, and McNamara decided to see for himself during another round-the-world tour, and arrived in Saigon on May 12.[12] Khanh explained his plans to McNamara the next day, calling for air and sea attacks against the North but acknowledging that since the United States would have to deal with retaliation from the North, it would have to choose the moment at which to begin.

Returning to Washington, McNamara, at Johnson's suggestion, delivered a report to a special National Security Council meeting on May 15, which a large bipartisan congressional delegation also attended. He told them roughly what the President wanted to hear. Khanh, he said, favored strikes against the North at some point but did "not feel that he should strike north before his security situation in the south is improved, possibly by this Fall." Some congressmen complained about their unfavorable mail regarding Vietnam, and some complained that our allies should do more, but none advocated stronger action by the United States. No one, apparently, mentioned the possibility of action against the North to the press, but Pentagon sources made clear once again that they thought much more would have to be done.[13] A few weeks earlier, when Oregon Senator Wayne Morse—rapidly emerging as a bitter critic of administration policy—had referred to the conflict as "McNamara's War," the Secretary had responded that he didn't "object to its being called 'McNamara's War.' I think it is a very important war and I am pleased to be identified with it and do whatever I can to win it."[14]

Simultaneously, the situation was complicated by a new crisis in Laos. During the winter of 1963–64 the Pathet Lao had continued to nibble at neutralist positions around the Plain of Jarres. Marshal Phoumi Nosavan, who still wanted to break up the coalition and turn to a military solution with American support, had visited General Khanh in Dalat in March and agreed to allow South Vietnamese troops to cross the border in pursuit of Viet Cong, a move desired by American military authorities but opposed by Souvanna Phouma. Ambassador Leonard Unger—the second in a series of three outstanding American ambassadors to Laos during this period—repeatedly argued that the United States should try to observe the Geneva Accords to the maximum extent possible, and advised against provocative but probably ineffective moves against the Ho Chi Minh trail, which might unleash the North Vietnamese against Souvanna.

On April 19, in an apparent effort to force the issue, several rightist Laotian officers arrested Premier Souvanna Phouma and neutralist leaders in Vientiane and tried to form a new rightist government. The CIA reported that the coup "was modeled on General Khanh's Saigon coup," and hoped to unite all anti-Communist forces and, perhaps, force American intervention against the Pathet Lao in a replay of the events of 1960–1961.[15] Although Phoumi repudiated the coup under American pressure and Souvanna was reconfirmed in power, the Pathet Lao in early May responded—as they had a year earlier after the assassination of Quinim Pholsema—by expanding the territory under their control. This led Souvanna Phouma to agree to American reconnaissance flights over the Plain of Jarres.[16]

The Laotian crisis was the fourth replay of an annual spring event—a right-wing provocation, followed by Pathet Lao retaliation on the Plain of Jarres—and for the fourth consecutive year Washington discussed immediate war. The Pathet Lao renewed their offensive on May 16, and on May 20 a State Department spokesman suggested that we might once more dispatch a fleet to the area or troops to Thailand. President Johnson asked McGeorge Bundy on May 20 to prepare two plans, one to stiffen the South Vietnamese and one an "integrated political-military plan for graduated action against the North."[17] The CIA began writing an estimate of possible Communist reaction, a State Department group prepared a congressional resolution to authorize action, and Douglas Cater of the White House Staff drafted a presidential speech. Rusk on May 21 warned Lodge that the United States might take action against the North to compel observance of the 1962 Geneva Accords. On the same day the State Department announced that the United States would begin armed reconnaissance in Laos.[18] Senior officials, including Rusk and U.N. Ambassador Stevenson, went on a major public relations offensive designed to impress the world with American firmness.[19]

The administration's senior national security team met three times on Sunday and Monday, May 24–25, with the President joining them for one meeting. Rusk favored immediate, dramatic action to force a Pathet Lao withdrawal in Laos—or, as both he and McNamara bizarrely put it, to "force the removal of Pathet Lao forces from Laos." "U.S. pressure would be exerted first to restore the Plaine des Jarres in Laos to the neutralists, force the removal of Pathet Lao forces from Laos, and then deal with North Vietnam." Later Rusk suggested that

Johnson make a new speech "to counter public reports that the President is not acting because of the upcoming elections"—which, of course, was true.

McNamara repeatedly tried to focus the discussion on the consequences of bombing North Vietnam. We could not stop North Vietnamese or Chinese intervention in Indochina from the air, he said, and we would need American ground forces. His Assistant Secretary for International Security Affairs, John McNaughton, had recently estimated that the United States might have to meet a North Vietnamese invasion of the South with seven American divisions. McNamara suggested that the President favored "interlarding"—the insertion of about 500 Americans into responsible positions in the South Vietnamese army and government—as an alternative to armed action, but Lodge, Taylor, and McNamara himself all rejected this idea as neo-colonial. Taylor wanted to give Khanh more time, but McNamara speculated that the United States might not be able to wait more than a few weeks.[20] When the President joined Rusk, McNamara, Taylor, McGeorge Bundy, and McCone for another meeting that evening, Johnson said he wanted to be ready, if necessary, to begin attacks on North Vietnam at once. First, however, he wanted to propose a U.N. peacekeeping mission, which, should it fail, would be followed by American action, undertaken with the objective of restoring peace.[21]

On May 25 McGeorge Bundy wrote Johnson a memo highly reminiscent of his November 1961 memorandum to Kennedy, once more adding his voice to the consensus in favor of intervention. He suggested that an immediate decision "that the US cannot tolerate the loss of Southeast Asia to Communism," combined with deployments to implement it, "gives the best present chance of avoiding the actual use of such force." Bundy laid out a full scenario, beginning with a Honolulu conference and a U.N. initiative, even though the United States would never get its way in the Security Council. After the United Nations failed to act, the United States could consult with SEATO allies, seek a congressional resolution, and bomb North Vietnam. At the same time, both Lodge and Michael Forrestal, who had just visited South Vietnam for two weeks, reported that some dramatic step against the North was necessary to energize the South Vietnamese. Johnson on May 26 ordered a Honolulu meeting within a week, to include Rusk, McNamara, Taylor, and McCone.[22]

That night Johnson apparently stayed up late thinking about Vietnam, and the next day he had lengthy and revealing conversations about the subject with McGeorge Bundy and his old friend Senator Russell. "It looks to me like we're getting into another Korea," he told Bundy. "I don't see what we can hope to get out of there with, once we're committed . . . I don't think it's worth fighting for." Yet despite these doubts, Johnson reaffirmed the assumptions upon which American policy was based. "If you start running from the Communists they just chase you right into the kitchen," he said. A recent Mansfield memo, he said, was "just as milktoast as it can be—got no spine at all." Bundy agreed that running would have a bad effect on "everyone in that part of the world."

Saying that he did not know what he would do in the President's shoes, Bundy commented, "You're constantly looking for some way of stiffening this thing that doesn't involve escalation." Threatening action without having decided upon it, as Kennedy had done over Laos, might no longer work. Touching on another critical point, Bundy suggested that Vietnam become an all-volunteer assignment for Americans. "Well, you wouldn't have a corporal's guard, would you?" Johnson replied. "I just don't know," said Bundy. "If that's true then I'm not sure we're the country to do this job."

Johnson's talk with Russell lasted much longer. Now sixty-six years old, Russell was one of the most intelligent and capable legislators of the Lost generation, and he had been Johnson's mentor when Johnson came to the Senate in 1948. Known mainly as the leader of the white southerners opposed to civil rights legislation—a subject which he and Johnson almost never discussed—Russell had a long memory and a good understanding of many military and foreign policy issues. A skeptical middle-American nationalist, he frequently remarked to Johnson that while it was a great mistake ever to have become involved in Indochina, he did not know how to get out.

Now, in the midst of a long conversation, Russell touched on several very important issues and made some potentially valuable suggestions. He dismissed the situation in Laos as a joke, citing the very low level of actual fighting. He agreed with Johnson that Communist China would probably intervene if the United States entered the war in Vietnam, and he expected the situation to be worse than Korea, because, he noted accurately, the "physical configuration" of Korea had made it difficult for the Communists to carry out guerrilla warfare. He also dismissed the idea that bombing could stop the infiltration of enemy troops in South Vietnam any more than they had in Korea. While acknowledging McNamara's intelligence, he argued that McNamara had become too opinionated and that he might not know as much about the people and history of the region as he should. Russell clearly would have been greatly relieved to hear that the United States was not going to war in South Vietnam. And while he made no definite recommendation to withdraw, repeating again and again that all the alternatives were terrible, he did suggest how the United States might extricate itself, by allowing a government to come to power that might invite us out.[23]

Johnson shared Russell's doubts about the worth of South Vietnam and Laos as such, but he still rejected Mansfield's alternatives to intervention—adopting de Gaulle's proposal for neutralization, going to the United Nations, or calling a conference. He said he had delayed action because the American people seemed to know little about the situation and care even less, but he quoted his foreign policy team to the effect that more dominoes would fall if South Vietnam were lost, and he rejected dissenting views. "They'd impeach a President who'd run out, wouldn't they?" he asked. When Russell replied that a new government might invite us out, Johnson asked whether that wouldn't look bad in the eyes of the world. Subsequent conversations revealed that Johnson saw this more as a grave danger than as an opportunity.

Russell had been among those senators who had been relieved to hear from Kennedy in late April 1961 that the United States was not intervening in Laos. A few days after Johnson's conversation with Russell, Senator George Smathers of Florida told Johnson that all the southern Democrats opposed a war in Southeast Asia. Thus, as Johnson pointed out in reply, while some conservative and centrist Republicans—including Barry Goldwater, Richard Nixon, and Nelson Rockefeller—favored intervention, southern Democrats (and some liberal Democrats) did not. And indeed, later events showed a lack of real enthusiasm in the Congress for war in Indochina, despite a general willingness to support the administration. But while Johnson recognized that the country was far from ready to intervene and hoped to postpone action until after the election, he rejected every alternative to intervention.[24]

Johnson had two more long conversations about Vietnam over the

next few days. In a remarkably cordial talk, Robert Kennedy emphasized the need to work at least as hard on the political aspects of the
situation as on the military ones, and Smathers remembered General
MacArthur's strictures against a land war in Asia. But after Johnson
stressed the danger to Indonesia and even India should South Vietnam
fall and the need to stand up to the Communists, Smathers replied that
in the end Johnson would have to do what he thought best for the
country and the Free World, whatever the American people thought.[25]

And once again, in response to the President's obvious concern,
Washington decided over the next two weeks that the situation was not
quite so critical after all. The administration announced the Honolulu
conference on May 28, and Johnson on that day warned Canadian
Prime Minister Lester Pearson that the United States might have to undertake "carefully limited" action against North Vietnam."[26] But having stepped to the brink, Johnson immediately drew back. First, after
several more meetings on Laos, the administration decided to try to
solve the problem diplomatically—albeit without a Geneva conference—and to demand merely a Pathet Lao withdrawal to the lines of
May 16.[27] On May 30, at an interdepartmental meeting to prepare for
Honolulu, Harlan Cleveland of the U.N. mission remarked that it
would be difficult to convince the rest of the world of the wisdom of
acting against the North, and McNamara replied that he, Rusk, and
the President had all been worrying about this as well. And on the next
day, Undersecretary of State George Ball—who as we shall see had
grave doubts about the whole enterprise—wrote Rusk, who was on his
way to Saigon and Honolulu, in an apparent effort to exert a moderat-
ing influence.

Ball reported that the President on May 27 had met with him and
Walter Lippmann, who had pushed the case for neutralization. After
Lippmann left, Ball said, Johnson asked how he could remain a man of
peace and carry the country with him if action led to escalation "under
conditions where the rest of the world would regard us as being wrong-
headed." Ball, who undoubtedly had encouraged this fear, now told
Rusk "that the President will not act hastily and that he is by no means
tied to a scenario of the kind that was being considered when you left,"
and raised several serious questions about the wisdom of escalation
himself.[28]

In a press conference on June 2 the President began with Vietnam.

Following Bundy's suggestions closely, he declared that "America keeps her word," "the issue is the future of Southeast Asia as a whole," and "our purpose is peace." He also read the whole text of Eisenhower's letter of October 25, 1954, offering assistance to President Diem, and argued that he himself was following the same policy. Asked whether the United States was preparing to "move the Vietnam war into the North," he replied—falsely—"I know of no plans that have been made to that effect."[29] Representative Melvin Laird publicly stated that McNamara had briefed House committees on plans to take the war to the North. This statement was true, but Johnson defended his version on the grounds that he had as yet made no decision.[30]

The Pentagon, meanwhile, was planning for war. The Joint Staff in early May had prepared a long paper for the Chiefs outlining two separate but possibly sequential series of actions employing different capabilities. Both plans assumed that North Vietnam could and very possibly would call off the insurgencies in South Vietnam and Laos in response to appropriate measures by the United States, and neither gave any attention whatever to the guerrilla campaign in South Vietnam. The first revolved around OPLAN 37–64, which had been developed in response to NSAM 288 of March 17, and relied upon Laotian and South Vietnamese forces to the maximum extent possible. It called for air strikes against enemy positions in Laos and North Vietnam, carried out by South Vietnamese and Farmgate aircraft, including B-57 jet bombers that the Chiefs wanted to move into either Thailand or South Vietnam, and aerial mining of North Vietnamese ports, for which some South Vietnamese pilots were now receiving training. Even this plan, however, called for prepositioning large U.S. Marine and Army forces in Thailand, and the alert of further forces to meet Communist retaliation. Several comments also discussed the severely limited indigenous capabilities on which the plan had to rely.

OPLAN 99–64, which CINCPAC had developed nearly a year earlier in response to the June 1963 Laos crisis, included more serious and overt American actions, such as large-scale bombing of targets in North Vietnam, a naval blockade or quarantine, and, ultimately, "commitment of US and allied ground forces to Laos and North Vietnam as appropriate." The Joint Staff paper referred more than once to the possibility of escalation into "a CINCPAC OPLAN 32–64 (Phase III or IV) situation." OPLAN 32–64 provided for the "overall defense of Southeast Asia," probably against China as well as North Vietnam. McGeorge Bundy received a copy of this plan from General Taylor's aide, Colonel Smith.[31] The Chiefs on June 6 apparently discussed two plans—perhaps the same two—one calling for three to four brigades to seize towns along the Mekong, and another that would have moved seven divisions in three phases into Thailand, Laos, and South Vietnam.[32] The emphasis upon Thailand suggests that the Chiefs were planning to make a stand along the Mekong, as they had envisioned back in 1961 when Laos was the immediately threatened target.

Generals LeMay and Greene wanted to commit the administration to a massive air war against the North. On June 2 they submitted a memorandum to their Chairman, Maxwell Taylor, expressing their concern over "a lack of definition, even a confusion," concerning American objectives and possible courses of action in Southeast Asia. In order to ensure the termination of "North Vietnamese support of the subversive efforts in Laos and South Vietnam," they proposed a sweeping military objective: "the destruction of North Vietnamese will and capabilities as necessary to compel the Democratic Government of Vietnam [DRV] to cease providing support to the insurgencies in South Vietnam and Laos." Destruction "as necessary" implied that the United States should go to the limit of American capabilities—including nuclear weapons—in order to secure its objectives, and six months later the Chiefs became more explicit on this point. If conventional weapons failed to do enough damage, nuclear weapons could.

The Chiefs complained that "some current thinking appears to dismiss this objective in favor of a lesser objective, on visualizing limited military action which, hopefully, would cause the North Vietnamese to decide to terminate their subversive support" of those insurgencies. "The Joint Chiefs of Staff consider that this lesser objective just described is an inadequate objective," they continued, "*but would agree as an initial measure to pursue a course of action to achieve this lesser objective.*"[33] Even these two most warlike Chiefs were agreeing to limited initial objectives provided that the civilians were essentially willing to impose destruction "as necessary."

Two days of meetings in Honolulu on June 1–2 revealed the extent of the administration's plans, but eventually reached a consensus against immediate action. McNamara seemed inclined to push for an early, dramatic step, but somewhat to his surprise, General Westmoreland—

whom everyone expected to take over for Harkins in the near future—described the military situation as "tenuous, but far from hopeless." And indeed, while total Viet Cong incidents of all kinds averaged 471 a week during May—a figure slightly higher than the previous year—armed attacks averaged just 37 per week, or less than half the average of a year before. McNamara initially disagreed, arguing that the situation was "approaching the hopeless category," but Rusk, Lodge, and Westmoreland all implied that the situation could continue as it was for at least some months, and McNamara concluded "that there is no great pressure for drastic action at this time." Only McCone dissented.

Westmoreland also noted an interesting paradox: "The number of GVN operations rose dramatically above the rate of increase of VC initiated incidents, *but there was no corresponding increase of population or area under government control. In fact, government control continues to decline.* This establishes the fact that there is no direct relationship of operating tempo and extension of control."[34] Westmoreland, astonishingly, was confirming the longstanding observation of Hilsman, Serong, and several other observers: that the South Vietnamese, as advised by the Americans, were not undertaking operations that would really solve the counterinsurgency problem. But neither later in 1964, when Westmoreland took over from Harkins, nor beginning in 1965, when he commanded American troops, did the general draw the conclusion that American tactics had to change.

The next day, however, when the group began discussing actual military options, they made clear that major war might be in prospect. Action, McNamara, stated, would require the United States to "make major deployments . . . anticipate escalation, and call up some reserves," and to build a "political foundation," including a congressional resolution. General Taylor noted that the North Vietnamese could move in five divisions and the Chinese could supply many more, and posited a need for five to seven American divisions to meet the threat. Admiral Felt suggested that the United States would have to respond to North Vietnamese intervention with amphibious attacks on North Vietnam, and McNamara characterized this as "a possible, not probable reaction." While expressing the hope that "controlled, selective strikes" would prevent an attack on South Vietnam, McNamara and Rusk agreed that the United States had to be ready for anything, including the use of nuclear weapons. Felt went much further, arguing that "there was no possible way to hold off the communists on the ground without the use of tactical nuclear weapons," and that commanders needed the authority to use them, "as had been agreed in the various plans."[35] In short, while the senior civilians hoped to secure their objectives with limited military action, they seemed as willing as the Joint Chiefs to proceed to all-out war should that prove necessary.[36]

When the conferees returned to Washington on June 3, Bundy assured Johnson that Rusk and McNamara wanted to delay action "at least for several weeks, and possibly for quite a lot longer."[37] Johnson received a dissenting opinion from Lodge, who on June 5 sent a cable to Rusk and a letter to Johnson, asking once again for immediate, *deniable* strikes against the North to frighten Hanoi and strengthen Saigon, and doubting the wisdom of deploying seven American divisions on the Asian mainland as discussed in Honolulu. Over the past six months Lodge had suggested combining deniable strikes with proposals for the neutralization of both Vietnams, but Washington had never picked up on this idea. Given Johnson's extreme sensitivity to Lodge's views, the cable undoubtedly helped incline the President against drastic action during the remainder of 1964.[38]

The issue of further action refused to die because of new events in Laos. The United States had, as we have seen, begun reconnaissance flights over the Pathet Lao–held Plain of Jarres. Anti-aircraft fire apparently persuaded Ambassador Unger on June 4 to recommend that the flights be curtailed, but they continued, and on June 7 the Pentagon announced that the Pathet Lao had shot down two American fighters escorting the reconnaissance planes.[39] Unger, who had not secured Souvanna's approval for the armed escort, protested bitterly that he had no idea what to say now, and recommended against a retaliatory strike.[40]

Rusk, McNamara, and even Harriman were suddenly desperate to prove that the United States would not stand by in the face of enemy action, and in meetings on June 7–8 they persuaded a reluctant President Johnson to order a retaliatory strike. McNamara in particular insisted that the administration simply had to back up its many strong statements with deeds.[41] Rusk in another meeting on June 10 called shrilly for stronger action in Laos, but Bundy replied that the United States did not want to bring things to a head militarily there, and that Taylor would resign as Chairman of the Joint Chiefs rather than put troops in the Plain of Jarres. Two weeks later, Bundy warned Johnson that Rusk needed a rest and implied that the Secretary was on the verge of a nervous breakdown.[42] The same meeting also decided—partly on the advice of Attorney General Robert Kennedy—not to seek a congressional resolution authorizing action in Southeast Asia until circumstances required it. McNamara even suggested a new press campaign "to avoid building up public pressure for drastic action."[43]

Significantly, Souvanna Phouma and the Laotians themselves showed during the months to come that they could cope with the Pathet Lao without overt American assistance. On June 23 Souvanna asked for American airlift and tactical air support for an operation designed to recapture some territory from the Pathet Lao. In the end the United States provided only airlift, but a series of attacks on the Pathet Lao during July won back substantial territory. By August the military situation had quieted down, and Souvanna even attended lengthy meetings of the three factions in Paris. The Pathet Lao now claimed that the coalition had broken down and refused to recognize Souvanna Phouma as Prime Minister—a refusal that emerged as the main stumbling block to reconvening the Geneva conference. Souvanna, with American help, had forced the Communists onto the defensive both politically and militarily, and by the end of the year he was emerging as a staunch American ally.[44]

Desperate to make a firm stand despite the President's reluctance to change policy, the administration began a press campaign to intimidate North Vietnam. "In the minds of officials here," the *New York Times* reported on June 20 in language that Rusk had repeatedly used, "the United States commitment to the security of Southeast Asia is now unlimited and comparable with the commitment of West Berlin . . . Washington sees no way of negotiating a compromise."[45] On June 22 the *Times* reported from Saigon that the United States was completing new air bases in Thailand and in Da Nang, South Vietnam, preparing, if need be, for an all-out confrontation with China. "The Honolulu meeting and subsequent White House decisions are understood to have emphasized that the United States stands ready to meet Communist China head-on rather than be forced out of Southeast Asia," the story reported accurately.[46] On June 29 President Johnson confirmed that the United States would risk war to achieve its objectives in Asia. The administration apparently made these statements to reinforce a warning delivered during the same month by the Canadian ICC Commissioner Blair Seaborn to North Vietnamese Prime Minister Pham Van Dong in Hanoi that the DRV faced "the greatest devastation" if the conflict should escalate—a warning whose text remains classified.[47]

Although the United States did not know it, Ho Chi Minh and Mao Zedong were already preparing their response. In June Mao told a high North Vietnamese military leader, "Your business is my business and my business is your business," and suggested fighting the enemy together. In July—in a trip that the United States does not seem to have learned about—Chinese Foreign Minister Zhou Enlai visited Hanoi for discussions with Ho and the Pathet Lao. The Sino-Soviet split was as bitter as ever, and Mao had no intention of backing down against the United States and yielding to the "revisionist" line.[48]

Johnson, of course, was now focusing most of his attention upon legislative battles and the coming election. In his greatest triumph, the Senate during the third week of June voted to end debate on the Civil Rights Act, and passed it by a vote of 73 to 27, with Senator Barry Goldwater—the victor in the California Republican primary, and the clear front-runner for the Republican nomination—among the opposition. Economic news showed unemployment at a four-year low, and the President frequently gave credit to the recent tax cut. Goldwater, meanwhile, was making it very easy for Johnson to present himself as a man of peace, suggesting for example that the United States might use low-yield nuclear weapons to defoliate parts of Vietnam—an idea that drew an immediate blast from U.N. Secretary General U Thant.[49] Johnson was still delaying action on another critical campaign decision: the selection of his Vice President. Robert Kennedy—despite his intense and fully returned dislike for Johnson, whom he had never trusted—had in the months since November persuaded himself that he deserved the job. Johnson, who never had any intention of giving it to him, floated various other possibilities, including McNamara and Kennedy's brother-in-law Sargent Shriver, but delayed any decision. Kennedy by June was thinking seriously of running for the Senate from the state of New York, but he apparently counted so heavily on the vice-presidential possibility that he announced in the last few days of June that he would *not* run for the Senate.

Politics and Southeast Asia intersected after Goldwater's surprise victory over the liberal Nelson Rockefeller in the California primary. Ambassador Lodge on June 18 suddenly wrote Rusk that he was resigning to help the new moderate Republican hope, Governor William Scranton of Pennsylvania. The moment to choose a new ambassador to Saigon had finally come, and Johnson made a revealing and fateful decision.

Two weeks before, in anticipation of Lodge's resignation, Bundy on June 6 had given Johnson six recommendations for his successor: Peace Corps Director and Kennedy in-law Sargent Shriver, McNamara's deputy Roswell Gilpatric, McNamara himself, the lesser-known William Gaud of AID, Robert Kennedy, and Bundy himself. With the exception of Gaud, every one of these choices would have given the impression that the job had the highest priority, and all but Gaud had also risen to prominence in the Kennedy administration. Although Johnson had already found the suggestion of Robert Kennedy "wild," Bundy argued that Kennedy would welcome the challenge, and that he would "give a picture of idealism and peace-seeking which our cause will badly need, especially if we have to move to stronger measures." Bundy's offer to take the job himself indicated a commendable willingness to tackle an enormously difficult task, but also suggests that he already had serious doubts about continuing indefinitely in his present position.[50]

On the morning of June 15 Johnson told a shocked Bundy that he was rejecting these suggestions in favor of another distinguished figure closely associated with his predecessor: Chairman of the Joint Chiefs General Maxwell Taylor. Bundy protested the appointment of a military man, but Johnson replied that it was a "military job . . . He's our top military man . . . I'm not sure that the administration has as much respect on Vietnam as Taylor would have on Vietnam. I believe anything in his name, signed to, would carry some weight with nearly anyone." Johnson told a more sympathetic McNamara that Taylor could "give us the best protection with all the forces that want to make that a political war . . . I think we're going to have to make a decision pretty promptly and we're going to have to send him out there and then kind of support what he thinks we ought to do."[51] Johnson immediately began relying on Taylor's imprimatur to justify administration policy, and at the turn of the year the general's recommendations played a critical role in moving Johnson from peace into war. Neither Bundy nor McNamara ever pointed out that Kennedy, had he accepted Taylor's recommendations, would have put combat troops into South Vietnam in 1961.

The choice solved two organizational problems in Saigon, since McNamara and the Pentagon could hardly deny Taylor the complete authority over the country team which Nolting and Lodge had never received, and Lodge's departure finally cleared the way for Harkins's replacement by Westmoreland. To help administer the country team and mollify Rusk, Johnson appointed Rusk's close associate, Deputy Undersecretary for Political Affairs U. Alexis Johnson, as deputy ambassador. Johnson, like Rusk, had been fully committed to whatever American action was necessary to stop Communist advances in Asia since the time of the Korean War. At the Pentagon, Army Chief of Staff Earle Wheeler replaced Taylor as Chairman of the Joint Chiefs.

The administration also used Taylor's appointment to define a new public policy which, with one major exception, carried it through the November election. Rusk, McNamara, Bundy, and President Johnson had painted themselves into a somewhat uncomfortable corner during June. Their actions in Laos and their constant declaration of sweeping American objectives and American willingness to take all necessary steps to secure them had made Vietnam and Laos the major foreign policy story of these months. The administration had no other major foreign policy initiatives in progress, and the broader East-West issues that had dominated the Kennedy years were getting almost no attention. Remarkably enough, Khrushchev and East German leader Walter Ulbricht on June 12 signed a new treaty of friendship and assistance, finally and officially backing away from the threat to sign a separate peace treaty that would end Western rights in Berlin that had hung over the West since 1958, but the news barely caused a ripple in Washington. Firmness in Southeast Asia had become what Kennedy had never allowed it to be: the centerpiece of administration foreign policy.

With Goldwater now almost certainly the Republican candidate, however, the administration tacked back in the direction of peace. Lodge's resignation helped set the tone for the shift, partly because the ambassador made clear that he wanted to prevent Goldwater from getting the nomination for fear of what he might do in foreign affairs. Lodge now repeatedly declared that American policy was on the right track, and the administration made known through James Reston that

Taylor's appointment did not mean that the administration had decided to carry the war north, and that it preferred to follow a middle course that would avoid either a spectacular offensive or a spectacular defeat.[52] Domestic news helped shift the nation's attention. With Goldwater only weeks from the nomination, moderate Republicans scrambled frantically to find an alternative, while former President Eisenhower, contradicting himself almost daily, seemed unable to decide whether he could support the bellicose Arizona senator or not. And another huge domestic story broke on June 23, when the civil rights workers James Chaney, Andrew Goodman, and Michael Schwerner disappeared near Philadelphia, Mississippi, and the FBI, at President Johnson's orders, dispatched hundreds of agents to investigate their disappearance.

In Saigon, however, General Khanh was losing support, and continued to push the administration toward more forceful action that would secure his position. On July 19, less than two weeks after Taylor arrived and about a week after Goldwater's nomination, Khanh called publicly for the liberation of the North. After several more days of such talk—heavily reported in the American press—Taylor on July 23 speculated that Khanh was trying to take advantage of Goldwater's nomination to push the United States into action, and warned that the South Vietnamese might actually opt for negotiation if we did not agree. After several days of discussions in Washington, Taylor received permission to discuss possible, eventual action against the North, to make an immediate announcement of substantial increases in the American advisory effort, and to propose a series of South Vietnamese and Farmgate air strikes against enemy infiltration routes in Laos. In response to a request from McNamara, the Joint Chiefs were now recommending these measures, as well as deniable strikes against North Vietnam itself, as actions designed to support the counterinsurgency effort and "relieve the current frustration of South Vietnamese leaders." Khanh expressed pleasure about planned increases in the American presence on July 27, but made clear that many South Vietnamese still doubted American intentions and feared that the United States wanted to negotiate. Bombing the North, he suggested, might immediately persuade Ho Chi Minh of the need to negotiate and bring the long war to an end.[53] The President in a news conference on July 24 rejected de Gaulle's latest call for neutralization, and Washington announced the dispatch of 5,000 new advisers on July 27.[54]

Johnson saw the Joint Chiefs again on July 31, and turned down recommendations for immediate action against the North. Citing both the political turmoil in Saigon and his own still-uncertain position as Kennedy's unelected successor, he called this "a hell of a poor time in which to carry on an adventure—to strike back."[55] But the momentum of events now gave the United States the chance make the dramatic gesture that Khanh had long demanded and that McNamara and Rusk had wanted for some time.

Since March, as we have seen, U.S. forces had been assisting South Vietnamese in the planning and execution of OPLAN 34A, the new operations plan for sabotage operations against North Vietnam, including hit-and-run attacks along the North Vietnamese coast. These attacks had encountered fierce North Vietnamese resistance, and McNamara himself in late July was suggesting that they try offshore gunfire instead of landing sabotage teams. Meanwhile, American destroyers had been carrying out classified DeSoto patrols along the North Vietnamese coast to collect electronic intelligence. These missions had also accomplished very little, since the North Vietnamese prudently turned their radar off when the destroyers approached, but the new CINCPAC, Admiral Ulysses S. Grant Sharp, wanted to continue them partly to prepare for possible further action against North Vietnam.[56]

On the night of July 30–31, South Vietnamese patrol boats planning to land teams on two North Vietnamese islands—Hon Me and Hon Nieu—encountered fire from shore before landing, and conducted a brief offshore bombardment instead. Meanwhile, an American destroyer, the *Maddox*, had left Taiwan on a DeSoto patrol on July 28, scheduled to reach the North Vietnamese coast on August 1. American authorities in Saigon and Honolulu had decided that the 34A and DeSoto missions would not interfere with one another. On August 1 the destroyer passed within several miles of the islands that the South Vietnamese had bombarded. It continued its patrol the next day.

On the afternoon of August 2 the *Maddox* detected North Vietnamese patrol boats approaching at high speed, and set out for the open sea. The North Vietnamese boats followed, closing range with apparent intent to attack. According to North Vietnamese sources, they had received a mistaken, unauthorized order to do so, and failed to receive a message recalling them until it was too late.[57] The *Maddox* eventually opened fire as three boats continued to approach, seriously damaging one boat, but not sinking it.[58] The action concluded at about dawn Washington time, and by late morning President Johnson was discussing it with Rusk, Ball, General Wheeler, and McNamara's new deputy, Cyrus Vance.

Johnson, who now enjoyed a commanding lead over Barry Goldwater at the polls, was growing in confidence day by day in foreign as well as domestic affairs. On August 1, in a conversation with George Smathers, he spoke proudly about his policies toward Panama, Cuba, and Brazil, where he believed he had proven his liberal critics entirely wrong. He was also relying increasingly upon McNamara, whom he sounded out on the same day about assuming special responsibilities within the cabinet amounting virtually to those of a prime minister.[59]

The meeting of August 2 concluded that a local North Vietnamese commander had ordered the attack and decided not to retaliate, but also instructed Wheeler to continue the patrol. An intercept of the message recalling the North Vietnamese may have influenced this decision.[60] More critically, either in this meeting or in another one at the White House on the same day, officials, including Cyrus Vance, *specifically approved new 34A attacks for the night of August 3.*[61] Both McGeorge Bundy and President Johnson himself had concluded that the North Vietnamese were responding directly to the 34A attack of July 30–31, and one inevitably suspects that the White House was purposely courting another incident.[62] And indeed, by the morning of August 4 in Washington, the President and the Secretary of Defense were already discussing how to retaliate against North Vietnam *if* the patrol was attacked.[63]

In Saigon, Maxwell Taylor complained that Khanh would take American inaction as further proof of American evil intentions and fear of the North Vietnamese. He suggested a policy of attacking North Vietnamese patrol boats whenever encountered in international waters, and mining their harbors.[64] McNamara told George Ball that Taylor was overreacting, and Rusk cabled Taylor that it seemed more prudent to confine action against the North to 34A operations until the security situation in the South improved, but McNamara also wrote orders under the President's signature continuing the U.S. naval patrol.[65] Khanh, confirming Taylor's fears, argued that the United States had to take stronger action to show that it was not a paper tiger, while Washington denied Hanoi's truthful accusations about the shelling of North Vietnamese islands.[66]

Following the President's orders, the *Maddox* and another destroyer, the *C. Turner Joy*, began a new patrol in the same area on August 3, with escort from fighter aircraft from the carrier *Ticonderoga*. That night South Vietnamese boats made the newly approved 34A attack on coastal positions, although well to the south of the area the American destroyers were now patrolling. Admiral Johnson, the commander of the Seventh Fleet, now suggested that the DeSoto patrol terminate after August 4, but Admiral Moorer, the Pacific Fleet commander, ordered four more days of patrols to "adequately demonstrate U.S. resolve to assert our legitimate rights in these international waters." The Joint Chiefs agreed.[67]

On the early morning of August 4—the early evening of August 4 in the Gulf of Tonkin—Washington and Captain Herrick of the *Maddox* were informed of radio intercepts indicating that North Vietnamese vessels were preparing to make another attack. The intercept did not specify the target, and the target may have been another anticipated 34A raid, not the destroyers.[68] By 9:30 AM McNamara was meeting with various Joint Staff officers in the Pentagon and discussing sweeping retaliatory options, including air strikes and aerial mining of harbors in North Vietnam. The President was keeping right on top of the situation, and at 9:43 McNamara called to tell him that Admiral Sharp wanted to send the destroyers even closer to shore—a move Johnson rejected.[69] A little over an hour later McNamara called again to report that the destroyers had sighted two unidentified vessels and three unidentified aircraft, and that the carrier *Ticonderoga* had launched planes to meet them. He laid out an ambitious list of retaliatory options, including attacks on North Vietnamese POL (petroleum, oil, and lubricants) dumps, bridges, and "other prestige targets." The "sightings" actually referred to radar contacts, not visual sightings, but it is unlikely that Johnson understood this.[70] When McNamara met with Rusk, McGeorge Bundy, and the Joint Chiefs of Staff sometime after 11:00, he asked General LeMay not only for retaliatory options but for other further actions, "with special emphasis on reinforcements, such as the movement of B-57 [jet bombers] into South Vietnam." The Secretary apparently wanted to make an unmistakable demonstration of American willingness to act.

Although sonar contacts led those on the *Maddox* sincerely to think that it was under attack for some time during the evening of August 4, and although both destroyers fired at presumed targets and even concluded that they had sunk two vessels, Edmund Moise's exhaustive analysis of the evidence makes it impossible to believe that any attack actually occurred that night. Radio intercepts which McNamara later cited to prove that one did seem clearly to refer to the earlier incident of August 2.[71] Washington, however, believed that an attack had taken place as of lunchtime, when President Johnson approved "a firm, swift retaliatory strike" but rejected mining harbors or bombing the major port of Haiphong. The strike eventually targeted North Vietnamese naval bases and a POL facility in Vinh. At 3:00 PM McNamara specifically asked the Joint Chiefs to prepare retaliation for 7:00 PM—that is, dawn in Vietnam. He had obviously seized upon the opportunity to deliver the message he had been pleading for at least since June: that the United States was ready to act, not only now in retaliation for the attacks that had reportedly taken place, but also in the future, and to the extent necessary to defend South Vietnam. In addition, the President now agreed to submit the congressional resolution supporting action in Southeast Asia that the senior leadership had been planning since the spring. The State Department began preparing it that afternoon.[72]

The senior leadership, then, had clearly taken its critical decisions before about 2:00 PM, when a telephone call from Admiral Sharp, followed closely by a message from Captain Herrick on the *Maddox*, raised some doubts as to the extent—and possibly even the existence—of the second North Vietnamese attack. Herrick in particular reported that a review "makes many reported contacts and torpedoes fired appear doubtful" and perhaps simply the result of freak weather effects or over-eager sonar men. "Suggest complete evaluation before any action taken," he continued. Sharp initially insisted that an attack had occurred, but shortly after 4:00 PM he told McNamara there was a "slight possibility" that it had not. At about the same time, the *Ticonderoga*, whose planes had provided air cover during the night, reported that none of its pilots had seen any hostile boats, despite visibility of 2,000–3,000 yards. (One of the pilots, future Admiral James Stockdale, provided a detailed and compelling account of the action many years later.) But Captain Herrick reported that despite widespread confusion over sonar contacts and sightings of hostile PT boats, it was "certain that original ambush was bonafide."[73] None of Johnson's released telephone conversations suggest that McNamara ever raised these questions with the Commander in Chief.

McNamara, Cyrus Vance, and the Chiefs met at 4:47, under enormous pressure, to decide whether an attack had occurred or not. They concluded that it had for five reasons, two of which related to sightings of enemy lights by American destroyers and three of which related to intercepts of North Vietnamese communications relating to the "sacrifice" of two boats. In days to come, intelligence analysis apparently showed that these messages referred to the August 1 attack.[74] At 6:45 Johnson, McNamara, and Rusk briefed the bipartisan congressional leadership and Johnson announced his intention to ask for a congressional resolution of support. The President specifically stated that nine torpedoes had been fired toward American ships, and Rusk declared that we had been trying to send a message to Hanoi for months. Several leaders objected to the emphasis on the "limited" nature of American actions in a proposed statement, but only one—Senator Mansfield—questioned the general course of action.[75]

Johnson wanted to announce the strike on television before the East Coast population had gone to bed, but after American planes had struck their targets. Because of delays on the carriers, most of the planes had not yet been launched when the President addressed the nation at 11:36 PM EDT. The President had questioned the safety of going on the air while the strike was in progress, but McNamara had encouraged him to do so.[76] The strike inflicted heavy damage, but the North Vietnamese, warned by President Johnson's announcement, downed two American planes, killing one pilot and capturing the other.[77] The President's telephone conversations show that he handled the whole crisis rather matter-of-factly, interspersing his brief talks with McNamara with longer talks on congressional matters, his choice of a running mate, and the discovery—on this very same eventful day—of the bodies of James Chaney, Andrew Goodman, and Michael Schwerner in Mississippi.

The next morning, August 5, McGeorge Bundy told an NSC staff meeting that while the evidence for the first attack was "pretty good," "on the second one the amount of evidence we have today is less than

we had yesterday . . . This much seemed certain: There was an attack
. . . This matter may be of some importance since Hanoi has denied
making the second attack." When Douglas Cater, who had not apparently been privy to earlier plans for a congressional resolution, said that
he had not thought the logic of the proposed resolution through carefully and did not understand "how an attack on US forces specifically
justified a resolution in favor of maintenance of freedom in Southeast
Asia," Bundy "jokingly told him perhaps the matter should not be
thought through too far. For his own part, he welcomed the recent
events as justification for a resolution the Administration had wanted
for some time."[78]

Congress received the Gulf of Tonkin Resolution on August 5 and
passed it on August 7 with only two dissenting senatorial votes, those
of Wayne Morse of Oregon and Ernst Gruening of Alaska. Section 1
declared that North Vietnam had "repeatedly" attacked American vessels on the high seas and approved and supported "the determination
of the President" to take all necessary measures to prevent further such
attacks. Section 2 declared that the United States was prepared, "as the
President determines, to take all necessary steps, including the use of
armed force, to assist any member or protocol state of the South East
Asia Collective Defense Treaty requiring assistance in defense of its
freedom." Section 3 stated that the resolution would lapse either in
response to a presidential declaration that the peace and security of
Southeast Asia were secure, or as a result of a new congressional resolution. (The administration submitted this provision despite its belief
that the resolution was not, in fact, required, either to undertake the retaliatory action against North Vietnam or for any military action the
President might decide to carry out.)[79]

The administration—led by McNamara, who assumed the responsibility for explaining what had happened to the Congress and the public—was determined to secure support for future action as part of an
attempt to intimidate the Chinese and North Vietnamese, and Mc-
Namara deliberately lied in order to make the North Vietnamese action
as provocative as possible. Not only did he repeatedly state that the destroyers had been making a "routine patrol" rather than carrying on an
intelligence mission, but he also denied, in response to direct questions
from Senator Wayne Morse of Oregon—whom a Pentagon source had

tipped off regarding the 34A attacks—that the Navy had any knowledge of offensive actions by the South Vietnamese.[80]

The House approved the measure with apparent unanimity,[81] and the Senate recorded only two dissenting votes, those of Morse of Gruening. Morse, who spoke repeatedly and at length, argued that the United States and the South Vietnamese were provoking the escalation of the war, and chillingly predicted the loss of the war and the repudiation of the administration that undertook it. More significant, however, was the extremely restrained enthusiasm of the House and Senate as a whole. Again and again, senators and representatives explained that they were voting in support of the President's authority to retaliate against attacks, but without advocating any additional action, much less arguing for war. Two leading southern Democrats, Senators Russell of Georgia and Stennis of Mississippi, mentioned their decade-old reservations about American involvement in Indochina. Republicans George Aiken of New Hampshire and Frank Carlson of Kansas expressed their concerns over the wisdom of American policy, as did Democrat Frank Church of Idaho. Senator Gaylord Nelson of Wisconsin actually wanted to introduce an amendment stating that American policy remained limited to "the provision of aid, training assistance, and military advice," and that Congress "should continue to attempt to avoid a direct military involvement in the southeast Asian conflict." Representative Melvin Laird of Wisconsin asked the administration to decide between escalation and the Gaullist policy of negotiation and withdrawal.[82]

Senator Fulbright of Arkansas, who loyally managed the resolution on the Senate floor and repeated McNamara's reassurances again and again, dissuaded Nelson from offering his amendment. According to subsequent testimony, he wanted to pass the resolution as quickly as possible in order to help the President in the campaign against Goldwater, whom most Democrats and many Republicans viewed as dangerously extreme in foreign affairs. Several senators, including Democrat Daniel Brewster of Maryland, Republican John Sherman Cooper of Kentucky, and Fulbright himself, expressed grave reservations about the possibility of becoming involved in land war in Asia, but Fulbright assured the Senate that he expected the President to consult with Congress again, should any such step become necessary.[83]

By initiating 34A attacks and simultaneously authorizing DeSoto patrols, the administration had brought about one brief military confrontation between North Vietnamese and American forces. The second, spurious attack had then become the pretext for retaliation, a congressional resolution authorizing war, and the movement of additional U.S. air assets into South Vietnam. Essentially, the administration had managed to validate publicly its new concept of the war: that the source of the trouble lay in North Vietnam, and that action against North Vietnam could bring it to an end. But had Washington not begun covert attacks upon the North Vietnamese coast early in the year and carried out simultaneous, provocative DeSoto patrols, no confrontation would have taken place, and it would have been far more difficult to pass a resolution.

During August the administration tried to project the image of a firm, appropriate, carefully limited policy designed to deter and, if necessary, to repel Communist aggression, just as previous administrations had done during the Second World War, the Korean conflict, and throughout the era of the Cold War. To reinforce this message, the United States actually accused the North Vietnamese of aggression in the Security Council of the United Nations, and Johnson explained our position in letters to British Prime Minister Hume and to Khrushchev.[84] All told, the episode seemed to reinforce the image of responsible leadership that Johnson wanted to convey, especially in contrast to his electoral opponent. As Reston pointed out, the whole crisis—like the Bay of Pigs and the Cuban missile crisis—illustrated the enormous power of the modern Presidency, and thereby heightened the importance of the election. "The Congress," he wrote, "was free in theory only. In practice, despite the private reservations of many members, it had to go along . . . it had the choice of helping him or helping the enemy, which is no choice at all." And who, Reston asked, could be trusted with this enormous new power—Johnson or Goldwater?[85]

The events of the first week in August also conformed to a scenario that the Pentagon had envisaged since January 1964: that South Vietnamese covert operations against the North could lead to enemy retaliation, and hence to American bombing of the North as an additional measure of pressure. They enabled the Chiefs, with presidential concurrence, to begin implementing critical aspects of OPLAN 37–64, developed during the spring as a means of putting pressure on the North

Vietnamese. On the same day that President Johnson ordered the retaliatory strike, several squadrons of American jet aircraft flew to South Vietnam: six F-102s and eight F-100s to Da Nang, six new reconnaissance planes to Tan Son Nhut, and, most important, thirty-six B-57 jet bombers to Bien Hoa. Other planes landed in newly constructed airports in Thailand.

By the weekend Hanson Baldwin of the *New York Times* wrote that these moves were designed to deter and contain Communist China. They had exactly the opposite effect. Rightly convinced that Washington wanted to fight, the leadership in Hanoi met several days later and began planning to send North Vietnamese army units into the South in the following year. On August 5—just one day after the American strikes—Zhou Enlai cabled Ho and asked him to "investigate the situation, work out countermeasures, and be prepared to fight." By August 7 thirty-nine MIG 15/17 jet fighters had flown from Chinese bases to Phuc Yen airfield north of Hanoi. Le Duan, the most militant leader of the North Vietnamese politburo, visited Mao Zedong and received promises of assistance and advice to take on the Americans directly until they were willing to negotiate.[86] And the Chinese prepared aggressively for possible American escalation against China itself, moving four air divisions and one anti-aircraft division into areas bordering on North Vietnam.[87]

The Soviet Union made a much more measured response, one that clearly distinguished itself from Peking and showed more interest in a peaceful settlement, as in Laos. *Pravda* specifically distanced itself from a Chinese official who commented that "war in Southeast Asia would not be such a bad thing," and Khrushchev—only months away from his fall—sent Johnson a carefully worded letter disclaiming any direct knowledge of the incidents and calling for steps to remove "a threat to peace." Johnson replied that the United States "will always be prompt and firm in its positive reply to acts of aggression, and our power is equal to any such test." Realizing that both sides were prepared to fight, Moscow began to adjust its policy accordingly.[88] Khrushchev's fall in October, however, immediately changed the situation. In November 1964 North Vietnamese Prime Minister Pham Van Dong visited Moscow and received pledges of support should the United States attack North Vietnam. By the turn of the year Hanoi had both of its major patrons behind it.[89]

Just as Admiral Felt had predicted in December 1963, the introduction of 34A raids against South Vietnam had rapidly led to North Vietnamese retaliation against both South Vietnam and the United States, and hence to further escalation. War with North Vietnam was only one small step away. Johnson seemed to have moved well down the path laid down by the bureaucracy and Kennedy's senior advisers—further, certainly, than Kennedy had ever agreed to go. But having established his image of firm and confident leadership and created the basis for more action at some future date, Johnson temporarily lost interest in escalation. While he had found it expedient to approve a single retaliatory strike, he also wanted to present himself to the electorate as the more peaceful and cautious candidate. Thus he ordered the suspension of 34A operations, apparently in order to avoid further incidents. As we shall see, he remained cautious in subsequent weeks, stressing the need to strengthen the Saigon government and rejecting action before the election. "If the roof falls in," he remarked at one point, "I will have been proved wrong, but I am going to take the chance that it won't."[90] The President was determined to move at his own pace, and not for another six months, until February 1965, did he actually cross the threshold between peace and war. Never, however, did he evince any real interest in any long-term alternative to escalation, and when the time came he showed that he fully shared the assumptions of his senior advisers.

12

Planning for War
September–December 1964

★

The Tonkin Gulf strikes had aimed partly at boosting South Vietnamese morale and strengthening the Khanh government's resolve, but Khanh's efforts to take advantage of them ushered in a new political crisis. During his seven months in power, Khanh had apparently failed to build a stable following among any of the major contending political groups: the Can Lao remnants of the Diem regime, the Dai Viet nationalist party that had ties to certain generals, and the Buddhists, who retained their ability to mobilize large crowds of demonstrators in South Vietnam's major cities. On August 16 Khanh suddenly promulgated the Vung Tau charter (a new constitution) and assumed the presidency of South Vietnam, replacing Big Minh (who had officially remained Chief of State while under house arrest). Within two weeks, the Buddhists—led once again by the venerable Thich Tri Quang—had organized large-scale demonstrations against him, claiming that he had put himself in the hands of Can Lao and Dai Viet cliques and threatening large-scale passive resistance. Some Buddhist demonstrators attacked American offices in Da Nang as well. After about five days of demonstrations, Khanh during the last week of August tacked back toward the Buddhists, but promptly began worrying about a Dai Viet coup. The general's nerves were giving away under the strain, and Taylor and Alexis Johnson had to go to the resort town of Dalat on August 31 to meet him. Shocked by the chaos, Ambassador Taylor bluntly threatened to withdraw American support if Khanh could not show more leadership. In Washington, McGeorge Bundy on August 31 suggested to President Johnson that the United States consider landing "a limited number of Marines" to guard American installations.

Khanh finally returned to Saigon on September 4, claiming support from the Buddhists and planning a civilian cabinet. The next day, after releasing some arrested demonstrators, he removed some Dai Viet generals from power. Taylor seemed quite alarmed by Khanh's concessions to the Buddhists, whom the general claimed had now committed themselves to the war for the first time. Oddly, however, Washington sources claimed that Khanh had consulted Taylor on every step, and that the ambassador had endorsed concessions to dissident elements.[1]

Taylor returned to Washington for a regular consultation on September 6. Military and civilian proposals for further action had been accumulating rapidly since the Tonkin Gulf attacks. The President himself had kicked off this process on August 10, asking for proposals for further action "with maximum results and minimum danger."[2] William Bundy on August 13 suggested resuming and acknowledging both 34A operations and DeSoto patrols, preparing for joint U.S.-GVN air attacks against infiltration targets, cross-border operations into Laos, and planning for American air attacks against the North after January 1. The Joint Chiefs on August 14 endorsed these proposals, provided Bundy's stronger suggestions were "implemented as necessary . . . with the objective of destroying the DRV will and capabilities to continue support of insurgent forces in Laos and South Vietnam." Once again the Chiefs were insisting on the maximum application of American power should such prove necessary.[3]

In Saigon, General Westmoreland and Ambassador Taylor went further. Westmoreland on August 15 warned CINCPAC Admiral Sharp and General Wheeler that the North Vietnamese might respond to the Tonkin Gulf strikes by seizing the initiative on the ground. Whole units might be infiltrated for a surprise attack on Da Nang—destroying a new American air base—or Hue. He therefore recommended stationing a Marine battalion landing team off Da Nang, ready to land within six hours, and alerting the rest of a Marine Expeditionary Force (MEF) and an Army brigade to follow almost at once to secure Tan Son Nhut and Bien Hoa airfields as well. He also recommended the immediate deployment of logistics forces to prepare for "possible receipt of U.S. combat forces." During the next year Westmoreland's concern for the defense of South Vietnam emerged as a critical element in American planning, ensuring that the United States would deploy ground forces as soon as it began bombing the North, and contributing to restrictions on the scope of the initial bombing campaign.

Taylor and CINCPAC endorsed these recommendations, and CINCPAC suggested establishing an American base in South Vietnam. By August 20 a Marine battalion was afloat and ready to land off Da Nang.[4] Taylor on August 18 recommended resuming 34A operations, DeSoto patrols, and U-2 flights over North Vietnam, but delaying, if possible, further air strikes against North Vietnam until January 1, 1965. That, he argued, would give Khanh time to make sufficient pacification progress around Saigon so as to free *at least three division equivalents* of South Vietnamese troops to take up defensive positions in I Corps. If the situation deteriorated more rapidly, he suggested a course of action B, involving a new round of air strikes against the North.[5]

The August political crisis led both the Chiefs and Taylor to propose a more abbreviated timetable. The Chiefs on August 27—less General Wheeler, who was absent—declared that "an accelerated program of actions" was now "essential to prevent a complete collapse of the US position in Southeast Asia." Proposed actions against the North began with anti-infiltration strikes but went on to include aerial mining of North Vietnamese ports, a naval quarantine or blockade of North Vietnam *and Cambodia,* an all-out air attack on North Vietnam, amphibious and airborne operations against the North Vietnamese coast, and the commitment of American ground forces as required.[6] After the Chiefs' recommendations leaked, a Pentagon spokesman on September 5 denied that they had formally been made.[7]

The Army and the Air Force were beginning to split over the proper American strategy. General Harold K. Johnson, the new Army Chief of Staff, submitted a paper on September 25 recommending a variety of more intense efforts within South Vietnam, including more effective pacification and psychological operations. General LeMay on October 9 replied sharply, complaining that the Army memorandum "obscures what the Joint Chiefs of Staff have repeatedly acknowledged as the real problem—the DRV." For the whole of his tenure in office LeMay had repeatedly claimed that the Air Force could solve major military problems alone—most notably with respect to both Laos and Cuba in 1961. Westmoreland's presence in Saigon, however, and his now-approved recommendations for Marine and Army deployments, had already ensured that all three services would participate in the war.[8]

American authorities were now looking at South Vietnamese politics from a new perspective. Astonishingly, Taylor on September 6 commented that if the government continued "to seek a broadened consensus involving and attempting to encompass all or most of the minority elements"—an outcome which at first glance the United States might have been expected to favor—it would in due course "become susceptible to an accommodation with the Liberation Front." A truly representative government would not share American objectives. Thus the United States, he argued, had better abandon hope of a better government and act at once, beginning attacks against the North within two or three months. After about December 1, attacks would have the purpose of "holding the GVN together, or raising morale and creating conditions required for a negotiated settlement of hostilities on favorable terms."[9] John McNaughton, McNamara's Assistant Secretary for International Security Affairs, made similar recommendations on September 3. Even these actions might fail, he argued, and the United States might have to be content with having demonstrated its willingness to act.[10]

By the time Taylor met with the President and the senior foreign policy and military leadership on September 9, a consensus had emerged rejecting "substantial escalation before October, at the earliest" but calling for a new round of potentially provocative steps—34A attacks, DeSoto patrols, action against the Laotian corridor, and "retaliation against North Vietnamese moves that might easily lead to stronger action."[11] This time Generals Greene and LeMay had apparently insisted upon having their views heard, and McNamara explained that while these two chiefs believed extensive air strikes to be immediately necessary, Taylor did not. After very extensive questioning of Taylor—whom Johnson clearly still regarded as the man whose recommendations he had to consider most carefully—the President "said that in his judgment the proper answer to those advocating immediate and extensive action against the North was that we should not do this until our side could defend itself in the streets of Saigon." The President's phraseology was perhaps too frank: the "proper answer" did not necessarily mean the "true answer." After his reelection and inauguration, Johnson stopped insisting upon a stronger government. When the President asked "if anyone doubted whether it was worth all this effort," Taylor, Wheeler, McCone, and Rusk—"with considerable force"—argued that the United States could not afford a Communist victory.

Administration sources painted a highly misleading picture for the press, claiming that Taylor had given a "cautiously optimistic" report. Johnson himself referred in a press conference to "continued progress," Taylor told the press that the military situation "remained essentially normal," and both refused to discuss the possible widening of the war.[12] On Sunday, September 13, Tad Szulc actually wrote in the *New York Times* that any notion of escalating the war with American air power "was discarded out of hand," and that Taylor and Johnson both regarded it as "militarily useless."[13]

Alas, the political crisis worsened even before Taylor returned to Saigon. When Khanh, confirming his shift toward the Buddhists, planned to replace several anti-Buddhist generals, one of his main targets, IV Corps commander General Duong Van Duc, occupied strategic positions in Saigon and began a coup on September 13. Khanh initially asked Chargé d'Affaires Alexis Johnson for U.S. Marines to restore order—a request Johnson promptly refused—but managed to overcome the coup peacefully with the help of Air Force Commander Nguyen Cao Ky and the Catholic Young Turk Nguyen Van Thieu. By September 18 the situation appeared to be under control, but Khanh was still moving every night to protect himself, and he told Taylor on September 18 that he could not appoint a single commander of the Hop Tac pacification operation in the provinces around Saigon, since such an authority would be able to execute a coup virtually at will. Both Taylor in Saigon and Rusk in Washington warned that the United States might have to withdraw its support if turmoil continued. In the *New York Times*, the conservative columnist C. L. Sulzberger suggested that the United States would have to accept neutralization after the election.[14]

With Saigon in chaos and the election only weeks away, President Johnson halted the momentum of escalation on September 19, after two destroyers on a new DeSoto patrol reported firing upon radar contacts. At a noon meeting the Joint Chiefs recommended hitting POL (petroleum, oil, and lubricant) storage sites in the Hanoi-Haiphong area and simultaneously hitting the MIGs at Phuc Yen airfield, and McNamara and Rusk called for less drastic strikes. But when senior principals met with Johnson at 2:30, the President expressed justified skepticism over the evidence of an attack on the destroyers, "and made it clear that he was not interested in rapid escalation on so frail evidence and with a very fragile government in South Vietnam." Having established himself as a strong leader in August, the President apparently preferred to maintain a peaceful image in September.

The next day the President remained skeptical despite the united efforts of McNamara and Rusk to convince him that an attack had taken place. Johnson seemed to be growing in confidence, and one suspects that questions about the August 4 attack had now reached him, too. He listened with interest to George Ball's recommendation against resuming the DeSoto patrols, and eventually asked Ball and General Wheeler to prepare arguments against and for the patrols. In a press conference on September 21 the President took credit for overruling some of his advisers who wanted a retaliatory strike, and made clear he was not sure what had happened.[15]

The political situation in South Vietnam continued to deteriorate. On September 24 Montagnard troops in Darlac province revolted against the South Vietnamese, briefly occupying the town of Banmethuot. American Special Forces advisers eventually helped settle the dispute.[16] As September gave way to October both Taylor and the CIA produced devastating estimates of the situation. Taylor cited the breakdown of governmental authority in both urban and rural areas, the CIA reported that pacification had essentially come to a halt, and both cited growing anti-Americanism among virtually all political groups. Two weeks later General Westmoreland also argued that a "fairly effective government" in South Vietnam was a prerequisite to successful action against the North.[17]

The true military situation within South Vietnam seemed to figure less than ever in Washington's calculations. While no senior official seemed to be paying much attention, what was actually happening in the second half of 1964 presented a fascinating and critically important paradox. Beginning in June 1964—about the time that Westmoreland finally replaced Harkins—MACV's weekly reports began to show increases in ARVN large-scale (battalion-size or higher) operations. Such operations, which had averaged just over 50 a week during the second half of 1963, rose to a weekly average of 65 in June 1964, 70 in August, and 80 in November. These operations had an increasingly conventional orientation, and most of them were listed as "search and clear" operations rather than "clear and hold" measures in support of pacification. Less than half of them reported any contact with the enemy, showing that the problems Hilsman had reported more than two years earlier persisted. They enjoyed greater support from the growing American aircraft presence in South Vietnam. But since Viet Cong anti-aircraft capabilities continued to improve, American planes and helicopters suffered more and more hits from ground fire, with 10–30 typical for a single week. Westmoreland made another innovation, stationing several batteries of .155 howitzers in heavily populated Delta areas to provide quick-reaction fire when hamlets were attacked.[18]

Viet Cong attacks, meanwhile, never reached the levels of the summer and fall of 1963. Weekly averages of 100, 84, 118, and 100 for the months of June through September 1963 fell to 36, 37, 26, and 28 a year later. VC terrorism and sabotage increased so much, however, that the total number of reported incidents of enemy activity rose from weekly averages of 347 and 414 in August and September 1963 to 562 and 739 a year later. Incidents and attacks rose in I and II Corps, which had seemed on their way to security in mid-1963. To some extent VC attacks seem to have decreased during 1964 simply because the Viet Cong had eliminated the government's presence from much of the countryside. But the Viet Cong continued to stage damaging attacks and ambushes in provinces like Binh Duong—the site of ill-fated Operation Sunrise—and Hau Nghia on the Cambodian border.

Most significantly, perhaps, MACV reports never showed any significant headway in the pacification campaign. In July weekly summaries of activity in the "critical provinces" around Saigon frequently noted heavy VC activity in heavily populated Hau Nghia, Long An, Dinh Tuong, Binh Duong, and the central coastal provinces of Quang Ngai and Binh Dinh. In six critical provinces, a report noted on July 27, severe VC attacks diverted security forces, time, and energy from the pacification effort. A series of August reports noted few or no gains in pacification, and one even said the nation's attention had been diverted by the events in the Tonkin Gulf. A report on August 17 noted that not one hamlet in Long An met the American six-point criteria, and that recruiting qualified pro-government personnel had become almost impossible. And on August 31 MACV made another painful change in the format of the Headway Report. "Effective with this report," it read, "paragraph 5, critical provinces, is eliminated from MACV military report . . . MACV considers minimum elapsed time of one month neces-sary for objective, meaningful reports on pacification progress or lack thereof." The Embassy concurred.

Things did not improve in September or October. "Several US sector advisors," MACV noted on October 12, "feel that key ARVN com-manders have not provided necessary command guidance and show lit-tle interest in or understanding of pacification concepts." A Hop Tac council had now been formed to handle the critical provinces around Saigon, but it was clearly making little progress, and a Headway Re-port eventually acknowledged that it had no influence in the field. Paci-fication, in any case, continued to refer simply to intensified search-and-destroy missions in populated areas—not to a permanent ARVN presence among the people, the only tactic that could really contest the Viet Cong in its struggle for human and economic resources.

And despite the ARVN's increased aggressiveness—at least on pa-per—and the fall in Viet Cong attacks, the South Vietnamese Army had begun to melt away. In September MACV reported that several divi-sions were down to 82 percent of authorized strength.[19] Westmoreland in November reported that many ARVN companies had been going into action with just 50–70 soldiers—less than 50 percent of autho-rized strength—although he claimed to have reversed the trend.[20] Re-ports in November still listed about ten battalions as not combat effec-tive.[21]

American strategy had failed to do anything to halt, much less re-verse, the spread of the Viet Cong in the countryside. But in Saigon, Honolulu, and Washington, military authorities—like their civilian superiors—reacted to the deteriorating situation by calling for action against North Vietnam. "Pacification of South Vietnam," Westmore-land wrote on November 24, "is not likely to succeed as long as the VC receive extensive external direction and support. History has shown that it is impossible to close a frontier, and especially one configured like Vietnam, by physical means against an enemy determined to pene-trate. *Consequently, Hanoi must be induced by military means and psychological pressures to make a conscious decision to curtail support in its own national interest.*"[22] Saigon and Washington civilians were equally bereft of new ideas.

By the fall, McNamara, Rusk, Taylor, McNaughton, William Bundy, and McGeorge Bundy had already committed themselves to action against North Vietnam as the solution to these problems, and each of these men definitely viewed Vietnam as the main issue in American foreign policy. Undersecretary of State George Ball, however, did not share these views. In late September and early October Ball, working alone at his home late in the evenings, dictated into a tape recorder one of the most remarkable strategic appreciations ever written by an American. In so doing, he established a place in world history alongside the Athenian Nicias, the Frenchman Talleyrand, the Germans Bernhard von Bulow and Prince Max of Baden, and Britain's Earl of Chatham: those who tried, and failed, to save their homelands from disastrous courses of action. Ball's approach to the problem differed from those of his colleagues for several reasons. Concerned primarily with European affairs, he still saw Vietnam in the context of a broader diplomatic picture. As an international lawyer during the 1950s with numerous French clients, he had seen the French struggling with Indochina and had lived through several periods of French military optimism. And as a member of the Strategic Bombing Survey after the Second World War, he had developed a well-founded skepticism regarding the potential effects of air power.

Ball's memo, which he completed on October 5, initially declared that "our primary motive in supporting the Government of South Vietnam is unquestionably political . . . to make clear to the whole Free World that we will assist any nation that asks us for our help in defending itself against Communist aggression." Then he immediately listed critical differences between South Vietnam now and Korea in 1950—an analogy which clearly was playing a big role in Rusk's thinking, in particular. The United Nations was not behind the United States in South Vietnam; the South Korean government in 1950 was relatively stable; the South Koreans had defended themselves enthusiastically; and the Korean War had begun with a massive land invasion.

Ball then questioned, trenchantly and persuasively, all the arguments for bombing the North. He argued that it would probably not raise South Vietnamese morale for very long; that Hanoi would probably not give up its efforts in the South in response; and that bombing, without improvement in the political and military situation in the South, would not increase American bargaining power. A Pentagon War Game of September 8–11 had revealed that "exhausting" the current list of ninety-four targets would not "cripple Hanoi's capability for increasing support of the Viet Cong." Hanoi would more probably respond by sending as many as 60,000 men into South Vietnam, and the Chinese might join them. Such a North Vietnamese or Chinese move would immediately require American ground troops to meet it, altering the nature of the war, with major repercussions in Asian, European, and American public opinion. It would also, he argued, create almost immediate pressure to use tactical nuclear weapons, with far more serious consequences internationally and domestically, including, possibly, the intervention of the Soviet Union. As we have seen, the sequence of events Ball sketched out had been accepted since the mid-1950s by American military planners, who even now fully expected, if necessary, to carry it out.

Ball then argued that while escalation might indeed show America's willingness to stand by its commitments, it would raise severe doubts about American judgment among many allies. In Asia, even Thailand would certainly prefer to avoid involvement in a major war, while neutrals would probably welcome a political solution. The Japanese, he claimed, doubted that the United States could hold South Vietnam, and would certainly prefer a political solution to escalation threatening war with China. Most less-developed countries would certainly prefer a negotiated settlement to an air campaign against North Vietnam, and even the major European allies, while maintaining a "correct" attitude of public support, would become very concerned by any prolonged American involvement.

Under the circumstances, Ball concluded, the United States needed realistically to assess the costs and benefits of a political solution to the war before taking further action. He listed, for the record, the provisions that a settlement should "ideally" include: an end to North Vietnamese support for the insurgency, an independent government in South Vietnam that could thereby deal with the insurgency, and the right of the South Vietnamese to request allied assistance. But only one determined to ignore the thrust of the memorandum could argue, as Robert McNamara now does, that Ball really thought the United States should try to secure these maximum objectives.[23] In fact, Ball immediately stated that "sustained military pressure on the North" would *not* enable the United States to secure these objectives, but rather would force Washington into a large international conference pressuring us to withdraw. An immediate, private negotiation, he suggested, would force the United States to concede a political role to the Viet Cong, but might also offer the hope of some real guarantees for South Vietnamese independence.

In the short run, Ball recommended making clear to the South Vietnamese and the world that the next step really depended on them, and thereby allowing them to create either a government that could fight the insurgency effectively or a neutralist regime that might settle the conflict politically. He favored either talks between Saigon and the National Liberation Front (NLF) or broader talks to confirm the neutralization either of South Vietnam or of Indochina or Southeast Asia as a whole. Although Ball did not want to enlist President de Gaulle's help directly—partly, perhaps, because he found himself directly at odds with the general over NATO matters—he was, in essence, endorsing the solution that de Gaulle had been advocating since 1961.

"It may be observed," Ball concluded, "that I have dwelt at length on the probable reaction of other countries to alternative lines of action."

> This is not because I believe that in formulating our foreign policy we should be unduly preoccupied with what others want us to do . . . But our present policy has been justified primarily on political grounds. It has been defended on the proposition that America cannot afford to promote a settlement in South Vietnam without first demonstrating the superiority of its own military power . . .
>
> What I am urging is that our Southeast Asian policy be looked at in all of its aspects and in the light of our total world situation. It is essential that this be done before we commit military forces to a line of action that could put events in the saddle and destroy our freedom to choose the policies that are at once the most effective and the most prudent.[24]

The memorandum had an immediate impact. Ball wanted President Johnson to read it, but he sent it initially only to McNamara, Rusk, and McGeorge Bundy, trusting one of them to pass it on. They did not immediately respond, but Rusk gave it wider circulation within the State Department, and it clearly had an important effect upon William Bundy, who was about to propose new courses of action himself.

William Bundy at this very moment found himself involved in a public controversy. On September 29 the *New York Times* had reported from Tokyo that he had spoken publicly of the possible need to widen the war, reaffirmed our unshakable commitment, and rejected any new negotiations until Hanoi observed existing agreements. Since on the very same day President Johnson, in Manchester, New Hampshire, had rejected, at least for the moment, bombing the North or sending "American boys to do the fighting for Asian boys," this created something of a stir. Three days later two *Times* stories had specifically contrasted Johnson's unwillingness to escalate "as long as the Government there cannot even protect its own police station in a bloodless coup" with the opinions of "sub-cabinet officials" who wanted to use more naval patrols to provoke an incident and expand the war—a course William Bundy himself had advocated some weeks earlier.[25]

On October 19—just days after the first Communist Chinese nuclear explosion, the Labour Party election victory in Britain, and the fall of Khrushchev—William Bundy wrote a new memorandum on choices for Southeast Asia for Rusk, McNamara, Ball, and his brother. It began by noting a deterioration in the situation within South Vietnam since March, when Bundy had first begun writing scenarios for an expanded war, and a stiffening of the Communist position. Then, echoing Ball's memorandum, he argued that South Vietnam should *not* be regarded as a critical test of American ability to defend allies, because of its many unique and difficult features. Since the world understood that the South Vietnamese might lack the will to defend themselves, he wrote, "the *general* world consequences of the loss of South Vietnam and Laos probably could be made bearable." Even within Asia, he suggested "that the domino theory is much too pat," although he feared the consequences in Thailand and South Korea. More important, he accepted Ball's arguments that major European allies would doubt America's judgment in the event of a major war in Southeast Asia.

Like Ball, Bundy balanced his relatively optimistic estimate of the consequences of a defeat with a chilling picture of the possible consequences of going all out for a victory. The recent war game, he wrote, had "reached a point where major ground forces on our side, and/or the use of tactical nuclear weapons, were required to counter a ground reaction estimated as likely from North Vietnam alone."[26] The Chinese might respond in kind to such measures. American's worldwide military posture would suffer, and the South Vietnamese government might still fail to improve. Unlike Ball, Bundy argued that the United States should take some additional military action in an effort to strengthen its bargaining position, but he anticipated that this would lead to serious, worldwide pressure to reconvene a Geneva conference. There the United States would have to agree to some kind of neutral regime, or at least a legal political role for the NLF. He regarded this scenario, combined with new steps to reassure Thailand, as the best alternative to "systematic pressures on the North."[27] Bundy continued to push this approach for the next month.

Washington took no new decisions for the remainder of the month, as the President's campaign secured an obviously unassailable lead over Barry Goldwater. On Sunday, November 1—two days before the election—a Communist mortar attack on the Bien Hoa airfield devastated the recently augmented American air capability in South Vietnam, destroying five B-57 jet bombers and damaging thirteen as well as several other aircraft. Exactly half the bomber force dispatched in early August was destroyed or damaged. Ambassador Taylor, CINCPAC Admiral Sharp, and the Joint Chiefs all regarded this as the event that would set off full-scale war. Taylor asked for an immediate strike against the MIG jets at Phuc Yen airfield in retaliation, and military authorities prepared to order the Marine landing force to land at Da Nang as the first step in deployments of American ground forces. The Chiefs specifically asked for an immediate, all-out attack on the ninety-four-target list, beginning with a B-52 strike against Phuc Yen and preceded by the landing of Army and Marine units at Bien Hoa, Da Nang, and Tan Son Nhut airfield near Saigon to provide security.[28]

The President—in a meeting of which no record survives—decided on the afternoon of November 1 not to undertake a retaliatory strike. In a message to Taylor later that day Rusk explained that "in this one case we are invariably affected by election timing" but anticipated that policy might change during the next few weeks. Taylor rather truculently made clear that he believed the attack called for retaliation, but opposed both the use of U.S. aircraft in South Vietnam and the landing of security forces—at least until escalation began.[29] Having appointed Taylor to increase political support for whatever action the United States might take, Johnson was now gambling that he could discount the ambassador's recommendations for the time being. In a further meeting on November 2, Johnson apparently authorized a planning exercise led by William Bundy to examine future courses of action.

During the last two months the issue of action against North Vietnam had become deeply intertwined with the sudden emergence of a

Communist Chinese nuclear capability. On September 15—about a month before the Chinese actually exploded a device—Johnson, McNamara, Rusk, Bundy, and McCone had discussed responses to such a contingency. They tended to reject a preemptive strike to destroy the Chinese capability, but—in McCone's words—"if for other reasons we should find ourselves in military hostilities at any level with the Chinese Communists, we would expect to give very close attention to the possibility of an appropriate military action against Chinese nuclear facilities."[30] Now, as McNamara met with the Chiefs on November 2, he raised the same issue in connection with plans for war in Vietnam, and showed that he, like the Chiefs, was ready for the use of nuclear weapons:

> I want the Chiefs to reexamine the forces which would be required to support a major effort in South Vietnam and the logistics to back up these forces. I am sure that before anything is done the President will want to alert and move our forces prior to applying pressure against North Vietnam . . .
>
> What worries me is the long term picture of the capabilities of the 700 million people within the boundaries of China. We can't make the people in Southeast Asia any happier in the next 20 years than we are doing now. This means that we have a terrible problem facing us. The President being born in Texas is inclined to take some action. He wants to move, but he wants to be Goddamned sure of himself before he does so . . .
>
> After we have attacked the 94 targets in North Vietnam, I don't believe that we will be able to stop there. I would recommend that when that point is reached, we should strike against the Communist nuclear facilities. The nuclear capability of the ChiComs is a greater threat over a long time period. Therefore we shouldn't just look at the 94 target system if we propose to attack.

If China came into a ground war, McNamara continued, the United States would not immediately use nuclear weapons "just because the first few U.S. divisions might be forced back."[31]

On the next day the nation elected Lyndon Johnson to a full term of office, giving him 61 percent of the popular vote and 44 of the 50 states, plus the District of Columbia. (Goldwater carried South Carolina, Georgia, Alabama, Mississippi, Louisiana, and his native Arizona.) The Democrats also gained two senators, raising their total to 68, and 37 congressmen, for a total of 295 against 140 Republicans. In the twentieth century only the reelection of Franklin Roosevelt in 1936 had produced comparable figures both presidentially and congressionally.

Johnson—like Roosevelt in 1936—wanted to use these majorities to transform the United States domestically. But the planning exercise that he authorized on November 2—like Macon's Bill No. 2 in 1810, or Woodrow Wilson's *Lusitania* note in 1915, or the American note to Japan on November 26, 1941—became the crucial step in the country's entry into a new war. The National Security Council created a special working group to examine courses of action in Southeast Asia, chaired by William Bundy and including John McNaughton, the Assistant Secretary of Defense for International Security Affairs; Vice Admiral Lloyd Mustin, the senior operations officer of the Joint Chiefs of Staff (JCS); Harold Ford, the China-Asia officer of the CIA; and, at least in theory, McGeorge Bundy, who seems to have taken relatively little part. Various other State Department and CIA officials contributed to the work as well. Designed to examine various options, the working group during the next thirty days eventually produced a single recommendation. It received independent inputs from the Joint Chiefs of Staff, who in effect refused to delegate their authority to Admiral Mustin, and from Ambassador Maxwell Taylor. Rusk and McNamara intervened to shape the final recommendations midway through November, winnowing the various options down to one, and President Johnson approved it tentatively on December 3. Johnson still wanted to prevent the war from interfering with his domestic plans, and we shall see that he hesitated once again when asked to implement this recommendation. But his behavior in January and February proves that he understood exactly what he had approved in December, and he made no real effort to redefine the objectives or the strategy embodied in the working group's recommendations until at least 1968.

William Bundy initially laid out the work of the new group on November 3–4, while the nation was voting and registering the magnitude of Johnson's triumph. Part I, detailed to a team from the CIA, the Defense Intelligence Agency (DIA), and State's Bureau of Intelligence and Research (INR), was an intelligence assessment of the situation with enormous potential implications for various courses of action. Part II, which Bundy reserved for himself, attempted to define the broader stakes for the United States in South Vietnam and Laos, and the costs and benefits of various outcomes. Part III briefly summarized three options, A, B, and C: A, essentially a continuation of existing policy; B, an immediate, severe, and unyielding application of military pressure until the enemy agreed to American terms; and C, a more gradual, limited application of force, looking to relatively early peace talks. Part IV was designed to analyze possibilities for negotiation. Parts V–VII laid out options A, B, and C in detail. A planned section VIII, on actions elsewhere in Southeast Asia, seems never to have been written. Two final sections would lay out actions during the next thirty days and make recommendations.[32]

An initial round of drafts had been completed by approximately November 10. The CIA-DIA-INR intelligence assessment painted a gloomy picture of government instability, army factionalism, growing VC strength in the countryside, and the possibility of an imminent political collapse. It also concluded, however, that North Vietnam *could* reduce its support for the Viet Cong to the point that Saigon could begin to make progress, if it *chose* to do so. Although Hanoi saw victory almost within its grasp, it might draw back if the United States convinced it of its determination "to achieve its announced objectives regardless of the danger of war with Communist China and regardless of the international pressures that could be brought to bear against it."[33]

Perhaps because of the bleak prospects within South Vietnam and perhaps because of Ball's memorandum, other draft sections resisted the momentum for war that had been building at least since March— when Bundy on his own had prepared the report that became NSAM 288—and took a surprisingly cautious and peaceful line. Most striking in this respect was Bundy's original Part II, which echoed much of the logic—if not the precise language—of Ball's October 5 memorandum. Ball himself had met with Rusk, McNamara, and McGeorge Bundy on November 7 and found no sympathy whatever for his arguments. As he later recalled, McNamara seemed far more concerned that anyone would have dared put such heresies on paper than impressed by any of his arguments.[34] But Bundy's November 8–11 draft of Part II, "US Objectives and Stakes," certainly seemed to reflect Ball's views. In particular, Bundy emphasized the negative views of major European allies toward the war, and argued that that the United States could only guarantee its objective by "committing ourselves to whatever degree of military action would be required to defeat North Vietnam and probably

Communist China militarily," a commitment that would involve us in a ground war and possibly lead to the use of nuclear weapons "at some point." Bundy also substantially discounted the effects of the fall of South Vietnam. The domino theory, he said, was "at least oversimplified," and Thailand and Malaysia might both be saved from Communist domination in any case. He even took on Rusk's favorite analogy, arguing that "it cannot be concluded that the loss of South Vietnam would soon have the totally crippling effect in Southeast Asia and Asia generally that the loss of Berlin would have in Europe"—although, he conceded, it might.[35]

The early drafts of the various options, in which Bundy also played a key role, seemed to point toward a real scaling down of American objectives. Thus Michael Forrestal, now Rusk's special assistant for Southeast Asia, wrote a highly sophisticated analysis of option A—the recommendation to continue roughly along present lines—that seemed to take it quite seriously.[36] Although Bundy's original outline called for the Pentagon to produce the draft of option B—the maximum military option—he and John McNaughton eventually produced a draft of their own, while the Joint Chiefs both reserved and exercised the right to make suggestions. Because both Bundy and McNaughton seem to have been tilting toward option C, their B draft focused more upon distinguishing it from C than upon describing exactly what it would do, but the broad lines were clear. Essentially, option B called for exercising substantial and continuing pressure on North Vietnam—initially from the air—while refusing to engage in negotiations until Hanoi would meet American terms. Bundy defined these terms as "a restoration of the 1954 [Geneva] agreements," with more effective international machinery to enforce them, and said nothing about the election the agreements had called for. Partly perhaps because he was already tending toward option C, Bundy failed to address another huge issue: exactly how the South Vietnamese government would cope with the Viet Cong.

Both Bundy and McNaughton—who drafted a very specific section on the possibilities of escalation and counter-escalation—understood exactly how far matters might go. McNaughton anticipated deploying Marines in Da Nang as soon as air attacks began, to protect against a Viet Cong offensive. If the Chinese Air Force entered the war, the United States would attack "air bases, nuclear production facilities and other selected military targets in Communist China." (Bundy, earlier, had cited the possibility of the destruction of Communist China's nuclear capability as one of the "pros" of option B, echoing McNamara's November 2 statement to the Chiefs.) Most important, McNaughton acknowledged the presence of perhaps 65,000 North Vietnamese troops available for intervention in South Vietnam and/or Laos. In response, he called for the implementation of Phase III of OPLAN 32–64, including two divisions in Vietnam within sixty days and perhaps two divisions in Thailand as well. The plan called for air and naval strikes against North Vietnam, a naval blockade, and "an early ground attack northward to seize, liberate and occupy North Vietnam"—essentially a non-nuclear, more conventional version of Admiral Radford's 1956 plans. A Chinese counteroffensive, he continued, would mean full-scale war with China. All these proposals echoed the Chiefs' recommendations of November 4. Bundy also gave option B the best chance of achieving U.S. objectives, although he added that it posed the greatest risks of an expanded conflict.[37]

Bundy prepared option C with greater care, finishing a draft on November 8, circulating it two days later, and revising it in light of suggestions on November 13.[38] Read carefully, both drafts suggested that Bundy wanted to avoid escalation to full-scale war with North Vietnam and was willing to scale down American objectives somewhat to do so. In order to present a hopeful scenario, however, he indulged in some very wishful thinking.

The redraft—revised after comments from the rest of the group—actually raised American objectives in one key respect, dropping all reference to the Geneva Accords of 1954 and instead declaring that "an independent, secure South Vietnam" must be "reestablished." In subsequent months the administration stuck to these objectives, never offering simply to return to the 1954 agreements, although frequently giving the impression that it might do so. During an initial period of relatively limited military actions, such as air strikes against infiltration targets in Laos and North Vietnam, "a U.S. or multilateral ground force" would deploy "into the northern provinces of South Vietnam" to deter North Vietnamese intervention and cut down infiltration. Although Bundy's first draft anticipated that the situation in South Vietnam would continue to deteriorate, the redraft suggested that it might actually improve. Both drafts also discussed possible North Vietnamese counteraction, but focused on retaliation from the air and suggested that an enemy ground invasion was much less likely than under option B. (Oddly, the redraft referred only to a possible Chinese invasion, not to a North Vietnamese one.)

If the first round of limited actions did not improve the situation, Bundy foresaw bombing more targets from the ninety-four-target list, mining North Vietnamese ports, and establishing a naval quarantine. These steps, he suggested, would create tremendous pressure from world opinion to reconvene a Geneva conference, and the United States would have to accept it. And once talks began the United States would modify its terms, perhaps satisfying itself with less than ironclad guarantees that North Vietnamese support of the insurgency would cease. At best, he concluded, "we might judo our way to a settlement that might involve some modification [of our terms] but would give South Vietnam a fair chance to survive and get going." At worst, the South Vietnamese government might come apart, and we would have to fight alone, or—"more likely"—give up and withdraw. Other comments suggested that Bundy hoped either to save the situation or at least to administer some punishment to Hanoi and show American willingness to act before bowing to the inevitable. Option C, in short, seemed to aim at saving American face by making a show of force but avoiding a long-term commitment even if Washington had to abandon its main objectives.

Although the working group seems to have been designed to represent the involved agencies of the government, two other elements weighed in independently. On November 9 the Saigon Embassy pleaded once again for "air strikes against the DRV which will do damage to the sources of VC strength along the infiltration routes and to a limited degree in North Vietnam itself." Even if the government failed to improve, Taylor cabled two days later, he favored strikes against the North "to give pulmotor [respirator] treatment to a government in extremis and to make sure that the DRV does not get off unscathed in any settlement."[39] Although no one in Washington seems to have made the connection, Taylor was really endorsing Michael Forrestal's expanded option A rather than the more dramatic moves of option B or C.

The Joint Chiefs of Staff and the Joint Staff took quite a different line. On November 10 Admiral Mustin gave Bundy a biting Joint Staff critique of his draft of Part II, "US Objectives and Stakes," which had questioned the need to defend South Vietnam and pointed out the international and other difficulties associated with going to war. Echoing the policies developed under Eisenhower, the Joint Staff's comments bluntly denied that the U.S. decision should be influenced by the views of America's European allies, since the United States had already irrevocably committed itself to preserving South Vietnam. They also introduced what amounted to a new military theory of the war, claiming that the "defeat" of North Vietnam would *not* be necessary to ensure the termination of North Vietnamese support for the Viet Cong and the Pathet Lao, and implying that the termination of that support would enable the South Vietnamese government to defeat the insurgency. They argued that the risk of nuclear conflict should deter Chinese Communist intervention, while expressing a clear willingness to use nuclear weapons should the Chinese intervene. This paper is only one of many that show clearly that many military analysts, as well as some civilians, thought that North Vietnam could be induced or coerced to call off the insurgency without being totally destroyed.

The Joint Staff saw no possible fallback position in Southeast Asia should South Vietnam fall. In response to Bundy's comment that the United States would not enjoy support comparable to the Korean War, they replied, "we had no significant support in Korea other than verbal." They also rejected the idea that other nations could be adequately "reassured," and estimated that Thailand would go if South Vietnam fell. In conclusion, they argued that South Vietnam was indeed just as significant as Berlin symbolically, and more significant militarily. In further comments on November 14 Mustin argued that the United States should take whatever action was required in Southeast Asia "regardless of opinion in various other quarters."[40]

Meanwhile, the Chiefs themselves submitted a formal paper to McNamara on November 14 reiterating the recommendations they had made after Bien Hoa. They rejected Ambassador Taylor's call for merely retaliatory strikes. They wanted to begin by deploying Marine and Army troops around Da Nang, Tan Son Nhut airport in Saigon, and Bien Hoa; striking the MIGs at Phuc Yen with B-52s and hitting POL storage facilities in Hanoi within a few days; and proceeding to the full ninety-four-target list, as well as infiltration targets. The Chiefs optimistically estimated that "the DRV and CHICOMs would be unlikely to expand the conflict," but added that current CINCPAC OPLANs would enable the United States to meet anything the enemy could do. When escalation began a few months later, the Chiefs discovered that General Westmoreland did not share their sanguine views about the prospects of enemy retaliation, and that he actually *opposed* an immediate all-out air campaign until a long build-up had been completed. The Chiefs specifically asked that their views "be reflected by the Secretary of Defense in the joint State-Defense report being prepared on this subject," but McNamara simply replied on November 17 that the Chiefs' views would go to the President when the working group's report was presented, as indeed they did.[41] In a further comment the next day the Chiefs reiterated their view that pressure upon the North could "reduce, progressively, DRV support of the insurgencies in RVN and Laos to the extent necessary to tip the balance clearly in favor of the Governments of RVN and Laos." They said nothing about any need for more effective counterinsurgency within South Vietnam.[42]

Although the senior leadership was staying out of the planning process, a meeting on Chinese representation in the United Nations on November 18 foreshadowed the decisive influence that Rusk would shortly exert. Meeting with the President, U.N. Ambassador Adlai Stevenson recommended a shift toward a two-China policy. Rusk replied in terms he continued to repeat publicly and privately for the next three years: "The Secretary [Rusk] stated to the President that the matter of war and peace lay in the Pacific. If we appeared to falter before the Soviet Union and Communist China this would be interpreted as a reward for the track they have been following, and this would increase the chance of war. If we were to make a move that would signal to Peiping that we were weakening, this would increase our danger."

Any weakening in South Vietnam would of course have struck Rusk as an even more powerful signal of weakness. In an unusually blunt statement, the President let Stevenson know where he stood:

> The President said that Secretary Rusk's remarks impressed him; that perhaps better than abandoning our policy and inviting strong partisanship in Congress, the President said that what gave him pause was Secretary Rusk's statement that to change would be a pay-off for the Soviet and Chicom hard line.
>
> Stevenson said that he and others had felt for a long time that we should get the ChiComs into the community of nations—then you could manage them better.

The President noted that he did not pay the foreigners at the UN to advise him on foreign policy, but that he did pay Rusk and that he was inclined to listen to him.[43]

Johnson and Rusk wanted to defend South Vietnam *not* for the sake of allied opinion—much less because of American domestic politics—but because they thought it necessary to deter Communist China. The next day Johnson met with Vice President–elect Humphrey, Rusk, McNamara, and others, and Rusk suggested calling Taylor home for consultations preparatory to a presidential decision on December 1. At Johnson's request, William Bundy restated the three alternatives. McGeorge Bundy noted that the working group seemed to be focusing on option C and asked for presidential guidance, but McNamara remarked that work on option B was also well advanced. The Bundys and Rusk also reported that George Ball's "devil's advocate exercise" developing the alternative of negotiation and withdrawal had *not* advanced very far, instead of telling Johnson about Ball's memorandum. Ball, apparently intimidated by his own meeting with Rusk and McNamara, said nothing. Johnson merely remarked that he wanted the military fully consulted, since he could not explain any action to the congressional leadership otherwise.[44] The meeting did nothing to resolve the State-Pentagon split, much less to examine the problems associated with the various courses of action.

The working group's original drafts and further comments by civilian and military officials had revealed substantially different positions within the government, ranging from the Joint Chiefs' call for immediate, massive air strikes to a memorandum from several State and CIA officials recommending a renewed emphasis on the counterinsurgency program in the South.[45] Robert Johnson of State's Policy Planning Staff submitted a new defense of option A on November 18, arguing powerfully that none of the options would work without tremendous improvements in the counterinsurgency effort, and suggesting a small deployment of American ground troops within South Vietnam instead of a bombing campaign.[46] But William Bundy and John McNaughton now began narrowing the options in the direction of their preferred option C, while assessing its probable outcome more optimistically.

The day before the November 19 meeting McNaughton had finished a single, much-condensed redraft of "Courses of Action in Southeast

Asia" that pointed squarely toward option C.⁴⁷ The draft incorporated Bundy's pessimistic assumptions, repeating that the United States could not be certain of securing its maximum objectives in South Vietnam even if it undertook all-out war with North Vietnam or China, restating fallback objectives of creating a new defense line and explaining the reasons for our defeat, and repeating that the loss of South Vietnam might not be as serious in Southeast Asia and Asia generally as the loss of Berlin would be in Europe. McNaughton did, however, alter Bundy's analysis of European attitudes, claiming that both Britain and, "to a lesser extent, Germany, sympathize in principle with our whole policy of seeking to restrain Communist Chinese expansion," and that with respect to France "we are damned either way we go."

After a preparatory period during which the United States would retaliate against VC outrages, McNaughton wrote, option C would begin with new communications with Hanoi and Peking and

> additional graduated military moves against infiltration targets, first in Laos and then in the DRV, and then against other targets in North Vietnam . . . a steady deliberate approach . . . designed to give the US the option at any time to proceed or not, to escalate or not, and to quicken the pace or not . . . we would be indicating from the outset a willingness to negotiate in an affirmative sense, accepting the possibility that we might not achieve our full objectives.

And when McNaughton began developing the details of option C, he dropped any discussion of the introduction of American ground troops into South Vietnam or Thailand, referring only to the "removal of US dependents and taking security measures in SVN" before undertaking air strikes. Even when, as expected, Hanoi held firm and the United States moved on to the ninety-four-target list, aerial mining of North Vietnamese ports, and a naval quarantine, McNaughton foresaw only *possible* major additional deployments in the region. Should the Communists escalate in response, however, he apparently foresaw massive American action to meet them.

McNaughton had seems to have failed to persuade himself that option C would accomplish very much. His best imagined outcome—in brackets in the draft, as if to indicate its tentative character—read, "To avoid heavy risk and punishment, the DRV might feign compliance [with American demands] and settle for an opportunity to subvert the

South another day." At worst, South Vietnam might come apart anyway, or the United States might be faced "with the difficult decision whether to escalate on up to major conflict with China." Yet the draft recommended option C as less risky than option B and more likely than option A "to achieve at least part of our objectives," and as more likely to inspire confidence in American resolve even if it ended in the loss of South Vietnam.

Not a word of these deliberations had leaked to the press, but on November 23 the *New York Times* reported that Taylor was returning to Washington on November 26, and that he would request air strikes against infiltration targets, but not ground troops. The story, by David Halberstam—now based in Washington—said that Taylor was threatening to resign if he did not get his way, but that the President had not decided how far to go. One high official described Johnson as "something of a peacemonger." Since Taylor had made no such threat, Halberstam's sources seem to have been trying to put the responsibility for new action on him, which as we have seen had been Johnson's intention since he appointed him. Taylor confirmed his views in an interview with *Life* recommending air strikes, but his recommendations were not driving Washington's deliberations.[48]

Like McNaughton, William Bundy seemed to be discovering that the prospect going into a dubious war within a month could concentrate the mind nearly as wonderfully as that of being hanged in a fortnight. In his redraft of November 21 he tried very hard to assess the situation realistically and to weigh both the advantages and the disadvantages of all three possible courses of action. The critical preliminary section on objectives and stakes stuck largely to his original argument despite the objections of the Joint Staff and the Joint Chiefs, downplaying once again the probable effects even within Southeast Asia and noting the dangers of action, as well as inaction, with respect to American allies. Once again he concluded that the loss of South Vietnam might well *not* have an effect comparable to the loss of Berlin in Europe, but he added a footnote stating the contrary view of the Joint Staff.

Bundy still dismissed option A as anything more than a face-saving cover for defeat. Continuing indefinitely with present policies plus reprisals, he argued, would probably lead to talks within South Vietnam, a Communist-dominated coalition government, and a reunified Communist Vietnam. Despite the obvious increase in neutralism in South

Vietnam—particularly among the Buddhists—Bundy never considered the possibility that a South Vietnamese Souvanna Phouma might indeed emerge, and he ignored Robert Johnson's argument that option A might at least lead to a stalemate on the ground within South Vietnam. And at no time in his redraft did Bundy specifically refer to the argument that no action against the North would succeed unless the counterinsurgency program improved within South Vietnam. Instead, he roughly took the line of the Joint Chiefs, asserting that "if the DRV did in fact remove *wholly* its direction and support of the VC, the South Vietnamese could in time *probably* reduce the VC threat to manageable proportions."[49]

The section on option B seemed designed to make it somewhat more appealing, perhaps in recognition of the pressures coming from the Joint Chiefs. Calling once again for immediate, strong military actions, it substantially downplayed the possibility of North Vietnamese retaliation on the ground, and argued that Hanoi would most likely simply hold firm while the United States destroyed significant targets. This contrasted sharply with Bundy's and McNaughton's original drafts, which had noted the presence of 60,000 North Vietnamese troops ready to intervene. The redraft, moreover, also dropped the reference to the immediate introduction of ground troops in South Vietnam, and consigned any discussion of the implementation of American war plans to meet North Vietnamese and Chinese retaliation—should it occur—to an appendix. It also suggested that before deciding to invade North Vietnam the United States would consider scaling down its objectives based upon "the volume of international noise and desire for a peaceful settlement." These changes, in all probability, led the Joint Chiefs to repudiate option B as described in this memorandum.

Option C did refer to the possibility of deploying American or multinational forces into South Vietnam as a deterrent or a bargaining counter *immediately*, even before beginning retaliatory strikes, but made no firm recommendation. It called for a preliminary phase of retaliatory and anti-infiltration strikes combined with secret contacts with Hanoi and Peking, followed, if Hanoi held firm, by bombing of the ninety-four-target list, aerial mining, and a naval quarantine. Unspecified new deployments would accompany these measures, and the United States would meet escalation as necessary. Regarding American terms, Bundy said the United States would initially insist that Hanoi "cease its assistance to and direction of the VC," "that an independent and secure GVN be re-established," and "that there be adequate international supervising and verification machinery." But he made clear that the United States might well decide to settle for less. Furthermore, as *the best* possible outcome for option C, Bundy, echoed McNaughton, anticipating that North Vietnam might "feign compliance [with American terms] and settle for an opportunity to subvert the South another day."

Bundy—who ironically in March had drafted NSAM 288, establishing the objective of an independent, non-Communist South Vietnam—was now in effect trying to turn that into a maximum (and possibly unattainable) objective that the United States would have to abandon. While he avoided deciding in advance whether to risk full-scale war with China by escalating the war into North Vietnam if option C failed to secure a favorable settlement, his relatively calm estimate of the consequences of losing South Vietnam, combined with his references to the serious international consequences of escalation, reinforced his suggestion that the United States would have to settle for less than its preferred terms instead.

The Joint Chiefs counterattacked on November 23 in a memorandum for McNamara which directly raised the critical issue of American military planning for the first time. Referring to NSAM 288, they refused to contemplate any American objective other than "a stable and independent noncommunist government in the Republic of South Vietnam," and therefore rejected course A as offering no hope of attaining American objectives. They also pointed out, quite accurately, that course C failed to specify exactly how far we would go, when we would negotiate, or what our terms would be. As a substitute, they proposed course C', which would also use graduated military pressures but which—unlike Bundy's draft—would include "an advance decision to continue military pressures, if necessary, to the full limits of what military actions can contribute toward US national objectives." This time the reference to nuclear weapons was unmistakable. The Chiefs also rejected course B as described in Bundy's redraft, as "not a valid formulation of any authoritative views known to the Joint Chiefs of Staff," and proposed their own course B as a substitute for Bundy's: "a controlled program of intense military pressures against the DRV, swiftly yet deliberately applied . . . carried through, if necessary, to the full limits of what military actions can contribute toward US national objectives." An appendix indicated that the Chiefs wanted to begin with air strikes against POL targets in North Vietnam and the Phuc Yen MIG base.[50] While arguing that their course B was less likely to result in escalation than their redefined course C', the Chiefs accepted C' as a possible alternative. Faithful to the policies and strategies of the Eisenhower administration, the Chiefs remained firmly committed to the defense of Southeast Asia, *but only if higher authority would commit itself in advance to the use of nuclear weapons to secure this objective.*

Less than three weeks earlier, Senator Barry Goldwater—himself a Reserve Air Force major general—had gone down to a spectacular defeat, largely because of the widespread perception that he was far too willing to use nuclear weapons. The Chiefs, however, were sticking to the principle that had guided American military planning for at least ten years: that nuclear weapons should be regarded as a normal part of the American arsenal. The Chiefs' insistence on this point is also noteworthy given the central role of bombing in their recommendations and the limited effectiveness of conventional bombing at this time. They were already well aware of the limitations that bad weather would impose upon the bombing of the North during much of the year, and when the bombing campaign actually began in 1965, many key targets proved impossible to destroy until the introduction of guided "smart" bombs in 1972. The Air Force, however, had been basing its estimates of the effectiveness of bombing upon nuclear weapons since the 1950s at least.

The Executive Committee of the National Security Council—including Rusk, McNamara, McCone, General Wheeler of the JCS, Ball, the Bundy brothers, and Forrestal—met to consider the options at 5:00 P M on Tuesday, November 24. In order to decide upon a coherent policy and strategy, the ExCom had to settle the arguments with respect to both American objectives and the best means of achieving them. Could U.S. security interests, as Bundy had suggested, quite possibly survive the loss of South Vietnam, or were these interests, as the Joint Chiefs argued, worthy of any necessary sacrifice? Should the United States, as Bundy implied, moderate its policy to conform with allied opinion, or should it, as the Pentagon apparently believed, pursue its interests unilaterally? Most crucially, should the United States at some point abandon its maximum objectives, and what fallback position should it adopt? All these questions, with alternative answers, figured quite clearly—as we have seen—in the various proposals coming from the working group and the Joint Chiefs.

The meeting reached a "consensus" on several of the most important issues. "There was a consensus that the loss of South Vietnam would be somewhat more serious than stated in Section II of [Bundy's] draft paper," a summary stated, "and it would be at least in the direction of the Joint Staff view as stated in the footnote to page 7 of the draft"—that is, resulting in "the early loss of Southeast Asia and the progressive unraveling of the wider defense structures." Ball registered his dissent. Years later Bundy recalled that Rusk and McNamara had bluntly dismissed his relatively optimistic assessment of the consequences of South Vietnam's fall with the comment "It won't wash," just as they had summarily dismissed Ball's arguments in a meeting early in November.

This conclusion—so critical to the decision to go to war—reflected the paralysis that had infected the national security bureaucracy since the 1950s. The Pentagon's assessment was simply the last of many restatements of the policies developed during the Eisenhower administration. Realistically, the question of the consequences of the fall of South Vietnam—an almost entirely *political* issue, especially beyond Southeast Asia itself—should have fallen within the competence of the State Department, *which should have answered it not according to longstanding statements of policy but according to an up-to-date appreciation of current conditions.* In fact, the Department does not seem to have queried its missions around the world as to the consequences of the loss of South Vietnam in order to assess this question, but both Ball and William Bundy had produced relatively realistic assessments, based on their own personal knowledge of current diplomatic reality. Now, however, at the critical moment, their chief, Dean Rusk, had taken the other side. With respect to Southeast Asia, Rusk's personal convictions overrode any loyalty to his subordinates' views, because he believed, based upon the experience of the 1930s, that anything less than the resolute defense of South Vietnam would encourage Communist Chinese aggression. McNamara, meanwhile, had never questioned the Chiefs' definition of American objectives and stakes.

Option A received little attention, and Bundy recorded the consensus view that it would probably result in a worse negotiating outcome than either B or C. The meeting also decided that the South Vietnamese could in fact prevail in a "long" struggle with the Viet Cong if Hanoi would withdraw its effort. Only the JCS seemed definitely to believe that Hanoi played such a crucial role, but since the working group had dropped any insistence upon the need to improve counterinsurgency, the ExCom had to accept this assumption in order to endorse action against the North. The ExCom also optimistically discounted the probability of an actual military defeat or even a serious military setback in the South, "provided that adequate security measures were taken"—an implicit recognition, as we shall see, of the need for some American troops.

The bulk of the discussion focused upon the relative advantages and disadvantages of options B and C—and, crucially, the Chiefs' option C′, which in effect emerged as the preferred choice.[51] Regarding option B, Wheeler asked for immediate strikes against North Vietnamese airfields in order to make a sustained air campaign possible. When someone asked whether nuclear weapons might be used, McNamara said that he could not imagine such a case, but McGeorge Bundy predicted that under certain circumstances both military and political pressure for their use might arise. General Wheeler ruled them out as means of stopping North Vietnamese tanks from coming south—a possibility Rusk specifically raised—but said he might recommend them to save a threatened force, or to knock out a nuclear weapons production facility in China. LeMay was not present.

Option C foresaw an American effort, followed after a certain period by negotiations and, perhaps, a settlement that gave the United States much less than its stated objectives. But in the most important moment of the meeting, Rusk immediately rejected William Bundy's and Mc-Naughton's argument that the United States could improve its world position by making an effort in South Vietnam, even if it failed. Mc-Namara and McGeorge Bundy initially seemed to disagree with Rusk, but McGeorge Bundy in later comments appeared to reject early negotiations. Regarding the issue of an immediate deployment of ground forces, McNamara declared "that there was no military requirement for them" and suggested a massive air deployment instead—a literally unbelievable statement in light of the Bien Hoa attack. When Wheeler raised the need for base security and air defense, McNamara relented somewhat, and Rusk and McGeorge Bundy, echoing William Bundy, argued that ground troops might deter the enemy. The group decided to discuss the issue with Maxwell Taylor—but never did.

When the group began directly comparing options B and C, Rusk made another critical argument: that option C, if unsuccessful, could be followed by the JCS version, C', which committed the United States to whatever level of force turned out to be necessary. He specifically compared C' to the policy of the Cuban missile crisis—a misleading argument, as Rusk himself should have known, since Kennedy had in fact settled for less than Washington's maximum objectives and traded the missiles in Turkey for the Cuban ones rather than escalate militarily. Kennedy's strategy had actually followed the lines of option C: a display of military force followed by negotiation on the best terms available, largely because of the effects of war upon allied opinion.

Thirty years later, in the wake of the Gulf War and under the influence of the Weinberger and Powell Doctrines, which prescribe immediate, overwhelming force as the solution to any war, option B has struck one historian as a promising road not taken, and the selection of option C' has been called the critical mistake in the conduct of the Vietnam War.[52] Yet we shall see as we look at the history of the next few months that the idea of a knock-out blow was not implemented largely because it simply was not possible to implement. With the exception of General LeMay, the Chiefs did not believe that they could win the war without substantial deployments of American ground forces, and the Chiefs had never come down firmly in favor of an immediate all-out effort instead of a graduated one. Given the lack of a logistics base within South Vietnam, deployments would, and did, take many months to execute, and the Army and Marines, at least, were determined to make them. When bombing began a few months later, General Westmoreland made clear that he, too, wanted to keep attacks upon the North within limits, because he did not yet feel ready to cope with North Vietnamese retaliation on the ground. And as soon as American troops landed and became vulnerable, their need for tactical air support began to compete with plans for the strategic bombing of North Vietnam. In the end the Pentagon approved a somewhat gradual approach to the war, not because of cowardice, but because it really had no choice. What the Chiefs always insisted on was the civilians' promise that the United States would stick to its objectives and eventually use whatever force was necessary, and this was, in fact, the conclusion of the November 24 meeting and the subsequent planning process.

The critical disagreement between the JCS and the civilians related not to the pace of American military action against the North but to how far it would go, and specifically to whether it would eventually include the use of nuclear weapons, if necessary, to compel Hanoi to give up. In the end, as we shall see, that question was never completely clarified.

Maxwell Taylor arrived in Washington on November 26 with his own very different appreciation of the situation.[53] Taylor's memo, while advocating some air strikes, emphasized the situation within South Vietnam rather than action against the North. It pointed out bluntly that the situation had now deteriorated severely not only around Saigon and to the south but also in the northern provinces, which a year ago had been considered almost clean. The Viet Cong, he now admitted, was increasing its effectiveness and adopting new tactics, and infiltration had increased. The strength of the Viet Cong, he mused, remained a "mystery," if "our data on Viet Cong losses are even approximately correct." The Embassy was facing the facts, but it still did not understand that the armed Viet Cong represented only the tip of a large, well-organized iceberg that easily replaced losses.

Taylor listed three strategic necessities: an adequate government, an improved counterinsurgency campaign (to which the working group in Washington had given virtually no attention), and a campaign to "persuade or force the DRV to stop its aid to the Viet Cong and to use its directive powers to make the Viet Cong desist from their efforts to overthrow the government of South Vietnam." Taylor, like William Bundy, showed that he had obviously considered the possibility of failure. Thus he suggested that Washington might simply fight the war unilaterally against the North if the South Vietnamese failed to establish an effective government, but predicted that we would probably have to withdraw and lose the South after making the North pay a price.

Specifically, Taylor recommended beginning with anti-infiltration strikes and intensified maritime operations designed to strengthen the South Vietnamese government by improving morale. Then, he suggested, the United States might strike a bargain with the South Vietnamese civilian and military leadership. In recommendations eerily reminiscent of those he had submitted to Kennedy three years earlier, Taylor proposed that the South Vietnamese promise to maintain the authorized strength of military and police forces; replace incompetent commanders and province chiefs; suppress disorders and demonstrations (an apparent reference to the Buddhists); and, most critically, assume South Vietnamese responsibility for the *land* defense of South Vietnam, while the United States assumed responsibility for defense on air and sea. (Taylor's specific scenario for escalation, however, seemed to foresee the landing of a Marine expeditionary battalion and an Army brigade at some point.) Then, he thought, the United States might progressively escalate air attacks against North Vietnam, possibly until they had destroyed "all important fixed targets in North Vietnam" and secured "the interdiction of movement on all lines of communication"—a most optimistic assessment of American capabilities. Before leaving Saigon, Taylor had asked General Khanh and the civilian Prime Minister Tran Van Huong whether they would accept the risks of air attacks against the North, and they had replied in the affirmative.[54]

Taylor specifically opposed any negotiations "until the DRV is hurting" or letting "the DRV gain a victory in South Vietnam without having paid a disproportionate price," and proposed "keeping the GVN in the forefront of the combat and the negotiations." Thus he, like Bundy, envisioned a fallback position; but while Bundy's fallback involved a negotiated settlement and a coalition government, which world opinion would have preferred, Taylor apparently preferred a full-scale Communist military victory accompanied by widespread destruction within North Vietnam. *If* the South Vietnamese government improved and large-scale action against the North began, Taylor hoped to negotiate on the basis of a return to compliance with the 1954 Geneva Accords—including full American compliance with respect to personnel, involving the withdrawal of most of the Americans in the country. He said nothing, however, about elections.

Taylor joined the rest of the ExCom on Friday, November 27. The group agreed that the United States would probably not be able to continue fighting if the South Vietnamese government "collapsed or told us to get out," and the group apparently decided, as well, that a "neutralist" solution under which the United States might withdraw its forces had to be avoided until the Viet Cong had been defeated—effectively repudiating Taylor's own negotiating proposals. Taylor actually gave a slightly more optimistic report on the political situation, but rejected the conclusions of a relatively optimistic military report by General Westmoreland that did *not* call for immediate escalation. McNamara, who had thought for at least five months that the military situation was desperate, agreed with Taylor. The group clearly favored option A at once—that is, retaliatory strikes and perhaps some covert anti-infiltration strikes—and a move into the "first stages of option C" within the next two months. They did not, however, discuss the introduction of American combat troops, or discuss the distinction between option C and option C'.[55]

On the next day—November 28—McGeorge Bundy sent Johnson a book of papers on the working group's deliberations. In preparation for a meeting on December 1, he particularly recommended the "short summary"—apparently the condensed draft of "Courses of Action" that McNaughton had written on November 18—and Taylor's report. He said nothing about the arguments over the American stake in Vietnam, or about the critical distinction between option C and option C'.[56]

William Bundy on Sunday, November 29, circulated a revised "Draft Position Paper on Southeast Asia"—approved in general by Rusk, Taylor, McNaughton, and Forrestal—that condensed the previous options into one, reflecting the two ExCom meetings.[57] The redraft totally abandoned Bundy's original, careful analysis of the nature of American objectives in South Vietnam, and stated simply that United States objectives there were "unchanged." In fact, it defined them in the most sweeping terms yet:

1. Get Hanoi and North Vietnam (DRV) support and direction removed from South Vietnam, and, to the extent possible, obtain DRV cooperation in ending Viet Cong operations in SVN.

2. Re-establish an independent and secure South Vietnam with appropriate international safeguards, including the freedom to accept US and other external assistance as required.

3. Maintain the security of other non-Communist nations in southeast Asia including specifically the maintenance and observance of the Geneva Accords of 1962 in Laos.

The second objective meant that the United States would *not* settle for reestablishment of the 1954 Geneva Accords, which severely limited foreign assistance to South Vietnam.

Bundy then sketched out two phases of action apparently similar to option C. During Phase I, expected to last thirty days, the United

States would intensify existing actions, including armed reconnaissance strikes in Laos and reprisal strikes for major VC actions in the South. (An annex specified seven different types of VC actions requiring retaliation and listed seventeen separate reprisal targets in North Vietnam.) While the United States expected the South Vietnamese to end the political turmoil in Saigon, neither the position paper nor Bundy's proposed statement to the South Vietnamese suggested that the counterinsurgency program had to be fundamentally altered to achieve American objectives. After thirty days the United States would withdraw dependents and begin anti-infiltration strikes across the border. Then, if the South Vietnamese government improved its effectiveness "to an acceptable degree and Hanoi [did] not yield on acceptable terms," the United States would begin a second-phase program of graduated military pressures against the DRV, consisting "principally of progressively more serious air strikes, of a weight and tempo adjusted to the situation as it develops (possibly running from two to six months) . . . This could eventually lead to such measures as air strikes on all major military-related targets, aerial mining of DRV ports, and a US naval blockade of the DRV." This draft said nothing about ground troops.

"Concurrently," Bundy continued, "the US would be alert to any sign of yielding by Hanoi, and would be prepared to explore negotiated solutions that attain US objectives in an acceptable manner." With this sentence Bundy essentially committed the United States to whatever level of violence was necessary to achieve the maximum objectives stated at the outset—as the Chiefs had wanted—but without specifically promising to go to "the full limits of what military actions can contribute" to American objectives. In complete contrast to his own draft of option C, the idea of reducing our objectives had disappeared, and the draft embodied the Joint Chiefs' option C′ as defined in their paper of November 23. The only alternative Bundy now listed was the Pentagon's option B′, the initiation of immediate air strikes against North Vietnamese airfields and POL storage.

After two more days of ExCom meetings, the exact same group met with President Johnson—just back from Texas—and Vice President-elect Humphrey on December 1. Taylor took the lead at the meeting, presenting essentially the same case for action that he had put in writing a week earlier, and contributing to the impression that he, rather

23

With a bloodstained Jacqueline Kennedy on his left and Lady Bird Johnson on his right, President Lyndon Johnson was sworn in on Air Force One, after John Kennedy's assassination in Dallas, Texas, on November 22, 1963.

★

Despite criticism from U.N. Secretary General U Thant (32), the United States increased bombing of both the North and the South, and American Marines began counterinsurgency operations around Da Nang in March 1965 (33–34).

★

33

34

35

36

37

Faced with dissent in the late spring of 1965, Johnson browbeat Senate Foreign Relations Committee Chairman J. William Fulbright (35) and listened respectfully to Undersecretary of State George Ball (36). Meanwhile, McNamara went to Vietnam to discuss General William Westmoreland's request for more than 100,000 American troops (37).

★

38

Flying with a B-66 destroyer, F-105s bombed targets in North Vietnam (38), while American Marines patrolled rice paddies in search of Viet Cong (39). American casualties steadily increased, and in October 1967 a massive demonstration marched on the Pentagon to protest continuation of the war (40).

★

39

40

41

During the Tet Offensive in 1968, South Vietnamese civilians evacuated the village of My Tho in Dinh Tuong province (41), not far from the site of the Battle of Ap Bac five years earlier. Meanwhile, the Marines endured a long and bloody siege at Khe Sanh (42). After five more years of combat and protest, Henry Kissinger and his North Vietnamese counterpart, Le Duc Tho, met in Paris to sign a peace agreement on January 27, 1973 (43).

★

42

43

In late March 1975, South Vietnamese fled the Central Highlands as the North Vietnamese began their final offensive (44). Six weeks later helicopters picked up the last Americans from rooftops in Saigon, only hours before North Vietnamese tanks entered the city (45).

than the Washington bureaucracy, was pushing for new steps. Taylor's presentation—like the new draft "Position Paper on Southeast Asia"—omitted all the most serious questions raised by Ball's October memorandum and Bundy's working group drafts, particularly the questions about the true stakes in South Vietnam, the attitudes of America's allies, and the consequences of escalation. Under Kennedy this would not have mattered so much, because Kennedy himself never failed to raise these questions during any serious discussions of Southeast Asia. Johnson in this meeting also raised some of these questions, but merely to argue for further delay rather than to propose a new policy.

As a careful reader of the nation's major newspapers, Johnson knew that Buddhist and student demonstrations against the Saigon government had broken out during the last ten days, calling the future of the government and American policy in general into question. Four days earlier a White House source at the LBJ ranch had told reporters that "no great, horrendous decision" was likely to result from Taylor's visit, and Johnson had personally confirmed this the next day at a press conference, noting that he had read stories about a planned expansion of the war many times during the last six months or so.[58] Now Johnson referred again and again to the necessity of doing something about the political problems in South Vietnam. Unlike the ExCom, he asked about the various political factions and the need to bring them together. At one point he even asked if the South Vietnamese were "drunk on [Joseph] Alsop" and oversold with respect to America's commitment to them, implying that they did not take their own responsibilities seriously enough. Expressing nostalgia for the good old days of Ngo Dinh Diem—whose demise he still regretted—Johnson insisted that the South Vietnamese had to shape up before we undertook any further action, and demanded that the United States remove its dependents. The President, indeed, was not prepared officially to abandon Kennedy's middle course of assisting the South rather than withdrawing or escalating. While it was easy to get in or out, he said at one point, it was hard to be patient. Later he put it differently: it was easy either to "sock"—to bomb—or to follow Wayne Morse's suggestion and withdraw.

The President also displayed, in his own way, considerable sensitivity to the question of allies. While he did not mention James Reston's dispatch from Moscow in the previous day's *New York Times,* which noted that London, Paris, and Moscow all opposed the expansion of the war in Vietnam, he repeatedly spoke of the need for far greater allied contributions before going ahead. And indeed, he did not commit himself even to begin *reprisal* strikes until we had more allies with us, our dependents had been withdrawn, and we had done "all we can" in South Vietnam. The President declined even to release even a relatively bland statement reaffirming a policy of "all possible and useful assistance" to the South Vietnamese.[59]

With an eye, perhaps, on the possibility of leaks, Johnson had avoided any detailed discussion of the planned second phase of escalation spelled out in the new "Position Paper on Southeast Asia," or of ground troop deployments. Johnson had, however, pronounced the papers "generally satisfactory." And when the ExCom met after the meeting to reconsider the draft, they made a seemingly minor change—one which guaranteed that a decision to begin bombing the North would plunge the United States into a full-scale war.

Bundy's November 29 draft—the paper presented to the President—had described the second-phase program of action as consisting "principally of progressively more serious air strikes, of a weight and tempo adjusted to the situation as it develops (possibly running from two to six months)," and conceivably leading to strikes on all major military targets, the aerial mining of North Vietnamese ports, and a naval quarantine. In a new draft on December 2, the ExCom transformed the first key sentence as follows: "Such a program would consist principally of progressively more serious air strikes, of a weight and tempo adjusted to the situation as it develops (possibly running from two to six months) *and of appropriate US deployments to handle any contingency.*"[60]

Interestingly enough, even Taylor's instructions for conversations with the South Vietnamese leaders about Phase II did not specifically mention the introduction of American troops. But an appendix to the new ExCom paper spelled out exactly what would happen when Phase II began, giving a schedule of American deployments and operations in Southeast Asia that seemed to reflect CINCPAC OPLAN 32–64.

According to the schedule, approximately 500 land-based American aircraft would redeploy to South Vietnam and elsewhere in Southeast Asia during the first few days after the initiation (D-Day) of Phase II, with many more to come. The 1,300-man Marine battalion that had been cruising off Da Nang ever since August would land on D+3, and the rest of the 3rd Marine Division—17,000 strong—would embark from Okinawa and Hawaii on D+2 and deploy during the next thirty-three days. On D+9 the Army's 173rd Airborne brigade—3,400 men strong—would leave Okinawa for South Vietnam, arriving within twenty days. The plans also foresaw the deployment of three full army divisions—the 82nd Airborne and the 1st and 2nd Infantry—to *Thailand* during the first sixty days of Phase II—presumably to protect Thailand and Laos against possible enemy retaliation—and other massive deployments to the western Pacific area to meet other possible contingencies. This plan, like certain earlier plans, may have assumed that North Vietnam and China might respond to Phase II bombing with a massive conventional invasion, and the troops in Thailand were designed to hold the western bank of the Mekong. More bombing would persuade or compel them to quit.

As we shall see, when Phase II actually began, the deployments to Thailand did not take place, as Westmoreland's demands for troops rapidly multiplied and Washington decided on a major ground war in South Vietnam. The Pentagon had apparently failed to coordinate long-planned deployments in Thailand with the State Department, where Thai reluctance to accept such deployments was already well known.[61] We have seen that numerous working group discussions had foreseen such deployments at the beginning of Phase II or even earlier, and these deployments were now official policy. McNamara had given up his efforts to avoid ground deployments. And when Johnson eventually approved Phase II bombing of North Vietnam, the initial troop movements into South Vietnam went off like clockwork. Alas, within a few months, demands for troops to establish security *within South Vietnam* increased rapidly enough to absorb *all* the designated divisions.

Nor was this all. Such deployments could indeed have been merely a security measure to protect American bases while bombing took place, followed, as William Bundy had foreseen in his original drafts of option C, by a conference and a settlement on the best terms available. But the new position paper retained the November 29 definition of America's objectives and the statement that the United States would negotiate only when the enemy was ready to concede them. Since the enemy in fact had no intention of yielding to those terms, these deployments in practice would become merely the first step in a process that could put at least seven divisions of Americans on the ground in Southeast Asia. Another tab of the military appendix—Tab 4—laid out "Possible US/Allied Countermoves" to North Vietnamese reactions. Should the North Vietnamese move two to five divisions into South Vietnam, it stated, the United States would immediately initiate an air interdiction campaign; mine North Vietnamese harbors and blockade North Vietnamese ports; undertake an "early" ground offensive, with consideration of "seizing and occupying some or all of NVN"; and make major new deployments to prepare for Chinese intervention.[62]

One could argue, in fact, that the planned deployments in South Vietnam and the projected offensive against the North were taking the place of nuclear weapons as the ultimate American weapon to secure U.S. objectives. For while Bundy's draft committed the United States to indefinite military action in pursuit of maximum American objectives, it did not incorporate the Chiefs' language committing Washington to "the full limits of what military actions can contribute toward US national objectives." While the paper specified American objectives, it did not specify exactly how far the United States would go to achieve them. If the political leaders ever decided that the national interest did not justify resort to the most extreme actions, they could always discard option C' and return to Bundy's option C, and negotiate for the best settlement available.

Eventually—in 1968 and in 1972—the Johnson and Nixon administrations did just that. Both those administrations *threatened* the use of nuclear weapons to varying degrees, and both may seriously have discussed it at one time or another, but such an option was not politically feasible either domestically or internationally. Kennedy in 1961 had shied away from war in Laos as soon as he realized that the United States would be outnumbered on the ground and that the military would count on nuclear weapons to redress the balance. He had also avoided war over the far more critical issue of Cuba partly because of the fear of nuclear escalation. Now Johnson, McNamara, Bundy, and Rusk had decided to go to war and hope for the best because they saw no alternative. In so doing, they tried to ignore the pitfalls of the policies and strategies the Eisenhower administration had left behind: that the United States had undertaken to defend many areas on the assumptions that nuclear weapons would be used as necessary and that nuclear weapons could be effective. The Joint Chiefs seemed to assume that these policies remained in force. The civilians, who wanted to preserve a nuclear option even if in practice they might never authorize it, failed to see, as Kennedy had in 1961, that the only alternatives to the use of nuclear weapons were an unpopular and indecisive conventional war on the one hand, or an immediate political solution on the other.

Indeed, although no one seems to have remarked upon it, the whole sequence of events in the fall of 1964 bore an eerie resemblance to the events of the fall of 1961. Then, too, the bureaucracy had presented the President with proposals for war in Southeast Asia. At that time Kennedy had eventually set a limit on the nature of the American commitment and defined carefully limited objectives. Because he had never realized that the new policy had not succeeded, he had never specifically developed an alternative. Johnson in his first year in office had opened the door to war much further by approving "an independent, non-Communist South Vietnam," free to accept American assistance, as a national objective back in March, and by securing the Gulf of Tonkin resolution in August. Various conversations during 1964, moreover, had shown that this President had no interest in any alternative policy. While he wanted to limit the domestic consequences of the war, he accepted the need for the United States to do whatever was necessary to stop Communist aggression in Southeast Asia. And thus, rather than insist on key changes in the language of the redrafted document—as Kennedy had done in 1961 and again in 1963—he took a different approach, embodied very clearly in the December 7 memo in which he approved the redrafted "Position Paper on Southeast Asia," with appendices, that put the United States on the road to war

> I have approved the attached paper on policy toward Southeast Asia as guidance for our work in this field in coming months, subject to such amendment and further development as I may approve from time to time. I have also approved the attached instructions to Ambassador Taylor . . . Taken together, these documents state my present position.
>
> I consider it a matter of the highest importance that the substance of this position should not become public except as I specifically direct.
>
> In discussions of relevant parts of these matters with foreign governments, I expect that every effort will be made to impress upon our foreign friends the importance of discretion, but I recognize that we cannot control what foreign governments say.

In the case of American officials the matter is different. The officers to whom this memorandum is directed are requested to take personal responsibility for the supervision of the execution of this policy and for insuring that knowledge of all parts of it within the Executive Branch is confined as narrowly as possible to those who have an immediate working need to know.[63]

Johnson, certainly, had authorized war in the near future without investigating the situation very thoroughly. But in that respect, as a recent biography makes quite clear, his decision did not differ from other major initiatives that he had taken, even in areas much closer to his heart. Early in 1964 he had launched his War on Poverty—one of the centerpieces of his administration—with only the vaguest notion of how that war would be fought.[64] The "Great Society" that he had proclaimed as a goal in May was equally undefined. At home and abroad, he wanted above all to complete the work, as he understood it, of his hero Franklin D. Roosevelt.[65] He had personally helped fill in the blanks of Roosevelt's National Youth Administration in Texas in the 1930s, and he counted on others to do the same now.[66] His goals revolved around the creation of abundance and justice at home and the defense of freedom abroad, and he had complete confidence, as events would show, in his nation's ability to achieve them. In all this he was utterly characteristic of his own generation, and he could therefore count upon their support.

The problem as Johnson now saw it was to integrate war in Vietnam into a larger picture, and to prevent it from standing in the way of other equally or more important tasks. The President had many other plans for his first few months, plans which he did not intend any controversies over Southeast Asia to disturb. During January he had to deliver his State of the Union and budget messages, and he planned also to begin presenting the most ambitious legislative agenda since the New Deal. In order to give these initiatives the maximum possible attention, Johnson had to conceal any dramatic changes in policy toward Southeast Asia from the American people. A domestic aide, Jack Valenti, recalled Johnson's comments in this period almost thirty years later:

I remember something he said [election] night in my presence, and said later in Washington to the rest of the staff, "We've got to shove in our stack, because mandates don't last long." He had the 89th Congress in mind. He had this huge canvas on which he was painting the Great Society and I do not believe, knowing Lyndon Johnson as well as I did, that he would contemplate at that time doing anything which would diminish or shrink or otherwise injure what he wanted to do domestically. I just don't believe that.[67]

Leaks, then, must be avoided at all costs, and December's newspapers did not hint that the administration was thinking about anything more than additional bombing of enemy infiltration routes. This, however, was not all. Back at the ranch a week later, on December 15, Johnson gave a not-for-direct-quotation interview to Tom Wicker of the *New York Times*. The President, Wicker informed his readers the next day, "plans no fundamental change in the United States' course of action in the guerrilla warfare in South Vietnam" and opposed expansion of the conflict.[68] On the same day the President was more forthcoming in an interview with an older *New York Times* reporter, Turner Catledge, in which he complained about the *Times* coverage and about younger reporters: "Whether we spread military operations across North Vietnam is yet to be decided. We certainly haven't decided against it. We've got to do whatever it takes, either to get a good settlement there, or to furnish a good face behind which we can withdraw. Again, withdrawal is not in the picture, certainly now."[69]

Events in South Vietnam, however, were not waiting upon Johnson's domestic program. During the remainder of December Johnson and American policy came under serious pressure on four different fronts. Within South Vietnam the political situation deteriorated, the Viet Cong undertook far more serious military operations, and terrorist acts against Americans led to new demands for immediate retaliation. Meanwhile, in Washington, a dreaded leak created new risks for the President. Whatever his preference, Johnson by the first week of January faced tremendous pressure to act at once. He decided to do so, but he implemented his decision so carefully that he managed to conceal the extent of the new American commitment not only from the public but from a number of subsequent historians as well.

13

Over the Edge
December 1964–March 1965

★

The December 2 plan for further action in Southeast Asia that Johnson had tentatively approved on December 7 called for immediate retaliation against any new Viet Cong terrorist acts against Americans, and for the implementation of Phase II of military action against South Vietnam—including a program of continuing air strikes and large and increasing ground deployments in South Vietnam and Thailand—within as little as thirty days, provided that the South Vietnamese made satisfactory progress toward a stable government. Returning to South Vietnam in early December, Ambassador Taylor immediately conveyed this message, and stories from both Saigon and Washington discussed the possibility of anti-infiltration bombing in Laos and South Vietnam.[1] The political situation in Saigon, however, continued to deteriorate.

In a new and ominous development, the role of the United States in South Vietnam was becoming a critical issue in South Vietnamese politics. During December the organized Buddhist opposition began a determined campaign to unseat the Huong government largely because of its closeness to the Americans.[2] This quite predictably provoked a counterattack from General Khanh and the Young Turk faction of the military, which included Generals Ky of the air force and Thieu of the army. The Young Turks began pressuring the High National Council—Saigon's official legislature—to remove several senior Buddhist officers, including Big Minh, from the active list. When the council refused, the generals on December 20 dissolved it and arrested some of its members, effectively destroying the authority of the civilian government.[3]

Although Taylor obviously favored the policies of the Young Turk generals against the Buddhists, he had also committed the United States to the formation of an effective civilian government. In Saigon, Taylor on December 20 quickly met with three Young Turk generals (but not Commander in Chief Khanh) and chewed them out like junior officers or West Point cadets. "Do you all understand English?" he asked. "I told you all clearly at General Westmoreland's dinner we Americans were tired of coups. Apparently I wasted my words. Maybe this is because something is wrong with my French because you evidently didn't understand."[4] Taylor told the generals to leave Huong in office and reverse course. They took offense, and during the next few days Taylor became involved in a bitter public conflict with Khanh. While the ambassador suggested that Khanh should leave the country, the South Vietnamese commander even suggested privately, as the *New York Times* reported, that American aid might not be necessary. In Washington, James Reston reported a widespread view that Khanh and the military, by refusing to allow the civilian government to operate freely or to govern the country themselves, were destroying the government's authority and thus weakening the argument that the United States was assisting a legally constituted state. Reston even suggested—as it turned out quite accurately—that the crisis faced Washington with a choice of abandoning its policy of assistance and either taking over the war itself under the Tonkin Gulf resolution or negotiating.[5]

Although no one seems to have remarked upon it at the time, the new crisis was remarkably similar to the events of September-October 1963, when the U.S. government tried to use aid to bend Diem and Nhu to its will, and they in return threatened to do without American help. Washington on December 21 authorized Taylor to delay any decisions on increased aid and suspend covert strikes against Laos and even within South Vietnam. Khanh and thirty-four other general officers, meanwhile, sent Huong and Chief of State Pham Khac Suu a letter on December 24 detailing Taylor's insults and asking them to declare Taylor *persona non grata* and oust him from the country. The State Department, in a cable drafted by William Bundy and approved by Rusk and McGeorge Bundy, immediately authorized Taylor to say that such a demand would "make it virtually impossible for USG to continue to support the GVN effort."[6] An alarmed General Westmoreland asked CINCPAC to alert the Marines to protect U.S. nationals in case of "anti-American activities of unknown intensity."[7]

Like the previous year's crisis, this one had also split the Americans in Saigon. In a December 25 cable for McCone, Rusk, McNamara, and McGeorge Bundy, the Saigon CIA station decided this time to take the bull by the horns and retaliate, in effect, for Lodge's dismissal of Richardson more than a year earlier. Taylor, the station chief said, was now "the focal point of all Vietnamese military anger and disappointment," and should "somehow be removed from the Vietnam scene."[8] On the day before, the CIA had reported that the generals acted partly out of fear that the United States would endorse a neutralist solution, but also because "with Mr. Taylor remaining as Ambassador the generals feel there is no hope of revitalizing the effort against the Viet Cong," because of his "inflexible attitude."[9] General Lansdale, now working at the White House as a consultant on unrelated matters, took this opportunity to suggest to McGeorge Bundy that American policy might benefit from the return of Rufus Phillips, Lucien Conein, John Paul Vann, and, by implication, himself, to Saigon.[10]

Before Washington could respond to this, the Viet Cong on December 25 weighed in dramatically, setting off a bomb at the Brinks Bachelor Officer's Quarters in Saigon that killed two Americans and injured fifty. Taylor and CINCPAC Admiral Sharp immediately asked for a retaliatory strike, if necessary without South Vietnamese participation. Washington hesitated, initially unsure that the Viet Cong were actually responsible or that such a strike could send much of a signal given the ongoing political crisis.[11] During the next three days State urged Taylor in effect to give in and allow Prime Minister Huong to make his own deal with the generals, and to begin working with the Young Turks as an alternative to Khanh.[12] On December 28 Taylor renewed his request for a retaliatory strike in a cable for Rusk, McNamara, McCone, and McGeorge Bundy. A high-level meeting in Washington on the same day failed to reach agreement, and Rusk and Bundy decided to fly to the LBJ Ranch to ask the President for a decision. McGeorge Bundy prepared a memo for LBJ coming down quite firmly in favor of retaliation as reflecting the December decisions, but Johnson refused to order the strike.[13] Meanwhile, several prominent newspapers around the country, including the *Minneapolis Star,* the *Providence Journal,* and the entire Hearst and Scripps-Howard chains, suggested that the time had come to acknowledge that we could no longer fulfill our commitment to South Vietnam and to give up.[14]

Bundy, Rusk, and Johnson evidently discussed the whole situation at some length on December 29, and Bundy drafted a cable reflecting Johnson's thinking that went to Taylor the next day. As it turned out, this document set in motion the implementation of Phase II, the plan for war against North Vietnam.

Johnson began by refusing to authorize reprisal bombings until American dependents had been evacuated and the security of American installations had improved. Then, presumably on the advice of McGeorge Bundy, he stressed the need for more effective communication with the South Vietnamese and asked "whether we are making full use of the kind of Americans who have shown a knack for this kind of communication in the past." He named no names, but Taylor could not possibly have mistaken the reference to Lansdale, Conein, and perhaps Phillips in his characterization of "men who are skillful with Vietnamese, even if they are not always the easiest men to handle in a country team."

Johnson's next point also seemed to reflect Bundy's long-standing feeling—shared by Michael Forrestal—that the American military had never given enough attention to adapting its plans to the situation in Vietnam. "Every time I get a military recommendation it seems to me that it calls for large-scale bombing. I have never felt that this war will be won from the air, and it seems to me that what is much more needed and would be more effective is a larger and stronger use of Rangers and Special Forces and Marines, or other appropriate military strength on the ground and on the scene." He promised to meet any request for more Americans in such a role. Subject either to movement on these four areas or persuasive arguments to the contrary, Johnson expressed willingness to begin the Phase I *reprisal* bombings called for in the December 2 NSC paper.[15]

It took a week—until January 6, 1965—for Taylor to submit his reply. Developments on several fronts raised the ante in the meantime. First, on December 27, several hundred Viet Cong seized the town of Binh Gia, near the coast in Phuoc Tuy province north of Saigon. During the next six days they not only held the town but ambushed several units dispatched to relieve it, eventually inflicting casualties of 158 South Vietnamese and 4 Americans killed and 77 South Vietnamese and 3 Americans missing.[16] Second, on December 30, the *Washington Post* columnist Joseph Alsop revealed that in November Taylor had asked for a retaliatory strike after the Bien Hoa attack and that Johnson had turned him down. If Johnson continued to refuse to act, Alsop wrote, "we shall learn by experience about what it would have been like if Kennedy had ducked the challenge in October, 1962."[17] On the very next day, Taylor, Alexis Johnson, and Westmoreland cabled the senior leadership that Khanh might emerge from the crisis in charge—an outcome that Taylor regarded as disastrous—and that the United States might as a result have to disengage from its present relationship with the government, shrinking MACV "to the status of a MAAG and USOM [the aid mission] to an economic-budgetary advisory group," while continuing to take responsibility "for the air and maritime defense of SVN against the DRV"—a reversion, in short, to the situation that had prevailed before Taylor's mission in November 1961. This, they wrote, might encourage the Saigon government to "walk on its own legs," but it might also lead it to make its own deal with the NLF. "This danger," they concluded, "could be offset if at the time we were engaged in reprisal attacks *or had initiated Phase II operations against the DRV.*" The Alsop column was Johnson's worst nightmare, since he had appointed Taylor ambassador to take advantage of his prestige, and he was sufficiently incensed to ask McGeorge Bundy to investigate the possibility that Taylor himself had leaked his November request. Bundy passed the request on to his brother William, who eventually provided a reassuring report.[18] Taylor remained one of the main symbols of Kennedy's prestige, and the Alsop column undoubtedly gave his recommendation greater weight.

Taylor's reply to the President's cable—an extraordinarily revealing summary both of the results of American policy to date and of the premises of further action—arrived on January 6. Its six sections occupy eighteen densely printed pages of the *Foreign Relations of the United States*[19] and make it one of the longest cables in the history of American diplomacy. It initially described

a seriously deteriorating situation characterized by continued political turmoil, irresponsibility and division within the armed forces, lethargy in the pacification program, some anti-US feeling which could grow, signs of mounting terrorism by VC directly at US personnel and deepening discouragement and loss of morale throughout SVN. Unless these conditions are somehow changed and trends reversed, we are likely soon to face a number of unpleasant developments ranging from anti-U.S. demonstrations, further civil disorders, and even political assassinations to the ultimate installation of a hostile govt which will ask us to leave while it seeks accommodation with the National Liberation Front and Hanoi.

Taylor identified three major problems: "lack of a stable government, inadequate security against the VC and nationwide war-weariness." He blamed the first on the unexpected "magnitude of the centrifugal political forces which had been kept under control by [Diem's] iron rule." More critically, Taylor then blamed the lack of security in the countryside almost entirely upon infiltration from the North, finally and definitely adopting the classic American Army view—which observers like Colonel Frank Serong and Roger Hilsman had rejected—that the VC were partisans supported from outside. "The ability of the VC to regenerate their strength and to maintain their morale," he wrote—referring to what he had described just six weeks earlier as one of the great mysteries of the war—"is to an important degree the result of infiltration from the logistical sanctuaries outside the country and from the sense of support and confidence this gives them." In making this argument Taylor relied upon a MACV study of October 31, 1964, which had estimated infiltration from the North since 1959 at 34,000 men—by coincidence, exactly the current estimate of VC guerrilla forces. Given the recognized need for a ten-to-one superiority in counterguerrilla operations, he argued, Saigon could not cope with this force.[20] Taylor continued to regard the 60,000–80,000 local guerrillas—20,000–40,000 fewer than earlier estimates—as insignificant. He did not try to explain how infiltration could explain the catastrophic deterioration of security all over the Mekong Delta. He conceded, however, that "effective pacification" required a coordinated effort that had so far been beyond the capacity of any Saigon government, and that it would take years to bring security to the countryside "by present methods at current rates of progress."

What could the United States do? Psychologically, he argued, "a few victories, military or political" could turn the situation around. Since we could not "change national characteristics, create leadership where it does not exist, raise large additional GVN forces or seal porous frontiers to infiltration," we had to add "something new . . . to make up for those things we cannot control." No government would get far, he said, "unless a new factor is added which will contribute to coalescing the political factions around and within the government and thus bolster its position."

Regarding pacification, Taylor—like the NSC working group of November-December—could not suggest anything new. The American advisory presence, he argued, had probably reached "the saturation point," and he did not recommend an increase. He rejected the use of American troops in a counterguerrilla role—a decision he justified at length in a later portion of the cable. Instead, he recommended initiating the air attacks called for under Phase II to accomplish four purposes: to persuade Hanoi that it would become "increasingly costly" to support the VC, to create an atmosphere for negotiations, to turn the South Vietnamese from feuding internally to attacking "the external source of their troubles," and to "restore U.S./GVN camaraderie." Phase II was not "a resort to use bombing to win on the Douhet theory," but an attempt to influence the will of North Vietnamese leaders, who "as practical men, cannot wish to see the fruits of ten years of labor destroyed by slowly escalating air attacks (which they cannot prevent) without trying to find some accommodation which will exorcise the threat."[21]

The later sections of the cable rejected Johnson's alternative suggestions one by one. Taylor argued that the prior evacuation of dependents was likely to cause panic, although he agreed on their evacuation when sustained attacks began. Regarding security for American installations, he reported that Westmoreland estimated that thirty-four battalions, or 75,000 additional U.S. personnel, would be required, "together with the necessary logistic support," to guard literally hundreds of vulnerable installations, and recommended new increases in South Vietnamese forces instead. He turned down the suggestion for Americans like Lansdale to work with the South Vietnamese, claiming that American personnel on duty "meet pretty well your description of 'sensitive, persistent and attentive Americans' . . . we definitely do not need more."

Lastly, responding to Johnson's suggestion of more innovative use of American ground forces, Taylor provided comments from Westmoreland and his staff. They paid essentially no attention to Johnson's comments regarding "Rangers and Special Forces and Marines," and rejected any substantial increases in the American advisory presence. As three possible alternatives they suggested providing 20,000–60,000

American troops as strategic reserves in the four corps zones; integrating 66,000 men (thirty-one battalions plus support) into ARVN units to provide an example; and using three divisions (75,000 men) to establish three secure enclaves at points along the coast. Taylor recommended against all these alternatives on the grounds that "their military value would be more than offset by their political liability":

> The Vietnamese have the manpower and the basic skills to win this war. What they lack is motivation. The entire advisory effort has been devoted to giving them both skill and motivation. If that effort has not succeeded there is less reason to think that U.S. combat forces would have the desired effect. In fact, there is good reason to believe that they would [have] the opposite effect by causing some Vietnamese to let the U.S. carry the burden while others, probably the majority would turn actively against us. Thus intervention with ground combat forces would at best buy time and would lead to ever increasing commitments until, like the French, we would be occupying an essentially hostile foreign country.

As we shall see, Taylor sincerely believed these arguments and opposed any substantial use of American forces, but Westmoreland, in fact, did not. Taylor in a previous cable had already called for the implementation of Phase II bombing of the North, but he may not have understood that the cryptic language of the December 2 NSC paper— that Phase II would also include "appropriate US deployments to handle any contingency"—was backed up by an appendix providing for multidivisional deployments in both South Vietnam and Thailand within a matter of months. But Westmoreland, who had been discussing such deployments with CINCPAC and the Chiefs, apparently did know, and despite a continuing conspiracy of silence on the issue of ground forces, senior officials in Washington seem to have understood this as well.

Taylor's demand for immediate action to prevent catastrophe was the event that Johnson had foreseen six months earlier when he had chosen Taylor as ambassador. When it arrived at the White House on the morning of January 6, Johnson restricted its distribution to McGeorge Bundy, McNamara, Rusk, and Ball, cutting out the rest of the State Department. The next day Taylor was advised to put the security designation NODIS/LOR on subsequent messages on this topic to facilitate their restricted handling.[22] Johnson and these four senior advisers met twice to discuss a reply on January 6 and 7, but only one fragmentary account of the first meeting survives. Bowing to the inevitable, Johnson edited McGeorge Bundy's draft reply, which went out on the evening of January 7, and agreed to begin reprisal bombings, subsequent to the withdrawal of dependents, and to begin planning for Phase II, but reserving any commitment as to its "timing and scale." It also implicitly reopened the November argument over American objectives, arguing that while no course of action might turn the situation in South Vietnam around, "we are convinced that it is of high importance to try." Bundy's original draft reply concurred in Taylor's recommendation against American combat troops, but the final version, edited by the President, omitted this reference, suggesting that the President understood and endorsed the idea that Phase II had to include combat troops as well. Johnson also expressed an intention to send someone to discuss certain issues with Taylor.[23]

From Monday, January 11, through Saturday, January 23, three more rounds of messages between Taylor and the White House brought the nation closer to war.[24] Taylor continued to ask for the early initiation of Phase II while resisting the prior evacuation of dependents and arguing that the United States might not be able to make reprisal strikes within twenty-four hours of Viet Cong outrages, as the President wished. The President's restrictions on information worked almost to perfection, and the press never learned that the government was talking about going to war. On January 13 the United States lost two jets in an anti-infiltration strike against a bridge inside Laos.[25] Domestic news, however, generally dominated these two weeks. Johnson sent major messages to Congress on January 14, 15, and 16, and the papers carried news of his poverty program on January 18. The President took the oath of office on January 20. The next day, meeting with the bipartisan congressional leadership, Johnson discussed plans to withdraw dependents, Rusk defined our objectives as limited to the 1954 and 1962 Geneva Accords, McNamara gave the new infiltration estimate as 19,000–34,000 men since 1959, but the President made only one brief reference to *possible* air strikes against the North. Johnson also said that "we have decided that more U.S. forces are not needed in South Vietnam short of a decision to go to full-scale war."[26]

The President wanted to let the decision to act slide for a while longer, but the administration's silence seemed to be having serious consequences on at least two fronts. First, although on January 18 several generals agreed to join the Huong cabinet and end the political crisis, the Buddhists over the next few days retaliated with anti-American statements and direct action against United States Information Service (USIS) libraries in Saigon and Hue.[27] By January 26–27 the Embassy had concluded that Khanh had allied himself with the Buddhist leadership in an attempt to replace the Huong government with one that would be "both weaker and more inclined towards negotiations with the Communists," and asked for permission to ask other generals to act against Khanh.[28] Meanwhile, the administration made a key decision in principle on another front. On January 27th General Westmoreland received permission to use American jets against Viet Cong forces in South Vietnam, but Washington required case-by-case approval from the Joint Chiefs, Ambassador Taylor, and the Vietnamese armed forces.[29]

And as the administration failed to give more than feeble hints of future action, support for an American withdrawal seemed to be growing. As early as January 7 an Associated Press survey of eighty-three senators had found only three who definitely supported widening the war, and just five others who thought that some American troops or action against the North might help bring the conflict to an end. Wayne Morse, Frank Church of Idaho, Ernest Gruening of Alaska, and the conservative maverick Allen Ellender of Louisiana all favored either neutralization or immediate withdrawal. On January 11 Senator Richard Russell commented after a long briefing from CIA Director McCone that we could not win without a stable government in Saigon and suggested that we should "re-evaluate" our role.[30] The lack of any real political pressure to go to war had never been more apparent. On that same day McGeorge Bundy saw the British journalist Henry Brandon, who actually accused the administration of following Russell and the columnist Walter Lippmann on Southeast Asia and abandoning the greater firmness of Kennedy.[31] In the last week of January sources in both Saigon and Washington briefed reporters on the new infiltration estimates of 19,000–34,000, but officials in Washington denied that these disclosures foreshadowed a change in policy.[32] Richard Nixon on January 26 declared publicly that an air and naval quarantine could win the war without either nuclear weapons or American ground troops.[33]

Concerned about the lack of a firm decision, McGeorge Bundy on January 26 asked Johnson for a meeting with himself and McNamara. Then, the next day, he gave the President a memorandum reflecting their common views in an effort to end a whole year of indecision and set the American military in motion at last.[34]

The memo—now famous as the "fork in the road" memorandum—used apocalyptic language in an attempt to force a decision.[35] "Both of us," Bundy wrote, "are now pretty well convinced that our current policy can lead only to disastrous defeat," and he laid two alternatives before the President: "to use our military power in the Far East and to force a change in Communist policy," or "to deploy all our resources along a track of negotiation, aimed at salvaging what little can be preserved." Bundy added that Dean Rusk, who was in Florida with the flu, wanted to continue trying to make the present policy work, but he omitted the third alternative, pushed in November by his brother and John McNaughton, of negotiating after some display of force.

But read carefully against the background of the previous two months, the memorandum asked only for a simple but critical change in the plan laid out in December: the immediate initiation of Phase II, to which Johnson had as yet evidently refused to commit himself. "Our December directives," Bundy wrote, "make it very plain that wider action against the Communists will not take place until we can get a [stable] government." Now, however, Bundy argued that the American failure to act was demoralizing both the South Vietnamese and Americans in Saigon. "The basic directive," he repeated, "says that we will not go further until there is a stable government, and no one has much hope that there is going to be a stable government while we sit still." Bundy and McNamara were simply taking the position that Taylor had enunciated in his long cable of January 6: that the United States had to begin Phase II immediately. (It was Phase II, of course, that the December directives to which Bundy referred had postponed until after a stable government had emerged.)

It took only one meeting of an hour and fifteen minutes between Johnson, McNamara, McGeorge Bundy, Rusk, Ball, and perhaps Johnson's friend Abe Fortas to secure the President's agreement. "Stable government or no stable government," Johnson said, "we'll do what we ought to do." He also reaffirmed his personal commitment to General Khanh, with whom Bundy thought the United States might have to keep working despite Taylor's opposite opinion.[36] Johnson also agreed that McGeorge Bundy would lead a small delegation to Saigon to investigate the situation and report.

The White House and Taylor hammered out the details of Bundy's visit—originally scheduled for February 3–6—between January 27 and February 1. While Taylor finally agreed in principle to the evacuation of dependents, he successfully resisted Bundy's suggestion that former Ambassador Lodge accompany him to talk to the Buddhists, who still revered Lodge for the role he had played in 1963. While they argued over the details, Khanh on January 26 seized power again and declared martial law, finally forcing Washington and Saigon to abandon their insistence upon civilian rule. Bundy, however, wrote Johnson on January 26 that he now shared the feeling that "this back-and-forth government in Saigon is a symptom, not a root cause of our problem."[37]

By the time Bundy left, he had made clear to Taylor what he thought the solution might be. "In general," he cabled on February 1, "I am primarily interested in coming away with a sense of what kind of pressures you and your senior subordinates feel can be effectively applied to the VC and Hanoi." He also raised the question of a U.S. or international force "along the DMZ [demilitarized zone] or elsewhere as appropriate as part of a Phase II action."[38] Johnson had tipped his hand even earlier: once the dependents had been removed, he had told Taylor on January 27, "I am determined to make it clear to all the world that the US will spare no effort and no sacrifice in doing its full part to turn back the Communists in Vietnam."[39] As Bundy's deputy Chester Cooper remarked in 1979, Johnson "damn well had decided what he was going to do."[40]

And as January gave way to February the administration still managed to keep any hint of its deliberations from getting into the newspapers. Announcing Bundy's trip on February 1, Johnson's Press Secretary, George Reedy, characterized it as a consultation with Taylor regarding the Saigon political crisis and the ambassador's role in it, and news stories made only passing references to the possibility of expanded military action. On the day before the announcement of Bundy's visit, Soviet Premier Aleksei Kosygin had announced a simultaneous visit to Hanoi, and sources speculated that this might lead to a Soviet negotiating initiative. The press was now talking more frankly about the increasing neutralist influence of the Buddhists upon Khanh.

When Johnson gave a press conference on February 4, he dodged a question about the possibility that the South Vietnamese might invite us to leave, and never mentioned the possibility of expanding the war.[41] A State Department legal adviser submitted a paper to William Bundy on February 6 premised on the idea that the United States would seek an early negotiated settlement, evidently quite unaware of the decision to escalate.[42]

Bundy and his party—including McNaughton and William Colby of the CIA—initially spent a relatively quiet and sobering February 4–6 in Saigon. During the first few days in February it had become clear that Khanh wanted to make an alliance with the Buddhists, open talks with the NLF, and become "the Sihanouk of South Vietnam," that is, a militantly nationalistic, neutralist head of state. Taylor had commented on February 3 that the mercurial general's efforts would lead either to prolonged civil unrest or to "a neutralist Khanh in a Sihanouk role," and that "both are unacceptable solutions from the point of view of the U.S." On February 4 Bundy, Taylor, and Alexis Johnson agreed to encourage the Young Turk generals, led by Thieu and Ky, to replace Khanh. Bundy went further in a telegram to Washington the next day, seeing no prospect of a government acceptable both to Washington and to the Buddhists. A civil war had begun within the existing civil war, he suggested, and "the construction of a government of national unity may well require sharp confrontation with the Buddhists before, during or after the construction job." On the same day, Bundy told his brother over the telephone that he did not expect to make any recommendations for immediate action upon his return because of "the fluidity of the local situation here."[43]

On his last day in Saigon Bundy met with Thich Thien Minh, a Buddhist leader. Although second-hand accounts have described this meeting as an encounter between two civilizations that failed to make contact, a recently declassified account of it shows that the Buddhist leader asked the United States to help form a good government, professed his anti-Communism, but also spoke at length about the enormous popular longing and need for peace.[44]

The American effort since 1961 had produced truly astonishing results. The Viet Cong, as Bundy learned in a briefing, were stronger and better equipped than ever, although MACV claimed that the ARVN had inflicted record casualties during January. Even more remarkably, the pro-American anti-Communist political forces within South Vietnam had steadily lost ground since mid-1963 not merely to the Communists but also to non-Communist neutralists led by the Buddhists, the only non-Communist political force that could deploy a mass following. Even General Khanh, whom Johnson had seized upon about a year earlier as America's man on the spot, had decided to become, not the next Ngo Dinh Diem or Phoumi Nosavan, but the next Norodom Sihanouk or Souvanna Phouma. South Vietnamese politics, indeed, now bore a remarkable and increasing resemblance to the Laotian situation in 1960–1961, in which the pro-American elements had also become isolated. And by an extraordinary coincidence, Marshal Phoumi Nosavan, the Eisenhower administration's Laotian protégé whom the Kennedy administration had jettisoned in favor of Souvanna Phouma, was mounting his own last, doomed coup against the Laotian government during the first week of February 1965. The coup led to renewed fighting among government forces, and then, after several months of maneuvering, to Phoumi's exile and final departure from the Laotian scene.[45]

Nor was this all. As in 1961, both the Soviet Union and America's major European allies very clearly wanted to settle the crisis in Southeast Asia through negotiations and not in a war. In Paris the French government had discussed a possible settlement both with newly accredited Chinese diplomats and with the North Vietnamese economic delegate Mai Van Bo. (The French still had formal diplomatic relations only with the Saigon government, not with Hanoi.) The French told the American Embassy that Mai Van Bo, the more forthcoming of their two Communist interlocutors, had expressed interest in reestablishing a neutral South Vietnam under the Geneva Accords.[46] The State Department had concluded, quite correctly, that Kosygin was visiting North Vietnam both to offer help with air defense and to promote a settlement that would strengthen Moscow's position vis-à-vis Peking in the Communist world.[47] The new Labour government in London was as yet taking a less forthright stand against war than its conservative predecessors four years earlier, but Bundy had already had to explain to President Johnson that Prime Minister Harold Wilson was unlikely to provide any real assistance, and events showed Wilson to be as uneasy as Macmillan had been.[48] Visiting Washington in January, Japanese Prime Minister Sato had suggested that Asia's problems should be solved by Asians themselves.[49] As in 1961, the United States could count on firm support, first, from its most dependent clients in the Far East—Thailand, the Philippines, and Nationalist China—and also from Australia and New Zealand. And the Secretary General of the United Nations, the Burmese U Thant, had been trying to arrange direct U.S.–North Vietnamese talks for about eight months.

Confronted by the Laotian civil war in 1961, John Kennedy, emphasizing the weakness of Phoumi Nosavan, the attitude of America's allies, and the enormous difficulties of fighting in Laos, had chosen neutralization instead of war and rejected the combined advice of the State and Defense Departments and the Joint Chiefs of Staff. The neutralist Souvanna Phouma had now become a staunch American ally in the struggle against the North Vietnamese, cooperating willingly, if covertly, in bombing raids along the border. Kennedy had always supported the neutrality both of Souvanna and of Sihanouk, and he had remarked on at least one occasion that neutralization would not work in South Vietnam *in the absence of such a figure there.* Now Khanh wanted to play exactly that role. In early March former Ambassador to Laos Leonard Unger—now working for William Bundy at State—did dare openly to make this analogy, suggesting that a Military Assistance Advisory Group and an aid program might adequately protect American interests in South Vietnam. "The example of Laos," he wrote, "suggests that if we ceased at once to take a negative view of neutrality and started working with the Government in company with like-minded friends we might be able to assure the continuation of a non-Communist South Viet-Nam."[50] No one picked up the hint.

Other things had changed since 1961. While Kennedy had discovered the enormous difficulties of deploying and sustaining troops within Laos then, now the United States was fully prepared to deploy troops and planes in South Vietnam—although here, too, logistical difficulties would take many months to overcome and would doom any chance of winning a quick and decisive victory. On the other hand, the international climate had changed dramatically in the four intervening years. The Berlin and German questions had lapsed into utter quiet. The missile gap was no longer an issue. The United States was about to take the lead in the space race. The Sino-Soviet split had widened considerably. The mood of the American people was far more confident, far more peaceful, and far more attuned to developments within American society itself than in 1961.

Kennedy throughout the whole of his presidency had refused to undertake war in Southeast Asia because of the difficulty of the job and because of the priority he had continually assigned to other tasks, most of them in foreign policy. First Berlin and the Congo, then Cuba, and finally, in 1963, the test ban and détente with the Soviet Union had been his priority. Meanwhile, he had invested a good deal of prestige in cultivating Third World nationalism. Johnson, too, had another huge task he wished to perform: the passage of the Great Society, which he was even now presenting to Congress, and of which he was determined to achieve as much as possible during the session of 1965. But Johnson, in contrast to Kennedy, had never really challenged the assumption of Rusk, Bundy, and McNamara that Communist aggression in South Vietnam presented a challenge which the United States would simply have to do its best to meet. He had allowed them to enshrine that view in NSAM 288 in March 1964, and he had signed on to a full-scale war plan designed to accomplish the task in December 1964. Subsequently he had delayed implementing that plan, both because of political turmoil in South Vietnam and because he did not want it to interfere with the presentation of the Great Society. Now, however, the moment for decision had arrived, and no evidence suggests that Johnson had ever really considered a negative decision.

Johnson, moreover, had never set himself any other long-term task in foreign affairs against which he, like Kennedy, might have weighed the danger of war in Southeast Asia. While anxious to establish himself as a man of peace, he had given no sustained attention in the fourteen months of his presidency to any specific issues on which progress with the Soviets might be made. Despite this, during the last month of 1964 Rusk, with McNamara's apparent help and approval, had reached an informal but potentially very important understanding with the Soviet Union. On November 30, December 2, and December 5, 1964, Rusk had informed Soviet Foreign Minister Gromyko that the United States was reducing its defense budget for fiscal 1966 (beginning July 1, 1965) to $1.25 billion less than the budget for fiscal 1965. Soviet Premier Kosygin, in a speech to the Supreme Soviet on December 9, had announced a reduction in Soviet military expenditures for 1965 and specifically linked it to the declared American reduction.[51] Washington had chosen not to publicize this informal agreement, but later events suggested that Kosygin regarded it as important. It could not possibly survive escalation in Vietnam.

As of February 6, Bundy in Saigon had not apparently decided to recommend immediate action against the North, preferring, apparently, to wait until the Embassy had managed to ease Khanh out of power. But in the predawn hours of February 7 the Viet Cong took a hand again. A mortar attack on the American airfield and advisory compound near Pleiku killed eight Americans and destroyed five more aircraft, and the VC struck two other airfields as well. The United States government immediately had to decide whether to go forward.

The National Security Council met at 7:45 in the evening on February 6, only hours after the attacks had taken place, with Senator Mansfield and House Speaker John McCormack in attendance. McNamara's deputy Cyrus Vance reported the unanimous recommendation from Saigon that the United States and the South Vietnamese undertake a joint retaliatory strike. Johnson made clear that he intended to evacuate American dependents immediately, and asked for comment. Ball, representing the State Department, wholeheartedly supported the strike despite Kosygin's presence in Hanoi. Mansfield courageously dissented, questioning the strength of the government in Saigon, raising the possibility of war with China, and stating his belief that "the results could be worse than Korea." Johnson responded in revealing terms:

> The President took the opposite opinion, emphasizing that he had kept the shotgun over the mantel and the bullets in the basement for a long time now, but that the enemy was killing his personnel and he could not expect them to continue their work if he did not authorize them to take steps to defend themselves. He commented that "cowardice has gotten us into more wars than response has." He particularly recalled the fact that we would not have gotten into World War I if we had been courageous in the early stages, nor World War II. He then said he realized that there was a risk of involving the Soviets and Chinese but that neither of these are friendly with us and the problem is to face up to them both.[52]

Leaving aside Johnson's rather questionable historical exposition—especially with regard to the First World War—this statement suggests that the President fully understood and accepted the implications of option C′, which he had approved in December: that the United States would pursue its objectives in South Vietnam despite the risks of escalation to general war.

On February 7, Saigon time, American and South Vietnamese planes flew strikes against four military targets in southern North Vietnam, but in a significant portent of things to come, bad weather allowed them actually to hit only one of them. Meeting once again with the NSC and congressional leaders, Johnson denied that any decision for further action had been reached, pending Bundy's return later that day, and announced that he was disregarding Ambassador Taylor's recommendation to restrike the three targets that had not been hit. When Mansfield asked whether the United Nations or a Geneva conference could discuss the situation, Johnson replied that nothing could be expected from the United Nations and Ball said that the United States needed a position of greater strength to go to Geneva.[53] Bundy returned that evening, met with Johnson, and presented his recommendations.

Like Taylor's massive cable of four weeks before and his own "fork in the road" memorandum, the memorandum Bundy presented on February 8 argued that greater American will might become the key to the situation. It acknowledged that the Communists were still gaining in the countryside, and even admitted that, after three years of American effort, no Vietnamese or American authorities were taking responsibility for providing security for areas that had been "'cleared' in crude military terms." Effectively admitting that neither Washington nor Saigon had a real counterinsurgency program in place, he tentatively proposed more Special Forces to fill the gap.

Bundy paid many compliments to Taylor's leadership, but proceeded to oppose him on a point of fundamental importance, suggesting that the United States prepare to work with a government led by Khanh and supported by the Buddhists. Khanh, he believed, "will pursue the fight against the Communists as long as he thinks he can count on U.S. help." Bundy also suggested that the Buddhists somehow had to be incorporated into the government.

The annex to the memo called for a new policy of "sustained reprisal," in which continuing air and naval action against the North would be justified by the whole Viet Cong terror campaign in the South. Taylor on the same day had already suggested such a program, "something like a Phase II," with a better internal and international "posture" and, he hoped, less pressure for negotiations.[54] Bundy's annex—whose original typeface suggests that it was the work of John McNaughton of the Pentagon—suggested that the program would begin slowly and increase gradually, but acknowledged that such a policy might quickly reach or exceed the level of military activity of December's Phase II. The annex, however, discreetly omitted any reference to American ground troops. To stop the campaign, the Communists would have to "stop enough of their activity in the South to permit the probable success of a determined pacification effort"—something which, as we have seen, did not yet exist at all. Reprisals would substantially depress the Viet Cong and, Bundy hoped, raise the morale of the South Vietnamese.

The annex also reopened the argument over American objectives that had apparently been settled in November. At that time, as we have seen, Rusk in particular had argued that the United States would never get any credit for trying and failing in South Vietnam, and the paper the President approved had rejected any halt in American military activity before U.S. objectives had been met. Now, however, Bundy argued that while the new policy had only a 25–75 percent chance of success, it would be worth it even if it failed.

The President essentially interpreted Bundy's recommendations as a plan to move to Phase II and accepted them at once. In another NSC meeting the next day, February 8, General Wheeler recommended an immediate attack on the North Vietnamese MIGs at Phuc Yen airfield. McNamara replied that this meant at least the initiation of Phase II, but that the United States could wait for several weeks. Johnson affirmed that the administration had chosen to go forward, and that he would tell the waiting congressional leadership that the United States was implementing its December decisions without waiting for a stable government.

Johnson then told the congressional leaders that he was beginning a program of defeating North Vietnamese aggression without escalating the war. When the conversation turned to the security of American bases, Wheeler described the difficulties and Johnson remarked that one could only stop such attacks by "sending a very large number of U.S. troops to Vietnam"—exactly what December's Phase II annexes called for. But when House Minority Leader (and future President) Gerald Ford asked whether the new program required new personnel,

Johnson replied disingenuously that our present needs were met, and that only an unexpected response would necessitate more men. After basing his actions both on the Tonkin Gulf resolution and on the powers of the presidency, Johnson concluded that the administration was trying to tell the American people as much as it could without harming the national interest. He "asked those present not to discuss publicly our military actions but he said they could say our actions would be kept at a manageable level"—surely a flexible euphemism.[55] Late that afternoon Johnson cabled Taylor that despite the lack of the strong government that Washington had demanded in December, he was now ready to carry out "our December plan for continuing action against North Vietnam with modifications up and down in tempo and scale," and authorized Taylor to discuss it with the South Vietnamese. Briefings downplayed the dangers of escalation. Reston reported the next day that both sides seemed to be acting with restraint, and that the United States did not expect "the powerful North Vietnamese divisions" to intervene in the South.[56]

In the next few days the nature of the problem that dominated the next six months of the Johnson administration began to emerge. The President did not want to share his decision to begin full-scale war against the Viet Cong and North Vietnam with the American people, but the decision was too big not to leak. McNamara on February 8 met with the Joint Chiefs and asked them to prepare an eight-week plan of action against the North, to include provision for the security of American bases and plans to counter North Vietnamese or Chinese intervention on the ground.[57] Two days later the *New York Times* carried a remarkably accurate story by its military correspondent, Hanson Baldwin, on the opinions of the Chiefs. Many military leaders, Baldwin reported, had believed since 1961 that both sustained bombing and ground action would be necessary to defeat the Communists in South Vietnam, but Maxwell Taylor, as Chief of Staff, had held them back. Now the Chiefs wanted sustained bombing against "sanctuaries," a unified U.S.–South Vietnamese command, and the use of American ground units, "as needed," in South Vietnam.[58] On February 9 Bundy wrote Mike Mansfield—who had weighed in with another prophetic memorandum of his own—that the administration was willing to run the risk of war with China, and implied a willingness to make a sacrifice at least equal to that of the Korean War. But the next day, when

Ambassador to Great Britain David Bruce advised Johnson against the use of American forces, Johnson simply remarked that the late Douglas MacArthur had given him the same advice on the day before his death the previous year.[59]

The Viet Cong, meanwhile, continued to force the pace. On the night of February 10–11 an explosion in a U.S. enlisted men's barracks in Qui Nhon on the central coast killed 21 more Americans. In another NSC meeting on February 10 the administration decided on another retaliatory strike, and McNamara recommended moving additional forces into Southeast Asia for political reasons. He also said, however, in response to a presidential question, that to guard American bases would require "at least 100,000 men, 44 battalions," and that such a large force would be unacceptable "for a variety of reasons." "At an appropriate time," Bundy commented, "we could publicly announce that we had turned a corner and changed our policy but no mention should be made now of such a decision." Bundy afterward told John McCone, McNamara, and Ball that "we were on the track of sustained and continuing operations against the North." But when the congressional leadership came in once again, Johnson simply described the new retaliatory strike and gave no hint that a sustained program had begun. And administration sources told the *New York Times* on February 11 that Johnson had resisted military advice "to continue raids against North Vietnam."[60]

On February 13 the White House cabled Taylor that the President had approved a program of "measured and limited air action jointly with the GVN against selected military targets in the DRV remaining south of the 19th parallel until further notice," probably involving multi-target strikes once or twice a week.[61] The cable also anticipated an announcement of the policy. Senior officials, moreover, seem to have firmed up their objectives in the week or so since McGeorge Bundy's return. The Bundy report had spoken of the possibility that bombing might fail to secure American objectives, but now, as they moved into Phase II, McGeorge Bundy, McNamara, and Johnson seem wholeheartedly to have embraced the premise of the December program: that the United States would take whatever military actions proved necessary to stop North Vietnamese aggression and face the risk of escalation. George Ball summarized Bundy's and McNamara's views in a

February 13 memorandum he had shown to them—a memo in which Ball himself stressed the dangers of escalation:

> McNamara and Bundy believe that we must pursue a course of increasing military pressure to the point where Hanoi is prepared to agree not only to stop infiltration from the North, but effectively to call off the insurgency in the South and withdraw those elements infiltrated in the past. To achieve this objective, they would accept the risks of substantial escalation, including the acceptance of ground warfare with Red China—although they believe it likely that we can achieve the desired objective without such a war. This view is shared by Maxwell Taylor.[62]

For the rest of the month of February the administration struggled to begin Phase II covertly while coping with increasing internal and international opposition and with a new crisis inside South Vietnam. In an apparently difficult high-level meeting on February 15 McNamara asked for an official decision to go into Phase II, but Johnson refused to make any new statement of policy either publicly or privately. Showing his stubborn and legalistic streak, the President evidently argued that since the United States had a long-standing policy of helping the South Vietnamese to resist aggression, it did not have to announce its new strategy.[63] The next day Bundy wrote Johnson looking for a way out.

Bundy suggested that the meeting had confused two questions: the firmness of Johnson's actual decision to undertake continuing action, and the wisdom of a public statement. Given Johnson's long hesitation, he said, "there is a deep-seated need," both in the Pentagon and in Saigon, "for assurance that the decision has in fact been taken." In another meeting that afternoon Johnson promised McNamara what he needed "to carry out our decision," but refused again to announce a new policy.[64] In an effort to begin building broad support, however, he invited former President Eisenhower to the White House on the next day.

In the meeting Eisenhower showed both that he had been kept well informed of the administration's policy and its rationale, and that he remained faithful to some of the key strategic concepts of his own administration. Thus he supported the concept of strikes against the North to boost South Vietnamese morale and to induce the North Vietnamese to change their policy. He agreed with Johnson that the United

States should not enter negotiations until it had won some victories, citing the example of Lincoln's delay in releasing the Emancipation Proclamation. Regarding the possibility of Chinese intervention, Eisenhower recommended repeating the threats of nuclear strikes which, he claimed, had brought about a settlement of the Korean War.[65] If the Chinese intervened with large forces, he suggested that the United States respond with massive air attacks against their supply lines, including the use of tactical nuclear weapons, rather than using large numbers of American troops. But Eisenhower endorsed General Wheeler's suggestion of one division south of the demilitarized zone, and said that if six or eight divisions had to go to Vietnam, "so be it."[66]

The Pentagon, meanwhile, was busily planning the implementation of Phase II. The Chiefs on February 11 recommended an eight-week program of four air strikes per week, and the deployment of nine fighter squadrons and thirty B-52s. They also recommended immediately deploying one Marine expeditionary battalion in Da Nang; deploying a brigade of the 25th Infantry Division to Thailand; alerting the rest of the third Marine Expeditionary Force (MEF; a division) and the 173d Airborne brigade for movement to Vietnam, and the rest of the 25th Division for Thailand; and considering the deployment of two more divisions south of the DMZ and in Thailand, respectively. Westmoreland initially replied three days later reiterating the need for Marines to guard the key Da Nang base and noting that the security situation was deteriorating in I, II, and III Corps, raising the possibility of a need to move to Phase II, OPLAN 32–64. CINCPAC concurred in his view.[67] The Chiefs on February 20 recommended the deployment of the whole MEF (39,000 men), committed to counterinsurgency combat operations; an Army division around Pleiku; a South Korean division; and four air squadrons. They expressed their judgment "that the needs of the military situation in South Vietnam have become primary, and direct military action appears to be imperative if defeat is to be avoided," and asked that Westmoreland's own planning "be held to the smallest possible U.S. military repeat military group," an obvious attempt to exclude Taylor.[68]

General Westmoreland took the last injunction literally and seriously. He replied on February 22 that he wanted to put the Marines in Da Nang, the Army division in Pleiku and Qui Nhon, and the Koreans elsewhere. But on the very same day Ambassador Taylor cabled Washington, "General Westmoreland and I agree that there is no need to consider deployments to SVN at this time except possibly for the protection of the airfield at Da Nang." Only in this way, Taylor argued, could the administration stick to existing policy (as he understood it) against ground troops, and he questioned whether American forces could do much better than the French in Asian guerrilla warfare.[69]

What delayed the actual implementation of Phase II was the ongoing political crisis in Saigon. Taylor on February 14 had referred to the difficulty of getting Saigon's concurrence for the program "in the condition of virtual no-government which exists in Saigon today." The Armed Forces Council had designated a civilian politician, Phan Huy Quat, to replace Huong as Prime Minister, but he faced the familiar problem of reconciling the military and the Buddhists.[70] Taylor got agreement from Thieu and Khanh on February 15 and from Quat the next day, and the administration planned the beginning of continuous air strikes for February 20.[71] But on February 19 General Lam Van Phat moved troops into Saigon in a coup against Khanh. Behind him was Colonel Pham Ngoc Thao, the old inspector of strategic hamlets and perennial coup plotter who is now assumed to have been a Viet Cong agent. Washington postponed the strike pending a resolution of the situation, and the Embassy supported an attempt by the Young Turks, Generals Thieu and Ky, to remove Khanh. This was the final crisis in Taylor's relations with the general, and Taylor prevailed. By February 23 he confidently expected Khanh to leave two days later, and based upon this, Washington ordered a strike for February 26.[72] But in another portent of difficulties that Washington had not foreseen, the February 26 strike had to be delayed because of bad weather.

Despite the two-week lull in bombing, the two retaliatory strikes on February 7 and February 11 had sounded the alarm among neutral nations and major American allies. French Foreign Minister Couve de Murville had seen Johnson to protest, and on the night of February 10, while the administration was planning to retaliate for the Qui Nhon bombing, British Prime Minister Harold Wilson called Johnson to ask to visit Washington and discuss the situation—much, perhaps, as the previous Labour party Prime Minister, Clement Attlee, had done in late 1950 after President Truman discussed the possible use of the atomic bomb in Korea. Johnson flatly refused to receive him, pointing out the support he was giving Wilson over the Malaysia-Indonesia crisis and the precarious pound sterling, and suggesting that they should simply support each other as loyal allies. A week later Wilson told Ambassador Bruce that he was concerned about the possibility of continuing air attacks without negotiations.[73]

More pressure came from U.N. Secretary General U Thant, who on February 16 reminded Adlai Stevenson that he had been trying to arrange bilateral U.S.–North Vietnam talks for over a year, and now suggested seven-power talks including both Vietnams, Communist China, Britain, France, the Soviets, and the United States. The next day Rusk saw British Foreign Secretary Michael Stewart, who told him that Moscow had approached London about resuming their role as co-chairmen of the Geneva conference and asking under what circumstances Washington would be ready to talk. Rusk replied, in what was rapidly becoming the American line, "that we would not consider negotiations unless we felt there was some possibility of a meaningful conclusion to them"—that is, until the enemy seemed ready to accept our terms. To meet the growing pressure, however, the administration decided to ask the British to suggest that the two co-chairmen simply ask the parties to state their views.[74]

More serious pressure emerged on February 24, when U Thant publicly assailed the United States government for withholding the truth about possible negotiations from the American people. "I am sure that the great American people, if only they knew the true facts and the background to the developments in South Vietnam, will agree with me that further bloodshed is unnecessary," he said. "The political and diplomatic method of discussions and negotiations alone can create conditions which will enable the United States to withdraw gracefully from that part of the world." The White House denied receiving any "proposals," and Rusk called U Thant that night to protest that bilateral talks were out of the question and that the American people were, indeed, fully informed. Once again insisting, in effect, on the fulfillment of American terms, Rusk complained that with respect to talks, "it was dangerous to consider only procedure without knowing whether anything could be accomplished through a procedure."[75]

At the same time, behind the scenes, several men within the administration began immediately to dissent from the hard-line course. Some of them, it would seem, did not really understand what had been decided back in December. George Ball and former Ambassador to

Moscow Llewellyn Thompson on February 13 had suggested that the United States should not in fact run the risk of Chinese intervention, and would instead have to go to a conference and salvage what we could get when intervention threatened—roughly the proposal of William Bundy and McNaughton which the senior leadership had rejected in November. McGeorge Bundy's staffer James C. Thomson Jr. on February 19 gave Bundy a strong argument for negotiation as "the only rational alternative."[76]

More seriously, Johnson on February 17 received a memo from his Vice President, Hubert Humphrey, which was the work of Humphrey and Thomas Hughes of State's Bureau of Intelligence and Research. Echoing many of Mansfield's long-standing arguments, Humphrey suggested that a full-scale attack on North Vietnam would critically undermine the rest of the administration's foreign policy. He also cited the unpopularity of the Korean War and declared that in this case "the chances of success are slimmer." He suggested that Johnson could and should cut his losses. The memorandum was prophetic and courageous, but it apparently enraged the President. Humphrey was dissenting from the policy that had been approved in his own presence at the National Security Council the previous December.[77] Having written the memorandum, Humphrey found himself excluded from the highest councils of the administration for months.

Two-time Democratic presidential candidate and current U.N. Ambassador Adlai Stevenson also dissented from administration policy. On February 17 he wrote President Johnson suggesting that the United States express willingness to enter into talks without preconditions. In a memorandum of March 1 Stevenson made clear that he would prefer to negotiate on a less favorable basis rather than to risk escalation and unfavorable international opinion by moving beyond strikes in southern North Vietnam. He apparently received no reply.[78]

By the end of February Phase II was finally ready to begin, complete with ground forces. CIA Director McCone saw Johnson on February 25 and warned him of a North Vietnamese build-up in Laos and southern North Vietnam. Johnson expressed his concern, and the next day, in a meeting with JCS Chairman General Wheeler, he approved the deployment of two Marine battalions in Da Nang, together with the immediate deployment of the headquarters of a full Marine Expeditionary Brigade. Johnson deferred a decision on the deployment of the rest of the brigade, and assigned the new units a "primary mission" of providing security for the airfield at Da Nang. As Wheeler informed CINCPAC Admiral Sharp, the President also agreed to "do everything possible to maximize our military efforts to reverse the present unfavorable situation," including beginning Rolling Thunder—the sustained bombing of the North—as soon as possible after February 27, using American jet aircraft against the enemy in South Vietnam, and various other measures.[79]

On February 26 the administration issued a White Paper that presented rather fragmentary evidence of increased North Vietnamese infiltration. Rolling Thunder officially began on March 2, 1965, making this D-Day for Phase II of the December program, although Washington made no announcement of it. The December annexes called for one Marine battalion landing team to land on D+3 and the remainder of the 3rd Marine Division to arrive within thirty days. Instead, two battalions of Marines landed on March 8—D+6—and the third battalion, making an entire Marine Expeditionary Brigade or MEB, just four days later. When Westmoreland on March 2 broke the news of the Marine deployments to two South Vietnamese generals—including the Catholic Nguyen Van Thieu—they immediately expressed concern over the reaction of the population in Da Nang, a stronghold of militant Buddhism. The Buddhists had, in fact, formed a committee calling for the withdrawal of foreign forces from Vietnam.[80] In another decision of enormous significance, Westmoreland on March 9 received authority to order American air power into combat in South Vietnam at will. On the same day, Washington finally agreed to drop the requirement for a South Vietnamese observer on Farmgate aircraft, and to repaint these planes with American insignia.[81]

As the American war in Vietnam began, the administration continued to mislead the public regarding both the timing and the scope of the decisions that it had taken. On March 3, after the first Rolling Thunder strikes, the White House, State Department and Defense Department refused to acknowledge any change in policy, but officials indicated privately that a continuing campaign had begun. Newspapers on March 7 reported the Pentagon's announcement of the landing of the Marines to guard the Da Nang base—"at the request of the South Vietnamese," a spokesman stated falsely—without any hint of further deployments.[82] Secretary Rusk on March 7 assured the nation that the

Marines would simply guard the Da Nang airfield and its Hawk missiles.[83]

As we have seen, the decisions reached in December 1964 and implemented beginning in February-March 1965 reflected long-held views of the need to resist Communist aggression in South Vietnam within the Pentagon and the State Department, and long-standing plans for doing so. The views identified North Vietnam as the source of aggression against the South and called for the deployment of all necessary military power to force the North to stop, if necessary by destroying the North itself. The plans accepted the risks of broader conflict, even with Communist China, and provided for military responses.

In principle, the Congress, the American public, and America's major allies agreed with the need to resist Communist expansion. Significantly, however, the public was already divided sharply on how far the United States should go to secure that goal in Southeast Asia. In a Senate debate on Vietnam during the second half of February 1965, the administration suddenly enjoyed considerable support, much of it from Republicans, and public opinion polls showed a substantial majority in support of the President's stated policies. Already, however, the opposition had shown more determination, and telegrams reaching the White House after the first retaliatory bombing strike had run twelve to one against it.[84] In short, the revelation that the United States government had decided in principle to do whatever was necessary to force North Vietnam to halt the insurgency—risking war with China if necessary—would in fact have been tremendously controversial.

The decision to conceal the decision the administration had made—like that decision itself—reflects the "lessons of the thirties" in a way that has never been appreciated. Johnson, Rusk, McNamara, Bundy, and the rest of the GI generation had been young men during the 1930s and 1940s, experiencing first hand the debate between advocates of appeasement or isolationism and advocates of interventionism. The war and its outcome had decisively vindicated interventionism, but had also left nearly all of them with a vastly oversimplified view of the proper response to aggression. Essentially, because the events of the 1930s in Asia and Europe had led to world war, the GI generation had come away believing that armed aggression anywhere had to be resisted immediately, both as a matter of right and because a failure to resist aggression would inevitably lead to more aggression. Winston Churchill, more than anyone else, had propagated this view in the best-selling first volume of his memoirs, *The Gathering Storm,* in which he had argued that firmness could actually have prevented the conflict.

Why Americans wanted so badly to believe that the Second World War might have been prevented is a question far outside the boundaries of this work, but the scholarship of recent decades gives little grounds for believing that either Nazi Germany or imperial Japan could have been *deterred* by anything the Western powers might have done.[85] Other nations could only stop those regimes from expanding by decisively *defeating* them, and this required the full support of those nations' publics, and—especially in Europe—the formation of a coalition of overwhelming power. Viewed in this light, President Roosevelt's strategy in the years 1939–1941, while hardly that which Churchill or Dean Rusk or Lyndon Johnson would have recommended in retrospect, becomes more, not less, astute. Roosevelt delayed intervention until the American public accepted the need for it, and until Hitler and the Japanese had helped create a coalition that could defeat them with overwhelming force.

Events as of March 1965 had *not* persuaded the American public of the wisdom of a major war in Southeast Asia, but that did not deter Johnson and his advisers, who justified their failure to announce the truth to their countrymen on the basis of the righteousness and necessity of their course. Having seen their nation overcome extraordinary obstacles in their youth, they truly could not bring themselves to confront the possibility of failure. President Johnson understood his countrymen's reluctance to act. As we shall see, the drama of the next five months of 1965—from March through July—revolves around the President's refusal, for as long as possible, to admit that the nation was embarking upon a major war. The President also wanted desperately to get as much Great Society legislation through the Congress as possible—a process which, as we shall see, was substantially complete by July. Meanwhile, the State Department had also realized the need to keep American policy in the lowest possible key, partly to maintain international confidence and partly to avoid any premature, irresistible pressure for negotiations.

The effects of Johnson's handling of the situation persist until this day. The President seems successfully to have persuaded the press and the public that he did not, in fact, decide to embark upon a major war until June and July. And so carefully did he cover his tracks and deceive even some high-level policymakers that this misconception has persisted, and even found its way into the works of various historians who have analyzed a two-part decision—first bombing, then ground forces—that never occurred.[86] In fact, the United States government made a single decision for war in principle in December 1964, decided to implement it in mid-February 1965, and began the implementation in March. Unfortunately, in deciding to go to war against the North, Washington and Saigon had moved further away than ever from a realistic understanding of the problems posed by the insurgency in the South. Having lost the war in the South Vietnamese countryside, they had chosen to begin a new war against the government, the society, and the regular army of North Vietnam, which in turn had secured powerful material and manpower support from Communist China and the Soviet Union.

14

War in Secret
March–June 1965

★

By setting Phase II of the December decisions in motion in early March, the President had committed American military power to the ultimate objective of an independent, non-Communist South Vietnam, free to accept foreign assistance as needed, and had given permission to the Pentagon, CINCPAC, and MACV to implement long-standing plans for action to meet the immediate threat in South Vietnam and to deal as necessary with North Vietnamese and Communist Chinese intervention. These plans called for the sustained bombing of North Vietnam, the introduction of at least three divisions of ground troops as soon as possible, and the use of the Navy both to interdict infiltration by sea and to provide fire support inside South Vietnam. Military authorities began implementing the plans during the spring of 1965.

President Johnson, however, remained determined to insist that the United States had not changed its policy of assisting the South Vietnamese. Johnson, as we have seen, had refused his advisers' repeated requests to explain his new policy in detail during February. In the event, the first bombing strikes against the North aroused relatively little protest and established Johnson's personal ascendancy over his advisers, who allowed themselves momentarily to believe that the war might be won with virtually no disruption of the national or international community. "We have certainly not persuaded Hanoi to leave its neighbors alone," McGeorge Bundy wrote Johnson on March 6, "but we have made a new beginning:

> Most important of all, we may be moving, with less friction than we anticipated, toward a situation in which international opinion may regard

our actions against the North as a natural reply against Viet Cong operations in the South. If this can be done . . . it will be most helpful to us
against guerrilla infiltration over the long run, whatever the eventual result in Vietnam.

My own view is that if this result is achieved . . . it will be your personal
achievement. You alone—against your noisiest advisers—made the basic
decision to present these actions within the framework of *a continuing
policy and a continuing purpose,* and not as major new departures.[1]

Johnson's closest advisers now accepted the need to conceal new departures from the American people and loyally collaborated in deceiv-
ing the public for the next four months. Meanwhile, the administration
also had to deal with international pressure for negotiation, and here,
too, Johnson in early April made a speech which repositioned Washington without in the least committing the United States to stop military
action until its goals had been achieved. Some administration figures
questioned aspects of the new policy. Undersecretary of State George
Ball tried to revise American objectives and design a new negotiating
strategy, and Ambassador Maxwell Taylor and his deputy, U. Alexis
Johnson, became concerned in March and April by the pace of American ground force deployments. Neither of these dissents had more than
a marginal impact upon policy. The Pentagon, supported whenever
necessary by the President, simply moved step by step to implement its
plans, deploying not only an initial stream of forces amounting to three
divisions but also logistics units dispatched in order to make way for
the deployment of many more in the second half of 1965 and beyond.
While the senior civilians focused upon domestic and international
opinion, the Pentagon was running the war.

Even before the approval of Phase II, on February 11, the Joint
Chiefs had recommended the immediate deployment of both a Marine
brigade and an Army brigade, and the alert of at least the remainder of
one division of both Marines and Army.[2] On March 2 President Johnson dispatched Army Chief of Staff General Harold Johnson to Vietnam to survey the situation and make recommendations for winning
the war.[3] On March 6 McGeorge Bundy told President Johnson that
the general's mission would focus on improvements in pacification.
"Last night," Bundy wrote chillingly, "Bob McNamara said for the
first time what many others have thought for a long time—that the Pentagon and the military have been going at this thing the wrong way
round from the very beginning: they have been concentrating on mili-

tary results against guerrillas in the field, when they should have been concentrating on intense police control from the individual villager on up."[4] General Johnson's mission did nothing to change the Army's emphasis.

By the time General Johnson reached Saigon, General Westmoreland had already concluded that the war had moved from a purely guerrilla war to "a more formalized military conflict," and Johnson heard a frightening account of South Vietnamese manpower shortages.[5] Johnson returned on March 14 with twenty-one recommendations, including two new American divisions to occupy bases in the central coast and the Central Highlands and an additional four-division ground force to man a line across the 17th parallel and through Laos to the Mekong. General Johnson and the other Chiefs met with the President on March 15, and the President told them that he wanted "the killing of Viet Cong intensified." About a month later General Johnson gave his own concept of pacification to the Chiefs. "Successful pacification," he said, had "three basic requirements . . . a. Find the enemy. b. Fix the enemy in place so that he can be engaged successfully. c. Fight and finish the enemy."[6] While General Johnson may later have developed doubts about the way in which the war was fought, his ideas at this time seem to have been completely conventional.[7]

On March 26 General Westmoreland completed a Commander's Estimate of the military situation in South Vietnam that built upon Johnson's report.[8] Westmoreland recommended new troop deployments and explained how they would help win the war. The estimate shows that Westmoreland fully shared the mistaken assumptions of his civilian superiors about how American military force might change the enemy's behavior. He not only took an almost purely military view of the problem the United States faced but also accepted the premise of Phase II: that North Vietnam directed the insurgency and could call it off at will. He assumed that "the basic strategy of retaliatory and punitive air strikes against North Vietnam will, in time, bring about the desired results, that is, the supply and support of the insurgency will be terminated by the DRV and hopefully the DRV/VC high command will direct the cessation of offensive operations," and he seemed to assume that this might take place by the end of 1965. To accomplish this, he recommended two separate deployments of American and perhaps allied forces—one definite, the other possible—designed to revolutionize the balance of ground forces within South Vietnam.

Westmoreland estimated that Viet Cong forces now totaled about 48,000 main force troops—a considerable increase during the last year—and perhaps 100,000 militia. He ignored the Viet Cong's political strength and the additional manpower available for reinforcement, but did estimate that infiltration and recruitment could conceivably raise VC strength to 245,000 by late 1965. A build-up of military and paramilitary South Vietnamese forces to nearly 650,000 men by late 1965 would not, he argued, improve the current "generally unsatisfactory military situation," and desertions would continue to rise. Without more help, a collapse of morale would probably lead the Saigon government to open peace talks, and the government would be vulnerable either to a general uprising or a North Vietnamese Army–led seizure of a provincial capital in the Highlands.

Westmoreland suggested that the deployment of just two American divisions could transform the situation. Rating an American Army battalion as equivalent to two South Vietnamese battalions—and a somewhat larger Marine battalion as equal to three—he argued that one division in northern II Corps (Binh Dinh and Quang Ngai provinces) could produce a "dramatic local reversal of the military trend." In the Central Highlands, another division "could fight the VC not in the jungle on his terms but from the air and with firepower and maneuver made possible by the best available mobility and communications means." Another brigade at Bien Hoa and Vung Tau just southeast of Saigon could help "carry the fight to the enemy." If the North Vietnamese infiltrated major units, the United States would "undoubtedly defeat" them. He also wanted a Marine brigade at Da Nang and another Marine battalion further north around Hue. He noted that the existing logistics base would not support even this force. As a possible additional option, Westmoreland, paralleling suggestions in the State Department during the preparation of the December plan, proposed an international force of five divisions—132,000 Americans and 33,000 Thais, Laotians, and ARVNs—to form a barrier along the 17th parallel and across Laos to the Mekong on the Thai border. But he did not seem to think this essential.

"Introducing three U.S. divisions onto the mainland of Southeast Asia," he wrote, "would so change the balance of power on the peninsula that the Communist choice would be limited to (1) whether they should sue for peace as quickly as possible to prevent the eventual loss of their present control over North Vietnam and northern Laos, or (2) take on the U.S. and its allies in a major war." He did not seem to doubt that they would select (1). He noted that it would take at least six months to position such a force owing to logistical problems, and thus concluded that "if bombing is not successful or takes effect very slowly, then the cordon may be desirable."

In contrast to recent JCS plans, which seemed to assume that bombing the North would lead to Chinese intervention and foresaw American intervention merely to hold a couple of enclaves in South Vietnam while defending the Mekong from Thailand, Westmoreland's estimate focused on the conventional defense of South Vietnam alone. This was far more realistic, but his concept of the relative worth of American enemy forces was not. In particular, he disregarded the extent to which the effectiveness of American forces would be degraded by operating within a hostile environment, and the enormous help which enemy riflemen received from elements of the North and South Vietnamese population who performed tasks American soldiers would have to perform for American troops.

His estimate paid relatively little attention to the internal problems of South Vietnam and practically none to the issue of regaining control of the countryside—especially in the Mekong Delta, which he essentially ignored. Westmoreland did plan, as he repeatedly stated, to solve the problem of bickering among South Vietnamese generals and increase the effectiveness of the ARVN by bringing it into an American-led unified command. But to terminate the war he counted on "the VC/DRV high command" to impose a unilateral cease-fire. This, in turn, should allow the Saigon government to reestablish control over the countryside. The problem of controlling the people—which had only gotten worse during three years of intense American advisory effort—would, apparently, solve itself.

Looking back at the war nine years later, General Harold Johnson spoke of an "underlying assumption" among both civilian and military leaders "that if the United States demonstrated a fairly hard line of support for South Vietnam . . . our power and prestige in the world would be so awesome that the other side would have really no alternative but to cave in." Westmoreland's estimate certainly seemed to reflect such a view.[9] In 1950 General Douglas MacArthur seems to have recommended intervention in the Korean War on the basis of similar assumptions of American operational superiority, only to abandon them within a few short weeks. "It is now apparent," MacArthur had cabled Washington on July 7, 1950, "that we are confronted in Korea with an aggressive and well-trained professional army" with "excellent" leadership and impressive tactical skill.[10] The North Vietnamese Army in 1965 was far more experienced than the North Koreans in 1950, but Westmoreland seemed to discount its effectiveness.

In response to the President's directive to find ways to kill more Viet Cong, the Joint Chiefs in the latter half of March were also pushing for more troops, "not simply to withstand the Viet Cong, but to gain effective operational superiority and assume the Offensive." They wanted to land the whole Marine Expeditionary Force at Da Nang—where roughly two-thirds of the MEF was already in place—with a mission of counterinsurgency combat as well as defense; to add an Army division around Pleiku and a South Korean division; and to deploy air squadrons for tactical air support. The Chiefs on March 17 cabled CINCPAC to begin upgrading logistics in South Vietnam, as General Johnson had also recommended, in order to support these and other additional deployments.[11] The Chiefs overruled the objections of General McConnell of the Air Force—LeMay's successor—who still wanted to avoid more than minimum ground deployments and to pursue Rolling Thunder more aggressively.[12] While Washington awaited Taylor's return for more consultation, MACV by March 27 asked for the immediate deployment of 18,000 security, logistics, and miscellaneous personnel; the rest of the MEF; and, probably, an additional nine to twelve Army battalions—a division plus an extra brigade—to go on the offensive from bases in coastal enclaves. Commenting on these requests, Taylor suggested that the United States needed some ground troops to end the war relatively quickly, but opposed using them on "search and destroy" missions, which might be ineffective and costly in casualties.[13]

Taylor met with McNamara and the Chiefs in Washington on March 29 and eventually agreed that third-country troops should be "introduced as rapidly as possible commensurate with political acceptability, logistic support, and useful missions for these forces." The ambassador also favored keeping new troops in coastal enclaves and keeping some in reserve offshore, but General Johnson disagreed. McNamara, typically, came down for Taylor's suggestion provisionally, while leaving the door wide open to proceed to deployments for pacification in the Central Highlands subsequently. He also stressed the political need for

South Korean forces, in which the President was very keenly inter-ested.[14] Describing this meeting to Alexis Johnson, Taylor quoted him-self as having said that three divisions "seemed high," and referred to Prime Minister Quat's doubts about more men and the presence of anti-American sentiment. McGeorge Bundy assured President Johnson that McNamara and Taylor were quite close together on deploy-ments.[15]

On April 1 McGeorge Bundy summarized the issues in a memoran-dum for the President before a meeting that day. He endorsed the re-quest for 10,000–20,000 logistics and support forces, and noted that most of the proposed two-to-three-division increment could not land for at least sixty days and that both Rusk and McNamara recom-mended deferring approval of the additional divisions until then. Con-curring, Bundy cited the "uncertain" South Vietnamese government and popular reaction to deployments and the need to test American troops in combat, but in fact the delay in *approval* did not slow down the deployment of the two divisions at all. At the meeting that day the President approved these recommendations and also gave permission to the Marines to engage in "counterinsurgency combat operations."[16]

The government also reached a temporary consensus with respect to the extent of Rolling Thunder, whose initial eight-week program would expire at the end of April. Although both CINCPAC Admiral Sharp and especially Air Force Chief of Staff McConnell had advocated bombing north of the 20th parallel at an early date, General Johnson of the Army obviously feared early Chinese intervention, and Westmore-land on March 27 cabled that he did not expect bombing the North to win the war. The Chiefs as a whole did not recommend a drastically ex-panded campaign. The strikes targeted barracks, bridges, and radar sites in southern North Vietnam, and the Chiefs apparently accepted McNamara's conclusion that it was not yet necessary to attack the MIGs at Phuc Yen airfield. While the Chiefs on April 6 acknowledged that the campaign had as yet failed significantly to curtail North Viet-namese military activities, they made no drastic recommendations to increase it. The major dissenter in Washington was CIA Director McCone, who argued on April 2 that the United States had to lift re-strictions on the bombing of the North in order to avoid a long and costly ground war.[17]

The highest officials of the administration remained quite determined to conceal their plans for ground troops from the public. Stories about the possibility of more American troops in South Vietnam came to a halt after General Johnson's mission in mid-March. The Selma-to-Montgomery civil rights march and two dramatic space flights took over the news late that month. When Taylor left Saigon on March 27, he said that the situation had "generally improved" since his last trip home and declined to discuss the question of additional troops. Washington officials said he had come to discuss the effectiveness of the bombing.[18] In a press conference on April 1, the day he approved the plans for more deployments, President Johnson responded as follows to a question about what General Taylor might have proposed:

> I know of no division in the American Government, I know of no far-reaching strategy that is being suggested or promulgated. I hear the commentators—I heard one yesterday and heard one today—talk about the dramatics of this situation, the great struggle that was coming about between various men and the top level conferences that were in the offing, where revolutionary decisions were being made, and I turned off one of my favorite networks and walked out of the room. Mrs. Johnson said, "What did you say?" And I said, "I didn't say anything but if you are asking me what I think, I would say God forgive them, because they know not what they do."[19]

On the same day, administration sources told the *New York Times* they saw no change in the strategy of bombing the North.[20]

At an NSC meeting on April 2 McGeorge Bundy laid down the law regarding statements to the press: "Under no circumstances should there be any reference to the movement of U.S. forces or other courses of action."[21] Rusk was even more explicit in another meeting without the President on Sunday, April 3:

> Secretary Rusk began by saying he thought Ambassador Taylor would now have an impression of the problem facing the political leadership in the United States on policy toward Vietnam. The President felt that he must not force the pace too fast or the Congress and public opinion, which had been held in line up to now through the President's strenuous efforts, would no longer support our actions in Vietnam. Ambassador Taylor agreed that he understood the situation in the United States. Secretary Rusk said he hoped Ambassador Taylor would therefore not be too specific in relating the Washington decisions to Prime Minister Quat.

The same meeting discussed the Marines' change of mission:

There was an agreement that the Marines should be used in 1) local counterinsurgency in a mobile posture and in 2) strike reaction, and that they should have an "active and aggressive posture." Secretary Rusk said later in the discussion that he did not yet want to give up the ability to describe their mission as defensive.[22]

These decisions were registered in NSAM 328 of April 6, which also recorded the President's desire that "premature publicity be avoided by all possible precautions," and that "these movements and changes should be understood as being gradual and wholly consistent with existing policy."[23] McNamara now asked the Chiefs for a plan to deploy two or three divisions into South Vietnam "at the earliest practicable date." On April 7 McNamara encouraged an executive session of the Senate Foreign Relations Committee to recognize "a difference between adding logistical personnel, engineer corps personnel . . . on the one hand, which I do not believe will lead to enlarging the war and, on the other hand, introducing major combat elements such as a division of personnel." The President, he said, would consult Congress before taking the latter step.[24]

The Washington news blackout succeeded fully, and Ambassador Taylor apparently decided to take additional precautions on the way home. Stopping in Honolulu to confer with CINCPAC, he told Admiral Sharp on April 3 that neither McNamara nor any other senior civilians, including the President, "were convinced of the need for divisions," and that they feared that Americans might become trapped inland and have to fight their way to the sea. It is hard to see any explanation for this statement—which Taylor recorded himself—other than as disinformation designed to prevent a leak of the administration's real plans. Sharp did not disagree when Taylor reported that the bombing would continue to avoid the Hanoi-Haiphong area for another three months.[25]

The Joint Chiefs on April 8 met with McNamara and the President for more than two hours. After McNamara gave a briefing on Rolling Thunder, General McConnell reported frankly that 432 bombs had failed to destroy a particular bridge. He also admitted, in response to the President's questions about the loss of two aircraft to enemy MIGs, that our flyers were inexperienced. "We played the first half of the game," Johnson said, "and the score is 21 to 0 against us; now I want you to tell me how to win . . . I want you to come back here next Tuesday and tell me how we are going to kill more Viet Cong." The President also affirmed that he intended to control operations tightly.[26] The Chiefs on April 12 ordered preparations for the deployment of the approved 18,000–20,000 logistics force followed by three divisions, of which one might be Korean.[27]

During the same weeks in which the administration was planning an expansion of the ground war, it also orchestrated a public relations campaign to emphasize its hopes for an early peace in response to both domestic and international pressure. The campaign was remarkably successful.

With respect to true negotiations—as with military strategy—the administration remained faithful in private to the position adopted in December 1964: that Washington "would be alert to any sign of yielding by Hanoi, and would be prepared to explore negotiated solutions that attain US objectives in an acceptable manner."[28] As we have seen, the administration in February had told the French and British that it did not plan to enter into negotiations until the enemy had shown that it was willing to meet our terms. In practice, as Ambassador Taylor and others had repeatedly noted, this meant that Washington had to avoid negotiations for some time, until American military pressure had had major effects upon the Viet Cong and the North.

At the beginning of Phase II, John McNaughton, the Assistant Secretary of Defense for International Security Affairs, tried to revive the less drastic approach that he and William Bundy had put forth unsuccessfully several months earlier. In a White House meeting and a long memorandum on March 9–10, McNaughton suggested that the risks of either an all-out bombing campaign or a massive ground deployment might be unacceptable, and that failure might involve either "undesirable escalation or defeat." Thus, while continuing a limited bombing campaign and deploying troops, the United States might prepare, at an appropriate moment, to accept an informal partition of South Vietnam. When the *Pentagon Papers* were published in 1971, a redraft of this memorandum attracted as much attention as any other single document because of McNaughton's breakdown of America's goals in Vietnam: 70 percent to avoid a humiliating defeat and protect our reputation as a guarantor, 20 percent to keep South Vietnam and adjacent territory "from Chinese hands," and 10 percent "to permit the people of South Vietnam to enjoy a better, freer way of life." That definition, however, seems to have aimed at suggesting—as William Bundy had in the fall—that the main American stake was intangible, and that the United States could escape with its prestige largely intact if it made a reasonable effort to achieve its goals.[29] But official policy was restated by the Joint Chiefs on March 15, writing McNamara that the United States should not go into negotiations until it had secured a strong military advantage.[30]

The American people and world opinion, however, hoped that American military intervention would rapidly lead to negotiations and peace, and from the moment that Rolling Thunder began the administration tried to show its interest in negotiations at an appropriate time. The *New York Times* reported both on March 6 and March 12 that Washington sought a settlement which would simply enable the South Vietnamese to work out their own problems, and hoped that the Soviets would once again, as in Laos, cooperate in reaching a settlement. But when U Thant on March 8 called for a seven-power conference—the United States, China, Britain, France, the Soviet Union, and the two Vietnams—to discuss the situation, the administration immediately rejected such talks until Hanoi had proved that it was prepared to stop its aggression. President Johnson gave a similar reply to Yugoslav President Tito on March 13, and Undersecretary Ball, swallowing his own views, attacked France on March 16 for making America's task more difficult.[31] A Gallup poll taken in mid-March showed the same number of respondents favoring sending more troops to South Vietnam on the one hand, and favoring immediate peace talks on the other.[32]

The administration suffered some public relations setbacks and challenges to its policy during the last week in March. On March 23 British Foreign Secretary Michael Stewart appeared at the National Press Club during his Washington visit and criticized the United States for using gas warfare in South Vietnam. The gas in question—originally reported by the Australian Associated Press correspondent Peter Arnett—was riot-control tear gas. Rusk brushed off a proposal by USIA Director Carl Rowan to promise not to use gas, and the administration's stance drew worldwide criticism and a highly skeptical op-ed piece from James Reston.[33] President Johnson on March 26 asked the NSC whether the gas story might have been a "Communist plot," an idea he often fell back upon in difficult moments, and six weeks later Mc-

George Bundy suggested to a high AP official that Arnett be replaced.[34] Meanwhile, on March 25 Peking announced that it would send both materiel and men to help the Viet Cong, if requested.[35]

Surveying the American press, the administration was particularly concerned by the editorials of the *New York Times,* where Robert Kleiman was repeatedly criticizing the premises and objectives of American policy, and by the views of Walter Lippmann, the most respected columnist in America, who wrote that South Vietnam did not constitute a vital American interest. McGeorge Bundy courted Lippmann aggressively beginning in mid-February, but had to report to Johnson a month later that he had had little success in bringing him around. The columnist, Bundy told Johnson on March 15, shared the "smug pessimism of [French Foreign Minister] Couve and U Thant," and wanted immediate negotiations. Johnson had Lippmann to lunch at the White House that very day, and Lippmann told him he had to offer the North an incentive to negotiate. Johnson kept Lippmann at the White House all afternoon, and even telephoned Bundy in his presence. "Mac," he said, "I've got Walter Lippmann over here and he says we're not doing the right thing. Maybe he's right." Lippmann was flattered, but two days later he told Bundy he favored a unified, Titoist Vietnam.[36]

The President on March 25 issued a statement of his own, declaring in carefully chosen words that the United States sought "no more than a return to the *essentials* of the Agreements of 1954—a reliable arrangement to guarantee the independence and security of all in southeast Asia."[37] The essentials, in American eyes, would probably not have included all-Vietnam elections, reunification, or the nearly complete withdrawal of American forces. On April 1 a conference of seventeen non-aligned nations at Belgrade opened up an opportunity for Washington by calling on all parties to start negotiations as soon as possible without any preconditions. The State Department immediately seized upon this suggestion as an alternative to U Thant's proposal for a three-month cease fire.[38] On April 4 James Reston wrote from Europe that most Europeans opposed our policy, and that liberal intellectuals now definitely expressed a preference for Kennedy, the less typical American, over Johnson.[39] The President decided to reply to the seventeen-nation proposal in a televised, well-publicized speech at Johns Hopkins University on April 7.

The Johns Hopkins speech epitomized the enormous strengths and weaknesses of the President who gave it and the GI generation of Americans to which he belonged. The war, Johnson argued, was an attack by North Vietnam on South Vietnam, with the objective of total conquest. Peking, the regime that had destroyed freedom in Tibet and attacked India and South Korea, was urging Hanoi on. The United States since 1954 had promised to defend South Vietnam, and failure would shake the confidence of people all over the globe "in the value of an American commitment and in the value of America's word." As Rusk had so often done, Johnson put the issue on a level with our commitments to Europe. "The central lesson of our time is that the appetite of aggression is never satisfied. To withdraw from one battlefield means only to prepare for the next. We must say in southeast Asia—as we did in Europe—in the words of the Bible: 'Hitherto shalt thou come, but no further.'"

Our new strategy, Johnson explained, did not represent a change in "purpose," but only in "what we believe that purpose requires." He did not, however, refer specifically to any elements of a new strategy beyond air attacks. And he stated very clearly the essence of American strategy: to persuade Hanoi that the war was futile:

> I wish it were possible to convince others with words of what we now find it necessary to say with guns and planes: Armed hostility is futile. Our resources are equal to any challenge. Because we fight for values and we fight for principles, rather than territory or colonies, our patience and our determination are unending.
>
> Once this is clear, then it should also be clear that the only path for reasonable men is the path of peaceful settlement.

Once again showing the American ambivalence about the Geneva Accords, Johnson defined the essence of a possible settlement in rather contradictory terms: "peace demands an independent South Vietnam—securely guaranteed and able to shape its own relationships to all others—free from outside interference—tied to no alliance—a military base for no other country."

Such a peace could be reached, he continued, in several ways: "in discussion or negotiation with the governments concerned; in large groups or in small ones; in the reaffirmation of old agreements or their strengthening with new ones . . . And we remain ready, with this purpose, for *unconditional discussions.*"[40] This carefully chosen phrase expressed a willingness to *exchange views* with any interested parties at once, but it did *not* express any willingness to negotiate based on the existing balance of power, or to cease military operations before that balance of power had changed. On the previous day Johnson and Mc-George Bundy had spent over an hour trying to persuade Lippmann that this speech represented a real peace offer, but Lippmann immediately grasped that it offered North Vietnam and the Viet Cong nothing but a chance to surrender.[41]

In the remainder of the speech Johnson spoke of the poverty and underdevelopment of Southeast Asia and offered North Vietnam a role in a massive effort to harness the Mekong River along the lines of the TVA—to which he specifically referred. He spoke of transforming Southeast Asia just as the Rural Electrification Administration had transformed the Hill Country of Texas during the 1930s.[42] Although he never mentioned the father figure and inspiration of his generation, Franklin Roosevelt, the whole speech read like an attempt to extend Roosevelt's work around the world, in defiance of any obstacles. To the GI generation, nothing was impossible.

> Our generation has a dream. It is a very old dream. But we have the power and now we have the opportunity to make that dream come true.
>
> For centuries nations have struggled among each other. But we dream of a world where disputes are settled by law and reason. And we will try to make it so.
>
> For most of history men have hated and killed one another in battle. But we dream of an end to war. And we will try to make it so.
>
> For all existence men have lived in poverty, threatened by hunger. But we dream of a world where all are fed and charged with hope. And we will help to make it so.
>
> The ordinary men and women of North Vietnam and South Vietnam—of China and India—of Russia and America—are brave people. They are filled with the same proportions of hate and fear, of love and hope. Most of them want the same things for themselves and their families. Most of them do not want their sons to ever die in battle, or to see their homes, or the homes of others, destroyed.
>
> Well, this can be their world yet. Man now has the knowledge—always before denied—to make this planet serve the real needs of the people who live on it.

Within the United States and even among some allies and neutrals, the speech had an effect far out of proportion to its substance. U Thant, the British government, and even the French government welcomed it.

The *New York Times* referred to the President's "willingness to negoti-ate," and most stories completely missed the critical distinction be-tween discussions and negotiations. This was all the more remarkable since the same distinction had played a critical role in the crisis in U.N.-Panamanian relations, when President Johnson in particular had im-mediately expressed willingness to "discuss" the Panama Canal treaty but had for many weeks refused to "negotiate" a new one. Mike Mans-field, who had continued to argue for an alternative policy in memo-randa for the President, also welcomed Johnson's offer. Two Gallup polls taken just before and just after the speech showed a public more divided than ever. Both showed small, roughly equal numbers of re-spondents favoring a number of options: withdrawal, a cease-fire and negotiations, the continuation of present policy, stepped-up military activity, and going "all out" with a declaration of war. But the share of respondents registering "no opinion" actually increased from 28 per-cent in the first poll to 39 percent in the second.[43]

Moscow and Peking denounced the terms, however, and Ho Chi Minh immediately dismissed "United States talk of negotiations as 'misleading'"—quite rightly, since Johnson hadn't offered negotiations at all—and repeated that the United States must withdraw as part of a settlement. Until Johnson's speech, Ho had still cherished hopes that even the bombing of the North might be the prelude to early negotia-tions—in other words, that Washington might actually be pursuing something like the original option C proposed by McNaughton and William Bundy. The President's address convinced Hanoi otherwise, and on April 13 North Vietnam stated its own terms.[44]

Hanoi, in contrast to Washington, claimed definitely to base its pro-posals for settlement on the 1954 Geneva Accords, whose provisions restricting aid to South Vietnam, affirming the unity of all Vietnam, and calling for all-Vietnam elections Washington refused to endorse. Hanoi stated a four-point program: first, the recognition of unity, sov-ereignty, and territorial integrity as basic rights of the Vietnamese peo-ple, and the withdrawal of American forces and the cessation of Ameri-can military activity within Vietnam; second, the respect of the military provisions of the 1954 Geneva Accords pending the "peaceful reuni-fication of Vietnam"; third, the settlement of the internal affairs of South Vietnam according to the program of the National Liberation Front, which called for a coalition government; and fourth, the peaceful reunification of the country under terms agreed upon by the Vietnamese themselves. These terms were no worse—and in some respects they were better—than the terms the Nixon administration eventually secured in 1973.[45] In the wake of Hanoi's statement, both U Thant and the American press suggested that both sides had in effect opened negotiations, albeit publicly, and spoke of the Geneva Accords as a possible basis for settlement.[46]

Having made what he regarded as a fair offer, however, Johnson dug in his heels and suddenly refused to listen respectfully to contrary opinions. On April 16 the White House announced that the President was too busy to keep previously scheduled appointments with Prime Minister Shastri of India and President Ayub Khan of Pakistan, neither of whom supported the escalation of the war. Officials confirmed that the President was unhappy with their opposition. A four-year effort to cultivate the Indian government went up in smoke, and five days later Shastri angrily canceled his whole trip to Washington and criticized American bombing at a Soviet-hosted forum. The administration also lost a chance to try to ease tensions between the two South Asian nations, which went to war later in the year.[47] In order to pursue the Vietnam War, Johnson had in effect reverted to the Eisenhower-Dulles policy of disregarding neutral opinion. The President was enjoying enormous prestige at home, however, and on April 23 Reston defended Johnson's dislike of state visits, suggesting that only he had the courage to act on feelings that his predecessors had shared.[48]

While talking peace, the administration moved forward in the war. Back in Saigon, Taylor on April 7 briefed Quat carefully on the introduction of additional Marines and logistics forces, and the South Vietnamese Prime Minister responded fairly favorably, while warning of the danger of nationalist reaction.[49] But Westmoreland on April 11 cabled CINCPAC and the Joint Chiefs asking for the immediate deployment of the 173rd Airborne brigade in the Bien Hoa–Vung Tau area east of Saigon—the unit listed back in December as the first Army unit to go to South Vietnam.[50] He apparently did not inform Maxwell Taylor. Meeting with the President again on April 13, the Chiefs recommended deploying three divisions and 180,000 men, but the President, citing congressional and enemy reaction, declared that "he was *never* going to agree *at this time* to 3 divisions; something else on a smaller scale would have to be tried." He did, however, approve the deployment of 5,000 more Marines and of the 173rd Airborne, and suggested that some "fat-bellied Colonels" from American Army Reserve Civil Affairs units might do some good in the provinces of South Vietnam.[51] Rusk foresaw trouble with Taylor over the 173rd Airborne, but Mc-Namara replied, "Someone has to make a decision. We are not doing enough here for [Hanoi] to give up direction of the war."[52] The President's reservations rapidly proved to be temporary.

Rusk's fears were accurate. From April 14 through April 17 Taylor dispatched at least seven messages to Washington protesting the deployment of the 173rd Airborne brigade as contrary to what had been decided in Washington, contrary to the assurances he had just given Quat, and unwise on its merits. The ambassador claimed that the military situation had actually improved since February and passed along comments from his deputy, Alexis Johnson, who had visited the Da Nang area and returned questioning the deployment of a "massive non-Vietnamese military force" amid this "volatile and hypersensitive people with strong xenophobic characteristics never far below the surface."[53] Washington was not disposed to listen. "The President," Bundy cabled Taylor on April 15,

> has repeatedly emphasized his personal desire for a strong experiment in the encadrement of U.S. troops with Vietnamese. He is also very eager to see prompt experiments in use of energetic teams of U.S. officials in support of provincial governments under unified U.S. leadership . . .
>
> On further troop deployments, President's belief is that current situation requires use of all practicable means of strengthening position in South Vietnam and that additional U.S. troops are important if not decisive reinforcement. He has not seen evidence of negative result of deployments to date, and does not wish to wait any longer than is essential for genuine GVN agreement.[54]

An official State-Defense message arrived the next day, confirming that President Johnson's reservations about even larger deployments—as expressed to the JCS and cited by Bundy—were not expected to last very long. It called for the experimental "encadrement" of American troops into Vietnamese forces; the deployment of the 173rd; the deployment of battalion or multi-battalion forces at two or three more coastal locations to undertake counterinsurgency operations, to be followed promptly, if successful, "by requests for additional US forces";

and several new medical, economic, and administrative programs, including the use of Army Civil Affairs personnel to create a stable government in the countryside.[55] Taylor compromised, essentially, in two replies on April 17.[56] He took note of the decision "that it is necessary to take a major part in the ground combat" and agreed to the new deployments, subject to South Vietnamese concurrence and necessary logistical preparations. But he rejected President Johnson's encadrement proposals as likely to arouse South Vietnamese opposition and claimed not to understand the Civil Affairs proposal. Together, he said, these would approximate a vote of no confidence in Quat's government. The President, in Texas, deferred a decision until McNamara could meet with Taylor and Westmoreland in Honolulu.[57]

The Honolulu conference of April 20 helped lead to a redefinition—although not really to a change—in the administration's strategy. In addition to settling the troop question, it explicitly defined, for the first time, the respective roles of ground troops and strategic bombing in the American attempt to win the war.

In Honolulu, McNamara, McNaughton, General Wheeler, Admiral Sharp, William Bundy, Taylor, and Westmoreland all agreed that bombing alone would not "break the will of Hanoi," but that a combination of a larger ground effort in the South and limited bombing of the North might achieve American objectives sometime between six months and two years hence. American strategy would rely upon a combination of "VC failure [not VC *defeat*] in the South" and "DRV pain in the North," attempting "to break the will of the DRV/VC by denying them victory." Although the words were not mentioned, such a strategy was clearly emerging as an alternative to all-out bombing and the use of nuclear weapons."[58]

To secure these goals, they agreed upon the pending deployments of 38,500 more Americans, including the 173rd Airborne brigade, another army brigade to follow, three more Marine battalions and air squadrons, and 18,000 in augmentations of existing units and logistics forces, with another possible 16,000 logistics troops to follow. Additional later deployments might include the rest of the 3rd MEF and an Army Airmobile division. In the air, they favored continuing the same pace and roughly the same target list for six to twelve months. None of the military leaders present dissented from this strategy, although Wheeler noted that some unidentified "Chiefs" favored heavier bombing. They also rejected President Johnson's encadrement proposals and cut the role of American Civil Affairs officers to a pilot project in three selected provinces.

The April 21 meeting at which McNamara presented these recommendations revealed some differences of opinion among senior officials over the nature of American strategy. McNamara requested more troops, initially for *defensive* purposes, that is, "to avoid serious losses of U.S. forces now deployed which he considered inadequate to meet the threat of a Viet Cong attack." These troops would also inflict casualties upon the enemy and release the ARVN for more offensive operations. Meanwhile, McNamara wanted to continue the bombing at roughly the current pace for six to twelve months. "The thrust of McNamara's statement and subsequent discussions," wrote the outgoing CIA Director, John McCone, was "to change the purpose of the bombing attacks on North Vietnam from one of causing the DRV to seek a negotiated settlement to one of continual harassment of lines of supply, infiltrations, etc., while the combination of SVN forces and U.S. forces were engaging in defeating the Viet Cong to such a point that the DRV and other interested Communist States would realize the hopelessness of the Viet Cong effort and therefore would seek a peaceful negotiation," perhaps within a year. McCone suggested prophetically that this "would present our ground forces with an increasingly difficult problem requiring more and more troops," and advocated an immediate attack against the Phuc Yen MIGs and all-out bombing of the North to force a solution.

"Are we pulling away from our theory that bombing will turn 'em off?" the President asked at one point. As always with Johnson—and with certain other Presidents as well—one cannot be quite sure whether this question referred to substance or to the need to *explain* what the United States was doing. "That wasn't our theory," McNamara replied. "We wanted to lift morale; we wanted to push them toward negotiation—we've done that."[59] Essentially, McNamara was right. Only the Air Force had ever proposed attempting to win the war with massive bombing alone. Plans developed and approved in November-December 1964 had called for the introduction of ground troops as soon as Phase II bombing began, not simply to protect bases, but to take the offensive—and McNamara was merely asking for the next (and hardly the last) step in the implementation of those plans. McGeorge Bundy noted during the same meeting that McNamara wanted to send a signal in the South, not the North, so as not to bring in the Chinese. The risks of Chinese intervention certainly seemed greater since April 3, when Chinese MIGs on Hainan Island in the Gulf of Tonkin had scrambled to engage passing American aircraft and one American had been lost.[60] But McNamara also seems to have taken statements by Westmoreland and Wheeler about the weakness of the position within South Vietnam to heart, and decided that it was necessary to postpone more drastic measures against North Vietnam until the United States had reinforced the South. And Westmoreland definitely wanted to avoid the risk even of full-scale North Vietnamese intervention for some time to come.

Senior officials considered a new intelligence estimate the next day. The estimate—evidently the product of a late night and considerable negotiation—argued that Hanoi would reinforce the South in response to new American deployments. Yet a later section, which McNamara highlighted during the meeting, speculated that the United States might change Hanoi's and Peking's minds about their staying power by reversing the tide of battle and inflicting heavy casualties over the next six to twelve months. Such a development, it argued, would face the North with a choice between a full-scale offensive against the South—perhaps with Chinese help—and negotiations, presumably on American terms. Given the risk that the offensive might lead to American moves against the North and against China, "perhaps using nuclear weapons," the authors saw "somewhat better than even" chances that the DRV and China would seek "at least a temporary political solution." Taylor, meanwhile, cabled that he saw no major risks of Communist reaction to the Honolulu program.[61] Strategy now depended explicitly upon the idea that North Vietnam faced greater risks and had less staying power than the United States.

At the meeting on April 22 that considered this estimate, McCone and McNamara reiterated their positions, and General Wheeler entirely supported the Honolulu program. He made no complaints about either the tempo or scope of the bombing of the North, supported both current and further future ground deployments, and recognized "a need for more air power in South Vietnam because their air power was getting used up." Although no one said so, various logistical difficulties were already slowing the build-up considerably.[62] President Johnson declined at the meeting to make any decisions before getting South

Vietnamese reaction. But that afternoon McNamara drafted a cable informing Taylor privately that Johnson was inclined to favor the Honolulu recommendations. The Chiefs, he added, had concluded that the ARVN could not build up enough forces to win the kind of "signal successes against the VC in the South" that would induce the North Vietnamese to stop supporting the insurgency.[63]

"The Johnson Administration," the New York Times reported on April 22, "disappointed by the absence of positive reaction to the President's offer of 'unconditional discussions' on Vietnam, will apparently shift its concentration to a greater effort to win the ground war in Vietnam."[64] McNamara himself gave a long not-for-attribution briefing to reporters that afternoon. He claimed that the administration was trying to improve the ratio of friendly to enemy ground forces entirely by mobilizing more South Vietnamese, and that this had been "the subject of the last Taylor visit and the Honolulu Conference." In a wide-ranging survey of diplomatic as well as political factors, McNamara claimed that even nations who criticized our policy would be deeply shaken if we abandoned South Vietnam, and ruled out neutralization and a coalition government. The Secretary of Defense also added a new element to the administration's strategy—a nuclear bluff. A New York Times reporter recorded his words as follows:

> We are NOT following a strategy that recognizes any sanctuary or *any weapons restriction*. But we would use nuclear weapons only after fully applying non-nuclear arsenal. In other words, if 100 planes couldn't take out a target, we wouldn't necessarily go to nuclear weapons; we would try 200 planes, and so on. But "inhibitions" on using nuclear are NOT "overwhelming." Conceded that would be a "gigantic step." Quote: "We'd use whatever weapons we felt necessary to achieve our objective, recognizing that one must offset against the price"—and the price includes all psychological, propaganda factors, etc. Also fallout on innocent. "Inconceivable" under current circumstances that nuclear would provide a net gain against the terrific price that would be paid. NOT inconceivable that the price would be paid in some future circumstances McN refuses to predict.[65]

These remarks made their way into the newspapers on April 25, setting off a worldwide flap, and McNamara amended his remarks publicly the next day. "There is no military requirement for nuclear weapons" in the present and foreseeable situation, he said, "and no useful purpose can be served by speculation on remote contingencies."[66] Yet his original threat could not have been accidental, and such threats apparently remained part of American strategy at least for the rest of the year. In secret contacts in Paris with North Vietnamese representative Mai Van Bo, American diplomat Edmund Gullion referred in August to the "fantastic strength we hoped not to use . . . No one who had not seen U.S. power could imagine its full potential."[67] And on December 2, 1965, McNamara referred in a telephone conversation with Johnson to certain "very dangerous alternatives that we can't even put in writing around here, [and] certainly don't want to talk to anyone else about."[68] The extent to which the Johnson and Nixon administrations actually considered the use of nuclear weapons during the Vietnam War remains an important topic for future investigation.

In a series of conversations between April 23 and April 27 Ambassador Taylor secured Prime Minister Quat's agreement to the new deployments, and the Joint Chiefs ordered the deployment of the 173rd Airborne brigade on April 30.[69] On April 27 McGeorge Bundy suggested to President Johnson that he delay approval of the additional Army brigade at Qui Nhon and Nha Trang, but that deployment was not expected before mid-June, and planning for it went ahead anyway.[70] In fact, although documentation remains scanty on this point, Washington seems to have agreed to deploy *two* additional Army brigades during June, one from the 1st Infantry Division and one from the 101st Airborne. The 173rd Airborne and three more Marine battalions landed in South Vietnam on May 6–7, and the headquarters of the Marine Expeditionary Force was established at Da Nang. At Westmoreland's suggestion, the Marines renamed their forces the Marine Amphibious Force, to avoid a linguistic association with the old French Expeditionary Force of pre-1954 days.[71] A month later, however, Westmoreland suffered a key setback when he tried to begin implementing another critical aspect of his plans: a unified command that would put the ARVN at his disposal. When the Joint Chiefs on May 20 asked CINCPAC to draw up a plan for a "joint coordinating staff," as approved by McNamara, Taylor immediately opposed the idea as "obnoxious to national pride." Admiral Sharp agreed, and Westmoreland on May 27 gave in.[72]

The administration also revisited the issue of peace talks in late April. On April 21 George Ball had pushed for negotiations rather than escalation at a top-level meeting, and Johnson gave Ball twenty-four hours to "pull a rabbit out of a hat." Ball dictated a memorandum advocating that the United States prepare to accept a settlement that fell short of our stated goals, "but still meets our basic objectives." He suggested prophetically that the United States could not compel North Vietnam to withdraw southern-born Viet Cong without totally destroying the North, or "exterminate" the Viet Cong in the South without prolonging the war to a length the American people would not tolerate. Reviewing Hanoi's four points, he conceded that the United States could not accept the unity of Vietnam (ignoring that the Geneva Accords of 1954 did) or endorse a political settlement according to the program of the NLF, but suggested that the United States might grant the NLF a political role if it disbanded militarily.[73] The memorandum had no effect upon the pending deployment decisions, but Johnson asked for further study.

Looking for reinforcements, Ball called on former Secretary of State Dean Acheson. No one could accuse Acheson of taking a soft line toward Communist expansion, but the Washington attorney agreed that Johnson was neglecting Europe because of Vietnam. Helped by a younger Washington attorney, Lloyd Cutler, Acheson went to work on a longer draft, and Ball submitted it on May 8 after consulting with several State Department and CIA officials. The White House had independently decided upon another public peace offensive. On May 10 Lippmann suggested to McGeorge Bundy that the United States halt the bombing for a few days during the celebrations of Buddha's birthday.[74] Perhaps coincidentally, the White House on the day of the Lippmann-Bundy lunch informed Saigon that it wanted to halt the bombing of North Vietnam for perhaps five days beginning on May 12, a period that would include Buddha's birthday, in order to "clear a path either toward restoration of peace or toward increased military action." The pause began on schedule at midnight, May 12, Saigon time, but the administration avoided any public announcement.[75] Not for three days did the American press discuss what had happened. The Soviet government, however, rebuffed American attempts to pass a message to Hanoi that said that the halt was an invitation to peace talks but that the American position had not changed.

Ball submitted a new peace plan on May 13, two days into the pause. It suggested that the Saigon government announce a halt to offensive military operations in the air and on the ground and offer an amnesty and elections to all Viet Cong willing to lay down their arms. Foreign troops would withdraw when officials of the Saigon government could move freely throughout Vietnam. The President, his senior advisers, and Acheson discussed Ball's plan and the end of the bombing halt at the White House on May 16. Johnson made clear that the bombing halt was a gesture to Senators Mansfield and Fulbright (and perhaps to Lippmann), and they agreed to resume in a day or two. Rusk, however, announced plans to forward the Acheson-Ball plan to Maxwell Taylor in the hope that the Quat government might be persuaded to launch it.[76] The bombing resumed on May 18, and Reston lauded Johnson for his patience. The administration, he claimed, favored "the right of self-determination for the South Vietnamese, even the right to create a coalition government with the Communists if they so desire, though Washington certainly does not desire this."[77]

Rusk evidently regarded the Acheson-Ball plan as too sensitive to telegram, and Ball's assistant Thomas Ehrlich personally took it to Saigon. Taylor and Alexis Johnson replied very negatively on May 20. In two separate documents, they explained that the Saigon government would insist upon the total disbandment of the Viet Cong, while the Viet Cong would never allow Saigon officials into areas it controlled. The present Saigon government could not present a very appealing or convincing political program to Viet Cong or neutrals and would not accept Viet Cong political participation, and was therefore bound to reject the plan, which might result in the overthrow of any government that accepted it. As it turned out, the Quat government was already running into trouble and had only weeks to live anyway. For the time being, the idea of early negotiations died.[78]

The administration emphasized its interest in "discussions" and refused to share its broader strategic plans with the public in order to maintain public support for as long as possible. Here analogies with the 1930s undoubtedly influenced the leadership's behavior in many ways. Johnson and Rusk, in particular, repeatedly stated that the failure of the Western powers to react to early moves by the Japanese and the Germans in Manchuria, China, the Rhineland, and Czechoslovakia had *brought about* the Second World War.[79] Today most historians would probably agree that Hitler and the Japanese were not likely to be deterred by the West, and thus that the real problem for the Western powers was not whether they could prevent the war but whether they chose the right circumstances and the right strategy with which to fight. The more specific analogy which seems to have influenced administration officials' behavior was their identification with Winston Churchill, who had warned of German aggression at an early stage. In real life, Churchill had spoken for only a minority of British opinion, and the British people had rallied behind him and his policies only after events had decisively proven his view of the danger to be correct. Franklin Roosevelt, meanwhile, had taken great care not to move beyond American public opinion in the critical years 1939–1941, and had not asked for a declaration of war until Pearl Harbor had been attacked.

Johnson, Rusk, and perhaps Bundy, however, seem to have felt that since they, like Churchill, understood the threat of aggression, they had both a right and a duty to act against it whether their countrymen shared their views or not. Rusk especially seems to have drawn emotional sustenance from a sense of himself as a lonely, embattled bulwark of peace, fending off carping critics. The greater good these men believed they served apparently justified keeping the American people and the Congress in the dark as long as possible. They and their countrymen paid dearly for this view in the years to come.

During April and May a new crisis broke out in the Dominican Republic. Since the assassination of General Trujillo in 1961, that island had lurched back and forth from left to right, and the Kennedy administration had regarded it as a critical danger zone in the fight against Communism in the hemisphere. On April 25 a left-leaning military coup took power, apparently with the intention of returning Juan Bosch, a liberal overthrown in the fall of 1963, to the presidency of the country. Within a week the United States had dispatched 14,000 American troops to Santo Domingo—initially to protect Americans, but subsequently to restore order and prevent a takeover by Communists who, President Johnson announced on May 2, had taken over the uprising. Johnson became obsessed with the situation during May, as the American troops tried to put a stop to the civil war.[80] Once again, the President—who did not wait for the Organization of American States to act—showed a willingness to deploy American power at once to meet a perceived Communist threat. By May 28 Reston was expressing some doubts about Johnson's leadership. "The men closest to the President in the cabinet and the White House staff," he wrote, "do not seem to be speaking plainly and bluntly to the President about the conduct and substance of some of his policies."[81] Johnson seemed indeed to be getting more and more confident in his own judgment and less inclined to listen to dissent. Bundy on May 1 had accepted an invitation to debate the administration's Vietnam policy at the University of Michigan later in the month, but Johnson insisted two weeks later that he withdraw. "I got into trouble with the President by agreeing to debate [the political scientist] Hans Morgenthau," Bundy recalled years later. "He just didn't want to dignify the opposition by debating."[82]

While preparing to deploy at least three divisions of ground forces, the administration once again argued over the scope of the bombing. We have seen that the civilian leadership, supported by Westmoreland, had resisted the Chiefs' recommendations to bomb the MIGs at Phuc Yen airfield during the spring. The Chiefs expressed further concern about SAM-2 missile sites detected around Hanoi and Haiphong beginning in early April, and on May 27 they recommended simultaneously striking the sites with low-level fighter aircraft and hitting the MIGs—now augmented with five Soviet IL-28 bombers—with B-52s.[83] McNamara remained reluctant to do this, just as he remained determined, for the most part, to avoid bombing targets within the Hanoi-Haiphong area. When he asked the intelligence community about Communist reaction to such strikes, the State Department immediately warned that the Chinese might respond by introducing their own air power, and McNamara turned the strikes down.[84]

CINCPAC Admiral Sharp attacked these decisions bitterly in his memoir, *Strategy for Defeat*, and blamed them entirely on the civilian leadership.[85] General Westmoreland wrote a similar critique in his memoirs, heaping particular scorn on John McNaughton, whom he quoted as having said (to someone else) that the North Vietnamese had no intention of using their SAMs.[86] Westmoreland added, however, that he had opposed all-out bombing of the North "until the South Vietnamese were prepared to cope with North Vietnamese reaction." This sentence does less than full justice to the position Westmoreland actually took in June 1965.

While acknowledging that the bombing of the North fell outside his authority—it was directed by CINCPAC—Westmoreland on June 11 raised the issue of B-52 strikes against Phuc Yen and their consequences. No Pentagon civilian could have expressed greater caution than he. "Once started," he cabled, "major offensive air operations in Hanoi-Haiphong area must include continuous neutralization of all DRV jet capable airfields." This in turn would bring the SAM-2s into play, and Westmoreland asked whether, "in this age of electronic marvels," there might be reasonably effective electronic alternatives to destroying the SAM sites. "Sustained US/GVN air operations in Hanoi-Haiphong areas seem a must, once [the] die is cast," he continued, and they were bound to lead to large-scale North Vietnamese intervention in the South, and, very possibly, Chinese Communist intervention in the air war. "Should this contingency eventuate, it raises an entirely new array of questions. Military answers to these questions are highly sensitive to several US national policy determinations. The latter include US attacks on Chicom bases, selective use of nuclear weapons, availability of allied real estate when allies have no choice in potentially escalatory actions envisioned above; and US willingness to mobilize for major war."

The Communists, he continued, might send several division equivalents into South Vietnam covertly, requiring more American air power to cope. The Soviets might also intervene in the air, at least covertly, and if the enemy mounted counter-air and interdiction operations of their own, American air requirements would escalate dramatically. Westmoreland discussed his reliance on tactical air power as a defensive weapon against the Viet Cong:

> Finally, ever increasing reliance of GVN ground forces on air fire power for prosecution of counterinsurgency operations is toll exacted by continuing instability and ineffectiveness in face of increasing insurgent military strength.
>
> All of foregoing considerations, to varying but major degree, influence the estimate of our basic ability to maintain a viable military posture in RVN and Southeast Asia, given the current status of forces and facilities available or projected to be made available to me. I am especially concerned about our air posture. Recent events and intelligence dramatically point out the growing strength of the VC. Where it was not available, timely application of massive air may or may not have changed results in our favor; but in sharply increasing percentage of RVNAF victories, massive air was the decisive factor.
>
> . . . Survival of GVN presence in number of more important areas of RVN is becoming more and more dependent upon air . . .

Though oversimplified, I see no practical alternative, short of nuclear war, to continuing as we are, preparing for the long haul by building up our forces and facilities with objective of gaining a qualitative and quantitative margin over the enemy which will wear him down.[87]

The MACV commander fully shared the Washington civilian leadership's fears of enemy escalation in return for heavier American bombing—all the more so because he was relying upon tactical air power to turn the tide of the ground war. He had already asked for B-52 strikes against suspected Viet Cong base areas within South Vietnam, which became a major element of American strategy. Only nuclear weapons, Westmoreland seemed to think—echoing a Joint Chiefs paper of more than a year earlier—could actually compel North Vietnam and China to give up quickly, and he apparently understood Washington's unwillingness to use them. He also understood, as McNamara undoubtedly did as well, that Chinese entry into the air war over North Vietnam would trigger immediate demands for an air campaign against Chinese bases and nuclear facilities, probably carried out in part with nuclear weapons.

The Saigon Embassy shared Westmoreland's opinion. Deputy Ambassador Johnson, cabling State on June 10—the day before Westmoreland's cable—argued that no amount of bombing alone would convince North Vietnam that it could not win, and that the United States must turn the tide in the South. While he favored an occasional strike in the Hanoi area to show that it remained vulnerable, he did not urge one at once. And he agreed that the Chinese would at the very least provide more MIGs, and perhaps begin operating from their own air bases, if the United States destroyed the MIGs now deployed at Phuc Yen. Yet another obstacle to all-out conventional bombing of the North emerged during the next year, when the Air Force discovered that its stocks of conventional bombs were insufficient for the Rolling Thunder program—yet more evidence that the Air Force had assumed since at least the 1950s that any major strategic bombing campaign would use nuclear weapons.[88]

Recent revelations show that the Chinese tried to warn the United States of their intentions, but that they left a greater degree of ambiguity than they had in 1950 over Korea. Zhou Enlai on April 2 gave Pakistani President Ayub Khan a four-point message for President Johnson.

While China would not provoke a war with the United States, the message said, it would meet any nation's request for help against imperialist aggression, and if its help led to American aggression against China, all-out war would result. Should that war break out, even nuclear weapons would not force China to quit, and the war would have no boundaries. President Johnson did not receive the warning because he canceled Ayub's invitation to the White House, but the Chinese delivered a slightly more cryptic version of it through the British on May 31. Passing the British report to President Johnson on June 4, McGeorge Bundy pointed out that the warning did not explain "at what point the Chinese might move in Vietnam itself in a way which would force us to act against China . . . the $64 question."[89]

And the Chinese were rapidly backing their words with deeds. In late April they agreed to send large numbers of road-building troops to North Vietnam, freeing their North Vietnamese Army (NVA) counterparts to work on improving the Ho Chi Minh trail into South Vietnam. In June they began sending large numbers of air defense personnel and equipment and railroad workers as well—forces that numbered 100,000 by the spring of 1966 and eventually reached more than 300,000 men. These enormous increments were certain to increase North Vietnamese capabilities and reduce the effectiveness of American air power, but American estimates made no mention of them as yet.[90]

By late May it was becoming impossible to hide the impending ground war. Hanson Baldwin on May 19 reported that the military might need 500,000 Americans and years of fighting to regain Vietnam from the Viet Cong. A few days later he listed several specific divisions likely to arrive, and said Saigon sources anticipated a full Army division in June. Then, in the last few days of May, the Viet Cong began a big series of major attacks all over the northern half of the country. They briefly seized a district town and staged a big ambush near Pleiku and reportedly killed nearly 400 ARVN in Quang Ngai. On June 6 a State Department spokesman confirmed that American troops were now participating in combat—almost exactly two months after Johnson had authorized them to do so.[91]

On June 7 Westmoreland took note of these developments in a message to the Joint Chiefs which announced, in effect, that South Vietnam was on the verge of losing the war. Westmoreland was now the key military strategist of the war, since only the MACV commander, and not CINCPAC or the Joint Chiefs, actually knew the situation on the ground first hand and appreciated the scope of the problem posed by the Viet Cong and, potentially, the North Vietnamese. The general confirmed reports of elements of the 325th Division of the NVA in northern II Corps, and of another NVA division across the border in Laos. The Viet Cong had staged major attacks in at least six provinces, showing better training and discipline and heavier firepower than ever before. The ARVN, meanwhile, was taking heavy casualties, experiencing increased desertion, and showing "signs of reluctance to take the offensive . . . in some cases their steadfastness under fire is coming into doubt." Planned new battalions had to be scrapped, and the South Vietnamese could not stand up to further North Vietnamese reinforcements without reinforcements of their own. "I see no course of action open to us except to reinforce our efforts in SVN with additional U.S. or third country forces as rapidly as is practical during the critical weeks ahead," Westmoreland wrote. "Additionally, studies must continue and plans developed to deploy even greater forces, if and when required, to attain our objectives or counter enemy initiatives."[92]

Because of Westmoreland's alarming language, and because this message recommended deployments that would definitely commit the United States to ground combat in the eyes of the American people and the world, several historians have treated this message as a decisive turning point in the war. Yet it was not. The specific deployments Westmoreland requested—the rest of the 3rd MEF; the remainder of authorized logistics forces; the Army Airmobile division, with further logistics forces, in the Central Highlands; a U.S. Corps headquarters; and a South Korean division—had all been discussed and tentatively scheduled for weeks. They would raise American combat infantry strength in South Vietnam to twenty-two battalions.

Not even the reference to the need for possible additional troops was new—but the message did mislead its readers regarding their purpose and significance. The additional deployments Westmoreland sketched out—the remainder of either the 1st Infantry Division or the 101st Airborne, and yet another Marine brigade—would bring United States and third-country strength up to a total of forty-four battalions, designed "to give us a substantial and hard-hitting offensive capability on the ground to convince the VC that they cannot win." But back in

February McNamara and others had cited forty-four battalions as the number of troops necessary merely to defend American installations in South Vietnam. As Hanson Baldwin's stories showed, the Pentagon realized very well that sustained offensive operations would require many more—as indeed they did.

Westmoreland's request for troops did mean, however, that the administration would now have to acknowledge that it was truly going to war in South Vietnam.

War in Public
June–July 1965

★

The Johnson administration had decided upon its objectives and strategy for the Vietnam War in November-December 1964: an independent, non-Communist South Vietnam, free to maintain an alliance with the United States, secured by whatever degree of military action against North Vietnam proved necessary. The Pentagon had planned, and the President had in principle approved, a bombing campaign against the North and a massive deployment of ground troops. Sustained bombing and deployments had begun in early March, and deployments had continued through the spring, limited mainly by the almost nonexistent logistics capacity of Vietnam. While some civilians may have hoped that the North Vietnamese would rapidly settle the war on American terms, the senior leadership had approved plans for a major war, and was fully prepared to fight it.

In public, the Johnson administration in the first five months of 1965 had described a rather different strategy, designed to allow the American people and America's allies abroad to face the future with some confidence. The President, to begin with, continued to argue that he was pursuing the policy of the two preceding administrations: helping to defend the independence of South Vietnam against foreign aggression. Under his firm guidance, McNamara and other administration officials became accustomed to delaying announcements of troop deployments for as long as possible, and consistently refusing to discuss future plans. Meanwhile, the administration, led by the President, proclaimed its willingness to enter into "unconditional discussions"—although *not* "negotiations"—with anyone, anytime, anywhere, and repeated time and again that the war could end whenever Hanoi "ceased its aggression." This line suggested that the conflict might actually end at any moment. It also matched the administration's strategic concept, since it ignored the problem that had begun the war and had steadily worsened during more than three years of intense American involvement: the increasing Viet Cong control of the people and countryside of South Vietnam, which was rapidly isolating the South Vietnamese government within cities and towns.

The day after Westmoreland's forty-four-battalion cable arrived on June 7, the State Department and the White House publicly confirmed—two months after the fact—that Westmoreland had the authority to commit American troops to combat. The next day, however, the White House tried "to counter the impression that the United States was embarking upon an expanded combat role against the Viet Cong," while the Viet Cong announced that they might ask for North Vietnamese or Chinese volunteers. Meanwhile, Taylor returned to Washington for more consultation.[1]

Two high-level meetings on June 8 and June 10 showed that Johnson was now practicing deception upon dissenters within his own administration, as well as on the public. Not only did the policymakers continue to make only the minimum necessary decisions to go forward, but their deliberations apparently allowed the few remaining skeptics to believe that policy might still stop short of large-scale war.

McNamara on June 8 pointed out that Westmoreland was asking for an immediate increase from the currently programmed 70,000 men by the end of August to 116,000, including 17,000 third-country troops, and possibly to 168,000 later on. But after Taylor and an unidentified State Department official—probably Ball or William Bundy—suggested that such troops might turn the conflict into a white man's war, McNamara spoke of a "limited cost and limited risk" option, apparently involving only five new battalions. A notetaker recorded that logistics would severely limit the number of troops that could be introduced by September in any case, and that McNamara's option turned out "to be almost identical with what the logistics will in any case permit."[2] In the second meeting on June 10, which several congressional leaders also attended, McNamara claimed to favor an increase to only 93,000 men.[3] And the next day—Friday, June 11—at a full NSC meeting, McNamara referred only to Westmoreland's near-term request for a total of twenty-three American battalions and 123,000 men, and said nothing about the general's possible additional requirements. In the same meeting Rusk repeated that there seemed to be no present possibility of talks. When Adlai Stevenson suggested asking U Thant to propose a cease-fire during negotiations, Johnson referred him to Rusk.[4] According to Taylor, Johnson on June 11 took both Westmoreland's recommendation and McNamara's five-battalion proposal home with him to the ranch for the weekend, but the President made no decision until another full week had passed.[5]

Showing even less candor than usual, officials on June 11 told the press only of plans to increase American troops to 73,000, and said they did not expect "the United States to assume the major war burden."[6] Matters looked very different in Saigon, and Westmoreland on June 12 asked for full authority to conduct offensive operations against any Viet Cong concentrations that might threaten American installations. "We have reached the point in Vietnam where we cannot avoid the commitment to combat of U.S. ground troops," he said. CINCPAC Admiral Sharp replied immediately that this message had "caused some consternation in Washington and, I might add, here." Westmoreland's existing authority to conduct "counterinsurgency combat operations" and to come to the aid of threatened South Vietnamese forces, Sharp explained, had been agreed upon in consultation with the President himself, and any attempt to redefine it might result in unwelcome restrictions.[7]

The Pentagon, meanwhile, had endorsed Westmoreland's troop request and then some. The Joint Chiefs on the very same June 12 asked McNamara for "a substantial further build-up of US and Allied forces in the RVN, at the most rapid rate feasible on an orderly basis," and endorsed Westmoreland's current requests with slight modifications, yielding a total of 117,000 Americans by sometime in the fall. The Chiefs on the same day cabled Westmoreland a plan for June and July, including two brigades from the Army's 1st Infantry Division and one from the 101st Airborne, with the 173rd Airborne retained in South Vietnam. They had already endorsed the Airmobile Division for August.[8]

While Washington discussed Westmoreland's request, many months of American efforts to establish a civilian government collapsed. On June 11 Young Turk South Vietnamese generals led by Air Marshal

Nguyen Cao Ky and Nguyen Van Thieu overthrew the Quat government and took power. The Embassy's reaction suggested that Ambassador Taylor and Alexis Johnson had given up on civilian government themselves. Although Taylor expressed some reservations about Ky's maturity—which became an international issue when Ky expressed great admiration for Adolf Hitler—the Embassy made no attempts, as it had during late 1964 or early 1965, to bring about a return to civilian rule. Both Washington spokesmen and the American press downplayed the significance of the change.[9]

On June 16 McNamara began a well-publicized press conference by announcing the activation of the new Airmobile Division, whose greatest contribution, he said, would be to improve combat readiness "in operations where terrain obstacles could give enemy guerrilla or light infantry forces an advantage over our standard combat formations." But he announced the deployment of only six more unidentified combat battalions and additional logistics forces to South Vietnam during the next few weeks, for a total of 75,000 troops. Asked whether more deployments would follow, he replied that he, Rusk, and the President "have repeatedly said that we will do whatever is necessary to achieve our objective in South Vietnam, and we won't do more than is necessary." He also exhibited photographs showing damage to bombed bridges and military installations in North Vietnam, and one petroleum installation. Asked whether new draft calls were required, he answered carefully, and, in retrospect, chillingly, "the deployment *of the troops I mentioned earlier* will not affect the draft calls in any way." Asked about the morale of South Vietnamese forces—whose decreasing combat effectiveness Westmoreland had cited in his still-secret request—McNamara replied, "They're fighting well, they are fighting hard, they are fighting effectively."[10] On the very next day, McNamara approved the Joint Chiefs' deployment schedule with only minor modifications, with total deployments of about 117,000 Americans and 20,000 third-country troops by November 1. One day later he secured the President's approval of the deployment of these forces at a meeting with Johnson, Rusk, and McGeorge Bundy. In an apparent effort to pretend that they had not, in fact, authorized approximately 117,000 American troops, those at the meeting also decided that brigades from the 1st and 101st Divisions *might* be withdrawn when the Airmobile Division arrived. A few days later McNaughton explained how the President might delay a formal decision on the Airmobile Division until July 10.[11]

Following what had become their standard operating procedure, Johnson, Rusk, McGeorge Bundy, and McNamara were moving to meet Westmoreland's and the Chiefs' requests while delaying any formal decision—much less the notification of the American public—for as long as possible. But in this case they seem to have gone one step further, withholding their decision even from second-level State Department officials who believed things were going too far. McNamara's claim at the June 8, 10, and 11 meetings that he opposed Westmoreland's entire request encouraged William Bundy and George Ball to reopen the question of American objectives. Ambassador Taylor had insisted in two meetings that even the Acheson Plan, under which the Viet Cong would become a political organization and lay down their arms, had to await a major improvement in the military situation, but Bundy and Ball went ahead nonetheless.[12]

Bundy began on June 11 with a cable to Saigon on behalf of both the Bureau of Intelligence and Research (INR) and the CIA, asking whether the military situation had really reached such a critical phase as reported in Westmoreland's June 7 cable. The Embassy replied a week later describing the near-catastrophic state of the ARVN and reiterating the need for new forces.[13] More daringly, Bundy on June 14 addressed a highly secret, personal letter to the ambassadors to Japan, Laos, Thailand, and South Korea, indicating that he regarded the future of the American commitment as an open question. The deterioration of the situation, he wrote, left the United States with three unpleasant alternatives: expanding the bombing at the risk of Chinese intervention; mining Haiphong harbor; or building up to 300,000 troops and running the risk of a white man's war. None of these, he suggested—in words which his superior Dean Rusk would surely have sharply questioned—would raise chances of success much above 30 percent, and he invited comments on his analysis and on the consequences of losing South Vietnam.[14] Pessimistic replies would have inclined Bundy toward suggesting a new policy, but in fact the replies generally held out hope that the existing level of effort would at least hold for some time, and—more influentially—reacted more favorably to the idea of American reinforcements than to heavy bombing of Hanoi and Haiphong or mining and blockade of North Vietnamese harbors.[15]

During the week in which President Johnson was studying Westmoreland's request, he decided to give his leading in-house critic some encouragement. On June 14 he telephoned George Ball, initially to ask for a paper summarizing the administration's negotiating efforts that he could pass to British Prime Minister Wilson. Then Johnson raised the issue of Ball's own proposals, which in April and May had foundered on the rocks of the Saigon Embassy's opposition to any negotiations. The President said he liked what Ball had been doing, "raising the red flag and saying we ought to give thought to different approaches." Johnson also said that he wanted to get dissenters like Mansfield and Fulbright on board, and asked for Ball's help in developing an agreed-upon policy.[16]

Four days later, on June 18, Johnson approved the first phase of Westmoreland's troop request, raising planned deployments to 117,000. On the same day, Ball, who apparently did not know about this step, gave Johnson a new memorandum trying to hold options open at least through the summer. Quoting Emerson that "things are in the saddle, and ride mankind," he suggested limiting total American troops to 100,000, using them both to hold off any forthcoming summer offensive and to test their effectiveness against the Viet Cong, and preparing plans *either* to step up the ground war further *or* to seek a negotiated solution on less than stated American objectives. Then, questioning whether even 500,000 men could achieve American objectives, Ball reviewed the experience of the French and of the United States, and drew some pessimistic, but qualified, conclusions:

> Ever since 1961—the beginning of our deep involvement in South Vietnam—we have met successive disappointments. We have tended to underestimate the strength and staying power of the enemy. We have tended to overestimate the effectiveness of our sophisticated weapons under jungle conditions. We have watched the progressive loss of territory to Viet Cong control. We have been unable to bring about the creation of a stable political base in Saigon.
>
> This is no one's fault. It is in the nature of the struggle.
>
> The French had much the same experience.
>
> They quoted the same kind of statistics that guide our opinions—statis-

tics as to the number of Viet Minh killed, the number of enemy defectors, the rate of enemy desertions, etc. . . .

This does not mean that we cannot succeed where the French did not; we have things running for us that the French did not have. But we cannot yet be sure—that is the reason for the trial period.[17]

Although Johnson had consistently rejected such views, he had to take Ball seriously. Ball and his former law partner and patron Adlai Stevenson might deal the President a serious blow should they leak their opposition to the press—which both to date had loyally failed to do—or, worse, make their opposition public. But by encouraging Ball to believe that the President shared some of his views, Johnson might spread the word that an early peace remained his goal, mollify his vocal and steadily multiplying critics, and win praise for the peaceful aspects of his policy. Ball would remain less likely to take his case to the press if he believed the President might at a suitable moment adopt his policy.

Developments in Congress, where Great Society legislation was moving toward passage, helped position Johnson as a wise moderate. Johnson on June 14 met with Senator Fulbright, the Chairman of the Foreign Relations Committee, and told him that he, Johnson, had resisted military plans to expand the war further and had tried and failed to start "unconditional discussions." In a major Senate speech the next day, Fulbright opposed escalation, and actually misrepresented Johnson's stated position to bring it closer to his own. The President, he said, "remains committed to the goal of ending the war at the earliest possible time by negotiations without preconditions. In so doing, he is providing the leadership appropriate to a great nation." In fact, of course, the Johnson administration opposed "negotiations" until the military balance had change drastically, and had offered nothing but "unconditional discussions." Then, in the last two weeks of June, two Republican House leaders, future Secretary of Defense Melvin Laird and future President Gerald Ford, opposed any concessions to the Viet Cong but also argued for winning the war with massive bombing, rather than the use of ground forces.[18]

The White House's problem in late June, as in April, consisted of preparing for a new round of escalation on the one hand while demonstrating its interest in peace on the other. Johnson was delighted with a memorandum McGeorge Bundy gave him on June 16 listing numerous

positive American responses to proposals for talks, and used it for ammunition in many subsequent meetings.[19] Johnson apparently asked
Bundy on June 19 to summarize the pros and cons of another bombing
pause, and Bundy's response clearly leaned against one.[20] Johnson also
asked Bundy to comment on a long, well-argued memorandum by the
Senate's most vociferous dove, Wayne Morse, arguing that the United
States should ask the United Nations to take over the Vietnam problem. Asking the U.N. to intervene sounded promising, but Bundy reported on June 24 that his brother Bill and even Ball opposed such
a move as likely to unsettle Saigon, encourage Hanoi, and force the Soviet Union to defend Hanoi's position.[21] When Johnson eventually
spoke on the twentieth anniversary of the United Nations in San Francisco on June 25, he merely asked the nations of the world "to bring to
the tables those who seem determined to make war."[22]

The President, meanwhile, was making a determined effort to forge
an illusory consensus among his advisers. On Monday, June 21, his
new press secretary, Bill Moyers—who was himself skeptical about
the war—called Ball to tell him that the President had read his latest
memorandum, and that he agreed "in substance" with it. "I told Mc-
Namara," Moyers quoted Johnson as saying, "that I would not make a
decision on this [going over 100,000 men], and not to assume that I am
willing to go overboard on this—I ain't. If there is no alternative, the
fellow here with the program [Ball] is the way I will probably go."
Johnson was lying: he had authorized 115,000 men three days earlier.[23]
But Ball, thus encouraged, submitted another memo suggesting that the
United States had no binding legal obligation to aid South Vietnam and
could decide to withdraw on political grounds.[24] Also on June 21, in a
telephone conversation with McNamara, Johnson expressed serious
doubts about the possibility of victory and the difficulty of maintaining
public support, but concluded, once again, that the United States could
not afford to leave South Vietnam.[25]

Senior officials, including Deputy Ambassador to South Vietnam
U. Alexis Johnson, met with the President late on June 23 to discuss a
number of diplomatic and military issues relating to Vietnam. Partly
because the top-level meeting of June 18 apparently remained a secret,
a gap was opening between the proposals of Ball and William Bundy
and the reality of administration policy. At this meeting Deputy Am-

bassador Johnson introduced an unusual note of skepticism about the wisdom of additional American deployments, and Ball took the opportunity to argue for stopping at 100,000 men and thinking hard about cutting American losses and making a stand in Thailand. This was the same argument that William Bundy and McNaughton had made the previous November, and Ball got the same response. "Rusk and McNamara objected: Thailand, they thought, could not be held if SVN had given up. Rather, Rusk said, we would end up with the only secure areas Australia, New Zealand, the Philippines, and NATO, with even India falling to the Communist Chinese." William Bundy found this an astonishing statement. McNamara then emerged suddenly as a great conciliator, suggesting that his plans for more forces might be combined with Ball's plans for more of a political effort, and President Johnson urged them to go ahead. The next day McNamara telephoned Ball and set up a meeting, saying "he suspected that when we are through we will find what we are thinking in terms of political settlement would fit well in what they are thinking of in expanded but limited military programs." The man who was known for doing the impossible wanted to square the circle.[26] McNamara and Ball apparently designated McNaughton and former Ambassador to Laos Leonard Unger to prepare parts of an agreed-on paper. Consciously or not, he was speaking disingenuously to Ball, since information at his disposal gave not the slightest reason to believe that peace talks could succeed for many months.

Having spoken to Ball, McNamara began preparing a document designed to embody a consensus recommendation for the next steps in three critical areas: the size of future ground force deployments, the future course of American bombing of North Vietnam, and the role of peace initiatives. Perhaps to assist in resolving the first issue, General Wheeler queried Westmoreland urgently on June 22. Wheeler asked Westmoreland immediately and personally to assess the need for additional U.S. forces and to recommend new actions in both South and North Vietnam. "You should know that thought here in some areas is to the effect that introduction of U.S. troop units over 10,000 [100,000] . . . will convert the war into a second Vietnamese/French war in which we would play the role of the French." Westmoreland replied firmly two days later: "By way of introduction, the premise behind whatever further actions we may undertake, either in SVN, or DRV, must be that we are in for the long pull. The struggle has become a war of attrition. *Short of decision to introduce nuclear weapons against sources and channels of enemy power, I see no likelihood of achieving a quick, favorable end to the war.*"[27]

Westmoreland then sketched out yet another increment of American forces following the two he had proposed on June 7, one which would retain both the 173rd Airborne brigade and the scheduled brigade of the 101st Airborne and add yet another U.S. division in III Corps. Proper administration and separation of the Americans from the population, he thought, could prevent them from taking over the role of the French. With respect to North Vietnam, he proposed the use of B-52s against some military targets, the interdiction of the railroad from Hanoi into China, the mining of Haiphong harbor, leafleting of North Vietnamese cities, and more armed reconnaissance to inhibit movement of supplies, as actions that would not provoke "unacceptable" Communist Chinese involvement. He concluded that he found it difficult, if not impossible, to imagine how the United States could deploy the necessary forces for the long haul without the "mobilization of manpower, industrial and training resources at least to a limited degree."

By the time this message arrived, McNaughton had drafted a memorandum for the President. He offered a list of proposed new military actions that combined Westmoreland's and the Chiefs' requests—and in some instances exceeded them—with new proposals for peace initiatives. He raised Westmoreland's troop request from thirty-four American battalions to forty (200,000 men total), and asked for the call-up of 100,000 reserves and the extension of tours of duty. He also proposed expanding all aspects of the air campaign, including armed reconnaissance against lines of communication with China, the bombing of war production facilities, the bombing and mining of Haiphong harbor, and, "as necessary," bombing of SAM sites and MIGs. New political proposals—drafted by Unger—included a series of initiatives designed "(a) to open a dialogue with Hanoi, Peking, and the VC looking toward a settlement in Vietnam, (b) to keep the Soviet Union from deepening its military involvement and support of North Vietnam until the time when settlement can be achieved, and (c) to cement the support for US policy by the US public, allies and friends, and to keep international opposition at a manageable level. *While our approaches may be rebuffed until the tide begins to turn, they nevertheless should be made.*" Specifically, they called for a frank approach to Moscow, an appeal to the United Nations, proposing a Geneva conference, initiating contacts with the NLF and the DRV, contacting the Chinese Communists if possible, consulting the British, Canadians, French, Indians, and U Thant, and perhaps making a bombing pause.[28] Rather than present the President with an either/or choice of war or peace, the memorandum seemed to be combining all the options simultaneously. McNaughton, of course, had shown skepticism about the feasibility of maximum American objectives at least since the fall, and the memorandum seemed to cast some doubt on the ultimate outcome, proposing these steps simply "to create conditions for a favorable settlement by demonstrating to the VC/DRV that the odds are against their winning."[29]

After further revisions, McNamara apparently circulated a new copy of this memorandum on Saturday, June 26. It drew a variety of sharp reactions, pushing the administration once again toward a reexamination of its ends and means. General Wheeler wanted to make sure that Westmoreland got enough forces to achieve the current stated objective: "to *prove* to the VC/DRV that they *cannot* win." Referring to the complete, two-part troop request that Westmoreland had made on June 7, totaling thirty-four U.S. and ten third-country infantry battalions, he asked Westmoreland on June 28 whether such forces would be sufficient to achieve this objective, and requested an immediate reply. Westmoreland began his answer two days later by reporting no indication that the enemy was modifying its policy or strategy, and continued, "the direct answer to your basic question is 'no' . . . The DRV/VC are too deeply committed to be influenced by anything but the application of overwhelming force." While the forty-four battalions might "reestablish the military balance by the end of December," they would not cause the enemy to back off.

By January, he continued, the requested forty-four battalions might enable friendly forces to take the initiative "in selected areas," but the enemy, of course, might reinforce its strength. Westmoreland had abandoned the optimism of his March Commander's Estimate, in which he had suggested that the sight of American forces might induce the North to abandon its objectives. "Instinctively," he continued, "we believe that there may be substantial additional US force requirements." He concluded once again that some form of mobilization seemed to be required and might have an excellent effect on Hanoi. Although McNamara took this cable into account, no copy appears to have reached either the State Department or the White House.[30]

During June Westmoreland had also begun trying out key elements of his strategy within South Vietnam. They revealed his strategic concept to be essentially identical to that of General Harkins: to destroy Viet Cong troops in their base areas with the help of massive American firepower. Indeed, the first major American initiatives hit some of the same areas with which Harkins, Diem, and Nhu had tried to deal three years earlier. Thus the first B-52 strike against supposed Viet Cong concentrations on June 17 hit an area near Ben Cat in Binh Duong province—the site of Operation Sunrise in 1962. Post-strike surveys found no evidence of many enemy casualties, but the Pentagon subsequently claimed that the strike had foiled a VC attack.[31] On June 29 a battalion of the 173rd Airborne brigade undertook the first major American search-and-destroy mission of the war, targeting fifty square miles of War Zone D, which a special South Vietnamese unit had tried and failed to pacify in 1962–1963, in a two-day strike. The mission, also including Australian and South Vietnamese troops, began with a huge artillery barrage—exactly the tactic Roger Hilsman had warned against two and a half years earlier because it destroyed surprise—and reportedly found lots of rice but very few Viet Cong. South Vietnamese soldiers showed no aggressiveness, and the United States lost one man killed and twenty-one wounded to snipers and booby traps. Officials said the operation would shake the confidence of the Viet Cong.[32]

A week later, after some B-52 strikes, the United States staged another 2,500-man sweep through War Zone D. On July 8, the second day of the sweep, the 173rd Airborne claimed to have inflicted 100 Viet Cong casualties, although they admitted seeing few bodies. But on June 10 the *New York Times* reported that the 173rd had lost ten killed and forty-two wounded, and that Australian troops said the reported enemy casualties were much too high. "At an earlier stage of the war," the story continued, "American advisers also insisted upon a body count before releasing results and derided the Vietnamese for their vague and generous method of counting Vietcong losses. More recently, however, the American command has been inclined to accept aerial estimates of enemy casualties. The command has also begun to calculate probable damage inflicted on the Viet Cong despite the absence of bodies or weapons."[33]

At long last, MACV had the opportunity to try out its tactics with American forces. Its premise, of course, was that American firepower and determination would make those tactics decisively successful, and thus MACV faced enormous pressure to report high casualties from the start. The daily accounts of B-52 and tactical air strikes against Viet Cong concentrations inevitably gave the American public the impression that the Viet Cong were taking a tremendous beating, but the insecurity of the entire country continued to plague U.S. forces as never before. The Viet Cong infiltrated the Da Nang air base, killed an American, and destroyed or damaged six planes on June 30, and mortared the American airfield in Soc Trang in the Delta on July 1. They also seized several more towns in the interior and ambushed relief columns before withdrawing.[34]

Although the Pentagon did not circulate any specific information on these operations to other agencies, some of the dissenters in the administration picked important facts out of the newspapers and used them for ammunition. George Ball evidently did not regard McNamara's June 26 draft as a "Ball-McNamara paper," and went to work on another statement of his own views with the help of William Bundy, who seemed to hope that Ball could have at least some impact. Ball began bluntly by denying that any combination of increased bombing and more ground troops could secure American objectives. He also argued that once the United States had lost a substantial number of lives, disengagement would become much more difficult. Thus he suggested that the President decide not to commit combat forces, and that the U.S. exit strategy begin with a demand for a government of national unity in Saigon, in place of the military government that had now been in power for two weeks. If this failed, he wanted to tell the new Ky government that the United States could not maintain its existing level of support, leading either to a declaration by Ky that South Vietnam would go it alone, or to a new government prepared to deal with the Viet Cong. Because the world knew "that the government in Saigon is a joke," Ball anticipated no unmanageable international consequences. He concluded frankly and powerfully:

> The position taken in this memorandum does not suggest that the United States should abdicate leadership in the cold war. But any prudent military commander carefully selects the terrain on which to stand and fight, and no great captain has ever been blamed for a successful tactical withdrawal . . .
> In my view, a deep commitment of United States forces in a land war in South Vietnam would be a catastrophic error. If ever there was an occasion for a tactical withdrawal, this is it.[35]

That afternoon, June 28, McGeorge Bundy called Ball to say that he, Rusk, McNamara, McNaughton, William Bundy, and Unger would meet the next afternoon after lunch to discuss Ball's paper. But the next morning William Bundy apparently learned from Rusk that at a luncheon meeting the President would be asked to approve the deployment of three more Marine battalions. Protesting that this decision, combined with the approval of the Airmobile Division, would raise troop strength to 125,000 men, Bundy asked for a postponement of the decision until after Ball's and McNamara's positions could be reviewed. But the luncheon meeting went ahead, the President approved the deployments, and Ball, although he may not have known it, wound up arguing a case that had now been doubly overtaken by events.[36] Not surprisingly, McNamara at the afternoon meeting hotly disputed Ball's argument, and William Bundy recorded the conclusion that Ball had suggested "the worst way to lose if it came to that." Now that the war was on, McNamara and Rusk were treating the political situation in Saigon as almost irrelevant.[37] Undaunted, Ball began drafting his argument yet again.[38]

All the parties were now pointing toward a meeting with Johnson on Friday, July 2. Ball on July 1 tried again, citing three events over the last few weeks that cast doubt on our ability to win the guerrilla war: a sneak Viet Cong attack on the Da Nang airfield, a B-52 raid that had missed VC concentrations, and the 173rd Airborne sweep through Zone D that had taken twenty-three casualties without making contact. He suggested freezing our commitment at 72,000 men (Johnson, as we have seen, had already authorized more than 120,000), approaching Hanoi through Paris, and offering the NLF some unspecified political role. In an appendix he surveyed the likely reaction of allies, suggesting that Thailand and South Korea—the most difficult cases— would respond to further proofs of American support, and concluding quite accurately, "We have not persuaded either our friends or allies that our further involvement is essential to the defense of freedom in the Cold War."[39]

More surprisingly, McGeorge Bundy on June 30 weighed in with a blunt, highly critical memorandum to McNamara commenting on his June 26 draft. That draft has never been located, but Bundy's comments make clear that it foresaw American deployments of more than forty battalions. They also show that Bundy had not forgotten the very troubling issue that he had discussed with McNamara on at least two previous occasions, and most recently on March 6: the question of whether the U.S. Army really understood how to fight this kind of war.

[The paper] proposes a doubling of our presently planned strength in South Vietnam, a tripling of our air effort in the north, and a new and very important program of naval quarantine. *It proposes this new land commitment at a time when our troops are entirely untested in the kind of warfare projected.* It proposes greatly extended air action when the value of the air action we have taken is sharply disputed. It proposes naval quarantine by mining at a time when nearly everyone agrees the real question is not in Hanoi, but in South Vietnam. My first reaction is that this program is rash to the point of folly.

. . . I see no reason to suppose that the Viet Cong will accommodate us by fighting the kind of war we desire . . .

Any expanded program needs to have a clear sense of its own internal momentum. The paper does not face this problem. If US casualties go up sharply, what further actions do we propose to take or not to take? More broadly still, what is the real object of the exercise? If it is to get to the conference table, what results do we seek there? Still more brutally, do we want to invest 200 thousand men to cover an eventual retreat? Can we not do that just as well where we are?[40]

Bundy also questioned the mining of Haiphong. He suggested that the United States consider a more drastic nuclear threat against North Vietnam, as proposed by former President Eisenhower.

For all his brilliance, McGeorge Bundy seems to have played an unwitting but critical role in the unfolding of American policy during the first half of 1965, simply because he had continued to assume the existence of options that formal, written decisions had actually foreclosed. When Bundy had helped persuade Johnson to initiate Phase II in February he had said nothing about ground forces, but Phase II, as described by the papers the President had approved in December, included the huge and open-ended build-up of American forces that was now under way. Similarly, he seems to have believed that the United States was embarked on the original McNaughton–William Bundy option C, under which Washington could continually reevaluate its objectives and its strategy, but it was really the revised option C', which called for whatever action proved necessary to secure American maximum objectives, to which the President had agreed. And Bundy had never realized—until now, perhaps—that McNamara lacked the ability, or perhaps even the intention, to change the manner in which the U.S. Army planned to fight this war. McNamara's new memo—like every such paper written since February—was really just another step in the *implementation* of an open-ended plan that Johnson had approved in principle in December and set in motion in February, and Bundy should certainly have realized by now that President Johnson, who had successively approved every troop request without dissent and had shown no interest in lesser American objectives, knew what he was doing. The memorandum did in any case raise critical questions, most notably that of the effectiveness of American troops, and it seems to have led McNamara to ask General Wheeler to prepare a study of the question of whether the requested forces would in fact enable the United States to win.

William Bundy, meanwhile, decided to suggest a "'Middle Way' Course of Action," based upon Ball's doubts—which he partially, but not completely, shared—and upon a more optimistic estimate of the military situation that he had heard from Alexis Johnson, who was consulting in Washington. Bundy now knew how many forces had actually been authorized, and he asked that the deployment of the Airmobile Division be postponed indefinitely, holding U.S. forces at 85,000 through the summer and testing both their effectiveness and the staying power of the South Vietnamese. He also asked to defer any expansion of the bombing campaign or the mining of Haiphong, while using air power to the maximum extent possible in the South. Meanwhile, he proposed discreet contacts with Hanoi and third-party contacts with the NLF designed to prepare for some unspecified settlement. With Westmoreland arguing that he could only hold the situation together with at least 175,000 men, this program had little chance of acceptance.[41]

Secretary Rusk also weighed in with a rare memo of his own on July 1—one which he did not show to William Bundy. As usual, he took the most extreme view of all of the stakes in Vietnam. "The central objective of the United States . . . must be to insure that North Vietnam not succeed in taking over or determining the future of South Vietnam by force. We must accomplish this objective without a general war *if possible*." Rusk took the administration's public line that the United States was fighting only the infiltrators from the North. He argued in effect for the current reinforcement schedule and level of bombing, and proposed the implementation of the Acheson Plan as soon as possible, "perhaps in the III and IV Corps," or in selected provinces around Saigon. The Secretary of State did not seem to realize that most of the populated countryside was now in Viet Cong hands.[42]

McNamara also submitted a revised version of his memorandum on July 1. It apparently cut back ground force recommendations slightly from the earlier drafts, endorsing only Westmoreland's two-stage, forty-four-battalion request of June 7 (the first stage of which had already been approved), although it quoted Westmoreland's June 30 statement that this alone would not cause the enemy to back off. It called again for 100,000 reserves and for the same sweeping series of actions against North Vietnam, which no other leading civilian adviser had endorsed. Negotiating initiatives, it repeated, "will pay off toward an actual settlement only after the tide begins to turn (unless we lower our sights considerably)"—a bow, in all probability, to McNaughton's views.

"I have just come from another long session in the State Department on the draft papers for discussion tomorrow," McGeorge Bundy wrote the President late on the afternoon of July 1. "I find that both Rusk and McNamara feel strongly that the George Ball paper should not be argued with you in front of any audience larger than yourself, Rusk, McNamara, Ball, and me. They feel that it is exceedingly dangerous to have this possibility reported in a wider circle. Moreover, both of them feel great reticence about expressing their own innermost thoughts to you in front of any larger group."[43]

Johnson agreed to the smaller meeting, and Bundy continued the discussion a few hours later.

The positions within the government are roughly as follows: McNamara and Ball honestly believe in their own recommendations, though Bob would readily accept advice to tone down those of his recommendations which move rapidly against Hanoi by bombing and blockade.

Dean Rusk leans toward the McNamara program, adjusted downward in this same way.

The second-level men in both State and Defense are not optimistic about the future prospects in Vietnam and are therefore very reluctant to see us move to a 44 battalion force with a call-up of reserves. So they would tend to cluster around the middle course suggested by my brother. They would like to see what happens this summer before getting much deeper in.

The Joint Chiefs are strongly in favor of going in even further than McNamara. Specifically they want now to take out the SAM site, the IL-28s, and the MIGs in the Hanoi area.

My hunch is that you will want to listen hard to George Ball and then reject his proposal. Discussion could then move to the narrower choice between my brother's course and McNamara's. The decision between them should be made in about ten days, which is the point at which McNamara would like a final go-ahead on the air mobile division.[44]

Read in the context of the previous four and a half years, these two memos tell us as much as we are ever likely to know about the four key men who led the United States into the Vietnam War: Johnson, Rusk, McNamara, and Bundy. The President had apparently made it quite clear to Bundy that he was not interested in following Ball's recommendations, although he carefully "listened hard" to them, as we have seen, to keep Ball on board and to give the impression that he favored the earliest possible negotiations. And the President would surely have agreed as to the dangers of allowing George Ball's views to leak into the newspapers by airing them before a larger group. Yet this, clearly, was not the only reason that Rusk and McNamara pushed for a meeting of only four participants.

All three leading subordinates—and especially Rusk and McNamara—now believed in the war and wanted to do the President's bidding. They had also accepted Johnson's way of doing business, which held every decision as closely as possible and tended to cut them off from their subordinates. The difficulty here, from Rusk and McNamara's perspective, was that their most important subordinates—William Bundy and John McNaughton—thought that Ball's proposals had to be taken very seriously indeed. While neither of these two men wanted at this time to throw in the towel and negotiate on the best terms available, both still believed, as they had when they produced the original planning papers in November 1964, that the result of the war in Vietnam was a very open question, and that the United States should not commit itself to achieving its maximum objectives, which they would have been prepared, if necessary, to scale down. Having repeatedly overwhelmed Ball in small-group meetings, Rusk and McNamara did not want to give him a chance to secure support from their subordinates in front of the President.

But if their own subordinates had become so skeptical in light of the steady decline in South Vietnamese performance, why did Rusk and McNamara stick so tightly to the maximum American objectives? In Rusk's case, we have seen time and time again ever since 1961 that this was a matter of faith. To him, South Vietnam was the test of American willingness to resist Communist aggression in Asia, and the United States must meet that test as it had done in Korea, and as Britain, France, and the United States had failed to do in Manchuria in 1931 and in Czechoslovakia in 1938. Should general war result, Rusk was willing to fight it.[45] And if America's allies were skeptical, that made it even more necessary for the United States to shoulder the burden of opposing and deterring the Chinese Communists. In a meeting on July 6 Rusk said that he expected hostile Soviet moves in Berlin in response to the war in Vietnam, but that he was not deterred.[46]

McNamara's case was more complex. Certainly he does not seem to have doubted as yet the American military's ability to deal with the Communists in Southeast Asia. During 1961 and early 1962 he had repeatedly endorsed plans for intervention in Laos or South Vietnam, and during 1963 he had loyally stood behind Generals Harkins and Krulak as they insisted that the American military was doing the job in an advisory role. But at the same time, McNamara from the summer of 1962 through the fall of 1963 had insisted on setting a time limit on the American commitment to South Vietnam and concluding the job by 1965—because President Kennedy wanted him to.

Now, in 1965, McNamara was trying to meet the needs of a new President who believed in the need to defend South Vietnam. He still had confidence in what the American military could do, and he seems never to have acquired any real understanding of insurgency and counterinsurgency or questioned the ground strategic concepts of West-moreland and the Chiefs. His role was now to implement the military's plans—with a few exceptions—in a way that met the political needs of the new President. The mystique that built up around McNamara should not obscure the essence of his role: implementing other men's plans, in pursuit of other men's objectives. Even years later, when Mc-Namara had developed deep doubts of his own, he behaved with complete loyalty.

As for Bundy, because he would never have committed himself so tightly to such a rigid objective, he seems not to have realized until too late that the President and the Secretaries of State and Defense had done just that. In any case, his relationship with Johnson had begun a terminal decline at the time of the Michigan teach-in debate fiasco. He knew that Johnson had never trusted him, and as it turned out, he had less than a year left on his job.

Johnson, McNamara, and Rusk—with Bundy's general support—had forged a personal bond around the cause of the war in South Vietnam. Sometime in 1966 or 1967 McNamara abandoned the other two, but by then Bundy had been replaced by Walt Rostow, who was every bit as committed to the war as Rusk. Most of the entire second level of the government struggled in vain against the top leadership for the whole of the Johnson presidency, winning its most important victory in March 1968, when Johnson partially halted the bombing, refused Westmoreland's request for another 200,000 American troops, and decided not to run for reelection. But that victory was only partial, and in the end Johnson bequeathed essentially the same war, the same objectives, and the same strategy to his successor.

When the four leaders met with Ball on July 2, Johnson made no overall decision. He did not have to, since no further troop deployments needed to be authorized for ten days. He did endorse a suggestion to send Averell Harriman on a semi-official visit to Moscow; he dispatched McNamara, Wheeler, and Henry Cabot Lodge, whom he had chosen as the next Ambassador to Vietnam, on another trip to Saigon to talk to Westmoreland about requirements for 1966; and he asked State to investigate more negotiating possibilities—which the Saigon Embassy, once again, flatly rejected.[47] The administration was remaining on course.

The administration could delay any new formal decision or announcement of further plans because all new deployments for July had already been approved. And July was a critical month for Great Society legislation, including both the Voting Rights Act and the Medicare program. Proceeding at a leisurely pace, the administration on July 3 cabled Taylor confirming that it was giving serious consideration to the forty-four-battalion request, and suggesting that McNamara visit South Vietnam beginning July 15. Taylor replied that he would be welcome sooner, since the issue of deployments was pressing.[48]

The cable also informed Taylor that Henry Cabot Lodge would replace him. The selection of Lodge, which President Johnson seems to have decided upon as early as March 1965, revealed a great deal about the President's priorities. Lodge in his earlier tour had shown no administrative talent, and McNamara and the Pentagon also still nursed a grudge against him dating back to the fall of 1963. But Lodge was a prominent Republican whom Kennedy had appointed to the same position, and Johnson seems to have been far more interested in political cover than in the contribution that the Embassy might or might not make to the war effort. Given the reservations about Lodge that Johnson had frequently expressed himself, the decision was shockingly cynical.[49]

While McNamara's trip seems to have been designed, like so many previous excursions, to lend an imprimatur of authenticity to decisions that had already been made, he sent a preliminary message to Taylor on July 7 that aimed to show skeptics and dissenters like William Bundy, McNaughton, and Ball that he had raised every significant question. He began by asking for military recommendations for deployments for the rest of the year, the probable requirements for 1966, and the "program of political contacts with the NLF, DRV, and Soviets which you propose as a complement to your military actions." Taylor had actually just rejected such contacts for the foreseeable future. McNamara then asked for assurances that recommended troop levels would "prove to the Viet Cong that they cannot win, and thereby force them to a settlement on our terms." This question included a critical logical fallacy: proving to the Viet Cong that they could not win might also simply persuade them that they had to persevere without victory until the United States gave up. He asked a broad range of additional military questions, including the desirability of some kind of barrier across the 17th parallel, and asked whether the Acheson Plan might be implemented in some part of the country. But he added, significantly, that decisions after his return to Washington "may well require" the declaration of a national emergency and a call-up of reserves.[50]

Three days later—before leaving—McNamara told the Chiefs the decision had already been made, and that 115,000 Americans would reach South Vietnam by September 1 and thirty-four battalions by November 1. He also sketched out a huge reserve call-up. "The Secretary of Defense," General Greene recorded, "further stated that the public was going to have to be softened up for whatever it would be necessary to do. That was the purpose of the trip which he was about to make . . . As usual, the Secretary was slightly condescending and impatient during his conference, giving me the impression that he was personally informing the Chiefs of an action which had already been decided upon and which he was communicating to the Chiefs only because he felt he had to."[51]

Greene also was not informed about another Pentagon project, a response to the military questions raised by McGeorge Bundy. On about July 2 McNamara apparently asked General Wheeler for assurances that the United States could win in Vietnam "if we do everything we can," and Wheeler turned the question over to a study group headed by his assistant, General Andrew Goodpaster. While Goodpaster undertook the task, John McNaughton provided him with some guidance. He told him, in effect, to assume that the United States would deploy forty-four U.S. and third-country battalions during 1965 and more in 1966, and asked him to grapple with the issue of North Vietnamese reinforcements in response, their effect on force ratios, and the continuing weakness of the ARVN. He also suggested, significantly, that the study group assume that Rolling Thunder would continue at the current level and that the United States would not mine North Vietnamese harbors. He raised the issue of the Ky government's ability to survive, but volunteered his own view that the war would continue as long as the South Vietnamese Army held together.

McNaughton wrote a critical paragraph that exemplified the dilemma, really, of any major military undertaking, but that failed to analyze it properly:

> One key question, of course, is what we mean by the words "assurance" and "win." My view is that the degree of "assurance" should be fairly

high—better than 75% (whatever that means). With respect to the word "win," this I think means that we succeed in demonstrating to the VC that they cannot win; this, of course, is victory for us only if it is, with a high degree of probability, a way station towards a favorable settlement in South Vietnam. I see such a favorable settlement as one in which the VC terrorism is substantially eliminated and, obviously, there are no longer large-scale VC attacks; the central South Vietnamese government (without having taken in the Communists) should be exercising fairly complete sovereignty over most of South Vietnam. I presume that we would rule out the ceding to the VC (either tacitly or explicitly) of large areas of the country.

McNaughton had broadly identified the two questions that planners of any major military operation must pose: first, the chances that it would have the desired *military* effect, and second, the chances that the desired military outcome would secure the *political* goal of the war. The 75 percent figure seems to refer to the former question, that is, whether American deployments would convince the Viet Cong that they could not win, at least while the Americans remained there (a point to which he returned in another memo). But the second question was an independent one, and McNaughton should have assigned a separate figure to it. Even a comparably optimistic figure of 75 percent would have left him with an overall probability of success of only about 55 percent, since these two independent probabilities have to be multiplied to get the overall chance of success. Reducing the probability of a settlement to 50 percent would have left his chances of victory at 37.5 percent. In fact, the chance of victory according to the equation he proposed was near zero, since the Viet Cong would never conclude that they must settle simply because they could not defeat American forces currently deployed, but would rather fight on and wait for the inevitable (in their view) day when those forces must leave.[52]

The Goodpaster study, submitted on July 14, certainly tried to lay McNaughton's doubts to rest. General Greene, who heard about it two days earlier, was furious because Wheeler had never discussed it with the Chiefs and because no Marine had taken part in it.[53] Significantly in light of later controversies, the study assumed that the United States would not invade North Vietnam—the one step which, in its authors' view, would bring about active Chinese and/or Soviet intervention—would not use nuclear or chemical weapons, and would not undertake the mass bombing of North Vietnamese civilians per se. The study's assumed strategy consisted, first, of relentless offensive military operations within South Vietnam, designed to force the Viet Cong and North Vietnamese forces to fight at a pace they could not sustain and thereby destroy them; and second, of an expanded bombing campaign against North Vietnamese lines of communication and POL stocks, *as well as the mining of North Vietnamese harbors,* which McNaughton had urged Goodpaster's group to discount. The study also advocated an immediate strike against North Vietnamese air defense capabilities and ground action against the Ho Chi Minh trail in Laos.

The study suggested that the forty-four battalions now requested should "establish superiority and turn the tide of battle in our favor"—something which Westmoreland had explicitly said they would *not* do. It added, however, that depending on DRV decisions to reinforce, anywhere from seven to thirty-five more battalions might be required. Even those estimates eventually proved much too low.

Should this strategy be pursued without restrictions, the authors of the study argued, we should "hopefully" be able to convince the Viet Cong and the North that they could not win and arrive at a settlement, or alternatively to reduce the insurgency to a level that the South Vietnamese might cope with alone. In sum, the authors clearly did not believe that the United States could win the war by bombing the North alone, although they assigned bombing the North a critical role in their strategy.

They raised some pointed questions about the effectiveness of American operations, and—like McNaughton—resorted to a species of statistical illogic to resolve them.

> The concept of tactical operations for the offensive within SVN is, at the present time, the heart of this problem, and the uncertainties that exist must be squarely recognized and acknowledged. With limited and local exceptions, the course of the war to date in SVN does not provide experience directly approximating what is now visualized. Lacking such operations, we cannot assert with certainty that tactics can be devised and operations conducted that will, in fact, put the DRV/VC battalions out of operation and keep them so. Nevertheless, several avenues of operation which are available permit a high order of confidence that such can be achieved.

a. Operations to locate and attack VC/DRV units to destroy them or render them ineffective as fighting units.

b. Operations to clear and occupy the base areas from which VC/DRV units operate and are supported.

c. Operations to establish major areas of strength, for example, in the central highlands or other major infiltration avenues, to interdict DRV support for the VC.

The logic of this list seemed to be that at least *one or two* of these options ought to prove effective, but that *all* of them would probably have to work to ensure victory. And even then, the authors acknowledged, another question remained to be answered: if the U.S. and third-country forces could put the enemy's battalion-sized units out of action, could South Vietnamese forces provide security to their territory and population with only advisory American assistance and limited support? This assumption, they argued, appeared reasonable, but deserved further study—a conclusion completely at variance with the totally negative experience of the last four years.

The study's authors, in short, argued that the war could be won within South Vietnam and along the Ho Chi Minh trail, helped by expanded bombing of the North and mining of Haiphong Harbor, as McNamara had already recommended. Operations against Laos, however, would in any event have to await a much larger American build-up. The study was the Pentagon's explanation of how American troops would win the war, and McNamara incorporated some of it into his final report. McGeorge Bundy received a copy of the study on July 21, confirming that McNamara saw it in some sense as a response to Bundy's "rash to the point of folly" memorandum of June 30.[54]

The President and the Secretary of State were pushing ahead. Rusk on July 15 asked the CIA for an estimate—whose drafters should be limited "to the absolute minimum for security reasons"—of North Vietnamese, Communist Chinese, and Soviet reactions to an increase of U.S. forces to 175,000 by November 1, a 225,000-man call-up of reserves, increases in draft calls and tours of duty, a $2–3 billion budget supplement, and possible air attacks on Hanoi and Haiphong.[55] The answers to these questions did not arrive, alas, until after McNamara's return. On July 16, the day that McNamara's discussions in South Vietnam began, his deputy, Cyrus Vance, met with President Johnson three times. The President expressed his intention to deploy thirty-four American battalions as requested, but explained that he could not possibly ask for more than $300–400 million in additional funds before January without killing his legislative program.[56] In Saigon, McNamara found Generals Ky and Thieu anxious to increase American forces all the way to the 200,000 mark, but desirous of keeping them away from populated areas. The South Vietnamese economy was now in shambles, with exports crippled by the war, and Ky and Thieu also wanted to double American dollar aid under the commodity import program for the next year. Meanwhile, they were concerned about the inflationary effect of the black market exchange rate.[57]

A number of chance occurrences marked the week before McNamara returned home. On July 14 a leading administration opponent of the war, Adlai Stevenson, collapsed and died in London. Stevenson had publicly supported Johnson's policies right until the end, but James Reston, in a *New York Times* obituary, referred to Stevenson's discomfort over both Vietnam and the Dominican Republic. Five days later President Johnson shocked the nation by replacing Stevenson with Supreme Court Justice Arthur J. Goldberg, allowing Johnson to fill the so-called Jewish seat on the Court (previously occupied by Louis Brandeis and Felix Frankfurter) with the Washington attorney Abe Fortas, who had provided Johnson with indispensable assistance during at least two earlier crises of his career.[58] On the day after Stevenson's death, Colonel Pham Ngoc Thao, the inveterate coup plotter and, almost certainly, VC agent who had gotten so much good American press in 1961 and 1962, was shot and killed during an attempt to arrest him in Saigon.[59]

Meanwhile, while McNamara visited Saigon, Ambassador-at-Large Averell Harriman—never in favor under Johnson, who had demoted him from Undersecretary for Political Affairs to Ambassador-at-Large—visited Moscow to discuss Vietnam with Soviet Premier Aleksei Kosygin. Apparently to promote the idea of its interest in negotiations, the administration added Belgrade, Bonn, London, and even New Delhi to his itinerary before he returned home.

Harriman and Kosygin made no progress on Vietnam, because Harriman loyally repeated the administration line with respect to the nature of the conflict, the need to punish the North from the air, and American willingness to open unconditional "discussions." But their talks show, in retrospect, how Vietnam had now overshadowed all the issues which in the Kennedy administration had enjoyed a vastly higher priority—and how the decision to pursue the war with maximum American objectives had deprived Washington of significant diplomatic opportunities.

When Harriman met with Kosygin for the first time on July 15, the Soviet Premier tried to restart the forward momentum of U.S.-Soviet relations. Kosygin immediately listed six areas in which he hoped to improve relations with Washington: the non-proliferation of nuclear weapons, an end to all nuclear tests, a reduction of nuclear weapons, cuts in overall military expenditures, increased trade, and increased personal contacts. But he specifically criticized the United States for having violated the understanding between Gromyko and Rusk and increasing its defense budget by $700 million to pay for the Vietnam War, while the Soviets cut their defense expenditures by $500 million rubles. Kosygin in this meeting declined to enter into much discussion about Vietnam, but repeatedly asked Harriman whether he really believed a real government existed in South Vietnam. Then, violating a taboo which Khrushchev had always respected, he related Vietnam to tensions in the international communist world:

> The US is aware, [Kosygin] said, that differences exist in the international Communist movement on questions of war and peace between the Chinese and the Soviets. He felt the US was doing all it can to prove Mao right and the Soviets wrong in this dispute. "You follow pro-Chinese policies," he said, and are responsible for tensions in the world and war in the East. People of that region are turning against the US and by your actions you prove the Chinese thesis that war is inevitable . . . He stated that he had never said this to anyone else and hoped that I would communicate it to President Johnson.[60]

Kosygin was much more forthcoming in a second conversation on July 21. Harriman reported that President Johnson had read the record of their earlier conversation, and conveyed vague assurances of the President's interest in disarmament, bilateral relations, and personal contacts—but no specific responses to Kosygin's six areas. But Kosygin expressed pleasure that Johnson was concerned by some of the same problems, and said he was convinced "that progress could be made on the[se] questions, if it were not for Vietnam." Should that problem be solved, he suggested, a bilateral or multilateral summit might lead to rapid progress in areas like non-proliferation and disarmament.

Since their first meeting, Harriman had received confirmation of the Rusk-Gromyko exchange over defense budgets, and he presented figures designed to show that the projected fiscal 1966 budget, while increased over 1965, would still be smaller than 1964. Kosygin was not particularly impressed, and suggested that the unilateral American decision to increase the budget violated the confidential understanding of the last year. Given the strategic arms race that was about to break out, the understanding on reduced defense budgets looms as a missed opportunity of major proportions.

When the two men returned to the topic of Vietnam, Kosygin urged the United States to deal directly with Hanoi, bypassing Peking, and to make a counterproposal to Hanoi's four points. "Our Vietnamese comrades," he said, "do not rule out a political settlement . . . Naturally, this would be on the basis of the retention of the 17th parallel." Kosygin, who had visited Vietnam only months earlier and who throughout these conversations showed a sophistication far superior to Khrushchev's, summarized the situation.

> The question of Vietnam will never be settled by force, he said. You will only have more bloodshed and, in the end the Vietnamese will finally liberate themselves from dependence on the U.S., as people have elsewhere. It would be a blot on the U.S. and the responsibility would inescapably lie on the president who, by force of circumstances, is responsible for all American actions. It seems to me that this would not be in his interest or in the interest of the American people.[61]

After visiting West Germany, Harriman on July 29 met with Yugoslav President Tito, who was already emerging as a leader of the nonaligned movement. After Harriman explained the American position, Tito replied that Yugoslavia regarded the Vietnam situation as a danger to peace. "It is necessary in the first place," he said, "for the U.S. to cease bombing North Vietnam. This policy is extremely unpopular in the whole world, especially for humanitarian reasons . . . The U.S. should announce that it is going to discontinue bombing and that it is prepared for talks on the basis of the 1954 Geneva agreements." Then the Yugoslav leader said that he would like to talk frankly.

He believes that the U.S., which desires peace, should at this juncture . . . demonstrate broadness of mind to international developments in general. The impression is often left that the U.S. is helping the most reactionary forces in the world . . . Tito said he was deeply impressed by President Kennedy's capacity to listen to others. When he was in Washington in 1963, Kennedy had asked about Tito's impressions of Latin America. Tito said he answered that many Latin Americans do not like the U.S. despite the aid being given because the U.S. was assisting various reactionary cliques who were in power. Tito said Kennedy agreed, pointing out that he had just withdrawn an ambassador from a Latin American country where a military putsch had just taken place. Kennedy's intention was to pursue progressive policies.[62]

There was not the slightest chance that the United States would agree to the strict observance of the 1954 Accords.

Harriman also visited London, where Prime Minister Wilson praised him for keeping the dialogue with the Soviet Union going but made no attempt to alter American policy. His trip, combined with numerous other indications over the last six months, showed clearly that all the world's major powers, including the British, French, Soviets, Indians, and Japanese, would have welcomed a bombing halt, a reconvened Geneva conference, and a settlement reflecting the balance of military and political power within South Vietnam itself. The conversations with Kosygin suggest that the détente which Kennedy had sought throughout his presidency, and which he had begun to achieve with the test ban treaty, might now have gone much further. Harriman, who had helped both President Roosevelt and President Kennedy establish a constructive relationship with the Soviets, would have welcomed a chance to pursue these opportunities, but he knew that his government, as yet, had no intention of doing so. The United States, without any significant enthusiastic support from the international community, had decided to fight the Vietnam War at the cost of major opportunities in East-West relations, and even at the risk of war with a major Communist power. A joint State-Defense paper prepared around this time foresaw possible escalation by the North Vietnamese and Chinese leading eventually to the use of American nuclear weapons.[63]

McNamara's final report, dated July 20—the day before he arrived home—began by stating this policy in so many words. "Our object in Vietnam," he began, "is to create conditions for a favorable outcome by demonstrating to the VC/DRV that the odds are against their win-ning . . . *if possible,* without causing the war to expand into one with China or the Soviet Union and in a way which preserves support of the American people and, *hopefully,* of our allies and friends." Continuing, he implied that reducing the insurgency to a manageable level (and per-suading the Viet Cong to become a political organization rather than a military one) was more likely without a cease-fire agreement than with one. Then he finessed the issue of scaling down American objectives: "We do not need now to address the question whether ultimately we would settle for something less than the nine fundamentals; because de-ployment of the forces recommended in paragraph 5 is prerequisite to the achievement of *any* acceptable settlement, and a decision can be made later, when bargaining becomes a reality, whether to compromise in any particular."[64]

McNamara's specific recommendations followed his July 1 draft closely: forty-three battalions by the end of the year, with another 100,000 possibly needed during 1966, and perhaps more later. Just how many more emerged from other parts of his memo: a two-year call-up of 235,000 reservists and national guardsmen, and an increase in regular forces of 375,000 men, yielding 600,000 new troops by the middle of 1966. The report described their eventual mission in lan-guage lifted directly from the Goodpaster study: "keeping the enemy at a disadvantage, maintaining a tempo such as to deny them time to recu-perate or regain their balance, and pressing the fight against VC/DRV main force units in South Vietnam to run them to the ground and destroy them," while also increasing enemy supply requirements and making enemy lines of communication insecure. McNamara recom-mended increasing Rolling Thunder sorties slowly from 2,500 to 4,000 a month, but dropped the proposals for immediate attacks around Ha-noi and Haiphong and the mining of Haiphong harbor. Continuing his attempts to reconcile the irreconcilable, McNamara also repeated his recommendations for expanded contacts with Hanoi and the NLF, while noting that Taylor, Alexis Johnson, and Ambassador-designate Lodge all rejected this proposal.

McNamara also tried to discount any negative political impact of large American forces, quoting Thieu and Ky that the people knew the United States did not intend to create a colony. He was optimistic re-garding Chinese reaction to the new program, but discussed the possibility of North Vietnamese intervention without explaining exactly how the United States would meet it. He conceded that U.S. forces would not be numerous enough to make a difference in a guerrilla conflict, but argued that they could make "a significant difference" in the "'Third-Stage' or conventional war" that seemed to be evolving. But then he faced up to the logic of this argument: that the best his program could do would be to force the VC back into the kind of campaign they had waged from 1960 through 1964. In such a case, he suggested, "A fairly large number of US (or perhaps 'international') forces may be required to stay in Vietnam."

President Johnson met with his senior advisers on Wednesday, July 21, and with the Joint Chiefs on Thursday, July 22, to discuss these recommendations. He spent the weekend at Camp David, where he convened a small meeting of domestic advisers on Sunday, July 25. Two long meetings on Monday, July 26, dealt with plans to hit several SAM sites around Hanoi, after a SAM had downed an American plane. On Tuesday, July 27, Johnson explained his decision to the National Security Council and the congressional leadership, and on Wednesday, July 28, he announced it at a press conference.

McGeorge Bundy's preliminary memorandum to Johnson on the morning of July 21 treated the military decisions as a settled question, and these meetings—read against the background of the previous eight months—bear out his view. Although George Ball received for the first time an opportunity to argue his position before an audience of both senior and second-level officials, Johnson used the meetings largely to bring Ball's isolation into relief and to hone arguments against his position. The truly critical decisions the meetings had to reach involved not the administration's policy and strategy in Vietnam itself but the presentation of the decision to the American public and the mobilization of American armed forces to carry it out. And here, once again, Johnson moved as cautiously as possible, actively enlisting the cooperation of the congressional leadership in his attempts to downplay the significance of what he was doing.

The first meeting on July 21 began with an hour-long discussion outside the President's hearing. It included five State Department representatives (Rusk, Ball, William Bundy, Unger, and Lodge), three from Defense (McNamara, Vance, and McNaughton), General Wheeler from the Chiefs, two from the CIA (Admiral William Raborn, the new director, and Richard Helms), two from the NSC (McGeorge Bundy and Chester Cooper), USIA Director Carl Rowan, and Bill Moyers and Jack Valenti of Johnson's own staff. McNamara handed out, and later collected, copies of his report. While laying out the planned deployments and proposed reserve call-ups, he said nothing about bombing the North. Lodge immediately opposed the proposed contacts with Hanoi and the NLF as likely to encourage the enemy, and McGeorge Bundy supported him. Rusk talked about the need to explain the call-up of reserves to the American people, and offered to take the lead himself.

When Johnson entered the room, McNamara summarized his recommendations again, and the President turned, instinctively, to the issue of explaining them to the public:

> The President indicated that, *when the time came to call up the reserves,* he wanted a full statement of the situation in Vietnam which required additional US troops. What consequences are likely to flow from a call-up? (The McNamara paper gives no sense of victory, but rather of a continuing stalemate.) Why can't we get more third country troops? What are the alternatives available to us? We could tell the GVN that we are leaving, but is this an option we wish to pursue at this time? If we pull out of Vietnam now, will we have to call up more troops and suffer more casualties at some later date? *We have explored all initiatives for a peaceful settlement, to an extent, perhaps, that we might already look weak.* In short, what are our present options, why do we select the recommended number of troops rather than more or fewer? What will this increased force accomplish?[65]

In response, McNamara and especially General Wheeler explained that the American forces would take the offensive against Viet Cong main-force units. Admiral Raborn reported the CIA's view that the enemy would avoid major battles, but McNamara replied that if they did, "the ARVN could proceed with pacification activities and consolidate its oil spots." He did not suggest just why the ARVN would suddenly reverse the trend in the countryside that had persisted for about five years, and no one asked. After the meeting, Chester Cooper wrote Bundy that the United States would in fact need a massive pacification effort in addition to McNamara's program.[66] Then Johnson asked if anyone dissented from McNamara's recommendations, and Ball spoke up, suggesting that the United States take some short-term losses rather than run the risk of a major war. Johnson's reply showed him at his consensus-building best, and reaffirmed the belief that had determined his policies since early 1964: "The President felt that Mr. Ball clearly identified the dangers before us, *but did not get the impression that Mr. Ball opposes the McNamara report.* The President wanted to minimize the dangers of this enterprise but *felt that he had no other choice.* He would seriously like to explore other alternatives, now or as we proceed."

To Rusk, nothing had changed over the last four years. The Secretary of State volunteered that "if we had met the challenge posed in 1961 by sending 50,000 men to South Vietnam, Hanoi may have hesitated to proceed with its actions against the South . . . We should probably have committed ourselves heavier in 1961."[67] Even though North Vietnam was already sending troops south in response to the American build-up, Rusk clung to his version of the lesson of the 1930s: that firmness alone could deter Communist aggression anywhere in the world. After further discussion that raised, but did not really settle, some important military issues, Johnson adjourned the meeting until 2:30 in the afternoon, when Ball would again take the floor.

Drawing on his memorandum of late June, Ball compared aid to South Vietnam to "giving cobalt treatment to a terminal cancer case." Johnson replied that "the situation was serious. He regretted that we were embroiled in Vietnam. But we *are* there." He then asked two important questions: Could Westerners fight successfully in Vietnam? And could the United States fight on behalf of a constantly changing government?

Rather than answer those questions, Bundy, Rusk, and Mc Namara—for at least the third time—rejected Ball's proposals *seriatim.* Bundy called the "cancer analogy" weak, and said we could decide if our policy was wrong after giving it a try. Rusk stressed the dangers if the Communist world came to doubt our will. "It is more important," he said, "to convince the Communist leadership [that we will see it through] than to worry about the opinion of non-Communist countries"—a notable attitude for the senior diplomat of the entire Western alliance. "I am more optimistic than some of my colleagues," he said. "I don't believe the VC have made large advances among the Vietnamese people." McNamara once again endorsed Rusk's views of the consequences of cutting our losses and implied that a further 100,000 men could pacify the country within two years. General Wheeler, correcting him, said the United States might make "definite progress" within three years. Lodge also rejected Ball's pessimism and referred specifically to the Munich analogy. Concluding, Johnson asked those present to "constantly remind the people that we are doing other things besides bombing." The decision had obviously been made, and Ball acknowledged that he had had his "day in court."

The two meetings, while reestablishing a consensus and addressing the question of how to sell administration policy, had not directly addressed what now loomed as the most difficult question, the reserve call-up. In a memo written late on July 21, McGeorge Bundy mentioned that the President had told McNamara that he could ask for only $300–400 million in new funds now, and reported that McNamara did not think he could pay for the planned call-up with less than $2 billion.[68] Johnson apparently decided to address this over the weekend at Camp David with some of his domestic advisers.

The *New York Times* on July 22 published a picture of the previous day's meeting, predicted several more, and expected a troop increase. A Saigon story accurately reported that MACV expected to increase to over 200,000 men by early 1966.[69] At noon that day the President met with McNamara and Vance, the Joint Chiefs, the three service secretaries, and his trusted friend Clark Clifford, who had already emerged as an opponent of escalation.

Contrary to the argument of H. R. McMaster in *Dereliction of Duty*, President Johnson at this meeting did not restrict the options that the Chiefs could discuss, much less imply that McNamara's existing request represented a limit beyond which he would not go. The President gave each Chief a careful hearing and used them as sounding boards for some of Ball's suggestions and objections—although no one from the State Department attended. Chief of Naval Operations Admiral David MacDonald insisted that "sooner or later we will force them to the conference table," and suggested that our allies would lose faith in us if we did not act. McNamara volunteered that the current new 100,000-man increment might easily be matched by a second 100,000 early in 1966. (JCS plans completed at the end of July foresaw nearly 300,000 Americans in South Vietnam by the end of 1966).[70] When Johnson asked whether the North Vietnamese would match American escalation, General Wheeler said they would risk only two divisions, so as not to leave themselves open to an invasion of the North. "From the military point of view," he added, "we can handle, *if we are determined to do so,* China and North Vietnam"—an obvious reference to nuclear weapons. MacDonald specifically recommended both 100,000-man increments, unspecified increases in air attacks on North Vietnam, and appropriate reserve call-ups and draft calls.

General McConnell of the Air Force also called for expanding the bombing campaign to include "all military targets available to us in North Vietnam." But even with this and Westmoreland's troop requests, he was vague about what the United States would accomplish. "With these forces properly employed, and cutting off their supplies," he said, "we can do better than we're doing." Marine Corps Commandant General Greene made the most specific bombing recommendations, calling for strikes against POL, the MIGs, the IL-28s, and industrial targets. He also asked for 80,000 more Marines in addition to Westmoreland's request, and for a blockade of Haiphong and neutral Cambodia. (Valenti's record says nothing about mining Haiphong harbor.) Greene estimated that the war would last five years and require 500,000 troops, and said, "I think the U.S. people will back you."[71]

General Johnson of the Army also saw a "long-term" problem and referred briefly to the difficult political situation in South Vietnam. The President rejected his assurances that Red China would not intervene, and the general admitted that we would face "another ball game" if they did. President Johnson eventually inquired about casualties and intelligence, and asked McGeorge Bundy to summarize the case against the war, which Bundy did. Wheeler said that some American or international forces would have to remain in Vietnam indefinitely—again, a critical point, since it meant the United States could not offer to return to the 1954 Geneva Accords. "If we can secure the military situation," Wheeler concluded in a classic restatement of the Pentagon's view, "it seems likely that we can get some kind of stable government." When a skeptical Clark Clifford asked what the result of carrying out the military plan would be, Wheeler replied that "it would accomplish the political objective of maintaining South Vietnam as a free and independent State."[72]

Later that afternoon Johnson met again with Wheeler and roughly the same group of senior civilians from the day before. Johnson apparently still intended to call up reserves, but expressed more concern about playing the matter in low key, partly to avoid putting too much pressure on Moscow and Peking to assist Hanoi. McNamara said he could cut the military services' request for $12 billion by at least half. Rusk still seemed to think that both China and Russia might easily intervene if the United States unleashed all-out bombing against Hanoi. McNamara argued that bombing Haiphong would not end the war. For different reasons, the Secretaries of State and Defense obviously planned to stop the Joint Chiefs' recommendation for expanded bombing—one which Westmoreland would probably have opposed as well. Johnson also argued that the administration had to publicize its peace proposals more heavily, and confirmed his intention to speak to Congress the next day. Press Secretary Moyers, briefing the press, denied any discussions of a reserve call-up—as it turned out, a significant straw in the wind.[73]

Significantly, the President avoided keeping any records of the meetings at which major decisions were actually reached. On Friday, July 23, he met for two more hours with Rusk, McNamara, McGeorge Bundy, Ball, Wheeler, his domestic aide Horace Busby, and Moyers, but no record of this meeting has survived.[74] McNamara, however, seems to have presented three plans. All of them would deploy 175,000 men by the end of the year, but the first would call up reserves and announce the deployment of another 100,000 in 1966; the second would announce the deployment of only 55,000 additional troops at this time and ask for reserve call-up authority in December; and the third would avoid any reserve call-up at all.[75] Johnson apparently decided to combine the least threatening aspects of the second and third, which McNamara had described as a program that would minimize "the actions which might induce Communist China or the Soviet Union to take initiatives they might not otherwise undertake." That night the Secretary of the Navy told Marine Corps Commandant General Greene that no reserve call-up would take place, and McNamara told the Joint Chiefs the same thing at lunch the next day, adding that any supplemental budget request would have to wait until January. Picking up from Thursday's meeting, he suggested that mobilization and a debate might provoke an extreme reaction from the Russians and the Chinese. Challenged by Admiral MacDonald, McNamara "smilingly replied that mobilization of the Reserves would indeed cause considerable debate, that a lot of minority votes would result, that there was certain to be a strong vote against a call-up, and that the Communists might get the wrong impression regarding division among our ranks."[76] On the same day the State Department cabled Saigon that early the following week Johnson was expected to announce deployments along the lines Mc-Namara had discussed.[77]

Johnson entertained several guests at Camp David over the weekend, including the new Ambassador to the United Nations, Arthur Goldberg, McNamara, and Clark Clifford. Clifford, who had been deeply impressed by Ball's presentation the previous Wednesday and had spoken with him on Thursday evening, pleaded for an attempt to reduce public discussion of Vietnam, wait out the summer monsoon, and look for a way out. The alternative, he argued, was a five-year, 50,000-casualty war that China and Russia would never allow the United States to win, and a "catastrophe for my country."[78] Clifford's dissent may have encouraged Johnson to play the next round of deployments in the lowest possible key. On Sunday McNamara apparently told Johnson that the Pentagon could in fact provide the necessary forces for Vietnam without a reserve call-up.[79]

Before Johnson could announce any new policy, another crisis erupted when a Soviet-supplied (and probably Soviet-crewed) SAM missile shot down an American fighter over North Vietnam on July 24. Taylor immediately recommended retaliation, and the President, the Vice President (included in a major Vietnam meeting for the first time in many months), and senior advisers spent most of the late afternoon and early evening of July 26 trying to decide what to do. The same meeting also rejected Ambassador Goldberg's proposal for a new Security Council resolution calling for peace. The President ultimately approved strikes against two sites located some miles from the Hanoi area, in order to make it possible to continue attacks on various targets on the Rolling Thunder list. In a sad portent of things to come, military authorities eventually concluded that at least one of the sites, and possibly both, were empty, and the United States lost six planes during the attack.[80] In one respect, however, American firmness had been successful. Unbeknownst to Washington, the Chinese government in mid-July had reneged on an earlier project and declined to provide MIG pilots to the North Vietnamese.[81]

On the same evening, July 26, State cabled to Saigon the text of an expected statement by a high-ranking American official explaining the new American decisions in Vietnam. The statement referred to the meetings of the last few days, reaffirmed American objectives, and announced that a total of thirty-four American battalions would reach South Vietnam by November, raising forces to 170,000 men. It also reported an approach from Ambassador Goldberg to U Thant in the hope of bringing about peace, and laid out a new version of American terms:

> . . . the U.S. looks forward to the day when relations between North Vietnam and South Vietnam can be worked out by peaceful means—including a free decision by the peoples of all Vietnam on the matter of reunification. These principles imply and include the use of free election under international supervision, just as soon as the end of aggression permits.
>
> These purposes in essence are the purposes of the Geneva Agreements of 1954. The failure of the 1954 Agreements was not in purpose but in practice—not in the quality of the objectives, but in the effectiveness of the instruments. When there is a new settlement in Southeast Asia, it must be based on stronger and more lasting guarantees than those of 1954.[82]

The reference to elections under international supervision was, as Taylor and Alexis Johnson explained to Thieu and Ky, designed to avoid having any such elections, since "Communists never have accepted international supervision of elections and can be expected to oppose in future."[83] The emphasis on stronger guarantees than in 1954 was obviously designed to lay the foundation for the indefinite presence of American troops, which McNamara had recognized as necessary.

Yet this statement was never made. By the time the NSC met at 5:40 PM the next day, Johnson had reverted to form, deciding to make the least threatening statement possible consistent with a bare minimum of short-term accuracy. At that meeting, which Wheeler attended for the Chiefs, Rusk repeated that the other side had shown no interest in talks. Then McNamara said that a total of just twenty-eight—not thirty-four—new battalions were now necessary, and that the administration needed a billion dollars now and more in January. After a whole month's frenzied debate, Johnson was not even willing to acknowledge the full McNamara program for the remainder of 1965.

Ambassador Lodge then told the meeting that the Senate Foreign Relations Committee had questioned him sharply over the need for a ten-to-one ratio in counterguerrilla war, noting what an astronomical number of American troops this would require. General Wheeler replied that the mobility and firepower of American and South Vietnamese forces might reduce the necessary ratio to four to one. "With the additional forces to be sent to South Vietnam," he continued, "General Westmoreland believes we can hold our present position and possibly move back into areas now contested." Westmoreland had said nothing of the kind. Referring to a map showing VC-controlled areas, Rusk argued arbitrarily that it overstated enemy gains.

Johnson then carefully stated five choices before the United States. The first was "to use our massive power, including SAC, to bring the enemy to his knees," which less than 10 percent of "our people" urged. (In fact, no one had proposed such a strategy.) The second was simply to leave, but "most people feel our national honor is at stake and that we must keep our commitments there," as made, he said, by Eisenhower, Kennedy, and himself. The third was to leave forces at their present levels and take more casualties. The fourth was to ask Congress for everything the United States might need, including "money, authority to call up the reserves, acceptance of the deployment of more combat battalions." Although many favored this course, it would allow Hanoi "to ask the Chinese Communists and the Soviets to increase aid and add to their existing commitments."

Thus the administration had chosen the fifth alternative, "to do what is necessary to meet the present situation, but not to be unnecessarily provocative to either the Russians or the Communist Chinese." The United States would provide the men Westmoreland said he needed (although McNamara had, in effect, lied about that by implying that only twenty-eight battalions would go by January), but would not "brag about what we are doing nor thunder at the Chinese Communists and the Russians." Holding until January, the President said, would give Ambassadors Lodge and Goldberg and "the diplomats" a chance to work. "If Russia, England, etc. wouldn't get all excited about calling up reserves," he said, "I would do it right now." When he asked if anyone questioned this decision, no one did.[84] The President was announcing William Bundy's policy while executing McNamara's.

Six senators and four representatives then joined the senior leadership, and the President laid out the alternatives again, focusing on the choice between numbers four and five. Questioned repeatedly by Representative Gerald Ford, Johnson eventually admitted that "under alternative four he would have to get a new bill and a great big reserve plan and go through a big process. Under five we would simply put $1.8 billion or whatever into the appropriation bills on the Senate side and then get in order for January." Pushed by Representative Leslie Arends, McNamara acknowledged that thirteen more battalions would still leave Westmoreland with an additional requirement of "further forces" before January 1. Senator Mansfield once again read a statement expressing his concern over the decision, but announced that he would support it. He submitted another brilliant critique of the policy the next day, reporting grave doubts among a most distinguished group of senators.[85] Pushed by the Republican Bourke Hickenlooper of Iowa, who clearly wanted more forceful action, Johnson confirmed that "now settlement was not a practical problem, because the Communists thought they were winning." Speaker John McCormack concluded the meeting with a promise of united support from "all true Americans." When the leadership left, Johnson spoke briefly to Rusk, McNamara, Bundy, and three personal aides. He remarked "that we were prolonging the agony for 90 days and that he wanted a statement of 700 words, the essence of which would be that he was giving Westmoreland what he needed. Secretary McNamara repeated the thirteen battalion, 50,000 men figure, and expressed his confidence on the handling of the matter."[86]

The next day, Wednesday, July 28, Johnson opened his press conference with a somewhat longer statement laying out the nation's goals and stakes in South Vietnam. He confirmed the dispatch of the Airmobile division—a decision he had made about six weeks earlier—and other troops raising American strength to 125,000 men. "Additional forces will be needed later," he said, "and they will be sent as requested." He reiterated at some length his readiness for "unconditional discussions" and described a new appeal to U Thant. And he closed with an expression of deep regret at the need to send young Americans into war.

> It is now my opportunity to help every child get an education, to help every Negro and every American citizen have an equal opportunity, to help every family get a decent home, and to help bring healing to the sick and dignity to the old . . .
>
> But I also know, as a realistic public servant, that as long as there are men who hate and destroy, we must have the courage to resist, or we will

see it all, all that we have built, all that we hope to build, all of our dreams for freedom—all, *all* will be swept away on the flood of conquest.

So, too, this shall not happen. We will stand in Vietnam.[87]

The statement worked brilliantly. The *New York Times* lead story gave equal play to the 50,000-man increase (actually only half of what was planned) and the President's eagerness for discussions, and even referred, erroneously, to American "offers to negotiate." Members of Congress, especially those who had expressed reservations, were reported "relieved" by the course the President had chosen, and Mansfield praised the President for speaking in a "calm and deliberately measured manner" and for seeking "an honorable settlement." Tom Wicker wrote on July 30 that the President wanted simply to raise the United States to a position of equality with the Viet Cong, and then to negotiate. Even Walter Lippmann telephoned George Ball on July 30 and gave Johnson credit for "quite an advance in his press conference." Ball agreed that it was "quite a breakthrough" and assured Lippmann that events were not yet in the saddle.[88]

In the same press conference, Johnson announced his choice of Abe Fortas for the Supreme Court. Two days later, on July 30, he signed the Medicare Bill in Independence, Missouri, and presented former President Truman with Medicare Card no. 1. The Congress had already passed the Voting Rights Act and a huge Education Bill. Johnson had a 65 percent approval rating. The Gemini program, the next step on the way to the moon, had just completed a spectacular mission, including a space walk. The economy had been steadily expanding for four years and five months. Unemployment was 4.5 percent; annual inflation was less than 1 percent. The deficit for the fiscal year ending June 30, 1965, was $3.8 billion (less than $20 billion even in 1997 dollars). One U.S. dollar bought four Deutschmarks and 360 Japanese yen. The Interstate Highway System was well on its way to completion. *The Sound of Music* was the most popular movie of the year. America's colleges—with the sole exception of the University of California at Berkeley—were filled with well-dressed, industrious, and obedient undergraduates, and in June, in a cover story on the Palisades, California, high school class of 1965, *Time* had announced that American youth seemed to be on the verge of a new golden age.

No one knew that a whole era of American history was over.

16

Bad History, Wrong War

★

From the time of the Geneva conference of 1954 through the moment of the American decision to go to war in Vietnam in 1965, Indochina had figured as one of many battlegrounds in the Cold War. There as elsewhere, successive administrations tried to prevent the further spread of Communism, first economically and politically, then through an advisory role, and finally with direct military intervention. All these measures reflected the containment policy that the United States followed for more than four decades after the Second World War, and President Johnson therefore found it easy to claim, as he frequently did, that he was merely continuing his predecessors' policies. Yet the simple formula of "containment" could be applied in many different ways. Johnson's foreign policy differed in subtle but critical ways from Kennedy's, and therefore led him to take the steps that Kennedy had consistently rejected.

Despite the sweeping rhetoric of his inaugural address, Kennedy never regarded the Cold War as a simple matter of opposing Communism wherever it appeared. Certainly he built up the American military substantially and contemplated military intervention in certain key areas—most notably in Cuba—but we have seen that military moves were never more than one part of his strategy. Throughout his tenure, he paid at least as much attention to keeping in step with major European allies, improving America's reputation among emerging nations, and looking for areas of agreement with the Soviet Union. The recently released transcripts of the ExCom meetings during the Cuban missile crisis show how those particular considerations decisively inclined him against war even in October 1962, and led him to a peaceful solution of the crisis.[1] Even then, faced with the opportunity to eliminate Fidel Castro with the initial support of the American people, the President concluded that the possibility of Soviet retaliation in Berlin and the likely negative reaction of European allies made the risk of war too great. Here, too, he found himself in opposition to many of his senior civilian and military advisers, but his approach prevailed and successfully removed Soviet missiles from Cuba while laying the foundation for improved relations with Moscow.

Similar considerations had played a critical role in Kennedy's 1961 decision to seek the neutralization of Laos. Confronted repeatedly with proposals for intervention, he had always referred to the opposition of the British and the French and the lack of enthusiasm among Congress and the American people for war in Southeast Asia. He had also kept the basic strategic facts of the situation firmly in mind: that North Vietnam and China could respond to any American intervention with the infusion of hundreds of thousands of men. The American involvement in South Vietnam grew dramatically under his Presidency, but he never regarded it as anything but a liability. We shall never know what he would have decided had he realized that the pro-Western position in South Vietnam was collapsing, but we do know how he had handled a similar situation in Laos, and that he rejected several proposals for American troops in South Vietnam.

We also know that Kennedy would never have made a decision to fight in Southeast Asia in isolation from his broader foreign policy goals. Such a decision would have divided him, as it divided Johnson, from many important American allies and neutrals, and would have temporarily destroyed the prospect of improving relations with the Soviets. While Johnson was aware of these problems, he never allowed them significantly to influence his policy. The record of Kennedy's term in office suggests that they would have influenced him very heavily indeed.

The Johnson administration took a much more straightforward approach to the containment of Communism. Its decision to fight in South Vietnam in 1965 grew above all out of an obsession with avoiding the mistakes, as administration leaders saw them, of the 1930s. Had Britain, France, and the United States opposed the initial stages of German and Japanese aggression, these men believed, the Second

World War would not have taken place. Those like Churchill who had vainly called for such a policy during the 1930s had been right, and now they were determined to act as they thought Churchill would have done, even if they could not build an overwhelming consensus among the American people behind such a course of action.[2] In light of their experience, Johnson, McNamara, Rusk, and Taylor seemed to feel, they had no other option. In their own way, they felt they were doing what their leader Franklin Roosevelt had done. But this view ignored crucial aspects of Roosevelt's policies and strategies. Had they understood Roosevelt's moves more clearly, they might have been able to see Vietnam in a different light.

Confronted by the threat of German and Japanese expansion in the late 1930s and early 1940s, Roosevelt had not rushed blindly to confront these nations, but had gradually altered his policy to meet the changing circumstances that the United States faced. Roosevelt, like many Americans and, certainly, most Englishmen, seems to have regarded the Munich agreement of 1938 as a reasonable risk to try to secure peace. In September 1939 he and most Americans apparently believed that Britain and France could once again defeat Germany. The United States, in any case, had little military weight to throw into the scales. After the war both Roosevelt's partisans and his detractors argued that he had decided at a very early date, and certainly by the fall of 1940, to enter the war in Europe; but recent treatments have cast a great deal of doubt on this view.

Rather than try to get the United States into the war as soon as possible, Roosevelt seems to have tailored American commitments to American and Allied capabilities. In the summer of 1940 he hesitated to aid Britain both because his military leadership advised against it and because he truly did not know if Britain could hold out. When he did agree to send fifty destroyers, he secured bases that moved the American defense perimeter out into the Atlantic and promises that the British fleet would sail to America should Germany invade Britain in return. And during the first half of 1941 he concentrated on securing Britain and the Atlantic as a kind of forward defense position, without necessarily having any clear idea how Nazi Germany would be defeated.

Roosevelt's policy seemed to change after Germany attacked the Soviet Union. If the Soviets could resist the attack—and he was relatively optimistic on this point—then the United States might enter the war as part of a coalition that could deploy overwhelming force. In the weeks after the attack he became much more aggressive in stating his goals, taking offensive naval action in the Atlantic, and—crucially as it turned out—demanding that Japan withdraw from its advanced positions in the Pacific. The cut-off of Japanese petroleum imports led to the attack on Pearl Harbor on December 7, and to American entry into the war. With the combined resources of the USSR, Britain, and the United States, the defeat of the Axis was virtually assured. Roosevelt did not secure this result by opposing the Japanese and the Germans at the earliest possible opportunity, nor could he have. Instead, he waited until the nature of the threat they posed had become clear, and until their aggression had created a coalition that could deploy overwhelming power against them.[3]

Rather than appreciate the actual genius of Roosevelt's strategy and the contingency of its success, the next two generations of American leaders tried to apply oversimplified lessons of the 1930s and 1940s to the very different situation of the Cold War. They assumed, first of all, that the Soviet leaders were likely to resort to all-out war against the West if they thought they might have a reasonable chance of success. In fact, in my opinion, future historians will eventually conclude that neither the United States nor the Soviet Union could ever have risked all-out war against the other during the Cold War. Each in its own way was invulnerable to the other: the Soviets protected by manpower and their vast spaces, the United States by the oceans. Of course, both nations—first the United States, and then the Soviets—developed the capacity to inflict enormous (and eventually, virtually total) destruction upon each other with nuclear weapons, but neither could ever make use of this capability without running unacceptable risks to itself. In the Second World War the Axis powers were vulnerable to total defeat and occupation. In the Cold War the Americans and Soviets were not.

"War," wrote Clausewitz, "can be of two kinds, in the sense that either the objective is to *overthrow the enemy*—to render him politically helpless or militarily impotent, thus forcing him to sign whatever peace we please; or *merely to occupy some of his frontier-districts* so that we can annex them or use them for bargaining at the peace negotiations."[4] American military planning always treated a possible war with the Communist powers as falling with the first type, but in practice, since neither side could afford even to try to destroy the other, the Cold War became a limited war of the second type in which both sides, after securing their most important spheres of influence in the late 1940s and early 1950s, fought for influence in "frontier districts" in the absence of serious peace negotiations, which did not come about until the collapse of Communism. The conflict was usually political but occasionally military. Because these conflicts at the periphery could not produce decisive results in the overall struggle, the American people tolerated them only if they were successful, not too costly, and relatively brief. Even the Korean War exceeded these guidelines, although geographical and political factors enabled the United States to secure its original objective. And no administration ever found it possible to employ nuclear weapons in such a war, despite official policy and military doctrine. Fifty-five years after Hiroshima it is not clear that they are, indeed, useable weapons of war.

Conventional wisdom arises for many reasons and meets many needs. It must bear some relation to observed fact. In the wake of a crisis, it shows a strong tendency to vindicate the leaders who have brought the crisis to a successful conclusion. In the modern era of mass media, it tends to become more simplistic and, often, more emotional. During the 1950s and the 1960s the conventional wisdom regarding the origins of the Second World War and the appropriate response to the Cold War showed all these features. It provided a more than adequate basis for arming to deter the Soviet threat and for building and maintaining the Western alliance. But it was unsubtle, oversimplified, and in many ways naive. It failed to take account of many strategic and political realities, and one consequence was the catastrophe of the Vietnam War.

The Vietnam War was, inevitably, another limited war, in which the United States never sought the overthrow even of North Vietnam, much less of China or the Soviet Union. But here the United States never had any chance of achieving its objective of an "independent, non-Communist South Vietnam" at a remotely acceptable cost. As George Ball in particular argued so powerfully, South Vietnam was not a place to confront the Communists successfully.

Militarily, MACV's strategy and tactics could not, as it turned out, defeat the enemy. General Westmoreland, as we have seen, believed that American forces could decisively defeat Viet Cong and North Vietnamese main-force units with combined operations including ground forces, helicopters, and tactical air power. Such operations, which American forces conducted for about five years, from 1965 through 1970, and which South Vietnamese forces continued to conduct in 1971–1972 with American tactical air support, undoubtedly killed many enemy soldiers, but never decisively destroyed the enemy's capability to fight. The vast majority of American operations, like the vast majority of ARVN operations in the years 1961–1964, never made contact with the enemy. When main-force engagements occurred—as they did for the first time in the battle of the Ia Drang Valley in November 1965—they were very costly to both sides.

The tactical problem was compounded, as Westmoreland and the Pentagon had always acknowledged that it might be, by North Vietnam's reinforcement of the Viet Cong with more DRV troops. General Wheeler's casual reassurances during the late July meetings in Washington that the North would not dare send large forces into the South—and that American forces would "cream" them if they did—turned out to be wrong. As a result, demands for American forces rose rapidly. The July decisions raised American troop strength to about 184,000 by the end of 1965, but in December CINCPAC requested 221,000 *additional* troops in South Vietnam by the end of 1966. McNamara in March 1966 approved an even larger increase to 415,000 by the end of the year and 425,000 by June 1967. The Joint Chiefs, finding it impossible to meet these goals without a reserve call-up—which McNamara and Johnson still refused to make—scaled the 1966 figures back by about 47,000 men. McNamara, meanwhile, estimated in June 1966 that North Vietnamese strength in South Vietnam had doubled. At the end of the year he put enemy strength in South Vietnam at 275,000, including 54,000 North Vietnamese regulars.[5]

When Westmoreland tried to take the offensive against the most important enemy base areas—including the Iron Triangle north of Saigon and War Zones C and D—in early 1967, the North Vietnamese countered with attacks across the demilitarized zone. These attacks failed with heavy casualties, but their consequences were summarized as follows by Pentagon historians some years later:

> By the end of May [1967], enemy efforts to invade the northern provinces of South Vietnam had been repulsed, at least for the time being. But the

enemy, although thwarted in the north, had contributed to the disruption of offensive operations of free world forces elsewhere in South Vietnam. The redeployments made to reinforce positions on the DMZ had deprived commanders of troops urgently needed to fulfill their missions. Actually, even before this diversion of forces had taken place, the general offensive had bogged down. Forces available were simply not adequate to the task at hand. Major operations such as CEDAR FALLS and JUNCTION CITY had required the massing of from 25 to 30 battalions, which could not be spared from other tasks such as providing security for populated areas and LOCs. *The result was that combat operations against enemy main forces and bases could not be sustained.*[6]

Neither Westmoreland nor the Pentagon ever took sufficient account of the ways in which the hostile, Viet Cong–dominated landscape of South Vietnam degraded the capabilities of American forces by tying up large numbers of Americans in security duty. Westmoreland responded to the situation by requesting two more huge increments of troops that would raise total forces to 678,000 by mid-1969. After lengthy discussions during which McNamara actually proposed scaling down American objectives, President Johnson in July 1967 approved a total of nearly 540,000 American troops for South Vietnam.[7] During the second half of 1967 Westmoreland insisted upon dropping Viet Cong political cadres from official estimates of the enemy's strength to make the case that the United States was winning the war.[8]

During 1968 and 1969—beginning with the January 1968 Tet Offensive—the North Vietnamese and the Viet Cong launched offensives on an unprecedented scale, making these the two heaviest years of fighting and increasing both American and enemy casualties substantially. Contrary to a widely held view, the Tet Offensive marked the beginning, not the end, of the heaviest period of the war.[9] But despite all this, an interdepartmental study undertaken in the early weeks of the Nixon administration—NSSM-1—concluded that the United States had never inflicted casualties at a rate that the enemy could not replace.[10] Westmoreland's original strategic concept, based upon the destruction of enemy main-force units, had failed. It is very difficult to see how options like invasions of Laos or North Vietnam could have changed the calculus of the ground war, all the more so since we now know that China had prepared to intervene if the United States crossed the 17th parallel.[11]

Meanwhile, Westmoreland continued to leave the job of pacifying and protecting the population largely to the South Vietnamese. Not until 1967 did the Civil Operations and Rural Development (CORDS) program begin a sustained attack on the pacification problem, and it had only intermittent effectiveness. The Marines tried to pacify certain areas of I Corps with combined action platoons, but Westmoreland stopped this program.[12] Pacification operations, in any case, hardly ever had more than temporary effectiveness. As Eric Bergerud has shown in an important provincial study, after 1969 American troops on pacification missions frequently reduced the level of Viet Cong activity and improved population security, but the effects of these operations hardly ever survived the departure of American troops.[13] Despite temporary successes, Americans never found a way either decisively to reduce the entrenched political strength of the Viet Cong, which in the late 1950s and early 1960s had mobilized a high percentage of the most committed elements of the South Vietnamese population, or to increase the confidence of the people in the weak, heavily penetrated Saigon government.

The American failure to reduce enemy capabilities, which became obvious to the American public when the Viet Cong managed to mount its biggest offensive three years into the war, ultimately undermined public support and forced the Johnson and Nixon administrations to de-escalate the conflict and open peace talks. Indeed, we have seen that the Johnson administration realized from the beginning that the American people did not feel strongly enough about South Vietnam to send 300,000–500,000 men there for perhaps five years. That was why Johnson all the way through 1965 took such care to announce only the minimum deployments necessary, and to suggest that the administration favored a quick settlement. When the scale of the commitment finally became apparent in 1967, increasing numbers of Americans argued that the United States should either win the war rapidly—which it could not do—or abandon it; and after the Tet Offensive, most of the passion aroused by the war turned against the government, and, tragically, against the military. By 1969 opposition to the war was significantly reducing the effectiveness of the American forces.

The scale of the effort required and the lack of success eventually began to undermine, rather than support, the war's broader objectives. As Ball and McNaughton had tried to point out in 1964–1965, the United

States was fighting to preserve its credibility and the integrity of its commitments, but the long-term failure to achieve its objective despite the commitment of enormous resources undermined its credibility and threatened its ability to fulfill other commitments. Meanwhile, active international support for the American effort remained limited to a few staunchly anti-Communist Asian nations such as Nationalist China, Thailand, the Philippines, South Korea, and Australia. Washington purchased troops from South Korea and the Philippines at exorbitant rates, undoubtedly strengthening the military regime in Seoul and the Marcos government in the Philippines, which eventually proclaimed itself a dictatorship in 1972.

The "independent, non-Communist South Vietnam" that the United States sought required a strong non-Communist government. The Saigon government and the ARVN undoubtedly became somewhat stronger from 1965 through 1975—but never strong enough. In the spring of 1966 the government had to crush another neutralist Buddhist revolt, supported by portions of the ARVN, in the I Corps area.[14] That was the end of organized non-Communist opposition to the regime, although a peace candidate made a remarkable showing in the 1967 presidential elections, and found himself jailed as a result. The war moved hundreds of thousands—perhaps millions—of South Vietnamese civilians from the countryside to urban areas, where some of them became more reliable supporters of the government. But the Viet Cong, although weakened by Tet and the battles of 1968–1969, remained strong in much of the countryside, and regained a great deal of ground after the Communist Easter Offensive of 1972, which would probably have won the war for Hanoi without American advisers and American air power. Thus, to secure the return of American POWs in 1972, President Nixon and Henry Kissinger had to conclude an agreement that actually put the Viet Cong on an equal footing with the Saigon government. Viet Cong agents also continued to penetrate the very highest levels of the Saigon government.[15] And in 1975, when President Thieu tried to cope with the last North Vietnamese offensive by making a tactical withdrawal from the Highlands, most of the ARVN completely collapsed. To win the war, the United States had both to remove the military threat of enemy main-force units and to create a stable South Vietnamese government that could outdo the Viet Cong in maintaining the allegiance and mobilizing the resources of South Vietnamese society. It failed to do either one.

One great irony of the Vietnam war, nearly forty years after it began and thirty years after it ended, is its essential lack of effect upon the Cold War. Although the war undoubtedly undermined allied public confidence in the United States, it never really shook the foundations of the Western alliance. And because the United States was fighting a Vietnamese insurgency and a North Vietnamese Communist state—albeit supported by international Communism—even the fall of South Vietnam had few repercussions outside of Indochina, where Laos and Cambodia also came under Communist rule.[16] The war, however, stopped progress in Soviet-American relations for four critical years, during which the arms race entered a new and very important phase. Only in the Nixon administration did serious arms control talks begin, and their achievements were inevitably limited by the drastically expanded scale of the Soviet and American nuclear arsenals. At no time in the 1970s and 1980s did the two superpowers discover an arms control expedient nearly as effective as the informal Rusk-Gromyko understanding of 1964 on reduced defense budgets, which the Vietnam War brought to an end in the spring of 1965.

EPILOGUE
Tragedy and History

★

On July 26, 1965—as President Johnson announced, officially and for the first time, that the United States was fighting the war in Vietnam to victory—an eighteen-year-old boy named David Kaiser hiked to the top of Angels Landing in Zion National Park, in the red rock country of southern Utah. Surrounded by massive red and gray mountains and dazzled by the sun, he was deeply thrilled by his first encounter with his country's landscape, which he almost consciously associated with the greatness of his nation and its government. The United States had saved the world from Nazism in the Second World War and from Communism in the 1940s and 1950s. The government had moved to wipe out segregation, the great national shame he had despised all his life, and was working to end poverty. The Cuban missile crisis had tamed the Soviet Union, and standing firm in Vietnam would tame Chinese Communism. While he had not read President Johnson's April 7 speech carefully, none of it would have struck him as excessively ambitious or grandiose. In short, like so many of his contemporaries, he was proud to be a citizen of the greatest nation on earth, and glad to assume the burden of defending freedom around the globe. He did not know that the world of his childhood had come to an end seven weeks earlier, on his eighteenth birthday, when General Westmoreland had asked for forty-four battalions to fight the war, and he had no idea as he gazed upon this great American Olympus that his parents' generation had just made a catastrophic mistake.

Throughout their lives, those Americans born roughly in the first quarter of the twentieth century—whose ages at that moment ranged from forty to sixty-four—had helped the federal government solve enormous foreign and domestic problems, and now that they dominated the government themselves, they eagerly sought new challenges. Since their earliest adulthood, the government had provided them both with tasks to accomplish and with appropriate rewards. In the Civilian Conservation Corps they had cleared forests and built parks, in the PWA and WPA they had built bridges and schools, and in the Second World War American men and women had decisively tipped the material and military balance in favor of freedom. After the war, this GI generation had received unprecedented but well-deserved rewards: the GI Bill of Rights, which turned college into a normal middle-class experience; mortgages at 4 percent interest; an expanding economy; and taxes that bore most heavily on the next-oldest generation. They had willingly assumed the burden of defending freedom from Communism all over the world. The next-younger Silent generation had not dared to emerge from their shadow. Meanwhile, the GIs were raising a new, very numerous generation, confident that their offspring would follow the path they had laid out—and only a tiny few of those offspring had thus far thought to question that assumption.

All that, now, was about to change, because of the war upon which the GIs had decided to embark—a challenge which they lacked the wisdom to understand, or the tactical expertise to fight successfully, or the perspective to appreciate in its true significance. And chance had played another cruel trick on the United States, by striking down the man who combined the characteristic energy and courage of his contemporaries with the wisdom to recognize tasks whose costs would inevitably outweigh any possible benefits, and who had refused to begin that war again and again.

In comparison with many others I suffered very little from the Vietnam War. While I eventually became one of the 8 million of my contemporaries who did military service during the conflict, I was not one of the 2 million who actually served in Vietnam, much less one of the 1.6 million who experienced combat, or the hundreds of thousands of wounded, or the 59,000 who died.[1] Yet the war irrevocably changed me by beginning to show me my nation as it really was: not a new and unique civilization marching ever forward down the road to progress, but a great nation like every other, driven, at bottom, more by emotion than by reason, cursed at the moment by an excess of certainty, and liable to make mistakes on the same scale as its triumphs.

By the time I began this book in 1990, I had spent twenty-five years studying and writing about European history, and this helped me see this American tragedy in a broader perspective. The United States of 1965 was all too similar in these critical respects to Periclean Athens, or Britain in the 1770s, or late-eighteenth-century France, or imperial Germany—all of them nations that overreached their greatness and left behind stories that could inspire pity and terror for centuries to come. And several of the greatest studies of the outbreaks of such wars had been written by men who had lived through them as citizens of the nations that had suffered the most from their own errors, including Thucydides, Luigi Albertini, and Fritz Fischer. They had dared to look clearly at their countries' greatest mistakes, realizing as they did so that they were doing no more and no less than trying to see their leaders and their fellow citizens in all their humanity, and thus to understand those who had done wrong.[2]

Such national catastrophes also call forth particular kinds of heroism, and the history of the United States in Vietnam is replete with inspiration as well as tragedy. Many high-ranking Americans, as we have seen, did their best to prevent the war, and many quickly spoke out against it, often at great cost to themselves. Others, including career military officers, protested, both privately and publicly, the way in which the war was being fought, leading in more than one case to the end of a distinguished military career. Some seized upon the war as an occasion to restate the great principles upon which the United States was founded, or to try to hold their own country accountable to the rules they had helped establish in other wars. But by far the greatest number simply bore the burden of their countrymen's mistakes and did what they could in the situation in which they found themselves. All of them deserve our thanks.

Thirty-two years after my first visit, having completed this book, I returned to Zion Canyon, hiked to the top of Angels Landing again, and found that the same magnificent landscape now inspired very different feelings. The proud, confident patriotism of my youth now seemed to be the effect of a particular moment in history, the reflection of a special national consensus that could not in any event have lasted much longer.

Not only were the certainties of that extraordinary year 1965 much too simple to have endured, but the facile national consensus of the post-war era had created an emotional and spiritual hunger that was beginning to burst forth uncontrollably. A season of civic achievement was giving way to a season of individual awakening, and political certainty was making way for political skepticism. Had the Vietnam War not opened all our eyes, something else surely would have—but I shall always regret that both Americans and Vietnamese had to pay such a price.

The massive rock mountains now inspired more humility than pride. Carved by the Virgin River over many millions of years, they had loomed over the whole of human history, and would undoubtedly remain as they were for thousands of generations to come. And meanwhile, in just three decades, the Vietnam War, horrible and tragic though it was, had retreated into the background of American life. Having brought one era of American history suddenly and dramatically to an end, it had begun another that was probably less than halfway through even as the century drew to a close. The disintegration of the civic order that the war had begun still continues, and seems to be leading inexorably to some new and unforeseeable crisis. In that crisis my own generation will finally discover its true destiny, while our children face it wherever the front lines turn out to be. The outcome of that crisis will probably create some new civic consensus, a new set of certainties, and new social roles. And these new institutions and beliefs will prevail for perhaps two decades more, only to be rejected by still younger Americans in a seasonal cycle likely to persist through the whole of American and human history.

★ DEDICATED TO ★

LOST GENERATION
Justice Hugo Black
Benjamin A. Cohen
Senator Ernst Gruening
Senator Wayne Morse
General Matthew Ridgway, USA

GI GENERATION
George Ball
Art Buchwald
Clark Clifford
Paul Kattenburg
Senator Mike Mansfield
Senator Eugene McCarthy
General David Shoup, USMC
Telford Taylor

SILENT GENERATION
Sam Adams
Colonel William Corson, USMC
Daniel Ellsberg
Colonel David Hackworth, USA
Lieutenant Colonel Anthony Herbert, USA
Dr. Martin Luther King Jr.
Eartha Kitt
Admiral James Stockdale, USN

BOOM GENERATION
Muhammad Ali
Ken Berez
Sam Brown
Ron Kovic
Ronald Ridenhour
Oliver Stone
Hugh Thompson
the American prisoners of war
the wounded
the 59,000 names on the Wall
and the thousands of other American heroes,
living and dead, of the war in Vietnam

Abbreviations ★ Notes ★ Acknowledgments ★ Index

Abbreviations

★

CASEA	Courses of Action in Southeast Asia
CMH	Center for Military History, Washington, D.C.
DD	*Declassified Documents Quarterly*
FRUS	*Foreign Relations of the United States*
GP, MCHC	Greene papers, Marine Corps Historical Center, Washington, D.C.
HB	History Backup section, William Westmoreland papers, LBJ Library
HJ, MHI	Harold Johnson papers, Military History Institute
JFK	John F. Kennedy Library
LBJ	Lyndon B. Johnson Library
LC	Library of Congress
MHI	Military History Institute, Carlisle, Pa.
MP	Memos to the President
MUSTD	Major United States Troop Deployment
NA	National Archives
NDU	National Defense University Library
NSF	National Security Files
PP	Pentagon Papers, Senator Gravel edition
VN	Vietnam
VPSF	Vice-Presidential Security Files
WM	Warnke-McNaughton papers, LBJ Library

Notes

★

Introduction

1. See David Halberstam, *The Best and the Brightest* (New York, 1972), based mainly on interviews; George McT. Kahin, *Intervention: How America Became Involved in Vietnam* (Garden City, N.Y., 1986), which provided some important new documentation on the Johnson years; and William Gibbons's multivolume history, *The U.S. Government and the Vietnam War* (Princeton, 1984–1995), whose earlier volumes also drew on only a very small base of declassified documents.
2. Marc Trachtenberg has discovered the same pattern with respect to more crucial issues of nuclear weapons and European defense. See Trachtenberg, *A Constructed Peace: The Making of the European Settlement, 1945–1963* (Princeton, 1999).
3. William Strauss and Neil Howe, *Generations: The History of America's Future, 1584 to 2069* (New York, 1991); see also their *The Fourth Turning* (New York, 1996).
4. Thucydides, *History of the Peloponnesian War,* trans. Rex Warner (New York, 1988), p. 364.

1. The Eisenhower Administration and Indochina, 1954–1960

1. See esp. John Lewis Gaddis, *Strategies of Containment* (New York, 1982), pp. 127–197.
2. On the Eisenhower administration's decision not to intervene, see esp. Melanie Billings-Yun, *Decision Against War: Eisenhower and Dien Bien Phu, 1954* (New York, 1988); Ronald H. Spector, *Advice and Support: The Early Years, 1941–1960* (Washington, 1983), pp. 191–214; and David L. Anderson, *Trapped by Success: The Eisenhower Administration and Vietnam, 1953–1961* (New York, 1991), pp. 17–64.

3. *FRUS*, 1952–54, XII, pt. 1, pp. 696–703. (Documents in the 1952–54 series are not numbered. Documents in subsequent series will be cited by number.)

4. Ibid., pp. 724–733.

5. For the text of the treaty see *United States Treaties*, VI, p. 81. See also Kahin, *Intervention*, pp. 71–75.

6. *FRUS*, 1952–54, XII, pt. 1, pp. 1062–72 (emphasis added). American military authorities, however, made no immediate plans to meet these military objectives, apparently because they preferred in the case of Communist aggression to retaliate directly against Communist China rather than undertake local defense. See Chairman of the JCS Admiral Arthur W. Radford's statement to the NSC, Jan. 13, 1954, *FRUS*, 1955–57, XXI, 4.

7. *FRUS*, 1955–57, I, 206, 245.

8. Ibid., XIX, 6 (Jan. 7, 1955).

9. Robert Buzzanco, *Masters of War: Military Dissent and Politics in the Vietnam Era* (New York, 1996), pp. 25–54, notes that the Joint Chiefs opposed intervening in Indochina for most of the early 1950s. His argument that they never favored it, however, cannot be reconciled with this and many other later documents.

10. *FRUS*, 1955–57, XIX, 254.

11. Ibid., XIX, 66.

12. Ibid., I, 328, 329, 330. I have taken the liberty of interpreting some ellipses in these documents to refer to nuclear weapons. The editors have kindly used them in such a way as to rule out any other interpretation.

13. Ibid., I, 332.

14. Ibid., I, 333.

15. Ibid., I, 332 (minutes of meeting) and 333 (Radford's paper).

16. Ibid., XXI, 118 (meeting of Aug. 30), 119 (NSC 5612/1, Sept. 5).

17. Eisenhower, at Dulles's suggestion, changed "military objectives" to "national objectives" at this point.

18. See NSC 5707/8, June 3, 1957, *FRUS*, 1957–59, 119, 120.

19. NSC 5809, April 2, 1958, *FRUS*, 1958–60, XVI, 12 (emphasis added).

20. *FRUS*, 1958–60, XVI, 65.

21. Townsend Hoopes, *The Devil and John Foster Dulles* (Boston, 1973), pp. 316–317.

22. *FRUS*, 1955–57, XXI, 225.

23. *FRUS*, 1955–57, XXI, 119, and 1958–60, XVI, 12. A few months later the Department of State became alarmed when Sihanouk established diplomatic relations with Communist China. Ibid., XVI, 76.

24. See the editors' introduction to *FRUS*, 1958–60, XVI, pp. vi–viii, on the limitations in the documentary base upon which they were allowed to draw.

25. These may be followed at length in *FRUS*, 1958–60, XVI.

26. Ibid., microfiche supplement (hereafter m.s.), pt. 1, 310 (emphasis added).

27. Bernard Fall, *Anatomy of a Crisis: The Laotian Crisis of 1960–1961* (Garden City, N.Y., 1969), pp. 66–74.

28. *FRUS, 1958–60*, XXI, 119.

29. Ibid., 409.

30. Fall, *Anatomy of a Crisis*, pp. 75–89.

31. *FRUS, 1958–60*, XVI, 159.

32. The elections chose only 21 out of 59 seats, and the NLHX Party, the Pathet Lao's political arm, won 9 of them. They and their neutralist allies controlled 21 after the election.

33. Ibid., 169, 174, 180, 183, 192.

34. Ibid., 195, 203, 204, 205, 217.

35. Fall, *Anatomy of a Crisis*, pp. 122–146. Fall, who was probably the leading Western expert on Indochina at the time, was also on the scene during the attack.

36. *FRUS, 1958–60*, XVI, 230, 232, 253, 254, 257, 260, 263, 264, 271, 272.

37. Ibid., 309, 310, 312.

38. Ibid., 313, 315, 318. The editors of *FRUS* had to delete the specific reference to the CIA, but in this and various subsequent telegrams, no other interpretation suggests itself.

39. His telegram as published in *FRUS* (ibid., 319) includes the following: "For past few weeks rumors also rife Vientiane that *[less than one line of source text not declassified]* has throughout crisis been guiding CDNI friends from *[less than one line of source text not declassified]* nearby, that CDNI to avenge Ambassador Smith's dismissal of *[less than one line of source text not declassified]* had determined [to] have Ambassador Smith shipped out as soon as new CDNI-military government formed. Phoui confessed he himself had wondered whether such rumors not essentially true. I explained to him again that *[less than one line of source text not declassified]* had not been dismissed but had gone in normal rotation. Phoui merely remarked that *[less than one line of source text not declassified]* had made no secret of fact that he had not been due to leave for another two months." General Phoumi Nosavan said he had "solemn assurances not from Ambassador Smith but from US authorities Vientiane most directly concerned that aid would go on regardless [of] Ambassador Smith's contrary recommendation and, in any event, FAL had on hand 3-month advance allocation funds." Smith specifically said that he did not think that General Heintges, the head of the Program Evaluation Office and senior military adviser, had given these assurances to Phoumi.

40. Ibid., 322, 327 (on Sarit and Phoumi), 329, 336, 337, 338, 351. Even CIA Director Allen Dulles acknowledged that the elections had been

rigged. Phoumi referred to his cousin Sarit by the courtesy title "Uncle," which many Americans erroneously interpreted literally.

41. Ibid., 354, 355.
42. Ibid., 373, 375, and m.s., pt. 2, 476.
43. See ibid., 367, 377, 379, 384, 391, and m.s., pt. 2, 438, 505.
44. Ibid., 396, 397, 398, 399, 400.
45. Ibid., 415, 416, 418.
46. Ibid., 421, 426, 429, 430, 431, 432, 434, 444.
47. Ibid., 438, 349, 440, 446, 447, 448, 450.
48. Ibid., 462, 463, 464.
49. Ibid., 467, 469, 472, 473, 474, 476.
50. Ibid., 486, and m.s., pt. 2, 675.
51. Ibid., 487.
52. Ibid., 485, 490.
53. Ibid., 492.
54. Ibid., 493, 495.
55. Ibid., 497.
56. Ibid., m.s., pt. 2, 690.
57. A deletion occurs at this point in the record.
58. Ibid., 498 (emphasis added).
59. *FRUS*, 1961–63, XXIV, 1, 2.
60. Ibid., 3.
61. Accounts of the meeting by Kennedy himself, Gen. Wilton Persons, and Herter are ibid., 7, 8, 9. See also Fred I. Greenstein and Richard H. Immerman, "What Did Eisenhower Tell Kennedy about Indochina? The Politics of Misperception," *Journal of American History*, Sept. 1992, pp. 568–587, which includes notes by Clark Clifford and Robert McNamara.
62. See Strauss and Howe, *Generations*, pp. 247–260.
63. See the recent book by Marc Trachtenberg, *A Constructed Peace: The Making of the European Settlement, 1945–1963* (Princeton, 1999), pp. 146–200.
64. See Eisenhower's memo to Dulles, Sept. 8, 1953, *FRUS*, 1952–54, II, pt. 1, pp. 460–463, and many comments by Eisenhower during NSC meetings reported in the same volume.
65. George F. Kennan, *Memoirs, 1950–1963* (Boston, 1972), pp. 185–187.

2. No War in Laos, January–June 1961

1. Strauss and Howe, in *Generations*, pp. 261–278, date the birth years of this generation as 1901–1924, but in my opinion many Americans born in the 1901–1904 period are more typical of the previous Lost generation.
2. The accusation that Democrats actually stole the election—now a tenet

of Republican dogma—has little evidentiary basis. A detailed study of the voting in Illinois in 1960 concluded that Kennedy won that state fairly, and even a shift of Illinois to the Republican column would not have changed the result. See Edmund F. Kallina Jr., *Courthouse over White House: Chicago and the Presidential Election of 1960* (Orlando, 1988).

3. The author of the most recent sensational best-seller devoted to Kennedy made a calculated and avowed decision to ignore that documentation, with results of predictably dubious validity: Seymour Hersh, *The Dark Side of Camelot* (Boston, 1997); see also Hersh, "May-Zelikow Confidential," *Diplomatic History* 22, no. 4 (Fall 1998), pp. 654–661, in which Hersh explicitly discounts archival sources.

4. *FRUS, 1961–63*, XXIV, 10, 12; VIII, 11; and see CM-85–61, JFK, NSF, Countries, Laos: General, 2/16/61–2/19/61.

5. Harold W. Chase and Allen H. Lerman, eds., *Kennedy and the Press: The News Conferences* (New York, 1965), p. 25.

6. *FRUS, 1961–63*, XXIV, 13. Kennedy apparently kept no record of this talk in the White House. The farcical aspects of Laotian politics and the peaceful character of the people immediately struck most observers in Laos, and also emerged in various press reports, even those of *Time* magazine, despite its generally tough line against Asian Communism. See, e.g., *Time*, Feb. 3, 1961.

7. Isaiah Berlin oral history, JFK.

8. *FRUS, 1960–63*, XXIV, 14, 15. Deptel 840 to Vientiane, ibid., 15. Charles "Chip" Bohlen, the former ambassador to Moscow who had become a special assistant to Rusk, proposed the approach to Moscow.

9. Ibid., 17, 20.

10. Ibid., 19.

11. Prince Sihanouk of Cambodia had refused even a personal appeal from Kennedy, leading the *New York Times* of Feb. 26 (sec. 1, p. 16) to brand the President's "first serious venture into personal diplomacy" a failure.

12. Edward J. Marolda and Oscar P. Fitzgerald, *The United States Navy and the Vietnam Conflict*, II (Washington, 1986), p. 60.

13. The March 9 meeting is *FRUS, 1960–63*, XXIV, 25; see also a March 3 meeting and its results, ibid., 22. The agreed military measures included an airlift of 14 Marine helicopters, their crews, and maintenance personnel to Udorn, Thailand, on the Laotian border. See Marolda and Fitzgerald, *The Navy and Vietnam*, II, pp. 60–61.

14. *FRUS, 1960–63*, XXIV, 31.

15. No contemporary minutes of this meeting have come to light, but see Arthur M. Schlesinger Jr., *A Thousand Days* (Boston, 1965), pp. 332–333, and Edwin O. Guthman and Jeffrey Shulman, eds., *Robert Kennedy: In His Own Words* (New York, 1988), pp. 246–248.

16. On Rostow's role see Montague Kern, Patricia W. Levering, and Ralph

B. Levering, *The Kennedy Crises: The Press, the Presidency, and Foreign Policy* (Chapel Hill, 1983), pp. 40–41.

17. *FRUS, 1960–63*, XXIV, 35.
18. Marolda and Fitzgerald, *The Navy and Vietnam*, II, p. 61.
19. *FRUS, 1960–63*, XXIV, 36; *New York Times*, March 24.
20. *Time*, March 31, 1961, pp. 7–10.
21. *New York Times*, March 24.
22. *New York Times*, April 5, editorial page.
23. Alistair Horne, *Harold Macmillan*, II (New York, 1989), pp. 292–293.
24. FRUS, 1960–63, XXIV, 42.
25. *New York Times*, March 27; March 28.
26. FRUS, 1960–63, XXIV, 43, 43n, 44.
27. Ibid., 47, 48.
28. Chalmers Roberts, *First Rough Draft* (New York, 1973), pp. 192–195.
29. *FRUS, 1960–63*, XXIV, 52, 53, 55.
30. Ibid., 58, 59, and see Ambassador Brown's and Acting Secretary of State Chester Bowles's calls for intervention on April 26, ibid., 60, 61.
31. Ibid., 63.
32. Minutes are in JFK, NSF, Chester V. Clifton series, Conferences with the President, vol. 1.
33. Strauss and Howe, *Generations*, dated the Lost generation as those born from 1883 to 1900, but the years 1900–1904 saw the birth of a number of prominent Americans, including John Steinbeck, Charles Lindbergh, and George F. Kennan, whose character and views were far more typical of the Lost than of the younger GIs. Mansfield, born in 1903, is thus an equivocal figure in this analysis. Dirksen, Russell, Saltonstall, Hickenlooper, and Bridges were all born before 1900.
34. *FRUS, 1960–63*, XXIV, 68. The NSC meeting, of which we lack any record, reached no definite decisions and agreed to pursue the cease-fire negotiations. Ibid. See also *New York Times*, April 30.
35. Ibid., 74, 72, 73.
36. On the Chiefs' views, see ibid., 76. Rostow's unsigned and undated paper, along with partially declassified versions of some of the Chiefs' appreciations, are in JFK, NSF, Laos: General, Defense Papers, 5/61. The tone and many of the specific arguments closely resemble those of other memos by Rostow during 1961. LeMay argued that while the United States should not introduce ground troops, it should demand a cease-fire, bomb Hanoi if need be, and prepare for the presumably nuclear war with China that might result. "I believe that war with China is inevitable if we are determined to take decisive action in Southeast Asia," he wrote, and he blamed American "failure" in Korea on our failure to knock out "primary sources of supply."
37. See notes on this meeting by Colonel Burris, Vice President Johnson's military aide, LBJ, VPSF, National Security Council Records of Action,

and *FRUS*, 1960–63, XXIV, 77. Treasury Secretary Douglas Dillon suggested "the dispatch of troops to Thailand plus high level personal assurances, perhaps by the Vice President," to achieve this purpose.

38. JFK, NSF, Laos: General, 5/1–5/8/61.
39. Chase and Lerman, *Kennedy and the Press*, pp. 73–74; *New York Times*, May 6, 1961.
40. Arthur Krock papers, Mudd Library, Princeton University, memo of May 5, box 1, book III.
41. *FRUS*, 1960–63, XXIV, 84.
42. Ibid., 85, 86.
43. Ibid., 93, 95. Rusk's disagreements with the British and French, and talk of further SEATO intervention, found their way into *New York Times* dispatches from Geneva as well. See front-page stories of May 14–17, written by London correspondent Drew Middleton, who was attending the opening weeks of the conference.
44. *FRUS*, 1960–63, XXIV, 103.
45. Ibid., 106.
46. On Khrushchev see Vladislav Zubok and Constantine Pleshakov, *Inside the Kremlin's Cold War* (Cambridge, Mass., 1996), pp. 236–258.
47. *FRUS*, 1960–63, XXIV, 107, 108.
48. Kennedy, Reston wrote in the *Times* on June 6, came away convinced "of the importance of strengthening the nation's defenses and its relations with its allies . . . the President's reaction was to confirm rather than minimize his opposition to the present trend of Soviet policy and to increase his determination to look to the defenses of the United States." The deep gulf between the two sides disturbed him.
49. Chase and Lerman, *Kennedy and the Press*, p. 87.
50. *FRUS*, 1960–63, XXIV, 111, 111nn.
51. Ibid., 113.
52. Ibid., 114.
53. *New York Times*, June 19, p. 1; June 22, p. 1.

3. A New Effort in Vietnam, January–August 1961

1. I am treating the Eisenhower administration's policy toward South Vietnam in relatively little detail, thanks partly to the existence of two excellent books on the subject: Ronald H. Spector's *Advice and Support* and David L. Anderson's *Trapped by Success*.
2. Anderson, *Trapped by Success*, pp. 65–119.
3. These figures are from John D. Montgomery, *The Politics of Foreign Aid: American Experience in Southeast Asia* (New York, 1962), pp. 281–284. See also Spector, *Advice and Support*, pp. 306–307; Kahin, *Intervention*, pp. 85–88.
4. *FRUS*, 1958–60, I, 45, 56.

5. See Spector, *Advice and Support,* pp. 308–316.
6. Larry E. Cable, *Conflict of Myths: The Development of American Counterinsurgency Doctrine and the Vietnam War* (New York, 1986), esp. pp. 3–7, 113–180.
7. See Spector, *Advice and Support,* pp. 262–282, 295–302, 310–320.
8. Ibid., pp. 320–325. General Williams supported Diem's proposals for the Civil Guard.
9. See Anderson, *Trapped by Success,* pp. 175–184, and Durbrow oral history, LBJ.
10. See William Duiker, "The Revolutionary Path: The Life of Ho Chi Minh," forthcoming, ch. 15. I am grateful to Professor Duiker for sharing this important work with me prior to its publication.
11. For a summary see William Duiker, "Waging Revolutionary War," in Jayne S. Werner and Luu Doan Huynh, eds., *The Vietnam War: Vietnamese and American Perspectives* (Armonk, N.Y., 1993), pp. 27–29.
12. On the highly acrimonious controversy between Durbrow and Williams see *FRUS,* 1958–60, I, 140, 141, 167.
13. Ibid., 211.
14. Durbrow to Parsons, Nov. 8, ibid., 214.
15. Ibid., 185.
16. Ibid., 197, 198 (Lansdale memo of Sept. 20), 202 (Deptel 581, Oct. 7).
17. Ibid., 203, 204, 205, 207.
18. See Spector, *Advice and Support,* pp. 369–371, and *FRUS,* 1958–60, I, 218, 219, 222, 225, 226, 227, 229.
19. *FRUS,* 1958–60, I, 230, 238, 241, 245, 251.
20. Messages of Dec. 9 and 10, 1961, ibid., 264; Lansdale memo of Dec. 14, ibid., 265, 265n. Lansdale figured as Alden Pyle in Graham Greene's *The Quiet American* and as Colonel Hillandale in Eugene Burdick and William J. Lederer's mammoth best-seller *The Ugly American.*
21. Ibid., 271, 273, 274.
22. *FRUS,* 1961–63, I, 1.
23. Spector, *Advice and Support,* pp. 371–373, also notes that the plan essentially restated long-held American military views.
24. Lansdale's report is in *United States–Vietnam Relations, 1945–1967* (Washington, 1971), XI, pp. 1–13.
25. Rostow oral history, JFK.
26. Two accounts of the meeting are in *FRUS,* 1961–63, I, 3, 4.
27. Ibid., 5, 6. On January 30 Kennedy also approved the financing of the proposed increases in the ARVN and Civil Guard, although the U.S. government did not yet inform Diem of this. JFK, NSF, VN, box 195.
28. *FRUS,* 1961–63, I, 11, 18, 20.
29. *FRUS,* 1961–63, VIII, 17.
30. Ibid., 18.

31. Ibid., 57.
32. Rostow oral history, JFK.
33. JFK, NSF, VN, General, 1/61–3/61, box 193.
34. *FRUS*, 1961–63, I, 24 (Rostow for the President, April 3, 1961), 27, 29, 30, 53.
35. See *U.S.-Vietnam Relations*, XI, pp. 22–35; *FRUS*, 1961–63, I, 31; and JFK, NSF, VN, II/11 and II/11a. Summarizing the history of South Vietnam since 1954, Lansdale played fast and loose with critical facts, stating that Britain and the Soviet Union, the co-chairs of the Geneva conference of 1954, had decided in late 1955 to postpone nationwide elections indefinitely because of the growing political strength of Diem in the South, and identifying all the 10,000 VC guerrillas as infiltrators from the North. He also argued that the Communists were now trying new political tactics because the government had had more success against the guerrillas during January and February.
36. The first draft, dated April 26, is in *U.S.-Vietnam Relations*, XI, pp. 43–57; the second, including major additions and changes provided by the State Department, is *FRUS*, 1961–63, I, 42; and the final draft is in *U.S.-Vietnam Relations*, XI, pp. 88–130.
37. Lansdale specifically attributed these suggestions to the CIA, and the psychological suggestions to USIA, in a May 1 memo for the task force: JFK, NSF, VN, IV/1. For Rostow's comments see *FRUS*, 1961–63, I, 51, and for Kennedy's approval see ibid., 52.
38. Ibid., 40, 52.
39. *FRUS*, 1960–63, I, 29, 33, 39, 42.
40. *U.S.-Vietnam Relations*, XI, pp. 58–61.
41. *FRUS*, 1960–63, I, 43.
42. See *U.S.-Vietnam Relations*, XI, pp. 131, 157–158; and message, JCS to CINCPAC, 111853Z May 61, LBJ, VPSF, box 10, Program for South Vietnam.
43. *New York Times*, May 5, p. 1.
44. *FRUS*, 1961–63, I, 46, and *U.S.-Vietnam Relations*, XI, pp. 67–68.
45. Chase and Lerman, *Kennedy and the Press*, pp. 73–76.
46. *FRUS*, 1961–63, I, 51, 52.
47. See Kennedy's letter, dated May 8, in *U.S.-Vietnam Relations*, XI, pp. 132–135, and *FRUS*, 1961–63, I, 54, 55.
48. *U.S.-Vietnam Relations*, XI, pp. 155–156.
49. *FRUS*, 1961–63, I, 54n6, 57.
50. JFK, NSF, VN, VIII/10 (Saigon 1767, May 18); *FRUS*, 1961–63, I, 64.
51. *FRUS*, 1961–63, I, 62.
52. *U.S.-Vietnam Relations*, XI, pp. 167–172.
53. Saigon 1817 and Saigon 1821, May 30 and May 31, 1961, JFK, NSF, VN, box 193.

54. Saigon 1838, ibid.

55. *FRUS*, 1961–63, I, 92.

56. See *Time*, July 28, p. 25; Aug. 4, p. 18 (cover story); Aug. 25, p. 25; and *Newsweek*, July 31, p. 43; Aug. 21, p. 21.

57. These issues may be followed in *FRUS*, 1961–63, I, 69, 71, 73, 78, 92, 113, 114, 116; and *U.S.-Vietnam Relations*, XI, pp. 178–226, 241–244.

58. Cover story of Aug. 4.

59. See U. Alexis Johnson, *The Right Hand of Power* (Englewood Cliffs, N.J., 1984), pp. 91–94, 266–325. Walter P. McConaughy had succeeded J. Graham Parsons as Assistant Secretary of State for Far Eastern Affairs on April 3, but Johnson took the lead in policy toward Southeast Asia.

60. See JFK, NSF, VN, General, 6/19/61–6/30/61, box 193.

61. *FRUS*, 1961–63, XXIV, 122.

62. See ibid., 120, 121, 125, 126, for this paper and its development.

63. Eight days later Lemnitzer confirmed in writing that, despite some improvements, "the Lao Army is not yet an effective fighting force." Ibid., 132.

64. Ibid., 127; for the earlier part of the meeting see *FRUS*, 1961–63, XIV, 52.

65. *FRUS*, 1960–63, XXIV, 128.

66. Ibid., 129.

67. Ibid., 130, 137, 139.

68. See Robert Johnson memo for Rostow, July 5, 1961, and Rostow for Rusk, July 13, JFK, NSF, VN, General, 7/5–7/13/61, box 193, and *FRUS*, 1961–63, I, 85.

69. *FRUS*, 1961–63, XXIV, 134.

70. Ibid., I, 94; see also Maxwell D. Taylor, *The Uncertain Trumpet* (New York, 1959), pp. 137–139. Taylor's book was not the polemic on behalf of conventional war that it is often portrayed as. Most of his recommendations dealt with strategic nuclear offense and defense, and he even referred to the need, in certain cases, for tactical nuclear weapons in limited wars.

71. *FRUS*, 1961–63, I, 98.

72. Ibid., XXIV, 141.

73. Ibid., 145.

74. See Johnson's July 26 memo for Rostow, ibid., 146, which refers to a CIA estimate of reactions to the panhandle operation. An unsigned estimate of friendly reaction to the seizure of the Red River Delta is in DD, 1981, and Johnson's memo also notes that this was under consideration.

75. See, e.g., Taylor for Kennedy, July 26, 1961, *FRUS*, 1961–63, I, 104.

76. *FRUS*, 1961–63, I, 107.

77. See, e.g., the columns by James Reston on July 26 and Arthur Krock on July 27 in the *New York Times*, suggesting that the Soviets might con-

cede the Western allies a corridor to Berlin in return for recognition of the Oder-Neisse frontier between Germany and Poland.

78. Bundy's minutes of the meeting are in *FRUS, 1961–63,* XXIV, 148, 161n1.

79. Ben Bradlee, *A Good Life* (New York, 1995), pp. 218–219.

80. *FRUS, 1961–63,* XXIV, 151, 152, 155; I, 112.

81. Ibid., XXIV, 157, 158, 160, 162.

82. Ibid., 163.

83. Ibid., I, 117, 120. The South Vietnamese were already sending small teams of Special Forces across the border, as reported in the *New York Times,* Aug. 13, p. 1.

84. *FRUS, 1961–63,* XXIV, 154, 161.

85. Ibid., 165, 166.

86. Ibid., 167, 168; *New York Times,* Aug. 25, p. 9.

87. *FRUS, 1961–63,* XXIV, 167, 168, 169, 171.

88. The candidates, in addition to Souvanna himself, were Quinim Pholsema, Pheng Phongsavong, Khamsouk Keola, Sisoumang, Khamsing, General Heuan, and Khampham Boupa.

89. Ibid., 172. See also 173, NSAM (National Security Action Memorandum) 80, formally recording these decisions.

90. Harriman papers, LC, box 519, Vietnam, General, 1961.

4. War or Peace? September–November 1961

1. See *FRUS, 1961–63,* XIV, 141 (meeting of Sept. 5, 1961), 147 (Kennedy for Rusk, Sept. 12). See also the *New York Times,* Sept. 14, reporting Kennedy's and some of his aides' statements that their purpose was "to arm the country for negotiations, not for an unqualified and unreasoning skid toward a showdown . . . Mr. Kennedy is now said to be determined not to let another month slip by" without taking a diplomatic initiative.

2. *FRUS, 1961–63,* XIV, 180, 191, 201, 202. See also the account of Ambassador to Yugoslavia George Kennan's talk with his Soviet counterpart in Belgrade, 175, 175n2.

3. Ibid., 184, 185, 189, 207.

4. *FRUS, 1961–63,* XXIII, 74.

5. Ibid., I, 207.

6. *New York Times,* Nov. 18.

7. Cottrell memo, Sept. 1, JFK, NSF, VN, General, 9/01, box 194, and *FRUS, 1961–63,* I, 122, 127, 130.

8. *FRUS, 1961–63,* I, 131, 134.

9. Ibid., 133, and see ibid., XXIV, 176 (Bangkok 345 of Sept. 7), for the Bangkok talks.

10. Ibid., I, 131, and see 128 for Rostow's assistant Robert Johnson's original suggestion along these lines.
11. *New York Times*, Sept. 26.
12. *FRUS*, 1961–63, I, 135, 138; and messages, MAAG Saigon to CINCPAC, Sept. 21 and 25, JFK, NSF, VN, General, 9/61, box 194.
13. *FRUS*, 1961–63, I, 139.
14. Ibid., 140.
15. Ibid., 142.
16. *New York Times*, Oct. 2.
17. *FRUS*, 1961–63, I, 147.
18. The Secretary argued, first, that Senator Fulbright would never approve, and added that "the basic question of U.S. military action itself has not been decided." Ibid., XXIII, 9, 10.
19. Ibid., I, 145.
20. Documentation on these efforts is spotty. See JFK, NSF, Laos, General, box 131; and JFK, NSF, Regional Security File, Southeast Asia, General, 1961.
21. Rostow oral history, JFK.
22. *FRUS*, 1961–63, XXIV, 195.
23. The other, of course, was the Attorney General.
24. The Chiefs rejected this recommendation. See Wheeler for Lemnitzer, Sept. 13, 1961, National Archives, RG 218, JMF 9155.3/3360 Vietnam (7 Sept. 61).
25. *FRUS*, 1961–63, I, 144; *U.S.-Vietnam Relations*, XI, pp. 297–311.
26. Robert F. Futrell with Martin Blumenson, *The United States Air Force in Southeast Asia: The Advisory Years to 1965* (Washington, 1981), pp. 79–80.
27. Parts of the paper are printed in two different volumes of *FRUS*, 1961–63: I, 204, and XXIV, 155. Rostow's paper on Laos is XXIV, 205.
28. *FRUS*, 1961–63, I, 156, 156n. Unfortunately no record of the October 11 meeting survives.
29. Ibid., 157.
30. See *FRUS*, 1961–63, XIV, 164. Vol. XIV covers all these developments in great detail.
31. Ibid., 165.
32. Ben Bradlee, *Conversations with Kennedy* (New York, 1975), p. 15.
33. *FRUS*, 1961–63, XIV, 168, 170; *New York Times*, Oct. 7.
34. Krock papers, Mudd Library, box 1 (emphasis added). I am indebted to Marc Trachtenberg for this reference.
35. *New York Times*, Oct. 12.
36. See Halberstam, *The Best and the Brightest*, p. 76, and Reston's column of June 10, 1979, which cannot be reconciled with his memoirs, *Deadline: A Memoir* (New York, 1992), p. 291. Reston apparently first

made this point in a 1966 television interview, again without specifically quoting Kennedy regarding Vietnam. See *New York Times*, Jan. 18, 1966.

37. Maxwell D. Taylor, *Swords and Plowshares* (New York, 1972), pp. 225–226.

38. *FRUS, 1961–63*, I, 163.

39. Ibid., 168.

40. *Time*, Oct. 27, p. 33. (The Oct. 27 issue was published on Oct. 21.)

41. The conversation and the report are in *FRUS, 1961–63*, I, 174, 210.

42. Ibid., 157, 161, 164, 171, 172, and JFK, NSF, VN, General, 10/16/61–10/19/61, box 194 (CIA TDCS of Oct. 17).

43. *FRUS, 1961–63*, I, 177, 178, 185, 192, 210. Regarding Diem's request for Lansdale, a State Department official wrote, "No. No. NO!"

44. *The Pentagon Papers*, Senator Gravel ed. (Boston, 1971) (hereafter PP), II, pp. 651–652; *FRUS, 1961–63*, I, 171.

45. *FRUS, 1961–63*, I, 174, 175, 182, 188.

46. Three days later McGeorge Bundy cabled Taylor in Bangkok at the President's request and asked him not to leak this recommendation. Bundy's effort was successful, and even *Time*, which would have been delighted to report Taylor's actual recommendation, said (Nov. 3, p. 13) that the general's "preliminary report" had taken no position on troops. Ibid., 198.

47. *FRUS, 1961–63*, I, 191, 192, 198, 201; *New York Times*, Oct. 28, 1961, p. 28.

48. *U.S.-Vietnam Relations*, XI, pp. 331–342.

49. Rostow oral history, JFK. In Honolulu on October 16—on the way to Saigon—Rostow had suggested that CINCPAC prepare a plan for the "limited but systematic harassment by U.S. naval and air power of North Vietnam," and Felt provided such a report on November 2. *FRUS, 1961–63*, I, 170, 206.

50. Although only Taylor signed the report, he later wrote that Rostow helped draft it. Taylor, *Swords and Plowshares*, pp. 243–244.

51. *FRUS, 1961–63*, I, 210.

52. Ibid., XXIV, 211, 212.

53. Ibid., 213, 214, 215, 217, 218, 219.

54. *FRUS, 1961–63*, I, 207, 211.

55. *Newsweek*, Nov. 13, 1961, p. 25.

56. *FRUS, 1961–63*, I, 211.

57. See the *New York Times* stories by Hanson Baldwin, who often provided the American military's views, July 6, July 31, Aug. 1, Aug. 13, Aug. 14, and Sept. 4, all reporting military unhappiness with McNamara on various issues.

58. Bundy's draft is *FRUS, 1961–63*, I, 214; on his talk with Lemnitzer see ibid., 217.

59. Ibid., 225.
60. Ibid., 222. Johnson still expected nothing more from the Geneva talks than "a settlement on the basis of a very weak and unsatisfactory Souvanna Phouma government."
61. Ibid., 226.
62. The draft and Lemnitzer's brief notes of the meeting are ibid., 228, 232.
63. *New York Times*, Nov. 10, p. 1.
64. *U.S.-Vietnam Relations*, XI, pp. 359–366 (emphasis added).
65. *FRUS*, 1961–63, I, 233.
66. Lemnitzer's notes are ibid., 236. We unfortunately lack any fuller record of this meeting.
67. Ibid., 244.
68. Ibid., 239.
69. Ibid., 247.
70. *New York Times*, Nov. 8.
71. Ibid., 209, and JFK, NSF, VN, General, 11/11/61–11/13/61, box 195.
72. *FRUS*, 1961–63, I, 242, 242n. Johnson regretted having given Galbraith a copy of draft instructions for Nolting.
73. Ibid., 252.
74. Ibid., 253.
75. It was typical of Rusk suddenly to take the President's side in the midst of a meeting, although he had taken a very hard-line position in two recent conversations with the British and French ambassadors, speaking quite negatively about the course of the Laos negotiations, and telling the French ambassador that we would not be bound by the attitude of our allies in Southeast Asia. Ibid., 241, 243.
76. See Joint Chiefs of Staff for Chairman, JCS, Nov. 14, 1961, NA, RG 218, JMF 9155.3/9105 Vietnam (13 Oct. 61).
77. *FRUS*, 1961–63, I, 254. The notes were written by Col. Howard Burris, Vice President Johnson's military aide.
78. Ibid., 256. On Goodwin's departure see Richard N. Goodwin, *Remembering America* (New York, 1988), pp. 209–213.
79. Week in Review, p. 1.
80. Chase and Lerman, *Kennedy and the Press*, p. 143.

5. Limiting the Commitment, November 1961–November 1962

1. See Lansdale's memo for Taylor, Oct. 23, 1961, *FRUS*, 1961–63, I, 185, and Nolting's instructions, *U.S.-Vietnam Relations*, XI, pp. 400–405.
2. *FRUS*, 1961–63, I, 266, 270.
3. Ibid., 278.
4. *U.S.-Vietnam Relations*, XI, pp. 419–421.
5. *New York Times*, Nov. 25, p. 1; Dec. 1, p. 1; *FRUS*, 1961–63, I, 277.

6. *FRUS*, 1961–63, I, 285, 286, 289 (emphasis added); and see Wheeler memo, Nov. 28, 1961, NA, RG 218, JMF 9155.3/9105 Vietnam (13 Oct. 61), sec. II.

7. *FRUS*, 1961–63, I, 305, 307, 308.

8. Ibid., 326, 341.

9. Wheeler for Lemnitzer, Sept. 13, NA, RG 218, JMF 9155.3/3360 Vietnam (7 Sept. 61).

10. JCS 131850Z Nov. 61 to CINCPAC and CINCPAC 141212Z to JCS, ibid., JMF 9155.3/9105 Vietnam (13 Nov. 61), sec. I.

11. *FRUS*, 1961–63, I, 245, 271, 284, 301, 312, 317, 327, 328; II, 17. Taylor's memo of Nov. 27 (284) went to Kennedy, Rusk, McNamara, Lemnitzer, and other high officials. Passages relating to relations between MACV and the CIA have been deleted from the published versions of these documents.

12. Ibid., I, 318, 330, 331; II, 9.

13. Ibid., II, 17, 19, 25, 40.

14. *Small Wars Manual, United States Marine Corps, 1940* (Manhattan, Kan., n.d.), pp. 11–12.

15. *FRUS*, 1961–63, I, 336, 342.

16. Ibid., 326.

17. *U.S.-Vietnam relations*, XII, pp. 448–454.

18. *FRUS*, 1961–63, XXIV, 221 (Nov. 6). This was an eyes-only cable for Rusk and Kennedy.

19. Ibid., 241.

20. Ibid., 223, 264; and *New York Times*, Jan. 6, p. 2.

21. *FRUS*, 1961–63, XXIV, 258, 269 (Bagley memo of Jan. 5, JCS memo of Jan. 5).

22. *New York Times*, Feb. 9, p. 1; Feb. 12, p. 1; Feb. 14, p. 1.

23. Chase and Lerman, *Kennedy and the Press*, pp. 182–183.

24. *New York Times*, Feb. 19, p. 20; Feb. 21, p. 1; March 7, p. 29.

25. *FRUS*, 1961–63, XXIV, 297. The Vietnam portion of the briefing has never been printed: it may be found in JFK, NSF, Clifton series, Conferences with the President, 1/25/61–2/27/62.

26. *New York Times*, March 7, 1962, p. 1; *FRUS*, 1961–63, XXIII, 8–24.

27. Records of these conversations are in Airgram 184, Vientiane, March 30, 1962, Harriman papers, LC, box 529.

28. *FRUS*, 1961–63, XXIV, 318.

29. Felt and Lemnitzer presented these arguments to McNamara in Honolulu on March 21; see ibid., 311, and Bagley for Taylor, April 3, 324.

30. Ibid., VII, 146 et seq.

31. Ibid., XV, 1, 2, 8, 10, 15, 16, 17, 18, 19, 24, 25, 27, 29.

32. *New York Times*, Feb. 25, Week in Review, p. 3; on the content of other stories see below.

33. *New York Times,* Feb. 25, p. 1; March 2, p. 1; March 18, p. 1.

34. John M. Newman, *JFK and Vietnam* (New York, 1992), p. 207.

35. *New York Times,* April 1, Week in Review.

36. *FRUS,* 1961–63, II, 145.

37. As Galbraith told me in 1990, he was sent in the knowledge that he did not suffer from an open mind. Interview with John Kenneth Galbraith.

38. *U.S.-Vietnam Relations,* XI, pp. 406–418 (telegrams of Nov. 20 and 21).

39. *FRUS,* 1961–63, I, 282, 290.

40. On the previous day, Kennedy had also received a long memo on Asia from Chester Bowles—now Ambassador-at-Large—which also argued that the United States was unlikely to win a decisive victory in South Vietnam and should prepare for a negotiated settlement. Ibid., II, 141, 142. Arthur Schlesinger gave Kennedy Bowles's memo, but one cannot be sure that Kennedy read it, if only because of its length.

41. See *FRUS,* 1961–63, II, 141, 148.

42. *U.S.-Vietnam Relations,* XII, pp. 464–465 (JCSM-282-2, April 13).

43. *FRUS,* 1961–63, II, 158, 164.

44. Ibid., 176, 178n.

45. Ibid., 183, 192.

46. See Gibbons, *The U.S. Government and the Vietnam War,* II, pp. 122–123; and LBJ, Ball papers, telephone conversations, I/15 (April 26) and I/17 (May 1).

47. *New York Times,* May 12, p. 1.

48. Quoted in Newman, *JFK and Vietnam,* p. 254. Newman's source is George Allen, a CIA analyst who was present at the meeting. Allen has informed me, however, that McNamara did not clear the room before asking this question, as Newman alleges. Interview with George Allen, Dec. 8, 1995.

49. *FRUS,* 1961–63, XXIV, 326.

50. Ibid., 327–341.

51. *FRUS,* 1961–63, XXIII, 436.

52. Ibid., 346, 349, 352, 353.

53. The story appeared on May 12, p. 1.

54. If Phase III led to limited war, Hilsman suggested, "the most effective move would be an early negotiated settlement, before either casualties or frustrations get out of hand." *FRUS,* 1961–63, XXIII, 356, 359.

55. Ibid., 354, 355.

56. Ibid., 360, 362, 363, 366; Michael Forrestal oral history, interview of July 28, 1964, JFK; *New York Times,* May 13, 14, 15, p. 1 stories. Forrestal describes the Hilsman-Lemnitzer incident.

57. *FRUS,* 1961–63, XXIV, 368.

58. *New York Times,* May 17, p. 1; May 18, p. 1.

59. *FRUS,* 1961–63, XXIV, 370, 377, 378, 379.

60. See ibid., 381n.

61. Ibid., 383, 384.
62. Ibid., 387, 389, 390, 391, 392, 393, 394. The President initially opposed resuming aid to Phoumi, partly because of the balance-of-payments crisis: ibid., 395.
63. Ibid., XXIV, 396, 398; XXIII, 451.
64. Ibid., XXIII, 454, 455; XXIV, 406; *New York Times,* July 28, p. 1. See also Guthman and Shulman, *Robert Kennedy: In His Own Words,* p. 260, in which Kennedy recalled in 1964 that he had in fact promised to take the troops out in 60 days, something he denied in the memo he wrote in July 1962 for circulation to senior officials.
65. *FRUS, 1961–63,* II, 248.
66. Gilpatric oral history, LBJ.
67. Carl Kaysen, who worked in the White House as one of Bundy's deputies and dealt with the Pentagon on many other matters, says today that Kennedy frequently gave McNamara oral instructions. To judge from McNamara's book *In Retrospect: The Tragedy and Lessons of Vietnam* (New York, 1995), McNamara has no recollection of any such conversation now, or, indeed, much independent recollection of anything about Vietnam that is not reflected in the public record.
68. See Gibbons, *The U.S. Government and the Vietnam War,* II, pp. 126–129.
69. *FRUS, 1961–63,* VII, 68, 106.
70. Duiker, "The Revolutionary Path," ch. 15.
71. *FRUS, 1961–63,* XXIV, 410 (emphasis added).
72. Ibid.
73. Ibid., 241, 253; Forrestal for Dungan, Aug. 3, 1962, John M. Newman papers, JFK.
74. Qiang Zhai, "Beijing and the Vietnam Conflict, 1964–1965: New Chinese Evidence," *Cold War International History Project Bulletin,* nos. 6–7 (Winter 1995–96), pp. 233–250.
75. See *FRUS, 1961–63,* XXV, passim, esp. 112, 119.
76. Ibid., XII, 310 (memo by Chester Bowles), 312.
77. Despite some deletions which the CIA successfully insisted upon, this may be followed ibid., 241–298.
78. *FRUS, 1961–63,* X, 234, 265, 266, 274, 278, 290.
79. Ibid., 304, 319, 363–368, 380, 382, 385, 386. See also the fine article by James G. Hershberg, "Before 'The Missiles of October': Did Kennedy Plan a Military Strike against Cuba?" *Diplomatic History* 14, no. 2 (Spring 1990), pp. 163–198.
80. Hershberg, "Before 'The Missiles of October,'" pp. 184–190. Hershberg notes that Kennedy had publicly given only three possible pretexts for action: an attack on Guantanamo or elsewhere, the installation of Soviet offensive weapons, or Cuban support for subversion elsewhere.
81. See Admiral George Anderson, oral history, JFK.

82. The most thorough account is now Ernest R. May and Philip Zelikow, eds., *The Kennedy Tapes* (Cambridge, Mass., 1997), which includes the transcripts of most ExCom meetings.
83. Robert Kennedy immediately commented, "That's a surprise!"
84. *FRUS*, 1961–63, XI, 94.
85. See McGeorge Bundy, *Danger and Survival* (New York, 1988), pp. 425–436.
86. *New York Times,* Oct. 28. Walter Lippmann had already called publicly for a trade.
87. Ibid., Oct. 29, p. 1.
88. *FRUS*, 1961–63, XV, 153, conversation of Nov. 14. Adenauer argued on the contrary that Khrushchev had proved himself untrustworthy.
89. "In Time of Crisis," *Saturday Evening Post,* Dec. 8, 1962.

6. The War in Vietnam, 1962

1. As Minh explained to General Taylor during his visit: *FRUS*, 1961–63, I, 177.
2. McGarr to Secretary of Defense, 220821Z Oct. 61, NA, RG 218, JMF 9155.3/9105 Vietnam (26 Oct. 61) sec. 1; see also *FRUS*, 1961–63, I, 337n2.
3. *FRUS*, 1961–63, I, 325.
4. McGarr for Lemnitzer, Dec. 20, and McGarr for Felt, Dec. 21, ibid., 331, 333.
5. Ibid., 337.
6. Ibid., II, 13.
7. McGarr for Felt, Feb. 8, 1962, NA, RG 218, JMF 9155.3/9105 South Vietnam (31 Oct. 61).
8. *FRUS*, 1961–63, I, 334. Kennedy was informed of this procedure and gave his tacit consent on December 21.
9. Roger Hilsman, *To Move a Nation* (New York, 1967), pp. 50–54, 424–427.
10. *FRUS*, 1961–63, II, 42.
11. Ibid., VIII, 67 (Jan. 11), 69.
12. *FRUS*, 1961–63, II, 54.
13. Ibid., II, 32, 39, 67, 77.
14. Ibid., II, 244.
15. Ibid., I, 264, 265, 275; II, 41, 43, 125, 169, 170, 174.
16. Ibid., II, 236, 250, 251, 256, 260, 262, 263.
17. Ibid., 270, 271, 292, 294.
18. *New York Times,* March 7, p. 3; *FRUS*, 1961–63, II, 157.
19. The "Lessons Learned" collection, together with the remarkable reports of Australian Colonel Serong, is vol. 1 of the History Backup section (hereafter HB) of the William Westmoreland papers, LBJ.

20. HB, I/11, I/27.
21. HB, I/35.
22. *FRUS*, 1961–63, II, 244.
23. These took place in Tay Ninh province in January, as described by Hilsman; in Binh Duong province, March 9–11; Kien Hoa and Dinh Tuong, March 7–14; Kien Hoa again, April 4–5; Darlac, Tuyen Duc, and Quang Duc, April 12–27; and War Zone D in mid-June.
24. See "Lessons Learned," HB, XV/49, and the CIA situation report on this operation of Sept. 1, 1962, Newman papers, JFK. (The Newman collection is filed chronologically, with one folder per month, 1961–1963.)
25. *Newsweek,* Jan. 29, 1962, p. 43.
26. *FRUS*, 1961–63, II, 229.
27. See "Lessons Learned," nos. 15, 21, HB, I/31, I/45.
28. *FRUS*, 1961–63, II, 244.
29. Futrell with Blumenson, *The Advisory Years,* p. 145.
30. The lengthy conversation is in *FRUS*, 1961–63, II, 277.
31. See Newman, *JFK and Vietnam,* pp. 240–255.
32. Futrell with Blumenson, *The Advisory Years,* p. 152.
33. On the Honolulu meeting, see *FRUS*, 1961–63, II, 298; on the air support increase, ibid., 333. Some Nationalist Chinese pilots were also apparently added. See also Futrell with Blumenson, *The Advisory Years,* p. 140.
34. *FRUS*, 1961–63, II, 300, 320.
35. Report of Jan. 4, 1963, Newman papers, JFK.
36. Qiang, "Beijing and the Vietnam Conflict," p. 235.
37. His arrival was reported in the *New York Times,* Aug. 4, 1962, p. 4.
38. Harkins to Thuan, Oct. 5, 1962, Newman papers, JFK.
39. See "Report of PBT Ranger Operations in Zone D," March 30, 1963, Newman papers, JFK; see also *New York Times,* Nov. 21 and Dec. 4, 1962, and Futrell with Blumenson, *The Advisory Years,* p. 156.
40. Newman Papers, JFK.
41. *Vital Speeches of the Day,* Dec. 15, 1962, pp. 157–160.
42. See the classic works by Douglas Pike, *Viet Cong: The Organization and Techniques of the National Liberation Front of South Vietnam* (Cambridge, Mass., 1966), esp. pp. 85–118; and Jeffrey Race, *War Comes to Long An* (Berkeley, 1972), pp. 106–130.
43. Pike, *Viet Cong,* p. 115.
44. Sam Adams, *War Without Windows: An Intelligence Memoir* (South Royalton, Vt., 1994), pp. 41–87.
45. On this problem see General Cao Van Vien and General Dong Van Khuyen, *Reflections on the Vietnam War* (Washington, 1980), pp. 1–18.
46. Race, *War Comes to Long An,* pp. 106–130.
47. *FRUS*, 1961–63, I, 299; II, 98.
48. Ibid., II, 51.

49. South Vietnam Operation Plan and Border Control Plan, 8 Nov. 1961, NA, RG 218, JMF 9155.3/9105 Vietnam (8 Nov. 61).
50. *FRUS*, 1961–63, I, 337.
51. The plan, filed under JCS 9155.3/9105 (22 Feb. 1962), National Archives, RG 218, was declassified at my request.
52. *FRUS*, 1961–63, I, 13.
53. Ibid., II, 114.
54. See Hilsman's statements of Jan. 1963, ibid., III, 4.
55. Ibid., III, 93.
56. May 4, 1962, Newman papers, JFK.
57. *New York Times*, March 29, p. 1; April 1, p. 3; April 4, Week in Review; April 8, p. 3; Deptel 1173, April 4, 1962, JFK, NSF, VN, General, 4/1/62–4/10/62, box 196.
58. *FRUS*, 1961–63, II, 139.
59. *New York Times*, May 13, 1962.
60. HB, I/41; MACV to JCS, 081020Z Sept. 1962, Newman papers, JFK.
61. JCS, Operations Directorate, Situation Report, Nov. 28, 1962, Newman papers, JFK.
62. "The Implementation of the Strategic Hamlet Program," Newman papers, JFK. Newman filed this document under September 1962, although internal evidence clearly dates it at least six months later.
63. *FRUS*, 1961–63, III, 5, meeting of Jan. 2, 1963.
64. Ibid., II, 98, 16.
65. Ibid., II, 113; Hilsman memo, March 19, 1962, Newman papers, JFK.
66. *FRUS*, 1961–63, II, 204, 205.
67. Newman, *JFK and Vietnam*, pp. 248–249.
68. *FRUS*, 1961–63, II, 210, 211, 212, 216. The Saigon office of the Agency for International Development (AID) was known as the United States Operations Mission (USOM).
69. Ibid., 223, 225.
70. Ibid., 225, 231
71. Ibid., 242, 245.
72. Ibid., 248.
73. Ibid., 279.
74. Harkins oral history, LBJ (Nov. 10, 1981).
75. *FRUS*, 1961–63, II, 282, 202.
76. Ibid., 303, 314.
77. See ibid., 319, for Taylor's memo; a version including the informative maps and tables, CM-117–62, Nov. 17, has been declassified by the National Archives at my request.
78. Duiker, "The Revolutionary Path," ch. 15.
79. Interview with Senator Mike Mansfield, July 30, 1996.
80. *FRUS*, 1961–63, II, 69, 70.
81. Ibid., 93. *Newsweek* articles of Nov. 6, Jan. 29, and Feb. 19, by the cor-

respondents Robert Elegant and François Sully, had argued that Diem had lost touch with the people and refused to make necessary changes.

82. See Bigart's stories of March 13 and March 17, and Saigon 1215, March 23, 1962, JFK, NSF, VN, March 23–April 1.
83. *FRUS,* 1961–63, II, 159, 162, 167, 169.
84. Ibid., 218, 219.
85. *New York Times,* July 25, 1962.
86. *FRUS,* 1961–63, II, 268.
87. *New York Times,* Dec. 3, 1962, p. 12.
88. This was Mansfield's private opinion, conveyed indirectly to the State Department and subsequently to Kennedy. See *FRUS,* 1961–63, II, 334.
89. Ibid., 331.
90. Interview with Mike Mansfield, July 30, 1996.
91. See Duiker, "Waging Revolutionary War," pp. 30–31.
92. *New York Times,* May 13; *Newsweek,* May 28, p. 40.
93. *New York Times,* Aug. 8, p. 1; Neil Sheehan, *A Bright Shining Lie: John Paul Vann and America in Vietnam* (New York, 1988), pp. 79–91.
94. Sheehan, *Bright Shining Lie,* p. 93, confirms this figure.
95. Ibid., 117–120; *New York Times,* Oct. 6.
96. Neil Sheehan has described every detail of the Battle of Ap Bac, and we need not retrace his steps.
97. Sheehan, *Bright Shining Lie,* pp. 209–265.
98. JFK, NSF, VN, IX/7, 7a, 7b, 9.
99. Ibid., IX/11c.
100. *New York Times,* western ed., Jan. 8, 1963, editorial page. Despite the New York newspaper strike that blacked out the regular edition of the *Times,* the column drew widespread comment.
101. HB, I/61.
102. Strauss and Howe characterize the Silents as an adaptive or Artist generation, whose childhood during a great national crisis—in this case, the Depression and the Second World War—leave them sensitive to others feelings but always somewhat uncertain of their own. See *Generations,* pp. 279–294.

7. A Gathering Storm, January–July 1963

1. See *New York Times,* Sept. 28, 1962, p. 2, and the unattributed story by David Binder, Dec. 15, which makes many of the same points.
2. Futrell, *The Advisory Years,* p. 161.
3. *FRUS,* 1961–63, III, 15 (memo of Jan. 17).
4. For Harkins's plan of Jan. 19, 1963, and Felt's Jan. 25 endorsement for the JCS, see ibid., 18. The $234 million included $18 million for training the Montagnards. On the Farmgate augmentation see ibid., 16.
5. Ibid., 26.

6. Ibid., 27, 29.
7. Ibid., 33, 45, 50.
8. Harriman oral history, JFK.
9. *FRUS,* 1961–63, III, 66, 71, 100.
10. Telegram of March 26, ibid., 67.
11. Harkins argued that the South Vietnamese were conducting an appropriate mix of large- and small-scale operations, that the Comprehensive Plan and National Campaign Plan fulfilled the requirement for a plan, and that although the hamlet program might have moved too quickly in some areas, "strategic hamlets have proven effective regardless of standards or location." He dismissed Hilsman and Forrestal's recommendations for exerting more influence upon Diem as not recognizing "the Vietnamese personality or the modus operandi of President Diem and family. They have been tried in the past with largely negative results." CINCPAC 092320Z March 1963 for JCS, Newman papers, JFK.
12. This program was being slowly and laboriously transferred from CIA to military control.
13. Thus on March 18 Nolting cabled Harriman regarding a forthcoming General Accounting Office report criticizing both American aid operations and some GVN officials. "As it now stands," he wrote, "continued foreign press criticism of the GVN and US policy here, followed by the Mansfield report and signs of reluctance and disillusionment on the part of certain segments of US opinion, have without doubt encouraged coup plotting, have made the government here tighten up rather than liberalize, and have encouraged the enemy." *FRUS,* 1961–63, III, 63; cf. I, 56, the presidential program of May 1961.
14. MACV J-3 1046, 21 Feb. 63, Newman papers, JFK.
15. Report of 14 March 1963, HB, I/61.
16. *FRUS,* 1961–63, III, 41, and Harkins to Thuan, March 11, Newman papers, JFK (and see Harkins to General Ty, Feb. 18, ibid.). See also CIA Station Chief John Richardson's report of conversations with Nhu and Thuan, April 12, Newman papers, JFK (parts of this conversation, with significant deletions, are in *FRUS,* 1961–63, III, 88).
17. Newman papers, JFK.
18. Harkins to Felt, April 12, Newman papers, JFK.
19. *Washington Post,* March 18, A19.
20. Ibid., March 30, p. A11.
21. *New York Times,* April 13, p. 4; April 18, p. 3; April 19, p. 2; April 22, p. 2.
22. *Time,* May 17, pp. 40–41.
23. *FRUS,* 1961–63, III, 68, 81, 82.
24. Ibid., 88, and see Richardson's full record, April 12, Newman papers, JFK. The CIA apparently insisted that the published record eliminate any reference to Richardson's existence, and it reads like a monologue.

25. *FRUS,* 1961–63, III, 85, 87, 91.
26. Ibid., 99.
27. Ibid., 101, 102, 124.
28. Ibid., 77. Thompson also referred to Ap Bac as a "reverse."
29. John Mecklin, *Mission in Torment* (New York, 1965), pp. 129–151; Pierre Salinger, *With Kennedy* (New York, 1966), pp. 326–327; *FRUS,* 1961–63, III, 107 (May 3, 1963). This instruction was hand-delivered by Arthur Sylvester, McNamara's press chief, at a May 6 Honolulu conference.
30. One was shot down over the Plain of Jarres in November.
31. *FRUS,* 1961–63, XXIV, 427, 432, 435, 437, 440, 441, 443.
32. Conversations of Feb. 25 and 27, ibid., 443, 444.
33. Ibid., XXII, 174.
34. Ibid., XXIV, 448.
35. Ibid., 449, 451, 452.
36. Ibid., VII, 109, 127. This volume, on Basic National Security Policy, shows that the makers of the film *Dr. Strangelove* (1964) were very well informed about current strategic debates.
37. Ibid., VII, 125.
38. Ibid., XXII, 458, 459, 460.
39. Ibid., 462, 463, 464, 465, 466.
40. See the column by Kennedy's friend Charles Bartlett, *Chicago Sun-Times,* May 11, 1963, and Anderson's informative oral history, JFK. Anderson convincingly argued that events during the Cuban missile crisis were not the reason he was relieved. According to McGeorge Bundy's recollection, McNamara wanted to remove both Anderson and LeMay, but had to choose between them. Interview with McGeorge Bundy, Nov. 4, 1994.
41. *FRUS,* 1961–63, III, 73, 97.
42. "South Vietnam Operations-Intelligence Summary," April 29, 1963, JMF 9155.3/2200 (7 Jan. 63), National Archives.
43. CINCPAC Booklet for SecDef Meeting, May 6, Newman papers, JFK.
44. *FRUS,* 1961–63, III, 107.
45. *Time,* May 17, 1963, p. 40.
46. *FRUS,* 1961–63, III, 26, 107; Marolda and Fitzgerald, *The Navy and Vietnam,* II, pp. 334–335. See also notes of JCS meeting, May 14, HJ, MHI.
47. *Washington Post,* May 12, p. 1.
48. *FRUS,* 1961–63, III, 122, 127, 128.
49. Ibid., 126.
50. Chase and Lerman, *Kennedy and the Press,* pp. 447–448.
51. *FRUS,* 1961–63, III, 123.
52. A nearly complete set of the 1963 reports, filed chronologically amidst a great deal of other material, can be found in the Newman papers, JFK.

53. See the Headway Reports of May 10, 16, 24, and 31, 1963, Newman papers, JFK.
54. Headway Report, MACV 132025Z June, Newman papers, JFK.
55. See General Ty's order, June 18, Newman papers, JFK; and *FRUS*, 1961–63, III, 209, 209n.
56. "An Informal Appreciation of the Status of the Strategic Hamlet Program," June 1, 1963, copy in my possession.
57. *New York Times*, May 5, Week in Review.
58. Ernest R. May, *The Truman Administration and China, 1945–1949* (New York, 1975), pp. 81–82.
59. See *FRUS*, 1961–63, VII, 279, 285, 286, 288.
60. For the text of the speech see *Public Papers of the President, John F. Kennedy, 1963* (Washington, 1964), pp. 459–464; on the drafting, Theodore C. Sorensen, *Kennedy* (New York, 1965), pp. 730–731; on views of the test ban, *FRUS*, VII, 290, 291; on the role of the senators, *FRUS*, 1961–63, VII, 292. *FRUS* gives no indication that a merely atmospheric and underwater ban had been receiving any serious consideration from the executive branch at that time.
61. *New York Times*, April 28, Week in Review, p. 1.
62. *FRUS*, 1961–63, XXIV, 477, is Forrestal's memo for the President and the State-Defense Paper. A another copy of the paper, which I discovered in the Harriman papers, LC, was declassified by the Department of State with fewer deletions.
63. *FRUS*, 1961–63, XXIV, 478, 479, 481, 482.

8. The Buddhist Crisis and the Cable of August 24, 1963

1. See the initial American reports, *FRUS*, 1961–63, III, 112, 116, 117, 118, and the much later account of Ambassador to the United Nations Buu Hoi, Oct. 2, 1963, ibid., IV, 168.
2. See Ellen Hammer, *A Death in November* (New York, 1987); William Colby, *Lost Victory* (Chicago, 1989); Richard M. Nixon, *No More Vietnams* (New York, 1985); and Francis X. Winters, *The Year of the Hare* (Athens, Ga., 1997).
3. *FRUS*, 1961–63, III, 129, 131, 139.
4. Ibid., 138, 140, 141, 132, 144, 145, 146, 148, 149; *New York Times*, May 29, p. 5; June 2, p. 2.
5. *FRUS*, 1961–63, III, 149, 151, 153, 157, 158, 161, and *New York Times*, June 10, p. 1; see also Saigon telegram 1140, June 10, Newman papers, JFK.
6. *FRUS*, 1961–63, III, 163, 164, 167.
7. See ibid., 169, and Michael Forrestal's two oral history interviews, JFK and LBJ Libraries.

8. *FRUS,* 1961–63, III, 175.
9. Ibid., 168, 169, 170, 172, 177, 178.
10. *New York Times,* June 22, p. 6; July 3, p. 1.
11. Interview with William Trueheart, Nov. 1991.
12. *FRUS,* 1961–63, III, 181, 184, 185, 186, 190, 192, 193.
13. Ibid., 200, 202, 203, 205.
14. *New York Times,* July 3, p. 8.
15. *FRUS,* 1961–63, III, 219, 220; *New York Times,* July 14, p. 1; William W. Prochnau, *Once Upon a Distant War* (New York, 1995), pp. 326–331.
16. *FRUS,* 1961–63, III, 226, 227; *New York Times,* July 16–18, p. 1 stories.
17. *FRUS,* 1961–63, III, 228, 229, 230, 232, 233, 235, 237.
18. Ibid., VII, 316–353.
19. Ibid., VII, 318, 327.
20. Chase and Lerman, *Kennedy and the Press,* p. 461.
21. *New York Times,* July 21, Week in Review; *Time,* July 19, p. 33.
22. *FRUS,* 1961–63, III, 207; meetings of July 3, July 8, July 15, HJ, MHI.
23. *FRUS,* 1961–63, III, 207; Headway Reports, Newman papers, JFK.
24. Headway Reports of July 26 and Aug. 2, Newman papers, JFK.
25. *New York Times,* July 22, p. 1; July 27, p. 1; July 28, p. 4.
26. *FRUS,* 1961–63, III, 243, 244, 245.
27. *Time,* Aug. 9, 1963. The story even hinted that Diem and Mme. Nhu had a sexual relationship. On the genesis of the story and Mohr's coverage in general see Kim Willenson, ed., *The Bad War* (New York, 1987), pp. 171–177.
28. *FRUS,* 1961–63, III, 247, 248; *New York Times,* Aug. 8, p. 1.
29. *FRUS,* 1961–63, III, 105, 246.
30. Ibid., 256. Another paper gave a lengthy survey of potentially key personalities in a coup. Interestingly enough, no fewer than ten M-24 tanks and a dozen armored personnel carriers had been assigned to the Presidential Guard to ward off a coup.
31. TDCS 3/655,517, July 12, 1963, Newman papers, JFK.
32. *FRUS,* 1961–63, III, 250, 251, 252.
33. Ibid., 253.
34. Ibid., 253n.
35. *New York Times,* Aug. 15, p. 1.
36. *FRUS,* 1961–63, III, 257.
37. Ibid., 207.
38. Ibid., 259n.
39. CINCPAC 172325Z Aug. to JCS, DD, 1975, 267B.
40. *FRUS,* 1961–63, III, 255.
41. Ibid., summarizing Saigon 203 of Aug. 10, and 259.
42. Ibid., 260, and see *U.S.-Vietnam Relations,* III, IV.b.4., pp. 15–16.

43. See *FRUS*, 1961–63, III, 268; *New York Times*, Aug. 16–21.
44. *FRUS*, 1961–63, III, 268, 269.
45. *New York Times*, Aug. 22; Aug. 23.
46. *FRUS*, 1961–63, III, 270.
47. Ibid., 273, 274.
48. Ibid., 276. CIA cable, "Frustration and discontent among Vietnamese Army officers," Aug. 23, 1963, declassified at my request. The CIA has deleted virtually all identifying information from this cable, as well as the source of the information.
49. Ibid.
50. *New York Times*, Aug. 24, p. 1.
51. *FRUS*, 1961–63, III, 281.
52. See Taylor to Gilpatric, March 13, 1970, and Gilpatric to Taylor, March 20, 1970, Taylor papers, NDU, box 50.
53. *FRUS*, 1961–63, III, 282.
54. These events may be followed in *FRUS*, 1958–60, XVII, 298–310.
55. *New York Times*, Aug. 16, p. 2.
56. Sheehan, *Bright Shining Lie*, pp. 359–360.
57. Interview with William Trueheart, Nov. 1991.
58. *FRUS*, 1961–63, III, 284, 285. Washington learned about Harkins's conversation with Don only from Admiral Felt in Honolulu, not directly.
59. Ibid., 285, 286. Ball explained the change to Forrestal as follows on Sunday morning: "They're going to talk directly to the generals and not talk to Diem at all." They agreed that Kennedy did not have to be consulted, but Forrestal promised to inform him in Hyannis Port. LBJ, Ball papers, Vietnam, I/40.
60. Guthman and Shulman, *Robert Kennedy: In His Own Words*, pp. 396–397; William J. Rust, *Kennedy and Vietnam* (New York, 1985), p. 119; Taylor, *Swords and Plowshares*, p. 293; interview with McGeorge Bundy, Nov. 4, 1994.
61. According to Hilsman, a junior USIA officer used too much of Hilsman's own briefing to the press, including speculation (also reported in the *Times*) about American policy, in preparing this broadcast. Lodge, who was scheduled to meet Diem that day for the first time, was extremely upset. See *FRUS*, 1961–63, III, 287; see also Hilsman, *To Move a Nation*, pp. 489–490; Mecklin, *Mission in Torment*, pp. 193–195.
62. Two sets of records of the meetings for this week are now available. Records by Hilsman and Bromley Smith of the NSC staff may be found in *FRUS*, 1961–63, III, 289 (Aug. 26), 303 (Aug. 27); and IV, 1 (Aug. 28), 6 (also Aug. 28), 15 (Aug. 29), 26 (Aug. 30), and 37 (Aug. 31). Krulak's accounts of these meetings in the Taylor papers, NDU, box 51A, which have been declassified at my request, are usually more coherent and informative. More of Bromley Smith's records, which tend to be shorter, are at JFK.

63. Frederick Nolting, *From Trust to Tragedy* (New York, 1988), pp. 124–125.

64. *FRUS, 1961–63*, III, 293, 295, 305.

65. Ibid., 297, 300, 306.

66. Ibid., 307.

67. See ibid., IV, 4n6.

68. Ibid., III, 309.

69. Ibid., IV, 4.

70. Ibid., IV, 5. Rusk, Ball, Harriman, and Hilsman all transcribed many of their telephone conversations.

71. Queried in 1992, McGeorge Bundy denied having any notes of such a meeting.

72. *FRUS, 1961–63*, IV, 6, 6n; see also Aug. 28, 1963, telephone conversations, Harriman papers, LC. Forrestal immediately called Harriman to convey the President's remark.

73. *FRUS, 1961–63*, IV, 8. A second personal message from Kennedy to Lodge reaffirmed the policy of the telegrams of August 24 and 25, but added, "I trust you will not hesitate to recommend delay or change in plans if at any time you think it wise," and reaffirmed Washington's confidence in Harkins. Ibid., 9.

74. Ibid., 12, 13.

75. *New York Times*, Aug. 27, p. 3; Aug. 28, p. 1; Aug. 29, p. 3; *FRUS, 1961–63*, III, 294, 299. CIA cable, "Comments of Ngo Dinh Nhu on possible changes in U.S. policy toward South Vietnam," Aug. 27, 1963, declassified at my request. The CIA has deleted virtually all identifying information from this cable, as well as the source of the information.

76. *FRUS, 1961–63*, IV, 10; CIA cable, distributed Aug. 24, "Plans of Hanoi to increase military pressure in South Vietnam," recently declassified at my request. The CIA has deleted virtually all identifying information from this cable, as well as the source of the information.

77. *New York Times*, Aug. 26, p. 1; Aug. 27, pp. 1, 3; Aug. 28, p. 1; Aug. 29, p. 1.

78. Ibid., Aug. 29, p. 1; *FRUS, 1961–63*, IV, 15. Szulc declined in February 1996 to identify his sources, but recalled that all his stories had been multi-sourced.

79. *FRUS, 1961–63*, IV, 16, 18, 18n.

80. Ibid., 26n7.

81. Ibid., III, 258.

82. See Mieczyslaw Maneli, *War of the Vanquished* (New York, 1971), pp. 120–126.

83. *FRUS, 1961–63*, IV, 19, 20, 23, 48.

84. Thao—now generally assumed to have been a VC agent, as was widely suspected at the time—had reported that Generals Khiem, Khanh, and Big Minh were waiting for someone else to act. As others argued, his re-

port probably did not prove anything because no one trusted him. See ibid., 22.

85. Ibid., 32, 33.

86. Ibid., 46. For some reason the telegram describing these conversations did not go out until September 2.

87. *FRUS*, 1961–63, II, 35.

88. This comes from Krulak's record, *U.S.-Vietnam Relations*, XI, pp. 540–544. See also *FRUS*, 1961–63, IV, 37.

89. Gibbons, *The U.S. Government and the Vietnam War*, II, p. 161.

90. *FRUS*, 1961–63, IV, 43.

91. Chase and Lerman, *Kennedy and the Press*, pp. 485–486 (emphasis added).

9. The Coup, August–November 1963

1. *U.S.-Vietnam Relations*, III, IV.b.4, p. 42.

2. *FRUS*, 1961–63, IV, 54, 56, 57, 63, 66, 70. Hilsman suggested to Lodge that he use the threat of a congressional aid cut-off in his talks with Diem.

3. Ibid., 44. Although Geoffrey Warner, in "The United States and the Fall of Diem, Part II: The Death of Diem," *Australian Outlook* 28, no. 4 (1974), pp. 3–17, published an account of this conversation based upon d'Orlandi's diary, the *FRUS* editors have still deleted their names.

4. *FRUS*, 1961–63, IV, 58, 60.

5. Ibid., 72.

6. Ibid., 77.

7. Ibid., 76.

8. *New York Times*, Sept. 9, p. 1; Chase and Lerman, *Kennedy and the Press*, pp. 487–488; *FRUS*, 1961–63, III, 80.

9. Reports by Col. Bryce F. Denno, July 19; Lt. Col. Richard Powell, Sept. 9; Brig. Gen. Delk Oden, Sept. 9; and Col. Wilbur Wilson, III Corps adviser, Sept. 11, all in Newman papers, JFK.

10. *FRUS*, 1961–63, IV, 82 (Krulak's report) and 83 (meeting of Sept. 10). See also Krulak's own record of this meeting, Taylor papers, NDU, box 50.

11. According to Krulak's record, Mendenhall went further, saying that he and Trueheart agreed that the war could not be won under the Diem government.

12. None of the three note-takers at the meeting recorded this remark, but it has found its way into several subsequent histories and was recently confirmed by Phillips himself. It may be significant that Krulak's record omits Harriman from the list of participants. The next day Krulak, counterattacking, gave Bundy a rather unconvincing memo attempting to refute what Phillips had said about the situation in Long An province. JFK,

NSF, VN, box 199. Krulak's memo acknowledged 38 armed attacks and 256 total incidents involving strategic hamlets in Long An province.

13. *FRUS, 1961–63*, IV, 85.
14. Ibid., 93. On Rusk's role in the China White Paper see Warren I. Cohen, *Dean Rusk* (Totowa, N.J., 1980), pp. 39–41.
15. *FRUS, 1961–63*, III, 86.
16. Ibid., IV, 88, 89; *New York Times*, Sept. 11, pp. 1, 42.
17. *FRUS, 1961–63*, IV, 93, 94.
18. Ibid., 97.
19. Chase and Lerman, *Kennedy and the Press*, pp. 490–496.
20. *FRUS, 1961–63*, IV, 102, 111.
21. *FRUS, 1961–63*, IV, 96.
22. Ibid., 130, 134, 136, 138, 139.
23. Ibid., 104, 120. This real-life incident appears to be the origin of Seymour Hersh's fantastic story that Kennedy asked Lansdale to go to Saigon as CIA station chief to arrange Diem's assassination—a story which the record makes clear is without foundation. I informed Hersh—well before the publication of his book—that the White House calendar shows that Lansdale never saw Kennedy during 1963. See Hersh, *The Dark Side of Camelot*, pp. 426–428.
24. *New York Times*, Sept. 15, pp. 1, 4.
25. See Mecklin, *Mission in Torment*, pp. 222–223.
26. See *FRUS, 1961–63*, IV, 114, for cables that generally followed Hilsman's papers.
27. The telegram is ibid., 125; on the meetings, see 113, 115, 120n.
28. *New York Times*, Sept. 16, p. 2; *FRUS*, IV, 117. Halberstam seemed to quote from Phillips's June report on the strategic hamlet program as a whole, which no one in the White House had ever seen.
29. Ibid., 124, 125. To Harriman's horror, Rusk initially designated not Hilsman but U. Alexis Johnson, the Deputy Undersecretary for Political Affairs and Rusk's right-hand man, as the State Department representative.
30. See *FRUS, 1961–63*, IV, 126, and Saigon 557, Sept. 22, Newman papers, JFK.
31. McNamara memo, DD, 1982, 446B; USOM memo, Sept. 1, JFK, NSF, VN; Halberstam article, Sept. 16, 1963.
32. Alsop also took a parting shot at the young Saigon press corps before his departure, blaming them, in part, for Diem and Nhu's unfortunate views. See Alsop's columns, *Washington Post*, Sept. 16, 18, 20, 23.
33. *FRUS, 1961–63*, IV, 143.
34. See Maneli, *War of the Vanquished*, pp. 140–152.
35. About six months later Michael Forrestal told his oral history interviewer that Kennedy had always hoped that Diem might mend his ways. JFK.

36. *FRUS*, 1961–63, III, 258.
37. Ibid., IV, 54. Lippmann's Sept. 3 column appeared in the *Washington Post*, p. A13.
38. *FRUS*, 1961–63, III, 87.
39. "But this type of solution, laden with domestic political dynamite, lay well in the future—if it could be achieved at all." *Newsweek*, Sept. 23, 1963, pp. 25–26. Jonathan Alter of *Newsweek* provided me with the original documentation naming Hilsman, and this is the first available proof that Hilsman actually regarded neutralization of South Vietnam as a possibility at that time, as he has subsequently claimed. This dispatch also reported administration pressure on Mansfield not to speak out for neutralization.
40. *FRUS*, 1961–63, XXIV, 488, 489.
41. "Observations on Vietnam and Cuba," JFK, President's Office Files, box 128, 1. The memo might even have been written after Nov. 1.
42. *FRUS*, 1961–63, IV, 144; *New York Herald Tribune*, Sept. 23.
43. *FRUS*, 1961–63, IV, 150, 154, 158, 159, 160. McNamara, *In Retrospect*, pp. 74–75, supplies the names of Honey and Asta. Taylor also saw Big Minh, who spoke despairingly of the political and military situation; ibid., 162. Taylor ignored this conversation in *Swords and Plowshares*, pp. 326–327.
44. For these reports see Newman papers, JFK.
45. *FRUS*, 1961–63, IV, 163.
46. For the full text of the report see *U.S.-Vietnam Relations*, XII, pp. 554–573.
47. JFK, tape 114/A49, cassettes 2 and 3.
48. Although McNamara heard the tape of the Oct. 2 meeting as he prepared his book, *In Retrospect,* his account of this meeting (pp. 79–80) is extremely inaccurate.
49. See *FRUS*, 1961–63, IV, 169, 172, 174 (the meetings), 170 (the public statement of Oct. 2). On Forrestal and Sullivan's protests and McNamara's instructions to Bundy, see Gibbons, *The U.S. Government and the Vietnam War*, II, pp. 186–187; Chester Cooper, *The Lost Crusade* (New York, 1970), pp. 264–265; and Forrestal oral history, LBJ.
50. A partial tape has been released: JFK, tape 114/A50/2.
51. JFK, tape 114/A50/3.
52. *FRUS*, 1961–63, IV, 171, 177, 178, 192. Bundy seems to have been replying to another query from Lodge as well, one which the editors of *Foreign Relations* could not find.
53. Ibid., 181.
54. Ibid., 182.
55. On other reactions see Kern, Levering, and Levering, *The Kennedy Crises*, pp. 179–181.
56. *FRUS*, 1961–63, IV, 190.

57. JCS 051824Z Oct. 1963 to CINCPAC, Newman papers, JFK.

58. LBJ, Ball papers, Vietnam, telephone conversation, Oct. 4, 10:20 AM (emphasis added). The transcriber used strings of characters—e.g., "We #*&$ that up"—as substitutes for profanity. For many other examples of Kennedy using such language, see Bradlee, *Conversations with Kennedy.*

59. Clark Clifford with Richard Holbrooke, *Counsel to the President* (New York, 1991), p. 304.

60. Chase and Lerman, *Kennedy and the Press,* pp. 500–501, 508.

61. He also reported that Nhu was publicly continuing to advocate a reduced American presence. *FRUS,* 1961–63, IV, 184, 186.

62. *New York Times,* Oct. 4, p. 1; Oct. 5, p. 1.

63. *FRUS,* 1961–63, IV, 191, 193, 197, 203, 204, 207. The reports were submitted on Oct. 16 and 23.

64. Ibid., 195n.

65. Ibid., 171, 177, 178, 192.

66. Memo for record, Nov. 7, 1963, LBJ, NSF, VN, I/85c. Declassified at my request.

67. *FRUS,* 1961–63, IV, 206, 207n5.

68. Ibid., 209, 213, 214, 215.

69. *U.S.-Vietnam Relations,* XII, pp. 579–590.

70. *FRUS,* 1961–63, IV, 227.

71. Ibid., 240.

72. Ibid., 211, 216, 225.

73. Historical Division, Joint Secretariat, Joint Chiefs of Staff, *The Joint Chiefs of Staff and the War in Vietnam, 1960–1968* (Washington, 1971), I, ch. 7, pp. 24–25. (Each chapter of this work is paginated separately.)

74. Guthman and Shulman, *Robert Kennedy: In His Own Words,* pp. 400, 402–403.

75. Lodge claimed that Diem's statement in French—"Je ne vais pas servir"—made no sense, but to me it seems clear enough.

76. *FRUS,* 1961–63, IV, 220, 221.

77. Ibid., 234, 235, 236.

78. Ibid., 242.

79. Ibid., 240, 247.

80. Tape recording, meeting of Oct. 30, JFK, tape 118/A54.

81. *FRUS,* 1961–63, IV, 249, 249n.

82. Ibid., 262.

83. Ibid., 251–253, 255–260, 263–275.

84. See Hammer, *A Death in November,* pp. 312–323; William Colby, *Lost Victory* (Chicago, 1989); and Richard Nixon, *No More Vietnams* (New York, 1985), pp. 62–73.

85. Stuck in Washington, Lansdale in the late summer of 1963 had begun promoting the idea that Nhu—a self-styled intellectual—might accept a

position at Harvard. On Lansdale's views see Gibbons, *The U.S. Government and the Vietnam War*, II, pp. 165–166. Phillips has recently confirmed to me that he shared this view.

86. JFK, cassette M/2.

87. As maintained, scandalously, by Hersh in *The Dark Side of Camelot*.

88. See *FRUS, 1961–63*, IV, 224, 225, 245, 332. On the munitions shortage see John Schlight, *The War in South Vietnam: The Years of the Offensive, 1965–1968* (Washington, 1988), pp. 69, 79, 117, 155.

89. Ibid., 15n5.

90. See Zubok and Pleshakov, *Inside the Kremlin's Cold War*, pp. 269–271.

91. Six weeks later, in his September 19 talk with Ambassador to West Germany George McGhee, Kennedy expressed the hope that Germany's opposition to détente might ease—thinking, perhaps, of Adenauer's finally impending retirement—and, McGhee thought, seemed to agree that German reunification was more likely after a relaxation of current tensions. Harriman memo, July 30, 1963, Harriman papers, LC, box 541; *FRUS, 1961–63*, XV, 202, 214.

92. Kennan, *Memoirs, 1950–1963*, p. 317.

93. Guthman and Shulman, *Robert Kennedy: In His Own Words*, pp. 390–392.

94. *FRUS, 1961–63*, IV, 311, 313. Forrestal even saw the editorial writer Robert Kleiman to try to change his views, unsuccessfully.

95. Ibid., XXIII, 111, 114, 119.

96. Chase and Lerman, *Kennedy and the Press*, p. 516.

97. *New York Times*, Nov. 13, p. 1; *FRUS, 1961–63*, IV, 312.

98. *New York Times*, Nov. 16, p. 1.

99. Meeting of Nov. 18, HJ, MHI.

100. Newman papers, JFK.

101. FRUS, 1961–63, III, 207; IV, 82, 218.

102. Robert Komer, an NSC staffer, was responsible for the Middle East and South Asia.

103. Adlai Stevenson had been booed and struck with signs on a visit to Dallas on October 24.

104. Memo by William Y. Smith, Taylor papers, NDU, box 25. Declassified at my request.

10. A Decision for War, November 1963–April 1964

1. The best works on Johnson are the multivolume biographies by Robert Dallek, *Lone Star Rising* (New York, 1991) and *Flawed Giant* (New York, 1998); and by Robert Caro, *The Path to Power* (New York, 1982), and *Means of Ascent* (New York, 1990). Although parts of Caro's first volume are some of the most extraordinary American history ever written, the level of his analysis falls off drastically in volume 2.

Dallek is far more concise, far more balanced, and, best of all, managed to bring his task to completion, something which Caro, alas, will have difficulty doing at his current pace. Lloyd C. Gardner, *Pay Any Price: Lyndon Johnson and the Wars for Vietnam* (Chicago, 1995) is a provocative attempt to relate Vietnam to other parts of Johnson's career.

2. *New York Times,* Nov. 28, p. 21.

3. See LBJ, NSF, MP, I/84 et seq.; see, e.g., I/75, Dec. 1, 1964; I/73, Dec. 2; and I/61, Dec. 6, on Dean Acheson, who, Bundy reported, had "no use for less developed countries, the UN, Adlai Stevenson, or George Kennan."

4. Johnson, of course, met many foreign leaders who came to Washington for Kennedy's funeral, but without any opportunity to have serious discussions.

5. *FRUS, 1961–63,* XV, 247, 248, 249, 250, 253, 254.

6. LBJ, NSF, MP, I/47, I/46, I/44.

7. *New York Times,* Jan. 1, p. 3; Jan. 2, p. 1; Jan. 3, p. 1.

8. LBJ, NSF, MP, vol. 1, Jan. 13.

9. Ibid., IV/28–28a, May 14.

10. Ibid., VII/63, VII/26; and *FRUS, 1961–63,* XIII, 63, on the Wilson visit.

11. Anderson oral history, JFK. This testimony is all the more remarkable since McNamara, with Kennedy's approval, had relieved Anderson as Chief of Naval Operations in the spring of 1963.

12. H. R. Haldeman's published diaries give a good account of Nixon's work habits. Actually Nixon relaxed slightly more than Johnson, since he sometimes watched sports events on television, which Johnson never did.

13. See the appointment calendars of the two Presidents at their respective presidential libraries.

14. Report of May 23, 1961, LBJ, VPSF, Vice President's Visit to Southeast Asia (I).

15. See reports of March 16, March 20, Aug. 13, and Aug. 17, 1962, LBJ, VPSF, box 6.

16. "Certainly," he had told the ExCom on August 31 after Kattenburg's famous remarks, "the US itself could not pull a coup and certainly there were bad situations in South Vietnam. However, there were bad situations in the U.S. It was difficult to live with [Louisiana Congressman and subcommittee chairman] Otto Passman, but we couldn't pull a coup on him." See *FRUS, 1961–63,* IV, 37, and Forrestal oral history, LBJ.

17. Johnson actually was much more impressed with the possibility that Kennedy had died in retaliation for assassination plots against Castro.

18. On Johnson and Hilsman see William Bundy oral history, LBJ.

19. *FRUS, 1961–63,* IV, 330.

20. Ibid., 336, 337n.

21. *New York Times,* Dec. 6, p. 10.

22. See notes of JCS meeting of Nov. 29, HJ, MHI.
23. *FRUS, 1961–63,* IV, 331, 331n1. John Newman, in *JFK in Vietnam,* pp. 445–449, argues that the revised draft called for plans for American action against North Vietnam. As we shall see, this interpretation is not consistent with subsequent events, although such plans rapidly emerged.
24. Exactly what Kennedy approved has, scandalously, not been entirely declassified. For a sanitized version see *FRUS, 1961–63,* XXIV, 481, 482. A copy of an earlier, similar list of proposed operations in a June 17, 1963, memo for the President from the Harriman papers includes the declassification of the South Vietnamese cross-border operations and one or two other actions, which the *FRUS* versions do not.
25. This quote was given to me on condition of anonymity; the speaker has since died.
26. See Headway Reports, MACV 080320Z Nov., 150233Z Nov., 060300Z Dec., 130350Z Dec., 200315Z Dec., 270053Z Dec., Newman papers, JFK; and 1311601Z Nov. and 290248Z Nov., CMH (the last two, missing from the Newman papers, were provided to me by Vincent Demma).
27. *FRUS, 1961–63,* IV, 352, 369.
28. Ibid., 366.
29. See *FRUS, 1961–63,* XXIII, 125; IV, 334, 341, 344, 358, 359, 365, 367.
30. JCS meeting of Dec. 2, HJ, MHI.
31. *FRUS, 1961–63,* IV, 340, 351, 354.
32. *The Joint Chiefs and the War,* I, ch. 8, p. 18 (emphasis added).
33. Meeting of Dec. 9, HJ, MHI.
34. LBJ, conversation 1195.
35. *New York Times,* Nov. 28, p. 17; Dec. 13, p. 1; Jan. 2, 1964, p. 2; Jan. 3, p. 22; Jan. 15, p. 30; March 27, p. 26.
36. *FRUS, 1961–63,* IV, 370.
37. Ibid., 373.
38. Ibid., 374 (McNamara's report), 376.
39. Ibid., 347, and see two State Department memos of Dec. 11 and Vientiane 682 of Dec. 13, LBJ, NSF, Laos, I/81 and I/104.
40. Marolda and Fitzgerald, *The Navy and Vietnam,* II, p. 337 (emphasis added).
41. *FRUS, 1961–63,* IV, 372, 374. A copy of the State-Defense CIA message of Jan. 16, 1964, confirms that Johnson was briefed: LBJ, MP, II/366. It is dated Jan. 23.
42. PP, III, p. 151.
43. *The Joint Chiefs and the War,* I, ch. 8, pp. 20–21.
44. *FRUS, 1964–68,* I, 13, 14, 14n4. Exactly why what the President approved has never been declassified and why it was omitted from the *Pentagon Papers* are extremely interesting questions.

45. Data on Viet Cong activity come from the weekly Headway Reports, available through 1963 in the Newman papers, JFK, and at CMH. Vincent Demma of CMH graciously provided me with some reports. On the political consequences of the coup, see Pike, *Viet Cong*, pp. 163–164.

46. Duiker, "The Revolutionary Path," ch. 15.

47. Presidential Counsel Theodore Sorensen—who had already decided to leave the White House—took a slightly different line. While also rejecting neutralization at present and declaring that Democrats could not abandon the commitment to maintaining South Vietnamese independence, he suggested to Johnson "that you continue to emphasize that the South Vietnamese have the primary responsibility for winning the war—so that if during the next four months the new government fails to take the necessary political, economic, social and military actions, it will be their choice and not our betrayal or weakness that loses that area." *FRUS, 1964–68,* I, 2, 8; 1961–63, IV, 355; for Sorensen's memo of Jan. 14 see LBJ, NSF, VN, II/127a.

48. Meetings of Jan. 7 and Jan. 20, HJ, MHI, and PP, III, pp. 496–8.

49. *New York Times,* Jan. 28, p. 1; Jan. 29, p. 32. The Jan. 29 edition includes a full text of McNamara's statement. See also Feb. 19, p. 1.

50. *FRUS, 1964–68,* I, 34, 36.

51. Lodge had reported that the Italian ambassador, d'Orlandi, had passed such rumors along to him on January 20. See Kahin, *Intervention,* p. 198.

52. See Saigon 1307, Jan. 15, 1964; Saigon 1398, Jan. 26; and Saigon 1469, Feb. 1, LBJ, NSF, VN, vols. II–III.

53. PP, III, pp. 307–308.

54. Harkins oral history, MHI. To my knowledge no text has ever quoted this critical statement, which confirms Kahin's argument in *Intervention,* pp. 189–202.

55. *FRUS, 1964–68,* I, 19.

56. "One thing is for sure," Harkins commented ruefully, "with this coup, we've gone through all the eligible general officers." See Harkins's cables, MACV 300305Z Jan. and 300430Z Jan. to Taylor, DD, 1975, 156C and 156D.

57. See CIA, "Appraisal of General Khanh," March 20, 1964, LBJ, NSF, VN, VI/49.

58. *FRUS, 1964–68,* I, 30.

59. *FRUS, 1964–68,* I, 54, 55, 56; *New York Times,* Feb. 22, pp. 1, 3; see also Feb. 25, p. 1.

60. *FRUS, 1964–68,* I, 34.

61. It should be noted that even Hilsman was now focusing on conventional action against North Vietnam. In a farewell memo on March 14 he argued for an immediate military buildup in Southeast Asia, "improving

our capability to take whatever military steps may be necessary to halt Communist aggression in the area." He too seems to have believed that the United States could buy time to make things work in South Vietnam by intimidating the Communist powers. Ibid., 90.

62. Ibid., 57. Some references to nuclear weapons have been deleted from this document, but the Chiefs' reply and the surrounding context make it easy to identify them.

63. Emphasis added. For McNamara's memo and the Chiefs' reply, see *FRUS, 1964–68*, I, 57, 66.

64. March 1 meeting, HJ, MHI.

65. JCSM-168–64, in JCS 2343/330, declassified at my request.

66. Annex A, Appendix B, JCSM-174–64, declassified at my request.

67. Douglas Pike, in *PAVN: People's Army of Vietnam* (Novato, Calif., 1986), p. 190, gives a 1965 estimate of 400,000 men.

68. See Cable, *Conflict of Myths*, passim, and *FRUS, 1964–68*, I, 65, calling for attacks into Laos, Cambodia, and North Vietnam.

69. On LeMay, MacDonald, and Greene, see *The Joint Chiefs and the War*, I, ch. 9, pp. 2–9.

70. Ibid., p. 8, and meeting of March 1, HJ, MHI.

71. For this draft see DD, 1975, 157A.

72. Bundy memo, March 2, and Saigon 1715, March 9, LBJ, NSF, VN, IV–V.

73. LBJ, telephone conversations, March 2, 11:00 AM, #2301.

74. Ibid., March 4, 1:48 PM, #2345.

75. *FRUS, 1964–68*, I, 67.

76. See meeting of March 2, HJ, MHI.

77. Memo for record, March 4, GP, MCHC (emphasis added).

78. March 24, 7:26 PM, #2640–1. The President added that Taylor did not believe another "Korean type operation" would result, but that Greene and LeMay did think so, while MacDonald came down in the middle and Wheeler "didn't say much."

79. Greene memo, GP, MCHC; *FRUS, 1964–68*, I, 70, 71, 72.

80. For this draft see LBJ, NSF, VN, V/43. An interesting section on negotiations, which he subsequently dropped, recognized that to secure its objectives the United States would have to ask for *more* than observance of the 1954 Geneva Accords, including a removal of the limitations upon foreign assistance to South Vietnam, effective international policing of South Vietnam's borders, and dropping the provision for all-Vietnam elections.

81. *New York Times*, March 1, Week in Review, p. 8.

82. Telephone conversation, March 9, 9:45 PM, #2441.

83. McNamara press conference, *Newsweek* dispatch of March 12, *Newsweek* files.

84. *FRUS, 1964–68*, I, 77; *New York Times*, March 10, p. 1; March 14, p. 1.

85. Norman dispatches, March 12 and 13, *Newsweek* files.

86. *FRUS, 1964–68*, I, 82, 84. Bundy dropped his section on negotiating terms, although he made clear that the United States should insist upon a South Vietnam that could continue to avoid the all-Vietnam elections called for in the 1954 Accords.

87. Memo for record, March 16 and 17, GP, MCHC.

88. *FRUS, 1964–68*, I, 84, 86, 87.

89. Ibid., 92 (cable of March 20).

90. Ibid., 91, 92 (March 19 and 20.)

91. Ibid., 101, 102; Greene memos for record, March 27, April 11, April 17, GP, MCHC.

92. See JCSM 298–64, April 14 (JCS 2343/345–3), with enclosures, and CSAM 203–64, March 31, both declassified at my request.

93. *FRUS, 1964–68*, I, 99, 100. For the Headway Reports of March 23 and the remainder of 1964, see University Publications of America microfilms, *Records of the Military Assistance Command, Vietnam,* reel 2.

94. "Tell Bill [Bundy] his one commission as my appointee is to be damn sure [Lodge's] recommendations are either carried out or I know about it," Johnson told McGeorge Bundy on March 20. Telephone conversations, #2574.

95. *FRUS, 1964–68*, I, 54, 71, 86, 112, 116, 128, 178.

96. This remarkable memo is LBJ, NSF, MP, I/33. See also *FRUS, 1964–68*, I, 100. It reveals one of the most striking examples of McNamara's ability to hold and profess opposite views at the same time.

97. Harkins complained that Lodge was insisting that he clear all his meetings with General Khanh with Deputy Chief of Mission David Nes, and not with Lodge himself. Rusk agreed with Lodge in principle, but added optimistically that Harkins's calls might be discussed with Lodge "alongside the other important business that you and he should be transacting on a regular basis." *FRUS, 1964–68*, I, 133, 144, 144n.

98. MACV 141029Z Feb. 1964, CMH.

99. Nes to Forrestal, April 7 and May 6, Nes papers, LBJ.

100. See JCSM-298–64 and enclosures.

101. The claims of H. R. McMaster, in *Dereliction of Duty: Johnson, McNamara, the Joint Chiefs of Staff, and the Lies that Led to Vietnam* (New York, 1997), are not supported by newly available documentation. The Chiefs in early 1964 seem to have had no idea what the war would require.

11. To the Tonkin Gulf, April–August 1964

1. See Goodwin, *Remembering America*, pp. 244–246. Several Kennedy loyalists regarded this as a tremendous step backward for American policy toward Latin America.

2. LBJ, conversation of Jan. 10, #1305.
3. Conversations with Richard Russell and McGeorge Bundy, Jan. 10, #1305, #1307, #1309.
4. *FRUS*, 1964–68, I, 41.
5. See Howard Palfrey Jones, *Indonesia: The Possible Dream* (New York, 1971), pp. 188–232, 262–351.
6. See *FRUS*, 1961–63, XX, passim, on the Congo crisis under Kennedy; and Piero Gleijeses, "'Flee! The White Giants are Coming!': The United States, the Mercenaries, and the Congo, 1964–65," *Diplomatic History* 18, no. 2 (spring 1994), pp. 207–237.
7. LBJ, NSF, MP, Feb. 25, 1964, I/106a.
8. LBJ, NSF, countries, Cambodia, I/90, Deptel 991 to Saigon; I/68 and I/65, Deptel 610, 630, Jan. 4 and 6; I/21, Circular 1506, Feb. 14; I/5, Deptel 585, Feb. 28; II/157, Forrestal for the President, March 22; II/164, Rusk for Butler, March 22.
9. *FRUS*, 1964–68, XXX, 4 (conversation of Jan. 18).
10. Ibid., I, 59, 94, 96, 105.
11. Ibid., I, 110, 111, 116, 118, 119, 120, and see William Bundy's memo for record, April 27, and Rusk's Secto 74, April 20, LBJ, NSF, VN, VII/182, VII/179.
12. *FRUS*, 1964–68, I, 136, 137, 138, 140, 141, 142
13. Ibid., I, 154, 155; *New York Times*, May 16, 1964, p. 1; May 17, Week in Review, pp. 1, 3.
14. *New York Times*, April 25, p. 2.
15. LBJ, NSF, Laos, II/159, II/157, II/119, II/105.
16. These events can be followed in LBJ, NSF, Laos, II. Ambassador Unger continually warned that excessive American action in violation of the Geneva Accords might trigger North Vietnamese moves that only American intervention could meet. Like Souvanna himself, he suggested that there would be no lasting political solution in Laos without a settlement in Vietnam. On the coup see the CIA report of April 19, II/91.
17. *FRUS*, 1964–68, I, 167. Bundy refers to this conversation in this memo of May 22, but we have no information on the conversation itself as yet.
18. Even Harriman, who was now generally excluded from decisions on Southeast Asia, endorsed strong action in a memo for Rusk, rejecting de Gaulle's calls for a reconvened Geneva conference. *FRUS*, 1964–68, I, 164; Harriman memo of May 22, LBJ, NSF, Laos, V/206; Unger to Rusk, May 20, ibid., IV/6; *New York Times*, May 22, p. 1.
19. *New York Times*, May 22, pp. 1, 34; May 23, p. 1.
20. *FRUS*, 1964–68, I, 172; see also William Sullivan's and McNaughton's memos of May 24, ibid., 170, 171.
21. Goodpaster memo for record, May 25, 1964, "Four Meetings on Extension of Operations Against North Vietnam, 24–25 May," CJCS File 091

Vietnam (25 May 64), National Archives, RG 218 (declassified at my request).

22. *FRUS, 1964–68*, I, 173, 178, 181.
23. Russell appeared to be thinking that the Buddhist leader Thich Tri Quang might be allowed to come to power, although he did not name him. Russell repeated this suggestion to McCone some months later. Greene memo for record, Oct. 31, GP, MCHC.
24. The conversations with Bundy and Russell have been published in Michael R. Beschloss, ed., *Taking Charge: The Johnson White House Tapes, 1963–64* (New York, 1997), pp. 363–370.
25. Conversations of May 28 (#3539) and June 1 (#3602–3604). Smathers also blamed McNamara for the administration's apparent eagerness for war. The Kennedy conversation is in Beschloss, *Taking Charge,* pp. 374–378.
26. *FRUS, 1964–68,* I, 173, 182.
27. See Tosec 36, May 29, and Bundy for Johnson, May 30, LBJ, NSF, Laos, VI/146, VI/146a. Bundy assured Johnson that Stevenson, Robert Kennedy, and Harriman had fully agreed.
28. *FRUS, 1964–68,* I, 184, 185.
29. *Public Papers of the President, Lyndon B. Johnson, 1963–64,* I, pp. 377–379.
30. LBJ, telephone conversations with Bundy and Rusk, June 2, #3612–3614.
31. LBJ, NSF, Laos, V/187.
32. Meeting of June 6, JP, MHI.
33. A few days later Taylor submitted his personal opinion that civilian authority might begin with an even more restricted option—"demonstrative strikes against limited military targets"—and that the Chiefs should prepare this option as well. *FRUS, 1964–68,* I, 191, 199 (emphasis added).
34. Ibid., I, 188 (emphasis added).
35. PP, III, p. 175, quoting from a fuller record.
36. *FRUS, 1964–68,* I, 188, 189.
37. The President did authorize an American approach to the Thai government regarding a plan to seize the Mekong River towns. *FRUS, 1964–68,* I, 192; meeting of June 5, JP, MHI.
38. *FRUS, 1964–68,* I, 198, 200. Seven divisions had been the maximum US force in Korea.
39. LBJ, NSF, Laos, VI/71.
40. LBJ, NSF, Aides Files, McGeorge Bundy, I/22.
41. Ibid., I/24.
42. Ibid., I/14, and LBJ, NSF, MP, June 24, V/13.
43. This portion of the meeting is in *FRUS, 1964–68,* I, 210. Another long,

unrecorded meeting on June 15 apparently decided against a resolution as well; see ibid., 214n2. The CIA may have a record of this meeting in Director McCone's files.

44. These developments can be followed in LBJ, NSF, Laos, VII–X, esp. William Bundy for the President, June 28, VII/119; McGeorge Bundy for the President, June 28, VII/117; James Thompson for McGeorge Bundy, July 23, VIII/156; Deptel 99 to Vientiane, June 29, VIII/9; Vientiane 276, Aug. 9, IX/40; "Laos Situation," Sept. 18, X/97a.

45. *FRUS*, 1964–68, I, 214, 215.

46. *New York Times*, June 22, p. 1.

47. See *FRUS*, 1964–68, I, 222, and Kahin, *Intervention*, p. 213.

48. Qiang, "Beijing and the Vietnam Conflict," p. 235.

49. *New York Times*, May 27, p. 1.

50. Bundy's suggestion of RFK eventually appeared in James Reston's column of June 17, probably increasing the President's doubts about Bundy's discretion. *FRUS*, 1964–68, I, 204; *New York Times*, June 17, p. 42.

51. Conversations of June 15–16, cited by Beschloss, *Taking Charge*, pp. 407–411.

52. *New York Times*, June 24, p. 36; June 28, p. 1; June 30, p. 1.

53. *FRUS*, 1964–68, I, 242, 243, 245, 246, 248, 249.

54. *New York Times*, July 25, p. 1; July 28, p. 1.

55. Memo for record, July 31, GP, MCHC.

56. All other sources on these operations and the Tonkin Gulf incidents have been superseded by Edwin E. Moise, *Tonkin Gulf and the Escalation of the Vietnam War* (Chapel Hill, 1996). See also Marolda and Fitzgerald, *The Navy and Vietnam*, II, pp. 393–408. Both works decisively undermine the picture presented by McNamara in *In Retrospect*, pp. 128–132.

57. Moise, *Tonkin Gulf*, pp. 73–74.

58. Ibid., pp. 84–86.

59. Telephone conversations, Aug. 1, #4603–4604.

60. Moise, *Tonkin Gulf*, p. 90, and see *FRUS*, 1964–68, I, 257, 258, 259.

61. LBJ, Gibbons papers, State Documents 1960–64, I/15, Michael Forrestal for Rusk, Aug. 8. Forrestal complained that responsible State Department officials had not been informed of this decision.

62. See Johnson's telephone conversation with Robert Anderson, Aug. 3, in Beschloss, *Taking Charge*, p. 493. LBJ, Ball papers, telephone conversations, I/79, Aug. 3, reports Bundy's conclusion.

63. Beschloss, *Taking Charge*, pp. 495–497.

64. *FRUS*, 1964–68, I, 262.

65. LBJ, Ball papers, telephone conversations, I/76, and *FRUS*, 1964–68, I, 271.

66. *New York Times*, Aug. 4, p. 1, two stories.

67. Marolda and Fitzgerald, *The Navy and Vietnam*, II, 421–425; Gibbons, *The U.S. Government and the Vietnam War*, II, p. 288.

68. Moise, *Tonkin Gulf,* pp. 112–113.
69. Beschloss, *Taking Charge,* p. 496.
70. LBJ, telephone conversations, #4662a.
71. See Moise, *Tonkin Gulf,* pp. 106–207, esp. 203–207.
72. *FRUS, 1964–68,* I, 272, 273, 274, 275, 276; Gibbons, *The U.S. Government and the Vietnam War,* II, pp. 292–293.
73. See Gibbons, *The U.S. Government and the Vietnam War,* II, pp. 289–292.
74. Ibid.
75. *FRUS, 1964–68,* I, 280.
76. Beschloss, *Taking Charge,* pp. 503–504.
77. Moise, *Tonkin Gulf,* pp. 214–231.
78. *FRUS, 1964–68,* I, 290. Apparently relying on anecdotal evidence, Halberstam severely distorted the tone of this exchange in *The Best and the Brightest,* pp. 503–504.
79. Gibbons, *The U.S. Government and the Vietnam War,* II, pp. 302–303, 306–307.
80. Ibid., pp. 310–313.
81. William Gibbons points out that the unanimity was only apparent, since two congressmen, the Democrat Adam Clayton Powell of New York—who described himself as a pacifist—and the maverick Republican Eugene Siler of Kentucky, who had earlier opposed the entire American effort in South Vietnam, refused to vote for it.
82. Ibid., pp. 308–310, 316–330.
83. Ibid., pp. 322–330.
84. *FRUS, 1964–68,* I, 282, 288, 294, 302. No. 282 erroneously describes a telegram to British Prime Minister *Macmillan,* who had resigned some months earlier.
85. *New York Times,* Aug. 9, p. 8.
86. Duiker, "The Revolutionary Path," ch. 15.
87. Futtrell and Blumenson, *The Advisory Years to 1965,* pp. 229–230; *New York Times,* Aug. 9, Week in Review, p. 3; Qiang, "Beijing and the Vietnam Conflict," p. 235.
88. Ilya Gaiduk, *The Soviet Union and the Vietnam War* (Chicago, 1996), pp. 12–21.
89. Duiker, "The Revolutionary Path," ch. 15.
90. Memo for record, Sept. 12, GP, MCHC.

12. Planning for War, September–December 1964

1. *FRUS, 1964–68,* I, 317, 321, 325, 328, 330, 332, 333, 335. *New York Times,* Aug. 24, p. 1; Aug. 27, p. 3; Sept. 6, p. 1.
2. *FRUS, 1964–68,* I, 307.
3. Ibid., I, 313, 316.

4. HB, VII/74, 150123Z Aug.; VII/91, 20 Aug.; PP, III, 179; *FRUS, 1964–68*, I, 318.

5. *FRUS*, I, 319.

6. See Appendix B and Enclosure B to JCS 2339/149, JCS records (declassified at my request.)

7. *FRUS, 1964–68*, I, 331; PP, III, 186, 187, 188; *New York Times*, Sept. 5, p. 1.

8. See CSAM 499–64, 25 Sept., JCSM 9155.3 (25 Sept. 64), and Memo by Chief of Staff, U.S. Air Force, Oct. 9, ibid., declassified at my request.

9. *FRUS, 1964–68*, I, 331.

10. PP, III, 188.

11. *FRUS, 1964–68*, I, 342.

12. Ibid., I, 343; *New York Times*, Sept. 10, pp. 1, 13.

13. Week in Review, p. 3.

14. *FRUS, 1964–68*, I, 347, 348, 349, 350, 351, 352, 354, 355; *New York Times*, Sept. 15, p. 1; Sept. 16, p. 30.

15. *FRUS*, I, 356; *New York Times*, Sept. 20, p. 1; Sept. 22, p. 1.

16. *FRUS, 1964–68*, I, 359; Headway Reports of Sept. 28 and Oct. 5, MACV records.

17. *FRUS, 1964–68*, I, 366 (Taylor cable of Sept. 30), 367 (Forrestal for Bundy, Sept. 30), 368 (Special National Intelligence Estimate, Oct. 1), 382.

18. Westmoreland for Taylor, Nov. 24, DD, 1977, no. 288E.

19. MACV 211045Z Sept. 64, Headway Reports, MACV records.

20. Westmoreland for Taylor, Nov. 24, DD, 1977, no. 288E.

21. Headway Reports, MACV records.

22. DD, 1977, 288e (emphasis added).

23. See McNamara, *In Retrospect,* p. 157. While willing in his memoir to admit his own mistakes, McNamara generally fails to give any credit to those who disagreed with him at the time.

24. Ball published his memo in the *Atlantic Monthly,* July 1972, pp. 36–49.

25. *New York Times*, Sept. 29, p. 1; Oct. 2, pp. 14, 36. On Bundy's advocacy see Gibbons, *The U.S. Government and the Vietnam War,* III, pp. 12–13.

26. Bundy added, "(Check this for accuracy)" in his text. I have been unable to find any specific record of this war game.

27. LBJ, NSF, Countries, Southeast Asia, IV/85.

28. JCSM-933–64, Nov. 4, 1964, JCS records (declassified at my request); see also *FRUS*, I, 393, 394, 395.

29. *FRUS*, I, 396, 397, 398.

30. *FRUS*, XXX, 49. The same meeting also decided to raise the issue of joint action against the Chinese with the Soviets, but Soviet Ambassador Dobrynin declined to pick up Bundy's hint on Sept. 25; ibid., 53.

31. Memo for record, Nov. 2, GP, MCHC.

32. *FRUS,* 1964–68, I, 403, and see PP, III, pp. 588–590.

33. The authors also suggested that bombing would not be able to cripple North Vietnam's overwhelmingly agricultural and decentralized economy, and anticipated that North Vietnamese leaders would willingly suffer "some damage to the country" in a test of wills. Draft of Nov. 13, LBJ, NSF, VN, Nov. 1964, Courses of Action in Southeast Asia (hereafter CASEA), I/4.

34. See George Ball, *The Past Has Another Pattern* (New York, 1982), pp. 383–384.

35. See LBJ, NSF, VN, Nov. 1964, CASEA, I/15 and I/16, for this draft.

36. Draft of Nov. 8, LBJ, WM, II/22.

37. See LBJ, NSF, VN, CASEA, I/23–25.

38. See the Nov. 8 draft, PP, III, 226, and the Nov. 13 draft, LBJ, NSF, VN, CASEA, I/27.

39. *FRUS,* 1964–68, I, 408, 409.

40. PP, III, 228, 231.

41. *FRUS,* 1964–68, I, 411.

42. PP, III, 234.

43. *FRUS,* 1964–68, XXX, 66.

44. *FRUS,* 1964–68, I, 417.

45. See the note by Robert Johnson covering a memo from Harold Ford and George Carver, Nov. 19, LBJ, WM, IV/2.

46. LBJ, WM, III/20 (declassified at my request).

47. LBJ, NSF, VN, Southeast Asia Memos, IV/67.

48. *New York Times,* Nov. 23, p. 1.

49. *FRUS,* 1964–68, I, 418 (emphasis added).

50. Ibid., I, 420, and see *The Joint Chiefs and the War,* I, ch. 14, p. 29.

51. For an account of the discussion apparently based on William Bundy's handwritten notes—which I have not seen—see PP, III, pp. 236–239. The conclusions are in *FRUS,* 1964–68, I, 424.

52. See McMaster, *Dereliction of Duty,* pp. 179–196.

53. *FRUS,* 1964–68, I, 426.

54. Ibid., I, 425.

55. Ibid., I, 427.

56. LBJ, NSF, MP, VII/74.

57. This is printed in PP, III, 246.

58. *New York Times,* Nov. 28, p. 1; Nov. 29, p. 69.

59. The draft statement is LBJ, NSF, MP, McGeorge Bundy, VII/53f.

60. *FRUS,* 1964–68, I, 433 (draft of Dec. 2), emphasis added.

61. See Forrestal's "Analysis of Option A," LBJ, WM, II/22, Nov. 8.

62. Portions of these appendixes were recently declassified at my request; they are LBJ, NSF, MP, McGeorge Bundy, VII/53a–n.

63. *FRUS,* 1964–68, I, 440.

64. Dallek, *Flawed Giant,* pp. 74–80.

65. Ibid., p. 83.
66. Caro, *The Path to Power,* pp. 344–368.
67. Ted Gittinger, ed., *The Johnson Years: A Vietnam Round Table* (Austin, Tex., 1993), p. 44.
68. Dec. 16, p. 1, and see Reston's column, p. 42.
69. Krock papers, Mudd Library, memo of Dec. 15, box 1, book III.

13. Over the Edge, December 1964–March 1965

1. *New York Times,* Dec. 11, p. 3; Dec. 12, p. 1:8.
2. Ibid., Dec. 13, p. 1.
3. *FRUS, 1964–68,* I, 451.
4. DD, 1979, 433D; see also *FRUS, 1964–68,* I, 451.
5. *New York Times,* Dec. 23, pp. 1, 26; Dec. 24, p. 1.
6. *FRUS, 1964–68,* I, 456, 457, 464, 465.
7. Kahin, *Intervention,* p. 258.
8. DD, 1979, 132c.
9. Ibid., 132a.
10. *FRUS, 1964–68,* I, 466, Dec. 24.
11. Ibid., I, 468, 469.
12. Ibid., I, 470, 471 (telegrams of 26 Dec.). State also turned down Taylor's request to warn Huong that the United States could not cooperate with a government headed or controlled by Khanh.
13. Ibid., I, 472, 473, 474, 475.
14. LBJ, NSF, MUSTD, I/138, James Greenfield, Dec. 31, 1964.
15. *FRUS, 1964–68,* I, 478 (Dec. 30, 1964).
16. *New York Times,* Jan. 6, p. 3.
17. *Washington Post,* Dec. 30, 1964.
18. The cable is *FRUS, 1964–68,* I, 478 (emphasis added). Johnson's request is LBJ, NSF, Histories, MUSTD, I/134a, McGeorge Bundy for Johnson, Jan. 2.
19. FRUS, 1964–68, II, 9–14.
20. Ibid., I, 392.
21. The Italian air power theorist Guido Douhet argued in the 1920s that strategic bombing alone could win wars.
22. See ibid., II, 15, 18.
23. The draft is LBJ, NSF, VN, NODIS/LOR, I(B)/36b; the final reply is *FRUS, 1964–68,* II, 19.
24. *FRUS, 1964–68,* II, 22, 27, 28, 33, 34.
25. The administration on January 15 refused to say whether it still felt bound by the 1962 accords, but on January 18 argued that Communist violations justified the strike. *New York Times,* Jan. 14, p. 1; Jan. 15, p. 1; Jan. 16, p. 1; Jan. 19, p. 1.
26. *FRUS, 1964–68,* II, 30.

27. *New York Times*, Jan. 19, p. 1; Jan. 21, p. 11; Jan. 22, p. 3; Jan. 23, p. 1; Jan. 24, p. 1.
28. *FRUS, 1964–68*, II, 38; LBJ, NSF, VN, NODIS/LOR, I(A)/52, Jan. 27.
29. Schlight, *The Years of the Offensive*, p. 17.
30. *New York Times*, Jan. 7, p. 1; Jan. 12, p. 1.
31. LBJ, NSF, MP, McGeorge Bundy, VIII/102.
32. *New York Times*, Jan. 23, p. 3; Jan. 27, p. 2.
33. Ibid., Jan. 27, p. 1.
34. Interview with McGeorge Bundy, 1994.
35. *FRUS, 1964–68*, II, 42
36. Quoted in Gibbons, *The U.S. Government and the Vietnam War*, III, p. 51, on the basis of Bundy's very fragmentary notes of the meeting.
37. *FRUS, 1964–68*, I, 39.
38. Ibid., II, 56; see also 44, 45, 47, 52, 54.
39. Ibid., II, 44.
40. Gibbons, *The U.S. Government and the Vietnam War*, III, p. 51.
41. *New York Times*, Feb. 2, p. 1; Feb. 3, p. 1; Feb. 5, pp. 1, 14.
42. LBJ, NSF, WM, V/11, Carl Salans to William Bundy.
43. *FRUS, 1964–68*, II, 58, 59, 63, 64, 66, 68, 72; see also 69 (Special National Intelligence Estimate, Feb. 4).
44. Memo of conversation, Feb. 6, 1965, LBJ, NSF, International Meetings and Travel File, Trip, McGeorge Bundy—Saigon, I/5. Declassified at my request.
45. This may be followed in detail in LBJ, NSF, Laos, XIV–XV.
46. *FRUS, 1964–68*, II, 45.
47. LBJ, NSF, WM, box 8, V/10, 2/5/65, Grant for Green; see also Gaiduk, *The Soviet Union and the Vietnam War*, pp. 22–30.
48. *FRUS, 1964–68*, I, 438, Dec. 5, 1964.
49. *New York Times*, Jan. 13, p. 1.
50. LBJ, Gibbons papers, III/11, Unger for Ball.
51. LBJ, MP, XII/11a, XII/11, 11b, and 11c.
52. *FRUS, 1964–68*, II, 76, 77, 78. no. 76, by William Colby, is by far the most thorough record and includes LBJ's statement.
53. *New York Times*, Feb. 8, pp. 1., 15, 16; *FRUS, 1964–68*, II, 80, 81.
54. *FRUS, 1964–68*, II, 79; Bundy's memo is 84.
55. Ibid., II, 87; see also 86, 88.
56. *New York Times*, Feb. 9, p. 13.
57. *The Joint Chiefs and the War*, II, 18–5.
58. *New York Times*, Feb. 10, p. 8. Baldwin also reported that about two years previously the Navy and the Air Force had proposed a program of air strikes and a naval blockade against the North.
59. *FRUS, 1964–68*, II, 94, 96.
60. Ibid., II, 97, 98, 99; *New York Times*, Feb. 12, p. 1.
61. *FRUS, 1964–68*, II, 115.

62. Ibid., II, 113.

63. LBJ, McGeorge Bundy papers, Meetings on Vietnam, Feb. 15. The President complained bitterly about a Tad Szulc story saying that the administration did plan to make a statement.

64. *FRUS, 1964–68*, II, 124, 128.

65. Thanks to Eisenhower and Dulles this has become one of the most venerable myths of the Cold War, although documentary sources do not support it. See Roger Dingman, "Atomic Diplomacy during the Korean War," *International Security* 13, no. 1 (Winter 1988–89), pp. 50–91.

66. *FRUS, 1964–68*, II, 133.

67. JCS 5147, 16160Z 65; MAC J3 4999, 171832Z Feb.; CINCPAC 180813Z Feb., LBJ, NSF, MUSTD, II/90, II/124, III/1b.

68. LBJ, Westmoreland papers, XIII/109, JCS 201953Z Feb. 65 to Sharp and Westmoreland.

69. LBJ, Westmoreland papers, XIII/121, 221655Z Feb. to Sharp and Wheeler; *FRUS, 1964–68*, II, 153. In his memoirs Westmoreland writes that he shared Taylor's reservations about ground forces, "but to a lesser degree," and claims at this time to have favored only the deployment of two Marine battalions. General William C. Westmoreland, *A Soldier Reports* (New York, 1976), p. 123.

70. *FRUS, 1964–68*, II, 116.

71. Ibid., II, 119; LBJ, NSF, VN, NODIS/LOR, I(A)/30, Saigon 2632, Feb. 17.

72. LBJ, NSF, VN, NODIS/LOR, I(A)/18, Saigon 2720; I(B)/8, Deptel 1805, 2/23/65.

73. *FRUS, 1964–68*, II, 103, 131.

74. Ibid., II, 135; LBJ, Gibbons papers, II/16 (Stevenson–U Thant conversation, Feb. 16); LBJ, NSF, VN, NODIS/LOR, I(A)/89, I(B)/65–66.

75. Walter Johnson, ed., *The Papers of Adlai E. Stevenson* (Boston, 1979), VIII, pp. 663–665.

76. *FRUS, 1964–68*, II, 113; LBJ, NSF, MUSTD, II/5a.

77. *FRUS, 1964–68*, II, 134.

78. *Papers of Adlai E. Stevenson*, VIII, pp. 702–704, 722–724.

79. *FRUS, 1964–68*, II, 165, 168, 170.

80. LBJ, Westmoreland papers, XIV/15, MAC J00 6394, March 2; *New York Times*, Feb. 28, p. 1.

81. Schlight, *The Years of the Offensive*, pp. 18–21.

82. *New York Times*, March 1, p. 1; March 3, p. 1.

83. Gibbons, *The U.S. Government and the Vietnam War*, III, pp. 123–124.

84. McGeorge Bundy to Johnson, Feb. 9, 1965, LBJ, MUSTD, I/65. On the congressional debate and public opinion see Gibbons, *The U.S. Government and the Vietnam War*, III, pp. 127–148.

85. I have treated this question with respect to Nazi Germany in two previ-

ous books: *Economic Diplomacy and the Origins of the Second World War* (Princeton, 1980), and *Politics and War: European Conflict from Philip II to Hitler* (Cambridge, Mass., 1990).

86. See Kahin, *Intervention;* Larry Berman, *Planning a Tragedy: The Americanization of the War in Vietnam* (New York, 1982); Brian Van der Mark, *Into the Quagmire: Lyndon Johnson and the Escalation of the Vietnam War* (New York, 1991).

14. War in Secret, March–June 1965

1. *FRUS*, 1964–68, II, 183.
2. At that time Army Chief of Staff General Harold Johnson had also asked for the deployment of one or two additional Army divisions in Thailand. Such deployments had figured in Pentagon plans developed in the fall and approved in principle by the President, but months earlier State Department officials had commented that the Thais did not want them. In the end Westmoreland found other uses for those troops. *The Joint Chiefs and the War,* II, ch. 18, pp. 7–8.
3. Gibbons, *The U.S. Government and the Vietnam War,* III, pp. 158–165.
4. *FRUS*, 1964–68, II, 183.
5. Ibid., II, 185, 186.
6. LBJ, NSF, MUSTD, III/18a, memo of April 13.
7. On Johnson's subsequent doubts see Lewis Sorley, "To Change a War: General Harold K. Johnson and the PROVN Study," *Parameters* 28, no. 1 (Spring 1998), pp. 93–109.
8. HB, XIV/83.
9. Johnson oral history, Aug. 1, 1974, MHI.
10. James F. Schnabel, *Policy and Direction: The First Year* (Washington, 1971), p. 83.
11. *FRUS*, 1964–68, II, 208; LBJ, NSF, MUSTD, II/50.
12. Schlight, *The Years of the Offensive,* p. 23.
13. *FRUS*, 1964–68, II, 218.
14. *The Joint Chiefs and the War,* II, ch. 19, p. 17. On the issue of third-country troops see Robert M. Blackburn, *Mercenaries and Lyndon Johnson's "More Flags"* (London, 1994), pp. 1–30.
15. *FRUS*, 1964–68, II, 220, 224.
16. Ibid., II, 228, 229, 230.
17. *The Joint Chiefs and the War,* II, ch. 18, pp. 10–26; Schlight, *The Years of the Offensive,* pp. 30–31; *FRUS*, 1964–68, II, 234.
18. *New York Times,* March 12, p. 1; March 13, p. 1; March 28, p. 1; March 29, p. 1.
19. *Public Papers of the President, Johnson, 1965,* I, pp. 370–371.
20. *New York Times,* April 2, p. 1.

21. *FRUS*, 1964–68, II, 232.

22. Ibid., II, 237; see also 238, 239. General Johnson's 21-point program included American and third-country reinforcements.

23. Ibid., II, 242.

24. Paul Hendrickson, *The Living and the Dead* (New York, 1996), pp. 163–165.

25. *FRUS*, 1964–68, II, 240.

26. Memo for record, April 8, GP, MCHC.

27. *The Joint Chiefs and the War*, II, ch. 21, pp. 3–4, 8–9.

28. *FRUS*, 1964–68, I, 433.

29. Ibid., II, 193, and see the redraft of March 24, PP, III, 253.

30. *The Joint Chiefs and the War*, II, ch. 28, pp. 4–5.

31. *New York Times*, March 6, p. 2; March 8, p. 1; March 9, p. 1; March 10, p. 1; March 14, p. 1; March 17, p. 1.

32. George H. Gallup, *The Gallup Poll* (New York, 1972), III, pp. 1932–33.

33. See *FRUS*, 1964–68, II, 216; *New York Times*, March 24, pp. 1, 7.

34. *FRUS*, 1964–68, II, 217; Bundy for Johnson, May 12, LBJ, NSF, MUSTD, IV/11a.

35. *New York Times*, March 25.

36. LBJ, MP, McGeorge Bundy, Feb. 17, VIII/10; March 15, IX/92; March 20, IX/81. Since the beginning of the year Bundy had had to make a weekly report to the President of all press contacts. See also Ronald Steel, *Walter Lippmann and the American Century* (Boston, 1980), pp. 560–561.

37. *Public Papers of the President, Johnson, 1965*, I, p. 319 (emphasis added).

38. See *New York Times*, April 2, p. 2; *FRUS*, 1964–68, II, 233.

39. *New York Times*, April 4, Week in Review, p. 10.

40. *Public Papers of the President, Johnson, 1965*, I, pp. 394–399 (emphasis added).

41. Steel, *Walter Lippmann*, pp. 563–565.

42. On Johnson's attempts to apply New Deal principles to Southeast Asia see Gardner, *Pay Any Price*, pp. 185–200.

43. *Gallup Poll*, III, pp. 1934–35, 1939–40.

44. Duiker, "The Revolutionary Path," ch. 15.

45. On reaction to Johnson's speech see *New York Times*, April 8, p. 1; April 9, p. 1; April 10, p. 1 and Week in Review, p. 1. For the four points see Kahin, *Intervention*, p. 326.

46. *New York Times*, April 16, p. 7; April 18, Week in Review, p. 1, April 20, p. 5.

47. *New York Times*, April 17, p. 1; April 21, p. 1.

48. *New York Times*, April 23, p. 34.

49. *FRUS*, 1964–68, II, 244.

50. HB, XV/31, 110825Z April 65.

51. Memo for record, April 14, GP, MCHC (emphasis added). The use of reserve colonels for civil affairs was one of President Johnson's favorite ideas, and Richard Holbrooke, then a young Foreign Service officer, heard it again the next year: see Willenson, ed., *The Bad War*, p. 148.

52. *FRUS, 1964–68*, II, 251; JCS 140051Z April 65, LBJ, NSF, MUSTD, III/26a.

53. *FRUS, 1964–68*, II, 252, 259, 260, 261; Saigon 3373, 14 April, LBJ, NSF, MUSTD, III/23a; Taylor 701 to JCS, 104000Z April, LBJ, HB XV/43; Saigon 3421, April 17, MUSTD, III/37a.

54. Deptel 2332 to Saigon, April 15, LBJ, NSF, VN, NODIS/LOR, II(B)/127; see also *FRUS, 1964–68*, II, 253.

55. *FRUS, 1964–68*, II, 256.

56. Ibid., II, 259, 260.

57. Ibid., II, 262.

58. Ibid., II, 164 (Taylor diary entry), 265 (McNamara for the President, April 21).

59. Ibid., II, 266.

60. Ibid., II, 250. It is not clear whether the American plane was downed by the Chinese or by an American missile.

61. Ibid., II, 268; LBJ, NSF, MUSTD, Saigon 3477, April 21, III/51a.

62. See Greene's memo for record of June 8, citing various deficiencies and shortages of equipment.

63. *FRUS, 1964–68*, II, 269, 271.

64. *New York Times*, April 22, p. 1.

65. Krock papers, Mudd Library, box 1.

66. *New York Times*, April 25, p. 1; April 27, pp. 1, 36.

67. *FRUS, 1964–68*, III, 120, conversation of Aug. 13.

68. LBJ, taped conversations, 1995 release.

69. *FRUS, 1964–68*, II, 270; Saigon 2397, April 24, MUSTD, III/60a; Saigon 3552, April 27, LBJ, NSF, VN, NODIS/LOR, II(A)/48; JCS 1141 to CINCPAC, 30 April, MUSTD, III/70a.

70. LBJ, NSF, MUSTD, III/66a; *The Joint Chiefs and the War*, II, ch. 21, pp. 17–18.

71. *The Joint Chiefs and the War*, II, ch. 21, p. 19.

72. *FRUS, 1964–68*, II, 311.

73. Ibid., II, 266, 267.

74. Compare LBJ, NSF, MP, X/47, and Steel, *Walter Lippmann*, p. 568, on this meeting.

75. *FRUS, 1964–68*, II, 288, 289, 291, 292.

76. Ibid., II, 300, 304.

77. *New York Times*, May 19, p. 46.

78. *FRUS, 1964–68*, II, 309.

79. See Yuen Foong Khong, *Analogies at War: Korea, Munich, Dien Bien Phu, and the Vietnam Decisions of 1965* (Princeton, 1992), pp. 174–205.
80. This is very clear from the President's daily diary, LBJ.
81. *New York Times,* May 28, p. 32.
82. Gibbons, *The U.S. Government and the Vietnam War,* III, p. 271.
83. *The Joint Chiefs and the War,* II, ch. 26, pp. 1–2.
84. *FRUS,* 1964–68, II, 328; see also 325, a June 2 memorandum from McNamara to Johnson recording the recommendations of Ambassadors Bruce (Britain) and Bohlen (France) and NATO Commander Lemnitzer against such strikes.
85. Admiral Ulysses S. Grant Sharp, *Strategy for Defeat* (San Rafael, Calif., 1978), pp. 95–104.
86. See Westmoreland, *A Soldier Reports,* pp. 119–122. It is my educated guess that McNaughton, if he said anything like this, referred not to the SAMs but to the IL-28 bombers the Russians also supplied, which the North Vietnamese never did, in fact, use.
87. HB, XVI/54, MACV 3052 110745Z Jun 65 (declassified at my request).
88. LBJ, NSF, MUSTD, V/2a (Saigon 4132, June 10).
89. Qiang, "Beijing and the Vietnam Conflict," p. 236; *FRUS,* 1964–68, III, 321.
90. Qiang, "Beijing and the Vietnam Conflict," pp. 236–237.
91. *New York Times,* May 18, p. 1; May 19, p. 1; May 23, p. 1; May 24, p. 1; May 31, p. 1; June 3, p. 1; June 5, p. 1; June 6, p. 1.
92. *FRUS,* 1964–68, II, 337.

15. War in Public, June–July 1965

1. *FRUS,* 1964–68, II, 339; *New York Times,* June 9, p. 1; June 10, p. 1.
2. *FRUS,* 1964–68, II, 338, 340.
3. Ibid., 343; Gibbons, *The U.S. Government and the Vietnam War,* III, pp. 286–288.
4. *FRUS,* 1964–68, II, 343.
5. Ibid., II, 338.
6. *New York Times,* June 12, p. 1.
7. HB, XVI/56.
8. LBJ, NSF, MUSTD, V/10a (JCS 112347Z June to CINCPAC), V/11a (memo for Secretary of Defense).
9. *FRUS,* 1964–68, II, 349, and III, 5; *New York Times,* June 12, p. 1.
10. LBJ, NSF, MUSTD, V/21a (emphasis added).
11. See Gibbons, *The U.S. Government and the Vietnam War,* III, p. 317; LBJ, NSF, MUSTD, V/54a, McNaughton memo (identified from the typeface).
12. *FRUS,* 1964–68, II, 338.

13. LBJ, NSF, MUSTD, V/7a; HB, XVI/66.
14. William Gibbons provided me with a copy of this letter.
15. Gibbons, *The U.S. Government and the Vietnam War,* III, pp. 332–340.
16. *FRUS,* 1964–68, III, 3.
17. Ibid., III, 7.
18. Gibbons, *The U.S. Government and the Vietnam War,* IV, pp. 303–308.
19. LBJ, NSF, MP, XI/65.
20. *FRUS,* 1964–68, III, 19.
21. Ibid., III, 10; LBJ, NSF, MP, XI/39.
22. *Public Papers of the President, Johnson, 1965,* II, p. 704.
23. The meeting of July 18 had left open the possibility that some of them might not remain in South Vietnam. In the end, they all did.
24. LBJ, NSF, MUSTD, V/55a, Ball memo of June 23, and Ball papers, telephone conversations, II/26.
25. This conversation was released in 1995, along with four others, because McNamara quoted from it in his memoirs.
26. *FRUS,* 1964–68, III, 16; 15 is a record by Richard Helms, who did not record this critical part of the discussion because President Johnson expressly forbade any discussion of it outside the meeting itself. See also LBJ, Ball papers, telephone conversations, II/28.
27. *FRUS,* III, 13, 17 (emphasis added).
28. Leonard Unger apparently contributed some of the political proposals. See Gibbons, *The U.S. Government and the Vietnam War,* III, p. 327n.
29. A June 24 draft of the McNaughton memo was supplied to me by William Gibbons.
30. *FRUS,* 1964–68, III, 28, 31.
31. *New York Times,* June 18, p. 1; June 19, p. 1; July 3, p. 3.
32. Ibid., June 30, p. 1; July 1, p. 3; July 2, p. 1.
33. Ibid., July 7, p. 1; July 9, p. 1; July 10, p. 1.
34. Ibid., July 1, p. 1; July 2, p. 1; July 6, p. 1; July 8, p. 1.
35. *FRUS,* 1964–68, III, 26.
36. See LBJ, Ball papers, telephone conversations, II/36, and Gibbons, *The U.S. Government and the Vietnam War,* p. 320.
37. Gibbons, *The U.S. Government and the Vietnam War,* p. 325.
38. McMaster, in *Dereliction of Duty,* p. 301, claims that McNamara lied to Wheeler about the topic of this meeting to keep him out of it. The conversations he quotes and the recollections of William Bundy do not support this. There really was no reason for Wheeler to attend a meeting discussing Ball's proposal for a reevaluation of American objectives and a withdrawal, and Wheeler certainly could not have been disappointed by the reception which Ball's proposals received.
39. *FRUS,* 1964–68, III, 40.
40. Ibid., III, 35 (emphasis added).

41. Ibid., III, 41.
42. Ibid., III, 40 (emphasis added).
43. Ibid., III, 42.
44. Ibid., III, 43.
45. As McNamara confirmed to Johnson on July 14: LBJ, taped conversations, 1995 release.
46. *FRUS, 1964–68,* XXX, 92.
47. Ibid., III, 46, 47, 53.
48. Ibid., III, 49; LBJ, NSF, VN, NODIS/LOR, II(B)/104e, July 4.
49. On the genesis of the appointment see LBJ, NSF, MP, IX/71 (March 24, 1965), and IX/50 (March 31), when the AP reported LBJ's plans.
50. *FRUS, 1964–68,* III, 54.
51. Memo of July 10, GP, MCHC.
52. PP, IV, pp. 291–293. The memo is undated but seems to have been written between July 2 and July 14, probably nearer the earlier date.
53. Memo of July 12, GP, MCHC. The Goodpaster study is LBJ, NSF, VN, XXXVII/413–413c.
54. *FRUS, 1964–68,* III, 69.
55. LBJ, NSF, VN, XXXVII/58, memo of July 15.
56. *FRUS, 1964–68,* III, 61.
57. Ibid., III, 60.
58. See Caro, *The Path to Power,* pp. 462–468, and *Means of Ascent,* pp. 369–384.
59. *New York Times,* July 22, p. 1.
60. LBJ, NSF, VN, Harriman talks on Vietnam, I/62 (Moscow 139, July 15).
61. Ibid., I/4 (Airgram A-151 from Moscow).
62. Ibid., I/5.
63. The study has not yet been declassified, but see *FRUS, 1964–68,* XXX, 92, 94, for discussions of it.
64. Ibid., III, 67 (emphasis added).
65. Ibid., III, 72 (here and in later quotation, emphasis added). This record, by Chester Cooper, captures the flavor of the meeting better than Valenti's notes, ibid., 71. Both documents also cover the afternoon session.
66. Ibid., III, 73.
67. The final sentence of the quotation is from the Valenti record.
68. *FRUS, 1964–68,* III, 74.
69. *New York Times,* July 22, pp. 1, 4.
70. Annex to JCSM-590–65, Aug. 5, 1965, JCS records (declassified at my request).
71. Greene's own record is his memo of July 22, GP, MCHC. Greene felt the President had treated him perfectly fairly.
72. *FRUS, 1964–68,* II, 76, and Greene memo.
73. *New York Times,* July 23, p. 1.
74. Presidential calendar, LBJ.

75. Gibbons, *The U.S. Government and the Vietnam War,* III, pp. 414–415.
76. Memo of July 24, GP, MCHC.
77. LBJ, NSF, VN, XXXVIII/115, Deptel 218.
78. *FRUS, 1964–68,* III, 87.
79. Gibbons, *The U.S. Government and the Vietnam War,* III, pp. 417–418, quoting William Bundy's unpublished manuscript.
80. *FRUS, 1964–68,* III, 87, 90.
81. Qiang, "Beijing and the Vietnam Conflict," p. 237.
82. *FRUS, 1964–68,* III, 89.
83. Ibid., III, 91.
84. Ibid., III, 93.
85. Ibid., III, 96. The other senators with whom he had met were the Democrats Richard Russell, Fulbright, and Sparkman and the Republicans George Aiken and John Sherman Cooper.
86. Ibid., III, 94.
87. *Public Papers of the President, Johnson,* 1965, II, pp. 794–798.
88. *New York Times,* July 29, p. 1 (two stories); July 30, p. 24; Ball papers, telephone conversations, 7/30 II/65.

16. Bad History, Wrong War

1. May and Zelikow, eds., *The Kennedy Tapes.*
2. Churchill himself had argued that the Second World War easily could and should have been prevented in the first volume of his memoirs, *The Gathering Storm* (Boston, 1948), e.g. pp. 37–38.
3. See Robert Divine, *Roosevelt and World War II* (Baltimore, 1969), pp. 1–48; Waldo Henrichs, *Threshold of War: Franklin D. Roosevelt and American Entry into World War II* (New York, 1988).
4. Carl von Clausewitz, *On War* (Princeton, 1976), p. 69.
5. *The Joint Chiefs and the War,* II, ch. 32, pp. 1–12.
6. Ibid., III, ch. 42, p. 12 (emphasis added).
7. Ibid., III, ch. 43, pp. 13–25.
8. See Sam Adams, *War of Numbers* (South Royalton, Vt., 1994), esp. pp. 94–321.
9. As shown very clearly by Ronald Spector in *After Tet: The Bloodiest Year in Vietnam* (New York, 1993).
10. See Guenter Lewy, *America in Vietnam* (New York, 1978), pp. 82–84.
11. See Chen Jian, "China's Involvement in the Vietnam War, 1964–69," and Qiang, "Beijing and the Vietnam Conflict," pp. 233–240.
12. On this aspect of the war see Francis J. West Jr., *The Village* (Madison, 1972); Al Hemingway, *Our War Was Different* (Annapolis, 1994).
13. Eric M. Bergerud, *The Dynamics of Defeat: The Vietnam War in Hau Nghia Province* (San Francisco, 1991).
14. Kahin, *Intervention,* pp. 412–432.

15. See Adams, *War of Numbers,* pp. 175–184.
16. Supporters of the war have argued that the American effort in South Vietnam gave nations like Thailand, Malaysia, and Singapore time to develop as non-Communist societies, and also have tried to connect the war to the fall of the increasingly Communist-influenced Sukarno government in Indonesia in 1965. None of the other mainland Southeast Asian nations, however, faced a comparable internal Communist threat, and in Indonesia the army won an incredibly bloody *political* victory over the Communists in 1965–1966, apparently executing hundreds of thousands of Indonesian Communists.

Epilogue: Tragedy and History

1. Figures are from Lawrence M. Baskir and William A. Strauss, *Chance and Circumstance: The Draft, the War, and the Vietnam Generation* (New York, 1978), p. 5.
2. Thucydides, *The Peloponnesian War;* Luigi Albertini, *The Origins of the War of 1914,* trans. Isabella Massey, 3 vols. (London, 1952–1957); Fritz Fischer, *Germany's Aims in the First World War* (London, 1967).

Acknowledgments

★

For the last nine years it has been my privilege to work in the Strategy and Policy Department of the Naval War College, and this book has been vastly improved as a result. Nowhere else could I have found twenty colleagues who were always not merely willing, but eager to hear the latest results of my research, to read drafts of chapters, and to help develop my thinking on the origins and course of wars. Special thanks go to Steve Ross, George Baer, Bill Fuller, Brad Lee, and Phil Meilinger, who read all or large portions of the manuscript and made excellent suggestions, and to my teaching partners—Jim Ponzo, Dan Phipps, Daryl King, Bob Larkin, Bill Goodwin, Lois Schoonover, Gary Tochet, and Dan Withers—who allowed me to interrupt them with new documents and never complained when my research threatened to overrun their half of the office. John Waghelstein and Richard Neustadt also kindly read parts of the manuscript.

I was assisted throughout by the staffs of the Kennedy and Johnson libraries, including Suzanne Forbes and Paul Agnew in Boston, and David Humphries, Mike Parish, and Regina Greenwell in Austin. The leadership of the LBJ Library—and, I would suppose, Mrs. Lyndon Johnson herself—deserve special thanks for their efforts to make documentation on the Johnson administration available as soon as possible. President Johnson, evidently, wanted his countrymen eventually to know all about his tenure in office, and the library he created has done its best to make this happen. I feel sure President Kennedy felt the same way, and I am glad that the Kennedy Library is finally catching up. I must also thank the Lyndon B. Johnson Foundation for its generous support of some of my research. Tina Lovato of the National Defense University Library was also very helpful, as was the Marine Corps Historical Center in Washington and the library of the Army War College at Carlisle. The State and Defense Departments graciously met most of my FOIA requests, but I cannot say the same for the Central Intelligence Agency. After waiting six years, it released only about 20 of the more than 300 documents I had requested, and it claimed, in effect, that it would never be able to supply accounts of the numerous conversations that William Colby and John Richardson, two CIA station chiefs in Saigon, had with Ngo Dinh Nhu. I believe it is fair to say that much important history will never be known if the Agency continues to treat the Freedom of Information Act in this way. On the eve of publication it provided a few more heavily redacted documents on appeal. Bob Schnare and his staff at the Naval War College were generous in their efforts to meet my needs. My old friend Catherine Hustead secured some of the photos at the National Archives.

Historians whose assistance I have appreciated include Robert Dallek; Marc Trachtenberg; William Duiker, who graciously allowed me to quote from his unfinished biography of Ho Chi Minh; Deborah Shapley; Ernest May; and above all that great Virginia gentleman William Gibbons, who has labored in these same vineyards far longer and with a far richer harvest than any of us, and who could always be counted on for encouragement, sound judgment, and good advice. He, too, read a good deal of the manuscript and made excellent suggestions. I also thank my agent, Michael Congdon, whose belief in the project never wavered, and the staff of Harvard University Press.

Illustration Credits

National Archives: Still Pictures Branch, 1, 7, 11, 12, 16, 27, 31, 33, 34, 37, 38, 39, 41, 42, 43

JFK Library: 2, 4, 5, 6, 8, 9, 10, 14, 20, 21, 23

LBJ Library: Yoichi R. Okamoto, 3, 13, 24, 25, 26, 30, 32, 35, 36; O. J. Rapp, 28; Frank Wolf, 40

CORBIS/Bettmann: 15, 17, 19, 44, 45

Archive Photos: 18, 22, 29

Index

★